S0-BNE-219

THE PLAYS OF EUGENE O'NEILL

VOLUME III

STRANGE INTERLUDE

DESIRE UNDER THE ELMS

LAZARUS LAUGHED

THE FOUNTAIN

THE MOON OF THE CARIBBEES

BOUND EAST FOR CARDIFF

THE LONG VOYAGE HOME

IN THE ZONE

ILE

WHERE THE CROSS IS MADE

THE ROPE

THE DREAMY KID

BEFORE BREAKFAST

THE PLAYS OF EUGENE O'NEILL VOLUME III

THE MODERN LIBRARY · NEW YORK

MODERN LIBRARY EDITION 1982

 PUBLISHED IN THE UNITED STATES BY RANDOM HOUSE, INC., NEW YORK. DISTRIBUTED IN CANADA BY RANDOM HOUSE OF CANADA LIMITED, TORONTO

MANUFACTURED IN THE UNITED STATES OF AMERICA

CONTENTS

STRANGE INTERLUDE

CHARACTERS

CHARLES MARSDEN

PROFESSOR HENRY LEEDS

NINA LEEDS, *his daughter*

EDMUND DARRELL

SAM EVANS

MRS. AMOS EVANS, *Sam's mother*

GORDON EVANS

MADELINE ARNOLD

FIRST PART

ACT ONE: Library, the Leeds' home in a small university town of New England—an afternoon in late summer.

ACT TWO: The same. Fall of the following year. Night.

ACT THREE: Dining room of the Evans' homestead in northern New York state—late spring of the next year. Morning.

ACT FOUR: The same as Acts One and Two. Fall of the same year. Evening.

ACT FIVE: Sitting room of small house Evans has rented in a seashore suburb near New York. The following April. Morning.

SECOND PART

ACT SIX: The same. A little over a year later. Evening.

ACT SEVEN: Sitting room of the Evans' apartment on Park Avenue. Nearly eleven years later. Early afternoon.

ACT EIGHT: Section of afterdeck of the Evans' cruiser anchored near the finish line at Poughkeepsie. Ten years later. Afternoon.

ACT NINE: A terrace on the Evans' estate on Long Island. Several months later. Late afternoon.

STRANGE INTERLUDE

FIRST PART—ACT ONE

SCENE: *The library of* PROFESSOR LEEDS' *home in a small university town in New England. This room is at the front part of his house with windows opening on the strip of lawn between the house and the quiet residential street. It is a small room with a low ceiling. The furniture has been selected with a love for old New England pieces. The walls are lined almost to the ceiling with glassed-in book-shelves. These are packed with books, principally editions, many of them old and rare, of the ancient classics in the original Greek and Latin, of the later classics in French and German and Italian, of all the English authors who wrote while* s *was still like an* ſ *and a few since then, the most modern probably being Thackeray. The atmosphere of the room is that of a cosy, cultured retreat, sedulously built as a sanctuary where, secure with the culture of the past at his back, a fugitive from reality can view the present safely from a distance, as a superior with condescending disdain, pity, and even amusement.*

There is a fair-sized table, a heavy armchair, a rocker, and an old bench made comfortable with cushions. The table, with the Professor's armchair at its left, is arranged toward the left of the room, the rocker is at center, the bench at right.

There is one entrance, a door in the right wall, rear.

It is late afternoon of a day in August. Sunshine, cooled and dimmed in the shade of trees, fills the room with a soothing light.

The sound of a MAID'S VOICE—*a middle-aged woman—explaining familiarly but respectfully from the right, and* MARSDEN *enters. He is a tall thin man of thirty-five, meticulously well-dressed in tweeds of distinctly English tailoring, his appearance that of an Anglicized New England gentleman. His face is too long for its width, his nose is high and narrow, his forehead broad, his mild blue eyes those of a dreamy self-analyst, his thin lips ironical and a bit sad. There is an indefinable feminine quality about him, but it is nothing apparent in either appearance or act. His manner is cool and poised. He speaks with a careful ease as one who listens to his own conversation. He has long fragile hands, and the stoop to his shoulders of a man weak muscularly, who has never liked athletics and has always been regarded as of delicate constitution. The main point about his personality is a quiet charm, a quality of appealing, inquisitive friendliness, always willing to listen, eager to sympathize, to like and to be liked.*

MARSDEN. (*standing just inside the door, his tall, stooped figure leaning back against the books—nodding back at the* MAID *and smiling kindly*) I'll wait in here, Mary. (*His eyes follow her for a second, then return to gaze around the room slowly with an appreciative relish for the familiar significance of the books. He smiles affectionately and his amused voice recites the words with a rhetorical resonance*) Sanctum Sanctorum! (*His voice takes on a monotonous musing quality, his eyes stare idly at his drifting thoughts*)

How perfectly the Professor's unique haven! . . .

(*He smiles*)

Primly classical . . . when New Englander meets Greek! . . .

(*Looking at the books now*)

He hasn't added one book in years . . . how old was I when I first came here? . . . six . . . with my father . . . father . . . how dim his face has grown! . . . he wanted to speak to me just before he died . . . the hospital . . . smell of iodoform in the cool halls . . . hot summer . . . I bent down . . . his voice had withdrawn so far away . . . I couldn't understand him . . . what son can ever understand? . . . always too near, too soon, too distant or too late! . . .

(*His face has become sad with a memory of the bewildered suffering of the adolescent boy he had been at the time of his father's death. Then he shakes his head, flinging off his thoughts, and makes himself walk about the room*)

What memories on such a smiling afternoon! . . . this pleasant old town after three months . . . I won't go to Europe again . . . couldn't write a line there . . . how answer the fierce question of all those dead and maimed? . . . too big a job for me! . . .

(*He sighs—then self-mockingly*)

But back here . . . it is the interlude that gently questions . . . in this town dozing . . . decorous bodies moving with circumspection through the afternoons . . . their habits affectionately chronicled . . . an excuse for weaving amusing words . . . my novels . . . not of cosmic importance, hardly . . .

(*Then self-reassuringly*)

but there is a public to cherish them, evidently . . . and I can write! . . . more than one can say of these modern sex-yahoos! . . . I must start work tomorrow . . . I'd like to use the Professor in a novel sometime . . . and his wife . . . seems impossible she's been dead six years . . . so aggressively his wife! . . . poor Professor! now it's Nina who bosses him . . . but that's different . . . she has bossed me, too, ever since she was a baby . . . she's a woman now . . . known love and death . . . Gordon brought down in flames . . . two days before the armistice . . . what fiendish irony! . . . his wonderful athlete's body . . . her lover . . . charred bones in a cage of twisted steel . . . no wonder she broke down . . . Mother said she's become quite queer lately . . . Mother seemed jealous of my concern . . . why have I never fallen in love with Nina? . . . could I? . . . that way . . . used to dance her on my knee . . . sit her on my lap . . . even now she'd never think anything about it . . . but sometimes the scent of her hair and skin . . . like a dreamy drug . . . dreamy! . . . there's the rub! . . . all dreams with me! . . . my sex life among the phantoms! . . .

(*He grins torturedly*)

Why? . . . oh, this digging in gets nowhere . . . to the devil with sex! . . . our impotent pose of today to beat the loud drum on fornication! . . . boasters . . . eunuchs parading with the phallus!

. . . giving themselves away . . . whom do they fool? . . . not even themselves! . . .

(*His face suddenly full of an intense pain and disgust*)

Ugh! . . . always that memory! . . . why can't I ever forget? . . . as sickeningly clear as if it were yesterday . . . prep school . . . Easter vacation . . . Fatty Boggs and Jack Frazer . . . that house of cheap vice . . . one dollar! . . . why did I go? . . . Jack, the dead game sport . . . how I admired him! . . . afraid of his taunts . . . he pointed to the Italian girl . . . "Take her!" . . . daring me . . . I went . . . miserably frightened . . . what a pig she was! . . . pretty vicious face under caked powder and rouge . . . surly and contemptuous . . . lumpy body . . . short legs and thick ankles . . . slums of Naples . . . "What you gawkin' about? Git a move on, kid" . . . kid! . . . I *was* only a kid! . . . sixteen . . . test of manhood . . . ashamed to face Jack again unless . . . fool! . . . I might have lied to him! . . . but I honestly thought that wench would feel humiliated if I . . . oh, stupid kid! . . . back at the hotel I waited till they were asleep . . . then sobbed . . . thinking of Mother . . . feeling I had defiled her . . . and myself . . . forever! . . .

(*Mocking bitterly*)

"Nothing half so sweet in life as love's young dream," what? . . .

(*He gets to his feet impatiently*)

Why does my mind always have to dwell on that? . . . too silly . . . no importance really . . . an incident such as any boy of my age . . .

(*He hears someone coming quickly from the right and turns expectantly.* PROFESSOR LEEDS *enters, a pleased relieved expression fighting the flurried worry on his face. He is a small, slender man of fifty-five, his hair gray, the top of his head bald. His face, prepossessing in spite of its too-small, over-refined features, is that of a retiring, studious nature. He has intelligent eyes and a smile that can be ironical. Temperamentally timid, his defense is an assumption of his complacent, superior manner of the classroom toward the world at large. This defense is strengthened by a natural tendency toward a prim provincialism where practical present-day considerations are con-*

cerned (though he is most liberal—even radical—in his tolerant understanding of the manners and morals of Greece and Imperial Rome!) This classroom poise of his, however, he cannot quite carry off outside the classroom. There is an unconvincing quality about it that leaves his larger audience—and particularly the PROFESSOR *himself—subtly embarrassed. As* MARSDEN *is one of his old students, whom, in addition, he has known from childhood, he is perfectly at ease with him.*)

MARSDEN. (*holding out his hand—with unmistakable liking*) Here I am again, Professor!

PROFESSOR LEEDS. (*shaking his hand and patting him on the back—with genuine affection*) So glad to see you, Charlie! A surprise, too! We didn't expect you back so soon! (*He sits in his chair on the left of the table while* MARSDEN *sits in the rocker.*) (*Looking away from* MARSDEN *a moment, his face now full of selfish relief as he thinks*)

Fortunate, his coming back . . . always calming influence on Nina . . .

MARSDEN. And I never dreamed of returning so soon. But Europe, Professor, is the big casualty they were afraid to set down on the list.

PROFESSOR LEEDS. (*his face clouding*) Yes, I suppose you found everything completely changed since before the war. (*He thinks resentfully*)

The war . . . Gordon! . . .

MARSDEN. Europe has "gone west"—(*He smiles whimsically*) to America, let's hope! (*Then frowningly*) I couldn't stand it. There were millions sitting up with the corpse already, who had a family right to be there— (*Then matter-of-factly*) I was wasting my time, too. I couldn't write a line. (*Then gaily*) But where's Nina? I must see Nina!

PROFESSOR LEEDS. She'll be right in. She said she wanted to finish thinking something out— You'll find Nina changed, Charlie, greatly changed! (*He sighs—thinking with a trace of guilty alarm*)

The first thing she said at breakfast . . . "I dreamed of Gordon"

. . . as if she wanted to taunt me! . . . how absurd! . . . her eyes positively glared! . . .

(*Suddenly blurting out resentfully*) She dreams about Gordon.

MARSDEN. (*looking at him with amused surprise*) Well, I'd hardly call that a change, would you?

PROFESSOR LEEDS. (*thinking, oblivious to this remark*)

But I must constantly bear in mind that she's not herself . . . that she's a sick girl . . .

MARSDEN. (*thinking*)

The morning news of Gordon's death came . . . her face like gray putty . . . beauty gone . . . no face can afford intense grief . . . it's only later when sorrow . . .

(*With concern*) Just what do you mean by changed, Professor? Before I left she seemed to be coming out of that horrible numbed calm.

PROFESSOR LEEDS. (*slowly and carefully*) Yes, she has played a lot of golf and tennis this summer, motored around with her friends, and even danced a good deal. And she eats with a ravenous appetite. (*Thinking frightenedly*)

Breakfast . . . "dreamed of Gordon" . . . what a look of hate for me in her eyes! . . .

MARSDEN. But that sounds splendid! When I left she wouldn't see anyone or go anywhere. (*Thinking pityingly*)

Wandering from room to room . . . her thin body and pale lost face . . . gutted, love-abandoned eyes! . . .

PROFESSOR LEEDS. Well, now she's gone to the opposite extreme! Sees everyone—bores, fools—as if she'd lost all discrimination or wish to discriminate. And she talks interminably, Charlie—intentional nonsense, one would say! Refuses to be serious! Jeers at everything!

MARSDEN. (*consolingly*) Oh, that's all undoubtedly part of the effort she's making to forget.

PROFESSOR LEEDS. (*absent-mindedly*) Yes. (*Arguing with himself*)

Shall I tell him? . . . no . . . it might sound silly . . . but it's terrible to be so alone in this . . . if Nina's mother had lived

. . . my wife . . . dead! . . . and for a time I actually felt released! . . . wife! . . . help-meet! . . . now I need help! . . . no use! . . . she's gone! . . .

MARSDEN. (*watching him—thinking with a condescending affection*)

Good little man . . . he looks worried . . . always fussing about something . . . he must get on Nina's nerves. . . .

(*Reassuringly*) No girl could forget Gordon in a hurry, especially after the shock of his tragic death.

PROFESSOR LEEDS. (*irritably*) I realize that. (*Thinking resentfully*)

Gordon . . . always Gordon with everyone! . . .

MARSDEN. By the way, I located the spot near Sedan where Gordon's machine fell. Nina asked me to, you know.

PROFESSOR LEEDS. (*irritated—expostulatingly*) For heaven's sake, don't remind her! Give her a chance to forget if you want to see her well again. After all, Charlie, life must be lived and Nina can't live with a corpse forever! (*Trying to control his irritation and talk in an objective tone*) You see, I'm trying to see things through clearly and unsentimentally. If you'll remember, I was as broken up as anyone over Gordon's death. I'd become so reconciled to Nina's love for him—although, as you know, I was opposed at first, and for fair reasons, I think, for the boy, for all his good looks and prowess in sport and his courses, really came of common people and had no money of his own except as he made a career for himself.

MARSDEN. (*a trifle defensively*) I'm sure he would have had a brilliant career.

PROFESSOR LEEDS. (*impatiently*) No doubt. Although you must acknowledge, Charlie, that college heroes rarely shine brilliantly in after life. Unfortunately, the tendency to spoil them in the university is a poor training—

MARSDEN. But Gordon was absolutely unspoiled, I should say.

PROFESSOR LEEDS. (*heatedly*) Don't misunderstand me, Charlie! I'd be the first to acknowledge— (*A bit pathetically*) It isn't Gordon,

Charlie. It's his memory, his ghost, you might call it, haunting Nina, whose influence I have come to dread because of the terrible change in her attitude toward me. (*His face twitches as if he were on the verge of tears—he thinks desperately*)

I've got to tell him . . . he will see that I acted for the best . . . that I was justified. . . .

(*He hesitates—then blurts out*) It may sound incredible, but Nina has begun to act as if she hated me!

MARSDEN. (*startled*) Oh, come now!

PROFESSOR LEEDS. (*insistently*) Absolutely! I haven't wanted to admit it. I've refused to believe it, until it's become too appallingly obvious in her whole attitude toward me! (*His voice trembles.*)

MARSDEN. (*moved—expostulating*) Oh, now you're becoming morbid! Why, Nina has always idolized you! What possible reason—?

PROFESSOR LEEDS. (*quickly*) I can answer that, I think. She has a reason. But why she should blame me when she must know I acted for the best— You probably don't know, but just before he sailed for the front Gordon wanted their marriage to take place, and Nina consented. In fact, from the insinuations she lets drop now, she must have been most eager, but at the time— However, I felt it was ill-advised and I took Gordon aside and pointed out to him that such a precipitate marriage would be unfair to Nina, and scarcely honorable on his part.

MARSDEN. (*staring at him wonderingly*) You said that to Gordon? (*Thinking cynically*)

A shrewd move! . . . Gordon's proud spot, fairness and honor! . . . but was it honorable of you? . . .

PROFESSOR LEEDS. (*with a touch of asperity*) Yes, I said it, and I gave him my reason. There *was* the possibility he might be killed, in the flying service rather more than a possibility, which needless to say, I did not point out, but which Gordon undoubtedly realized, poor boy! If he were killed, he would be leaving Nina a widow, perhaps with a baby, with no resources, since he was penniless, except what pension she might get from the government; and all this while she was still at an age when a girl, especially one of Nina's charm and beauty, should have all of life before her. Decidedly, I told him, in justice to Nina, they must wait until he had come back and begun to establish his position in the world. That was the square thing. And Gordon was quick to agree with me!

MARSDEN. (*thinking*)

> The square thing! . . . but we must all be crooks where happiness is concerned! . . . steal or starve! . . .

(*Then rather ironically*) And so Gordon told Nina he'd suddenly realized it wouldn't be fair to her. But I gather he didn't tell her it was your scruple originally?

PROFESSOR LEEDS. No, I asked him to keep what I said strictly confidential.

MARSDEN. (*thinking ironically*)

> Trusted to his honor again! . . . old fox! . . . poor Gordon! . . .

But Nina suspects now that you—?

PROFESSOR LEEDS. (*startled*) Yes. That's exactly it. She knows in some queer way. And she acts toward me exactly as if she thought I had deliberately destroyed her happiness, that I had hoped for Gordon's death and been secretly overjoyed when the news came! (*His voice is shaking with emotion*) And there you have it, Charlie—the whole absurd mess! (*Thinking with a strident accusation*)

> And it's true, you contemptible . . . !

(*Then miserably defending himself*)

> No! . . . I acted unselfishly . . . for her sake! . . .

MARSDEN. (*wonderingly*) You don't mean to tell me she has accused you of all this?

PROFESSOR LEEDS. Oh, no, Charlie! Only by hints—looks—innuendos. She knows she has no real grounds, but in the present state of her mind the real and the unreal become confused—

MARSDEN. (*thinking cynically*)

> As always in all minds . . . or how could men live? . . .

(*Soothingly*) That's just what you ought to bear in your mind—the state of hers—and not get so worked up over what I should say is a combination of imagination on both your parts. (*He gets to his feet as he hears voices from the right*) Buck up! This must be Nina coming. (*The* PROFESSOR *gets to his feet, hastily composing his features into his bland, cultured expression.*)

MARSDEN. (*thinking self-mockingly but a bit worried about himself*)

> My heart pounding! . . . seeing Nina again! . . . how sentimental . . . how she'd laugh if she knew! . . . and quite rightly . . . absurd for me to react as if I loved . . . that way . . . her dear old Charlie . . . ha! . . .

(*He smiles with bitter self-mockery*)

PROFESSOR LEEDS. (*thinking worriedly*)

> I hope she won't make a scene . . . she's seemed on the verge all day . . . thank God, Charlie's like one of the family . . . but what a life for me! . . . with the opening of the new term only a few weeks off! . . . I can't do it . . . I'll have to call in a nerve specialist . . . but the last one did her no good . . . his outrageous fee . . . he can take it to court . . . I absolutely refuse . . . but if he should bring suit? . . . what a scandal . . . no, I'll have to pay . . . somehow . . . borrow . . . he has me in a corner, the robber! . . .

NINA. (*enters and stands just inside the doorway looking directly at her father with defiant eyes, her face set in an expression of stubborn resolve. She is twenty, tall with broad square shoulders, slim strong hips and long beautifully developed legs—a fine athletic girl of the swimmer, tennis player, golfer type. Her straw-blond hair, framing her sunburned face, is bobbed. Her face is striking, handsome rather than pretty, the bone structure prominent, the forehead high, the lips of her rather large mouth clearly modelled above the firm jaw. Her eyes are beautiful and bewildering, extraordinarily large and a deep greenish blue. Since* GORDON'S *death they have a quality of continually shuddering before some terrible enigma, of being wounded to their depths and made defiant and resentful by their pain. Her whole manner, the charged atmosphere she gives off, is totally at variance with her healthy outdoor physique. It is strained, nerve-racked, hectic, a terrible tension of will alone maintaining self-possession. She is dressed in smart sport clothes. Too preoccupied with her resolve to remember or see* MARSDEN, *she speaks directly to her father in a voice tensely cold and calm*) I have made up my mind, Father.

PROFESSOR LEEDS. (*thinking distractedly*)

What does she mean? . . . oh, God help me! . . .

(*Flustered—hastily*) Don't you see Charlie, Nina?

MARSDEN. (*troubled—thinking*)

She has changed . . . what has happened? . . .

(*He comes forward toward her—a bit embarrassed but affectionately using his pet name for her*) Hello, Nina Cara Nina! Are you trying to cut me dead, young lady?

NINA. (*turning her eyes to* MARSDEN, *holding out her hand for him to shake, in her cool, preoccupied voice*) Hello, Charlie. (*Her eyes immediately return to her father*) Listen, Father!

MARSDEN. (*standing near her, concealing his chagrin*)

That hurts! . . . I mean nothing! . . . but she's a sick girl . . . I must make allowance . . .

PROFESSOR LEEDS. (*thinking distractedly*)

That look in her eyes! . . . hate! . . .

(*With a silly giggle*) Really, Nina, you're absolutely rude! What has Charlie done?

NINA. (*in her cool tone*) Why, nothing. Nothing at all. (*She goes to him with a detached, friendly manner*) Did I seem rude, Charlie? I didn't mean to be. (*She kisses him with a cool, friendly smile*) Welcome home. (*Thinking wearily*)

What has Charlie done? . . . nothing . . . and never will . . . Charlie sits beside the fierce river, immaculately timid, cool and clothed, watching the burning, frozen naked swimmers drown at last. . . .

MARSDEN. (*thinking torturedly*)

Cold lips . . . the kiss of contempt! . . . for dear old Charlie! . . .

(*Forcing a good-natured laugh*) Rude? Not a bit! (*Banteringly*) As I've often reminded you, what can I expect when the first word you ever spoke in this world was an insult to me. "Dog" you said, looking right at me—at the age of one! (*He laughs. The* PROFESSOR *laughs nervously.* NINA *smiles perfunctorily.*)

NINA. (*thinking wearily*)

The fathers laugh at little daughter Nina . . . I must get away! nice Charlie doggy . . . faithful . . . fetch and carry . . . bark softly in books at the deep night. . . .

PROFESSOR LEEDS. (*thinking*)

What is she thinking? . . . I can't stand living like this! . . .

(*Giggle gone to a twitching grin*) You are a cool one, Nina! You'd think you'd just seen Charlie yesterday!

NINA. (*slowly—coolly and reflectively*) Well, the war is over. Coming back safe from Europe isn't such an unusual feat now, is it?

MARSDEN. (*thinking bitterly*)

A taunt . . . I didn't fight . . . physically unfit . . . not like Gordon . . . Gordon in flames . . . how she must resent my living! . . . thinking of me, scribbling in press bureau . . . louder and louder lies . . . drown the guns and the screams . . . deafen the world with lies . . . hired choir of liars! . . .

(*Forcing a joking tone*) Little you know the deadly risks I ran, Nina! If you'd eaten some of the food they gave me on my renovated transport, you'd shower me with congratulations! (*The* PROFESSOR *forces a snicker.*)

NINA. (*coolly*) Well, you're here, and that's that. (*Then suddenly expanding in a sweet, genuinely affectionate smile*) And I *am* glad, Charlie, always glad you're here! You know that.

MARSDEN. (*delighted and embarrassed*) I hope so, Nina!

NINA. (*turning on her father—determinedly*) I must finish what I started to say, Father. I've thought it all out and decided that I simply must get away from here at once—or go crazy! And I'm going on the nine-forty tonight. (*She turns to* MARSDEN *with a quick smile*) You'll have to help me pack, Charlie! (*Thinking with weary relief*)

Now that's said . . . I'm going . . . never come back . . . oh, how I loathe this room! . . .

MARSDEN. (*thinking with alarm*)

What's this? . . . going? . . . going to whom? . . .

PROFESSOR LEEDS. (*thinking—terrified*)

Going? . . . never come back to me? . . . no! . . .

(*Desperately putting on his prim severe manner toward an unruly pupil*) This is rather a sudden decision, isn't it? You haven't mentioned before that you were considering—in fact, you've led me to believe that you were quite contented here—that is, of course I mean for the time being, and I really think—

MARSDEN. (*looking at* NINA—*thinking with alarm*)

Going away to whom? . . .

(*Then watching the* PROFESSOR *with a pitying shudder*)

He's on the wrong tack with his professor's manner . . . her eyes seeing cruelly through him . . . with what terrible recognition! . . . God, never bless me with children! . . .

NINA. (*thinking with weary scorn*)

The Professor of Dead Languages is talking again . . . a dead man lectures on the past of living . . . since I was born I have been in his class, loving-attentive, pupil-daughter Nina . . . my ears numb with spiritless messages from the dead . . . dead words droning on . . . listening because he is my cultured father . . . a little more inclined to deafness than the rest (let me be just) because he is my father . . . father? . . . what is father? . . .

PROFESSOR LEEDS. (*thinking—terrified*)

I must talk her out of it! . . . find the right words! . . . oh, I know she won't hear me! . . . oh, wife, why did you die, you would have talked to her, she would have listened to you! . . .

(*Continuing in his professor's superior manner*) —and I really think, in justice to yourself above all, you ought to consider this step with great care before you definitely commit yourself. First and foremost, there is your health to be taken into consideration. You've been very ill, Nina, how perilously so perhaps you're not completely aware, but I assure you, and Charlie can corroborate my statement, that six months ago the doctors thought it might be years before—and yet, by staying home and resting and finding healthy outdoor recreation among your old friends, and keeping your mind occupied with the routine of managing the household— (*He forces a prim playful smile*) and managing me, I might add!—you have wonderfully improved and I think it most ill-advised in the hottest part of August, while you're really still a convalescent—

NINA. (*thinking*)

Talking! . . . his voice like a fatiguing dying tune droned on a beggar's organ . . . his words arising from the tomb of a soul in puffs of ashes . . .

(*Torturedly*)

Ashes! . . . oh, Gordon, my dear one! . . . oh, lips on my lips, oh, strong arms around me, oh, spirit so brave and generous and gay! . . . ashes dissolving into mud! . . . mud and ashes! . . . that's all! . . . gone! . . . gone forever from me! . . .

PROFESSOR LEEDS. (*thinking angrily*)

Her eyes . . . I know that look . . . tender, loving . . . not for me . . . damn Gordon! . . . I'm glad he's dead! . . .

(*A touch of asperity in his voice*) And at a couple of hours' notice to leave everything in the air, as it were— (*Then judicially*) No, Nina, frankly, I can't see it. You know I'd gladly consent to anything in the world to benefit you, but—surely, you can't have reflected!

NINA. (*thinking torturedly*)

Gordon darling, I must go away where I can think of you in silence! . . .

(*She turns on her father, her voice trembling with the effort to keep it in control—icily*) It's no use talking, Father. I *have* reflected and I am going!

PROFESSOR LEEDS. (*with asperity*) But I tell you it's quite impossible! I don't like to bring up the money consideration but I couldn't possibly afford— And how will you support yourself, if I may ask? Two years in the University, I am sorry to say, won't be much use to you when applying for a job. And even if you had completely recovered from your nervous breakdown, which it's obvious to anyone you haven't, then I most decidedly think you should finish out your science course and take your degree before you attempt— (*Thinking desperately*)

No use! . . . she doesn't hear . . . thinking of Gordon . . . she'll defy me . . .

NINA. (*thinking desperately*)

I must keep calm . . . I mustn't let go or I'll tell him everything . . . and I mustn't tell him . . . he's my father . . .

(*With the same cold calculating finality*) I've already had six months' training for a nurse. I will finish my training. There's a doctor I know at a sanitarium for crippled soldiers—a friend of Gordon's. I wrote to him and he answered that he'll gladly arrange it.

PROFESSOR LEEDS. (*thinking furiously*)

Gordon's friend . . . Gordon again! . . .

(*Severely*) You seriously mean to tell me you, in your condition, want to nurse in a soldiers' hospital! Absurd!

MARSDEN (*thinking with indignant revulsion*)

Quite right, Professor! . . . her beauty . . . all those men . . . in their beds . . . it's too revolting! . . .

(*With a persuasive quizzing tone*) Yes, I must say I can't see you as a peace-time Florence Nightingale, Nina!

NINA. (*coolly, struggling to keep control, ignoring these remarks*) So you see, Father, I've thought of everything and there's not the slightest reason to worry about me. And I've been teaching Mary how to take care of you. So you won't need me at all. You can go along as if nothing had happened—and really, nothing will have happened that hasn't already happened.

PROFESSOR LEEDS. Why, even the manner in which you address me—the tone you take—proves conclusively that you're not yourself!

NINA. (*her voice becoming a bit uncanny, her thoughts breaking through*) No, I'm not myself yet. That's just it. Not all myself. But I've been becoming myself. And I must finish!

PROFESSOR LEEDS. (*with angry significance—to* MARSDEN) You hear her, Charlie? She's a sick girl!

NINA. (*slowly and strangely*) I'm not sick. I'm too well. But they are sick and I must give my health to help them to live on, and to live on myself. (*With a sudden intensity in her tone*) I must pay for my cowardly treachery to Gordon! You should understand this, Father, you who— (*She swallows hard, catching her breath*) (*Thinking desperately*)

I'm beginning to tell him! . . . I mustn't! . . . he's my father! . . .

PROFESSOR LEEDS. (*in a panic of guilty fear, but defiantly*) What do you mean? I am afraid you're not responsible for what you're saying.

NINA. (*again with the strange intensity*) I must pay! It's my plain duty! Gordon is dead! What use is my life to me or anyone? But I must make it of use—by giving it! (*Fiercely*) I must learn to give myself, do you hear—give and give until I can make that gift of myself for a man's happiness without scruple, without fear, without joy except in his joy! When I've accomplished this I'll have found myself, I'll know how to start in living my own life again! (*Appealing to them with a desperate impatience*) Don't you see? In the name of the commonest decency and honor, I owe it to Gordon!

PROFESSOR LEEDS. (*sharply*) No, I can't see—nor anyone else! (*Thinking savagely*)

I hope Gordon is in hell! . . .

MARSDEN. (*thinking*)

Give herself? . . . can she mean her body? . . . beautiful body . . . to cripples? . . . for Gordon's sake? . . . damn Gordon! . . .

(*Coldly*) What do you mean, you owe it to Gordon, Nina?

PROFESSOR LEEDS. (*bitterly*) Yes, how ridiculous! It seems to me when you gave him your love, he got more than he could ever have hoped—

NINA. (*with fierce self-contempt*) I gave him? What did I give him? It's what I didn't give! That last night before he sailed—in his arms until my body ached—kisses until my lips were numb—knowing all that night—something in me knowing he would die, that he would never kiss me again—knowing this so surely yet with my cowardly brain lying, no, he'll come back and marry you, you'll be happy ever after and feel his children at your breast looking up with eyes so much like his, possessing eyes so happy in possessing you! (*Then violently*) But Gordon never possessed me! I'm still Gordon's silly virgin! And Gordon is muddy ashes! And I've lost my happiness forever! All that last night I knew he wanted me. I knew it was only the honorable code-bound Gordon, who kept commanding from his brain, no, you mustn't, you must respect her, you must wait till you have a marriage license! (*She gives a mocking laugh.*)

PROFESSOR LEEDS. (*shocked*) Nina! This is really going too far!

MARSDEN. (*repelled—with a superior sneer*) Oh, come now, Nina! You've been reading books. Those don't sound like your thoughts.

NINA. (*without looking at him, her eyes on her father's—intensely*) Gordon wanted me! I wanted Gordon! I should have made him take me! I knew he would die and I would have no children, that there would be no big Gordon or little Gordon left to me, that happiness was calling me, never to call again if I refused! And yet I did refuse! I didn't make him take me! I lost him forever! And now I am lonely and not pregnant with anything at all, but—but loathing! (*She hurls this last at her father—fiercely*) Why did I refuse? What was that cowardly something in me that cried, no, you mustn't, what would your father say?

PROFESSOR LEEDS. (*thinking—furiously*)

What an animal! . . . and my daughter! . . . she doesn't get it from me! . . . was her mother like that? . . .

(*Distractedly*) Nina! I really can't listen!

NINA. (*savagely*) And that's exactly what my father did say! Wait, he told Gordon! Wait for Nina till the war's over, and you've got a good job and can afford a marriage license!

PROFESSOR LEEDS. (*crumbling pitifully*) Nina! I—!

MARSDEN. (*flurriedly—going to him*) Don't take her seriously, Professor! (*Thinking with nervous repulsion*)

> Nina has changed . . . all flesh now . . . lust . . . who would dream she was so sensual? . . . I wish I were out of this! . . . I wish I hadn't come here today! . . .

NINA. (*coldly and deliberately*) Don't lie any more, Father! To-day I've made up my mind to face things. I know now why Gordon suddenly dropped all idea of marriage before he left, how unfair to me he suddenly decided it would be! Unfair to me! Oh, that's humorous! To think I might have had happiness, Gordon, and now Gordon's child— (*Then directly accusing him*) You told him it'd be unfair, you put him on his honor, didn't you?

PROFESSOR LEEDS. (*collecting himself—woodenly*) Yes. I did it for your sake, Nina.

NINA. (*in the same voice as before*) It's too late for lies!

PROFESSOR LEEDS. (*woodenly*) Let us say then that I *persuaded* my-self it was for your sake. That may be true. You are young. You think one can live with truth. Very well. It is also true I was jealous of Gordon. I was alone and I wanted to keep your love. I hated him as one hates a thief one may not accuse nor punish. I did my best to prevent your marriage. I was glad when he died. There. Is that what you wish me to say?

NINA. Yes. Now I begin to forget I've hated you. You were braver than I, at least.

PROFESSOR LEEDS. I wanted to live comforted by your love until the end. In short, I am a man who happens to be your father. (*He hides his face in his hands and weeps softly*) Forgive that man!

MARSDEN. (*thinking timidly*)

In short, forgive us our possessing as we forgive those who possessed before us . . . Mother must be wondering what keeps me so long . . . it's time for tea . . . I must go home . . .

NINA. (*sadly*) Oh, I forgive you. But do you understand now that I must somehow find a way to give myself to Gordon still, that I must pay my debt and learn to forgive myself?

PROFESSOR LEEDS. Yes.

NINA. Mary will look after you.

PROFESSOR LEEDS. Mary will do very well, I'm sure.

MARSDEN. (*thinking*)

Nina has changed . . . this is no place for me . . . Mother is waiting tea. . . .

(*Then venturing on an uncertain tone of pleasantry*) Quite so, you two. But isn't this all nonsense? Nina will be back with us in a month, Professor, what with the depressing heat and humidity, and the more depressing halt and the lame!

PROFESSOR LEEDS. (*sharply*) She must stay away until she gets well. This time I do speak for her sake.

NINA. I'll take the nine-forty. (*Turning to* MARSDEN—*with a sudden girlishness*) Come on upstairs, Charlie, and help me pack! (*She grabs him by the hand and starts to pull him away.*)

MARSDEN. (*shrugging his shoulders—confusedly*) Well—I don't understand this!

NINA. (*with a strange smile*) But some day I'll read it all in one of your books, Charlie, and it'll be so simple and easy to understand that I won't be able to recognize it, Charlie, let alone understand it! (*She laughs teasingly*) Dear old Charlie!

MARSDEN. (*thinking in agony*)

God damn in hell . . . dear old Charlie! . . .

(*Then with a genial grin*) I'll have to propose, Nina, if you continue to be my severest critic! I'm a stickler for these little literary conventions, you know!

NINA. All right. Propose while we pack. (*She leads him off, right.*)

PROFESSOR LEEDS. (*blows his nose, wipes his eyes, sighs, clears his throat, squares his shoulders, pulls his coat down in front, sets his tie straight, and starts to take a brisk turn about the room. His face is washed blandly clean of all emotion*)

Three weeks now . . . new term . . . I will have to be looking over my notes. . . .

(*He looks out of window, front*)

Grass parched in the middle . . . Tom forgotten the sprinkler . . . careless . . . ah, there goes Mr. Davis of the bank . . . bank . . . my salary will go farther now . . . books I really need . . . all bosh two can live as cheaply as one . . . there are worse things than being a trained nurse . . . good background of discipline . . . she needs it . . . she may meet rich fellow there . . . mature . . . only students here for her . . . and their fathers never approve if they have anything. . . .

(*He sits down with a forced sigh of peace*)

I am glad we had it out . . . his ghost will be gone now . . . no more Gordon, Gordon, Gordon, love and praise and tears, all for Gordon! . . . Mary will do very well by me . . . I will have more leisure and peace of mind . . . and Nina will come back home . . . when she is well again . . . the old Nina! . . . my little Nina! . . . she knows and she forgave me . . . she said so . . . said! . . . but could she really? . . . don't you imagine? . . . deep in her heart? . . . She still must hate? . . . oh, God! . . . I feel cold . . . alone! . . . this home is abandoned! . . . the house is empty and full of death! . . . there is a pain about my heart! . . .

(*He calls hoarsely, getting to his feet*) Nina!

NINA'S VOICE. (*her voice, fresh and girlish, calls from upstairs*) Yes, Father. Do you want me?

PROFESSOR LEEDS. (*struggling with himself—goes to door and calls with affectionate blandness*) No. Never mind. Just wanted to remind you to call for a taxi in good time.

NINA'S VOICE. I won't forget.

PROFESSOR LEEDS. (*looks at his watch*)

Five-thirty just . . . nine-forty, the train . . . then . . . Nina no more! . . . four hours more . . . she'll be packing . . . then good-bye . . . a kiss . . . nothing more ever to say to each other . . . and I'll die in here some day . . . alone . . . gasp, cry out for help . . . the president will speak at the funeral . . . Nina will be here again . . . Nina in black . . . too late! . . .

(*He calls hoarsely*) Nina! (*There is no answer*)

In other room . . . doesn't hear . . . just as well . . .

(*He turns to the bookcase and pulls out the first volume his hands come on and opens it at random and begins to read aloud sonorously like a child whistling to keep up his courage in the dark*)

"Stetit unus in arcem
Erectus capitis victorque ad sidera mittit
Sidereos oculos propiusque adspectat Olympum
Inquiritque Iovem;" . . .

CURTAIN

ACT TWO

SCENE: *The same as Scene One,* PROFESSOR LEEDS' *study. It is about nine o'clock of a night in early fall, over a year later. The appearance of the room is unchanged except that all the shades, of the color of pale flesh, are drawn down, giving the windows a suggestion of lifeless closed eyes and making the room seem more withdrawn from life than before. The reading lamp on the table is lit. Everything on the table, papers, pencils, pens, etc., is arranged in meticulous order.*

MARSDEN *is seated on the chair at center. He is dressed carefully in an English made suit of blue serge so dark as to seem black, and which, combined with the gloomy brooding expression of his face, strongly suggests one in mourning. His tall, thin body sags wearily in the chair, his head is sunk forward, the chin almost touching his chest, his eyes stare sadly at nothing.*

MARSDEN. (*his thoughts at ebb, without emphasis, sluggish and melancholy*)

Prophetic Professor! . . . I remember he once said . . . shortly after Nina went away . . . "some day, in here, . . . you'll find me" . . . did he foresee? . . . no . . . everything in life is so contemptuously accidental! . . . God's sneer at our self-importance! . . .

(*Smiling grimly*)

Poor Professor! he was horribly lonely . . . tried to hide it . . . always telling you how beneficial the training at the hospital would be for her . . . poor old chap! . . .

(*His voice grows husky and uncertain—he controls it—straightens himself*)

What time is it? . . .

(*He takes out his watch mechanically and looks at it*)

Ten after nine. . . . Nina ought to be here. . . .

(*Then with sudden bitterness*)

Will she feel any real grief over his death, I wonder? . . . I doubt it! . . . but why am I so resentful? . . . the two times I've visited the hospital she's been pleasant enough . . . pleasantly evasive! . . . perhaps she thought her father had sent me to spy on her . . . poor Professor! . . . at least she answered his letters . . . he used to show them to me . . . pathetically overjoyed . . . newsy, loveless scripts, telling nothing whatever about herself . . . well, she won't have to compose them any more . . . she never answered mine . . . she might at least have acknowledged them . . . Mother thinks she's behaved quite inexcusably . . .

(*Then jealously*)

I suppose every single damned inmate has fallen in love with her! . . . her eyes seemed cynical . . . sick with men . . . as though I'd looked into the eyes of a prostitute . . . not that I ever have . . . except that once . . . the dollar house . . . hers were like patent leather buttons in a saucer of blue milk! . . .

(*Getting up with a movement of impatience*)

The devil! . . . what beastly incidents our memories insist on cherishing! . . . the ugly and disgusting . . . the beautiful things we have to keep diaries to remember! . . .

(*He smiles with a wry amusement for a second—then bitterly*)

That last night Nina was here . . . she talked so brazenly about giving herself . . . I wish I knew the truth of what she's been doing in that house full of men . . . particularly that self-important young ass of a doctor! . . . Gordon's friend! . . .

(*He frowns at himself, determinedly puts an end to his train of thought and comes and sits down again in the chair—in sneering, conversational tones as if he were this time actually addressing another person*)

Really, it's hardly a decent time, is it, for that kind of speculation . . . with her father lying dead upstairs? . . .

(*A silence as if he had respectably squelched himself—then he pulls out his watch mechanically and stares at it. As he does so a noise of a car is heard approaching, stopping at the curb beyond the garden. He jumps to his feet and starts to go to door—then hesitates confusedly)*

No, let Mary go . . . I wouldn't know what to do . . . take her in my arms? . . . kiss her? . . . right now? . . . or wait until she? . . .

(*A bell rings insistently from the back of the house. From the front voices are heard, first* NINA'S, *then a man's.* MARSDEN *starts, his face suddenly angry and dejected*)

Someone with her! . . . a man! . . . I thought she'd be alone! . . .

(MARY *is heard shuffling to the front door which is opened. Immediately, as* MARY *sees* NINA, *she breaks down and there is the sound of her uncontrolled sobbing and choking, incoherent words drowning out* NINA'S *voice, soothing her.*)

NINA. (*as* MARY'S *grief subsides a trifle, her voice is heard, flat and toneless*) Isn't Mr. Marsden here, Mary? (*She calls*) Charlie!

MARSDEN. (*confused—huskily*) In here—I'm in the study, Nina. (*He moves uncertainly toward the door.*)

NINA. (*comes in and stands just inside the doorway. She is dressed in a nurse's uniform with cap, a raglan coat over it. She appears older than in the previous scene, her face is pale and much thinner, her cheek bones stand out, her mouth is taut in hard lines of a cynical scorn. Her eyes try to armor her wounded spirit with a defensive stare of disillusionment. Her training has also tended to coarsen her fiber a trifle, to make her insensitive to suffering, to give her the nurse's professionally callous attitude. In her fight to regain control of her nerves she has over-striven after the cool and efficient poise, but she is really in a more highly strung, disorganized state than ever, although she is now more capable of suppressing and concealing it. She remains strikingly handsome and her physical appeal is enhanced by her pallor and the mysterious suggestion about her of hidden experience. She stares at* MARSDEN *blankly and speaks in queer flat tones*) Hello, Charlie. He's dead, Mary says.

MARSDEN. (*nodding his head several times—stupidly*) Yes.

NINA. (*in same tones*) It's too bad. I brought Doctor Darrell. I thought there might be a chance. (*She pauses and looks about the room—thinking confusedly*)

His books . . . his chair . . . he always sat there . . . there's his table . . . little Nina was never allowed to touch anything . . . she used to sit on his lap . . . cuddle against him . . . dreaming into the dark beyond the windows . . . warm in his arms before the fireplace . . . dreams like sparks soaring up to die in the cold dark . . . warm in his love, safe-drifting into sleep . . . "Daddy's girl, aren't you?" . . .

(*She looks around and then up and down*)

His home . . . my home . . . he was my father . . . he's dead . . .

(*She shakes her head*)

Yes, I hear you, little Nina, but I don't understand one word of it. . . .

(*She smiles with a cynical self-contempt*)

I'm sorry, Father! . . . you see you've been dead for me a long time . . . when Gordon died, all men died . . . what did you feel for me then? . . . nothing . . . and now I feel nothing . . . it's too bad . . .

MARSDEN. (*thinking woundedly*)

I hoped she would throw herself in my arms . . . weeping . . . hide her face on my shoulder . . . "Oh, Charlie, you're all I've got left in the world . . ."

(*Then angrily*)

Why did she have to bring that Darrell with her?

NINA. (*flatly*) When I said good-bye that night I had a premonition I'd never see him again.

MARSDEN. (*glad of this opening for moral indignation*) You've never tried to see him, Nina! (*Then overcome by disgust with himself—contritely*) Forgive me! It was rotten of me to say that!

NINA. (*shaking her head—flatly*) I didn't want him to see what he would have thought was me. (*Ironically*) That's the other side of it you couldn't dissect into words from here, Charlie! (*Then suddenly asking a necessary question in her nurse's cool, efficient tones*) Is he upstairs? (*Marsden nods stupidly*) I'll take Ned up. I might as well. (*She turns and walks out briskly*).

MARSDEN. (*staring after her—dully*)

That isn't Nina. . . .

(*Indignantly*)

They've killed her soul down there! . . .

(*Tears come to his eyes suddenly and he pulls out his handkerchief and wipes them, muttering huskily*)

Poor old Professor! . . .

(*Then suddenly jeering at himself*)

For God's sake, stop acting! . . . it isn't the Professor! . . . dear old Charlie is crying because she didn't weep on his shoulder . . . as he had hoped! . . .

(*He laughs harshly—then suddenly sees a man outside the doorway and stares—then calls sharply*) Who's that?

EVANS. (*his voice embarrassed and hesitating comes from the hall*) It's all right. (*He appears in the doorway, grinning bashfully*) It's me—I, I mean—Miss Leeds told me to come in here. (*He stretches out his hand awkwardly*) Guess you don't remember me, Mr. Marsden. Miss Leeds introduced us one day at the hospital. You were leaving just as I came in. Evans is my name.

MARSDEN. (*who has been regarding him with waning resentment, forces a cordial smile and shakes hands*) Oh, yes. At first I couldn't place you.

EVANS. (*awkwardly*) I sort of feel I'm butting in.

MARSDEN. (*beginning to be taken by his likable boyish quality*) Not at all. Sit down. (*He sits in the rocker at center as* EVANS *goes to the bench at right.* EVANS *sits uncomfortably hunched forward, twiddling his hat in his hands. He is above the medium height, very blond, with guileless, diffident blue eyes, his figure inclined to immature lumbering outlines. His face is fresh and red-cheeked, handsome in a boyish fashion. His manner is bashful with women or older men, coltishly playful with his friends. There is a lack of self-confidence, a lost and strayed appealing air about him, yet with a hint of some unawakened obstinate force beneath his apparent weakness. Although he is twenty-five and has been out of college three years, he still wears the latest in collegiate clothes and as he looks younger than he is, he is always mistaken for an undergraduate and likes to be. It keeps him placed in life for himself.*)

MARSDEN. (*studying him keenly—amused*)

This is certainly no giant intellect . . . overgrown boy . . . likable quality though . . .

EVANS. (*uneasy under* MARSDEN's *eyes*)

Giving me the once-over . . . seems like good egg . . . Nina says he is . . . suppose I ought to say something about his books, but I can't even remember a title of one . . .

(*He suddenly blurts out*) You've known Nina—Miss Leeds—ever since she was a kid, haven't you?

MARSDEN. (*a bit shortly*) Yes. How long have you known her?

EVANS. Well—really only since she's been at the hospital, although I met her once years ago at a Prom with Gordon Shaw.

MARSDEN. (*indifferently*) Oh, you knew Gordon?

EVANS. (*proudly*) Sure thing! I was in his class! (*With admiration amounting to hero-worship*) He sure was a wonder, wasn't he?

MARSDEN. (*cynically*)

Gordon über alles and forever! . . . I begin to appreciate the Professor's viewpoint . . .

(*Casually*) A fine boy! Did you know him well?

EVANS. No. The crowd he went with were mostly fellows who were good at sports—and I always was a dud. (*Forcing a smile*) I was always one of the first to get bounced off the squad in any sport. (*Then with a flash of humble pride*) But I never quit trying, anyway!

MARSDEN. (*consolingly*) Well, the sport hero usually doesn't star after college.

EVANS. Gordon did! (*Eagerly—with intense admiration*) In the war! He was an ace! And he always fought just as cleanly as he'd played football! Even the Huns respected him!

MARSDEN. (*thinking cynically*)

This Gordon worshipper must be the apple of Nina's eye!

(*Casually*) Were you in the army?

EVANS. (*shamefacedly*) Yes—infantry—but I never got to the front—never saw anything exciting. (*Thinking glumly*)

Won't tell him I tried for flying service . . . wanted to get in Gordon's outfit . . . couldn't make the physical exam. . . . never made anything I wanted . . . suppose I'll lose out with Nina, too . . .

(*Then rallying himself*)

Hey, you! . . . what's the matter with you? . . . don't quit! . . .

MARSDEN. (*who has been staring at him inquisitively*) How did you happen to come out here tonight?

EVANS. I was calling on Nina when your wire came. Ned thought I better come along, too—might be of some use.

MARSDEN. (*frowning*) You mean Doctor Darrell? (EVANS *nods*) Is he a close friend of yours?

EVANS. (*hesitatingly*) Well, sort of. Roomed in the same dorm with me at college. He was a senior when I was a freshman. Used to help me along in lots of ways. Took pity on me, I was so green. Then about a year ago when I went to the hospital to visit a fellow who'd been in my outfit I ran into him again. (*Then with a grin*) But I wouldn't say Ned was close to anyone. He's a dyed-in-the-wool doc. He's only close to whatever's the matter with you! (*He chuckles—then hastily*) But don't get me wrong about him. He's the best egg ever! You know him, don't you?

MARSDEN. (*stiffly*) Barely. Nina introduced us once. (*Thinking bitterly*)

He's upstairs alone with her . . . I hoped it would be I who . . .

EVANS.

Don't want him to get the wrong idea of Ned . . . Ned's my best friend . . . doing all he can to help me with Nina . . . he thinks she'll marry me in the end . . . God, if she only would! . . . I wouldn't expect her to love me at first . . . be happy only to take care of her . . . cook her breakfast . . . bring it up to her in bed . . . tuck the pillows behind her . . . comb her hair for her . . . I'd be happy just to kiss her hair! . . .

MARSDEN. (*agitated—thinking suspiciously*)

What are Darrell's relations with Nina? . . . close to what's the matter with her? . . . damned thoughts! . . . why should I care? . . . I'll ask this Evans . . . pump him while I have a chance . . .

(*With forced indifference*) Is your friend, the Doctor, "close" to Miss Leeds? She's had quite a lot the matter with her since her breakdown, if that's what interests him! (*He smiles casually.*)

EVANS. (*gives a start, awakening from his dream*) Oh—er—yes. He's always trying to bully her into taking better care of herself. but she only laughs at him. (*Soberly*) It'd be much better if she'd take his advice.

MARSDEN. (*suspiciously*) No doubt.

EVANS. (*pronounces with boyish solemnity*) She isn't herself, Mr. Marsden. And I think nursing all those poor guys keeps the war before her when she ought to forget it. She ought to give up nursing and be nursed for a change, that's my idea.

MARSDEN. (*struck by this—eagerly*) Exactly my opinion. (*Thinking*)

If she'd settle down here . . . I could come over every day . . . I'd nurse her . . . Mother home . . . Nina here . . . how I could work then! . . .

EVANS. (*thinking*)

He certainly seems all for me . . . so far! . . .

(*Then in a sudden flurry*)

Shall I tell him? . . . he'll be like her guardian now . . . I've got to know how he stands . . .

(*He starts with a solemn earnestness*) Mr. Marsden, I—there's something I ought to tell you, I think. You see, Nina's talked a lot about you. I know how much she thinks of you. And now her old man—(*He hesitates in confusion*) I mean, her father's dead—

MARSDEN (*in a sort of panic—thinking*)

What's this? . . . proposal? . . . in form? . . . for her hand? . . . to me? . . . Father Charlie now, eh? . . . ha! . . . God what a fool! . . . does he imagine she'd ever love him? . . . but she might . . . not bad looking . . . likable, innocent . . . something to mother . . .

EVANS. (*blundering on regardless now*) I know it's hardly the proper time—

MARSDEN. (*interrupting—dryly*) Perhaps I can anticipate. You want to tell me you're in love with Nina?

EVANS. Yes, sir, and I've asked her to marry me.

MARSDEN. What did she say?

EVANS. (*sheepishly*) Nothing. She just smiled.

MARSDEN. (*with relief*) Ah. (*Then harshly*) Well, what could you expect? Surely you must know she still loves Gordon?

EVANS. (*manfully*) Sure I know it—and I admire her for it! Most girls forget too easily. She ought to love Gordon for a long time yet. And I know I'm an awful wash-out compared to him—but I love her as much as he did, or anyone could! And I'll work my way up for her—I know I can!—so I can give her everything she wants. And I wouldn't ask for anything in return except the right to take care of her. (*Blurts out confusedly*) I never think of her—that way—she's too beautiful and wonderful—not that I don't hope she'd come to love me in time—

MARSDEN. (*sharply*) And just what do you expect me to do about all this?

EVANS. (*taken aback*) Why—er—nothing, sir. I just thought you ought to know. (*Sheepishly he glances up at ceiling, then down at floor, twiddling his hat.*)

MARSDEN. (*thinking—at first with a grudging appreciation and envy*)

He thinks he means that . . . pure love! . . . it's easy to talk . . . he doesn't know life . . . but he might be good for Nina . . . if she were married to this simpleton would she be faithful? . . . and then I? . . . what a vile thought! . . . I don't mean that! . . .

(*Then forcing a kindly tone*) You see, there's really nothing I can do about it. (*With a smile*) If Nina will, she will—and if she won't, she won't. But I can wish you good luck.

EVANS. (*immediately all boyish gratitude*) Thanks! That's darn fine of you, Mr. Marsden!

MARSDEN. But I think we'd better let the subject drop, don't you? We're forgetting that her father—

EVANS. (*guiltily embarrassed*) Yes—sure—I'm a damn fool! Excuse me! (*There is the noise of steps from the hall and* DOCTOR EDMUND DARRELL *enters. He is twenty-seven, short, dark, wiry, his movements rapid and sure, his manner cool and observant, his dark eyes analytical. His head is handsome and intelligent. There is a quality about him, provoking and disturbing to women, of intense passion which he has rigidly trained himself to control and set free only for the objective satisfaction of studying his own and their reactions; and so he has come to consider himself as immune to love through his scientific understanding of its real sexual nature. He sees* EVANS *and* MARSDEN, *nods at* MARSDEN *silently, who returns it coldly, goes to the table and taking a prescription pad from his pocket, hastily scratches on it.*)

MARSDEN. (*thinking sneeringly*)

Amusing, these young doctors! . . . perspire with the effort to appear cool! . . . writing a prescription . . . cough medicine for the corpse, perhaps! . . . good-looking? . . . more or less . . . attractive to women, I dare say. . . .

DARRELL. (*tears it off—hands it to* EVANS) Here, Sam. Run along up the street and get this filled.

EVANS. (*with relief*) Sure. Glad of the chance for a walk. (*He goes out, rear*).

DARRELL. (*turning to* MARSDEN) It's for Nina. She's got to get some sleep tonight. (*He sits down abruptly in the chair at center,* MARSDEN *unconsciously takes the* PROFESSOR's *place behind the table. The two men stare at each other for a moment,* DARRELL *with a frank probing, examining look that ruffles* MARSDEN *and makes him all the more resentful toward him*)

> This Marsden doesn't like me . . . that's evident . . . but he interests me . . . read his books . . . wanted to know his bearing on Nina's case . . . his novels just well-written surface . . . no depth, no digging underneath . . . why? . . . has the talent but doesn't dare . . . afraid he'll meet himself somewhere . . . one of those poor devils who spend their lives trying not to discover which sex they belong to! . . .

MARSDEN.

> Giving me the fishy, diagnosing eye they practice at medical school . . . like freshmen from Ioway cultivating broad A's at Harvard! . . . what is his specialty? . . . neurologist, I think . . . I hope not psychoanalyst . . . a lot to account for, Herr Freud! . . . punishment to fit his crimes, be forced to listen eternally during breakfast while innumerable plain ones tell him dreams about snakes . . . pah, what an easy cure-all! . . . sex the philosopher's stone . . . "O Oedipus, O my king! The world is adopting you!" . . .

DARRELL.

> Must pitch into him about Nina . . . have to have his help . . . damn little time to convince him . . . he's the kind you have to explode a bomb under to get them to move . . . but not too big a bomb . . . they blow to pieces easily . . .

(*Brusquely*) Nina's gone to pot again! Not that her father's death is a shock in the usual sense of grief. I wish to God it were! No, it's a shock because it's finally convinced her she can't feel anything any more. That's what she's doing upstairs now—trying to goad herself into feeling something!

MARSDEN. (*resentfully*) I think you're mistaken. She loved her father—

DARRELL. (*shortly and dryly*) We can't waste time being sentimental, Marsden! She'll be down any minute, and I've got a lot to talk over with you. (*As* MARSDEN *seems again about to protest*) Nina has a real affection for you and I imagine you have for her. Then you'll want as much as I do to get her straightened out. She's a corking girl. She ought to have every chance for a happy life. (*Then sharply driving his words in*) But the way she's conditioned now, there's no chance. She's piled on too many destructive experiences. A few more and she'll dive for the gutter just to get the security that comes from knowing she's touched bottom and there's no farther to go!

MARSDEN. (*revolted and angry, half-springs to his feet*) Look here, Darrell, I'll be damned if I'll listen to such a ridiculous statement!

DARRELL. (*curtly—with authority*) How do you know it's ridiculous? What do you know of Nina since she left home? But she hadn't been nursing with us three days before I saw she really ought to be a patient; and ever since then I've studied her case. So I think it's up to you to listen.

MARSDEN. (*freezingly*) I'm listening. (*With apprehensive terror*)

> Gutter . . . has she . . . I wish he wouldn't tell me! . . .

DARRELL. (*thinking*)

> How much need I tell him? . . . can't tell him the raw truth about her promiscuity . . . he isn't built to face reality . . . no writer is outside of his books . . . have to tone it down for him . . . but not too much! . . .

Nina has been giving way more and more to a morbid longing for martyrdom. The reason for it is obvious. Gordon went away without —well, let's say marrying her. The war killed him. She was left suspended. Then she began to blame herself and to want to sacrifice herself and at the same time give happiness to various fellow war-victims by pretending to love them. It's a pretty idea but it hasn't worked out.

Nina's a bad actress. She hasn't convinced the men of her love—or herself of her good intentions. And each experience of this kind has only left her more a prey to a guilty conscience than before and more determined to punish herself!

MARSDEN. (*thinking*)

What does he mean? . . . how far did she? . . . how many? . . .

(*Coldly and sneeringly*) May I ask on what specific actions of hers this theory of yours is based?

DARRELL. (*coldly in turn*) On her evident craving to make an exhibition of kissing, necking, petting—whatever you call it—spooning in general—with any patient in the institution who got a case on her! (*Ironically—thinking*)

Spooning! . . . rather a mild word for her affairs . . . but strong enough for this ladylike soul. . . .

MARSDEN. (*bitterly*)

He's lying! . . . what's he trying to hide? . . . was he one of them? . . . her lover? . . . I must get her away from him . . . get her to marry Evans! . . .

(*With authority*) Then she mustn't go back to your hospital, that's certain!

DARRELL. (*quickly*) You're quite right. And that brings me to what I want you to urge her to do.

MARSDEN. (*thinking suspiciously*)

He doesn't want her back . . . I must have been wrong . . . but there might be many reasons why he'd wish to get rid of her . . .

(*Coldly*) I think you exaggerate my influence.

DARRELL. (*eagerly*) Not a bit. You're the last link connecting her with the girl she used to be before Gordon's death. You're closely associated in her mind with that period of happy security, of health and peace of mind. I know that from the way she talks about you. You're the only person she still respects—and really loves. (*As* MARSDEN *starts guiltily and glances at him in confusion—with a laugh*)

Oh, you needn't look frightened. I mean the sort of love she'd feel for an uncle.

MARSDEN. (*thinking in agony*)

Frightened? . . . was I? . . . only person she loves . . . and then he said "love she'd feel for an uncle" . . . Uncle Charlie now! . . . God damn him! . . .

DARRELL. (*eyeing him*)

Looks damnably upset . . . wants to evade all responsibility for her, I suppose . . . he's that kind . . . all the better! . . . he'll be only too anxious to get her safely married. . . .

(*Bluntly*) And that's why I've done all this talking. You've got to help snap her out of this.

MARSDEN. (*bitterly*) And how, if I may ask?

DARRELL. There's only one way I can see. Get her to marry Sam Evans.

MARSDEN. (*astonished*) Evans? (*He makes a silly gesture toward the door—thinking confusedly*)

Wrong again . . . why does he want her married to . . . it's some trick. . . .

DARRELL. Yes, Evans. He's in love with her. And it's one of those unselfish loves you read about. And she is fond of him. In a maternal way, of course—but that's just what she needs now, someone she cares about to mother and boss and keep her occupied. And still more important, this would give her a chance to have children. She's got to find normal outlets for her craving for sacrifice. She needs normal love objects for the emotional life Gordon's death blocked up in her. Now marrying Sam ought to do the trick. Ought to. Naturally, no one can say for certain. But I think his unselfish love, combined with her real liking for him, will gradually give her back a sense of security and a feeling of being worth something to life again, and once she's got that, she'll be saved! (*He has spoken with persuasive feeling. He asks anxiously*) Doesn't that seem good sense to you?

MARSDEN. (*suspicious—dryly non-committal*) I'm sorry but I'm in no position to say. I don't know anything about Evans, for one thing.

DARRELL. (*emphatically*) Well, I do. He's a fine healthy boy, clean and unspoiled. You can take my word for that. And I'm convinced he's got the right stuff in him to succeed, once he grows up and buckles down to work. He's only a big kid now, but all he needs is a little self-confidence and a sense of responsibility. He's holding down a fair job, too, considering he's just started in the advertising game—enough to keep them living. (*With a slight smile*) I'm prescribing for Sam, too, when I boost this wedding.

MARSDEN. (*his snobbery coming out*) Do you know his family—what sort of people?—

DARRELL. (*bitingly*) I'm not acquainted with their social qualifications, if that's what you mean! They're upstate country folks—fruit growers and farmers, well off, I believe. Simple, healthy people, I'm sure of that although I've never met them.

MARSDEN. (*a bit shamefacedly—changing the subject hastily*) Have you suggested this match to Nina?

DARRELL. Yes, a good many times lately in a half-joking way. If I were serious she wouldn't listen, she'd say I was prescribing. But I think what I've said has planted it in her mind as a possibility.

MARSDEN. (*thinking suspiciously*)

Is this Doctor her lover? . . . trying to pull the wool over my eyes? . . . use me to arrange a convenient triangle for him? . . .

(*Harshly—but trying to force a joking tone*) Do you know what I'm inclined to suspect, Doctor? That you may be in love with Nina yourself?

DARRELL. (*astonished*) The deuce you do! What in the devil makes you think that? Not that any man mightn't fall in love with Nina. Most of them do. But I didn't happen to. And what's more I never could. In my mind she always belongs to Gordon. It's probably a reflection of her own silly fixed idea about him. (*Suddenly, dryly and harshly*) And I couldn't share a woman—even with a ghost! (*Thinking cynically*)

Not to mention the living who have had her! . . . Sam doesn't know about them . . . and I'll bet he couldn't believe it of her even if she confessed! . . .

MARSDEN. (*thinking baffledly*)

Wrong again! . . . he isn't lying . . . but I feel he's hiding something . . . why does he speak so resentfully of Gordon's memory? . . . why do I sympathize? . . .

(*In a strange mocking ironic tone*) I can quite appreciate your feeling about Gordon. I wouldn't care to share with a ghost-lover myself. That species of dead is so invulnerably alive! Even a doctor couldn't kill one, eh? (*He forces a laugh—then in a friendly confidential tone*) Gordon is too egregious for a ghost. That was the way Nina's father felt about him, too. (*Suddenly reminded of the dead man—in penitently sad tones*) You didn't know her father, did you? A charming old fellow!

DARRELL. (*hearing a noise from the hall—warningly*) Sstt! (NINA *enters slowly. She looks from one to the other with a queer, quick, inquisitive stare, but her face is a pale expressionless mask drained of all emotional response to human contacts. It is as if her eyes were acting on their own account as restless, prying, recording instruments. The two men have risen and stare at her anxiously.* DARRELL *moves back and to one side until he is standing in relatively the same place as* MARSDEN *had occupied in the previous scene while* MARSDEN *is in her father's place and she stops where she had been. There is a pause. Then just as each of the men is about to speak, she answers as if they had asked a question.*)

NINA. (*in a queer flat voice*) Yes, he's dead—my father—whose passion created me—who began me—he is ended. There is only his end living—his death. It lives now to draw nearer me, to draw me nearer, to become my end! (*Then with a strange twisted smile*) How we poor monkeys hide from ourselves behind the sounds called words!

MARSDEN. (*thinking frightenedly*)

How terrible she is! . . . who is she? . . . not my Nina! . . .

(*As if to reassure himself—timidly*) Nina! (DARRELL *makes an impatient gesture for him to let her go on. What she is saying interests him and he feels talking it out will do her good. She looks at* MARSDEN *for a moment startledly as if she couldn't recognize him.*)

NINA. What? (*Then placing him—with real affection that is like a galling goad to him*) Dear old Charlie!

MARSDEN.

Dear damned Charlie! . . . She loves to torture! . . .

(*Then forcing a smile—soothingly*) Yes, Nina Cara Nina! Right here!

NINA. (*forcing a smile*) You look frightened, Charlie. Do I seem queer? It's because I've suddenly seen the lies in the sounds called words. You know—grief, sorrow, love, father—those sounds our lips make and our hands write. You ought to know what I mean. You work with them. Have you written another novel lately? But, stop to think, you're just the one who couldn't know what I mean. With you the lies have become the only truthful things. And I suppose that's the logical conclusion to the whole evasive mess, isn't it? Do you understand me, Charlie? Say lie— (*She says it, drawing it out*) L-i-i-e! Now say life. L-i-i-f-e! You see! Life is just a long drawn out lie with a sniffling sigh at the end! (*She laughs.*)

MARSDEN. (*in strange agony*)

She's hard! . . . like a whore! . . . tearing your heart with dirty finger nails! . . . my Nina! . . . cruel bitch! . . . some day I won't bear it! . . . I'll scream out the truth about every woman! no kinder at heart than dollar tarts! . . .

(*Then in a passion of remorse*)

Forgive me, Mother! . . . I didn't mean all! . . .

DARRELL. (*a bit worried himself now—persuasively*) Why not sit down, Nina, and let us two gentlemen sit down?

NINA. (*smiling at him swiftly and mechanically*) Oh, all right, Ned. (*She sits at center. He comes and sits on the bench.* MARSDEN *sits by the table. She continues sarcastically*) Are you prescribing for me again, Ned? This is my pet doctor, Charlie. He couldn't be happy in heaven unless God called him in because He'd caught something! Did you ever know a young scientist, Charlie? He believes if you pick a lie to pieces, the pieces are the truth! I like him because he's so inhuman. But once he kissed me—in a moment of carnal weakness! I was as startled as if a mummy had done it! And then he looked so disgusted with himself! I had to laugh! (*She smiles at him with a pitying scorn.*)

DARRELL. (*good-naturedly smiling*) That's right! Rub it in! (*Ruffled but amused in spite of it*)

I'd forgotten about that kiss . . . I was sore at myself afterwards . . . she was so damned indifferent! . . .

NINA. (*wanderingly*) Do you know what I was doing upstairs? I was trying to pray. I tried hard to pray to the modern science God. I thought of a million light years to a spiral nebula—one other universe among innumerable others. But how could that God care about our trifling misery of death-born-of-birth? I couldn't believe in Him, and I wouldn't if I could! I'd rather imitate His indifference and prove I had that one trait at least in common!

MARSDEN. (*worriedly*) Nina, why don't you lie down?

NINA. (*jeeringly*) Oh, let me talk, Charlie! They're only words, remember! So many many words have jammed up into thoughts in my poor head! You'd better let them overflow or they'll burst the dam! I wanted to believe in any God at any price—a heap of stones, a mud image, a drawing on a wall, a bird, a fish, a snake, a baboon—or even a good man preaching the simple platitudes of truth, those Gospel words we love the sound of but whose meaning we pass on to spooks to live by!

MARSDEN. (*again—half-rising—frightenedly*) Nina! You ought to stop talking. You'll work yourself into— (*He glances angrily at* DARRELL *as if demanding that, as a doctor, he do something.*)

NINA. (*with bitter hopelessness*) Oh, all right!

DARRELL. (*answering his look—thinking*)

You poor fool! . . . it'll do her good to talk this out of her system
. . . and then it'll be up to you to bring her around to Sam . . .

(*Starts toward the door*) Think I'll go out and stretch my legs.

MARSDEN. (*thinking—in a panic*)

I don't want to be alone with her! . . . I don't know her! . . .
I'm afraid! . . .

(*Protestingly*) Well—but—hold on—I'm sure Nina would rather—

NINA. (*dully*) Let him go. I've said everything I can ever say—to him. I want to talk to you, Charlie. (DARRELL *goes out noiselessly with a meaning look at* MARSDEN*—a pause.*)

MARSDEN. (*thinking tremblingly*)

Here . . . now . . . what I hoped . . . she and I alone . . . she
will cry . . . I will comfort her . . . why am I so afraid? . . .
whom do I fear? . . . is it she? . . . or I? . . .

NINA. (*suddenly, with pity yet with scorn*) Why have you always been so timid, Charlie? Why are you always afraid? What are you afraid of?

MARSDEN. (*thinking in a panic*)

She sneaked into my soul to spy! . . .

(*Then boldly*)

Well then, a little truth for once in a way! . . .

(*Timidly*) I'm afraid of—of life, Nina.

NINA. (*nodding slowly*) I know. (*After a pause—queerly*) The mistake began when God was created in a male image. Of course, women would see Him that way, but men should have been gentlemen enough, remembering their mothers, to make God a woman! But the God of Gods—the Boss—has always been a man. That makes life so perverted, and death so unnatural. We should have imagined life as created in the birth-pain of God the Mother. Then we would understand why we, Her children, have inherited pain, for we would know that our life's rhythm beats from Her great heart, torn with the agony of love and birth. And we would feel that death meant reunion with Her, a passing back into Her substance, blood of Her blood again, peace of Her peace! (MARSDEN *has been listening to her fascinatedly. She gives a strange little laugh*) Now wouldn't that be more logical and satisfying than having God a male whose chest thunders with egotism and is too hard for tired heads and thoroughly comfortless? Wouldn't it, Charlie?

MARSDEN. (*with a strange passionate eagerness*) Yes! It would, indeed! It would, Nina!

NINA. (*suddenly jumping to her feet and going to him—with a horrible moaning desolation*) Oh, God, Charlie, I want to believe in something! I want to believe so I can feel! I want to feel that he is dead—my father! And I can't feel anything, Charlie! I can't feel anything at all! (*She throws herself on her knees beside him and hides her face in her hands on his knees and begins to sob—stifled torn sounds.*)

MARSDEN. (*bends down, pats her head with trembling hands, soothes her with uncertain trembling words*) There—there—don't—Nina, please—don't cry—you'll make yourself sick—come now—get up—do! (*His hands grasping her arms he half-raises her to her feet, but, her face still hidden in her hands, sobbing, she slips on to his lap like a little girl and hides her face on his shoulder. His expression becomes transported with a great happiness—in an ecstatic whisper*)

As I dreamed . . . with a deeper sweetness! . . .

(*He kisses her hair with a great reverence*)

There . . . this is all my desire . . . I am this kind of lover . . . this is my love . . . she is my girl . . . not woman . . . my little girl . . . and I am brave because of her little girl's pure love . . . and I am proud . . . no more afraid . . . no more ashamed of being pure! . . .

(*He kisses her hair again tenderly and smiles at himself—then soothingly with a teasing incongruous gaiety*) This will never do, Nina Cara Nina—never, never do, you know—I can't permit it!

NINA. (*in a muffled voice, her sobbing beginning to ebb away into sighs—in a young girl's voice*) Oh, Charlie, you're so kind and comforting! I've wanted you so!

MARSDEN. (*immediately disturbed*)

Wanted? . . . wanted? . . . not that kind of wanted . . . can she mean? . . .

(*Questioning hesitatingly*) You've wanted me, Nina?

NINA. Yes,—awfully! I've been so homesick. I've wanted to run home and 'fess up, tell how bad I've been, and be punished! Oh, I've got to be punished, Charlie, out of mercy for me, so I can forgive myself! And now Father dead, there's only you. You will, won't you —or tell me how to punish myself? You've simply got to, if you love me!

MARSDEN. (*thinking intensely*)

If I love her! . . . oh, I do love her! . . .

(*Eagerly*) Anything you wish, Nina—anything!

NINA. (*with a comforted smile, closing her eyes and cuddling up against him*) I knew you would. Dear old Charlie! (*As he gives a wincing start*) What is it? (*She looks up into his face.*)

MARSDEN. (*forcing a smile—ironically*) Twinge—rheumatics—getting old, Nina. (*Thinking with wild agony*)

Dear old Charlie! . . . descended again into hell! . . .

(*Then in a flat voice*) What do you want to be punished for, Nina?

NINA. (*in a strange, far-away tone, looking up not at him but at the ceiling*) For playing the silly slut, Charlie. For giving my cool clean body to men with hot hands and greedy eyes which they called love! Ugh! (*A shiver runs over her body.*)

MARSDEN. (*thinking with sudden agony*)

Then she did! . . . the little filth! . . .

(*In his flat voice*) You mean you— (*Then pleadingly*) But not—Darrell?

NINA. (*with simple surprise*) Ned? No, how could I? The war hadn't maimed him. There would have been no point in that. But I did with others—oh, four or five or six or seven men, Charlie. I forget—and it doesn't matter. They were all the same. Count them all as one, and that one a ghost of nothing. That is, to me. They were important to themselves, if I remember rightly. But I forget.

MARSDEN. (*thinking in agony*)

But why? . . . the dirty little trollop! . . . why? . . .

(*In his flat voice*) Why did you do this, Nina?

NINA. (*with a sad little laugh*) God knows, Charlie! Perhaps I knew at the time but I've forgotten. It's all mixed up. There was a desire to be kind. But it's horribly hard to give anything, and frightful to receive! And to give love—oneself—not in this world! And men are difficult to please, Charlie. I seemed to feel Gordon standing against a wall with eyes bandaged and these men were a firing squad whose eyes were also bandaged—and only I could see! No, I was the blindest! I would not see! I knew it was a stupid, morbid business, that I was more maimed than they were, really, that the war had blown my heart and insides out! And I knew too that I was torturing these tortured men, morbidly super-sensitive already, that they loathed the cruel mockery of my gift! Yet I kept on, from one to one, like a stupid, driven animal until one night not long ago I had a dream of Gordon diving down out of the sky in flames and he looked at me with such sad burning eyes, and all my poor maimed men, too, seemed staring out of his eyes with a burning pain, and I woke up crying, my own eyes burning. Then I saw what a fool I'd been—a guilty fool! So be kind and punish me!

MARSDEN. (*thinking with bitter confusion*)

I wish she hadn't told me this . . . it has upset me terribly! . . . I positively must run home at once . . . Mother is waiting up . . . oh, how I'd love to hate this little whore! . . . then I could punish!

. . . I wish her father were alive . . . "now he's dead there's only you," she said . . . "I've wanted you," . . .

(*With intense bitterness*)

Dear old Father Charlie now! . . . ha! . . . that's how she wants me! . . .

(*Then suddenly in a matter-of-fact tone that is mockingly like her father's*) Then, under the circumstances, having weighed the pros and cons, so to speak, I should say that decidedly the most desirable course—

NINA. (*drowsily—her eyes shut*) You sound so like Father, Charlie.

MARSDEN. (*in the tone like her father's*) —is for you to marry that young Evans. He is a splendid chap, clean and boyish, with real stuff in him, too, to make a career for himself if he finds a help-meet who will inspire him to his best efforts and bring his latent ability to the surface.

NINA. (*drowsily*) Sam is a nice boy. Yes, it would be a career for me to bring a career to his surface. I would be busy—surface life—no more depths, please God! But I don't love him, Father.

MARSDEN. (*blandly—in the tone like her father's*) But you like him, Nina. And he loves you devotedly. And it's time you were having children—and when children come, love comes, you know.

NINA. (*drowsily*) I want children. I must become a mother so I can give myself. I am sick of sickness.

MARSDEN. (*briskly*) Then it's all settled?

NINA. (*drowsily*) Yes. (*Very sleepily*) Thank you, Father. You've been so kind. You've let me off too easily. I don't feel as if you'd punished me hardly at all. But I'll never, never do it again, I promise —never, never!— (*She falls asleep and gives a soft little snore.*)

MARSDEN. (*still in her father's tones—very paternally—looking down*) She's had a hard day of it, poor child! I'll carry her up to her room. (*He rises to his feet with* NINA *sleeping peacefully in his arms. At this moment* SAM EVANS *enters from the right with the package of medicine in his hand.*)

EVANS. (*grinning respectfully*) Here's the— (*As he sees* NINA) Oh! (*Then excitedly*) Did she faint?

MARSDEN. (*smiling kindly at* EVANS—*still in her father's tones*) Sssh! She's asleep. She cried and then she fell asleep—like a little girl. (*Then benignantly*) But first we spoke a word about you, Evans, and I'm sure you have every reason to hope.

EVANS. (*overcome, his eyes on his shuffling feet and twiddling cap*) Thanks—I—I really don't know how to thank—

MARSDEN. (*going to door—in his own voice now*) I've got to go home. My mother is waiting up for me. I'll just carry Nina upstairs and put her on her bed and throw something over her.

EVANS. Can't I help you, Mr. Marsden?

MARSDEN. (*dully*) No. I cannot help myself. (*As* EVANS *looks puzzled and startled he adds with an ironical, self-mocking geniality*) You'd better call me just Charlie after this. (*He smiles bitterly to himself as he goes out.*)

EVANS. (*looks after him for a moment—then cannot restrain a joyful, coltish caper—gleefully*) Good egg! Good old Charlie! (*As if he had heard or guessed,* MARSDEN'S *bitter laugh comes back from the end of the hallway.*)

CURTAIN

ACT THREE

SCENE: *Seven months or so later—the dining room of the* EVANS' *homestead in northern New York state—about nine o'clock in the morning of a day in late spring of the following year.*

The room is one of those big, misproportioned dining rooms that are found in the large, jigsaw country houses scattered around the country as a result of the rural taste for grandeur in the eighties. There is a cumbersome hanging lamp suspended from chains over the exact center of the ugly table with its set of straightbacked chairs set back at spaced intervals against the walls. The wall paper, a repulsive brown, is stained at the ceiling line with damp blotches of mildew, and here and there has started to peel back where the strips join. The floor is carpeted in a smeary brown with a dark red design blurred into it. In the left wall is one window with starched white curtains looking out on a covered side porch, so that no sunlight ever gets to this room and the light from the window, although it is a beautiful warm day in the flower garden beyond the porch, is cheerless and sickly. There is a door in the rear, to left of center, that leads to a hall opening on the same porch. To the right of door a heavy sideboard, a part of the set, displaying some "company" china and glassware. In the right wall, a door leading to the kitchen. NINA *is seated at the foot of the table, her back to the window, writing a letter. Her whole personality seems changed, her face has a contented expression, there is an inner calm about her. And her personal appearance has changed in kind, her face and figure have filled out, she is prettier in a conventional way and less striking and unusual; nothing remains of the strange fascination of her face except her unchangeably mysterious eyes.*

NINA. (*reading what she has just written over to herself*)

It's a queer house, Ned. There is something wrong with its psyche, I'm sure. Therefore you'd simply adore it. It's a hideous old place, a faded gingerbread with orange fixin's and numerous lightning rods. Around it are acres and acres of apple trees in full bloom, all white and pinkish and beautiful, like brides just tripping out of church with the bridegroom, Spring, by the arm.

Which reminds me, Ned, that it's over six months since Sam and I were married and we haven't seen hide nor hair of you since the ceremony. Do you think that is any nice way to act? You might at least drop me a line. But I'm only joking. I know how busy you must be now that you've got the chance you've always wanted to do research work. Did you get our joint letter of congratulation written after we read of your appointment?

But to get back to this house. I feel it has lost its soul and grown resigned to doing without it. It isn't haunted by anything at all—and ghosts of some sort are the only normal life a house has—like our minds, you know. So although last evening when we got here at first I said "obviously haunted" to myself, now that I've spent one night in it I know that whatever spooks there may once have been have packed up their manifestations a long time ago and drifted away over the grass, wisps of mist between the apple trees, without one backward glance of regret or recollection. It's incredible to think Sam was born and spent his childhood here. I'm glad he doesn't show it! We slept last night in the room he was born in. Or rather he slept, I couldn't. I lay awake and found it difficult to breathe, as if all the life in the air had long since been exhausted in keeping the dying living a little longer. It was hard to believe anyone had ever been born alive there. I know you're saying crossly "She's still morbid" but I'm not. I've never been more normal. I feel contented and placid.

(*Looking up from the letter, thinking embarrassedly*)

Should I have told him? . . . no . . . my own secret . . . tell no one . . . not even Sam . . . why haven't I told Sam? . . . it'd do him so much good . . . he'd feel so proud of himself, poor dear . . . no . . . I want to keep it just my baby . . . only mine . . . as long as I can . . . and it will be time enough to let Ned know when I go to New York . . . he can suggest a good obstetrician . . . how delighted he'll be when he hears! . . . he always said it would be the best thing for me . . . well, I do feel happy when I think . . . and I love Sam now . . . in a way . . . it will be his baby too . . .

(*Then with a happy sigh, turns back to letter*)

But speaking of Sam's birth, you really must meet his mother sometime. It's amazing how little she is like him a strange woman from the bit I saw of her last night. She has been writing Sam regularly once a week ever since she's known we were married, the most urgent invitations to visit her. They were really more like commands, or prayers. I suspect she is terribly lonely all by herself in this big house. Sam's feeling toward her puzzles me. I don't believe he ever mentioned her until her letters began coming or that he'd ever have come to see the poor woman if I hadn't insisted. His attitude rather shocked me. It was just as though he'd forgotten he had a mother. And yet as soon as he saw her he was sweet enough. She seemed dreadfully upset to see Charlie with us, until we'd explained it was thanks to his kindness and in his car we were taking this deferred honeymoon. Charlie's like a fussy old woman about his car, he's afraid to let Sam or me drive it—

MARSDEN. (*enters from the rear. He is spruce, dressed immaculately, his face a bit tired and resigned, but smiling kindly. He has a letter in his hand*) Good morning. (*She gives a start and instinctively covers the letter with her hand.*)

NINA. Good morning. (*Thinking amusedly*)

If he knew what I'd just written . . . poor old Charlie! . . .

(*Then indicating the letter he carries*) I see you're an early correspondent, too.

MARSDEN. (*with sudden jealous suspicion*)

Why did she cover it up like that? . . . whom is she writing to? . . .

(*Coming toward her*) Just a line to Mother to let her know we've not all been murdered by rum-bandits. You know how she worries.

NINA. (*thinking with a trace of pitying contempt*)

Apron strings . . . still his devotion to her is touching . . . I hope if mine is a boy he will love me as much . . . oh, I hope it is a boy . . . healthy and strong and beautiful . . . like Gordon! . . .

(*Then suddenly sensing* MARSDEN'S *curiosity—perfunctorily*) I'm writing to Ned Darrell. I've owed him one for ages. (*She folds it up and puts it aside.*)

MARSDEN. (*thinking glumly*)

I thought she'd forgotten him . . . still I suppose it's just friendly . . . and it's none of my business now she's married. . . .

(*Perfunctorily*) How did you sleep?

NINA. Not a wink. I had the strangest feeling.

MARSDEN. Sleeping in a strange bed, I suppose. (*Jokingly*) Did you see any ghosts?

NINA. (*with a sad smile*) No, I got the feeling the ghosts had all deserted the house and left it without a soul—as the dead so often leave the living— (*She forces a little laugh*) if you get what I mean.

MARSDEN. (*thinking worriedly*)

Slipping back into that morbid tone . . . first time in a long while . . .

(*Teasingly*) Hello! Do I hear graveyards yawning from their sleep —and yet I observe it's a gorgeous morning without, the flowers are flowering, the trees are treeing with one another, and you, if I mistake not, are on your honeymoon!

NINA. (*immediately gaily mocking*) Oh, very well, old thing! "God's in his heaven, all's right with the world!" And Pippa's cured of the pip! (*She dances up to him.*)

MARSDEN. (*gallantly*) Pippa is certainly a pippin this morning!

NINA. (*kisses him quickly*) You deserve one for that! All I meant was that ghosts remind me of men's smart crack about women, you can't live with them and can't live without them. (*Stands still and looks at him teasingly*) But there you stand proving me a liar by every breath you draw! You're ghostless and womanless—and as sleek and satisfied as a pet seal! (*She sticks out her tongue at him and makes a face of superior scorn*) Bah! That for you, 'Fraid-cat Charlie, you slacker bachelor! (*She runs to the kitchen door*) I'm going to bum some more coffee! How about you?

MARSDEN. (*with a forced smile*) No, thank you. (*She disappears into the kitchen—thinking with bitter pain*)

Ghostless! . . . if she only knew . . . that joking tone hides her real contempt! . . .

(*Self-mockingly*)

"But when the girls began to play 'Fraid-cat Charlie ran away!"

(*Then rallying himself*)

Bosh! . . . I haven't had such thoughts . . . not since their marriage . . . happy in her happiness . . . but is she happy? . . . in the first few months she was obviously playing a part . . . kissed him too much . . . as if she'd determined to make herself a loving wife . . . and then all of a sudden she became contented . . . her face filled out . . . her eyes lazily examined peace . . . pregnant . . . yes, she must be . . . I hope so. . . . Why? . . . for her sake . . . my own, too . . . when she has a child I know I can entirely accept . . . forget I have lost her . . . lost her? . . . silly ass! . . . how can you lose what you never possessed? . . . except in dreams! . . .

(*Shaking his head exasperatedly*)

Round and round . . . thoughts . . . damn pests! . . . mosquitoes of the soul . . . whine, sting, suck one's blood . . . why did I invite Nina and Sam on this tour . . . it's a business trip with me, really . . . I need a new setting for my next novel . . . "Mr. Marsden departs a bit from his familiar field" . . . well, there they were stuck in the Professor's house . . . couldn't afford a vacation . . . never had a honeymoon . . . I've pretended to be done up every night so they could . . . I've gone to bed right after dinner so they could be alone and . . . I wonder if she can really like him . . . that way? . . .

(*The sound of* EVANS' *voice and his mother's is heard from the garden.* MARSDEN *goes over and carefully peers out*)

Sam with his mother . . . peculiar woman . . . strong . . . good character for a novel . . . no, she's too somber . . . her eyes are the saddest . . . and, at the same time, the grimmest . . . they're coming in . . . I'll drive around the country a bit . . . give them a chance for a family conference . . . discuss Nina's pregnancy, I suppose . . . does Sam know? . . . he gives no indication . . . why do wives hide it from their husbands? . . . ancient shame . . . guilty of continuing life, of bringing fresh pain into the world . . .

(*He goes out, rear. The outside door in the hall is heard being opened and* EVANS *and his mother evidently meet* MARSDEN *as he is about to go out. Their voices, his voice explaining, are heard, then the outer door being opened and shut again as* MARSDEN *departs. A moment later* EVANS *and his mother enter the dining room.* SAM *looks timorously happy, as if he could not quite believe in his good fortune and had constantly to reassure himself about it, yet he is riding the crest of the wave, he radiates love and devotion and boyish adoration. He is a charming-looking fresh boy now. He wears a sweater and linen knickers, collegiate to the last degree. His mother is a tiny woman with a frail figure, her head and face, framed in iron-gray hair, seeming much too large for her body, so that at first glance she gives one the impression of a wonderfully made, lifelike doll. She is only about forty-five but she looks at least sixty. Her face with its delicate features must have once been of a romantic, tender, clinging-vine beauty, but what has happened to her has compressed its defenseless curves into planes, its mouth into the thin line around a locked door, its gentle chin has been forced out aggressively by a long reliance on clenched teeth. She is very pale. Her big dark eyes are grim with the prisoner-pain of a walled-in soul. Yet a sweet loving-kindness, the ghost of an old faith and trust in life's goodness, hovers girlishly, fleetingly, about the corners of her mouth and softens into deep sorrow the shadowy grimness of her eyes. Her voice jumps startlingly in tone from a caressing gentleness to a blunted flat assertiveness, as if what she said then was merely a voice on its own without human emotion to inspire it.*)

EVANS. (*as they come in—rattling on in the cocksure boastful way of a boy showing off his prowess before his mother, confident of thrilled adulation*) In a few years you won't have to worry one way or another about the darned old apple crop. I'll be able to take care of you then. Wait and see! Of course, I'm not making so much now. I couldn't expect to. I've only just started. But I'm making good, all right, all right—since I got married—and it's only a question of time when— Why, to show you, Cole—he's the manager and the best egg ever—called me into his office and told me he'd had his eye on me, that my stuff was exactly what they wanted, and he thought I had the makings of a real find. (*Proudly*) How's that? That's certainly fair enough, isn't it?

MRS. EVANS. (*vaguely—she has evidently not heard much of what he said*) That's fine, Sammy. (*Thinking apprehensively*)

> I do hope I'm wrong! . . . but that old shiver of dread took me the minute she stepped in the door! . . . I don't think she's told Sammy but I got to make sure. . . .

EVANS. (*seeing her preoccupation now—deeply hurt—testily*) I'll bet you didn't hear a word I said! Are you still worrying about how the darn old apples are going to turn out?

MRS. EVANS. (*with a guilty start—protestingly*) Yes, I did hear you, Sammy—every word! That's just what I was thinking about—how proud I am you're doing so wonderful well!

EVANS. (*mollified but still grumbling*) You'd never guess it from the gloomy way you looked! (*But encouraged to go on*) And Cole asked me if I was married—seemed to take a real personal interest—said he was glad to hear it because marriage was what put the right kind of ambition into a fellow—unselfish ambition—working for his wife and not just himself— (*Then embarrassedly*) He even asked me if we were expecting an addition to the family.

MRS. EVANS. (*seeing this is her chance—quickly—forcing a smile*) I've been meaning to ask you that myself, Sammy. (*Blurts out apprehensively*) She—Nina—she isn't going to have a baby, is she?

EVANS. (*with an indefinable guilty air—as if he were reluctant to admit it*) I—why—you mean, is she now? I don't think so, Mother. (*He strolls over to the window whistling with an exaggeratedly casual air, and looks out.*)

MRS. EVANS. (*thinking with grim relief*)

He don't know . . . there's that much to be thankful for, anyway. . . .

EVANS. (*thinking with intense longing*)

If that'd only happen! . . . soon! . . . Nina's begun to love me . . . a little . . . I've felt it the last two months . . . God, it's made me happy! . . . before that she didn't . . . only liked me . . . that was all I asked . . . never dared hope she'd come to love me . . . even a little . . . so soon . . . sometimes I feel it's too good to be true . . . don't deserve it . . . and now . . . if that'd happen . . . then I'd feel sure . . . it'd be there . . . half Nina, half me . . . living proof! . . .

(*Then an apprehensive note creeping in*)

And I know she wants a baby so much . . . one reason why she married me . . . and I know she's felt right along that then she'd love me . . . really love me . . .

(*Gloomily*)

I wonder why . . . ought to have happened before this . . . hope it's nothing wrong . . . with me! . . .

(*He starts, flinging off his thought—then suddenly clutching at a straw, turns hopefully to his mother*) Why did you ask me that, Mother? D'you think—?

MRS. EVANS. (*hastily*) No, indeed! I don't think she is! I wouldn't say so at all!

EVANS. (*dejectedly*) Oh—I thought perhaps— (*Then changing the subject*) I suppose I ought to go up and say hello to Aunt Bessie.

MRS. EVANS. (*her face becoming defensive—in blunted tones, a trifle pleadingly*) I wouldn't, Sammy. She hasn't seen you since you were eight. She wouldn't know you. And you're on your honeymoon, and old age is always sad to young folks. Be happy while you can! (*Then pushing him toward door*) Look here! You catch that friend, he's just getting his car out. You drive to town with him, give me a chance to get to know my daughter-in-law, and call her to account for how she's taking care of you! (*She laughs forcedly.*)

EVANS. (*bursting out passionately*) Better than I deserve! She's an angel, Mother! I know you'll love her!

MRS. EVANS. (*gently*) I do already, Sammy! She's so pretty and sweet!

EVANS. (*kisses her—joyously*) I'll tell her that. I'm going out this way and kiss her good-bye. (*He runs out through the kitchen door.*)

MRS. EVANS. (*looking after him—passionately*)

He loves her! . . . he's happy! . . . that's all that counts! . . . being happy!

(*Thinking apprehensively*)

If only she isn't going to have a baby . . . if only she doesn't care so much about having one . . . I got to have it out with her . . . got to! . . . no other way . . . in mercy . . . in justice . . . this has got to end with my boy . . . and he's got to live happy! . . .

(*At the sound of steps from the kitchen she straightens up in her chair stiffly.*)

NINA. (*comes in from the kitchen, a cup of coffee in her hand, smiling happily*) Good morning— (*She hesitates—then shyly*) Mother. (*She comes over and kisses her—slips down and sits on the floor beside her.*)

MRS. EVANS. (*flusteredly—hurriedly*) Good morning! It's a real fine day, isn't it? I ought to have been here and got your breakfast, but I was out gallivanting round the place with Sammy. I hope you found everything you wanted.

NINA. Indeed I did! And I ate so much I'm ashamed of myself! (*She nods at the cup of coffee and laughs*) See. I'm still at it.

MRS. EVANS. Good for you!

NINA. I ought to apologize for coming down so late. Sam should have called me. But I wasn't able to get to sleep until after daylight somehow.

MRS. EVANS. (*strangely*) You couldn't sleep? Why? Did you feel anything funny—about this house?

NINA. (*struck by her tone—looks up*) No. Why? (*Thinking*)

How her face changes! . . . what sad eyes! . . .

MRS. EVANS. (*thinking in an agony of apprehension*)

Got to start in to tell her . . . got to . . .

NINA. (*apprehensive herself now*)

That sick dead feeling . . . when something is going to happen . . . I felt it before I got the cable about Gordon . . .

(*Then taking a sip of coffee, and trying to be pleasantly casual*) Sam said you wanted to talk to me.

MRS. EVANS. (*dully*) Yes. You love my boy, don't you?

NINA. (*startled—forcing a smile, quickly*) Why, of course! (*Reassuring herself*)

No, it isn't a lie . . . I do love him . . . the father of my baby . . .

MRS. EVANS. (*blurts out*) Are you going to have a baby, Nina?

NINA. (*she presses* MRS. EVANS' *hand—simply*) Yes, Mother.

MRS. EVANS. (*in her blunt flat tones—with a mechanical rapidity to her words*) Don't you think it's too soon? Don't you think you better wait until Sammy's making more money? Don't you think it'll be a drag on him and you? Why don't you just go on being happy together, just you two?

NINA. (*thinking frightenedly*)

What is behind what she's saying? . . . that feeling of death again! . . .

(*Moving away from her—repulsed*) No, I don't think any of those things, Mrs. Evans. I want a baby—beyond everything! We both do!

MRS. EVANS. (*hopelessly*) I know. (*Then grimly*) But you can't!

You've got to make up your mind you can't! (*Thinking fiercely—even with satisfaction*)

Tell her! . . . make her suffer what I was made to suffer! . . . I've been too lonely! . . .

NINA. (*thinking with terrified foreboding*)

I knew it! . . . Out of a blue sky . . . black! . . .

(*Springing to her feet—bewilderedly*) What do you mean? How can you say a thing like that?

MRS. EVANS. (*reaching out her hand tenderly, trying to touch* NINA) It's because I want Sammy—and you, too, child—to be happy. (*Then as* NINA *shrinks away from her hand—in her blunted tones*) You just can't.

NINA. (*defiantly*) But I can! I have already! I mean—I am, didn't you understand me?

MRS. EVANS. (*gently*) I know it's hard. (*Then inexorably*) But you can't go on!

NINA. (*violently*) I don't believe you know what you're saying! It's too terrible for you—Sam's own mother—how would you have felt if someone—when you were going to have Sam—came to you and said—?

MRS. EVANS. (*thinking fiercely*)

Now's my chance! . . .

(*Tonelessly*) They did say it! Sam's own father did—my husband! And I said it to myself! And I did all I could, all my husband could think of, so's I wouldn't—but we didn't know enough. And right to the time the pains come on. I prayed Sammy'd be born dead, and Sammy's father prayed, but Sammy was born healthy and smiling, and we just had to love him, and live in fear. He doubled the torment of fear we lived in. And that's what you'd be in for. And Sammy, he'd go the way his father went. And your baby, you'd be bringing it into torment. (*A bit violently*) I tell you it'd be a crime—a crime worse than murder! (*Then recovering—commiseratingly*) So you just can't, Nina!

NINA. (*who has been listening distractedly—thinking*)

Don't listen to her! . . . feeling of death! . . . what is it? . . . she's trying to kill my baby! . . . oh, I hate her! . . .

(*Hysterically resentful*) What do you mean? Why don't you speak plainly? (*Violently*) I think you're horrible! Praying your baby would be born dead! That's a lie! You couldn't!

MRS. EVANS. (*thinking*)

I know what she's doing now . . . just what I did . . . trying not to believe . . .

(*Fiercely*)

But I'll make her! . . . she's got to suffer, too! . . . I been too lonely! . . . she's got to share and help me save my Sammy! . . .

(*With an even more blunted flat relentless tonelessness*) I thought I was plain, but I'll be plainer. Only remember it's a family secret, and now you're one of the family. It's the curse on the Evanses. My husband's mother—she was an only child—died in an asylum and her father before her. I know that for a fact. And my husband's sister, Sammy's aunt, she's out of her mind. She lives on the top floor of this house, hasn't been out of her room in years, I've taken care of her. She just sits, doesn't say a word, but she's happy, she laughs to herself a lot, she hasn't a care in the world. But I remember when she was all right, she was always unhappy, she never got married, most people around here were afraid of the Evanses in spite of their being rich for hereabouts. They knew about the craziness going back, I guess, for heaven knows how long. I didn't know about the Evanses until after I'd married my husband. He came to the town I lived in, no one there knew about the Evanses. He didn't tell me until after we were married. He asked me to forgive him, he said he loved me so much he'd have gone mad without me, said I was his only hope of salvation. So I forgave him. I loved him an awful lot. I said to myself, I'll be his salvation—and maybe I could have been if we hadn't had Sammy born. My husband kept real well up to then. We'd swore we'd never have children, we never forgot to be careful for two whole years. Then one night we'd both gone to a dance, we'd both had a little punch to drink, just enough—to forget—driving home in the moonlight—that moonlight!—such little things at the back of big things!

NINA. (*in a dull moan*) I don't believe you! I won't believe you!

MRS. EVANS. (*drones on*) My husband, Sammy's father, in spite of all he and I fought against it, he finally gave in to it when Sammy was only eight, he couldn't keep up any more living in fear for Sammy, thinking any minute the curse might get him, every time he was sick, or had a headache, or bumped his head, or started crying, or had a nightmare and screamed, or said something queer like children do naturally. (*A bit stridently*) Living like that with that fear is awful torment! I know that! I went through it by his side! It nearly drove me crazy, too—but I didn't have it in my blood! And that's why I'm telling you! You got to see you can't, Nina!

NINA. (*suddenly breaking out—frenziedly*) I don't believe you! I don't believe Sam would ever have married me if he knew—!

MRS. EVANS. (*sharply*) Who said Sammy knew? He don't know a single thing about it! That's been the work of my life, keeping him from knowing. When his father gave up and went off into it I sent Sammy right off to boarding school. I told him his father was sick, and a little while after I sent word his father was dead, and from then on until his father did really die during Sammy's second year to college, I kept him away at school in winter and camp in summers and I went to see him, I never let him come home. (*With a sigh*) It was hard, giving up Sammy, knowing I was making him forget he had a mother. I was glad taking care of them two kept me so busy I didn't get much chance to think then. But here's what I've come to think since, Nina: I'm certain sure my husband might have kept his mind with the help of my love if I hadn't had Sammy. And if I'd never had Sammy I'd never have loved Sammy—or missed him, would I?—and I'd have kept my husband.

NINA. (*not heeding this last—with wild mockery*) And I thought Sam was so normal—so healthy and sane—not like me! I thought he'd give me such healthy, happy children and I'd forget myself in them and learn to love him!

MRS. EVANS. (*horrified, jumping to her feet*) Learn to? You told me you did love Sammy!

NINA. No! Maybe I almost have—lately—but only when I thought of his baby! Now I hate him! (*She begins to weep hysterically.* MRS. EVANS *goes to her and puts her arms around her.* NINA *sobs out*) Don't touch me! I hate you, too! Why didn't you tell him he must never marry!

MRS. EVANS. What reason could I give, without telling him everything? And I never heard about you till after you were married. Then I wanted to write to you but I was scared he might read it. And I couldn't leave her upstairs to come away to see you. I kept writing Sammy to bring you here right off, although having him come frightened me to death for fear he might get to suspect something. You got to get him right away from here, Nina! I just kept hoping you wouldn't want children right away—young folks don't nowadays—until I'd seen you and told you everything. And I thought you'd love him like I did his father, and be satisfied with him alone.

NINA. (*lifting her head—wildly*) No! I don't! I won't! I'll leave him!

MRS. EVANS. (*shaking her, fiercely*) You can't! He'd go crazy sure then! You'd be a devil! Don't you see how he loves you?

NINA. (*breaking away from her—harshly*) Well, I don't love him! I only married him because he needed me—and I needed children! And now you tell me I've got to kill my—oh, yes, I see I've got to, you needn't argue any more! I love it too much to make it run that chance! And I hate it too, now, because it's sick, it's not my baby, it's his! (*With terrible ironic bitterness*) And still you can dare to tell me I can't even leave Sam!

MRS. EVANS. (*very sadly and bitterly*) You just said you married him because he needed you. Don't he need you now—more'n ever? But I can't tell you not to leave him, not if you don't love him. But you oughtn't to have married him when you didn't love him. And it'll be your fault, what'll happen.

NINA. (*torturedly*) What will happen?—what do you mean?—Sam will be all right—just as he was before—and it's not my fault anyway!—it's not my fault! (*Then thinking conscience-strickenly*)

> Poor Sam . . . she's right . . . it's not his fault . . . it's mine . . . I wanted to use him to save myself . . . I acted the coward again . . . as I did with Gordon . . .

MRS. EVANS. (*grimly*) You know what'll happen to him if you leave him—after all I've told you! (*Then breaking into intense pleading*) Oh, I'd get down on my knees to you, don't make my boy run that risk! You got to give one Evans, the last one, a chance to live in this world! And you'll learn to love him, if you give up enough for him! (*Then with a grim smile*) Why, I even love that idiot upstairs, I've taken care of her so many years, lived her life for her with my life, you might say. You give your life to Sammy, then you'll love him same as you love yourself. You'll have to! That's sure as death! (*She laughs a queer gentle laugh full of amused bitterness.*)

NINA. (*with a sort of dull stupid wonderment*) And you've found peace?—

MRS. EVANS. (*sardonically*) There's peace in the green fields of Eden, they say! You got to die to find out! (*Then proudly*) But I can say I feel proud of having lived fair to them that gave me love and trusted in me!

NINA. (*struck—confusedly*) Yes—that's true, isn't it? (*Thinking strangely*)

> Lived fair . . . pride . . . trust . . . play the game! . . . who is speaking to me . . . Gordon! . . . oh, Gordon, do you mean I must give Sam the life I didn't give you? . . . Sam loved you too . . . he said, if we have a boy, we'll call him Gordon in

Gordon's honor . . . Gordon's honor! . . . what must I do now in your honor, Gordon? . . . yes! . . . I know! . . .

(*Speaking mechanically in a dull voice*) All right, Mother. I'll stay with Sam. There's nothing else I can do, is there, when it isn't his fault, poor boy! (*Then suddenly snapping and bursting out in a despairing cry*) But I'll be so lonely! I'll have lost my baby! (*She sinks down on her knees at* MRS. EVANS' *feet—piteously*) Oh, Mother, how can I keep on living?

MRS. EVANS. (*thinking miserably*)

Now she knows my suffering . . . now I got to help her . . . she's got a right to have a baby . . . another baby . . . sometime . . . somehow . . . she's giving her life to save my Sammy . . . I got to save her! . . .

(*Stammeringly*) Maybe, Nina—

NINA. (*dully and resentfully again now*) And how about Sam? You want him to be happy, don't you? It's just as important for him as it is for me that I should have a baby! If you know anything at all about him, you ought to see that!

MRS. EVANS. (*sadly*) I know that. I see that in him, Nina. (*Gropingly*) There must be a way—somehow. I remember when I was carrying Sam, sometimes I'd forget I was a wife, I'd only remember the child in me. And then I used to wish I'd gone out deliberate in our first year, without my husband knowing, and picked a man, a healthy male to breed by, same's we do with stock, to give the man I loved a healthy child. And if I didn't love that other man nor him me where would be the harm? Then God would whisper: "It'd be a sin, adultery, the worst sin!" But after He'd gone I'd argue back again to myself, then we'd have a healthy child, I needn't be afraid! And maybe my husband would feel without ever knowing how he felt it, that I wasn't afraid and that child wasn't cursed and so he needn't fear and I could save him. (*Then scornfully*) But I was too afraid of God then to have ever done it! (*Then very simply*) He loved children so, my poor husband did, and the way they took to him, you never saw anything like it, he was a natural born father. And Sammy's the same.

NINA. (*as from a distance—strangely*) Yes, Sammy's the same. But I'm not the same as you. (*Defiantly*) I don't believe in God the Father!

MRS. EVANS. (*strangely*) Then it'd be easy for you. (*With a grim smile*) And I don't believe in Him, neither, not any more. I used to be a great one for worrying about what's God and what's devil, but I got richly over it living here with poor folks that was being punished for no sins of their own, and me being punished with them for no sin but loving much. (*With decision*) Being happy, that's the nearest we can ever come to knowing what's good! Being happy, that's good! The rest is just talk! (*She pauses—then with a strange austere sternness*) I love my boy, Sammy. I could see how much he wants you to have a baby. Sammy's got to feel sure you love him—to be happy. Whatever you can do to make him happy is good—is good, Nina! I don't care what! You've got to have a healthy baby—sometime—so's you can both be happy! It's your rightful duty!

NINA. (*confusedly—in a half-whisper*) Yes, Mother. (*Thinking longingly*)

I want to be happy! . . . it's my right . . . and my duty! . . .

(*Then suddenly in guilty agony*)

Oh, my baby . . . my poor baby . . . I'm forgetting you . . . desiring another after you are dead! . . . I feel you beating against my heart for mercy . . . oh! . . .

(*She weeps with bitter anguish.*)

MRS. EVANS. (*gently and with deep sympathy*) I know what you're suffering. And I wouldn't say what I just said now only I know us two mustn't see each other ever again. You and Sammy have got to forget me. (*As* NINA *makes a motion of protest—grimly and inexorably*) Oh, yes, you will—easy. People forget everything. They got to, poor people! And I'm saying what I said about a healthy baby so's you will remember it when you need to, after you've forgotten—this one.

NINA. (*sobbing pitifully*) Don't! Please, Mother!

MRS. EVANS. (*with sudden tenderness—gathering* NINA *up in her arms, brokenly*) You poor child! You're like the daughter of my sorrow! You're closer to me now than ever Sammy could be! I want you to be happy! (*She begins to sob, too, kissing* NINA'S *bowed head.*)

CURTAIN

ACT FOUR

SCENE: *An evening early in the following winter about seven months later. The* PROFESSOR'S *study again. The books in the cases have never been touched, their austere array shows no gaps, but the glass separating them from the world is gray with dust, giving them a blurred ghostly quality. The table, although it is the same, is no longer the* PROFESSOR'S *table, just as the other furniture in the room, by its disarrangement, betrays that the* PROFESSOR'S *well-ordered mind no longer trims it to his personality. The table has become neurotic. Volumes of the Encyclopedia Britannica mixed up with popular treatises on Mind Training for Success, etc., looking startlingly modern and disturbing against the background of classics in the original, are slapped helter-skelter on top of each other on it. The titles of these books face in all directions, no one volume is placed with any relation to the one beneath it—the effect is that they have no connected meaning. The rest of the table is littered with an ink bottle, pens, pencils, erasers, a box of typewriting paper, and a typewriter at the center before the chair, which is pushed back, setting the rug askew. On the floor beside the table are an overflowing wastepaper basket, a few sheets of paper and the rubber cover for the typewriter like a collapsed tent. The rocking chair is no longer at center but has been pulled nearer the table, directly faces it with its back to the bench. This bench in turn has been drawn much closer, but is now placed more to the rear and half-faces front, its back squarely to the door in the corner.*

EVANS *is seated in the* PROFESSOR'S *old chair. He has evidently been typing, or is about to type, for a sheet of paper can be seen in the machine. He smokes a pipe, which he is always relighting whether it needs it or not, and which he bites and shifts about and pulls in and out and puffs at nervously. His expression is dispirited, his eyes shift about, his shoulders are collapsed submissively. He seems much thinner, his face drawn and sallow. The collegiate clothes are no longer natty, they need pressing and look too big for him.*

EVANS. (*turns to his typewriter and pounds out a few words with a sort of aimless desperation—then tears the sheet out of the machine with an exclamation of disgust, crumples it up and throws it violently on the floor, pushing his chair back and jumping to his feet*) Hell! (*He begins pacing up and down the room, puffing at his pipe, thinking tormentedly*)

No use . . . can't think of a darn thing . . . well, who could dope out a novel ad on another powdered milk, anyway? . . . all the stuff been used already . . . Tartars conquering on dried mares' milk . . . Metchnikoff, eminent scientist . . . been done to death . . . but simply got to work out something or . . . Cole said, what's been the matter with you lately? . . . you started off so well . . . I thought you were a real find, but your work's fallen off to nothing . . .

(*He sits down on the edge of the bench nearby, his shoulders hunched—despondently*)

Couldn't deny it . . . been going stale ever since we came back from that trip home . . . no ideas . . . I'll get fired . . . sterile . . .

(*With a guilty terror*)

in more ways than one, I guess! . . .

(*He springs to his feet as if this idea were a pin stuck in him—lighting his already lighted pipe, walks up and down again, forcing his thoughts into other channels*)

Bet the old man turns over in his grave at my writing ads in his study . . . maybe that's why I can't . . . bum influence . . . try tomorrow in my bedroom . . . sleeping alone . . . since Nina got sick . . . some woman's sickness . . . wouldn't tell me . . . too modest . . . still, there are some things a husband has a right to know . . . especially when we haven't . . . in five months

... doctor told her she mustn't, she said ... what doctor? ... she's never said ... what the hell's the matter with you, do you think Nina's lying? ... no ... but ...

(*Desperately*)

If I was only sure it was because she's really sick ... not just sick of me! ...

(*He sinks down in the rocking chair despondently*).

Certainly been a big change in her ... since that visit home ... what happened between Mother and her? ... she says nothing ... they seemed to like each other ... both of them cried when we left ... still, Nina insisted on going that same day and Mother seemed anxious to get rid of us ... can't make it out ... next few weeks Nina couldn't be loving enough ... I never was so happy ... then she crashed ... strain of waiting and hoping she'd get pregnant ... and nothing happening ... that's what did it ... my fault! ... how d'you know? ... you can't tell that! ...

(*He jumps to his feet again—walks up and down again distractedly*)

God, if we'd only have a kid! ... then I'd show them all what I could do! ... Cole always used to say I had the stuff, and Ned certainly thought so. ...

(*With sudden relieved excitement*)

By gosh, I was forgetting! ... Ned's coming out tonight ... forgot to tell Nina ... mustn't let her get wise I got him to come to look her over ... she'd hate me for swallowing my pride after he's never been to see us ... but I had to ... this has got my goat ... I've got to know what's wrong ... and Ned's the only one I can trust ...

(*He flings himself on chair in front of desk and, picking up a fresh sheet of paper, jams it into the machine*)

Gosh, I ought to try and get a new start on this before it's time ...

(*He types a sentence or two, a strained frown of concentration on his face.* NINA *comes silently through the door and stands just inside it looking at him. She has grown thin again, her face is pale and drawn, her movements are those of extreme nervous tension.*)

NINA. (*before she can stifle her immediate reaction of contempt and dislike*)

How weak he is! . . . he'll never do anything . . . never give me my desire . . . if he'd only fall in love with someone else . . . go away . . . not be here in my father's room . . . I even have to give him a home . . . if he'd disappear . . . leave me free . . . if he'd die . . .

(*Checking herself—remorsefully*)

I must stop such thoughts . . . I don't mean it . . . poor Sam! . . . trying so hard . . . loving me so much . . . I give so little in return . . . he feels I'm always watching him with scorn . . . I can't tell him it's with pity . . . how can I help watching him? . . . help worrying over his worry because of what it might lead to . . . after what his mother . . . how horrible life is! . . . he's worried now . . . he doesn't sleep . . . I hear him tossing about . . . I must sleep with him again soon . . . he's only home two nights a week . . . it isn't fair of me . . . I must try . . . I must! . . . he suspects my revulsion . . . it's hurting him . . . oh, poor dead baby I dared not bear, how I might have loved your father for your sake! . . .

EVANS. (*suddenly feeling her presence, jerks himself to his feet—with a diffident guilty air which is noticeable about him now whenever he is in her presence*) Hello, dear. I thought you were lying down. (*Guiltily*) Did the noise of my typing bother you? I'm terribly sorry!

NINA. (*irritated in spite of herself*)

Why is he always cringing? . . .

(*She comes forward to the chair at center and sits down—forcing a smile*) But there's nothing to be terribly sorry about! (*As he stands awkward and confused, like a schoolboy who has been called on to recite and cannot and is being "bawled out" before the class, she forces a playful tone*) Goodness, Sam, how tragic you can get about nothing at all!

EVANS. (*still forced to justify himself—contritely*) I know it isn't pleasant for you having me drag my work out here, trying to pound out rotten ads. (*With a short laugh*) Trying to is right! (*Blurts out*) I wouldn't do it except that Cole gave me a warning to buck up—or get out.

NINA. (*stares at him, more annoyed, her eyes hardening, thinking*)

Yes! . . . he'll always be losing one job, getting another, starting with a burst of confidence each time, then . . .

(*Cutting him with a careless sneering tone*) Well, it isn't a job to worry much about losing, is it?

EVANS. (*wincing pitiably*) No, not much money. But I used to think there was a fine chance to rise there—but of course that's my fault, I haven't made good— (*He finishes miserably*) somehow.

NINA. (*her antagonism giving way to remorseful pity*)

What makes me so cruel? . . . he's so defenseless . . . his mother's baby . . . poor sick baby! . . . poor Sam!

(*She jumps to her feet and goes over to him.*)

EVANS. (*as she comes—with a defensive, boastful bravery*) Oh, I can get another job just as good, all right—maybe a lot better.

NINA. (*reassuringly*) Certainly, you can! And I'm sure you're not going to lose this one. You're always anticipating trouble. (*She kisses him and sits on the arm of his chair, putting an arm around his neck and pulling his head on to her breast*) And it isn't your fault, you big goose, you! It's mine. I know how hard it makes everything for you, being tied to a wife who's too sick to be a wife. You ought to have married a big strapping, motherly—

EVANS. (*in the seventh heaven now—passionately*) Bunk! All the other women in the world aren't worth your little finger! It's you who ought to have married someone worth while, not a poor fish like me! But no one could love you more than I do, no matter what he was!

NINA. (*presses his head on her breast, avoiding his eyes, kisses him on the forehead*) And I love you, Sam. (*Staring out over his head—with loving pity, thinking*)

I almost do . . . poor unfortunate boy! . . . at these moments

. . . as his mother loves him . . . but that isn't enough for him . . . I can hear his mother saying, "Sammy's got to feel sure you love him . . . to be happy." . . . I must try to make him feel sure . . .

(*Speaking gently*) I want you to be happy, Sam.

EVANS. (*his face transformed with happiness*) I am—a hundred times more than I deserve!

NINA. (*presses his head down on her breast so he cannot see her eyes—gently*) Ssshh. (*Thinking sadly*)

I promised her . . . but I couldn't see how hard it would be to let him love me . . . after his baby . . . was gone . . . it was hard even to keep on living . . . after that operation . . . Gordon's spirit followed me from room to room . . . poor reproachful ghost! . . .

(*With bitter mockery*)

Oh, Gordon, I'm afraid this is a deeper point of honor than any that was ever shot down in flames! . . . what would your honor say now? . . . "Stick to him! . . . play the game!" . . . oh, yes, I know . . . I'm sticking . . . but he isn't happy . . . I'm trying to play the game . . . then why do I keep myself from him? . . . but I was really sick . . . for a time after . . . since then, I couldn't . . . but . . . oh, I'll try . . . I'll try soon . . .

(*Tenderly—but having to force herself to say it*) Doesn't my boy want to sleep with me again—sometime soon?

EVANS. (*passionately—hardly able to believe his ears*) Oh, it'd be wonderful, Nina! But are you sure you really want me to—that you'll feel well enough?

NINA. (*repeats his words as if she were memorizing a lesson*) Yes, I want you to. Yes, I'll feel well enough. (*He seizes her hand and kisses it in a passionately grateful silence—she thinks with resigned finality*)

There, Sammy's mother and Gordon . . . I'll play the game . . . it will make him happy for a while . . . as he was in those weeks after we'd left his mother . . . when I gave myself with a mad pleasure in torturing myself for his pleasure! . . .

(*Then with weary hopelessness*)

He'll be happy until he begins to feel guilty again because I'm not pregnant . . .

(*With a grim bitter smile*)

Poor Sam, if he only knew the precautions . . . as if I wouldn't die rather than take the slightest chance of that happening! . . . ever again . . . what a tragic joke it was on both of us! . . . I wanted my baby so! . . . oh, God! . . . his mother said . . . "You've got to have a healthy baby . . . sometime . . . it's your rightful duty" . . . that seemed right then . . . but now . . . it seems cowardly . . . to betray poor Sam . . . and vile to give myself . . . without love or desire . . . and yet I've given myself to men before without a thought just to give them a moment's happiness . . . can't I do that again? . . . when it's a case of Sam's happiness? . . . and my own? . . .

(*She gets up from beside him with a hunted movement*) It must be half past eight. Charlie's coming to bring his suggestions on my outline for Gordon's biography.

EVANS. (*his bliss shattered—dejectedly*)

Always happens . . . just as we get close . . . something comes between . . .

(*Then confusedly*) Say, I forgot to tell you Ned's coming out to-night.

NINA. (*astonished*) Ned Darrell?

EVANS. Sure. I happened to run into him the other day and invited him and he said Saturday evening. He couldn't tell what train. Said never mind meeting him.

NINA. (*excitedly*) Why didn't you tell me before, you big booby! (*She kisses him*) There, don't mind. But it's just like you. Now someone'll have to go down to the store. And I'll have to get the spare room ready. (*She hurries to the doorway. He follows her.*)

EVANS. I'll help you.

NINA. You'll do nothing of the kind! You'll stay right downstairs and bring them in here and cover up my absence. Thank heavens,

Charlie won't stay long if Ned is here. (*The doorbell rings—excitedly*) There's one of them now. I'll run upstairs. Come up and tell me if it's Ned—and get rid of Charlie. (*She kisses him playfully and hurries out.*)

EVANS. (*looking after her—thinks*)

She seems better tonight . . . happier . . . she seems to love me . . . if she'll only get all well again, then everything will . . .

(*The bell rings again*)

I must give Ned a good chance to talk to her . . .

(*He goes out to the outer door—returns a moment later with* MARSDEN. *The latter's manner is preoccupied and nervous. His face has an expression of anxiety which he tries to conceal. He seems a prey to some inner fear he is trying to hide even from himself and is resolutely warding off from his consciousness. His tall, thin body stoops as if a part of its sustaining will had been removed.*)

EVANS. (*with a rather forced welcoming note*) Come on in. Charlie. Nina's upstairs lying down.

MARSDEN. (*with marked relief*) Then by all means don't disturb her. I just dropped in to bring back her outline with the suggestions I've made. (*He has taken some papers out of his pocket and hands them to* EVANS) I couldn't have stayed but a minute in any event. Mother is a bit under the weather these days.

EVANS. (*perfunctorily*) Too bad. (*Thinking vindictively*)

Serve her right, the old scandal-monger, after the way she's gossiped about Nina! . . .

MARSDEN. (*with assumed carelessness*) Just a little indigestion. Nothing serious but it annoys her terribly. (*Thinking frightenedly*)

That dull pain she complains of . . . I don't like it . . . and she won't see anyone but old Doctor Tibbetts . . . she's sixty-eight . . . I can't help fearing . . . no! . . .

EVANS. (*bored—vaguely*) Well, I suppose you've got to be careful of every little thing when you get to her age.

MARSDEN. (*positively bristling*) Her age? Mother isn't so old!

EVANS. (*surprised*) Over sixty-five, isn't she?

MARSDEN. (*indignantly*) You're quite out there! She's still under sixty-five—and in health and spirits she isn't more than fifty! Everyone remarks that! (*Annoyed at himself*)

Why did I lie to him about her age? . . . I must be on edge . . . Mother is rather difficult to live with these days, getting me worried to death, when it's probably nothing . . .

EVANS. (*annoyed in his turn—thinking*)

Why all the fuss? . . . as if I gave a damn if the old girl was a million! . . .

(*Indicating the papers*) I'll give these to Nina first thing in the morning.

MARSDEN. (*mechanically*) Righto. Thank you. (*He starts to go toward door—then turns—fussily*) But you'd better take a look while I'm here and see if it's clear. I've written on the margins. See if there's anything you can't make out. (EVANS *nods helplessly and begins reading the sheets, going back beneath the lamp.*)

MARSDEN. (*looking around him with squeamish disapproval*)

What a mess they've made of this study . . . poor Professor! . . . dead and forgotten . . . and his tomb desecrated . . . does Sam write his ads here of a week-end now? . . . the last touch! . . . and Nina labors with love at Gordon's biography . . . whom the Professor hated! . . . "life is so full of a number of things!" . . . why does everyone in the world think they can write? . . . but I've only myself to blame . . . why in the devil did I ever suggest it to her? . . . because I hoped my helping her while Sam was in the city would bring us alone together? . . . but I made the suggestion before she had that abortion performed! . . . how do you know she did? . . . because I know! . . . there are psychic affinities . . . her body confessed . . . and since then, I've felt an aversion . . . as if she were a criminal . . . she is! . . . how could she? . . . why? . . . I thought she wanted a child . . . but evidently I don't know her . . . I suppose, afraid it would spoil her figure . . . her flesh . . . her power to enslave men's senses . . . mine . . . and I had hoped . . . looked forward to her becoming a mother . . . for my peace of mind. . . .

(*Catching himself—violently*)

Shut up! . . . what a base creature I'm becoming! . . . to have such thoughts when Mother is sick and I ought to be thinking only of her! . . . and it's none of my damn business, anyway! . . .

(*Glaring at* EVANS *resentfully as if he were to blame*)

Look at him! . . . he'll never suspect anything! . . . what a simple-simon! . . . he adored Gordon as a newsboy does a champion pugilist! . . . and Nina writes of Gordon as if he had been a demi-god! . . . when actually he came from the commonest people! . . .

(*He suddenly speaks to* EVANS *with a really savage satisfaction*) Did I tell you I once looked up Gordon's family in Beachampton? A truly deplorable lot! When I remembered Gordon and looked at his father I had either to suspect a lover in the wood pile or to believe in an Immaculate Conception . . . that is, until I saw his mother! Then a stork became the only conceivable explanation!

EVANS. (*who has only half-heard and hasn't understood, says vaguely*) I never saw his folks. (*Indicating the papers*) I can make this all out all right.

MARSDEN. (*sarcastically*) I'm glad it's understandable!

EVANS. (*blunderingly*) I'll give it to Nina—and I hope your mother is feeling better tomorrow.

MARSDEN. (*piqued*) Oh, I'm going. Why didn't you tell me if I was interrupting—your writing!

EVANS. (*immediately guilty*) Oh, come on, Charlie, don't get peevish, you know I didn't mean— (*The bell rings.* EVANS *stammers in confusion, trying at a nonchalant air*) Hello! That must be Ned. You remember Darrell? He's coming out for a little visit. Excuse me. (*He blunders out of the door.*)

MARSDEN. (*looking after him with anger mixed with alarmed suspicion and surprise*)

Darrell? . . . what's he doing here? . . . have they been meeting? . . . perhaps he was the one who performed the . . . no, his idea was she ought to have a child . . . but if she came and begged him? . . . but why should Nina beg not to have a baby? . . .

(*Distractedly*)

Oh, I don't know! . . . it's all a sordid mess! . . . I ought to be going home! . . . I don't want to see Darrell! . . .

(*He starts for the door—then struck by a sudden thought, stops*)

Wait . . . I could ask him about Mother . . . yes . . . good idea . . .

(*He comes back to the middle of the room, front, and is standing there when* DARRELL *enters, followed by* EVANS. DARRELL *has not changed in appearance except that his expression is graver and more thoughtful. His manner is more convincingly authoritative, more mature. He takes in* MARSDEN *from head to foot with one comprehensive glance.*)

EVANS. (*awkwardly*) Ned, you remember Charlie Marsden?

MARSDEN. (*holding out his hand, urbanely polite*) How are you, Doctor?

DARRELL. (*shaking his hand—briefly*) Hello.

EVANS. I'll go up and tell Nina you're here, Ned. (*He goes, casting a resentful glance at* MARSDEN.)

MARSDEN. (*awkwardly, as* DARRELL *sits down in the chair at center, goes over and stands by the table*) I was on the point of leaving when you rang. Then I decided to stop and renew our acquaintance. (*He stoops and picks up one sheet of paper, and puts it back carefully on the table.*)

DARRELL. (*watching him—thinking*)

Neat . . . suspiciously neat . . . he's an old maid who seduces himself in his novels . . . so I suspect . . . I'd like a chance to study him more closely. . . .

MARSDEN. (*thinking resentfully*)

What a boor! . . . he might say something! . . .

(*Forcing a smile*) And I wanted to ask a favor of you, a word of advice as to the best specialist, the very best, it would be possible to consult—

DARRELL. (*sharply*) On what?

MARSDEN. (*almost naïvely*) My mother has a pain in her stomach.

DARRELL. (*amused—dryly*) Possibly she eats too much.

MARSDEN. (*as he bends and carefully picks another sheet from the floor to place it as carefully on the table*) She doesn't eat enough to keep a canary alive. It's a dull, constant pain, she says. She's terribly worried. She's terrified by the idea of cancer. But, of course, that's perfect rot, she's never been sick a day in her life and—

DARRELL. (*sharply*) She's showing more intelligence about her pain than you are.

MARSDEN. (*bending down for another sheet, his voice trembling with terror*) I don't understand—quite. Do you mean to say you think—?

DARRELL. (*brutally*) It's possible.

(*He has pulled out his pen and a card and is writing. Thinking grimly*)

> Explode a bomb under him, as I did once before . . . only way to get him started doing anything. . . .

MARSDEN. (*angrily*) But—that's nonsense!

DARRELL. (*with satisfaction—unruffledly*) People who are afraid to face unpleasant possibilities until it's too late commit more murders and suicides than— (*Holds out card*) Doctor Schultz is your man. Take her to see him—tomorrow!

MARSDEN. (*bursting out in anger and misery*) Damn it, you're condemning her without—! (*He breaks down chokingly*) You've no damn right!— (*He bends down, trembling all over, to pick up another piece of paper.*)

DARRELL. (*genuinely astonished and contrite*)

> And I thought he was so ingrown he didn't care a damn about anyone! . . . his mother . . . now I begin to see him . . .

(*He jumps from his chair and going to* MARSDEN *puts a hand on his shoulder—kindly*) I beg your pardon, Marsden. I only wanted to drive it in that all delay is dangerous. Your mother's pain may be due to any number of harmless causes, but you owe it to her to make sure. Here. (*He hands out the card.*)

MARSDEN. (*straightens up and takes it, his eyes grateful now—humbly*) Thank you. I'll take her to see him tomorrow. (EVANS *comes in.*)

EVANS. (*to* MARSDEN, *blunderingly*) Say, Charlie, I don't want to hurry you but Nina wants some things at the store before it closes, and if you'd give me a lift—

MARSDEN. (*dully*) Of course. Come along. (*He shakes hands with* DARRELL) Good night, Doctor—and thank you.

DARRELL. Good night. (MARSDEN *goes, followed by* EVANS.)

EVANS. (*turns in the doorway and says meaningly*) Nina'll be right down. For Pete's sake, have a good heart-to-heart talk with her, Ned!

DARRELL. (*frowning—impatiently*) Oh—all right! Run along. (EVANS *goes.* DARRELL *remains standing near the table looking after them, thinking about* MARSDEN)

Queer fellow, Marsden . . . mother's boy still . . . if she dies what will he do? . . .

(*Then dismissing* MARSDEN *with a shrug of his shoulders*)

Oh, well, he can always escape life in a new book. . . .

(*He moves around the table examining its disorder critically, then sits down in armchair—amused.*)

Evidences of authorship . . . Sam's ads? . . . isn't making good, he said . . . was I wrong in thinking he had stuff in him? . . . hope not . . . always liked Sam, don't know why exactly . . . said Nina'd gotten into a bad state again . . . what's happened to their marriage? . . . I felt a bit sorry for myself at their wedding . . . not that I'd ever fallen . . . but I did envy him in a way . . . she always had strong physical attraction for me . . . that time I kissed her . . . one reason I've steered clear since . . . take no chances on emotional didos . . . need all my mind on my work . . . got rid of even that slight suspicion . . . I'd forgotten all about her . . . she's a strange girl . . . interesting case . . . I should have kept in touch on that account . . . hope she'll tell me about herself . . . can't understand her not having child . . . it's so obviously the sensible thing . . .

(*Cynically*)

Probably why . . . to expect common sense of people proves you're lacking in it yourself! . . .

NINA. (*enters silently. She has fixed herself up, put on her best dress, arranged her hair, rouged, etc.—but it is principally her mood that has changed her, making her appear a younger, prettier person for the moment.* DARRELL *immediately senses her presence, and, looking up, gets to his feet with a smile of affectionate admiration. She comes quickly over to him saying with frank pleasure*) Hello, Ned. I'm certainly glad to see you again—after all these years!

DARRELL. (*as they shake hands—smiling*) Not as long as all that, is it? (*Thinking admiringly*)

Wonderful-looking as ever . . . Sam is a lucky devil! . . .

NINA. (*thinking*)

Strong hands like Gordon's . . . take hold of you . . . not like Sam's . . . yielding fingers that let you fall back into yourself . . .

(*Teasingly*) I ought to cut you dead after the shameful way you've ignored us!

DARRELL. (*a bit embarrassedly*) I've really meant to write. (*His eyes examining her keenly*)

Been through a lot since I saw her . . . face shows it . . . nervous tension pronounced . . . hiding behind her smile . . .

NINA. (*uneasy under his glance*)

I hate that professional look in his eyes . . . watching symptoms . . . without seeing me . . .

(*With resentful mockery*) Well, what do you suspect is wrong with the patient now, Doctor? (*She laughs nervously*) Sit down, Ned. I suppose you can't help your diagnosing stare. (*She turns from him and sits down in the rocker at center.*)

DARRELL. (*quickly averting his eyes—sits down—jokingly*) Same old unjust accusation! You were always reading diagnosis into me, when what I was really thinking was what fine eyes you had, or what a becoming gown, or—

NINA. (*smiling*) Or what a becoming alibi you could cook up! Oh, I know you! (*With a sudden change of mood she laughs gaily and naturally*) But you're forgiven—that is, if you can explain why you've never been to see us.

DARRELL. Honestly, Nina, I've been so rushed with work I haven't had a chance to go anywhere.

NINA. Or an inclination!

DARRELL. (*smiling*) Well—maybe.

NINA. Do you like the Institute so much? (*He nods gravely*) Is it the big opportunity you wanted?

DARRELL. (*simply*) I think it is.

NINA. (*with a smile*) Well, you're the taking kind for whom opportunities are made!

DARRELL. (*smiling*) I hope so.

NINA. (*sighing*) I wish that could be said of more of us— (*Then quickly*) —meaning myself.

DARRELL. (*thinking with a certain satisfaction*)

> Meaning Sam . . . that doesn't look hopeful for future wedded bliss! . . .

(*Teasingly*) But I heard you were "taking an opportunity" to go in for literature—collaborating with Marsden.

NINA. No, Charlie is only going to advise. He'd never deign to appear as co-author. And besides, he never appreciated the real Gordon. No one did except me.

DARRELL. (*thinking caustically*)

> Gordon myth strong as ever . . . root of her trouble still . . .

(*Keenly inquisitive*) Sam certainly appreciated him, didn't he?

NINA. (*not remembering to hide her contempt*) Sam? Why, he's the exact opposite in every way!

DARRELL. (*caustically thinking*)

These heroes die hard . . . but perhaps she can write him out of her system. . . .

(*Persuasively*) Well, you're going ahead with the biography, aren't you? I think you ought to.

NINA. (*dryly*) For my soul, Doctor? (*Listlessly*) I suppose I will. I don't know. I haven't much time. The duties of a wife— (*Teasingly*) By the way, if it isn't too rude to inquire, aren't you getting yourself engaged to some fair lady or other?

DARRELL. (*smiling—but emphatically*) Not on your life! Not until after I'm thirty-five, at least!

NINA. (*sarcastically*) Then you don't believe in taking your own medicine? Why, Doctor! Think of how much good it would do you!— (*Excitedly with a hectic sarcasm*) —if you had a nice girl to love—or was it learn to love?—and take care of—whose character you could shape and whose life you could guide and make what you pleased, in whose unselfish devotion you could find peace! (*More and more bitterly sarcastic*) And you ought to have a baby, Doctor! You will never know what life is, you'll never be really happy until you've had a baby, Doctor—a fine, healthy baby! (*She laughs a bitter, sneering laugh.*)

DARRELL. (*after a quick, keen glance, thinking*)

Good! . . . she's going to tell . . .

(*Meekly*) I recognize my arguments. Was I really wrong on every point, Nina?

NINA. (*harshly*) On every single point, Doctor!

DARRELL. (*glancing at her keenly*) But how? You haven't given the baby end of it a chance yet, have you?

NINA. (*bitterly*) Oh, haven't I? (*Then bursts out with intense bitterness*) I'll have you know I'm not destined to bear babies, Doctor!

DARRELL. (*startledly*)

What's that? . . . why not? . . .

(*Again with a certain satisfaction*)

Can she mean Sam? . . . that he . . .

(*Soothingly—but plainly disturbed*) Why don't you begin at the beginning and tell me all about it? I feel responsible.

NINA. (*fiercely*) You are! (*Then wearily*) And you're not. No one is. You didn't know. No one could know.

DARRELL. (*in same tone*) Know what? (*Thinking with the same eagerness to believe something he hopes*)

She must mean no one could know that Sam wasn't . . . but I might have guessed it . . . from his general weakness . . . poor unlucky devil . . .

(*Then as she remains silent—urgingly*) Tell me. I want to help you, Nina.

NINA. (*touched*) It's too late, Ned. (*Then suddenly*) I've just thought—Sam said he happened to run into you. That isn't so, is it? He went to see you and told you how worried he was about me and asked you out to see me, didn't he? (*As* DARRELL *nods*) Oh, I don't mind! It's even rather touching. (*Then mockingly*) Well, since you're out here professionally, and my husband wants me to consult you, I might as well give you the whole case history! (*Wearily*) I warn you it isn't pretty, Doctor! But then life doesn't seem to be pretty, does it? And, after all, you aided and abetted God the Father in making this mess. I hope it'll teach you not to be so cocksure in future. (*More and more bitterly*) I must say you proceeded very unscientifically, Doctor! (*Then suddenly starts her story in a dull monotonous tone recalling that of* EVANS' *mother in the previous Act*) When we went to visit Sam's mother I'd known for two months that I was going to have a baby.

DARRELL. (*startled—unable to hide a trace of disappointment*) Oh, then you actually were? (*Thinking disappointedly and ashamed of himself for being disappointed*)

All wrong, what I thought . . . she was going to . . . then why didn't she? . . .

NINA. (*with a strange happy intensity*) Oh, Ned, I loved it more than I've ever loved anything in my life—even Gordon! I loved it so it seemed at times that Gordon must be its real father, that Gordon must have come to me in a dream while I was lying asleep beside Sam! And I was happy! I almost loved Sam then! I felt he was a good husband!

DARRELL. (*instantly repelled—thinking with scornful jealousy*)

> Ha! . . . the hero again! . . . comes to her bed! . . . puts horns on poor Sam! . . . becomes the father of his child! . . . I'll be damned if hers isn't the most idiotic obsession I ever . . .

NINA. (*her voice suddenly becoming flat and lifeless*) And then Sam's mother told me I couldn't have my baby. You see, Doctor, Sam's great-grandfather was insane, and Sam's grandmother died in an asylum, and Sam's father had lost his mind for years before he died, and an aunt who is still alive is crazy. So of course I had to agree it would be wrong—and I had an operation.

DARRELL. (*who has listened with amazed horror—profoundly shocked and stunned*) Good God! Are you crazy, Nina? I simply can't believe! It would be too hellish! Poor Sam, of all people! (*Bewilderedly*) Nina! Are you absolutely sure?

NINA. (*immediately defensive and mocking*) Absolutely, Doctor! Why? Do you think it's I who am crazy? Sam looks so healthy and sane, doesn't he? He fooled you completely, didn't he? You thought he'd be an ideal husband for me! And poor Sam's fooling himself too because he doesn't know anything about all this—so you can't blame him, Doctor!

DARRELL. (*thinking in a real panic of horror—and a flood of protective affection for her*)

> God, this is too awful! . . . on top of all the rest! . . . how did she ever stand it! . . . she'll lose her mind too! . . . and it's my fault! . . .

(*Getting up, comes to her and puts his hands on her shoulders, standing behind her—tenderly*) Nina! I'm so damn sorry! There's only one possible thing to do now. You'll have to make Sam give you a divorce.

NINA. (*bitterly*) Yes? Then what do you suppose would be his finish? No, I've enough guilt in my memory now, thank you! I've got to stick to Sam! (*Then with a strange monotonous insistence*) I've promised Sam's mother I'd make him happy! He's unhappy now because he thinks he isn't able to give me a child. And I'm unhappy because I've lost my child. So I must have another baby—somehow—don't you think, Doctor?—to make us both happy? (*She looks up at him pleadingly. For a moment they stare into each other's eyes—then both turn away in guilty confusion.*)

DARRELL. (*bewilderedly thinking*)

That look in her eyes . . . what does she want me to think? . . . why does she talk so much about being happy? . . . am I happy? . . . I don't know . . . what is happiness? . . .

(*Confusedly*) Nina, I don't know what to think.

NINA. (*thinking strangely*)

That look in his eyes . . . what did he mean? . . .

(*With the same monotonous insistence*) You must know what to think. I can't think it out myself any more. I need your advice—your *scientific* advice this time, if you please, Doctor. I've thought and thought about it. I've told myself it's what I ought to do. Sam's own mother urged me to do it. It's sensible and kind and just and good. I've told myself this a thousand times and yet I can't quite convince something in me that's afraid of something. I need the courage of someone who can stand outside and reason it out as if Sam and I were no more than guinea pigs. You've got to help me, Doctor! You've got to show me what's the sane—the truly sane, you understand!—thing I must do for Sam's sake, and my own.

DARRELL. (*thinking confusedly*)

What do I have to do? . . . this was all my fault . . . I owe her something in return . . . I owe Sam something . . . I owe them happiness! . . .

(*Irritably*)

Damn it, there's a humming in my ears! . . . I've caught some fever . . . I swore to live coolly . . . let me see. . . .

(*In a cold, emotionless professional voice, his face like a mask of a doctor*) A doctor must be in full possession of the facts, if he is to advise. What is it precisely that Sam's wife has thought so much of doing?

NINA. (*in the same insistent tone*) Of picking out a healthy male about whom she cared nothing and having a child by him that Sam would believe was his child, whose life would give him confidence in his own living, who would be for him a living proof that his wife loved him. (*Confusedly, strangely and purposefully*)

This doctor is healthy. . . .

DARRELL. (*in his ultra-professional manner—like an automaton of a doctor*) I see. But this needs a lot of thinking over. It isn't easy to prescribe—(*Thinking*)

I have a friend who has a wife . . . I was envious at his wedding . . . but what has that to do with it? . . . damn it, my mind won't work! . . . it keeps running away to her . . . it wants to mate with her mind . . . in the interest of Science? . . . what damned rot I'm thinking! . . .

NINA. (*thinking as before*)

This doctor is nothing to me but a healthy male . . . when he was Ned he once kissed me . . . but I cared nothing about him . . . so that's all right, isn't it, Sam's Mother?

DARRELL. (*thinking*)

Let me see. . . . I am in the laboratory and they are guinea pigs . . . in fact, in the interest of science, I can be for the purpose of this experiment, a healthy guinea pig myself and still remain an observer . . . I observe my pulse is high, for example, and that's obviously because I am stricken with a recurrence of an old desire . . . desire is a natural male reaction to the beauty of the female . . . her husband is my friend. . . . I have always tried to help him . . .

(*Coldly*) I've been considering what Sam's wife told me and her reasoning is quite sound. The child can't be her husband's.

NINA. Then you agree with Sam's mother? She said: "Being happy is the nearest we can ever come to knowing what good is!"

DARRELL. I agree with her decidedly. Sam's wife should find a healthy father for Sam's child at once. It is her sane duty to her husband. (*Worriedly thinking*)

Have I ever been happy? . . . I have studied to cure the body's unhappiness . . . I have watched happy smiles form on the lips of the dying . . . I have experienced pleasure with a number of women I desired but never loved . . . I have known a bit of honor and a trifle of self-satisfaction . . . this talk of happiness seems to me extraneous . . .

NINA. (*beginning to adopt a timid, diffident, guilty tone*) This will have to be hidden from Sam so he can never know! Oh, Doctor, Sam's wife is afraid!

DARRELL. (*sharply professional*) Nonsense! This is no time for timidity! Happiness hates the timid! So does Science! Certainly Sam's wife must conceal her action! To let Sam know would be insanely cruel of her—and stupid, for then no one could be the happier for her act! (*Anxiously thinking*)

Am I right to advise this? . . . yes, it is clearly the rational thing to do . . . but this advice betrays my friend! . . . no, it saves him! . . . it saves his wife . . . and if a third party should know a little happiness . . . is he any poorer, am I any the less his friend because I saved him? . . . no, my duty to him is plain . . . and my duty as an experimental searcher after truth . . . to observe these three guinea pigs, of which I am one . . .

NINA. (*thinking determinedly*)

I must have my baby! . . .

(*Timidly—gets from her chair and half-turns toward him—pleadingly*) You must give his wife courage, Doctor. You must free her from her feeling of guilt.

DARRELL. There can only be guilt when one deliberately neglects one's manifest duty to life. Anything else is rot! This woman's duty is to save her husband and herself by begetting a healthy child! (*Thinking guiltily and instinctively moving away from her*)

I am healthy . . . but he is my friend . . . there is such a thing as honor! . . .

NINA. (*determinedly*)

I must take my happiness! . . .

(*Frightenedly—comes after him*) But she is ashamed. It's adultery. It's wrong.

DARRELL. (*moving away again—with a cold sneering laugh of impatience*) Wrong! Would she rather see her husband wind up in an asylum? Would she rather face the prospect of going to pot mentally, morally, physically herself through year after year of devilling herself and him? Really, Madame, if you can't throw overboard all such irrelevant moral ideas, I'll have to give up this case here and now!

NINA. (*thinking frightenedly*)

Who is talking? . . . is he suggesting me? . . . but you know very well I can't be the one, Doctor! . . . why not, you're healthy and it's a friendly act for all concerned . . . (*Determinedly*) I must have my baby! . . .

(*Going further toward him—she can now touch him with her hand*) Please, Doctor, you must give her strength to do this right thing that seems to her so right and then so wrong! (*She puts out her hand and takes one of his.*)

DARRELL. (*thinking frightenedly*)

Whose hand is this? . . . it burns me . . . I kissed her once . . . her lips were cold . . . now they would burn with happiness for me! . . .

NINA. (*taking his other hand and slowly pulling him around to face her, although he does not look at her—pleadingly*) Now she feels your strength. It gives her the courage to ask you, Doctor, to suggest the father. She has changed, Doctor, since she became Sam's wife. She can't bear the thought now of giving herself to any man she could neither desire nor respect. So each time her thoughts come to the man she must select they are afraid to go on! She needs your courage to choose!

DARRELL. (*as if listening to himself*)

Sam is my friend . . . well, and isn't she your friend? . . . her two hands are so warm! . . . I must not even hint at my desire! . . .

(*Judicially calm*) Well, the man must be someone who is not unattractive to her physically, of course.

NINA. Ned always attracted her.

DARRELL. (*thinking frightenedly*)

What's that she said? . . . Ned? . . . attracts? . . .

(*In same tone*) And the man should have a mind that can truly understand—a scientific mind superior to the moral scruples that cause so much human blundering and unhappiness.

NINA. She always thought Ned had a superior mind.

DARRELL. (*thinking frightenedly*)

Did she say Ned? . . . she thinks Ned . . . ?

(*In same tone*) The man should like and admire her, he should be her good friend and want to help her, but he should not love her—although he might, without harm to anyone, desire her.

NINA. Ned does not love her—but he used to like her and, I think, desire her. Does he now, Doctor?

DARRELL. (*thinking*)

Does he? . . . who is he? . . . he is Ned! . . . Ned is I! . . . I desire her! . . . I desire happiness! . . .

(*Tremblingly now—gently*) But, Madame, I must confess the Ned you are speaking of is I, and I am Ned.

NINA. (*gently*) And I am Nina, who wants her baby. (*Then she reaches out and turns his head until his face faces hers but he keeps his eyes down—she bends her head meekly and submissively—softly*) I should be so grateful, Ned. (*He starts, looks up at her wildly, makes a motion as though to take her in his arms, then remains fixed for a moment in that attitude, staring at her bowed head as she repeats submissively*) I should be so humbly grateful.

DARRELL. (*suddenly falling on his knees and taking her hand in both of his and kissing it humbly—with a sob*) Yes—yes, Nina—yes—for your happiness—in that spirit! (*Thinking—fiercely triumphant*)

I shall be happy for a while! . . .

NINA. (*raising her head—thinking—proudly triumphant*)

I shall be happy! . . . I shall make my husband happy! . . .

CURTAIN

ACT FIVE

SCENE: *The sitting room of a small house* EVANS *has rented in a seashore suburb near New York. It is a bright morning in the following April.*

The room is a typical sitting room of the quantity-production bungalow type. Windows on the left look out on a broad porch. A double doorway in rear leads into the hall. A door on right, to the dining room. NINA *has tried to take the curse of offensive, banal newness off the room with some of her own things from her old home but the attempt has been half-hearted in the face of such overpowering commonness, and the result is a room as disorganized in character as was the* PROFESSOR'S *study in the last Act.*

The arrangement of the furniture follows the same pattern as in preceding scenes. There is a Morris chair and a round golden oak table at left of center, an upholstered chair, covered with bright chintz at center, a sofa covered with the same chintz at right.

NINA *is sitting in the chair at center. She has been trying to read a book but has let this drop listlessly on her lap. A great change is noticeable in her face and bearing. She is again the pregnant woman of Act Three but this time there is a triumphant strength about her expression, a ruthless self-confidence in her eyes. She has grown stouter, her face has filled out. One gets no impression of neurotic strain from her now, she seems nerveless and deeply calm.*

NINA. (*as if listening for something within her—joyfully*)

There! . . . that can't be my imagination . . . I felt it plainly . . . life . . . my baby . . . my only baby . . . the other never really lived . . . this is the child of my love! . . . I love Ned! . . . I've loved him ever since that first afternoon . . . when I went to him . . . so scientifically! . . .

(*She laughs at herself*)

Oh, what a goose I was! . . . then love came to me . . . in his arms . . . happiness! . . . I hid it from him . . . I saw he was frightened . . . his own joy frightened him . . . I could feel him fighting with himself . . . during all those afternoons . . . our wonderful afternoons of happiness! . . . and I said nothing . . . I made myself be calculating . . . so when he finally said . . . dreadfully disturbed . . . "Look here, Nina, we've done all that is necessary, playing with fire is dangerous" . . . I said, "You're quite right, Ned, of all things I don't want to fall in love with you!" . . .

(*She laughs*)

He didn't like that! . . . he looked angry . . . and afraid . . . then for weeks he never even phoned . . . I waited . . . it was prudent to wait . . . but every day I grew more terrified . . . then just as my will was breaking, his broke . . . he suddenly appeared again . . . but I held him to his aloof doctor's pose and sent him away, proud of his will power . . . and sick of himself with desire for me! . . . every week since then he's been coming out here . . . as my doctor . . . we've talked about our child wisely, dispassionately . . . as if it were Sam's child . . . we've never given in to our desire . . . and I've watched love grow in him until I'm sure . . .

(*With sudden alarm*)

But am I? . . . he's never once mentioned love . . . perhaps I've been a fool to play the part I've played . . . it may have turned him against me . . .

(*Suddenly with calm confidence*)

No . . . he does . . . I feel it . . . it's only when I start thinking, I begin to doubt . . .

(*She settles back and stares dreamily before her—a pause*)

There . . . again . . . his child! . . . my child moving in my life . . . my life moving in my child . . . the world is whole and perfect . . . all things are each other's . . . life is . . . and this is beyond reason . . . questions die in the silence of this peace . . . I am living a dream within the great dream of the tide . . . breathing in the tide I dream and breathe back my dream into the tide . . . suspended in the movement of the tide, I feel life move in me, suspended in me . . . no whys matter . . . there is no why . . . I am a mother . . . God is a Mother . . .

(*She sighs happily, closing her eyes. A pause.* EVANS *enters from the hallway in rear. He is dressed carefully but his clothes are old ones —shabby collegiate gentility—and he has forgotten to shave. His eyes look pitiably harried, his manner has become a distressingly obvious attempt to cover up a chronic state of nervous panic and guilty conscience. He stops inside the doorway and looks at her with a pitiable furtiveness, arguing with himself, trying to get up his courage*)

Tell her! . . . go on! . . . you made up your mind to, didn't you? . . . don't quit now! . . . tell her you've decided . . . for her sake . . . to face the truth . . . that she can't love you . . . she's tried . . . she's acted like a good sport . . . but she's beginning to hate you . . . and you can't blame her . . . she wanted children . . . and you haven't been able . . .

(*Protesting feebly*)

But I don't know for certain . . . that that's my fault . . .

(*Then bitterly*)

Aw, don't kid yourself, if she'd married someone else . . . if Gordon had lived and married her . . . I'll bet in the first month she'd . . . you'd better resign from the whole game . . . with a gun! . . .

(*He swallows hard as if he were choking back a sob—then savagely*)

Stop whining! . . . go on and wake her up! . . . say you're willing to give her a divorce so she can marry some real guy who can give her what she ought to have! . . .

(*Then with sudden terror*)

And if she says yes? . . . I couldn't bear it! . . . I'd die without her! . . .

(*Then with a somber alien forcefulness*)

All right . . . good riddance! . . . I'd have the guts to bump off then, all right! . . . that'd set her free . . . come on now! . . . ask her! . . .

(*But his voice begins to tremble uncertainly again as he calls*) Nina.

NINA. (*opens her eyes and gazes calmly, indifferently at him*) Yes?

EVANS. (*immediately terrified and beaten—thinking*)

I can't! . . . the way she looks at me! . . . she'd say yes! . . .

(*Stammering*) I hate to wake you up but—it's about time for Ned to come, isn't it?

NINA. (*calmly*) I wasn't asleep.

(*Thinking as if she found it hard to concentrate on him, to realize his existence*)

This man is my husband . . . it's hard to remember that . . . people will say he's the father of my child. . . .

(*With revulsion*)

That's shameful! . . . and yet that's exactly what I wanted! . . . wanted! . . . not now! . . . now I love Ned! . . . I won't lose him! . . . Sam must give me a divorce . . . I've sacrificed enough of my life . . . what has he given me? . . . not even a home . . . I had to sell my father's home to get money so we could move near his job . . . and then he lost his job! . . . now he's depending on Ned to help him get another! . . . my love! . . . how shameless! . . .

(*Then contritely*)

Oh, I'm unjust . . . poor Sam doesn't know about Ned . . . and it was I who wanted to sell the place . . . I was lonely there . . . I wanted to be near Ned. . . .

EVANS. (*thinking in agony*)

What's she thinking? . . . probably lucky for me I don't know! . . .

(*Forcing a brisk air as he turns away from her*) I hope Ned brings that letter he promised me to the manager of the Globe company. I'm keen to get on the job again.

NINA. (*with scornful pity*) Oh, I guess Ned will bring the letter. I asked him not to forget.

EVANS. I hope they'll have an opening right off. We can use the money. (*Hanging his head*) I feel rotten, living on you when you've got so little.

NINA. (*indifferently but with authority, like a governess to a small boy*) Now, now!

EVANS. (*relieved*) Well, it's true. (*Then coming to her—humbly ingratiating*) You've felt a lot better lately, haven't you, Nina?

NINA. (*with a start—sharply*) Why?

EVANS. You look ever so much better. You're getting fat. (*He forces a grin.*)

NINA. (*curtly*) Don't be absurd, please! As a matter of fact, I don't feel a bit better.

EVANS. (*thinking despondently*)

> Lately, she jumps on me every chance she gets . . . as if everything I did disgusted her! . . .

(*He strays over to the window and looks out listlessly*) I thought we'd get some word from Charlie this morning saying if he was coming down or not. But I suppose he's still too broken up over his mother's death to write.

NINA. (*indifferently*) He'll probably come without bothering to write. (*Vaguely—wonderingly*)

> Charlie . . . dear old Charlie . . . I've forgotten him, too. . . .

EVANS. I think that's Ned's car now. Yes. It's stopping. I'll go out and meet him. (*He starts for the door in rear.*)

NINA. (*sharply, before she can restrain the impulse*) Don't be such a fool!

EVANS. (*stops—stammers confusedly*) What—what's the matter?

NINA. (*controlling herself—but irritably*) Don't mind me. I'm nervous. (*Thinking guiltily*)

> One minute I feel ashamed of him for making such a fool of himself over my lover . . . the next minute something hateful urges me to drive him into doing it! . . .

(*The maid has answered the ring and opened the outer door.* NED

DARRELL *comes in from the rear. His face looks older. There is an expression of defensive bitterness and self-resentment about his mouth and eyes. This vanishes into one of desire and joy as he sees* NINA. *He starts toward her impulsively*) Nina! (*Then stops short as he sees* EVANS.)

NINA. (*forgetting* EVANS, *gets to her feet as if to receive* DARRELL *in her arms—with love*) Ned!

EVANS. (*affectionately and gratefully*) Hello, Ned! (*He holds out his hand which* DARRELL *takes mechanically.*)

DARRELL. (*trying to overcome his guilty embarrassment*) Hello, Sam. Didn't see you. (*Hurriedly reaching in his coat pocket*) Before I forget, here's that letter. I had a talk over the phone with Appleby yesterday. He's pretty sure there's an opening—(*With a condescension he can't help*)—but you'll have to get your nose on the grindstone to make good with him.

EVANS. (*flushing guiltily—forcing a confident tone*) You bet I will! (*Then gratefully and humbly*) Gosh, Ned, I can't tell you how grateful I am!

DARRELL. (*brusquely, to hide his embarrassment*) Oh, shut up! I'm only too glad.

NINA. (*watching* EVANS *with a contempt that is almost gloating—in a tone of curt dismissal*) You'd better go and shave, hadn't you, if you're going to town?

EVANS. (*guiltily, passing his hand over his face—forcing a brisk, purposeful air*) Yes, of course. I forgot I hadn't. Excuse me, will you? (*This to* DARRELL. EVANS *hurries out, rear.*)

DARRELL. (*as soon as he is out of earshot—turning on* NINA *accusingly*) How can you treat him that way? It makes me feel—like a swine!

NINA. (*flushing guiltily—protestingly*) What way? (*Then inconsequentially*) He's always forgetting to shave lately.

DARRELL. You know what I mean, Nina! (*Turns away from her—thinking bitterly*)

What a rotten liar I've become! . . . and he trusts me absolutely! . . .

NINA. (*thinking frightenedly*)

Why doesn't he take me in his arms? . . . oh, I feel he doesn't love me now! . . . he's so bitter! . . .

(*Trying to be matter-of-fact*) I'm sorry, Ned. I don't mean to be cross but Sam does get on my nerves.

DARRELL. (*thinking bitterly*)

Sometimes I almost hate her! . . . if it wasn't for her I'd have kept my peace of mind . . . no good for anything lately, damn it! . . . but it's idiotic to feel guilty . . . if Sam only didn't trust me! . . .

(*Then impatiently*)

Bosh! . . . sentimental nonsense! . . . end justifies means! . . . this will have a good end for Sam, I swear to that! . . . why doesn't she tell him she's pregnant? . . . what's she waiting for? . . .

NINA. (*thinking passionately, looking at him*)

Oh, my lover, why don't you kiss me? . . .

(*Imploringly*) Ned! Don't be cross with me, please!

DARRELL. (*fighting to control himself—coldly*) I'm not cross, Nina. Only you must admit these triangular scenes are, to say the least, humiliating. (*Resentfully*) I won't come out here again!

NINA. (*with a cry of pain*) Ned!

DARRELL. (*thinking exultantly at first*)

She loves me! . . . she's forgotten Gordon! . . . I'm happy! . . . do I love her? . . . no! . . . I won't! . . . I can't! . . . think what it would mean to Sam! . . . to my career! . . . be objective about it! . . . you guinea pig! . . . I'm her doctor . . . and Sam's . . . I prescribed child for them . . . that's all there is to it! . . .

NINA. (*torn between hope and fear*)

What is he thinking? . . . he's fighting his love . . . oh, my lover! . . .

(*Again with longing*) Ned!

DARRELL. (*putting on his best professional air, going to her*) How do you feel today? You look as if you might have a little fever. (*He takes her hand as if to feel her pulse. Her hand closes over his. She looks up into his face. He keeps his turned away.*)

NINA. (*straining up toward him—with intense longing—thinking*)

I love you! . . . take me! . . . what do I care for anything in the world but you! . . . let Sam die! . . .

DARRELL. (*fighting himself—thinking*)

Christ! . . . touch of her skin! . . . her nakedness! . . . those afternoons in her arms! happiness! . . . what do I care for anything else? . . . to hell with Sam! . . .

NINA. (*breaking out passionately*) Ned! I love you! I can't hide it any more! I won't! I love you, Ned!

DARRELL. (*suddenly taking her in his arms and kissing her frantically*) Nina! Beautiful!

NINA. (*triumphantly—between kisses*) You love me, don't you? Say you do, Ned!

DARRELL. (*passionately*) Yes! Yes!

NINA. (*with a cry of triumph*) Thank God! At last you've told me! You've confessed it to yourself! Oh, Ned, you've made me so happy! (*There is a ring from the front door bell.* DARRELL *hears it. It acts like an electric shock on him. He tears himself away from her. Instinctively she gets up too and moves to the lounge at right.*)

DARRELL. (*stupidly*) Someone—at the door. (*He sinks down in the chair by the table at left. Thinking torturedly*)

I said I loved her! . . . she won! . . . she used my desire! . . . but I don't love her! . . . I won't! . . . she can't own my life! . . .

(*Violently—almost shouts at her*) I don't, Nina! I tell you I don't!

NINA. (*the maid has just gone to the front door*) Sshh! (*Then in a triumphant whisper*) You do, Ned! You do!

DARRELL. (*with dogged stupidity*) I don't! (*The front door has been opened.* MARSDEN *appears in the rear, walks slowly and woodenly like a man in a trance into the room. He is dressed immaculately in deep mourning. His face is pale, drawn, haggard with loneliness and grief. His eyes have a dazed look as if he were still too stunned to comprehend clearly what has happened to him. He does not seem conscious of* DARRELL'S *presence at first. His shoulders are bowed, his whole figure droops.*)

NINA. (*thinking—in a strange superstitious panic*)

Black . . . in the midst of happiness . . . black comes . . . again . . . death . . . my father . . . comes between me and happiness! . . .

(*Then recovering herself, scornfully*)

You silly coward! . . . it's only Charlie! . . .

(*Then with furious resentment*)

The old fool! . . . what does he mean coming in on us without warning? . . .

MARSDEN. (*forcing a pitiful smile to his lips*) Hello, Nina. I know it's an imposition—but—I've been in such a terrible state since Mother—(*He falters, his face becomes distorted into an ugly mask of grief, his eyes water.*)

NINA. (*immediately sympathetic, gets up and goes to him impulsively*) There's no question of imposition, Charlie. We were expecting you. (*She has come to him and put her arms around him. He gives way and sobs, his head against her shoulder.*)

MARSDEN. (*brokenly*) You don't know, Nina—how terrible—it's terrible!—

NINA. (*leading him to the chair at center, soothingly*) I know, Charlie.

(*Thinking with helpless annoyance*)

Oh, dear, what can I say? . . . his mother hated me . . .
I'm not glad she's dead . . . but neither am I sorry . . .

(*With a trace of contempt*)

Poor Charlie . . . he was so tied to her apron strings . . .

(*Then kindly but condescendingly, comforting him*) Poor old Charlie!

MARSDEN. (*the words and the tone shock his pride to life. He raises his head and half-pushes her away—resentfully, thinking*)

Poor old Charlie! . . . damn it, what am I to her? . . . her old dog who's lost his mother? . . . Mother hated her . . . no, poor dear Mother was so sweet, she never hated anyone . . . she simply disapproved . . .

(*Coldly*) I'm all right, Nina. Quite all right now, thank you. I apologize for making a scene.

DARRELL. (*has gotten up from his chair—with relief—thinking*)

Thank God for Marsden . . . I feel sane again . . .

(*He comes to* MARSDEN*—cordially*) How are you, Marsden? (*Then offering conventional consolation, pats* MARSDEN'S *shoulder*) I'm sorry, Marsden.

MARSDEN. (*startled, looks up at him in amazement*) Darrell! (*Then with instdnt hostility*) There's nothing to be sorry about that I can discover! (*Then as they both look at him in surprise he realizes what he has said—stammeringly*) I mean—sorry—is hardly the right word—hardly—is it?

NINA. (*worriedly*) Sit down, Charlie. You look so tired. (*He slumps down in the chair at center mechanically.* NINA *and* DARRELL *return to their chairs.* NINA *looks across him at* DARRELL*—triumphantly—thinking*)

You do love me, Ned! . . .

DARRELL. (*thinking—answering her look—defiantly*)

I don't love you! . . .

MARSDEN. (*stares intensely before him. Thinking suspiciously—morbidly agitated*)

Darrell! . . . and Nina! . . . there's something in this room! . . . something disgusting! . . . like a brutal, hairy hand, raw and red, at my throat! . . . stench of human life! . . . heavy and rank! . . . outside it's April . . . green buds on the slim trees . . . the sadness of spring . . . my loss at peace in Nature . . .

her sorrow of birth consoling my sorrow of death . . . something human and unnatural in this room! . . . love and hate and passion and possession! . . . cruelly indifferent to my loss! . . . mocking my loneliness! . . . no longer any love for me in any room! . . . lust in this room! . . . lust with a loathsome jeer taunting my sensitive timidities! . . . my purity! . . . purity? . . . ha! yes, if you say prurient purity! . . . lust ogling me for a dollar with oily shoe button Italian eyes! . . .

(*In terror*)

What thoughts! . . . what a low scoundrel you are! . . . and your mother dead only two weeks! . . . I hate Nina! . . . that Darrell in this room! . . . I feel their desires! . . . where is Sam? . . . I'll tell him! . . . no, he wouldn't believe . . . he's such a trusting fool . . . I must punish her some other way . . .

(*Remorsefully*)

What? . . . punish Nina? . . . my little Nina? . . . why, I want her to be happy! . . . even with Darrell? . . . it's all so confused! . . . I must stop thinking! . . . I must talk! . . . forget! . . . say something! . . . forget everything! . . .

(*He suddenly bursts into a flood of garrulity*) Mother asked for you, Nina—three days before the end. She said, "Where is Nina Leeds now, Charlie? When is she going to marry Gordon Shaw?" Her mind was wandering, poor woman! You remember how fond she always was of Gordon. She used to love to watch the football games when he was playing. He was so handsome and graceful, she always thought. She always loved a strong, healthy body. She took such strict care of her own, she walked miles every day, she loved bathing and boating in the summer even after she was sixty, she was never sick a day in her life until—(*He turns on* DARRELL—*coldly*) You were right, Doctor Darrell. It was cancer. (*Then angrily*) But the doctor you sent me to, and the others he called in could do nothing for her—absolutely nothing! I might just as well have imported some witch doctors from the Solomon Islands! They at least would have diverted her in her last hours with their singing and dancing, but your specialists were at total loss! (*Suddenly with an insulting, ugly sneer, raising his voice*) I think you doctors are a pack of God-damned ignorant liars and hypocrites!

NINA. (*sharply*) Charlie!

MARSDEN. (*coming to himself—with a groan—shamefacedly*) Don't mind me. I'm not myself, Nina. I've been through hell! (*He seems about to sob—then abruptly springs to his feet, wildly*) It's this room! I can't stand this room! There's something repulsive about it!

NINA. (*soothingly*) I know it's ugly, Charlie. I haven't had a chance to fix it up yet. We've been too broke.

MARSDEN. (*confusedly*) Oh, it's all right. I'm ugly, too! Where's Sam?

NINA. (*eagerly*) Right upstairs. Go on up. He'll be delighted to see you.

MARSDEN. (*vaguely*) Very well. (*He goes to the door, then stops mournfully*) But from what I saw on that visit to his home, he doesn't love his mother much. I don't think he'll understand, Nina. He never writes to her, does he?

NINA. (*uneasily*) No—I don't know.

MARSDEN. She seemed lonely. He'll be sorry for it some day after she— (*He gulps*) Well— (*He goes.*)

NINA. (*in a sudden panic—thinking*)

Sam's mother! . . . "Make my boy, Sammy, happy!" . . . I promised . . . oh, why did Charlie have to remember her? . . .

(*Then resolutely*)

I can't remember her now! . . . I won't! . . . I've got to be happy! . . .

DARRELL. (*uneasily trying to force a casual conversation*) Poor Marsden is completely knocked off balance, isn't he? (*A pause*) My mother died when I was away at school. I hadn't seen her in some time, so her death was never very real to me; but in Marsden's case—

NINA. (*with a possessive smile of tolerance*) Never mind Charlie,

Ned. What do I care about Charlie? I love you! And you love me!

DARRELL. (*apprehensively, forcing a tone of annoyed rebuke*) But I don't! And you don't! You're simply letting your romantic imagination run away with you— (*Showing his jealous resentment in spite of himself*) —as you did once before with Gordon Shaw!

NINA. (*thinking*)

He is jealous of Gordon! . . . how wonderful that is! . . .

(*With provoking calm*) I loved Gordon.

DARRELL. (*irritably ignoring this as if he didn't want to hear it*) Romantic imagination! It has ruined more lives than all the diseases! Other diseases, I should say! It's a form of insanity! (*He gets up forcefully and begins to pace about the room. Thinking uneasily*)

Mustn't look at her . . . find an excuse and get away . . . and this time never come back! . . .

(*Avoiding looking at her, trying to argue reasonably—coldly*) You're acting foolishly, Nina—and very unfairly. The agreement we made has no more to do with love than a contract for building a house. In fact, you know we agreed it was essential that love mustn't enter into it. And it hasn't in spite of what you say. (*A pause. He walks about. She watches him. Thinking*)

She's got to come back to earth! . . . I've got to break with her! . . . bad enough now! . . . but to go on with it! . . . what a mess it'd make of all our lives! . . .

NINA. (*thinking tenderly*)

Let his pride put all the blame on me! . . . I'll accept it gladly! . . .

DARRELL. (*irritably*) Of course, I realize I've been to blame, too. I haven't been able to be as impersonal as I thought I could be. The trouble is there's been a dangerous physical attraction. Since I first met you, I've always desired you physically. I admit that now.

NINA. (*smiling tenderly—thinking*)

Oh, he admits that, does he? . . . poor darling! . . .

(*Enticingly*) And you still do desire me, don't you, Ned?

DARRELL. (*keeping his back turned to her—roughly*) No! That part of it is finished! (NINA *laughs softly, possessively. He whirls around to face her—angrily*) Look here! You're going to have the child you wanted, aren't you?

NINA. (*implacably*) My child wants its father!

DARRELL. (*coming a little toward her—desperately*) But you're crazy! You're forgetting Sam! It may be stupid but I've got a guilty conscience! I'm beginning to think we've wronged the very one we were trying to help!

NINA. You were trying to help me, too, Ned!

DARRELL. (*stammering*) Well—all right—let's say that part of it was all right then. But it's got to stop! It can't go on!

NINA. (*implacably*) Only your love can make me happy now! Sam must give me a divorce so I can marry you.

DARRELL. (*thinking suspiciously*)

Look out! . . . there it is! . . . marry! . . . own me! . . . ruin my career! . . .

(*Scornfully*) Marry? Do you think I'm a fool? Get that out of your head quick! I wouldn't marry anyone—no matter what! (*As she continues to look at him with unmoved determination—pleadingly*) Be sensible, for God's sake! We're absolutely unsuited to each other! I don't admire your character! I don't respect you! I know too much about your past! (*Then indignantly*) And how about Sam? Divorce him? Have you forgotten all his mother told you? Do you mean to say you'd deliberately—? And you expect me to—? What do you think I am?

NINA. (*inflexibly*) You're my lover! Nothing else matters. Yes, I remember what Sam's mother said. She said, "being happy is the nearest we can come to knowing what good is." And I'm going to be happy! I've lost everything in life so far because I didn't have the courage to take it—and I've hurt everyone around me. There's no use trying to think of others. One human being can't think of another. It's impossible. (*Gently and caressingly*) But this time I'm going to think of my own happiness—and that means you—and our child! That's quite enough for one human being to think of, dear, isn't it? (*She reaches out and takes his hand. A pause. With her other hand she gently pulls him around until he is forced to look into her eyes.*)

DARRELL. (*thinking fascinatedly*)

I see my happiness in her eyes . . . the touch of her soft skin! . . . those afternoons! . . . God, I was happy! . . .

(*In a strange dazed voice—as if it were forced out of him by an impulse stronger than his will*) Yes, Nina.

NINA. (*in a determined voice*) I've given Sam enough of my life! And it hasn't made him happy, not the least bit! So what's the good? And how can we really know that his thinking our child was his would do him any good? We can't! It's all guesswork. The only thing sure is that we love each other.

DARRELL. (*dazedly*) Yes. (*A noise from the hall and* EVANS *comes in from the rear. He sees their two hands together but mistakes their meaning.*)

EVANS. (*genially—with a forced self-confident air*) Well, Doc, how's the patient? I think she's much better, don't you—although she won't admit it.

DARRELL. (*at the first sound of* EVANS' *voice, pulls his hand from* NINA'S *as if it were a hot coal—avoiding* EVANS' *eyes, moving away from her jerkily and self-consciously*) Yes. Much better.

EVANS. Good! (*He pats* NINA *on the back. She shrinks away. His confidence vanishes in a flash. Thinking miserably*)

Why does she shrink away . . . if I even touch her? . . .

NINA. (*matter-of-factly*) I must see how lunch is coming on. You'll stay, of course, Ned?

DARRELL. (*struggling—shakenly*) No, I think I'd better—(*Thinking desperately*)

Got to go! . . . can't go! . . . got to go! . . .

EVANS. Oh, come on, old man!

NINA. (*thinking*)

He must stay . . . and after lunch we'll tell Sam. . . .

(*With certainty*) He'll stay. (*Meaningly*) And we want to have a long talk with you after lunch, Sam—don't we, Ned? (DARRELL *does not answer. She goes out, right.*)

EVANS. (*vaguely making talk*) I got Charlie to lie down. He's all in, poor guy. (*Then trying to face* DARRELL *who keeps looking away from him*) What did Nina mean, you want a long talk with me? Or is it a secret, Ned?

DARRELL. (*controlling an impulse toward hysterical laughter*) A secret? Yes, you bet it's a secret! (*He flings himself in the chair at left, keeping his face averted. His thoughts bitter and desperate like a cornered fugitive's.*)

This is horrible! . . . Sam thinks I'm finest fellow in world . . . and I do this to him! . . . as if he hadn't enough! . . . born under a curse! . . . I finish him! . . . a doctor! . . . God damn it! . . . I can see his end! . . . never forgive myself! . . . never forget! . . . break me! . . . ruin my career! . . .

(*More desperately*)

Got to stop this! . . . while there's time! . . . she said . . . after lunch, talk . . . she meant, tell him . . . that means kill him . . . then she'll marry me! . . .

(*Beginning to be angry*)

By God, I won't! . . . she'll find out! . . . smiling! . . . got me where she wants me! . . . then be as cruel to me as she is to him! . . . love me? . . . liar! . . . still loves Gordon! . . . her body is a trap! . . . I'm caught in it! . . . she touches my hand, her eyes get in mine, I lose my will! . . .

(*Furiously*)

By God, she can't make a fool of me that way! . . . I'll go away some place! . . . go to Europe! . . . study! . . . forget her in work! . . . keep hidden until boat sails so she can't reach me! . . .

(*He is in a state of strange elation by this time*)

Go now! . . . no! . . . got to spike her guns with Sam! . . . by

God, I see! . . . tell him about baby! . . . that'll stop her! . . . when she knows I've told him that, she'll see it's hopeless! . . . she'll stick to him! . . . poor Nina! . . . I'm sorry! . . . she does love me! . . . hell! . . . she'll forget! . . . she'll have her child! . . . she'll be happy! . . . and Sam'll be happy! . . .

(*He suddenly turns to* EVANS *who has been staring at him, puzzledly —in a whisper*) Look here, Sam. I can't stay to lunch. I haven't time, I've got a million things to do. I'm sailing for Europe in a few days.

EVANS. (*surprised*) You're sailing?

DARRELL. (*very hurriedly*) Yes—going to study over there for a year or so. I haven't told anyone. I came out today to say good-bye. You won't be able to reach me again. I'll be out of town visiting. (*Then elatedly*) And now for your secret! It ought to make you very happy, Sam. I know how much you've wished for it, so I'm going to tell you although Nina'll be furious with me. She was saving it to surprise you with at her own proper time— (*Still more elatedly*) —but I'm selfish enough to want to see you happy before I go!

EVANS. (*not daring to believe what he hopes—stammering*) What —what is it, Ned?

DARRELL. (*clapping him on the back—with strange joviality*) You're going to be a father, old scout, that's the secret! (*Then as* EVANS *just stares at him dumbly in a blissful satisfaction, he rattles on*) And now I've got to run. See you again in a year or so. I've said good-bye to Nina. Good-bye, Sam. (*He takes his hand and clasps it*) Good luck! Buckle down to work now! You've got the stuff in you! When I get back I'll expect to hear you're on the high-road to success! And tell Nina I'll expect to find you both happy in your child—both of you, tell her!—happy in your child! Tell her that, Sam! (*He turns and goes to the door. Thinking as he goes*)

That does it! . . . honorably! . . . I'm free! . . .

(*He goes out—then out the front door—a moment later his motor is heard starting—dies away.*)

EVANS. (*stares after him dumbly in the same state of happy stupefaction—mumbles*) Thank you—Ned. (*Thinking disjointedly*)

Why did I doubt myself? . . . now she loves me . . . she's loved me right along . . . I've been a fool . . .

(*He suddenly falls on his knees*)

Oh, God, I thank you!

(NINA *comes in from the kitchen. She stops in amazement when she sees him on his knees. He jumps to his feet and takes her in his arms with confident happiness and kisses her*) Oh, Nina, I love you so! And now I know you love me! I'll never be afraid of anything again!

NINA. (*bewildered and terror-stricken, trying feebly to push him away—thinking*)

Has he . . . has he gone crazy? . . .

(*Weakly*) Sam! What's come over you, Sam?

EVANS. (*tenderly*) Ned told me—the secret—and I'm so happy, dear! (*He kisses her again.*)

NINA. (*stammering*) Ned told you—what?

EVANS. (*tenderly*) That we're going to have a child, dear. You mustn't be sore at him. Why did you want to keep it a secret from me? Didn't you know how happy it would make me, Nina?

NINA. He told you we—we—you, the father—? (*Then suddenly breaking from him—wildly*) Ned! Where is Ned?

EVANS. He left a moment ago.

NINA. (*stupidly*) Left? Call him back. Lunch is ready.

EVANS. He's gone. He couldn't stay. He's got so much to do getting ready to sail.

NINA. Sail?

EVANS. Didn't he tell you he was sailing for Europe? He's going over for a year or so to study.

NINA. A year or so! (*Wildly*) I've got to call him up! No, I'll go in and see him right now! (*She takes a wavering step toward the door. Thinking in anguish*)

Go! . . . go to him! . . . find him! . . . my lover! . . .

EVANS. He won't be there, I'm afraid. He said we couldn't reach him, that he'd be visiting friends out of town until he sailed. (*Solicitously*) Why, do you have to see him about something important, Nina? Perhaps I could locate—

NINA. (*stammering and swaying*) No. (*She stifles an hysterical laugh*) No, nothing—nothing important—nothing is important—ha—! (*She stifles another laugh—then on the verge of fainting, weakly*) Sam! Help me—

EVANS. (*rushes to her, supports her to sofa at right*) Poor darling! Lie down and rest. (*She remains in a sitting position, staring blankly before her. He chafes her wrists*) Poor darling! (*Thinking jubilantly*)

Her condition . . . this weakness comes from her condition! . . .

NINA. (*thinking in anguish*)

Ned doesn't love me! . . . he's gone! . . . gone forever! . . . like Gordon! . . . no, not like Gordon! . . . like a sneak, a coward! . . . a liar! . . . oh, I hate him! . . . O Mother God, please let me hate him! . . . he must have been planning this! . . . he must have known it today when he said he loved me! . . .

(*Thinking frenziedly*)

I won't bear it! . . . he thinks he has palmed me off on Sam forever! . . . and his child! . . . he can't! . . . I'll tell Sam he was lying! . . . I'll make Sam hate him! . . . I'll make Sam kill him! . . . I'll promise to love Sam if he kills him! . . .

(*Suddenly turns to* EVANS*—savagely*) He lied to you!

EVANS. (*letting her wrists drop—appalled—stammers*) You mean—Ned lied about—?

NINA. (*in same tone*) Ned lied to you!

EVANS. (*stammers*) You're not—going to have a child—

NINA. (*savagely*) Oh, yes! Oh, yes, I am! Nothing can keep me from that! But you're—you're—I mean, you . . . (*Thinking in anguish*)

I can't say that to him! . . . I can't tell him without Ned to help me! . . . I can't! . . . look at his face! . . . oh, poor Sammy! . . . poor little boy! . . . poor little boy! . . .

(*She takes his head and presses it to her breast and begins to weep. Weeping.*) I mean, you weren't to know about it, Sammy.

EVANS. (*immediately on the crest again—tenderly*) Why? Don't you want me to be happy, Nina?

NINA. Yes—yes, I do, Sammy. (*Thinking strangely*)

Little boy! . . . little boy! . . . one gives birth to little boys! . . . one doesn't drive them mad and kill them! . . .

EVANS. (*thinking*)

She's never called me Sammy before . . . someone used to . . . oh, yes, Mother. . . .

(*Tenderly and boyishly*) And I'm going to make you happy from now on, Nina. I tell you, the moment Ned told me, something happened to me! I can't explain it, but—I'll make good now, Nina! I know I've said that before but I was only boasting. I was only trying to make myself think so. But now I say it knowing I can do it! (*Softly*) It's because we're going to have a child, Nina. I knew that you'd never come to really love me without that. That's what I was down on my knees for when you came in. I was thanking God—for our baby!

NINA. (*tremblingly*) Sammy! Poor boy!

EVANS. Ned said when he came back he'd expect to find us both happy—in our baby. He said to tell you that. You will be happy now, won't you, Nina?

NINA. (*brokenly and exhaustedly*) I'll try to make you happy, Sammy. (*He kisses her, then hides his head on her breast. She stares out over his head. She seems to grow older. Thinking as if she were repeating the words of some inner voice of life*)

Not Ned's child! . . . not Sam's child! . . . mine! . . . there!

. . . again! . . . I feel my child live . . . moving in my life . . . my life moving in my child . . . breathing in the tide I dream and breathe my dream back into the tide . . . God is a Mother. . . .

(*Then with sudden anguish*)

Oh, afternoons . . . dear wonderful afternoons of love with you, my lover . . . you are lost . . . gone from me forever! . . .

CURTAIN

SECOND PART—ACT SIX

SCENE: *The same—an evening a little over a year later. The room has undergone a significant change. There is a comfortable homey atmosphere as though now it definitely belonged to the type of person it was built for. It has a proud air of modest prosperity.*

It is soon after dinner—about eight o'clock. EVANS *is sitting by the table at left, glancing through a newspaper at headlines and reading an article here and there.* NINA *is in the chair at center, knitting a tiny sweater.* MARSDEN *is sitting on the sofa at right, holding a book which he pretends to be looking through, but glancing wonderingly at* EVANS *and* NINA.

There is a startling change in EVANS. *He is stouter, the haggard look of worry and self-conscious inferiority has gone from his face, it is full and healthy and satisfied. There is also, what is more remarkable, a decided look of solidity about him, of a determination moving toward ends it is confident it can achieve. He has matured, found his place in the world.*

The change in NINA *is also perceptible. She looks noticeably older, the traces of former suffering are marked on her face, but there is also an expression of present contentment and calm.*

MARSDEN *has aged greatly. His hair is gray, his expression one of a deep grief that is dying out into a resignation resentful of itself. He is dressed immaculately in dark tweed.*

NINA. (*thinking*)

I wonder if there's a draft in the baby's room? . . . maybe I'd better close the window? . . . oh, I guess it's all right . . . he needs lots of fresh air . . . little Gordon . . . he does remind me of Gordon . . . something in his eyes . . . my romantic imagination? . . . Ned said that . . . why hasn't Ned ever written?

. . . it's better he hasn't . . . how he made me suffer! . . . but I forgive him . . . he gave me my baby . . . the baby certainly doesn't look like him . . . everyone says he looks like Sam . . . how absurd! . . . but Sam makes a wonderful father . . . he's become a new man in the past year . . . and I've helped him . . . he asks me about everything . . . I have a genuine respect for him now . . . I can give myself without repulsion . . . I am making him happy . . . I've written his mother I'm making him happy . . . I was proud to be able to write her that . . . how queerly things work out! . . . all for the best . . . and I don't feel wicked . . . I feel good . . .

(*She smiles strangely*)

MARSDEN. (*thinking*)

What a change! . . . the last time I was here the air was poisoned . . . Darrell . . . I was sure he was her lover . . . but I was in a morbid state . . . why did Darrell run away? . . . Nina could have got Sam to divorce her if she really loved Darrell . . . then it's evident she couldn't have loved him . . . and she was going to have Sam's baby . . . Darrell's love must have seemed like treachery . . . so she sent him away . . . that must be it . . .

(*With satisfaction*)

Yes, I've got it straight now. . . .

(*With contemptuous pity*)

Poor Darrell . . . I have no use for him but I did pity him when I ran across him in Munich . . . he was going the pace . . . looked desperate . . .

(*Then gloomily*)

My running away was about as successful as his . . . as if one could leave one's memory behind! . . . I couldn't forget Mother . . . she haunted me through every city of Europe . . .

(*Then irritatedly*)

I must get back to work! . . . not a line written in over a year! . . . my public will be forgetting me! . . . a plot came to me yesterday . . . my mind is coming around again . . . I am beginning to forget, thank God! . . .

(*Then remorsefully*)

No, I don't want to forget you, Mother! . . . but let me remember . . . without pain! . . .

EVANS. (*turning over a page of his paper*) There's going to be the biggest boom before long this country has ever known, or I miss my guess, Nina.

NINA. (*with great seriousness*) Do you think so, Sammy?

EVANS. (*decidedly*) I'm dead sure of it.

NINA. (*with a maternal pride and amusement*)

Dear Sam . . . I can't quite believe in this self-confident business man yet . . . but I have to admit he's proved it . . . he asked for more money and they gave it without question . . . they're anxious to keep him . . . they ought to be . . . how he's slaved! . . . for me and my baby! . . .

EVANS. (*has been looking at* MARSDEN *surreptitiously over his paper*)

Charlie's mother must have hoarded up a half million . . . he'll let it rot in government bonds . . . wonder what he'd say if I proposed that he back me? . . . he's always taken a friendly interest . . . well, it's worth a bet, anyway . . . he'd be an easy partner to handle . . .

MARSDEN. (*staring at* EVANS *wonderingly*)

What a changed Sam! . . . I preferred him the old way . . . futile but he had a sensitive quality . . . now he's brash . . . a little success . . . oh, he'll succeed all right . . . his kind are inheriting the earth . . . hogging it, cramming it down their tasteless gullets! . . . and he's happy! . . . actually happy! . . . he has Nina . . . a beautiful baby . . . a comfortable home . . . no sorrow, no tragic memories . . . and I have nothing! . . . but utter loneliness! . . .

(*With grieving self-pity*)

If only Mother had lived! . . . how horribly I miss her! . . . my lonely home . . . who will keep house for me now? . . . it has got to be done sympathetically or I won't be able to work . . . I must write to Jane . . . she'll probably be only too glad . . .

(*Turning to* NINA) I think I'll write to my sister in California and ask her to come on and live with me. She's alone now that her youngest daughter is married, and she has very little money. And my hands are tied as far as sharing the estate with her is concerned. According to Mother's will, I'm cut off too if I give her a penny. Mother never got over her bitter feeling about Jane's marriage. In a way, she was right. Jane's husband wasn't much—no family or position or ability—and I doubt if she was ever happy with him. (*Sarcastically*) It was one of those love matches!

NINA. (*smiling—teasingly*) There's no danger of your ever making a love match, is there, Charlie?

MARSDEN. (*wincing—thinking*)

She can't believe any woman could possibly love me! . . .

(*Caustically*) I trust I'll never make that kind of a fool of myself, Nina!

NINA. (*teasingly*) Pooh! Aren't you the superior bachelor! I don't see anything to be so proud of! You're simply shirking, Charlie!

MARSDEN. (*wincing but forcing a teasing air*) You were my only true love, Nina. I made a vow of perpetual bachelorhood when you threw me over in Sam's favor!

EVANS. (*has listened to this last—jokingly*) Hello! What's this? I never knew you were my hated rival, Charlie!

MARSDEN. (*dryly*) Oh—didn't you really? (*But* EVANS *has turned back to his paper. Thinking savagely*)

That fool, too! . . . he jokes about it! . . . as if I were the last one in the world he could imagine . . .

NINA. (*teasingly*) Well, if I'm responsible, Charlie, I feel I ought to do something about it. I'll pick out a wife for you—guaranteed to suit! She must be at least ten years older than you, large and matronly and placid, and a wonderful cook and housekeeper—

MARSDEN. (*sharply*) Don't be stupid! (*Thinking angrily*)

She picks someone beyond the age! . . . she never imagines sex could enter into it! . . .

NINA. (*placatingly—seeing he is really angry*) Why, I was only picking out a type I thought would be good for you, Charlie—and for your work.

MARSDEN. (*sneeringly—with a meaning emphasis*) You didn't mention chaste. I couldn't respect a woman who hadn't respected herself!

NINA. (*thinking—stung*)

He's thinking of those men in the hospital . . . what a fool I was ever to tell him! . . .

(*Cuttingly*) Oh, so you think you deserve an innocent virgin!

MARSDEN. (*coldly—controlling his anger*) Let's drop me, if you please. (*With a look at her that is challenging and malicious*) Did I tell you I ran into Doctor Darrell in Munich?

NINA. (*startled—thinking frightenedly and confusedly*)

Ned! . . . he saw Ned! . . . why hasn't he told me before? . . . why did he look at me like that? . . . does he suspect? . . .

(*Trying to be calm but stammering*) You saw—Ned?

MARSDEN. (*with savage satisfaction*)

That struck home! . . . look at her! . . . guilty! . . . then I was right that day! . . .

(*Casually*) Yes, I chanced to run into him.

NINA. (*more calmly now*) Why on earth didn't you tell us before, Charlie?

MARSDEN. (*coolly*) Why? Is it such important news? You knew he was there, didn't you? I supposed he'd written you.

EVANS. (*looking up from his paper—affectionately*) How was the old scout?

MARSDEN. (*maliciously*) He seemed in fine feather—said he was having a gay time. When I saw him he was with a startling looking female—quite beautiful, if you like that type. I gathered they were living together.

NINA. (*cannot restrain herself—breaks out*) I don't believe it! (*Then immediately controlling herself and forcing a laugh*) I mean, Ned was always so serious-minded it's hard to imagine him messed up in that sort of thing. (*Thinking in a queer state of jealous confusion*)

Hard to imagine! . . . my lover! . . . oh, pain again! . . . Why? . . . I don't love him now . . . be careful! . . . Charlie's staring at me. . . .

MARSDEN. (*thinking—jealously*)

Then she did love him! . . . does she still? . . .

(*Hopefully*)

Or is it only pique? . . . no woman likes to lose a man even when she no longer loves him. . . .

(*With malicious insistence*) Why is that hard to imagine, Nina? Darrell never struck me as a Galahad. After all, why shouldn't he have a mistress? (*Meaningly*) He has no tie over here to remain faithful to, has he?

NINA. (*struggling with herself—thinking pitiably*)

He's right . . . why shouldn't Ned? . . . is that why he's never written? . . .

(*Airily*) I don't know what ties he has or hasn't got. It's nothing to me if he has fifty mistresses. I suppose he's no better than the rest of you.

EVANS. (*looking over at her—tenderly reproachful*) That isn't fair, Nina. (*Thinking proudly*)

I'm proud of that . . . never anyone before her . . .

NINA. (*looking at him—with real gratitude*) I didn't mean you, dear. (*Thinking—proudly*)

Thank God for Sammy! . . . I know he's mine . . . no jealousy . . . no fear . . . no pain . . . I've found peace . . .

(*Then distractedly*)

Oh, Ned, why haven't you written? . . . stop it! . . . what a fool I am! . . . Ned's dead for me! . . . oh, I hate Charlie! . . . why did he tell me? . . .

MARSDEN. (*looking at* EVANS*—contemptuously thinking*)

What a poor simpleton Sam is! . . . boasting of his virtue! . . . as if women loved you for that! . . . they despise it! . . . I don't want Nina to think I've had no experiences with women. . . .

(*Mockingly*) So then it's Sam who is the Galahad, eh? Really, Nina, you should have him put in the Museum among the prehistoric mammals!

EVANS. (*pleased—comes back kiddingly*) Well, I never had your chances, Charlie! I couldn't run over to Europe and get away with murder the way you have!

MARSDEN. (*foolishly pleased—admitting while denying*) Oh, I wasn't quite as bad as all that, Sam! (*Scornfully ashamed of himself—thinking*)

> Poor sick ass that I am! . . . I want them to think I've been a Don Juan! . . . how pitiful and disgusting! . . . I wouldn't have a mistress if I could! . . . if I could? . . . of course I could! . . . I've simply never cared to degrade myself! . . .

NINA. (*thinking—tormentedly*)

> The thought of that woman! . . . Ned forgetting our afternoons in nights with her! . . . stop these thoughts! . . . I won't give in to them! . . . why did Charlie want to hurt me? . . . is he jealous of Ned? . . . Charlie has always loved me in some queer way of his own . . . how ridiculous! . . . look at him! . . . he's so proud of being thought a Don Juan! . . . I'm sure he never even dared to kiss a woman except his mother! . . .

(*Mockingly*) Do tell us about all your various mistresses in foreign parts, Charlie!

MARSDEN. (*in confusion now*) I—I really don't remember, Nina!

NINA. Why, you're the most heartless person I've ever heard of, Charlie! Not remember even one! And I suppose there are little Marsdens—and you've forgotten all about them too! (*She laughs maliciously—*EVANS *laughs with her.*)

MARSDEN. (*still more confused—with a silly idiotic smirk*) I can't say about that, Nina. It's a wise father who knows his own child, you know!

NINA. (*frightenedly—thinking*)

> What does he mean? . . . does he suspect about the baby too? . . . I must be terribly careful of Charlie! . . .

EVANS. (*looking up from his paper again*) Did Ned say anything about coming back?

NINA. (*thinking—longingly*)

Come back? . . . oh, Ned, how I wish! . . .

MARSDEN. (*looking at her—meaningly*) No, he didn't say. I gathered he was staying over indefinitely.

EVANS. I'd sure like to see him again.

NINA. (*thinking*)

He has forgotten me . . . if he did come, he'd probably avoid me. . . .

MARSDEN. He spoke of you. He asked if I'd heard whether Nina had had her baby yet or not. I told him I hadn't.

EVANS. (*heartily*) Too bad you didn't know. You could have told him what a world-beater we've got! Eh, Nina?

NINA. (*mechanically*) Yes. (*Joyfully—thinking*)

Ned asked about my baby! . . . then he hadn't forgotten! . . . if he came back he'd come to see his baby! . . .

EVANS. (*solicitously*) Isn't it time to nurse him again?

NINA. (*starts to her feet automatically*) Yes, I'm going now. (*She glances at* MARSDEN, *thinking calculatingly*)

I must win Charlie over again . . . I don't feel safe . . .

(*She stops by his chair and takes his hand and looks into his eyes gently and reproachfully.*)

MARSDEN. (*thinking shamefacedly*)

Why have I been trying to hurt her? . . . my Nina! . . . I am nearer to her than anyone! . . . I'd give my life to make her happy! . . .

NINA. (*triumphantly*)

How his hand trembles! . . . what a fool to be afraid of Charlie! . . . I can always twist him round my finger! . . .

(*She runs her hand through his hair, and speaks as though she were hiding a hurt reproach beneath a joking tone*) I shouldn't like you any more, do you know it, after you've practically admitted you've philandered all over Europe! And I thought you were absolutely true to me, Charlie!

MARSDEN. (*so pleased he can hardly believe his ears*)

Then she did believe me! . . . she's actually hurt! . . . but I can't let her think . . .

(*With passionate earnestness, clasping her hand in both of his, looking into her eyes*) No, Nina! I swear to you!

NINA. (*thinking—cruelly*)

Pah! . . . how limp his hands are! . . . his eyes are so shrinking! . . . is it possible he loves me? . . . like that? . . . what a sickening idea! . . . it seems incestuous somehow! . . . no, it's too absurd! . . .

(*Smiling, gently releases her hand*) All right. I forgive you, Charlie. (*Then matter-of-factly*) Excuse me, please, while I go up and feed my infant, or we're due to hear some lusty howling in a moment. (*She turns away, then impulsively turns back and kisses* MARSDEN *with real affection*) You're an old dear, do you know it, Charlie? I don't know what I'd do without you! (*Thinking*)

It's true, too! . . . he's my only dependable friend . . . I must never lose him . . . never let him suspect about little Gordon . . .

(*She turns to go.*)

EVANS. (*jumping up, throwing his paper aside*) Wait a second. I'll come with you. I want to say good night to him. (*He comes, puts his arm about her waist, kisses her and they go out together.*)

MARSDEN. (*thinking excitedly*)

I almost confessed I loved her! . . . a queer expression came over her face . . . what was it? . . . was it satisfaction? . . . she didn't mind? . . . was it pleasure? . . . then I can hope? . . .

(*Then miserably*)

Hope for what? . . . what do I want? . . . If Nina were free, what would I do? . . . would I do anything? . . . would I wish to? . . . what would I offer her? . . . money? . . . she could get that from others . . . myself? . . .

(*Bitterly*)

What a prize! . . . my ugly body . . . there's nothing in me to attract her . . . my fame? . . . God, what a shoddy, pitiful! . . . but I might have done something big . . . I might still . . . if I had the courage to write the truth . . . but I was born afraid . . . afraid of myself . . . I've given my talent to making fools feel pleased with themselves in order that they'd feel pleased with me . . . and like me . . . I'm neither hated nor loved . . . I'm liked . . . women like me . . . Nina likes me! . . .

(*Resentfully*)

She can't help letting the truth escape her! . . . "You're an old dear, do you know it, Charlie?" Oh, yes, I know it . . . too damned well! . . . dear old Charlie! . . .

(*In anguish*)

Dear old Rover, nice old doggie, we've had him for years, he's so affectionate and faithful but he's growing old, he's getting cross, we'll have to get rid of him soon! . . .

(*In a strange rage, threateningly*)

But you won't get rid of me so easily, Nina! . . .

(*Then confusedly and shamefacedly*)

Good God, what's the matter with me! . . . since Mother's death I've become a regular idiot! . . .

EVANS. (*comes back from the right, a beaming look of proud parenthood on his face*) He was sleeping so soundly an earthquake wouldn't have made him peep! (*He goes back to his chair—earnestly*) He sure is healthy and husky, Charlie. That tickles me more than anything else. I'm going to start in training him as soon as he's old enough—so he'll be a crack athlete when he goes to college—what I wanted to be and couldn't. I want him to justify the name of Gordon and be a bigger star than Gordon ever was, if that's possible.

MARSDEN. (*with a sort of pity—thinking*)

His is an adolescent mind . . . he'll never grow up . . . well, in this adolescent country, what greater blessing could he wish for? . . .

(*Forcing a smile*) How about training his mind?

EVANS. (*confidently*) Oh, that'll take care of itself. Gordon was always near the top in his studies, wasn't he? And with Nina for a mother, his namesake ought to inherit a full set of brains.

MARSDEN. (*amused*) You're the only genuinely modest person I know, Sam.

EVANS. (*embarrassed*) Oh—me—I'm the boob of the family. (*Then hastily*) Except when it comes to business. I'll make the money. (*Confidently*) And you can bet your sweet life I will make it!

MARSDEN. I'm quite sure of that.

EVANS. (*very seriously—in a confidential tone*) I couldn't have said that two years ago—and believed it. I've changed a hell of a lot! Since the baby was born, I've felt as if I had a shot of dynamite in each arm. They can't pile on the work fast enough. (*He grins—then seriously*) It was about time I got hold of myself. I wasn't much for Nina to feel proud about having around the house in those days. Now—well—at least I've improved. I'm not afraid of my own shadow any more.

MARSDEN. (*thinking strangely*)

> Not to be afraid of one's shadow! . . . that must be the highest happiness of heaven! . . .

(*Flatteringly*) Yes, you've done wonders in the past year.

EVANS. Oh, I haven't even started yet. Wait till I get my chance! (*Glances at* MARSDEN *sharply, makes up his mind and leans forward toward him confidentially*) And I see my real chance, Charlie—lying right ahead, waiting for me to grab it—an agency that's been allowed to run down and go to seed. Within a year or so they'll be willing to sell out cheap. One of their people who's become a good pal of mine told me that in confidence, put it up to me. He'd take it on himself but he's sick of the game. But I'm not! I love it! It's great sport! (*Then putting a brake on this exuberance—matter-of-factly*) But I'll need a hundred thousand—and where will I get it? (*Looking at* MARSDEN *keenly but putting on a joking tone*) Any suggestion you can make, Charlie, will be gratefully received.

MARSDEN. (*thinking suspiciously*)

Does he actually imagine I . . . ? and a hundred thousand, no less! . . . over one-fifth of my entire . . . by jove, I'll have to throw cold water on that fancy! . . .

(*Shortly*) No, Sam, I can't think of anyone. Sorry.

EVANS. (*without losing any confidence—with a grin*)

Check! . . . That's that! . . . Charlie's out . . . till the next time! . . . but I'll keep after him! . . .

(*Contemplating himself with pride*)

Gee, I have changed all right! I can remember when a refusal like that would have ruined my confidence for six months!

(*Heartily*) Nothing to be sorry about, old man. I only mentioned it on the off chance you might know of someone. (*Trying a bold closing stroke—jokingly*) Why don't you be my partner, Charlie? Never mind the hundred thousand. We'll get that elsewhere. I'll bet you might have darn fine original ideas to contribute. (*Thinking—satisfied*)

There! . . . That'll keep my proposition pinned up in his mind! . . .

(*Then jumping to his feet—briskly*) What do you say to a little stroll down to the shore and back? Come on—do you good. (*Taking his arm and hustling him genially toward the door*) What you need is exercise. You're soft as putty. Why don't you take up golf?

MARSDEN. (*with sudden resistance pulls away—determinedly*) No, I won't go, Sam. I want to think out a new plot.

EVANS. Oh, all right. If it's a case of work, go to it! See you later. (*He goes out. A moment later the front door is heard closing.*)

MARSDEN. (*looks after him with a mixture of annoyance and scornful amusement*)

What a fount of meaningless energy he's tapped! . . . always on the go . . . typical terrible child of the age . . . universal slogan, keep moving . . . moving where? . . . never mind that . . . don't think of ends . . . the means are the end . . . keep moving! . . .

(*He laughs scornfully and sits down in* EVANS' *chair, picking up the paper and glancing at it sneeringly*)

It's in every headline of this daily newer testament . . . going . . . going . . . never mind the gone . . . we won't live to see it . . . and we'll be so rich, we can buy off the deluge anyway! . . . even our new God has His price! . . . must have! . . . aren't we made in His image? . . . or vice-versa? . . .

(*He laughs again, letting the paper drop disdainfully—then bitterly*)

But why am I so superior? . . . where am I going? . . . to the same nowhere! . . . worse! . . . I'm not even going! . . . I'm there! . . .

(*He laughs with bitter self-pity—then begins to think with amused curiosity*)

Become Sam's partner? . . . there's a grotesque notion! . . . it might revive my sense of humor about myself, at least . . . I'm the logical one to help him . . . I helped him to Nina . . . logical partner . . . partner in Nina? . . . what inane thoughts! . . .

(*With a sigh*)

No use trying to think out that plot tonight . . . I'll try to read. . . .

(*He sees the book he has been reading on the couch and gets up to get it. There is a ring from the front door.* MARSDEN *turns toward it uncertainly. A pause. Then* NINA'*s voice calls down the stairs.*)

NINA. The maid's out. Will you go to the door, Charlie?

MARSDEN. Surely. (*He goes out and opens the front door. A pause. Then he can be heard saying resentfully*) Hello, Darrell. (*And someone answering "Hello, Marsden" and coming in and the door closing.*)

NINA. (*from upstairs, her voice strange and excited*) Who is it, Charlie?

DARRELL. (*comes into view in the hall, opposite the doorway, at the foot of the stairs—his voice trembling a little with suppressed emotion*) It's I, Nina—Ned Darrell.

NINA. (*with a glad cry*) Ned! (*Then in a voice which shows she is trying to control herself, and is frightened now*) I—make yourself at home. I'll be down—in a minute or two. (DARRELL *remains standing looking up the stairs in a sort of joyous stupor.* MARSDEN *stares at him.*)

MARSDEN. (*sharply*) Come on in and sit down. (DARRELL *starts, comes into the room, plainly getting a grip on himself.* MARSDEN *follows him, glaring at his back with enmity and suspicion.* DARRELL *moves as far away from him as possible, sitting down on the sofa at right.* MARSDEN *takes* EVANS' *chair by the table.* DARRELL *is pale, thin, nervous, unhealthy looking. There are lines of desperation in his face, puffy shadows of dissipation and sleeplessness under his restless, harried eyes. He is dressed carelessly, almost shabbily. His eyes wander about the room, greedily taking it in.*)

DARRELL. (*thinking disjointedly*)

Here again! . . . dreamed of this house . . . from here, ran away . . . I've come back . . . my turn to be happy! . . .

MARSDEN. (*watching him—savagely*)

Now I know! . . . absolutely! . . . his face! . . . her voice! . . . they did love each other! . . . they do now! . . .

(*Sharply*) When did you get back from Europe?

DARRELL. (*curtly*) This morning on the Olympic. (*Thinking—cautiously*)

Look out for this fellow . . . always had it in for me . . . like a woman . . . smells out love . . . he suspected before . . .

(*Then boldly*)

Well, who gives a damn now? . . . all got to come out! . . . Nina wanted to tell Sam . . . now I'll tell him myself! . . .

MARSDEN. (*righteously indignant*)

What has brought him back? . . . what a devilish, cowardly trick to play on poor unsuspecting Sam! . . .

(*Revengefully*)

But I'm not unsuspecting! . . . I'm not their fool! . . .

(*Coldly*) What brought you back so soon? When I saw you in Munich you weren't intending—

DARRELL. (*shortly*) My father died three weeks ago. I've had to come back about his estate. (*Thinking*)

Lie . . . Father's death just gave me an excuse to myself . . . wouldn't have come back for that . . . came back because I love her! . . . damn his questions! . . . I want to think . . . before I see her . . . sound of her voice . . . seemed to burn inside my head . . . God, I'm licked! . . . no use fighting it . . . I've done my damnedest . . . work . . . booze . . . other women . . . no use . . . I love her! . . . always! . . . to hell with pride! . . .

MARSDEN. (*thinking*)

He has two brothers . . . they'll probably all share equally . . . his father noted Philadelphia surgeon . . . rich, I've heard . . .

(*With a bitter grin*)

Wait till Sam hears that! . . . he'll ask Darrell to back him . . . and Darrell will jump at it . . . chance to avert suspicion . . . conscience money, too! . . . it's my duty to protect Sam . . .

(*As he hears* NINA *coming down the stairs*)

I must watch them . . . it's my duty to protect Nina from herself . . . Sam is a simpleton . . . I'm all she has . . .

DARRELL. (*hearing her coming—in a panic—thinking*)

Coming! . . . in a second I'll see her! . . .

(*Terrified*)

Does she still love me? . . . she may have forgotten . . . no, it's my child . . . she can never forget that! . . .

(NINA *comes in from the rear. She has put on a fresh dress, her hair is arranged, her face newly rouged and powdered, she looks extremely pretty and this is heightened by the feverish state of mind she is in—a mixture of love, of triumphant egotism in knowing her lover has come back to her, and of fear and uncertainty in feeling her new peace, her certainties, her contented absorption in her child failing her. She hesitates just inside the door, staring into* DARRELL'S *eyes, thinking a fierce question.*)

NINA.

Does he still love me? . . .

(*Then triumphantly as she reads him*)

Yes! . . . he does! . . . he does! . . .

DARRELL. (*who has jumped to his feet—with a cry of longing*) Nina! (*Thinking with alarm now*)

She's changed! . . . changed! . . . can't tell if she loves! . . .

(*He has started to go to her. Now he hesitates. His voice taking on a pleading uncertain quality*) Nina!

NINA. (*thinking triumphantly—with a certain cruelty*)

He loves me! . . . he's mine . . . now more than ever! . . . he'll never dare leave me again! . . .

(*Certain of herself now, she comes to him and speaks with confident pleasure*) Hello, Ned! This is a wonderful surprise! How are you? (*She takes his hand.*)

DARRELL. (*taken aback—confusedly*) Oh—all right, Nina. (*Thinking in a panic*)

That tone! . . . as if she didn't care! . . . can't believe that! . . . she's playing a game to fool Marsden! . . .

MARSDEN. (*who is watching them keenly—thinking*)

She loves his love for her . . . she's cruelly confident . . . much as I hate this man I can't help feeling sorry . . . I know her cruelty . . . it's time I took a hand in this . . . what a plot for a novel! . . .

(*Almost mockingly*) Darrell's father died, Nina. He had to come home to see about the estate.

DARRELL. (*with a glare at* MARSDEN—*protestingly*) I was coming home anyway. I only intended to stay a year, and it's over that since—(*Intensely*) I was coming back anyway, Nina!

NINA. (*thinking with triumphant happiness*)

You dear, you! . . . as if I didn't know that! . . . oh, how I'd love to take you in my arms! . . .

(*Happily*) I'm awfully glad you've come, Ned. We've missed you terribly.

DARRELL. (*thinking—more and more at sea*)

She looks glad . . . but she's changed . . . I don't understand her . . . "we've missed" . . . that means Sam . . . what does that mean? . . .

(*Intensely, pressing her hand*) And I've missed you—terribly!

MARSDEN. (*sardonically*) Yes, indeed, Darrell, I can vouch for their missing you—Sam in particular. He was asking about you only a short while ago—how things were going with you when I saw you in Munich. (*Maliciously*) By the way, who was the lady you were with that day? She was certainly startling looking.

NINA. (*thinking—triumphantly mocking*)

A miss, Charlie! . . . he loves me! . . . what do I care about that woman? . . .

(*Gaily*) Yes, who was the mysterious beauty, Ned? Do tell us! (*She moves away from him and sits down at center.* DARRELL *remains standing.*)

DARRELL. (*glaring at* MARSDEN, *sullenly*) Oh, I don't remember—(*Thinking apprehensively with a bitter resentment*)

She doesn't give a damn! . . . if she loved me she'd be jealous! . . . but she doesn't give a damn! . . .

(*He blurts out resentfully at* NINA) Well, she was my mistress—for a time—I was lonely. (*Then with sudden anger turning on* MARSDEN) But what's all this to you, Marsden?

MARSDEN. (*coolly*) Absolutely nothing. Pardon me. It was a tactless question. (*Then with continued open malice*) But I was starting to say how Sam had missed you, Darrell. It's really remarkable. One doesn't encounter such friendship often in these slack days. Why, he'd trust you with anything!

NINA. (*wincing—thinking*)

That hurts . . . hurts Ned . . . Charlie is being cruel! . . .

DARRELL. (*wincing—in a forced tone*) And I'd trust Sam with anything.

MARSDEN. Of course. He is a person one can trust. They are rare. You're going to be amazed at the change in Sam, Darrell. Isn't he, Nina? He's a new man. I never saw such energy. If ever a man was bound for success Sam is. In fact, I'm so confident he is that as soon as he thinks the time is ripe to start his own firm I'm going to furnish the capital and become his silent partner.

DARRELL. (*puzzled and irritated—thinking confusedly*)

What's he driving at? . . . why doesn't he get the hell out and leave us alone? . . . but I'm glad Sam is on his feet . . . makes it easier to tell him the truth. . . .

NINA. (*thinking—worriedly*)

What's Charlie talking about? . . . it's time I talked to Ned . . . Oh, Ned, I do love you! . . . you can be my lover! . . . we won't hurt Sam! . . . he'll never know! . . .

MARSDEN. Yes, ever since the baby was born Sam's been another man—in fact, ever since he knew there was going to be a baby, isn't it, Nina?

NINA. (*agreeing as if she had only half-heard him*) Yes. (*Thinking*)

Ned's baby! . . . I must talk to him about our baby. . . .

MARSDEN. Sam is the proudest parent I've ever seen!

NINA. (*as before*) Yes, Sam makes a wonderful father, Ned. (*Thinking*)

Ned doesn't care for children . . . I know what you're hoping, Ned . . . but if you think I'm going to take Sam's baby from him, you're mistaken! . . . or if you think I'll run away with you and leave my baby . . .

MARSDEN. (*with the same strange driving insistence*) If anything happened to that child I actually believe Sam would lose his reason! Don't you think so, Nina?

NINA. (*with emphasis*) I know I'd lose mine! Little Gordon has become my whole life.

DARRELL. (*thinking—with a sad bitter irony*)

Sam . . . wonderful father . . . lose his reason . . . little Gordon! . . . Nina called my son after Gordon! . . . romantic imagination! . . . Gordon is still her lover! . . . Gordon, Sam and Nina! . . . and my son! . . . closed corporation! . . . I'm forced out! . . .

(*Then rebelling furiously*)

No! . . . not yet, by God! . . . I'll smash it up! . . . I'll tell Sam the truth no matter what! . . .

NINA. (*thinking with a strange calculation*)

I couldn't find a better husband than Sam . . . and I couldn't find a better lover than Ned . . . I need them both to be happy . . .

MARSDEN. (*with sudden despairing suspicion*)

Good God . . . after all, is it Sam's child? . . . mightn't it be Darrell's! . . . why have I never thought of that? . . . No! . . . Nina couldn't be so vile! . . . to go on living with Sam, pretending . . . and, after all, why should she, you fool? . . . there's no sense! . . . she could have gone off with Darrell, couldn't she? . . . Sam would have given her a divorce . . . there was no possible reason for her staying with Sam, when she loved Darrell, unless exactly because this was Sam's baby . . . for its sake . . .

(*Hectically relieved*)

Of course! . . . of course! . . . that's all right! . . . I love that poor baby now! . . . I'll fight for its sake against these two! . . .

(*Smilingly gets to his feet—thinking*)

I can leave them alone now . . . for they won't be alone, thanks to me . . . I leave Sam and his baby in this room with them . . . and their honor . . .

(*Suddenly raging*)

Their honor! . . . what an obscene joke! . . . the honor of a harlot and a pimp! . . . I hate them! . . . if only God would strike them dead! . . . now! . . . and I could see them die! . . . I would praise His justice! . . . His kindness and mercy to me! . . .

NINA. (*thinking—with horrified confusion*)

Why doesn't Charlie go? . . . What is he thinking? . . . I suddenly feel afraid of him! . . .

(*She gets to her feet with a confused pleading cry*) Charlie!

MARSDEN. (*immediately urbane and smiling*) It's all right. I'm going out to find Sam. When he knows you're here he'll come on the run, Darrell. (*He goes to the door. They watch him suspiciously*) And you two probably have a lot to talk over. (*He chuckles pleasantly and goes into the hall—mockingly warning*) We'll be back before long. (*The front door is heard slamming.* NINA *and* DARRELL *turn and look at each other guiltily and frighteningly. Then he comes to her and takes both of her hands uncertainly.*)

DARRELL. (*stammeringly*) Nina—I—I've come back to you—do you —do you still care—Nina?

NINA. (*giving way to his love passionately, as if to drown her fears*) I love you, Ned!

DARRELL. (*kisses her awkwardly—stammering*) I—I didn't know—you seemed so cold—damn Marsden—he suspects, doesn't he?—but it makes no difference now, does it? (*Then in a flood of words*) Oh, it's been hell, Nina! I couldn't forget you! Other women—they only made me love you more! I hated them and loved you even at the moment when—that's honest! It was always you in my arms—as you used to be—those afternoons—God, how I've thought of them—lying awake—recalling every word you said, each movement, each expression on your face, smelling your hair, feeling your soft body—(*Suddenly taking her in his arms and kissing her again and again—passionately*) Nina! I love you so!

NINA. And I've longed for you so much! Do you think I've forgotten those afternoons? (*Then in anguish*) Oh, Ned, why did you run away? I can never forgive that! I can never trust you again!

DARRELL. (*violently*) I was a fool! I thought of Sam! And that wasn't all! Oh, I wasn't all noble, I'll confess! I thought of myself and my career! Damn my career! A lot of good that did it! I didn't study! I didn't live! I longed for you—and suffered! I paid in full, believe me, Nina! But I know better now! I've come back. The time for lying is past! You've got to come away with me! (*He kisses her.*)

NINA. (*letting herself go, kissing him passionately*) Yes! My lover! (*Then suddenly resisting and pushing him away*) No! You're forgetting Sam—and Sam's baby!

DARRELL. (*staring at her wildly*) Sam's baby? Are you joking? Ours, you mean! We'll take him with us, of course!

NINA. (*sadly*) And Sam?

DARRELL. Damn Sam! He's got to give you a divorce! Let him be generous for a change!

NINA. (*sadly but determinedly*) He would be. You must be just to Sam. He'd give his life for my happiness. And this would mean his life. Could we be happy then? You know we couldn't! And I've changed, Ned. You've got to realize that. I'm not your old mad Nina. I still love you. I will always love you. But now I love my baby too. His happiness comes first with me!

DARRELL. But—he's mine, too!

NINA. No! You gave him to Sam to save Sam!

DARRELL. To hell with Sam! It was to make you happy!

NINA. So I could make Sam happy! That was in it too! I was sincere in that, Ned! If I hadn't been, I could never have gone to you that first day—or if I had, I'd never have forgiven myself. But as it is I don't feel guilty or wicked. I have made Sam happy! And I'm proud! I love Sam's happiness! I love the devoted husband and father in him! And I feel it's his baby—that we've made it his baby!

DARRELL. (*distractedly*) Nina! For God's sake! You haven't come to love Sam, have you? Then—I'll go—I'll go away again—I'll never come back—I tried not to this time—but I had to, Nina!

NINA. (*taking him in her arms—with sudden alarm*) No, don't go away, Ned—ever again. I don't love Sam! I love you!

DARRELL. (*miserably*) But I don't understand! Sam gets everything —and I have nothing!

NINA. You have my love. (*With a strange, self-assured smile at him*) It seems to me you're complaining unreasonably!

DARRELL. You mean—I can be—your lover again?

NINA. (*simply, even matter-of-factly*) Isn't that the nearest we can come to making everyone happy? That's all that counts.

DARRELL. (*with a harsh laugh*) And is that what you call playing fair to Sam?

NINA. (*simply*) Sam will never know. The happiness I have given him has made him too sure of himself ever to suspect me now. And as long as we can love each other without danger to him, I feel he owes that to us for all we've done for him. (*With finality*) That's the only possible solution, Ned, for all our sakes, now you've come back to me.

DARRELL. (*repulsed*) Nina! How can you be so inhuman and calculating!

NINA. (*stung—mockingly*) It was you who taught me the scientific approach, Doctor!

DARRELL. (*shrinking back from her—threateningly*) Then I'll leave again! I'll go back to Europe! I won't endure—! (*Then in a queer, futile rage*) You think I'll stay—to be your lover—watching Sam with my wife and my child—you think that's what I came back to you for? You can go to hell, Nina!

NINA. (*calmly—sure of him*) But what else can I do, Ned? (*Then warningly*) I hear them coming, dear. It's Sam, you know.

DARRELL. (*in a frenzy*) What else can you do? Liar! But I can do something else! I can smash your calculating game for you! I can tell Sam—and I will—right now—by God, I will!

NINA. (*quietly*) No. You won't, Ned. You can't do that to Sam.

DARRELL. (*savagely*) Like hell I can't! (*The front door is opened.* EVANS' *voice is immediately heard, even before he bounds into the room. He rushes up to* NED *hilariously, shakes his hand and pounds his back, oblivious to* DARRELL's *wild expression.*)

EVANS. You old son of a gun! Why didn't you let a guy know you were coming? We'd have met you at the dock, and brought the baby. Let me have a look at you! You look thinner. We'll fatten you up, won't we, Nina? Let us do the prescribing this time! Why didn't you let us know where you were, you old bum? We wanted to write you about the baby. And I wanted to boast about how I was getting on!

You're the only person in the world—except Nina and Charlie—I would boast about that to.

NINA. (*affectionately*) Mercy, Sam, give Ned a chance to get a word in! (*Looking at* NED *pityingly but challengingly*) He wants to tell you something, Sam.

DARRELL. (*crushed—stammers*) No—I mean, yes—I want to tell you how damn glad I am . . . (*He turns away, his face is screwed up in his effort to hold back his tears. Thinking miserably*)

I can't tell him! . . . God damn him, I can't! . . .

NINA. (*with a strange triumphant calm*)

There! . . . that's settled for all time! . . . poor Ned! . . . how crushed he looks! . . . I mustn't let Sam look at him! . . .

(*She steps between them protectingly*) Where's Charlie, Sam?

MARSDEN. (*appearing from the hall*) Here, Nina. Always here! (*He comes to her, smiling with assurance.*)

NINA. (*suddenly with a strange unnatural elation—looking from one to the other with triumphant possession*) Yes, you're here, Charlie—always! And you, Sam—and Ned! (*With a strange gaiety*) Sit down, all of you! Make yourselves at home! You are my three men! This is your home with me! (*Then in a strange half-whisper*) Ssshh! I thought I heard the baby. You must all sit down and be very quiet. You must not wake our baby. (*Mechanically, the three sit down, careful to make no noise—*EVANS *in his old place by the table,* MARSDEN *at center,* DARRELL *on the sofa at right. They sit staring before them in silence.* NINA *remains standing, dominating them, a little behind and to the left of* MARSDEN.)

DARRELL. (*thinking abjectly*)

I couldn't! . . . there are things one may not do and live with oneself afterwards . . . there are things one may not say . . . memory is too full of echoes! . . . there are secrets one must not reveal . . . memory is lined with mirrors! . . . he was too happy! . . . to kill happiness is a worse murder than taking life! . . . I gave him that happiness! . . . Sam deserves my happiness! . . . God bless you, Sam! . . .

(*Then in a strange objective tone—thinking*)

My experiment with the guinea pigs has been a success . . . the ailing ones, Sam, and the female, Nina, have been restored to health and normal function . . . only the other male, Ned, seems to have suffered deterioration.

(*Then bitterly humble*)

Nothing left but to accept her terms . . . I love her . . . I can help to make her happy . . . half a loaf is better . . . to a starving man. . . .

(*Glancing over at* EVANS*—bitterly gloating*)

And your child is mine! . . . your wife is mine! . . . your happiness is mine! . . . may you enjoy my happiness, her husband! . . .

EVANS. (*looking at* DARRELL *affectionately*)

Sure good to see Ned again . . . a real friend if there ever was one . . . looks blue about something . . . oh, that's right, Charlie said his old man had kicked in . . . his old man was rich . . . that's an idea . . . I'll bet he'd put up that capital . . .

(*Then ashamed of himself*)

Aw hell, what's the matter with me? . . . he's no sooner here than I start . . . he's done enough . . . forget it! . . . now anyway . . . he looks pretty dissipated . . . too many women . . . ought to get married and settle down . . . tell him that if I didn't think he'd laugh at me giving him advice . . . but he'll soon realize I'm not the old Sam he knew . . . I suppose Nina's been boasting about that already . . . she's proud . . . she's helped me . . . she's a wonderful wife and mother . . .

(*Looking up at her—solicitously*)

She acted a bit nervous just now . . . queer . . . like she used to . . . haven't noticed her that way in a long time . . . suppose it's the excitement of Ned turning up . . . mustn't let her get overexcited . . . bad for the baby's milk. . . .

MARSDEN. (*glancing furtively over his shoulder at* NINA*—broodingly thinking*)

She's the old queer Nina now . . . the Nina I could never fathom . . . her three men! . . . and we are! . . . I? . . . yes, more deeply than either of the others since I serve for nothing . . . a queer kind of love, maybe . . . I am not ordinary! . . . our child . . . what could she mean by that? . . . child of us three? . . . on the surface, that's insane . . . but I felt when she said it there was something in it . . . she has strange devious intuitions that tap the hidden currents of life . . . dark intermingling currents that become the one stream of desire . . . I feel, with regard to Nina, my life queerly identified with Sam's and Darrell's . . . her child is the child of our three loves for her . . . I would like to believe that . . . I would like to be her husband in a sense . . . and the father of a child, after my fashion . . . I could forgive her everything . . . permit everything . . .

(*Determinedly*)

And I do forgive! . . . and I will not meddle hereafter more than is necessary to guard her happiness, and Sam's and our baby's . . . as for Darrell, I am no longer jealous of him . . . she is only using his love for her own happiness . . . he can never take her away from me! . . .

NINA. (*more and more strangely triumphant*)

My three men! . . . I feel their desires converge in me! . . . to form one complete beautiful male desire which I absorb . . . and am whole . . . they dissolve in me, their life is my life . . . I am pregnant with the three! . . . husband! . . . lover! . . . father! . . . and the fourth man! . . . little man! . . . little Gordon! . . . he is mine too! . . . that makes it perfect! . . .

(*With an extravagant suppressed exultance*)

Why, I should be the proudest woman on earth! . . . I should be the happiest woman in the world! . . .

(*Then suppressing an outbreak of hysterical triumphant laughter only by a tremendous effort*)

Ha-ha . . . only I better knock wood . . .

(*She raps with both knuckles in a fierce tattoo on the table*)

before God the Father hears my happiness! . . .

EVANS. (*as the three turn to her—anxiously*) Nina? What's the matter?

NINA. (*controlling herself with a great effort comes to him—forcing a smile—puts her arms around him affectionately*) Nothing, dear. Nerves, that's all. I've gotten over-tired, I guess.

EVANS. (*bullying her—with loving authority*) Then you go right to bed, young lady! We'll excuse you.

NINA. (*quietly and calmly now*) All right, dear. I guess I do need to rest. (*She kisses him as she might kiss a big brother she loved—affectionately*) Good night, you bossy old thing, you!

EVANS. (*with deep tenderness*) Good night, darling.

NINA. (*she goes and kisses Charlie dutifully on the cheek as she might her father—affectionately*) Good night, Charlie.

MARSDEN. (*with a touch of her father's manner*) That's a good girl! Good night, dear.

NINA. (*she goes and kisses* DARRELL *lovingly on the lips as she would kiss her lover*) Good night, Ned.

DARRELL. (*looks at her with grateful humility*) Thank you. Good night. (*She turns and walks quietly out of the room. The eyes of the three men follow her.*)

CURTAIN

ACT SEVEN

SCENE: *Nearly eleven years later. The sitting room of the* EVANS' *apartment on Park Avenue, New York City—a room that is a tribute to* NINA'S *good taste. It is a large, sunny room, the furniture expensive but extremely simple. The arrangement of the furniture shown is as in previous scenes except there are more pieces. Two chairs are by the table at left. There is a smaller table at center, and a chaise longue. A large, magnificently comfortable sofa is at right.*

It is about one in the afternoon of a day in early fall. NINA *and* DARRELL *and their son,* GORDON, *are in the room.* NINA *is reclining on the chaise longue watching* GORDON *who is sitting on the floor near her, turning over the pages of a book.* DARRELL *is sitting by the table at left, watching* NINA.

NINA *is thirty-five, in the full bloom of her womanhood. She is slimmer than in the previous scene. Her skin still retains a trace of summer tan and she appears in the pink of physical condition. But as in the first act of the play, there is beneath this a sense of great mental strain. One notices the many lines in her face at second glance. Her eyes are tragically sad in repose and her expression is set and masklike.*

GORDON *is eleven—a fine boy with, even at this age, the figure of an athlete. He looks older than he is. There is a grave expression to his face. His eyes are full of a quick-tempered sensitiveness. He does not noticeably resemble his mother. He looks nothing at all like his father. He seems to have sprung from a line distinct from any of the people we have seen.*

DARRELL *has aged greatly. His hair is streaked with gray. He has grown stout. His face is a bit jowly and puffy under the eyes. The features have become blurred. He has the look of a man with no definite aim or ambition to which he can relate his living. His eyes are embittered and they hide his inner self-resentment behind a pose of cynical indifference.*

GORDON. (*thinking as he plays—resentfully*)

I wish Darrell'd get out of here! . . . why couldn't Mother let me run my own birthday? . . . I'd never had him here, you bet! . . . what's he always hanging 'round for? . . . why don't he go off on one of his old trips again . . . last time he was gone more'n a year . . . I was hoping he'd died! . . . what makes Mother like him so much? . . . she makes me sick! . . . I'd think she'd get sick of the old fool and tell him to get out and never come back! . . . I'd kick him out if I was big enough! . . . it's good for him he didn't bring me any birthday present or I'd smash it first chance I got! . . .

NINA. (*watching him—brooding with loving tenderness—sadly*)

No longer my baby . . . my little man . . . eleven . . . I can't believe it . . . I'm thirty-five . . . five years more . . . at forty a woman has finished living . . . life passes by her . . . she rots away in peace! . . .

(*Intensely*)

I want to rot away in peace! . . . I'm sick of the fight for happiness! . . .

(*Smiling with a wry amusement at herself*)

What ungrateful thoughts on my son's birthday! . . . my love for him has been happiness . . . how handsome he is! . . . not at all like Ned . . . when I was carrying him I was fighting to forget Ned . . . hoping he might be like Gordon . . . and he is . . . poor Ned, I've made him suffer a great deal . . . !

(*She looks over at* DARRELL*—self-mockingly*)

My lover! . . . so very rarely now, those interludes of passion . . . what has bound us together all these years? . . . love? . . . if he could only have been contented with what I was able to give him! . . . but he has always wanted more . . . yet never had the courage to insist on all or nothing . . . proud without being proud enough! . . . he has shared me for his comfort's sake with a little gratitude and a big bitterness . . . and sharing me has corrupted him! . . .

(*Then bitterly*)

No, I can't blame myself! . . . no woman can make a man happy who has no purpose in life! . . . why did he give up his career? . . . because I had made him weak? . . .

(*With resentful scorn*)

No, it was I who shamed him into taking up biology and starting the station at Antigua . . . if I hadn't he'd simply have hung around me year after year, doing nothing . . .

(*Irritatedly*)

Why does he stay so long? . . . over six months . . . I can't stand having him around me that long any more! . . . why doesn't he go back to the West Indies? . . . I always get a terrible feeling after he's been back a while that he's waiting for Sam to die! . . . or go insane! . . .

DARRELL. (*thinking—with an apathetic bitterness*)

What is she thinking? . . . we sit together in silence, thinking . . . thoughts that never know the other's thoughts . . . our love has become the intimate thinking together of thoughts that are strangers . . . our love! . . . well, whatever it is that has bound us together, it's strong! . . . I've broken with her, run away, tried to forget her . . . running away to come back each time more abject! . . . or, if she saw there was some chance I might break loose, she'd find some way to call me back . . . and I'd forget my longing for freedom, I'd come wagging my tail . . . no, guinea pigs have no tails . . . I hope my experiment has proved something! . . . Sam . . . happy and wealthy . . . and healthy! . . . I used to hope he'd break down . . . I'd watch him and read symptoms of insanity into every move he made . . . despicable? . . . certainly, but love makes one either noble or despicable! . . . he only grew healthier . . . now I've given up watching him . . . almost entirely . . . now I watch him grow fat and I laugh! . . . the huge joke has dawned on me! . . . Sam is the only normal one! . . . we lunatics! . . . Nina and I! . . . have made a sane life for him out of our madness! . . .

(*Watching* NINA—*sadly*)

Always thinking of her son . . . well, I gave him to her . . . Gordon . . . I hate that name . . . why do I continue hanging around here? . . . each time after a few months my love changes to bitterness . . . I blame Nina for the mess I've made of life . . .

NINA. (*suddenly turning on him*) When are you going back to the West Indies, Ned?

DARRELL. (*determinedly*) Soon!

GORDON. (*stops playing to listen—thinking*)

Gosh, I'm glad! . . . How soon, I wonder? . . .

NINA. (*with a trace of a sneer*) I don't see how you can afford to leave your work for such long periods. Don't you grow rusty?

DARRELL. (*looking at her meaningly*) My life work is to rust—nicely and unobtrusively! (*He smiles mockingly.*)

NINA. (*sadly—thinking*)

To rot away in peace . . . that's all he wants now, too! . . . and this is what love has done to us! . . .

DARRELL. (*bitterly*) My work was finished twelve years ago. As I believe you know, I ended it with an experiment which resulted so successfully that any further meddling with human lives would have been superfluous!

NINA. (*pityingly*) Ned!

DARRELL. (*indifferent and cynical*) But you meant my present dabbling about. You know better than to call that work. It's merely my hobby. Our backing Sam has made Marsden and me so wealthy that we're forced to take up hobbies. Marsden goes in for his old one of dashing off genteel novels, while I play at biology. Sam argued that golf would be healthier and less nonsensical for me, but you insisted on biology. And give it its due, it has kept me out in the open air and been conducive to travelling and broadening my mind. (*Then forcing a smile*) But I'm exaggerating. I really am interested, or I'd never keep financing the Station. And when I'm down there I do work hard, helping Preston. He's doing remarkable work already, and he's still in his twenties. He'll be a big man— (*His bitterness cropping up again*) at least if he takes my advice and never carries his experiments as far as human lives!

NINA. (*in a low voice*) How can you be so bitter, Ned—on Gordon's birthday?

DARRELL. (*thinking cynically*)

She expects me to love the child she deliberately took from me and gave to another man! . . . no, thank you, Nina! . . . I've been hurt enough! . . . I'll not leave myself open there! . . .

(*Regarding his son bitterly*) Every day he gets more like Sam, doesn't he?

GORDON. (*thinking*)

He's talking about me . . . he better look out! . . .

NINA. (*resentfully*) I don't think Gordon resembles Sam at all. He reminds me a great deal of his namesake.

DARRELL. (*touched on a sore spot—with a nasty laugh—cuttingly*) Gordon Shaw? Not the slightest bit in the world! And you ought to thank God he doesn't! It's the last thing I'd want wished on a boy of mine—to be like that rah-rah hero!

GORDON. (*thinking contemptuously*)

Boy of his! . . . He hasn't got a boy! . . .

NINA. (*amused and pleased by his jealousy*)

Poor Ned! . . . isn't he silly? . . . at his age, after all we've been through, to still feel jealous . . .

DARRELL. I'd much rather have him (*Pointing to* GORDON) grow up to be an exact duplicate of the esteemed Samuel!

GORDON. (*thinking resentfully*)

He's always making fun of my father! . . . he better look out! . . .

DARRELL. (*more and more mockingly*) And what could be fairer? The good Samuel is an A one success. He has a charming wife and a darling boy, and a Park Avenue apartment and a membership in an expensive golf club. And, above all, he rests so complacently on the proud assurance that he is self-made!

NINA. (*sharply*) Ned! You ought to be ashamed! You know how grateful Sam has always been to you!

DARRELL. (*bitingly*) Would he be grateful if he knew how much I'd really done for him?

NINA. (*sternly*) Ned!

GORDON. (*suddenly jumps up and confronts* DARRELL, *his fists clenched, trembling with rage, stammers*) You—shut up—making fun of my father!

NINA. (*in dismay*) Gordon!

DARRELL. (*mockingly*) My dear boy, I wouldn't make fun of your father for the world!

GORDON. (*baffledly—his lips trembling*) You—you did, too! (*Then intensely*) I hate you!

NINA. (*shocked and indignant*) Gordon! How dare you talk like that to your Uncle Ned!

GORDON. (*rebelliously*) He's not my uncle! He's not my anything!

NINA. Not another word or you'll be punished, whether it's your birthday or not! If you can't behave better than that, I'll have to phone to all your friends they mustn't come here this afternoon, that you've been so bad you can't have a party! (*Thinking remorsefully*)

Is this my fault? . . . I've done my best to get him to love Ned! . . . but it only makes him worse! . . . it makes him turn against me! . . . turn from me to Sam!

GORDON. (*sullenly*) I don't care! I'll tell Dad!

NINA. (*peremptorily*) Leave the room! And don't come near me again, do you hear, until you've apologized to Uncle Ned! (*Thinking angrily*)

Dad! . . . It's always Dad with him now! . . .

DARRELL. (*boredly*) Oh, never mind, Nina!

GORDON. (*going out—mutters*) I won't 'pologize—never! (*Thinking vindictively*)

I hate her too when she sides with him! . . . I don't care if she is my mother! . . . she has no right! . . .

(*He goes out, rear.*)

DARRELL. (*irritably*) What if he does hate me? I don't blame him! He suspects what I know—that I've acted like a coward and a weakling toward him! I should have claimed him no matter what happened to other people! Whose fault is it if he hates me, and I dislike him because he loves another father? Ours! You gave him to Sam and I consented! All right! Then don't blame him for acting like Sam's son!

NINA. But he shouldn't say he hates you. (*Thinking bitterly*)

Sam's! . . . he's becoming all Sam's! . . . I'm getting to mean nothing! . . .

DARRELL. (*sardonically*) Perhaps he realizes subconsciously that I am his father, his rival in your love; but I'm not his father ostensibly, there are no taboos, so he can come right out and hate me to his heart's content! (*Bitterly*) If he realized how little you love me any more, he wouldn't bother!

NINA. (*exasperatedly*) Oh, Ned, do shut up! I can't stand hearing those same old reproaches I've heard a thousand times before! I can't bear to hear myself making the same old bitter counter-accusations. And then there'll be the same old terrible scene of hate and you'll run away—it used to be to drink and women, now it's to the Station. Or I'll send you away, and then after a time I'll call you back, because I'll have gotten so lonely again living this lonely lie of my life, with no one to speak to except Sam's business friends and their deadly wives. (*She laughs helplessly*) Or else you'll get lonely in your lie a little before I do and come back again of your own desire! And then we'll kiss and cry and love each other again!

DARRELL. (*with an ironical grimace*) Or I might cheat myself into believing I'd fallen in love with some nice girl and get myself engaged to be married again as I did once before! And then you'd be jealous again and have to find some way of getting me to break it off!

NINA. (*forlornly amused*) Yes—I supposed the thought of a wife taking you away from me would be too much—again! (*Then helplessly*) Oh, Ned, when are we ever going to learn something about each other? We act like such brainless fools—with our love. It's always so wonderful when you first come back, but you always stay too long—or I always keep you too long! You never leave before we've come to the ugly bitter stage when we blame each other! (*Then suddenly forlornly tender*) Is it possible you can still love me, Ned?

DARRELL. (*mournfully smiling*) I must, or I'd never act this fool way, would I?

NINA. (*smiling back*) And I must love you. (*Then seriously*) After all, I can never forget that Gordon is the child of your love, Ned.

DARRELL. (*sadly*) You'd better forget that, for his sake and your own. Children have sure intuitions. He feels cheated of your love—by me. So he's concentrating his affections on Sam whose love he knows is secure, and withdrawing from you.

NINA. (*frightened—angrily*) Don't be stupid, Ned! That isn't so at all! I hate you when you talk that way!

DARRELL. (*cynically*) Hate me, exactly. As he does! That's what I'm advising you to do if you want to keep his love! (*He smiles grimly.*)

NINA. (*sharply*) If Gordon doesn't love you it's because you've never made the slightest attempt to be lovable to him! There's no earthly reason why he should like you, when you come right down to it, Ned! Take today, for instance. It's his birthday but you'd forgotten, or didn't care! You never even brought him a present.

DARRELL. (*with bitter sadness*) I did bring him a present. It's out in the hall. I bought him a costly delicate one so he could get full satisfaction and yet not strain himself when he smashed it, as he's smashed every present of mine in the past! And I left it out in the hall, to be given to him after I've gone because, after all, he is my son and I'd prefer he didn't smash it before my eyes! (*Trying to mock his own emotion back—with savage bitterness*) I'm selfish, you see! I don't want my son to be too happy at my expense, even on his birthday!

NINA. (*tormented by love and pity and remorse*) Ned! For God's sake! How can you torture us like that! Oh, it's too dreadful—what I have done to you! Forgive me, Ned!

DARRELL. (*his expression changing to one of pity for her—goes to her and puts his hand on her head—tenderly*) I'm sorry. (*With remorseful tenderness*) Dreadful, what you've done, Nina? Why, you've given me the only happiness I've ever known! And no matter what I may say or do in bitterness, I'm proud—and grateful, Nina!

NINA. (*looks up at him with deep tenderness and admiration*) Dearest, it's wonderful of you to say that! (*She gets up and puts her hands on his shoulders and looks into his eyes—tenderly in a sort of pleading*) Can't we be brave enough—for you to go away—now, on this note—sure of our love—with no ugly bitterness for once?

DARRELL. (*joyfully*) Yes! I'll go—this minute if you wish!

NINA. (*playfully*) Oh, you needn't go this minute! Wait and say good-by to Sam. He'd be terribly hurt if you didn't. (*Then seriously*) And will you promise to stay away two years—even if I call you back before then—and work this time, really work?

DARRELL. I'll try, Nina!

NINA. And then—surely come back to me!

DARRELL. (*smiling*) Surely—again!

NINA. Then good-by, dear! (*She kisses him.*)

DARRELL. Again! (*He smiles and she smiles and they kiss again.* GORDON *appears in the doorway at rear and stands for a moment in a passion of jealousy and rage and grief, watching them.*)

GORDON. (*thinking with a strange tortured shame*)

I mustn't see her! . . . pretend I didn't see her! . . . mustn't never let her know I saw her! . . .

(*He vanishes as silently as he had come.*)

NINA. (*suddenly moving away from* DARRELL, *looking around her uneasily*) Ned, did you see—? I had the queerest feeling just then that someone—

GORDON. (*his voice sounds from the hall with a strained casualness*) Mother! Uncle Charlie's downstairs. Shall he come right up?

NINA. (*startled, her own voice straining to be casual*) Yes, dear—

of course! (*Then worriedly*) His voice sounded funny. Did it to you? Do you suppose he—?

DARRELL. (*with a wry smile*) It's possible. To be on the safe side, you'd better tell him you kissed me good-by to get rid of me! (*Then angrily*) So Marsden's here again! The damned old woman! I simply can't go him any more, Nina! Why Gordon should take such a fancy to that old sissy is beyond me!

NINA. (*suddenly struck—thinking*)

Why, he's jealous of Gordon liking Charlie! . . .

(*Immediately all affectionate pity*)

Then he must love Gordon a little! . . .

(*Letting her pity escape her*) Poor Ned! (*She makes a movement toward him.*)

DARRELL. (*startled and afraid she may have guessed something he doesn't acknowledge to himself*) What? Why do you say that? (*Then rudely defensive*) Don't be silly! (*Resentfully*) You know well enough what I've always held against him! I wanted to put up all the money to back Sam when he started. I wanted to do it for Sam's sake—but especially for my child's sake. Why did Marsden absolutely insist on Sam letting him in equally? It isn't that I begrudge him the money he's made, but I know there was something queer in his mind and that he did it intentionally to spite me! (*From the hallway comes the sound of* MARSDEN'S *voice and* GORDON'S *greeting him vociferously as he lets him into the apartment. As* DARRELL *listens his expression becomes furious again. He bursts out angrily*) You're letting that old ass spoil Gordon, you fool, you! (MARSDEN *comes in from the rear, smiling, immaculately dressed as usual. He looks hardly any older except that his hair is grayer and his tall figure more stooped. His expression and the general atmosphere he gives out are more nearly like those of Act One. If not happy, he is at least living in comparative peace with himself and his environment.*)

MARSDEN. (*comes straight to* NINA) Hello, Nina Cara Nina! Congratulations on your son's birthday! (*He kisses her*) He's grown so much bigger and stronger in the two months since I've seen him. (*He turns and shakes hands with* DARRELL *coldly—with a trace of a patronizing air*) Hello, Darrell. Last time I was here you were leaving for the West Indies in a week but I see you're still around.

DARRELL. (*furious—with a mocking air*) And here you are around again yourself! You're looking comfortable these days, Marsden. I hope your sister is well. It must be a great comfort, having her to take your mother's place! (*Then with a harsh laugh*) Yes, we're two bad pennies, eh, Marsden?—counterfeits—fakes—Sam's silent partners!

NINA. (*thinking irritably*)

Ned's getting hateful again! . . . Poor Charlie! . . . I won't have him insulted! . . . he's become such a comfort . . . he understands so much . . . without my having to tell him . . .

(*Looking rebukingly at* DARRELL) Ned is sailing this week, Charlie.

MARSDEN. (*thinking triumphantly*)

He's trying to insult me . . . I know all he means . . . but what do I care what he says . . . she's sending him away! . . . intentionally before me! . . . it means he's finished! . . .

DARRELL. (*thinking resentfully*)

Is she trying to humiliate me before him? . . . I'll teach her! . . .

(*Then struggling with himself—remorsefully*)

No . . . not this time . . . I promised . . . no quarrel . . . remember . . .

(*Acquiescing—with a pleasant nod to* MARSDEN) Yes, I'm going this week and I expect to be gone at least two years this time—two years of hard work.

MARSDEN. (*thinking with scornful pity*)

His work! . . . what a pretense! . . . a scientific dilettante! . . . could anything be more pitiable? . . . poor chap! . . .

(*Perfunctorily*) Biology must be an interesting study. I wish I knew more about it.

DARRELL. (*stung yet amused by the other's tone—ironically*) Yes, so do I wish you did, Marsden! Then you might write more about life and less about dear old ladies and devilish bachelors! Why don't you write a novel about life sometime, Marsden? (*He turns his back on* MARSDEN *with a glance of repulsion and walks to the window and stares out.*)

MARSDEN. (*confusedly*) Yes—decidedly—but hardly in my line—(*Thinking in anguish—picking up a magazine and turning over the pages aimlessly*)

That . . . is . . . true! . . . he's full of poison! . . . I've never married the word to life! . . . I've been a timid bachelor of Arts, not an artist! . . . my poor pleasant books! . . . all is well! . . . is this well, the three of us? . . . Darrell has become less and less her lover . . . Nina has turned more and more to me . . . we have built up a secret life of subtle sympathies and confidences . . . she has known I have understood about her mere physical passion for Darrell . . . what woman could be expected to love Sam passionately? . . . some day she'll confide all about Darrell to me . . . now that he's finished . . . she knows that I love her without my telling . . . she even knows the sort of love it is. . . .

(*Passionately—thinking*)

My love is finer than any she has known! . . . I do not lust for her! . . . I would be content if our marriage should be purely the placing of our ashes in the same tomb . . . our urn side by side and touching one another . . . could the others say as much, could they love so deeply? . . .

(*Then suddenly miserably self-contemptuous*)

What! . . . platonic heroic at my age! . . . do I believe a word of that? . . . look at her beautiful eyes! . . . wouldn't I give anything in life to see them desire me? . . . and the intimacy I'm boasting about, what more does it mean than that I've been playing the dear old Charlie of her girlhood again? . . .

(*Thinking in anguish*)

Damned coward and weakling!

NINA. (*looking at him—pityingly—thinking*)

What does he always want of me? . . . me? . . . I am the only one who senses his deep hurt . . . I feel how life has wounded him . . . is that partly my fault, too? . . . I have wounded everyone . . . poor Charlie, what can I do for you? . . . if giving myself to you would bring you a moment's happiness, could I? . . . the idea used to be revolting . . . now, nothing about love seems important enough to be revolting . . . poor Charlie, he only thinks he ought to desire me! . . . dear Charlie, what a perfect lover he would make for one's old age! . . . what a perfect lover when one was past passion! . . .

(*Then with sudden scornful revulsion*)

These men make me sick! . . . I hate all three of them! . . . they disgust me! . . . the wife and mistress in me has been killed by them! . . . thank God, I am only a mother now! . . . Gordon is my little man, my only man! . . .

(*Suddenly*) I've got a job for you, Charlie—make the salad dressing for lunch. You know, the one I'm so crazy about.

MARSDEN. (*springs to his feet*) Righto! (*He puts his arm about her waist and they go out together laughingly, without a glance at* DARRELL.)

DARRELL. (*thinking dully*)

I mustn't stay to lunch . . . ghost at my son's feast! . . . I better go now . . . why wait for Sam? . . . what is there to say to him I can say? . . . and there's nothing about him I want to see . . . he's as healthy as a pig . . . and as sane . . . I was afraid once his mother had lied to Nina . . . I went upstate and investigated . . . true, every word of it . . . his great-grandfather, his grandmother, his father, were all insane . . .

(*Moving uneasily*)

Stop it! . . . time to go when those thoughts come . . . sail on Saturday . . . not come here again . . . Nina will soon be fighting Sam for my son's love! . . . I'm better out of that! . . . O Christ, what a mess it all is! . . .

GORDON. (*appears in the doorway in rear. He carries a small, expensive yacht's model of a sloop with the sails set. He is in a terrific state of conflicting emotions, on the verge of tears yet stubbornly determined*)

I got to do it! . . . Gosh, it's awful . . . this boat is so pretty . . . why did it have to come from him? . . . I can get Dad to buy me another boat . . . but now I love this one . . . but he kissed Mother . . . she kissed him . . .

(*He walks up defiantly and confronts* DARRELL *who turns to him in surprise*) Hey—Darrell—did you—? (*He stops chokingly.*)

DARRELL. (*immediately realizing what is coming—thinking with somber anguish*)

So this has to happen! . . . what I dreaded! . . . my fate is merciless, it seems! . . .

(*With strained kindliness*) Did what?

GORDON. (*growing hard—stammers angrily*) I found this—out in the hall. It can't be from anybody else. Is this—your present?

DARRELL. (*hard and defiant himself*) Yes.

GORDON. (*in a rage—tremblingly*) Then—here's what—I think of you! (*Beginning to cry, he breaks off the mast, bowsprit, breaks the mast in two, tears the rigging off and throws the dismantled hull at* DARRELL'*s feet*) There! You can keep it!

DARRELL. (*his anger overcoming him for an instant*) You—you mean little devil, you! You don't get that from me— (*He has taken a threatening step forward.* GORDON *stands white-faced, defying him.* DARRELL *pulls himself up short—then in a trembling voice of deeply wounded affection*) You shouldn't have done that, son. What difference do I make? It was never my boat. But it was your boat. You should consider the boat, not me. Don't you like boats for themselves? It was a beautiful little boat, I thought. That's why I—

GORDON. (*sobbing miserably*) It was awful pretty! I didn't want to do it! (*He kneels down and gathers up the boat into his arms again*) Honest I didn't. I love boats! But I hate you! (*This last with passionate intensity.*)

DARRELL. (*dryly*) So I've observed. (*Thinking with angry anguish*)

He hurts, damn him! . .

GORDON. No, you don't know! More'n ever now! More'n ever!

(*The secret escaping him*) I saw you kissing Mother! I saw Mother, too!

DARRELL. (*startled, but immediately forcing a smile*) But I was saying good-bye. We're old friends. You know that.

GORDON. You can't fool me! This was different! (*Explosively*) It would serve you good and right—and Mother, too—if I was to tell Dad on you!

DARRELL. Why, I'm Sam's oldest friend. Don't make a little fool of yourself!

GORDON. You are not his friend. You've always been hanging around cheating him—hanging around Mother!

DARRELL. Keep still! What do you mean cheating him?

GORDON. I don't know. But I know you aren't his friend. And sometime I'm going to tell him I saw you—

DARRELL. (*with great seriousness now—deeply moved*) Listen! There are things a man of honor doesn't tell anyone—not even his mother or father. You want to be a man of honor, don't you? (*Intensely*) There are things we don't tell, you and I! (*He has put his hand around* GORDON'*s shoulder impulsively*)

This is my son! . . . I love him! . . .

GORDON. (*thinking—terribly torn*)

Why do I like him now? . . . I like him awful! . . .

(*Crying*) We!—who d'you mean?—I've got honor!—more'n you!—you don't have to tell me!—I wasn't going to tell Dad anyway, honest I wasn't! We?—what d'you mean, we?—I'm not like you! I don't want to be ever like you! (*There is the sound of a door being flung open and shut and* EVANS' *hearty voice.*)

EVANS. (*from the entrance hall*) Hello, everybody!

DARRELL. (*slapping* GORDON *on the back*) Buck up, son! Here he is! Hide that boat or he'll ask questions. (GORDON *runs and hides the boat under the sofa. When* EVANS *enters,* GORDON *is entirely composed and runs to him joyfully.* EVANS *has grown stouter, his face is heavy now, he has grown executive and used to command, he automatically takes charge wherever he is. He does not look his age except that his hair has grown scanty and there is a perceptible bald spot on top. He is expensively tailored.*)

EVANS. (*hugging* GORDON *to him—lovingly*) How's the old son? How's the birthday coming along?

GORDON. Fine, Dad!

EVANS. Hello, Ned! Isn't this kid of mine a whopper for his age, though!

DARRELL. (*smiling strainedly*) Yes. (*Writhing—thinking*)

It hurts now! . . . to see my son his son! . . . I've had enough! . . . get out! . . . any excuse! . . . I can phone afterwards! . . . I'll yell out the whole business if I stay! . . .

I was just going, Sam. I've got to step around and see a fellow who lives near—biologist. (*He has gone to the door.*)

EVANS. (*disappointedly*) Then you won't be here for lunch?

DARRELL. (*thinking*)

I'll yell the truth into your ears if I stay a second longer . . . you damned lunatic! . . .

Can't stay. Sorry. This is important. I'm sailing in a few days—lots to do—see you later, Sam. So long—Gordon.

GORDON. (*as he goes out with awkward haste*) Good-bye—Uncle Ned. (*Thinking confusedly*)

Why did I call him that when I said I never would? . . . I know . . . must be because he said he's sailing and I'm glad . . .

EVANS. So long, Ned. (*Thinking—good-naturedly superior*)

Ned and his biology! . . . He takes his hobby pretty seriously! . . .

(*With satisfaction*)

Well, he can afford to have hobbies now! . . . his investment with me has made him a pile. . . .

Where's Mother, son?

GORDON. Out in the kitchen with Uncle Charlie. (*Thinking*)

I hope he never comes back! . . . why did I like him then? . . . it was only for a second . . . I didn't really . . . I never could! . . . why does he always call me Gordon as if he hated to? . . .

EVANS. (*sitting down at left*) I hope lunch is ready soon. I'm hungry as the devil, aren't you?

GORDON. (*absent-mindedly*) Yes, Dad.

EVANS. Come over here and tell me about your birthday. (GORDON *comes over.* EVANS *pulls him up on his lap*) How'd you like your presents? What'd you get from Uncle Ned?

GORDON. (*evasively*) They were all dandy. (*Suddenly*) Why was I named Gordon?

EVANS. Oh, you know all about that—all about Gordon Shaw. I've told you time and again.

GORDON. You told me once he was Mother's beau—when she was a girl.

EVANS. (*teasingly*) What do you know about beaus? You're growing up!

GORDON. Did Mother love him a lot?

EVANS. (*embarrassedly*) I guess so.

GORDON. (*thinking keenly*)

> That's why Darrell hates me being called Gordon . . . he knows Mother loved Gordon better'n she does him . . . now I know how to get back at him . . . I'll be just like Gordon was and Mother'll love me better'n him! . . .

And then that Gordon was killed, wasn't he? Am I anything like him?

EVANS. I hope you are. If when you go to college you can play football or row like Gordon did, I'll—I'll give you anything you ask for! I mean that!

GORDON. (*dreamily*) Tell me about him again, will you, Dad—about the time he was stroking the crew and the fellow who was Number Seven began to crack, and he couldn't see him but he felt him cracking somehow, and he began talking back to him all the time and sort of gave him his strength so that when the race was over and they'd won Gordon fainted and the other fellow didn't.

EVANS. (*with a fond laugh*) Why, you know it all by heart! What's the use of my telling you?

NINA. (*comes in from the rear while they are talking. She comes forward slowly—thinking resentfully*)

Does he love Sam more than he does me? . . . oh, no, he can't! . . . but he trusts him more! . . . he confides in him more! . . .

GORDON. Did you ever used to fight fellows, Dad?

EVANS. (*embarrassedly*) Oh, a little—when I had to.

GORDON. Could you lick Darrell?

NINA. (*thinking frightenedly*)

Why does he ask that? . . .

EVANS. (*surprised*) Your Uncle Ned? What for? We've always been friends.

GORDON. I mean, if you weren't friends, could you?

EVANS. (*boastfully*) Oh, yes, I guess so. Ned was never as strong as I was.

NINA. (*thinking contemptuously*)

Ned is weak. . . .

(*Then apprehensively*)

But you're getting too strong, Sam. . . .

GORDON. But Gordon could have licked you, couldn't he?

EVANS. You bet he could!

GORDON. (*thinking*)

She must have loved Gordon better'n Dad even! . . .

NINA. (*she comes forward to the chair at center, forcing a smile*) What's all this talk about fighting? That's not nice. For heaven's sake, Sam, don't encourage him—

EVANS. (*grinning*) Never mind the women, Gordon. You've got to know how to fight to get on in this world.

NINA. (*thinking pityingly*)

You poor booby! . . . how brave you are now! . . .

(*Softly*) Perhaps you're right, dear. (*Looking around*) Has Ned gone?

GORDON. (*defiantly*) Yes—and he's not coming back—and he's sailing soon!

NINA. (*with a shudder*)

Why does he challenge me that way? . . . and cling to Sam? . . . he must have seen Ned and me . . . he doesn't offer to come to my lap . . . he used to . . . Ned was right . . . I've got to lie to him . . . get him back . . . here . . . on my lap! . . .

(*With a sneer—to* EVANS) I'm glad Ned's gone. I was afraid he was going to be on our hands all day.

GORDON. (*eagerly, half-getting down from his father's lap*) You're glad—? (*Then cautiously thinking*)

She's cheating . . . I saw her kiss him. . . .

NINA. Ned's getting to be an awful bore. He's so weak. He can't get started on anything unless he's pushed.

GORDON. (*moving a little nearer—searching her face—thinking*)

She doesn't seem to like him so much . . . but I saw her kiss him! . . .

EVANS. (*surprised*) Oh, come now, Nina, aren't you being a little hard on Ned? It's true he's sort of lost his grip in a way but he's our best friend.

GORDON. (*moving away from his father again—resentfully—thinking*)

What's Dad standing up for him to her for? . . .

NINA. (*thinking triumphantly*)

That's right, Sam . . . just what I wanted you to say! . . .

(*Boredly*) Oh, I know he is but he gets on my nerves hanging around all the time. Without being too rude, I urged him to get back to his work, and made him promise me he wouldn't return for two years. Finally he promised—and then he became silly and sentimental and asked me to kiss him good-bye for good luck! So I kissed him to get rid of him! The silly fool!

GORDON. (*thinking—overjoyed*)

Then! . . . that's why! . . . that's why! . . . and he'll be gone two years! . . . oh, I'm so glad! . . .

(*He goes to her and looks up into her face with shining eyes*) Mother!

NINA. Dear! (*She takes him up on her lap and hugs him in her arms.*)

GORDON. (*kisses her*) There! (*Triumphantly thinking*)

That makes up for his kiss! . . . That takes it off her mouth. . . .

EVANS. (*grinning*) Ned must be falling for you—in his old age! (*Then sentimentally*) Poor guy! He's never married, that's the trouble. He's lonely. I know how he feels. A fellow needs a little feminine encouragement to help him keep his head up.

NINA. (*snuggling* GORDON'S *head against hers—laughing teasingly*) I think your hard-headed Dad is getting mushy and silly! What do you think, Gordon?

GORDON. (*laughing with her*) Yes, he's mushy, Mother! He's silly! (*He kisses her and whispers*) I'm going to be like Gordon Shaw, Mother! (*She hugs him fiercely to her, triumphantly happy.*)

EVANS. (*grinning*) You two are getting too hard-boiled for me. (*He laughs. They all laugh happily together.*)

NINA. (*suddenly overcome by a wave of conscience-stricken remorse and pity*)

Oh, I am hard on Ned! . . . poor dear generous Ned! . . . you told me to lie to your son against you . . . for my sake . . . I'm not worthy of your love! . . . I'm low and selfish! . . . but I do love you! . . . this is the son of our love in my arms! . . . oh, Mother God, grant my prayer that some day we may tell our son the truth and he may love his father! . . .

GORDON. (*sensing her thoughts, sits up in her lap and stares into her face, while she guiltily avoids his eyes—in fear and resentment. Thinking*)

She's thinking about that Darrell now! . . . I know! . . . she likes him too! . . . she can't fool me! . . . I saw her kissing! . . . she didn't think he was a silly fool then! . . . she was lying to Dad and me! . . .

(*He pushes off her lap and backs away from her.*)

NINA. (*thinking frightenedly*)

He read my thoughts! . . . I mustn't even think of Ned when he's around! . . . poor Ned! . . . no, don't think of him! . . .

(*Leaning forward toward* GORDON *with her arms stretched out entreatingly but adopting a playful tone*) Why, Gordon, what's come over you? You jumped off my lap as though you'd sat on a tack! (*She forces a laugh.*)

GORDON. (*his eyes on the floor—evasively*) I'm hungry. I want to see if lunch is nearly ready. (*He turns abruptly and runs out.*)

EVANS. (*in a tone of superior manly understanding, kindly but laying down the law to womanly weakness*) He's sick of being babied, Nina. You forget he's getting to be a big boy. And we want him to grow up a real he-man and not an old lady like Charlie. (*Sagaciously*) That's what's made Charlie like he is, I'll bet. His mother never stopped babying him.

NINA. (*submissively—but with a look of bitter scorn at him*) Perhaps you're right, Sam.

EVANS. (*confidently*) I know I am!

NINA. (*thinking with a look of intense hatred*)

Oh, Mother God, grant that I may some day tell this fool the truth! . . .

CURTAIN

ACT EIGHT

SCENE: *Late afternoon in late June, ten years later—the afterdeck of the* EVANS' *motor cruiser anchored in the lane of yachts near the finish line at Poughkeepsie. The bow and amidship of the cruiser are off right, pointed upstream. The portside rail is in the rear, the curve of the stern at left, the rear of the cabin with broad windows and a door is at right. Two wicker chairs are at left and a chaise longue at right. A wicker table with another chair is at center. The afterdeck is in cool shade, contrasted with the soft golden haze of late afternoon sunlight that glows on the river.*

NINA *is sitting by the table at center,* DARRELL *in the chair farthest left,* MARSDEN *in the chaise longue at right.* EVANS *is leaning over the rail directly back of* NINA, *looking up the river through a pair of binoculars.* MADELINE ARNOLD *is standing by his side.*

NINA'S *hair has turned completely white. She is desperately trying to conceal the obvious inroads of time by an over-emphasis on make-up that defeats its end by drawing attention to what it would conceal. Her face is thin, her cheeks taut, her mouth drawn with forced smiling. There is little left of her face's charm except her eyes which now seem larger and more deeply mysterious than ever. But she has kept her beautiful figure. It has the tragic effect of making her face seem older and more worn-out by contrast. Her general manner recalls instantly the* NINA *of Act Four, neurotic, passionately embittered and torn. She is dressed in a white yachting costume.*

DARRELL *seems to have "thrown back" to the young doctor we had seen at the house of* NINA'S *father in Act Two. He has again the air of the cool, detached scientist regarding himself and the people around him as interesting phenomena. In appearance, he is once more sharply defined, his face and body have grown lean and well-*

conditioned, the puffiness and jowls of the previous Act are gone. His skin is tanned almost black by his years in the tropics. His thick hair is iron-gray. He wears flannel pants, a blue coat, white buckskin shoes. He looks his fifty-one years, perhaps, but not a day more. MARSDEN *has aged greatly. The stoop of his tall figure is accentuated, his hair has grown whitish. He is an older image of the* MARSDEN *of Act Five, who was so prostrated by his mother's death. Now it is his sister's death two months before that has plunged him into despair. His present grief, however, is more resigned to its fate than the old. He is dressed immaculately in black, as in Act Five.*

EVANS *is simply* EVANS, *his type logically developed by ten years of continued success and accumulating wealth, jovial and simple and good-natured as ever, but increasingly stubborn and self-opinionated. He has grown very stout. His jowly broad face has a heavy, flushed, apoplectic look. His head has grown quite bald on top. He is wearing a yachting cap, blue yachting coat, white flannel pants, buckskin shoes.*

MADELINE ARNOLD *is a pretty girl of nineteen, with dark hair and eyes. Her skin is deeply tanned, her figure tall and athletic, reminding one of* NINA'S *when we first saw her. Her personality is direct and frank. She gives the impression of a person who always knows exactly what she is after and generally gets it, but is also generous and a good loser, a good sport who is popular with her own sex as well as sought after by men. She is dressed in a bright-colored sport costume.*

EVANS. (*nervous and excited—on pins and needles—lowering his binoculars impatiently*) Can't see anything up there! There's a damned haze on the river! (*Handing the binoculars to* MADELINE) Here, Madeline. You've got young eyes.

MADELINE. (*eagerly*) Thank you. (*She looks up the river through the glasses.*)

NINA. (*thinking—bitterly*)

Young eyes! . . . they look into Gordon's eyes! . . . he sees love in her young eyes! . . . mine are old now! . . .

EVANS. (*pulling out his watch*) Soon be time for the start. (*Comes forward—exasperatedly*) Of course, the damned radio has to pick out this time to go dead! Brand new one I had installed especially for this race, too! Just my luck! (*Coming to* NINA *and putting his hand on her shoulder*) Gosh, I'll bet Gordon's some keyed-up right at this moment, Nina!

MADELINE. (*without lowering the glasses*) Poor kid! I'll bet he is!

NINA. (*thinking with intense bitterness*)

That tone in her voice! . . . her love already possesses him! . . . my son! . . .

(*Vindictively*)

But she won't! . . . as long as I live! . . .

(*Flatly*) Yes, he must be nervous.

EVANS. (*taking his hand away, sharply*) I didn't mean nervous. He doesn't know what it is to have nerves. Nothing's ever got him rattled yet. (*This last with a resentful look down at her as he moves back to the rail.*)

MADELINE. (*with the calm confidence of one who knows*) Yes, you can bank on Gordon never losing his nerve.

NINA. (*coldly*) I'm quite aware my son isn't a weakling— (*Meaningly, with a glance at* MADELINE) even though he does do weak things sometimes.

MADELINE. (*without lowering the glasses from her eyes—thinking good-naturedly*)

Ouch! . . . that was meant for me! . . .

(*Then hurt*)

Why does she dislike me so? . . . I've done my best, for Gordon's sake, to be nice to her. . . .

EVANS. (*looking back at* NINA *resentfully—thinking*)

Another nasty crack at Madeline! . . . Nina's certainly become the prize bum sport! . . . I thought once her change of life was over she'd be ashamed of her crazy jealousy . . . instead of that it's got worse . . . but I'm not going to let her come between Gordon and Madeline . . . he loves her and she loves him . . . and her folks have got money and position, too . . . and I like her a lot . . . and, by God, I'm going to see to it their marriage goes through on schedule, no matter how much Nina kicks up! . . .

DARRELL. (*keenly observant—thinking*)

Nina hates this young lady . . . of course! . . . Gordon's girl . . . she'll smash their engagement if she can . . . as she did mine once . . . once! . . . thank God my slavery is over! . . . how did she know I was back in town? . . . I wasn't going to see her again . . . but her invitation was so imploring . . . my duty to Gordon, she wrote . . . what duty? . . . pretty late in the day! . . . that's better left dead, too! . . .

EVANS. (*looking at his watch again*) They ought to be lined up at the start any minute now. (*Pounding his fist on the rail—letting his pent-up feelings explode*) Come on, Gordon!

NINA. (*startled—with nervous irritation*) Sam! I told you I have a splitting headache! (*Thinking intensely*)

You vulgar boor! . . . Gordon's engagement to her is all your fault! . . .

EVANS. (*Resentfully*) I'm sorry. Why don't you take some aspirin? (*Thinking irritably*)

Nina in the dumps! . . . Charlie in mourning! . . . what a pair of killjoys! . . . I wanted to bring Gordon and his friends on board to celebrate . . . no chance! . . . have to take Madeline . . . stage a party in New York . . . leave this outfit flat . . . Nina'll be sore as the devil but she'll have to like it . . .

DARRELL. (*examining* NINA *critically—thinking*)

She's gotten into a fine neurotic state . . . reminds me of when I first knew her . . .

(*Then exultantly*)

Thank God, I can watch her objectively again . . . these last three years away have finally done it . . . complete cure! . . .

(*Then remorsefully*)

Poor Nina! . . . we're all deserting her . . .

(*Then glancing at* MARSDEN*—with a trace of a sneer*)

Even Marsden seems to have left her for the dead! . . .

MARSDEN. (*vaguely irritated—thinking*)

What am I doing here? . . . what do I care about this stupid race? . . . why did I let Nina bully me into coming? . . . I ought to be alone . . . with my memories of dear Jane . . . it will be two months ago Saturday she died . . .

(*His lips tremble, tears come to his eyes*)

MADELINE. (*with an impatient sigh, lowering the glasses*) It's no use, Mr. Evans, I can't see a thing.

EVANS. (*with angry disgust*) If only that damned radio was working!

NINA. (*exasperatedly*) For heaven's sake, stop swearing so much!

EVANS. (*hurt—indignantly*) What about it if I am excited? Seems to me you could show a little more interest without it hurting you, when it's Gordon's last race, his last appearance on a varsity! (*He turns away from her.*)

MADELINE. (*thinking*)

He's right . . . she's acting rotten . . . if I were Gordon's mother, I certainly wouldn't . . .

EVANS. (*turning back to* NINA*—resentfully*) You used to cheer loud enough for Gordon Shaw! And our Gordon's got him beat a mile, as an oarsman, at least! (*Turning to* DARRELL) And that isn't father stuff either, Ned! All the experts say so!

DARRELL. (*cynically*) Oh, come on, Sam! Surely no one could ever touch Shaw in anything! (*He glances at* NINA *with a sneer. Immediately angry at himself*)

What an idiot! . . . that popped out of me! . . . old habit! . . . I haven't loved her in years! . . .

NINA. (*thinking indifferently*)

Ned still feels jealous . . . that no longer pleases me . . . I don't feel anything . . . except that I must get him to help me. . . .

(*She turns to* DARRELL *bitterly*) Sam said "our" Gordon. He means his. Gordon's become so like Sam, Ned, you won't recognize him!

MADELINE. (*thinking indignantly*)

She's crazy! . . . he's nothing like his father! . . . he's so strong and handsome! . . .

EVANS. (*good-naturedly, with a trace of pride*) You flatter me, Nina. I wish I thought that. But he isn't a bit like me, luckily for him. He's a dead ringer for Gordon Shaw at his best.

MADELINE. (*thinking*)

Shaw . . . I've seen his picture in the gym . . . my Gordon is better looking . . . he once told me Shaw was an old beau of his mother's . . . they say she was beautiful once . . .

NINA. (*shaking her head—scornfully*) Don't be modest, Sam. Gordon *is* you. He may be a fine athlete like Gordon Shaw, because you've held that out to him as your ideal, but there the resemblance ceases. He isn't really like him at all, not the slightest bit!

EVANS. (*restraining his anger with difficulty—thinking*)

I'm getting sick of this! . . . she's carrying her jealous grouch too far! . . .

(*Suddenly exploding, pounds his fist on the rail*) Damn it, Nina, if you had any feeling you couldn't—right at the moment when he's probably getting into the shell— (*He stops, trying to control himself, panting, his face red.*)

NINA. (*staring at him with repulsion—with cool disdain*) I didn't say anything so dire, did I—merely that Gordon resembles you in character. (*With malice*) Don't get so excited. It's bad for your high blood pressure. Ask Ned if it isn't. (*Intensely—thinking*)

If he'd only die! . . .

(*Thinking—immediately*)

Oh, I don't mean that . . . I mustn't . . .

DARRELL. (*thinking keenly*)

There's a death wish . . . things have gone pretty far . . . Sam does look as if he might have a bad pressure . . . what hope that would have given me at one time! . . . no more, thank God! . . .

(*In a joking tone*) Oh, I guess Sam's all right, Nina.

EVANS. (*gruffly*) I never felt better. (*He jerks out his watch again*) Time for the start. Come on in the cabin, Ned, and shoot a drink.

We'll see if McCabe's getting the damned radio fixed. (*Passing by* MARSDEN *he claps him on the shoulder exasperatedly.*) Come on, Charlie! Snap out of it!

MARSDEN. (*startled out of his trance—bewilderedly*) Eh?—what is it?—are they coming?

EVANS. (*recovering his good nature—with a grin, taking his arm*) You're coming to shoot a drink. You need about ten, I think, to get you in the right spirit to see the finish! (*To* DARRELL *who has gotten up but is still standing by his chair*) Come on, Ned.

NINA. (*quickly*) No, leave Ned with me. I want to talk to him. Take Madeline—and Charlie.

MARSDEN. (*looking at her appealingly*) But I'm perfectly contented sitting— (*Then after a look in her eyes—thinking*)

> She wants to be alone with Darrell . . . all right . . . doesn't matter now . . . their love is dead . . . but there's still some secret between them she's never told me . . . never mind . . . she'll tell me sometime . . . I'm all she will have left . . . soon. . . .

(*Then stricken with guilt*)

> Poor dear Jane! . . . how can I think of anyone but you! . . . God, I'm contemptible! . . . I'll get drunk with that fool! . . . that's all I'm good for! . . .

MADELINE. (*thinking resentfully*)

> She takes a fine do-this-little-girl tone toward me! . . . I'll give in to her now . . . but once I'm married! . . .

EVANS. Come on then, Madeline. We'll give you a small one. (*Impatiently*) Charlie! Head up!

MARSDEN. (*with hectic joviality*) I hope it's strong poison!

EVANS. (*laughing*) That's the spirit! We'll make a sport out of you yet!

MADELINE. (*laughing, goes and takes* MARSDEN'*s arm*) I'll see you get home safe, Mr. Marsden! (*They go into the cabin,* EVANS *following them.* NINA *and* DARRELL *turn and look at each other wonderingly, inquisitively, for a long moment.* DARRELL *remains standing and seems to be a little uneasy.*)

DARRELL. (*thinking with melancholy interest*)

And now? . . . what? . . . I can look into her eyes . . . strange eyes that will never grow old . . . without desire or jealousy or bitterness . . . was she ever my mistress? . . . can she be the mother of my child? . . . is there such a person as my son? . . . I can't think of these things as real any more . . . they must have happened in another life. . . .

NINA. (*thinking sadly*)

My old lover . . . how well and young he looks . . . now we no longer love each other at all . . . our account with God the Father is settled . . . afternoons of happiness paid for with years of pain . . . love, passion, ecstasy . . . in what a far-off life were they alive! . . . the only living life is in the past and future . . . the present is an interlude . . . strange interlude in which we call on past and future to bear witness we are living! . . .

(*With a sad smile*) Sit down, Ned. When I heard you were back I wrote you because I need a friend. It has been so long since we loved each other we can now be friends again. Don't you feel that?

DARRELL. (*gratefully*) Yes. I do. (*He sits down in one of the chairs at left, drawing it up closer to her. Thinking cautiously*)

I want to be her friend . . . but I will never . . .

NINA. (*thinking cautiously*)

I must keep very cool and sensible or he won't help me. . . .

(*With a friendly smile*) I haven't seen you look so young and handsome since I first knew you. Tell me your secret. (*Bitterly*) I need it! I'm old! Look at me! And I was actually looking forward to being old! I thought it would mean peace. I've been sadly disillusioned! (*Then forcing a smile*) So tell me what fountain of youth you've found.

DARRELL. (*proudly*) That's easy. Work! I've become as interested in biology as I once was in medicine. And not selfishly interested, that's the difference. There's no chance of my becoming a famous biologist and I know it. I'm very much a worker in the ranks. But our Station is a "huge success," as Sam would say. We've made some damned important discoveries. I say "we." I really mean Preston.

You may remember I used to write you about him with enthusiasm. He's justified it. He *is* making his name world-famous. He's what I might have been—I did have the brains, Nina!—if I'd had more guts and less vanity, if I'd hewn to the line! (*Then forcing a smile*) But I'm not lamenting. I've found myself in helping him. In that way I feel I've paid my debt—that his work is partly my work. And he acknowledges it. He possesses the rare virtue of gratitude. (*With proud affection*) He's a fine boy, Nina! I suppose I should say man now he's in his thirties.

NINA. (*thinking with bitter sorrow*)

So, Ned . . . you remember our love . . . with bitterness! . . . as a stupid mistake! . . . the proof of a gutless vanity that ruined your career! . . . oh! . . .

(*Then controlling herself—thinking cynically*)

Well, after all, how do I remember our love? . . . with no emotion at all, not even bitterness! . . .

(*Then with sudden alarm*)

He's forgotten Gordon for this Preston! . . .

(*Thinking desperately*)

I must make him remember Gordon is his child or I can never persuade him to help me! . . .

(*Reproachfully*) So you have found a son while I was losing mine—who is yours, too!

DARRELL. (*struck by this—impersonally interested*) That's never occurred to me but now I think of it—(*Smiling*) Yes, perhaps unconsciously Preston is a compensating substitute. Well, it's done both of us good and hasn't harmed anyone.

NINA. (*with bitter emphasis*) Except your real son—and me—but we don't count, I suppose!

DARRELL. (*coolly*) Harmed Gordon? How? He's all right, isn't he? (*With a sneer*) I should say from all I've been hearing that he was your ideal of college hero—like his never-to-be-forgotten name-sake!

NINA. (*thinking resentfully*)

He's sneering at his own son! . . .

(*Then trying to be calculating*)

But I mustn't get angry . . . I must make him help me. . . .

(*Speaking with gentle reproach*) And am I the ideal of a happy mother, Ned?

DARRELL. (*immediately moved by pity and ashamed of himself*) Forgive me, Nina. I haven't quite buried all my bitterness. I'm afraid. (*Gently*) I'm sorry you're unhappy, Nina.

NINA. (*thinking with satisfaction*)

He means that . . . he still does care a little . . . if only it's enough to . . . !

(*Speaking sadly*) I've lost my son, Ned! Sam has made him all his. And it was done so gradually that, although I realized what was happening, there was never any way I could interfere. What Sam advised seemed always the best thing for Gordon's future. And it was always what Gordon himself wanted, to escape from me to boarding school and then to college, to become Sam's athletic hero—

DARRELL. (*impatiently*) Oh, come now, Nina, you know you've always longed for him to be like Gordon Shaw!

NINA. (*bursting out in spite of herself—violently*) He's not like Gordon! He's forgotten me for that—! (*Trying to be more reasonable*) What do I care whether he's an athlete or not? It's such nonsense, all this fuss! I'm not the slightest bit interested in this race today, for example! I wouldn't care if he came in last! (*Stopping herself—thinking frightenedly*)

Oh, if he should ever guess I said that! . . .

DARRELL. (*thinking keenly*)

Hello! . . . she said that as if she'd like to see him come last! . . . why? . . .

(*Then vindictively*)

Well, so would I! . . . it's time these Gordons took a good licking from life! . . .

MADELINE. (*suddenly appears in the door from the cabin, her face flushed with excitement*) They're off! Mr. Evans is getting something—it's terribly faint but—Navy and Washington are leading—Gordon's third! (*She disappears back in the cabin.*)

NINA. (*looking after her with hatred*)

Her Gordon! . . . she is so sure! . . . how I've come to detest her pretty face! . . .

DARRELL. (*thinking with a sneer*)

"Gordon's third!" . . . you might think there was no one else pulling the shell! . . . what idiots women make of themselves about these Gordons! . . . she's pretty, that Madeline! . . . she's got a figure like Nina's when I first loved her . . . those afternoons . . . age is beginning to tell on Nina's face . . . but she's kept her wonderful body! . . .

(*With a trace of malice—dryly*) There's a young lady who seems to care a lot whether Gordon comes in last or not!

NINA. (*trying to be sorrowful and appealing*) Yes. Gordon is hers now, Ned. (*But she cannot bear this thought—vindictively*) That is, they're engaged. But, of course, that doesn't necessarily mean— Can you imagine him throwing himself away on a little fool like that? I simply can't believe he really loves her! Why, she's hardly even pretty and she's deadly stupid. I thought he was only flirting with her—or merely indulging in a passing physical affair. (*She winces*) At his age, one has to expect—even a mother must face nature. But for Gordon to take her seriously, and propose marriage—it's too idiotic for words!

DARRELL. (*thinking cynically*)

Oh, so you'll compromise on his sleeping with her . . . if you have to . . . but she must have no real claim to dispute your ownership, eh? . . . you'd like to make her the same sort of convenient slave for him that I was for you! . . .

(*Resentfully*) I can't agree with you. I find her quite charming. It seems to me if I were in Gordon's shoes I'd do exactly what he has done. (*In confusion—thinking bitterly*)

In Gordon's shoes! . . . I always was in Gordon Shaw's shoes! . . . and why am I taking this young Gordon's part? . . . what is he to me, for God's sake? . . .

NINA. (*unheedingly*) If he marries her, it means he'll forget me! He'll forget me as completely as Sam forgot his mother! She'll keep him away from me! Oh, I know what wives can do! She'll use her body until she persuades him to forget me! My son, Ned! And your son, too! (*She suddenly gets up and goes to him and takes one of his hands in both of hers*) The son of our old love, Ned!

DARRELL. (*thinking with a strange shudder of mingled attraction and fear as she touches him*)

Our love . . . old love . . . old touch of her flesh . . . we're old . . . it's silly and indecent . . . does she think she still can own me? . . .

NINA. (*in the tone a mother takes in speaking to her husband about their boy*) You'll have to give Gordon a good talking to, Ned.

DARRELL. (*still more disturbed—thinking*)

Old . . . but she's kept her wonderful body . . . how many years since? . . . she has the same strange influence over me . . . touch of her flesh . . . it's dangerous . . . bosh, I'm only humoring her as a friend . . . as her doctor . . . and why shouldn't I have a talk with Gordon? . . . a father owes something to his son . . . he ought to advise him. . . .

(*Then alarmed*)

But I was never going to meddle again . . .

(*Sternly*) I swore I'd never again meddle with human lives, Nina!

NINA. (*unheedingly*) You must keep him from ruining his life.

DARRELL. (*doggedly—struggling with himself*) I won't touch a life that has more than one cell! (*Harshly*) And I wouldn't help you in this, anyway! You've got to give up owning people, meddling in their lives as if you were God and had created them!

NINA. (*strangely forlorn*) I don't know what you mean, Ned. Gordon is my son, isn't he?

DARRELL. (*with a sudden strange violence*) And mine! Mine, too! (*He stops himself. Thinking*)

Shut up, you fool! . . . is that the way to humor her? . . .

NINA. (*with strange quiet*) I think I still love you a little, Ned.

DARRELL. (*in her tone*) And I still love you a little, Nina. (*Then sternly*) But I will not meddle in your life again! (*With a harsh laugh*) And you've meddled enough with human love, old lady! Your time for that is over! I'll send you a couple of million cells you can torture without harming yourself! (*Regaining control—shamefacedly*) Nina! Please forgive me!

NINA. (*starts as if out of a dream—anxiously*) What were you saying, Ned? (*She lets go of his hand and goes back to her chair.*)

DARRELL. (*dully*) Nothing.

NINA. (*strangely*) We were talking about Sam, weren't we? How do you think he looks?

DARRELL. (*confusedly casual*) Fine. A bit too fat, of course. He looks as though his blood pressure might be higher than it ought to be. But that's not unusual in persons of his build and age. It's nothing to hope—I meant, to worry over! (*Then violently*) God damn it, why did you make me say hope?

NINA. (*calmly*) It may have been in your mind, too, mayn't it?

DARRELL. No! I've nothing against Sam. I've always been his best friend. He owes his happiness to me.

NINA. (*strangely*) There are so many curious reasons we dare not think about for thinking things!

DARRELL. (*rudely*) Thinking doesn't matter a damn! Life is something in one cell that doesn't need to think!

NINA. (*strangely*) I know! God the Mother!

DARRELL. (*excitedly*) And all the rest is gutless egotism! But to hell with it! What I started to say was, what possible reason could I have for hoping for Sam's death?

NINA. (*strangely*) We're always desiring death for ourselves or others, aren't we—while we while away our lives with the old surface ritual of coveting our neighbor's ass?

DARRELL. (*frightenedly*) You're talking like the old Nina now—when I first loved you. Please don't! It isn't decent—at our age! (*thinking in terror*)

The old Nina! . . . am I the old Ned? . . . then that means? . . . but we must not meddle in each other's lives again! . . .

NINA. (*strangely*) I am the old Nina! And this time I will not let my Gordon go from me forever!

EVANS. (*appears in the doorway of the cabin—excited and irritated*) Madeline's listening in now. It went dead on me. (*Raising the binoculars as he goes to the rail, he looks up the river*) Last I got, Gordon third, Navy and Washington leading. They're the ones to fear, he said—Navy especially. (*Putting down the glasses—with a groan*) Damned haze! My eyes are getting old. (*Then suddenly with a grin*) You ought to see Charlie! He started throwing Scotch into him as if he were drinking against time. I had to take the bottle away from him. It's hit him an awful wallop. (*Then looking from one to the other—resentfully*) What's the matter with you two? There's a race going on, don't you know it? And you sit like dead clams!

DARRELL. (*placatingly*) I thought someone'd better stay out here and let you know when they get in sight.

EVANS. (*relieved*) Oh, sure, that's right! Here, take the glasses. You always had good eyes. (DARRELL *gets up and takes the glasses and goes to the rail and begins adjusting them.*)

DARRELL. Which crew was it you said Gordon feared the most?

EVANS. (*has gone back to the cabin doorway*) Navy. (*Then proudly*) Oh, he'll beat them! But it'll be damn close. I'll see if Madeline's getting— (*He goes back in the cabin.*)

DARRELL. (*looking up the river—with vindictive bitterness—thinking*)

Come on, Navy! . . .

NINA. (*thinking bitterly*)

Madeline's Gordon! . . . Sam's Gordon! . . . the thanks I get for saving Sam at the sacrifice of my own happiness! . . . I won't have it! . . . what do I care what happens to Sam now? . . . I hate him! . . . I'll tell him Gordon isn't his child! . . . and threaten to tell Gordon too, unless! . . . he'll be in deadly fear of that! . . . he'll soon find some excuse to break their engagement! . . . he can! . . . he has the strangest influence over Gordon! . . . but Ned must back me up or Sam won't believe me! . . . Ned must tell him too! . . . but will Ned? . . . he'll be afraid of the insanity! . . . I must make him believe Sam's in no danger . . .

(*Intensely*) Listen, Ned, I'm absolutely sure, from things she wrote me before she died, that Sam's mother must have been deliberately lying to me about the insanity that time. She was jealous because Sam loved me and she simply wanted to be revenged, I'm sure.

DARRELL. (*without lowering glasses—dryly*) No. She told you the truth. I never mentioned it, but I went up there once and made a thorough investigation of his family.

NINA. (*with resentful disappointment*) Oh—I suppose you wanted to make sure so you could hope he'd go insane?

DARRELL. (*simply*) I needed to be able to hope that, then. I loved you horribly at that time, Nina—horribly!

NINA. (*putting her hands on his arm.*) And you don't—any more, Ned? (*Thinking intensely*)

Oh, I must make him love me again . . . enough to make him tell Sam! . . .

DARRELL. (*thinking strangely—struggling with himself*)

She'd like to own me again . . . I wish she wouldn't touch me . . . what is this tie of old happiness between our flesh? . . .

(*Harshly—weakly struggling to shake off her hands, without lowering the glasses*) I won't meddle again with human lives, I told you!

NINA. (*unheeding, clinging to him*) And I loved you horribly! I still do love you, Ned! I used to hope he'd go insane myself because I loved you so! But look at Sam! He's sane as a pig! There's absolutely no danger now!

DARRELL. (*thinking—alarmed*)

What is she after now—what does she want me for? . . .

(*Stiffly*) I'm no longer a doctor but I should say he's a healthy miss of Nature's. It's a thousand to one against it at this late day.

NINA. (*with sudden fierce intensity*) Then it's time to tell him the truth, isn't it? We've suffered all our lives for his sake! We've made him rich and happy! It's time he gave us back our son!

DARRELL. (*thinking*)

> Aha . . . so that's it! . . . tell Sam the truth? . . . at last! . . . by God, I'd like to tell him, at that! . . .

(*With a sneer*) Our son? You mean yours, my dear! Kindly count me out of any further meddling with—

NINA. (*unruffledly—obsessed*) But Sam won't believe me if I'm the only one to tell him! He'll think I'm lying for spite, that it's only my crazy jealousy! He'll ask you! You've got to tell him too, Ned!

DARRELL. (*thinking*)

> I'd like to see his face when I told him his famous oarsman isn't his son but mine! . . . that might pay me back a little for all he's taken from me! . . .

(*Harshly*) I've stopped meddling in Sam's life, I tell you!

NINA. (*insistently*) Think of what Sam has made us go through, of how he's made us suffer! You've got to tell him! You still love me a little, don't you, Ned? You must when you remember the happiness we've known in each other's arms! You were the only happiness I've ever known in life!

DARRELL. (*struggling weakly—thinking*)

> She lies! . . . there was her old lover, Gordon! . . . he was always first! . . . then her son, Gordon! . . .

(*With desperate rancor—thinking*)

> Come on, Navy! . . . beat her Gordons for me! . . .

NINA. (*intensely*) Oh, if I'd only gone away with you that time when you came back from Europe! How happy we would have been, dear! How our boy would have loved you—if it hadn't been for Sam!

DARRELL. (*thinking—weakly*)

> Yes, if it hadn't been for Sam I would have been happy! . . . I would have been the world's greatest neurologist! . . . my boy would have loved me and I'd have loved him! . . .

NINA. (*with a crowning intensity to break down his last resistance*) You must tell him, Ned! For my sake! Because I love you! Because you remember our afternoons—our mad happiness! Because you love me!

DARRELL. (*beaten—dazedly*) Yes—what must I do?—meddle again? (*The noise of* MADELINE'S *excited voice cheering and clapping her hands, of* MARSDEN'S *voice yelling drunkenly, of* EVANS', *all shouting, "Gordon! Gordon! Come on, Gordon!" comes from the cabin.* MARSDEN *appears swaying in the cabin doorway yelling "Gordon!" He is hectically tipsy.* DARRELL *gives a violent shudder as if he were coming out of a nightmare and pushes* NINA *away from him.*)

DARRELL. (*thinking—dazedly still, but in a tone of relief*)

> Marsden again! . . . thank God! . . . he's saved me! . . . from her! . . . and her Gordons! . . .

(*Turning on her triumphantly*) No, Nina—sorry—but I can't help you. I told you I'd never meddle again with human lives! (*More and more confidently*) Besides, I'm quite sure Gordon isn't my son, if the real deep core of the truth were known! I was only a body to you. Your first Gordon used to come back to life. I was never more to you than a substitute for your dead lover! Gordon is really Gordon's son! So you see I'd be telling Sam a lie if I boasted that I— And I'm a man of honor! I've proved that, at least! (*He raises his glasses and looks up the river—thinking exultantly*)

> I'm free! . . . I've beaten her at last! . . . now come on, Navy! . . . you've got to beat her Gordons for me! . . .

NINA. (*after staring at him for a moment—walking away from him—thinking with a dull fatalism*)

> I've lost him . . . he'll never tell Sam now . . . is what he said right? . . . is Gordon Gordon's? . . . oh, I hope so! . . . oh, dear, dead Gordon, help me to get back your son! . . . I must find some way. . . .

(*She sits down again.*)

MARSDEN. (*who has been staring at them with a foolish grin*) Hello, you two! Why do you look so guilty? You don't love each other any more! It's all nonsense! I don't feel the slightest twinge of jealousy. That's proof enough, isn't it? (*Then blandly apologetic*) Pardon me if I sound a bit pipped—a good bit! Sam said ten and then took the bottle away when I'd had only five! But it's enough! I've forgotten sorrow! There's nothing in life worth grieving about, I assure you, Nina! And I've gotten interested in this race now. (*He sings raucously*) "Oh, we'll row, row, row, right down the river! And we'll row, row, row—" Remember that old tune—when you were a little girl, Nina? Oh, I'm forgetting Sam said to tell you Gordon was on even terms with the leaders! A gallant spurt did it! Nip and tuck now! I don't care who wins—as long as it isn't Gordon! I don't like him since he's grown up! He thinks I'm an old woman! (*Sings*) "Row, row, row." The field against Gordon!

DARRELL. (*hectically*) Right! (*He looks through the glasses—excitedly*) I see a flashing in the water way up there! Must be their oars! They're coming! I'll tell Sam! (*He hurries into the cabin.*)

NINA. (*thinking dully*)

He'll tell Sam . . . no, he doesn't mean that . . . I must find some other way . . .

MARSDEN. (*walks a bit uncertainly to* NINA's *chair*) Gordon really should get beaten today—for the good of his soul, Nina. That Madeline is pretty, isn't she? These Gordons are too infernally lucky —while we others— (*He almost starts to blubber—angrily*) we others have got to beat him today! (*He slumps clumsily down to a sitting position on the deck by her chair and takes her hand and pats it*) There, there, Nina Cara Nina! Don't worry your pretty head! It will all come out all right! We'll only have a little while longer to wait and then you and I'll be quietly married! (*Thinking frightenedly*)

The devil! . . . what am I saying? . . . I'm drunk! . . . all right, all the better! . . . I've wanted all my life to tell her! . . .

Of course, I realize you've got a husband at present but, never mind, I can wait. I've waited a lifetime already; but for a long while now

I've had a keen psychic intuition that I wasn't born to die before— (EVANS *and* MADELINE *and* DARRELL *come rushing out of the cabin. They all have binoculars. They run to the rail and train their glasses up the river.*)

MADELINE. (*excitedly*) I see them! (*Grabbing his arm and pointing*) Look, Mr. Evans—there—don't you see?

EVANS. (*excitedly*) No—not yet— Yes! Now I see them! (*Pounding on the rail*) Come on, Gordon boy!

MADELINE. Come on, Gordon! (*The whistles and sirens from the yachts up the river begin to be heard. This grows momentarily louder as one after another other yachts join in the chorus as the crews approach nearer and nearer until toward the close of the scene there is a perfect pandemonium of sound.*)

NINA. (*with bitter hatred—thinking*)

How I hate her! . . .

(*Then suddenly with a deadly calculation—thinking*)

Why not tell her? . . . as Sam's mother told me? . . . of the insanity? . . . she thinks Gordon is Sam's son.

(*With a deadly smile of triumph*)

That will be poetic justice! . . . that will solve everything! . . . she won't marry him! . . . he will turn to me for comfort! . . . but I must plan it out carefully! . . .

MARSDEN. (*driven on—extravagantly*) Listen, Nina! After we're married I'm going to write a novel—my first real novel! All the twenty odd books I've written have been long-winded fairy tales for grown-ups—about dear old ladies and witty, cynical bachelors and quaint characters with dialects, and married folk who always admire and respect each other, and lovers who avoid love in hushed whispers! That's what I've been, Nina—a hush-hush whisperer of lies! Now I'm going to give an honest healthy yell—turn on the sun into the shadows of lies—shout "This is life and this is sex, and here are passion and hatred and regret and joy and pain and ecstasy, and these are men and women and sons and daughters whose hearts are weak and strong, whose blood is blood and not a soothing syrup!" Oh, I can do it, Nina! I can write the truth! I've seen it in you, your father, my mother, sister, Gordon, Sam, Darrell and myself. I'll write the book of us! But here I am talking while my last chapters are in the making—right here and now—(*Hurriedly*) You'll excuse me, won't you, Nina? I must watch—my duty as an artist! (*He scrambles to his feet and peers about him with a hectic eagerness.* NINA *pays no attention to him.*)

EVANS. (*exasperatedly, taking down his glasses*) You can't tell a damn thing—which is which or who's ahead—I'm going to listen in again. (*He hurries into the cabin.*)

NINA. (*with a smile of cruel triumph—thinking*)

I can tell her . . . confidentially . . . I can pretend I'm forced to tell her . . . as Sam's mother did with me . . . because I feel it's due to her happiness and Gordon's . . . it will explain my objection to the engagement . . . oh, it can't help succeeding . . . my Gordon will come back! . . . I'll see he never gets away again! . . .

(*She calls*) Madeline!

MARSDEN. (*thinking*)

Why is she calling Madeline? . . . I must watch all this carefully! . . .

EVANS. (*comes rushing out in wild alarm*) Bad news! Navy has drawn ahead—half a length—looks like Navy's race, he said— (*Then violently*) But what does he know, that damn fool announcer—some poor boob—!

MADELINE. (*excitedly*) He doesn't know Gordon! He's always best when he's pushed to the limit!

NINA. (*she calls more sharply*) Madeline!

DARRELL. (*turns around to stare at her—thinking*)

Why is she calling Madeline? . . . she's bound she'll meddle in their lives . . . I've got to watch her . . . well, let's see. . . .

(*He touches* MADELINE *on the shoulder*) Mrs. Evans is calling you, Miss Arnold.

MADELINE. (*impatiently*) Yes, Mrs. Evans. But they're getting closer. Why don't you come and watch?

NINA. (*not heeding—impressively*) There's something I must tell you.

MADELINE. (*in hopeless irritation*) But— Oh, all right. (*She hurries over to her, glancing eagerly over her shoulder towards the river*) Yes, Mrs. Evans?

DARRELL. (*moves from the rail toward them—thinking keenly*)

I must watch this . . . she's in a desperate meddling mood! . . .

NINA. (*impressively*) First, give me your word of honor that you'll never reveal a word of what I'm going to tell you to a living soul—above all not to Gordon!

MADELINE. (*looking at her in amazement—soothingly*) Couldn't you tell me later, Mrs. Evans—after the race?

NINA. (*sternly—grabbing her by the wrist*) No, now! Do you promise?

MADELINE. (*with helpless annoyance*) Yes, Mrs. Evans.

NINA. (*sternly*) For the sake of your future happiness and my son's I've got to speak! Your engagement forces me to! You've probably wondered why I objected. It's because the marriage is impossible. You can't marry Gordon! I speak as your friend! You must break your engagement with him at once!

MADELINE. (*cannot believe her ears—suddenly panic-stricken*) But why—why?

DARRELL. (*who has come closer—resentfully thinking*)

She wants to ruin my son's life as she ruined mine! . . .

NINA. (*relentlessly*) Why? Because—

DARRELL. (*steps up suddenly beside them—sharply and sternly commanding*) No, Nina! (*He taps* MADELINE *on the shoulder and draws her aside.* NINA *lets go of her wrist and stares after them in a sort of stunned stupor*) Miss Arnold, as a doctor I feel it my duty to tell you that Mrs. Evans isn't herself. Pay no attention to anything she may say to you. She's just passed through a crucial period in a woman's life and she's morbidly jealous of you and subject to queer delusions! (*He smiles kindly at her*) So get back to the race! And God bless you! (*He grips her hand, strangely moved.*)

MADELINE. (*gratefully*) Thank you. I understand, I think. Poor Mrs. Evans! (*She hurries back to the rail, raising her glasses.*)

NINA. (*springing to her feet and finding her voice—with despairing accusation*) Ned!

DARRELL. (*steps quickly to her side*) I'm sorry, Nina, but I warned you not to meddle. (*Then affectionately.*) And Gordon is—well—sort of my stepson, isn't he? I really want him to be happy. (*Then smiling good-naturedly*) All the same, I can't help hoping he'll be beaten in this race. As an oarsman he recalls his father, Gordon Shaw, to me. (*He turns away and raises his glasses, going back to the rail.* NINA *slumps down in her chair again.*)

EVANS. Damn! They all look even from here! Can you tell which is which, Madeline?

MADELINE. No—not yet—oh, dear, this is awful! Gordon!

NINA. (*looking about her in the air—with a dazed question*) Gordon?

MARSDEN. (*thinking*)

> Damn that Darrell! . . . if he hadn't interfered Nina would have told . . . something of infinite importance, I know! . . .

(*He comes and again sits on the deck by her chair and takes her hand*) Because what, Nina—my dear little Nina Cara Nina—because what? Let me help you!

NINA. (*staring before her as if she were in a trance—simply, like a young girl*) Yes, Charlie. Yes, Father. Because all of Sam's father's family have been insane. His mother told me that time so I wouldn't have his baby. I was going to tell Madeline that so she wouldn't marry Gordon. But it would have been a lie because Gordon isn't really Sam's child at all, he's Ned's. Ned gave him to me and I gave him to Sam so Sam could have a healthy child and be well and happy.

And Sam is well and happy, don't you think? (*Childishly*) So I haven't been such an awfully wicked girl, have I, Father?

MARSDEN. (*horrified and completely sobered by what he has heard—stares at her with stunned eyes*) Nina! Good God! Do you know what you're saying?

MADELINE. (*excitedly*) There! The one on this side! I saw the color on their blades just now!

EVANS. (*anxiously*) Are you sure? Then he's a little behind the other two!

DARRELL. (*excitedly*) The one in the middle seems to be ahead! Is that the Navy? (*But the others pay no attention to him. All three are leaning over the rail, their glasses glued to their eyes, looking up the river. The noise from the whistles is now very loud. The cheering from the observation trains can be heard.*)

MARSDEN. (*stares into her face with great pity now*) Merciful God, Nina! Then you've lived all these years—with this horror! And you and Darrell deliberately—?

NINA. (*without looking at him—to the air*) Sam's mother said I had a right to be happy too.

MARSDEN. And you didn't love Darrell then—?

NINA. (*as before*) I did afterwards. I don't now. Ned is dead, too. (*Softly*) Only you are alive now, Father—and Gordon.

MARSDEN. (*gets up and bends over her paternally, stroking her hair with a strange, wild, joyous pity*) Oh, Nina—poor little Nina—my Nina—how you must have suffered! I forgive you! I forgive you everything! I forgive even your trying to tell Madeline—you wanted to keep Gordon—oh, I understand that—and I forgive you!

NINA. (*as before—affectionately and strangely*) And I forgive you, Father. It was all your fault in the beginning, wasn't it? You mustn't ever meddle with human lives again!

EVANS. (*wildly excited*) Gordon's sprinting, isn't he? He's drawing up on that middle one!

MADELINE. Yes! Oh, come on, Gordon!

DARRELL. (*exultantly*) Come on, Navy!

EVANS. (*who is standing next to* NED, *whirls on him in a furious passion*) What's that? What the hell's the matter with you?

DARRELL. (*facing him—with a strange friendliness slaps him on the back*) We've got to beat these Gordons, Sam! We've got to beat—

EVANS. (*raging*) You—! (*He draws back his fist—then suddenly horrified at what he is doing but still angry, grabs* DARRELL *by both shoulders and shakes him*) Wake up! What the hell's got into you? Have you gone crazy?

DARRELL. (*mockingly*) Probably! It runs in my family! All of my father's people were happy lunatics—not healthy, country folk like yours, Sam! Ha!

EVANS. (*staring at him*) Ned, old man, what's the trouble? You said "Navy."

DARRELL. (*ironically—with a bitter hopeless laugh*) Slip of the tongue! I meant Gordon! Meant Gordon, of course! Gordon is always meant—meant to win! Come on, Gordon! It's fate!

MADELINE. Here they come! They're both spurting! I can see Gordon's back!

EVANS. (*forgetting everything else, turns back to the race*) Come on, boy! Come on, son! (*The chorus of noise is now a bedlam as the crews near the finish line. The people have to yell and scream to make themselves heard.*)

NINA. (*getting up—thinking with a strange, strident, wild passion*)

> I hear the Father laughing! . . . O Mother God, protect my son! . . . let Gordon fly to you in heaven! . . . quick, Gordon! . . . love is the Father's lightning! . . . Madeline will bring you down in flames! . . . I hear His screaming laughter! . . . fly back to me! . . .

(*She is looking desperately up into the sky as if some race of life and death were happening there for her.*)

EVANS. (*holding on to a stanchion and leaning far out at the imminent risk of falling in*) One spurt more will do it! Come on, boy, come on! It took death to beat Gordon Shaw! You can't be beaten either, Gordon! Lift her out of the water, son! Stroke! Stroke! He's gaining! Now! Over the line, boy! Over with her! Stroke! That's done it! He's won! He's won!

MADELINE. (*has been shrieking at the same time*) Gordon! Gordon! He's won! Oh, he's fainted! Poor dear darling! (*She remains standing on the rail, leaning out dangerously, holding on with one hand, looking down longingly toward his shell.*)

EVANS. (*bounding back to the deck, his face congested and purple with a frenzy of joy, dancing about*) He's won! By God, it was close! Greatest race in the history of rowing! He's the greatest oarsman God ever made! (*Embracing* NINA *and kissing her frantically*) Aren't you happy, Nina? Our Gordon! The greatest ever!

NINA. (*torturedly—trying incoherently to force out a last despairing protest*) No!—not yours!—mine!—and Gordon's!—Gordon is Gordon's!—he was my Gordon!—his Gordon is mine!

EVANS. (*soothingly, humoring her—kissing her again*) Of course he's yours, dear—and a dead ringer for Gordon Shaw, too! Gordon's body! Gordon's spirit! Your body and spirit, too, Nina! He's not like me, lucky for him! I'm a poor boob! I never could row worth a damn! (*He suddenly staggers as if he were very drunk, leaning on* MARSDEN *—then gives a gasp and collapses inertly to the deck, lying on his back.*)

MARSDEN. (*stares down at him stupidly—then thinking strangely*)

I knew it! . . . I saw the end beginning! . . .

(*He touches* NINA's *arm—in a low voice*) Nina—your husband! (*Touching* DARRELL *who has stood staring straight before him with a bitter ironical smile on his lips*) Ned—your friend! Doctor Darrell—a patient!

NINA. (*stares down at* EVANS*—slowly, as if trying to bring her mind back to him*) My husband? (*Suddenly with a cry of pain, sinks on her knees beside the body*) Sam!

DARRELL. (*looking down at him—thinking yearningly*)

Is her husband dead . . . at last? . . .

(*Then with a shudder at his thoughts*)

No! . . . I don't hope! . . . I don't! . . .

(*He cries*) Sam! (*He kneels down, feels of his heart, pulse, looks into his face—with a change to a strictly professional manner*) He's not dead. Only a bad stroke.

NINA. (*with a cry of grief*) Oh, Ned, did all our old secret hopes do this at last?

DARRELL. (*professionally, staring at her coldly*) Bosh, Mrs. Evans! We're not in the Congo that we can believe in evil charms! (*Sternly*) In his condition, Mr. Evans must have absolute quiet and peace of mind or— And perfect care! You must tend him night and day! And I will! We've got to keep him happy!

NINA. (*dully.*) Again? (*Then sternly in her turn, as if swearing a pledge to herself*) I will never leave his side! I will never tell him anything that might disturb his peace!

MARSDEN. (*standing above them—thinking exultantly*)

I will not have long to wait now! . . .

(*Then ashamed*)

How can I think such things . . . poor Sam! . . . he was . . . I mean he is my friend . . .

(*With assertive loyalty*) A rare spirit! A pure and simple soul! A good man—yes, a good man! God bless him! (*He makes a motion over the body like a priest blessing.*)

DARRELL. (*his voice suddenly breaking with a sincere human grief*) Sam, old boy! I'm so damned sorry! I will give my life to save you!

NINA. (*in dull anguish*) Save—again? (*Then lovingly, kissing* EVANS' *face*) Dear husband, you have tried to make me happy, I will give you my happiness again! I will give you Gordon to give to Madeline!

MADELINE. (*still standing on the rail, staring after* GORDON'S *shell*)

Gordon! . . . dear lover . . . how tired . . . but you'll rest in my arms . . . your head will lie on my breast . . . soon! . . .

CURTAIN

ACT NINE

*S*CENE: *Several months later. A terrace on the* EVANS' *estate on Long Island. In the rear, the terrace overlooks a small harbor with the ocean beyond. On the right is a side entrance of the pretentious villa. On the left is a hedge with an arched gateway leading to a garden. The terrace is paved with rough stone. There is a stone bench at center, a recliner at right, a wicker table and armchair at left.*

It is late afternoon of a day in early fall. GORDON EVANS *is sitting on the stone bench, his chin propped on his hands,* MADELINE *standing behind him, her arm about his shoulders.* GORDON *is over six feet tall with the figure of a trained athlete. His sun-bronzed face is extremely handsome after the fashion of the magazine cover American collegian. It is a strong face but of a strength wholly material in quality. He has been too thoroughly trained to progress along a certain groove to success ever to question it or be dissatisfied with its rewards. At the same time, although entirely an unimaginative code-bound gentleman of his groove, he is boyish and likable, of an even, modest, sporting disposition. His expression is boyishly forlorn, but he is making a manly effort to conceal his grief.*

MADELINE *is much the same as in the previous Act except that there is now a distinct maternal older feeling in her attitude toward* GORDON *as she endeavors to console him.*

MADELINE. (*tenderly, smoothing his hair*) There, dear! I know how horribly hard it is for you. I loved him, too. He was so wonderful and sweet to me.

GORDON. (*his voice trembling*) I didn't really realize he was gone—until out at the cemetery— (*His voice breaks.*)

MADELINE. (*kissing his hair*) Darling! Please don't!

GORDON. (*rebelliously*) Damn it, I don't see why he had to die! (*With a groan*) It was that constant grind at the office! I ought to have insisted on his taking better care of himself. But I wasn't home enough, that's the trouble. I couldn't watch him. (*Then bitterly*) But I can't see why Mother didn't!

MADELINE. (*reprovingly but showing she shares his feeling*) Now! You mustn't start feeling bitter toward her.

GORDON. (*contritely*) I know I shouldn't. (*But returning to his bitter tone*) But I can't help remembering how unreasonably she's acted about our engagement.

MADELINE. Not since your father was taken sick, she hasn't, dear. She's been wonderfully nice.

GORDON. (*in the same tone*) Nice? Indifferent, you mean! She doesn't seem to care a damn one way or the other any more!

MADELINE. You could hardly expect her to think of anyone but your father. She's been with him every minute. I never saw such devotion. (*Thinking*)

> Will Gordon ever get old and sick like that? . . . oh, I hope we'll both die before! . . . but I'd nurse him just as she did his father . . . I'll always love him! . . .

GORDON. (*consoled—proudly*) Yes, she sure was wonderful to him, all right! (*Then coming back to his old tone*) But—this may sound rotten of me—I always had a queer feeling she was doing it as a duty. And when he died, I felt her grief was—not from love for him—at least, only the love of a friend, not a wife's love. (*As if under some urgent compulsion from within*) I've never told you, but I've always felt, ever since I was a little kid, that she didn't really love Dad. She liked him and respected him. She was a wonderful wife. But I'm sure she didn't love him. (*Blurting it out as if he couldn't help it*) I'll tell you, Madeline! I've always felt she cared a lot for—Darrell. (*Hastily*) Of course, I might be wrong. (*Then bursting out*) No, I'm not wrong! I've felt it too strongly, ever since

I was a kid. And then when I was eleven—something happened. I've been sure of it since then.

MADELINE. (*thinking in amazement, but not without a queer satisfaction*)

> Does he mean that she was unfaithful to his father? . . . no, he'd never believe that . . . but what else could he mean? . . .

(*Wonderingly*) Gordon! Do you mean you've been sure that your mother was—

GORDON. (*outraged by something in her tone—jumping to his feet and flinging her hand off—roughly*) Was what? What do you mean, Madeline?

MADELINE. (*frightened—placatingly puts her arms around him*) I didn't mean anything, dear. I simply thought you meant—

GORDON. (*still indignant*) All I meant was that she must have fallen in love with Darrell long after she was married—and then she sent him away for Dad's sake—and mine, too, I suppose. He kept coming back every couple of years. He didn't have guts enough to stay away for good! Oh, I suppose I'm unfair. I suppose it was damned hard on him. He fought it down, too, on account of his friendship for Dad. (*Then with a bitter laugh*) I suppose they'll be getting married now! And I'll have to wish them good luck. Dad would want me to. He was game. (*With a bitter gloomy air*) Life is damn queer, that's all I've got to say!

MADELINE. (*thinking with a sort of tender, loving scorn for his boyish naïveté*)

> How little he knows her! . . . Mr. Evans was a fine man but . . . Darrell must have been fascinating once . . . if she loved any one she isn't the kind who would hesitate . . . any more than I have with Gordon . . . oh, I'll never be unfaithful to Gordon . . . I'll love him always! . . .

(*She runs her fingers through his hair caressingly—comfortingly*) You must never blame them, dear. No one can help love. We couldn't, could we? (*She sits beside him. He takes her in his arms.*

They kiss each other with rising passion. MARSDEN *comes in noiselessly from the garden, a bunch of roses and a pair of shears in his hands. He looks younger, calm and contented. He is dressed in his all black, meticulous, perfectly tailored mourning costume. He stands looking at the two lovers, a queer agitation coming into his face.*)

MARSDEN. (*scandalized as an old maid—thinking*)

I must say! . . . his father hardly cold in his grave! . . . it's positively bestial! . . .

(*Then struggling with himself—with a defensive self-mockery*)

Only it wasn't his father . . . what is Sam to Darrell's son? . . . and even if he were Sam's son, what have the living to do with the dead? . . . his duty is to love that life may keep on living . . . and what has their loving to do with me? . . . my life is cool green shade wherein comes no scorching zenith sun of passion and possession to wither the heart with bitter poisons . . . my life gathers roses, coolly crimson, in sheltered gardens, on late afternoons in love with evening . . . roses heavy with after-blooming of the long day, desiring evening . . . my life is an evening . . . Nina is a rose, my rose, exhausted by the long, hot day, leaning wearily toward peace. . . .

(*He kisses one of the roses with a simple sentimental smile—then still smiling, makes a gesture toward the two lovers*)

That is on another planet, called the world . . . Nina and I have moved on to the moon. . . .

MADELINE. (*passionately*) Dear one! Sweetheart!

GORDON. Madeline! I love you!

MARSDEN. (*looking at them—gaily mocking—thinking*)

Once I'd have felt jealous . . . cheated . . . swindled by God out of joy! . . . I would have thought bitterly, "The Gordons have all the luck!" . . . but now I know that dear old Charlie . . . yes, poor dear old Charlie!—passed beyond desire, has all the luck at last! . . .

(*Then matter-of-factly*)

But I'll have to interrupt their biological preparations . . . there are many things still to be done this evening . . . Age's terms of peace, after the long interlude of war with life, have still to be concluded . . . Youth must keep decently away . . . so many old wounds may have to be unbound, and old scars pointed to with pride, to prove to ourselves we have been brave and noble! . . .

(*He lets the shears drop to the ground. They jump startledly and turn around. He smiles quietly*) Sorry to disturb you. I've been picking some roses for your mother, Gordon. Flowers really have the power to soothe grief. I suppose it was that discovery that led to their general use at funerals—and weddings! (*He hands a rose to* MADELINE) Here, Madeline, here's a rose for you. Hail, Love, we who have died, salute you! (*He smiles strangely. She takes the rose automatically, staring at him uncomprehendingly.*)

MADELINE. (*thinking suspiciously*)

What a queer creature! . . . there's something uncanny! . . . oh, don't be silly! . . . it's only poor old Charlie! . . .

(*She makes him a mocking curtsey*) Thank you, Uncle Charlie!

GORDON. (*thinking with sneering pity*)

Poor old guy! . . . he means well . . . Dad liked him. . . .

(*Pretending an interest in the roses*) They're pretty. (*Then suddenly*) Where's Mother—still in the house?

MARSDEN. She was trying to get rid of the last of the people. I'm going in. Shall I tell her you want to see her? It would give her an excuse to get away.

GORDON. Yes. Will you? (MARSDEN *goes into the house on right.*)

MADELINE. You'd better see your mother alone. I'll go down to the plane and wait for you. You want to fly back before dark, don't you?

GORDON. Yes, and we ought to get started soon. (*Moodily*) Maybe it would be better if you weren't here. There are some things I feel I ought to say to her—and Darrell. I've got to do what I know Dad would have wanted. I've got to be fair. He always was to everyone all his life.

MADELINE. You dear, you! You couldn't be unfair to anyone if you tried! (*She kisses him*) Don't be too long.

GORDON. (*moodily*) You bet I won't! It won't be so pleasant I'll want to drag it out!

MADELINE. Good-bye for a while then.

GORDON. So long. (*He looks after her lovingly as she goes out right, rear, around the corner of the house. Thinking*)

Madeline's wonderful! . . . I don't deserve my luck . . . but, God, I sure do love her! . . .

(*He sits down on the bench again, his chin on his hands*)

It seems rotten and selfish to be happy . . . when Dad . . . oh, he understands, he'd want me to be . . . it's funny how I got to care more for Dad than for Mother . . . I suppose it was finding out she loved Darrell . . . I can remember that day seeing her kiss him . . . it did something to me I never got over . . . but she made Dad happy . . . she gave up her own happiness for his sake . . . that was certainly damn fine . . . that was playing the game . . . I'm a hell of a one to criticize . . . my own mother! . . .

(*Changing the subject of his thoughts abruptly*)

Forget it! . . . think of Madeline . . . we'll be married . . . then two months' honeymoon in Europe . . . God, that'll be great! . . . then back and dive into the business . . . Dad relied on me to carry on where he left off . . . I'll have to start at the bottom but I'll get to the top in a hurry, I promise you that, Dad! . . .

(NINA *and* DARRELL *come out of the house on the right. He hears the sound of the door and looks around. Thinking resentfully*)

Funny! . . . I can't stand it even now! . . . when I see him with Mother! . . . I'd like to beat him up! . . .

(*He gets to his feet, his face unconsciously becoming older and cold and severe. He stares accusingly at them as they come slowly toward him in silence.* NINA *looks much older than in the preceding Act. Resignation has come into her face, a resignation that uses no make-up, that has given up the struggle to be sexually attractive and look younger. She is dressed in deep black.* DARRELL'S *deep sunburn of the tropics has faded, leaving his skin a Mongolian yellow. He, too, looks much older. His expression is sad and bitter.)*

NINA. (*glancing at* GORDON *searchingly—thinking sadly*)

He sent for me to say good-bye . . . really good-bye forever this time . . . he's not my son now, nor Gordon's son, nor Sam's, nor Ned's . . . he has become that stranger, another woman's lover. . . .

DARRELL. (*also after a quick keen glance at* GORDON'S *face—thinking*)

There's something up . . . some final accounting . . .

(*Thinking resignedly*)

Well, let's get it over . . . then I can go back to work. . . . I've stayed too long up here . . . Preston must be wondering if I've deserted him. . . .

(*Then with a wondering sadness*)

Is that my son? . . . my flesh and blood? . . . staring at me with such cold enmity? . . . how sad and idiotic this all is! . . .

NINA. (*putting on a tone of joking annoyance*) Your message was a godsend, Gordon. Those stupid people with their social condolences were killing me. Perhaps I'm morbid but I always have the feeling that they're secretly glad someone is dead—that it flatters their vanity and makes them feel superior because they're living. (*She sits wearily on the bench.* DARRELL *sits on side of the recliner at right.*)

GORDON. (*repelled by this idea—stiffly*) They were all good friends of Dad's. Why shouldn't they be sincerely sorry? His death ought to be a loss to everyone who knew him. (*His voice trembles. He turns away and walks to the table. Thinking bitterly*)

She doesn't care a damn! . . . she's free to marry Darrell now! . . .

NINA. (*thinking sadly, looking at his back*)

He's accusing me because I'm not weeping . . . well, I did weep . . . all I could . . . there aren't many tears left . . . it was too bad Sam had to die . . . living suited him . . . he was so contented with himself . . . but I can't feel guilty . . . I helped him to live . . . I made him believe I loved him . . . his mind was perfectly sane to the end . . . and just before he died, he smiled at me . . . so gratefully and forgivingly, I thought . . . closing our life together with that smile . . . that life is dead . . . its regrets are dead . . . I am sad but there's comfort in the thought that now I am free at last to rot away in peace . . . I'll go and live in Father's old home . . . Sam bought that back . . . I suppose he left it to me . . . Charlie will come in every day to visit . . . he'll comfort and amuse me . . . we can talk together of the old days . . . when I was a girl . . . when I was happy . . . before I fell in love with Gordon Shaw and all this tangled mess of love and hate and pain and birth began! . . .

DARRELL. (*staring at* GORDON'S *back resentfully*)

It gets under my skin to see him act so unfeelingly toward his mother! . . . if he only knew what she's suffered for his sake! . . . the Gordon Shaw ideal passed on through Sam has certainly made my son an insensitive clod! . . .

(*With disgust*)

Bah, what has that young man to do with me? . . . compared to Preston he's only a well-muscled, handsome fool! . . .

(*With a trace of anger*)

But I'd like to jolt his stupid self-complacency! . . . if he knew the facts about himself, he wouldn't be sobbing sentimentally about Sam . . . he'd better change his tune or I'll certainly be tempted to tell him . . . there's no reason for his not knowing now . . .

(*His face is flushed. He has worked himself into a real anger.*)

GORDON. (*suddenly, having got back his control, turns to them—coldly*) There are certain things connected with Dad's will I thought I ought to— (*With a tinge of satisfied superiority*) I don't believe Dad told you about his will, did he, Mother?

NINA. (*indifferently*) No.

GORDON. Well, the whole estate goes to you and me, of course. I didn't mean that. (*With a resentful look at* DARRELL) But there is one provision that is peculiar, to say the least. It concerns you,

Doctor Darrell—a half-million for your Station to be used in biological research work.

DARRELL. (*his face suddenly flushing with anger*) What's that? That's a joke, isn't it? (*Thinking furiously*)

It's worse! . . . it's a deliberate insult! . . . a last sneer of ownership! . . . of my life! . . .

GORDON. (*coldly sneering*) I thought it must be a joke myself—but Dad insisted.

DARRELL. (*angrily*) Well, I won't accept it—and that's final!

GORDON. (*coldly*) It's not left to you but to the Station. Your supervision is mentioned but I suppose if you won't carry on, whoever is in real charge down there will be only too glad to accept it.

DARRELL. (*stupefied*) That means Preston! But Sam didn't even know Preston—except from hearing me talk about him! What had Sam to do with Preston? Preston is none of his business! I'll advise Preston to refuse it! (*Thinking torturedly*)

But it's for science! . . . he has no right to refuse! . . . I have no right to ask him to! . . . God damn Sam! . . . wasn't it enough for him to own my wife, my son, in his lifetime? . . . now in death he reaches out to steal Preston! . . . to steal my work! . . .

NINA. (*thinking bitterly*)

Even in death Sam makes people suffer . . .

(*Sympathetically*) It isn't for you—nor for Preston. It's for science, Ned. You must look at it that way.

GORDON. (*thinking resentfully*)

What a tender tone she takes toward him! . . . she's forgotten Dad already! . . .

(*With a sneer*) You'd better accept. Half-millions aren't being thrown away for nothing every day.

NINA. (*in anguish—thinking*)

How can Gordon insult poor Ned like that! . . . his own father! . . . Ned has suffered too much! . . .

(*Sharply*) I think you've said about enough, Gordon!

GORDON. (*bitterly, but trying to control himself—meaningly*) I haven't said all I'm going to say, Mother!

NINA. (*thinking—at first frightenedly*)

What does he mean? . . . does he know about Ned being . . . ?

(*Then with a sort of defiant relief*)

Well, what does it matter what he thinks of me? . . . he's hers now, anyway. . . .

DARRELL. (*thinking vindictively*)

I hope he knows the truth, for if he doesn't, by God, I'll tell him! . . . if only to get something back from Sam of all he's stolen from me! . . .

(*Authoritatively—as* GORDON *hesitates*) Well, what have you got to say? Your mother and I are waiting.

GORDON. (*furiously, taking a threatening step toward him*) Shut up, you! Don't take that tone with me or I'll forget your age— (*Contemptuously*) and give you a spanking!

NINA. (*thinking hysterically*)

Spanking! . . . the son spanks the father! . . .

(*Laughing hysterically*) Oh, Gordon, don't make me laugh! It's all so funny!

DARRELL. (*jumps from his chair and goes to her—solicitously*) Nina! Don't mind him! He doesn't realize—

GORDON. (*maddened, comes closer*) I realize a lot! I realize you've acted like a cur! (*He steps forward and slaps* DARRELL *across the face viciously.* DARRELL *staggers back from the force of the blow, his hands to his face.* NINA *screams and flings herself on* GORDON, *holding his arms.*)

NINA. (*piteously—hysterically*) For God's sake, Gordon! What would your father say? You don't know what you're doing! You're hitting your father!

DARRELL. (*suddenly breaking down—chokingly*) No—it's all right, son—all right—you didn't know—

GORDON. (*crushed, overcome by remorse for his blow*) I'm sorry—

sorry—you're right, Mother—Dad would feel as if I'd hit him—just as bad as if I'd hit him!

DARRELL. It's nothing, son—nothing!

GORDON. (*brokenly*) That's damn fine, Darrell—damn fine and sporting of you! It was a rotten, dirty trick! Accept my apology, Darrell, won't you?

DARRELL. (*staring at him stupidly—thinking*)

Darrell? . . . he calls me Darrell! . . . but doesn't he know? . . . I thought she told him. . . .

NINA. (*laughing hysterically—thinking*)

I told him he hit his father . . . but he can't understand me! . . . why, of course he can't! . . . how could he? . . .

GORDON. (*insistently holding out his hand*) I'm damned sorry! I didn't mean it! Shake hands, won't you?

DARRELL. (*doing so mechanically—stupidly*) Only too glad—pleased to meet you—know you by reputation—the famous oarsman—great race you stroked last June—but I was hoping the Navy would give you a beating.

NINA. (*thinking in desperate hysterical anguish*)

Oh, I wish Ned would go away and stay away forever! . . . I can't bear to watch him suffer any more! . . . it's too frightful! . . . yes, God the Father, I hear you laughing . . . you see the joke . . . I'm laughing too . . . it's all so crazy, isn't it? . . .

(*Laughing hysterically*) Oh, Ned! Poor Ned! You were born unlucky!

GORDON. (*making her sit down again—soothing her*) Mother! Stop laughing! Please! It's all right—all right between us! I've apologized! (*As she has grown calmer*) And now I want to say what I was going to say. It wasn't anything bad. It was just that I wanted you to know how fine I think you've both acted. I've known ever since I was a kid that you and Darrell were in love with each other. I hated the idea on Father's account—that's only natural, isn't it?—but I knew it was unfair, that people can't help loving each other any more than Madeline and I could have helped ourselves. And I saw how fair you both were to Dad—what a good wife you were, Mother—what a true friend you were, Darrell—and how damn much he loved you both! So all I wanted to say is, now he's dead, I hope you'll get married and I hope you'll be as happy as you both deserve—(*Here he breaks down, kissing her and then breaking away*) I've got to say good-bye—got to fly back before dark—Madeline's waiting. (*He takes* DARRELL'S *hand and shakes it again. They have both been staring at him stupidly*) Good-bye, Darrell! Good luck!

DARRELL. (*thinking sufferingly*)

Why does he keep on calling me Darrell . . . he's my boy . . . I'm his father . . . I've got to make him realize I'm his father! . . .

(*Holding* GORDON'S *hand*) Listen, son. It's my turn. I've got to tell you something—

NINA. (*thinking torturedly*)

Oh, he mustn't! . . . I feel he mustn't! . . .

(*Sharply*) Ned! First, let me ask Gordon a question. (*Then looking her son in the eyes, slowly and impressively*) Do you think I was ever unfaithful to your father, Gordon?

GORDON. (*startled, stares at her—shocked and horrified—then suddenly he blurts out indignantly*) Mother, what do you think I am—as rotten-minded as that! (*Pleadingly*) Please, Mother, I'm not as bad as that! I know you're the best woman that ever lived—the best of all! I don't even except Madeline!

NINA. (*with a sobbing triumphant cry*) My dear Gordon! You do love me, don't you?

GORDON. (*kneeling beside her and kissing her*) Of course!

NINA. (*pushing him away—tenderly*) And now go! Hurry! Madeline is waiting! Give her my love! Come to see me once in a while in the years to come! Good-bye, dear! (*Turning to* DARRELL, *who is standing with a sad resigned expression—imploringly*) Did you still want to tell Gordon something, Ned?

DARRELL. (*forcing a tortured smile*) Not for anything in the world! Good-bye, son.

GORDON. Good-bye, sir. (*He hurries off around the corner of the house at left, rear, thinking troubledly*)

> What does she think I am? . . . I've never thought that! . . . I couldn't! . . . my own mother! I'd kill myself if I ever even caught myself thinking . . . !

(*He is gone.*)

NINA. (*turns to* NED, *gratefully taking his hand and pressing it*) Poor dear Ned, you've always had to give! How can I ever thank you?

DARRELL. (*with an ironical smile—forcing a joking tone*) By refusing me when I ask you to marry me! For I've got to ask you! Gordon expects it! And he'll be so pleased when he knows you turned me down. (MARSDEN *comes out of the house*) Hello, here comes Charlie. I must hurry. Will you marry me, Nina?

NINA. (*with a sad smile*) No. Certainly not. Our ghosts would torture us to death! (*Then forlornly*) But I wish I did love you, Ned! Those were wonderful afternoons long ago! The Nina of those afternoons will always live in me, will always love her lover, Ned, the father of her baby!

DARRELL. (*lifting her hand to his lips—tenderly*) Thank you for that! And that Ned will always adore his beautiful Nina! Remember him! Forget me! I'm going back to work. (*He laughs softly and sadly*) I leave you to Charlie. You'd better marry him, Nina—if you want peace. And after all, I think you owe it to him for his life-long devotion.

MARSDEN. (*thinking uneasily*)

> They're talking about me . . . why doesn't he go? . . . she doesn't love him any more . . . even now he's all heat and energy and the tormenting drive of noon . . . can't he see she is in love with evening? . . .

(*Clearing his throat uneasily*) Do I hear my name taken in vain?

NINA. (*looking at* MARSDEN *with a strange yearning*)

Peace! . . . yes . . . that is all I desire . . . I can no longer imagine happiness . . . Charlie has found peace . . . he will be tender . . . as my father was when I was a girl . . . when I could imagine happiness . . .

(*With a girlish coquettishness and embarrassment—making way for him on the bench beside her—strangely*) Ned's just proposed to me. I refused him, Charlie. I don't love him any more.

MARSDEN. (*sitting down beside her*) I suspected as much. Then whom do you love, Nina Cara Nina?

NINA. (*sadly smiling*) You, Charlie, I suppose. I have always loved your love for me. (*She kisses him—wistfully*) Will you let me rot away in peace?

MARSDEN. (*strongly*) All my life I've waited to bring you peace.

NINA. (*sadly teasing*) If you've waited that long, Charlie, we'd better get married tomorrow. But I forgot. You haven't asked me yet, have you? Do you want me to marry you, Charlie?

MARSDEN. (*humbly*) Yes, Nina. (*Thinking with a strange ecstasy*)

I knew the time would come at last when I would hear her ask that! . . . I could never have said it, never! . . . oh, russet-golden afternoon, you are a mellow fruit of happiness ripely falling! . . .

DARRELL. (*amused—with a sad smile*) Bless you, my children! (*He turns to go.*)

NINA. I don't suppose we'll ever see you again, Ned.

DARRELL. I hope not, Nina. A scientist shouldn't believe in ghosts. (*With a mocking smile*) But perhaps we'll become part of cosmic positive and negative electric charges and meet again.

NINA. In our afternoons—again?

DARRELL. (*smiling sadly*) Again. In our afternoons.

MARSDEN. (*coming out of his day dream*) We'll be married in the afternoon, decidedly. I've already picked out the church, Nina—a gray ivied chapel, full of restful shadow, symbolical of the peace we have found. The crimsons and purples in the windows will stain our faces with faded passion. It must be in the hour before sunset when the earth dreams in afterthoughts and mystic premonitions of life's beauty. And then we'll go up to your old home to live. Mine wouldn't be suitable for us. Mother and Jane live there in memory. And I'll work in your father's old study. He won't mind me. (*From the bay below comes the roaring hum of an airplane motor.* NINA *and* DARRELL *jump startledly and go to the rear of the terrace to watch the plane ascend from the water, standing side by side.* MARSDEN *remains oblivious.*)

NINA. (*with anguish*) Gordon! Good-bye, dear! (*Pointing as the plane climbs higher moving away off to the left—bitterly*) See, Ned! He's leaving me without a backward look!

DARRELL. (*joyfully*) No! He's circling. He's coming back! (*The roar of the engine grows steadily nearer now*) He's going to pass directly over us! (*Their eyes follow the plane as it comes swiftly nearer and passes directly over them*) See! He's waving to us!

NINA. Oh, Gordon! My dear son! (*She waves frantically.*)

DARRELL. (*with a last tortured protest*) Nina! Are you forgetting? He's my son, too! (*He shouts up at the sky*) You're my son, Gordon! You're my— (*He controls himself abruptly—with a smile of cynical self-pity*) He can't hear! Well, at least I've done my duty! (*Then with a grim fatalism—with a final wave of his hand at the sky*) Good-bye, Gordon's son!

NINA. (*with tortured exultance*) Fly up to heaven, Gordon! Fly with your love to heaven! Fly always! Never crash to earth like my old Gordon! Be happy, dear! You've got to be happy!

DARRELL. (*sardonically*) I've heard that cry for happiness before, Nina! I remember hearing myself cry it—once—it must have been long ago! I'll get back to my cells—sensible unicellular life that floats in the sea and has never learned the cry for happiness! I'm going, Nina. (*As she remains oblivious, staring after the plane—thinking fatalistically*)

She doesn't hear, either. . . .

(*He laughs up at the sky*)

Oh, God, so deaf and dumb and blind! . . . teach me to be resigned to be an atom! . . .

(*He walks off, right, and enters the house.*)

NINA. (*finally lowering her eyes—confusedly*) Gone. My eyes are growing dim. Where is Ned? Gone, too. And Sam is gone. They're all dead. Where are Father and Charlie? (*With a shiver of fear she hurries over and sits on the bench beside* MARSDEN, *huddling against him*) Gordon is dead, Father. I've just had a cable. What I mean is, he flew away to another life—my son, Gordon, Charlie. So we're alone again—just as we used to be.

MARSDEN. (*putting his arm around her—affectionately*) Just as we used to be, dear Nina Cara Nina, before Gordon came.

NINA. (*looking up at the sky—strangely*) My having a son was a failure, wasn't it? He couldn't give me happiness. Sons are always their fathers. They pass through the mother to become their father again. The Sons of the Father have all been failures! Failing they died for us, they flew away to other lives, they could not stay with us, they could not give us happiness!

MARSDEN. (*paternally—in her father's tone*) You had best forget the whole affair of your association with the Gordons. After all, dear Nina, there was something unreal in all that has happened since you first met Gordon Shaw, something extravagant and fantastic, the sort of thing that isn't done, really, in our afternoons. So let's you and me forget the whole distressing episode, regard it as an interlude, of trial and preparation, say, in which our souls have been scraped clean of impure flesh and made worthy to bleach in peace.

NINA. (*with a strange smile*) Strange interlude! Yes, our lives are merely strange dark interludes in the electrical display of God the Father! (*Resting her head on his shoulder*) You're so restful, Charlie. I feel as if I were a girl again and you were my father and the Charlie of those days made into one. I wonder is our old garden the same? We'll pick flowers together in the aging afternoons of spring and summer, won't we? It will be a comfort to get home—to be old and to be home again at last—to be in love with peace together—to love each other's peace—to sleep with peace together—! (*She kisses him—then shuts her eyes with a deep sigh of requited weariness*) —to die in peace! I'm so contentedly weary with life!

MARSDEN. (*with a serene peace*) Rest, dear Nina. (*Then tenderly*) It has been a long day. Why don't you sleep now—as you used to, remember?—for a little while?

NINA. (*murmurs with drowsy gratitude*) Thank you, Father—have I been wicked?—you're so good—dear old Charlie!

MARSDEN. (*reacting automatically and wincing with pain—thinking mechanically*)

God damn dear old . . . !

(*Then with a glance down at* NINA'S *face, with a happy smile*)

No, God bless dear old Charlie . . . who, passed beyond desire, has all the luck at last! . . .

(NINA *has fallen asleep. He watches with contented eyes the evening shadows closing in around them.*)

CURTAIN

DESIRE UNDER THE ELMS

CHARACTERS

EPHRAIM CABOT

SIMEON, PETER, EBEN — *His sons*

ABBIE PUTNAM

Young Girl, Two Farmers, The Fiddler, A Sheriff, and other folk from the neighboring farms.

The action of the entire play takes place in, and immediately outside of, the Cabot farmhouse in New England, in the year 1850. The south end of the house faces front to a stone wall with a wooden gate at center opening on a country road. The house is in good condition but in need of paint. Its walls are a sickly grayish, the green of the shutters faded. Two enormous elms are on each side of the house. They bend their trailing branches down over the roof. They appear to protect and at the same time subdue. There is a sinister maternity in their aspect, a crushing, jealous absorption. They have developed from their intimate contact with the life of man in the house an appalling humaneness. They brood oppressively over the house. They are like exhausted women resting their sagging breasts and hands and hair on its roof, and when it rains their tears trickle down monotonously and rot on the shingles.

There is a path running from the gate around the right corner of the house to the front door. A narrow porch is on this side. The end wall facing us has two windows in its upper story, two larger ones on the floor below. The two upper are those of the father's bedroom and that of the brothers. On the left, ground floor, is the kitchen—on the right, the parlor, the shades of which are always drawn down.

DESIRE UNDER THE ELMS

PART ONE—SCENE ONE

*E*XTERIOR *of the farmhouse. It is sunset of a day at the beginning of summer in the year 1850. There is no wind and everything is still. The sky above the roof is suffused with deep colors, the green of the elms glows, but the house is in shadow, seeming pale and washed out by contrast.*

A door opens and EBEN CABOT *comes to the end of the porch and stands looking down the road to the right. He has a large bell in his hand and this he swings mechanically, awakening a deafening clangor. Then he puts his hands on his hips and stares up at the sky. He sighs with a puzzled awe and blurts out with halting appreciation.*

EBEN. God! Purty! (*His eyes fall and he stares about him frowningly. He is twenty-five, tall and sinewy. His face is well-formed, good-looking, but its expression is resentful and defensive. His defiant, dark eyes remind one of a wild animal's in captivity. Each day is a cage in which he finds himself trapped but inwardly unsubdued. There is a fierce repressed vitality about him. He has black hair, mustache, a thin curly trace of beard. He is dressed in rough farm clothes.*

He spits on the ground with intense disgust, turns and goes back into the house.

SIMEON *and* PETER *come in from their work in the fields. They are tall men, much older than their half-brother* [SIMEON *is thirty-nine and* PETER *thirty-seven*], *built on a squarer, simpler model, fleshier in body, more bovine and homelier in face, shrewder and more prac-*

tical. Their shoulders stoop a bit from years of farm work. They clump heavily along in their clumsy thick-soled boots caked with earth. Their clothes, their faces, hands, bare arms and throats are earth-stained. They smell of earth. They stand together for a moment in front of the house and, as if with the one impulse, stare dumbly up at the sky, leaning on their hoes. Their faces have a compressed, unresigned expression. As they look upward, this softens.)

SIMEON. (*grudgingly*) Purty.

PETER. Ay-eh.

SIMEON. (*suddenly*) Eighteen year ago.

PETER. What?

SIMEON. Jenn. My woman. She died.

PETER. I'd fergot.

SIMEON. I rec'lect—now an' agin. Makes it lonesome. She'd hair long's a hoss' tail—an' yaller like gold!

PETER. Waal—she's gone. (*This with indifferent finality—then after a pause*) They's gold in the West, Sim.

SIMEON. (*still under the influence of sunset—vaguely*) In the sky?

PETER. Waal—in a manner o' speakin'—thar's the promise. (*Growing excited*) Gold in the sky—in the West—Golden Gate—Californi-a!—Goldest West!—fields o' gold!

SIMEON. (*excited in his turn*) Fortunes layin' just atop o' the ground waitin' t' be picked! Solomon's mines, they says! (*For a moment they continue looking up at the sky—then their eyes drop.*)

PETER. (*with sardonic bitterness*) Here—it's stones atop o' the ground—stones atop o' stones—makin' stone walls—year atop o' year—him 'n' yew 'n' me 'n' then Eben—makin' stone walls fur him to fence us in!

SIMEON. We've wuked. Give our strength. Give our years. Plowed 'em under in the ground—(*he stamps rebelliously*)—rottin'—makin' soil for his crops! (*A pause*) Waal—the farm pays good for hereabouts.

PETER. If we plowed in Californi-a, they'd be lumps o' gold in the furrow!

SIMEON. Californi-a's t'other side o' earth, a'most. We got t' cal-c'late—

PETER. (*after a pause*) 'Twould be hard fur me, too, to give up what we've 'arned here by our sweat. (*A pause.* EBEN *sticks his head out of the dining-room window, listening.*)

SIMEON. Ay-eh. (*A pause*) Mebbe—he'll die soon.

PETER. (*doubtfully*) Mebbe.

SIMEON. Mebbe—fur all we knows—he's dead now.

PETER. Ye'd need proof.

SIMEON. He's been gone two months—with no word.

PETER. Left us in the fields an evenin' like this. Hitched up an' druv off into the West. That's plum onnateral. He hain't never been off this farm 'ceptin' t' the village in thirty year or more, not since he married Eben's maw. (*A pause. Shrewdly*) I calc'late we might git him declared crazy by the court.

SIMEON. He skinned 'em too slick. He got the best o' all on 'em. They'd never b'lieve him crazy. (*A pause*) We got t' wait—till he's under ground.

EBEN. (*with a sardonic chuckle*) Honor thy father! (*They turn, startled, and stare at him. He grins, then scowls*) I pray he's died. (*They stare at him. He continues matter-of-factly*) Supper's ready.

SIMEON *and* PETER. (*together*) Ayeh.

EBEN. (*gazing up at the sky*) Sun's downin' purty.

SIMEON *and* PETER. (*together*) Ay-eh. They's gold in the West.

EBEN. Ay-eh. (*Pointing*) Yonder atop o' the hill pasture, ye mean?

SIMEON *and* PETER. (*together*) In Californi-a!

EBEN. Hunh? (*Stares at them indifferently for a second, then drawls*) Waal—supper's gittin' cold. (*He turns back into kitchen.*)

SIMEON. (*startled—smacks his lips*) I air hungry!

PETER. (*sniffing*) I smells bacon!

SIMEON. (*with hungry appreciation*) Bacon's good!

PETER. (*in same tone*) Bacon's bacon! (*They turn, shouldering each other, their bodies bumping and rubbing together as they hurry clumsily to their food, like two friendly oxen toward their evening meal. They disappear around the right corner of house and can be heard entering the door.*)

CURTAIN

SCENE TWO

THE *color fades from the sky. Twilight begins. The interior of the kitchen is now visible. A pine table is at center, a cookstove in the right rear corner, four rough wooden chairs, a tallow candle on the table. In the middle of the rear wall is fastened a big advertising poster with a ship in full sail and the word "California" in big letters. Kitchen utensils hang from nails. Everything is neat and in order but the atmosphere is of a men's camp kitchen rather than that of a home.*

Places for three are laid. EBEN *takes boiled potatoes and bacon from the stove and puts them on the table, also a loaf of bread and a crock of water.* SIMEON *and* PETER *shoulder in, slump down in their chairs without a word.* EBEN *joins them. The three eat in silence for a moment, the two elder as naturally unrestrained as beasts of the field,* EBEN *picking at his food without appetite, glancing at them with a tolerant dislike.*

SIMEON. (*suddenly turns to* EBEN) Looky here! Ye'd oughtn't t' said that, Eben.

PETER. 'Twa'n't righteous.

EBEN. What?

SIMEON. Ye prayed he'd died.

EBEN. Waal—don't yew pray it? (*A pause.*)

PETER. He's our Paw.

EBEN. (*violently*) Not mine!

SIMEON. (*dryly*) Ye'd not let no one else say that about yer Maw! Ha! (*He gives one abrupt sardonic guffaw.* PETER *grins.*)

EBEN. (*very pale*) I meant—I hain't his'n—I hain't like him—he hain't me!

PETER. (*dryly*) Wait till ye've growed his age!

EBEN. (*intensely*) I'm Maw—every drop o' blood! (*A pause. They stare at him with indifferent curiosity.*)

PETER. (*reminiscently*) She was good t' Sim 'n' me. A good Step-maw's scurse.

SIMEON. She was good t' everyone.

EBEN. (*greatly moved, gets to his feet and makes an awkward bow to each of them—stammering*) I be thankful t' ye. I'm her—her heir. (*He sits down in confusion.*)

PETER. (*after a pause—judicially*) She was good even t' him.

EBEN. (*fiercely*) An' fur thanks he killed her!

SIMEON. (*after a pause*) No one never kills nobody. It's allus somethin'. That's the murderer.

EBEN. Didn't he slave Maw t' death?

PETER. He's slaved himself t' death. He's slaved Sim 'n' me 'n' yew t' death—on'y none o' us hain't died—yit.

SIMEON. It's somethin'—drivin' him—t' drive us!

EBEN. (*vengefully*) Waal—I hold him t' jedgment! (*Then scornfully*) Somethin'! What's somethin'?

SIMEON. Dunno.

EBEN. (*sardonically*) What's drivin' yew to Californi-a, mebbe? (*They look at him in surprise*) Oh, I've heerd ye! (*Then, after a pause*) But ye'll never go t' the gold fields!

PETER. (*assertively*) Mebbe!

EBEN. Whar'll ye git the money?

PETER. We kin walk. It's an a'mighty ways—Californi-a—but if yew was t' put all the steps we've walked on this farm end t' end we'd be in the moon!

EBEN. The Injuns'll skulp ye on the plains.

SIMEON. (*with grim humor*) We'll mebbe make 'em pay a hair fur a hair!

EBEN. (*decisively*) But t'aint that. Ye won't never go because ye'll wait here fur yer share o' the farm, thinkin' allus he'll die soon.

SIMEON. (*after a pause*) We've a right.

PETER. Two-thirds belongs t'us.

EBEN. (*jumping to his feet*) Ye've no right! She wa'n't yewr Maw! It was her farm! Didn't he steal it from her? She's dead. It's my farm.

SIMEON. (*sardonically*) Tell that t' Paw—when he comes! I'll bet ye a dollar he'll laugh—fur once in his life. Ha! (*He laughs himself in one single mirthless bark.*)

PETER. (*amused in turn, echoes his brother*) Ha!

SIMEON. (*after a pause*) What've ye got held agin us, Eben? Year arter year it's skulked in yer eye—somethin'.

PETER. Ay-eh.

EBEN. Ay-eh. They's somethin'. (*Suddenly exploding*) Why didn't ye never stand between him 'n' my Maw when he was slavin' her to her grave—t' pay her back fur the kindness she done t' yew? (*There is a long pause. They stare at him in surprise.*)

SIMEON. Waal—the stock'd got t' be watered.

PETER. 'R they was woodin' t' do.

SIMEON. 'R plowin'.

PETER. 'R hayin'.

SIMEON. 'R spreadin' manure.

PETER. 'R weedin'.

SIMEON. 'R prunin'.

PETER. 'R milkin'.

EBEN. (*breaking in harshly*) An' makin' walls—stone atop o' stone

—makin' walls till yer heart's a stone ye heft up out o' the way o' growth onto a stone wall t' wall in yer heart!

SIMEON. (*matter-of-factly*) We never had no time t' meddle.

PETER. (*to* EBEN) Yew was fifteen afore yer Maw died—an' big fur yer age. Why didn't ye never do nothin'?

EBEN. (*harshly*) They was chores t' do, wa'n't they? (*A pause—then slowly*) It was on'y arter she died I come to think o' it. Me cookin'—doin' her work—that made me know her, suffer her sufferin'—she'd come back t' help—come back t' bile potatoes—come back t' fry bacon—come back t' bake biscuits—come back all cramped up t' shake the fire, an' carry ashes, her eyes weepin' an' bloody with smoke an' cinders same's they used t' be. She still comes back—stands by the stove thar in the evenin'—she can't find it nateral sleepin' an' restin' in peace. She can't git used t' bein' free—even in her grave.

SIMEON. She never complained none.

EBEN. She'd got too tired. She'd got too used t' bein' too tired. That was what he done. (*With vengeful passion*) An' sooner'r later, I'll meddle. I'll say the thin's I didn't say then t' him! I'll yell 'em at the top o' my lungs. I'll see t' it my Maw gits some rest an' sleep in her grave! (*He sits down again, relapsing into a brooding silence. They look at him with a queer indifferent curiosity.*)

PETER. (*after a pause*) Whar in tarnation d'ye s'pose he went, Sim?

SIMEON. Dunno. He druv off in the buggy, all spick an' span, with the mare all breshed an' shiny, druv off clackin' his tongue an' wavin' his whip. I remember it right well. I was finishin' plowin', it was spring an' May an' sunset, an' gold in the West, an' he druv off into it. I yells "Whar ye goin', Paw?" an' he hauls up by the stone wall a jiffy. His old snake's eyes was glitterin' in the sun like he'd been drinkin' a jugful an' he says with a mule's grin: "Don't ye run away till I come back!"

PETER. Wonder if he knowed we was wantin' fur Californi-a?

SIMEON. Mebbe. I didn't say nothin' and he says, lookin' kinder queer an' sick: "I been hearin' the hens cluckin' an' the roosters crowin' all the durn day. I been listenin' t' the cows lowin' an' everythin' else kickin' up till I can't stand it no more. It's spring an' I'm feelin' damned," he says. "Damned like an old bare hickory tree fit on'y fur burnin'," he says. An' then I calc'late I must've looked a mite hopeful, fur he adds real spry and vicious: "But don't git no fool idee I'm dead. I've sworn t' live a hundred an' I'll do it, if on'y t' spite yer sinful greed! An' now I'm ridin' out t' learn God's message t' me in the spring, like the prophets done. An' yew git back t' yer plowin'," he says. An' he druv off singin' a hymn. I thought he was drunk—'r I'd stopped him goin'.

EBEN. (*scornfully*) No, ye wouldn't! Ye're scared o' him. He's stronger—inside—than both o' ye put together!

PETER. (*sardonically*) An' yew—be yew Samson?

EBEN. I'm gittin' stronger. I kin feel it growin' in me—growin' an' growin'—till it'll bust out—! (*He gets up and puts on his coat and a hat. They watch him, gradually breaking into grins.* EBEN *avoids their eyes sheepishly*) I'm goin' out fur a spell—up the road.

PETER. T' the village?

SIMEON. T' see Minnie?

EBEN. (*defiantly*) Ay-eh!

PETER. (*jeeringly*) The Scarlet Woman!

SIMEON. Lust—that's what's growin' in ye!

EBEN. Waal—she's purty!

PETER. She's been purty fur twenty year!

SIMEON. A new coat o' paint'll make a heifer out of forty.

EBEN. She hain't forty!

PETER. If she hain't, she's teeterin' on the edge.

EBEN. (*desperately*) What d'yew know—

PETER. All they is. . . . Sim knew her—an' then me arter—

SIMEON. An' Paw kin tell yew somethin' too! He was fust!

EBEN. D'ye mean t' say he . . .?

SIMEON. (*with a grin*) Ay-eh! We air his heirs in everythin'!

EBEN. (*intensely*) That's more to it! That grows on it! It'll bust soon! (*Then violently*) I'll go smash my fist in her face! (*He pulls open the door in rear violently.*)

SIMEON. (*with a wink at* PETER—*drawlingly*) Mebbe—but the night's wa'm—purty—by the time ye git thar mebbe ye'll kiss her instead!

PETER. Sart'n he will! (*They both roar with coarse laughter.* EBEN *rushes out and slams the door—then the outside front door—comes around the corner of the house and stands still by the gate, staring up at the sky.*)

SIMEON. (*looking after him*) Like his Paw.

PETER. Dead spit an' image!

SIMEON. Dog'll eat dog!

PETER. Ay-eh. (*Pause. With yearning*) Mebbe a year from now we'll be in Californi-a.

SIMEON. Ay-eh. (*A pause. Both yawn*) Let's git t'bed. (*He blows out the candle. They go out door in rear.* EBEN *stretches his arms up to the sky—rebelliously.*)

EBEN. Waal—thar's a star, an' somewhar's they's him, an' here's me, an' thar's Min up the road—in the same night. What if I does kiss her? She's like t'night, she's soft 'n' wa'm, her eyes kin wink like a star, her mouth's wa'm, her arms're wa'm, she smells like a wa'm plowed field, she's purty . . . Ay-eh! By God A'mighty she's purty, an' I don't give a damn how many sins she's sinned afore mine or who she's sinned 'em with, my sin's as purty as any one on 'em! (*He strides off down the road to the left.*)

SCENE THREE

IT IS *the pitch darkness just before dawn.* EBEN *comes in from the left and goes around to the porch, feeling his way, chuckling bitterly and cursing half-aloud to himself.*

EBEN. The cussed old miser! (*He can be heard going in the front door. There is a pause as he goes upstairs, then a loud knock on the bedroom door of the brothers*) Wake up!

SIMEON. (*startledly*) Who's thar?

EBEN. (*pushing open the door and coming in, a lighted candle in his hand. The bedroom of the brothers is revealed. Its ceiling is the sloping roof. They can stand upright only close to the center dividing wall of the upstairs.* SIMEON *and* PETER *are in a double bed, front.* EBEN'S *cot is to the rear.* EBEN *has a mixture of silly grin and vicious scowl on his face*) I be!

PETER. (*angrily*) What in hell's-fire . . . ?

EBEN. I got news fur ye! Ha! (*He gives one abrupt sardonic guffaw.*)

SIMEON. (*angrily*) Couldn't ye hold it 'til we'd got our sleep?

EBEN. It's nigh sunup. (*Then explosively*) He's gone an' married agen!

SIMEON *and* PETER. (*explosively*) Paw?

EBEN. Got himself hitched to a female 'bout thirty-five—an' purty, they says . . .

SIMEON. (*aghast*) It's a durn lie!

PETER. Who says?

SIMEON. They been stringin' ye!

EBEN. Think I'm a dunce, do ye? The hull village says. The preacher from New Dover, he brung the news—told it t'our preacher

—New Dover, that's whar the old loon got himself hitched—that's whar the woman lived—

PETER. (*no longer doubting—stunned*) Waal . . . !

SIMEON. (*the same*) Waal . . . !

EBEN. (*sitting down on a bed—with vicious hatred*) Ain't he a devil out o' hell? It's jest t' spite us—the damned old mule!

PETER. (*after a pause*) Everythin'll go t' her now.

SIMEON. Ay-eh. (*A pause—dully*) Waal—if it's done—

PETER. It's done us. (*Pause—then persuasively*) They's gold in the fields o' Californi-a, Sim. No good a-stayin' here now.

SIMEON. Jest what I was a-thinkin'. (*Then with decision*) S'well fust's last! Let's light out and git this mornin'.

PETER. Suits me.

EBEN. Ye must like walkin'.

SIMEON. (*sardonically*) If ye'd grow wings on us we'd fly thar!

EBEN. Ye'd like ridin' better—on a boat, wouldn't ye? (*Fumbles in his pocket and takes out a crumpled sheet of foolscap*) Waal, if ye sign this ye kin ride on a boat. I've had it writ out an' ready in case ye'd ever go. It says fur three hundred dollars t' each ye agree yewr shares o' the farm is sold t' me. (*They look suspiciously at the paper. A pause.*)

SIMEON. (*wonderingly*) But if he's hitched agen—

PETER. An' whar'd yew git that sum o' money, anyways?

EBEN. (*cunningly*) I know whar it's hid. I been waitin'—Maw told me. She knew whar it lay fur years, but she was waitin' . . . It's her'n—the money he hoarded from her farm an' hid from Maw. It's my money by rights now.

PETER. Whar's it hid?

EBEN. (*cunningly*) Whar yew won't never find it without me. Maw spied on him—'r she'd never knowed. (*A pause. They look at him suspiciously, and he at them*) Waal, is it fa'r trade?

SIMEON. Dunno.

PETER. Dunno.

SIMEON. (*looking at window*) Sky's grayin'.

PETER. Ye better start the fire, Eben.

SIMEON. An' fix some vittles.

EBEN. Ay-eh. (*Then with a forced jocular heartiness*) I'll git ye a good one. If ye're startin' t' hoof it t' Californi-a ye'll need somethin' that'll stick t' yer ribs. (*He turns to the door, adding meaningly*) But ye kin ride on a boat if ye'll swap. (*He stops at the door and pauses. They stare at him.*)

SIMEON. (*suspiciously*) Whar was ye all night?

EBEN. (*defiantly*) Up t' Min's. (*Then slowly*) Walkin' thar, fust I felt 's if I'd kiss her; then I got a-thinkin' o' what ye'd said o' him an' her an' I says, I'll bust her nose fur that! Then I got t' the village an' heerd the news an' I got madder'n hell an' run all the way t' Min's not knowin' what I'd do— (*He pauses—then sheepishly but more defiantly*) Waal—when I seen her, I didn't hit her—nor I didn't kiss her nuther—I begun t' beller like a calf an' cuss at the same time, I was so durn mad—an' she got scared—an' I jest grabbed holt an' tuk her! (*Proudly*) Yes, sirree! I tuk her. She may've been his'n—an' your'n, too—but she's mine now!

SIMEON. (*dryly*) In love, air yew?

EBEN. (*with lofty scorn*) Love! I don't take no stock in sech slop!

PETER. (*winking at* SIMEON) Mebbe Eben's aimin' t' marry, too.

SIMEON. Min'd make a true faithful he'pmeet! (*They snicker.*)

EBEN. What do I care fur her—'ceptin' she's round an' wa'm? The p'int is she was his'n—an' now she b'longs t' me! (*He goes to the door—then turns—rebelliously*) An' Min hain't sech a bad un. They's worse'n Min in the world, I'll bet ye! Wait'll we see this cow the Old Man's hitched t'! She'll beat Min, I got a notion! (*He starts to go out.*)

SIMEON. (*suddenly*) Mebbe ye'll try t' make her your'n, too?

PETER. Ha! (*He gives a sardonic laugh of relish at this idea.*)

EBEN. (*spitting with disgust*) Her—here—sleepin' with him—stealin' my Maw's farm! I'd as soon pet a skunk 'r kiss a snake! (*He goes out. The two stare after him suspiciously. A pause. They listen to his steps receding.*)

PETER. He's startin' the fire.

SIMEON. I'd like t' ride t' Californi-a—but—

PETER. Min might o' put some scheme in his head.

SIMEON. Mebbe it's all a lie 'bout Paw marryin'. We'd best wait an' see the bride.

PETER. An' don't sign nothin' till we does!

SIMEON. Nor till we've tested it's good money! (*Then with a grin*) But if Paw's hitched we'd be sellin' Eben somethin' we'd never git nohow!

PETER. We'll wait an' see. (*Then with sudden vindictive anger*) An' till he comes, let's yew 'n' me not wuk a lick, let Eben tend to thin's if he's a mind t', let's us jest sleep an' eat an' drink likker, an' let the hull damned farm go t' blazes!

SIMEON. (*excitedly*) By God, we've 'arned a rest! We'll play rich fur a change. I hain't a-going to stir outa bed till breakfast's ready.

PETER. An' on the table!

SIMEON. (*after a pause—thoughtfully*) What d'ye calc'late she'll be like—our new Maw? Like Eben thinks?

PETER. More'n' likely.

SIMEON. (*vindictively*) Waal—I hope she's a she-devil that'll make him wish he was dead an' livin' in the pit o' hell fur comfort!

PETER. (*fervently*) Amen!

SIMEON. (*imitating his father's voice*) "I'm ridin' out t' learn God's message t' me in the spring like the prophets done," he says. I'll bet right then an' thar he knew plumb well he was goin' whorin', the stinkin' old hypocrite!

SCENE FOUR

SAME as Scene Two—shows the interior of the kitchen with a lighted candle on table. It is gray dawn outside. SIMEON *and* PETER *are just finishing their breakfast.* EBEN *sits before his plate of untouched food, brooding frowningly.*

PETER. (*glancing at him rather irritably*) Lookin' glum don't help none.

SIMEON. (*sarcastically*) Sorrowin' over his lust o' the flesh!

PETER. (*with a grin*) Was she yer fust?

EBEN. (*angrily*) None o' yer business. (*A pause*) I was thinkin' o' him. I got a notion he's gittin' near—I kin feel him comin' on like yew kin feel malaria chill afore it takes ye.

PETER. It's too early yet.

SIMEON. Dunno. He'd like t' catch us nappin'—jest t' have somethin' t' hoss us 'round over.

PETER. (*mechanically gets to his feet.* SIMEON *does the same*) Waal —let's git t'wuk. (*They both plod mechanically toward the door before they realize. Then they stop short.*)

SIMEON. (*grinning*) Ye're a cussed fool, Pete—and I be wuss! Let him see we hain't wukin'! We don't give a durn!

PETER. (*as they go back to the table*) Not a damned durn! It'll serve t' show him we're done with him. (*They sit down again.* EBEN *stares from one to the other with surprise.*)

SIMEON. (*grins at him*) We're aimin' t' start bein' lilies o' the field.

PETER. Nary a toil 'r spin 'r lick o' wuk do we put in!

SIMEON. Ye're sole owner—till he comes—that's what ye wanted. Waal, ye got t' be sole hand, too.

PETER. The cows air bellerin'. Ye better hustle at the milkin'.

EBEN. (*with excited joy*) Ye mean ye'll sign the paper?

SIMEON. (*dryly*) Mebbe.

PETER. Mebbe.

SIMEON. We're considerin'. (*Peremptorily*) Ye better git t' wuk.

EBEN. (*with queer excitement*) It's Maw's farm agen! It's my farm! Them's my cows! I'll milk my durn fingers off fur cows o' mine! (*He goes out door in rear, they stare after him indifferently.*)

SIMEON. Like his Paw.

PETER. Dead spit 'n' image!

SIMEON. Waal—let dog eat dog! (EBEN *comes out of front door and around the corner of the house. The sky is beginning to grow flushed with sunrise.* EBEN *stops by the gate and stares around him with glowing, possessive eyes. He takes in the whole farm with his embracing glance of desire.*)

EBEN. It's purty! It's damned purty! It's mine! (*He suddenly throws his head back boldly and glares with hard, defiant eyes at the sky*) Mine, d'ye hear? Mine! (*He turns and walks quickly off left, rear, toward the barn. The two brothers light their pipes.*)

SIMEON. (*putting his muddy boots up on the table, tilting back his chair, and puffing defiantly*) Waal—this air solid comfort—fur once.

PETER. Ay-eh. (*He follows suit. A pause. Unconsciously they both sigh.*)

SIMEON. (*suddenly*) He never was much o' a hand at milkin', Eben wa'n't.

PETER. (*with a snort*) His hands air like hoofs! (*A pause.*)

SIMEON. Reach down the jug thar! Let's take a swaller. I'm feelin' kind o' low.

PETER. Good idee! (*He does so—gets two glasses—they pour out drinks of whisky*) Here's t' the gold in Californi-a!

SIMEON. An' luck t' find it! (*They drink—puff resolutely—sigh—take their feet down from the table.*)

PETER. Likker don't pear t' sot right.

SIMEON. We hain't used t' it this early. (*A pause. They become very restless.*)

PETER. Gittin' close in this kitchen.

SIMEON. (*with immense relief*) Let's git a breath o' air. (*They arise briskly and go out rear—appear around house and stop by the gate. They stare up at the sky with a numbed appreciation.*)

PETER. Purty!

SIMEON. Ay-eh. Gold's t' the East now.

PETER. Sun's startin' with us fur the Golden West.

SIMEON. (*staring around the farm, his compressed face tightened, unable to conceal his emotion*) Waal—it's our last mornin'—mebbe.

PETER. (*the same*) Ay-eh.

SIMEON. (*stamps his foot on the earth and addresses it desperately*) Waal—ye've thirty year o' me buried in ye—spread out over ye—blood an' bone an' sweat—rotted away—fertilizin' ye—richin' yer soul—prime manure, by God, that's what I been t' ye!

PETER. Ay-eh! An' me!

SIMEON. An' yew, Peter. (*He sighs—then spits*) Waal—no use'n cryin' over spilt milk.

PETER. They's gold in the West—an' freedom, mebbe. We been slaves t' stone walls here.

SIMEON. (*defiantly*) We hain't nobody's slaves from this out—nor nothin's slaves nuther. (*A pause—restlessly*) Speaking o' milk, wonder how Eben's managin'?

PETER. I s'pose he's managin'.

SIMEON. Mebbe we'd ought t' help—this once.

PETER. Mebbe. The cows knows us.

SIMEON. An' likes us. They don't know him much.

PETER. An' the hosses, an' pigs, an' chickens. They don't know him much.

SIMEON. They knows us like brothers—an' likes us! (*Proudly.*) Hain't we raised 'em t' be fust-rate, number one prize stock?

PETER. We hain't—not no more.

SIMEON. (*dully*) I was fergittin'. (*Then resignedly*) Waal, let's go help Eben a spell an' git waked up.

PETER. Suits me. (*They are starting off down left, rear, for the barn when Eben appears from there hurrying toward them, his face excited.*)

EBEN. (*breathlessly*) Waal—har they be! The old mule an' the bride! I seen 'em from the barn down below at the turnin'.

PETER. How could ye tell that far?

EBEN. Hain't I as far-sight as he's near-sight? Don't I know the mare 'n' buggy, an' two people settin' in it? Who else . . . ? An' I tell ye I kin feel 'em a-comin', too! (*He squirms as if he had the itch.*)

PETER. (*beginning to be angry*) Waal—let him do his own unhitchin'!

SIMEON. (*angry in his turn*) Let's hustle in an' git our bundles an' be a-goin' as he's a-comin'. I don't want never t' step inside the door agen arter he's back. (*They both start back around the corner of the house.* EBEN *follows them.*)

EBEN. (*anxiously*) Will ye sign it afore ye go?

PETER. Let's see the color o' the old skinflint's money an' we'll sign. (*They disappear left. The two brothers clump upstairs to get their bundles.* EBEN *appears in the kitchen, runs to window, peers out, comes back and pulls up a strip of flooring in under stove, takes out a canvas bag and puts it on table, then sets the floorboard back in place. The two brothers appear a moment after. They carry old carpet bags.*)

EBEN. (*puts his hand on bag guardingly*) Have ye signed?

SIMEON. (*shows paper in his hand*) Ay-eh. (*Greedily*) Be that the money?

EBEN. (*opens bag and pours out pile of twenty-dollar gold pieces*) Twenty-dollar pieces—thirty on 'em. Count 'em. (*Peter does so, arranging them in stacks of five, biting one or two to test them.*)

PETER. Six hundred. (*He puts them in bag and puts it inside his shirt carefully.*)

SIMEON. (*handing paper to* EBEN) Har ye be.

EBEN. (*after a glance, folds it carefully and hides it under his shirt—gratefully*) Thank yew.

PETER. Thank yew fur the ride.

SIMEON. We'll send ye a lump o' gold fur Christmas. (*A pause.* EBEN *stares at them and they at him.*)

PETER. (*awkwardly*) Waal—we're a-goin'.

SIMEON. Comin' out t' the yard?

EBEN. No. I'm waitin' in here a spell. (*Another silence. The brothers edge awkwardly to door in rear—then turn and stand.*)

SIMEON. Waal—good-by.

PETER. Good-by.

EBEN. Good-by. (*Then go out. He sits down at the table, faces the stove and pulls out the paper. He looks from it to the stove. His face, lighted up by the shaft of sunlight from the window, has an expression of trance. His lips move. The two brothers come out to the gate.*)

PETER. (*looking off toward barn*) Thar he be—unhitchin'.

SIMEON. (*with a chuckle*) I'll bet ye he's riled!

PETER. An' thar she be.

SIMEON. Let's wait 'n' see what our new Maw looks like.

PETER. (*with a grin*) An' give him our partin' cuss!

SIMEON. (*grinning*) I feel like raisin' fun. I feel light in my head an' feet.

PETER. Me, too. I feel like laffin' till I'd split up the middle.

SIMEON. Reckon it's the likker?

PETER. No. My feet feel itchin' t' walk an' walk—an' jump high over thin's—an'. . . .

SIMEON. Dance? (*A pause.*)

PETER. (*puzzled*) It's plumb onnateral.

SIMEON. (*a light coming over his face*) I calc'late it's 'cause school's out. It's holiday. Fur once we're free!

PETER. (*dazedly*) Free?

SIMEON. The halter's broke—the harness is busted—the fence bars is down—the stone walls air crumblin' an' tumblin'! We'll be kickin' up an' tearin' away down the road!

PETER. (*drawing a deep breath—oratorically*) Anybody that wants this stinkin' old rock-pile of a farm kin hev it. T'ain't our'n, no sirree!

SIMEON. (*takes the gate off its hinges and puts it under his arm*) We harby 'bolishes shet gates, an' open gates, an' all gates, by thunder!

PETER. We'll take it with us fur luck an' let 'er sail free down some river.

SIMEON. (*as a sound of voices comes from left, rear*) Har they comes! (*The two brothers congeal into two stiff, grim-visaged statues.* EPHRAIM CABOT *and* ABBIE PUTNAM *come in.* CABOT *is seventy-five, tall and gaunt, with great, wiry, concentrated power, but stoop-shouldered from toil. His face is as hard as if it were hewn out of a boulder, yet there is a weakness in it, a petty pride in its own narrow strength. His eyes are small, close together, and extremely near-sighted, blinking continually in the effort to focus on objects, their stare having a straining, ingrowing quality. He is dressed in his dismal black Sunday suit.* ABBIE *is thirty-five, buxom, full of vitality. Her round face is pretty but marred by its rather gross sensuality. There is strength and obstinacy in her jaw, a hard determination in her eyes, and about her whole personality the same unsettled, untamed, desperate quality which is so apparent in* EBEN.)

CABOT. (*as they enter—a queer strangled emotion in his dry cracking voice*) Har we be t' hum, Abbie.

ABBIE. (*with lust for the word*) Hum! (*Her eyes gloating on the house without seeming to see the two stiff figures at the gate*) It's purty—purty! I can't b'lieve it's r'ally mine.

CABOT. (*sharply*) Yewr'n? Mine! (*He stares at her penetratingly. She stares back. He adds relentingly*) Our'n—mebbe! It was lonesome too long. I was growin' old in the spring. A hum's got t' hev a woman.

ABBIE. (*her voice taking possession*) A woman's got t' hev a hum!

CABOT. (*nodding uncertainly*) Ay-eh. (*Then irritably*) Whar be they? Ain't thar nobody about—'r wukin'—r' nothin'?

ABBIE. (*sees the brothers. She returns their stare of cold appraising contempt with interest—slowly*) Thar's two men loafin' at the gate an' starin' at me like a couple o' strayed hogs.

CABOT. (*straining his eyes*) I kin see 'em—but I can't make out. . . .

SIMEON. It's Simeon.

PETER. It's Peter.

CABOT. (*exploding*) Why hain't ye wukin'?

SIMEON. (*dryly*) We're waitin' t' welcome ye hum—yew an' the bride!

CABOT. (*confusedly*) Huh? Waal—this be yer new Maw, boys. (*She stares at them and they at her.*)

SIMEON. (*turns away and spits contemptuously*) I see her!

PETER. (*spits also*) An' I see her!

ABBIE. (*with the conqueror's conscious superiority*) I'll go in an' look at *my* house. (*She goes slowly around to porch.*)

SIMEON. (*with a snort*) *Her* house!

PETER. (*calls after her*) Ye'll find Eben inside. Ye better not tell him it's *yewr* house.

ABBIE. (*mouthing the name*) Eben. (*Then quietly*) I'll tell Eben.

CABOT. (*with a contemptuous sneer*) Ye needn't heed Eben. Eben's a dumb fool—like his Maw—soft an' simple!

SIMEON. (*with his sardonic burst of laughter*) Ha! Eben's a chip o' yew—spit 'n' image—hard 'n' bitter's a hickory tree! Dog'll eat dog. He'll eat ye yet, old man!

CABOT. (*commandingly*) Ye git t' wuk!

SIMEON. (*as* ABBIE *disappears in house—winks at* PETER *and says tauntingly*) So that thar's our new Maw, be it? Whar in hell did ye dig her up? (*He and* PETER *laugh.*)

PETER. Ha! Ye'd better turn her in the pen with the other sows. (*They laugh uproariously, slapping their thighs.*)

CABOT. (*so amazed at their effrontery that he stutters in confusion*) Simeon! Peter! What's come over ye? Air ye drunk?

SIMEON. We're free, old man—free o' yew an' the hull damned farm! (*They grow more and more hilarious and excited.*)

PETER. An' we're startin' out fur the gold fields o' Californi-a!

SIMEON. Ye kin take this place an' burn it!

PETER. An' bury it—fur all we cares!

SIMEON. We're free, old man! (*He cuts a caper.*)

PETER. Free! (*He gives a kick in the air.*)

SIMEON. (*in a frenzy*) Whoop!

PETER. Whoop! (*They do an absurd Indian war dance about the old man who is petrified between rage and the fear that they are insane.*)

SIMEON. We're free as Injuns! Lucky we don't skulp ye!

PETER. An' burn yer barn an' kill the stock!

SIMEON. An' rape yer new woman! Whoop! (*He and* PETER *stop their dance, holding their sides, rocking with wild laughter.*)

CABOT. (*edging away*) Lust fur gold—fur the sinful, easy gold o' Californi-a! It's made ye mad!

SIMEON. (*tauntingly*) Wouldn't ye like us to send ye back some sinful gold, ye old sinner?

PETER. They's gold besides what's in Californi-a! (*He retreats back beyond the vision of the old man and takes the bag of money and flaunts it in the air above his head, laughing.*)

SIMEON. And sinfuller, too!

PETER. We'll be voyagin' on the sea! Whoop! (*He leaps up and down.*)

SIMEON. Livin' free! Whoop! (*He leaps in turn.*)

CABOT. (*suddenly roaring with rage*) My cuss on ye!

SIMEON. Take our'n in trade fur it! Whoop!

CABOT. I'll hev ye both chained up in the asylum!

PETER. Ye old skinflint! Good-by!

SIMEON. Ye old blood sucker! Good-by!

CABOT. Go afore I . . . !

PETER. Whoop! (*He picks a stone from the road.* SIMEON *does the same.*)

SIMEON. Maw'll be in the parlor.

PETER. Ay-eh! One! Two!

CABOT. (*frightened*) What air ye . . . ?

PETER. Three! (*They both throw, the stones hitting the parlor window with a crash of glass, tearing the shade.*)

SIMEON. Whoop!

PETER. Whoop!

CABOT. (*in a fury now, rushing toward them*) If I kin lay hands on ye—I'll break yer bones fur ye! (*But they beat a capering retreat before him,* SIMEON *with the gate still under his arm.* CABOT *comes back, panting with impotent rage. Their voices as they go off take up the song of the gold-seekers to the old tune of "Oh, Susannah!"*)

"I jumped aboard the Liza ship,
And traveled on the sea,
And every time I thought of home
I wished it wasn't me!
Oh! Californi-a,
That's the land fur me!
I'm off to Californi-a!
With my wash bowl on my knee."

(*In the meantime, the window of the upper bedroom on right is raised and* ABBIE *sticks her head out. She looks down at* CABOT*—with a sigh of relief.*)

ABBIE. Waal—that's the last o' them two, hain't it? (*He doesn't answer. Then in possessive tones*) This here's a nice bedroom, Ephraim. It's a r'al nice bed. Is it my room, Ephraim?

CABOT. (*grimly—without looking up*) Our'n! (*She cannot control a grimace of aversion and pulls back her head slowly and shuts the window. A sudden horrible thought seems to enter* CABOT'S *head*) They been up to somethin'! Mebbe—mebbe they've pizened the stock—r' somethin'! (*He almost runs off down toward the barn. A moment later the kitchen door is slowly pushed open and* ABBIE *enters. For a moment she stands looking at* EBEN. *He does not notice her at first. Her eyes take him in penetratingly with a calculating appraisal of his strength as against hers. But under this her desire is dimly awakened by his youth and good looks. Suddenly he becomes conscious of her presence and looks up. Their eyes meet. He leaps to his feet, glowering at her speechlessly.*)

ABBIE. (*in her most seductive tones which she uses all through this scene*) Be you—Eben? I'm Abbie— (*She laughs*) I mean, I'm yer new Maw.

EBEN. (*viciously*) No, damn ye!

ABBIE. (*as if she hadn't heard—with a queer smile*) Yer Paw's spoke a lot o' yew. . . .

EBEN. Ha!

ABBIE. Ye mustn't mind him. He's an old man. (*A long pause. They stare at each other*) I don't want t' pretend playin' Maw t' ye, Eben. (*Admiringly*) Ye're too big an' too strong fur that. I want t' be frens with ye. Mebbe with me fur a fren ye'd find ye'd like livin' here better. I kin make it easy fur ye with him, mebbe. (*With a scornful sense of power*) I calc'late I kin git him t' do most anythin' fur me.

EBEN. (*with bitter scorn*) Ha! (*They stare again,* EBEN *obscurely moved, physically attracted to her—in forced stilted tones*) Yew kin go t' the devil!

ABBIE. (*calmly*) If cussin' me does ye good, cuss all ye've a mind t'. I'm all prepared t' have ye agin me—at fust. I don't blame ye nuther. I'd feel the same at any stranger comin' t' take my Maw's place. (*He shudders. She is watching him carefully*) Yew must've cared a lot fur yewr Maw, didn't ye? My Maw died afore I'd growed. I don't remember her none. (*A pause*) But yew won't hate me long,

Eben. I'm not the wust in the world—an' yew an' me've got a lot in common. I kin tell that by lookin' at ye. Waal—I've had a hard life, too—oceans o' trouble an' nuthin' but wuk fur reward. I was a orphan early an' had t' wuk fur others in other folks' hums. Then I married an' he turned out a drunken spreer an' so he had to wuk fur others an' me too agen in other folks' hums, an' the baby died, an' my husband got sick an' died too, an' I was glad sayin' now I'm free fur once, on'y I diskivered right away all I was free fur was t' wuk agen in other folks' hums, doin' other folks' wuk till I'd most give up hope o' ever doin' my own wuk in my own hum, an' then your Paw come. . . . (CABOT *appears returning from the barn. He comes to the gate and looks down the road the brothers have gone. A faint strain of their retreating voices is heard: "Oh, Californi-a! That's the place for me." He stands glowering, his fist clenched, his face grim with rage.*)

EBEN. (*fighting against his growing attraction and sympathy—harshly*) An' bought yew—like a harlot! (*She is stung and flushes angrily. She has been sincerely moved by the recital of her troubles. He adds furiously*) An' the price he's payin' ye—this farm—was my Maw's, damn ye!—an' mine now!

ABBIE. (*with a cool laugh of confidence*) Yewr'n? We'll see 'bout that! (*Then strongly*) Waal—what if I did need a hum? What else'd I marry an old man like him fur?

EBEN. (*maliciously*) I'll tell him ye said that!

ABBIE. (*smiling*) I'll say ye're lyin' a-purpose—an' he'll drive ye off the place!

EBEN. Ye devil!

ABBIE. (*defying him*) This be my farm—this be my hum—this be my kitchen—!

EBEN. (*furiously, as if he were going to attack her*) Shut up, damn ye!

ABBIE. (*walks up to him—a queer coarse expression of desire in her face and body—slowly*) An' upstairs—that be my bedroom—an' my bed! (*He stares into her eyes, terribly confused and torn. She adds softly*) I hain't bad nor mean—'ceptin' fur an enemy—but I got t' fight fur what's due me out o' life, if I ever 'spect t' git it. (*Then putting her hand on his arm—seductively*) Let's yew 'n' me be frens, Eben.

EBEN. (*stupidly—as if hypnotized*) Ay-eh. (*Then furiously flinging off her arm*) No, ye durned old witch! I hate ye! (*He rushes out the door.*)

ABBIE. (*looks after him smiling satisfiedly—then half to herself, mouthing the word*) Eben's nice. (*She looks at the table, proudly*) I'll wash up *my* dishes now. (EBEN *appears outside, slamming the door behind him. He comes around corner, stops on seeing his father, and stands staring at him with hate.*)

CABOT. (*raising his arms to heaven in the fury he can no longer control*) Lord God o' Hosts, smite the undutiful sons with Thy wust cuss!

EBEN. (*breaking in violently*) Yew 'n' yewr God! Allus cussin' folks—allus naggin' 'em!

CABOT. (*oblivious to him—summoningly*) God o' the old! God o' the lonesome!

EBEN. (*mockingly*) Naggin' His sheep t' sin! T' hell with yewr God! (CABOT *turns. He and* EBEN *glower at each other.*)

CABOT. (*harshly*) So it's yew. I might've knowed it. (*Shaking his finger threateningly at him*) Blasphemin' fool! (*Then quickly*) Why hain't ye t' wuk?

EBEN. Why hain't yew? They've went. I can't wuk it all alone.

CABOT. (*contemptuously*) Nor noways! I'm wuth ten o' ye yit, old's I be! Ye'll never be more'n half a man! (*Then, matter-of-factly*) Waal—let's git t' the barn. (*They go. A last faint note of the "Californi-a" song is heard from the distance.* ABBIE *is washing her dishes.*)

CURTAIN

PART TWO—SCENE ONE

THE *exterior of the farmhouse, as in Part One—a hot Sunday afternoon two months later.* ABBIE, *dressed in her best, is discovered sitting in a rocker at the end of the porch. She rocks listlessly, enervated by the heat, staring in front of her with bored, half-closed eyes.*

EBEN *sticks his head out of his bedroom window. He looks around furtively and tries to see—or hear—if anyone is on the porch, but although he has been careful to make no noise,* ABBIE *has sensed his movement. She stops rocking, her face grows animated and eager, she waits attentively.* EBEN *seems to feel her presence, he scowls back his thoughts of her and spits with exaggerated disdain—then withdraws back into the room.* ABBIE *waits, holding her breath as she listens with passionate eagerness for every sound within the house.*

EBEN *comes out. Their eyes meet; his falter. He is confused, he turns away and slams the door resentfully. At this gesture,* ABBIE *laughs tantalizingly, amused but at the same time piqued and irritated. He scowls, strides off the porch to the path and starts to walk past her to the road with a grand swagger of ignoring her existence. He is dressed in his store suit, spruced up, his face shines from soap and water.* ABBIE *leans forward on her chair, her eyes hard and angry now, and, as he passes her, gives a sneering, taunting chuckle.*

EBEN. (*stung—turns on her furiously*) What air yew cacklin' 'bout?

ABBIE. (*triumphant*) Yew!

EBEN. What about me?

ABBIE. Ye look all slicked up like a prize bull.

EBEN. (*with a sneer*) Waal—ye hain't so durned purty yerself, be ye? (*They stare into each other's eyes, his held by hers in spite of himself, hers glowingly possessive. Their physical attraction becomes a palpable force quivering in the hot air.)*

ABBIE. (*softly*) Ye don't mean that, Eben. Ye may think ye mean it, mebbe, but ye don't. Ye can't. It's agin nature, Eben. Ye been fightin' yer nature ever since the day I come—tryin' t' tell yerself I hain't purty t'ye. (*She laughs a low humid laugh without taking her eyes from his. A pause—her body squirms desirously—she murmurs languorously*) Hain't the sun strong an' hot? Ye kin feel it burnin' into the earth—Nature—makin' thin's grow—bigger 'n' bigger—burnin' inside ye—makin' ye want t' grow—into somethin' else—till ye're jined with it—an' it's your'n—but it owns ye, too—an' makes ye grow bigger—like a tree—like them elums— (*She laughs again softly, holding his eyes. He takes a step toward her, compelled against his will*) Nature'll beat ye, Eben. Ye might's well own up t' it fust 's last.

EBEN. (*trying to break from her spell—confusedly*) If Paw'd hear ye goin' on. . . . (*Resentfully*) But ye've made such a damned idjit out o' the old devil. . . ! (ABBIE *laughs.*)

ABBIE. Waal—hain't it easier fur yew with him changed softer?

EBEN. (*defiantly*) No. I'm fightin' him—fightin' yew—fightin' fur Maw's rights t' her hum! (*This breaks her spell for him. He glowers at her*) An' I'm onto ye. Ye hain't foolin' me a mite. Ye're aimin' t' swaller up everythin' an' make it your'n. Waal, you'll find I'm a heap sight bigger hunk nor yew kin chew! (*He turns from her with a sneer.*)

ABBIE. (*trying to regain her ascendancy—seductively*) Eben!

EBEN. Leave me be! (*He starts to walk away.*)

ABBIE. (*more commandingly*) Eben!

EBEN. (*stops—resentfully*) What d'ye want?

ABBIE. (*trying to conceal a growing excitement*) Whar air ye goin'?

EBEN. (*with malicious nonchalance*) Oh—up the road a spell.

ABBIE. T' the village?

EBEN. (*airily*) Mebbe.

ABBIE. (*excitedly*) T' see that Min, I s'pose?

EBEN. Mebbe.

ABBIE. (*weakly*) What d'ye want t' waste time on her fur?

EBEN. (*revenging himself now—grinning at her*) Ye can't beat Nature, didn't ye say? (*He laughs and again starts to walk away.*)

ABBIE. (*bursting out*) An ugly old hake!

EBEN. (*with a tantalizing sneer*) She's purtier'n yew be!

ABBIE. That every wuthless drunk in the country has. . . .

EBEN. (*tauntingly*) Mebbe—but she's better'n yew. She owns up fa'r 'n' squar' t' her doin's.

ABBIE. (*furiously*) Don't ye dare compare. . . .

EBEN. She don't go sneakin' an' stealin'—what's mine.

ABBIE. (*savagely seizing on his weak point*) Your'n? Yew mean—my farm?

EBEN. I mean the farm yew sold yerself fur like any other old whore—my farm!

ABBIE. (*stung—fiercely*) Ye'll never live t' see the day when even a stinkin' weed on it'll belong t' ye! (*Then in a scream*) Git out o' my sight! Go on t' yer slut—disgracin' yer Paw 'n' me! I'll git yer Paw t' horsewhip ye off the place if I want t'! Ye're only livin' here 'cause I tolerate ye! Git along! I hate the sight o' ye! (*She stops, panting and glaring at him.*)

EBEN. (*returning her glance in kind*) An' I hate the sight o' yew! (*He turns and strides off up the road. She follows his retreating figure with concentrated hate. Old* CABOT *appears coming up from the barn. The hard, grim expression of his face has changed. He seems in some queer way softened, mellowed. His eyes have taken on a strange, incongruous dreamy quality. Yet there is no hint of physical weakness about him—rather he looks more robust and younger.* ABBIE *sees him and turns away quickly with unconcealed aversion. He comes slowly up to her.*)

CABOT. (*mildly*) War yew an' Eben quarrelin' agen?

ABBIE. (*shortly*) No.

CABOT. Ye was talkin' a'mighty loud. (*He sits down on the edge of porch.*)

ABBIE. (*snappishly*) If ye heerd us they hain't no need askin' questions.

CABOT. I didn't hear what ye said.

ABBIE. (*relieved*) Waal—it wa'n't nothin' t' speak on.

CABOT. (*after a pause*) Eben's queer.

ABBIE. (*bitterly*) He's the dead spit 'n' image o' yew!

CABOT. (*queerly interested*) D'ye think so, Abbie? (*After a pause, ruminatingly*) Me 'n' Eben's allus fit 'n' fit. I never could b'ar him noways. He's so thunderin' soft—like his Maw.

ABBIE. (*scornfully*) Ay-eh! 'Bout as soft as yew be!

CABOT. (*as if he hadn't heard*) Mebbe I been too hard on him.

ABBIE. (*jeeringly*) Waal—ye're gittin' soft now—soft as slop! That's what Eben was sayin'.

CABOT. (*his face instantly grim and ominous*) Eben was sayin'? Waal, he'd best not do nothin' t' try me 'r he'll soon diskiver. . . . (*A pause. She keeps her face turned away. His gradually softens. He stares up at the sky*) Purty, hain't it?

ABBIE. (*crossly*) I don't see nothin' purty.

CABOT. The sky. Feels like a wa'm field up thar.

ABBIE. (*sarcastically*) Air yew aimin' t' buy up over the farm too? (*She snickers contemptuously.*)

CABOT. (*strangely*) I'd like t' own my place up thar. (*A pause*) I'm gittin' old, Abbie. I'm gittin' ripe on the bough. (*A pause. She stares at him mystified. He goes on*) It's allus lonesome cold in the house—even when it's bilin' hot outside. Hain't yew noticed?

ABBIE. No.

CABOT. It's wa'm down t' the barn—nice smellin' an' warm—with the cows. (*A pause*) Cows is queer.

ABBIE. Like yew?

CABOT. Like Eben. (*A pause*) I'm gittin' t' feel resigned t' Eben—jest as I got t' feel 'bout his Maw. I'm gittin' t' learn to b'ar his softness—jest like her'n. I calc'late I c'd a'most take t' him—if he wa'n't sech a dumb fool! (*A pause*) I s'pose it's old age a-creepin' in my bones.

ABBIE. (*indifferently*) Waal—ye hain't dead yet.

CABOT. (*roused*) No, I hain't, yew bet—not by a hell of a sight—I'm sound 'n' tough as hickory! (*Then moodily*) But arter three score and ten the Lord warns ye t' prepare. (*A pause*) That's why Eben's come in my head. Now that his cussed sinful brothers is gone their path t' hell, they's no one left but Eben.

ABBIE. (*resentfully*) They's me, hain't they? (*Agitatedly*) What's all this sudden likin' ye've tuk to Eben? Why don't ye say nothin' 'bout me? Hain't I yer lawful wife?

CABOT. (*simply*) Ay-eh. Ye be. (*A pause—he stares at her desirously—his eyes grow avid—then with a sudden movement he seizes her hands and squeezes them, declaiming in a queer camp meeting preacher's tempo*) Yew air my Rose o' Sharon! Behold, yew air fair; yer eyes air doves; yer lips air like scarlet; yer two breasts air like two fawns; yer navel be like a round goblet; yer belly be like a heap o' wheat. . . . (*He covers her hand with kisses. She does not seem to notice. She stares before her with hard angry eyes.*)

ABBIE. (*jerking her hands away—harshly*) So ye're plannin' t' leave the farm t' Eben, air ye?

CABOT. (*dazedly*) Leave . . . ? (*Then with resentful obstinacy*) I hain't a-givin' it t' no one!

ABBIE. (*remorselessly*) Ye can't take it with ye.

CABOT. (*thinks a moment—then reluctantly*) No, I calc'late not. (*After a pause—with a strange passion*) But if I could, I would, by the Eternal! 'R if I could, in my dyin' hour, I'd set it afire an' watch it burn—this house an' every ear o' corn an' every tree down t' the last blade o' hay! I'd sit an' know it was all a-dying with me an' no one else'd ever own what was mine, what I'd made out o' nothin' with my own sweat 'n' blood! (*A pause—then he adds with a queer affection*) 'Ceptin' the cows. Them I'd turn free.

ABBIE. (*harshly*) An' me?

CABOT. (*with a queer smile*) Ye'd be turned free, too.

ABBIE. (*furiously*) So that's the thanks I git fur marryin' ye—t' have ye change kind to Eben who hates ye, an' talk o' turnin' me out in the road.

CABOT. (*hastily*) Abbie! Ye know I wa'n't. . . .

ABBIE. (*vengefully*) Just let me tell ye a thing or two 'bout Eben! Whar's he gone? T' see that harlot, Min! I tried fur t' stop him. Disgracin' yew an' me—on the Sabbath, too!

CABOT. (*rather guiltily*) He's a sinner—nateral-born. It's lust eatin' his heart.

ABBIE. (*enraged beyond endurance—wildly vindictive*) An' his lust fur me! Kin ye find excuses fur that?

CABOT. (*stares at her—after a dead pause*) Lust—fur yew?

ABBIE. (*defiantly*) He was tryin' t' make love t' me—when ye heerd us quarrelin'.

CABOT. (*stares at her—then a terrible expression of rage comes over his face—he springs to his feet shaking all over*) By the A'mighty God—I'll end him!

ABBIE. (*frightened now for Eben*) No! Don't ye!

CABOT. (*violently*) I'll git the shotgun an' blow his soft brains t' the top o' them elums!

ABBIE. (*throwing her arms around him*) No, Ephraim!

CABOT. (*pushing her away violently*) I will, by God!

ABBIE. (*in a quieting tone*) Listen, Ephraim. 'Twa'n't nothin' bad —on'y a boy's foolin'—'twa'n't meant serious—jest jokin' an' teasin'. . . .

CABOT. Then why did ye say—lust?

ABBIE. It must hev sounded wusser'n I meant. An' I was mad at thinkin'—ye'd leave him the farm.

CABOT. (*quieter but still grim and cruel*) Waal then, I'll horsewhip him off the place if that much'll content ye.

ABBIE. (*reaching out and taking his hand*) No. Don't think o' me!

Ye mustn't drive him off. 'Tain't sensible. Who'll ye get to help ye on the farm? They's no one hereabouts.

CABOT. (*considers this—then nodding his appreciation*) Ye got a head on ye. (*Then irritably*) Waal, let him stay. (*He sits down on the edge of the porch. She sits beside him. He murmurs contemptuously*) I oughtn't t' git riled so—at that 'ere fool calf. (*A pause*) But har's the p'int. What son o' mine'll keep on here t' the farm—when the Lord does call me? Simeon an' Peter air gone t' hell—an' Eben's follerin' 'em.

ABBIE. They's me.

CABOT. Ye're on'y a woman.

ABBIE. I'm yewr wife.

CABOT. That hain't me. A son is me—my blood—mine. Mine ought t' git mine. An' then it's still mine—even though I be six foot under. D'ye see?

ABBIE. (*giving him a look of hatred*) Ay-eh. I see. (*She becomes very thoughtful, her face growing shrewd, her eyes studying* CABOT *craftily.*)

CABOT. I'm gittin' old—ripe on the bough. (*Then with a sudden forced reassurance*) Not but what I hain't a hard nut t' crack even yet—an' fur many a year t' come! By the Etarnal, I kin break most o' the young fellers' backs at any kind o' work any day o' the year!

ABBIE. (*suddenly*) Mebbe the Lord'll give *us* a son.

CABOT. (*turns and stares at her eagerly*) Ye mean—a son—t' me 'n' yew?

ABBIE. (*with a cajoling smile*) Ye're a strong man yet, hain't ye? 'Tain't noways impossible, be it? We know that. Why d'ye stare so? Hain't ye never thought o' that afore? I been thinkin' o' it all along. Ay-eh—an' I been prayin' it'd happen, too.

CABOT. (*his face growing full of joyous pride and a sort of religious ecstasy*) Ye been prayin', Abbie?—fur a son?—t' us?

ABBIE. Ay-eh. (*With a grim resolution*) I want a son now.

CABOT. (*excitedly clutching both of her hands in his*) It'd be the blessin' o' God, Abbie—the blessin' o' God A'mighty on me—in my old age—in my lonesomeness! They hain't nothin' I wouldn't do fur ye then, Abbie. Ye'd hev on'y t' ask it—anythin' ye'd a mind t'!

ABBIE. (*interrupting*) Would ye will the farm t' me then—t' me an' it. . . ?

CABOT. (*vehemently*) I'd do anythin' ye axed, I tell ye! I swar it! May I be everlastin' damned t' hell if I wouldn't! (*He sinks to his knees pulling her down with him. He trembles all over with the fervor of his hopes*) Pray t' the Lord agen, Abbie. It's the Sabbath! I'll jine ye! Two prayers air better nor one. "An' God hearkened unto Rachel"! An' God hearkened unto Abbie! Pray, Abbie! Pray fur him to hearken! (*He bows his head, mumbling. She pretends to do likewise but gives him a side glance of scorn and triumph.*)

SCENE TWO

ABOUT *eight in the evening. The interior of the two bedrooms on the top floor is shown.* EBEN *is sitting on the side of his bed in the room on the left. On account of the heat he has taken off everything but his undershirt and pants. His feet are bare. He faces front, brooding moodily, his chin propped on his hands, a desperate expression on his face.*

In the other room CABOT *and* ABBIE *are sitting side by side on the edge of their bed, an old four-poster with feather mattress. He is in his night shirt, she in her nightdress. He is still in the queer, excited mood into which the notion of a son has thrown him. Both rooms are lighted dimly and flickeringly by tallow candles.*

CABOT. The farm needs a son.

ABBIE. I need a son.

CABOT. Ay-eh. Sometimes ye air the farm an' sometimes the farm be yew. That's why I clove t' ye in my lonesomeness. (*A pause. He pounds his knee with his fist*) Me an' the farm has got t' beget a son!

ABBIE. Ye'd best go t' sleep. Ye're gittin' thin's all mixed.

CABOT. (*with an impatient gesture*) No, I hain't. My mind's clear's a well. Ye don't know me, that's it. (*He stares hopelessly at the floor.*)

ABBIE. (*indifferently*) Mebbe. (*In the next room* EBEN *gets up and paces up and down distractedly.* ABBIE *hears him. Her eyes fasten on the intervening wall with concentrated attention.* EBEN *stops and stares. Their hot glances seem to meet through the wall. Unconsciously he stretches out his arms for her and she half rises. Then aware, he mutters a curse at himself and flings himself face downward on the bed, his clenched fists above his head, his face buried in the pillow.* ABBIE *relaxes with a faint sigh but her eyes remain fixed on the wall; she listens with all her attention for some movement from* EBEN.)

CABOT. (*suddenly raises his head and looks at her—scornfully*) Will ye ever know me—'r will any man 'r woman? (*Shaking his head*) No. I calc'late 't wa'n't t' be. (*He turns away.* ABBIE *looks at the wall. Then, evidently unable to keep silent about his thoughts, without looking at his wife, he puts out his hand and clutches her knee. She starts violently, looks at him, sees he is not watching her, concentrates again on the wall and pays no attention to what he says*) Listen, Abbie. When I come here fifty odd year ago—I was jest twenty an' the strongest an' hardest ye ever seen—ten times as strong an' fifty times as hard as Eben. Waal—this place was nothin' but fields o' stones. Folks laughed when I tuk it. They couldn't know what I knowed. When ye kin make corn sprout out o' stones, God's livin' in yew! They wa'n't strong enuf fur that! They reckoned God was easy. They laughed. They don't laugh no more. Some died hereabouts. Some went West an' died. They're all under ground—fur follerin' arter an easy God. God hain't easy. (*He shakes his head slowly*) An' I growed hard. Folks kept allus sayin' he's a hard man like 'twas sinful t' be hard, so's at last I said back at 'em: Waal then, by thunder, ye'll git me hard an' see how ye like it! (*Then suddenly*) But I give in t' weakness once. 'Twas arter I'd been here two year. I got weak—despairful—they was so many stones. They was a party leavin', givin' up, goin' West. I jined 'em. We tracked on 'n' on. We come t' broad medders, plains, whar the soil was black an' rich as gold. Nary a stone. Easy. Ye'd on'y to plow an' sow an' then set an' smoke yer pipe an' watch thin's grow. I could o' been a rich man—but somethin' in me fit me an' fit me—the voice o' God sayin': "This hain't wuth nothin' t' Me. Git ye back t' hum!" I got afeerd o' that voice an' I lit out back t' hum here, leavin' my claim an' crops t' whoever'd a mind t' take 'em. Ay-eh. I actoolly give up what was rightful mine! God's hard, not easy! God's in the stones! Build my church on a rock—out o' stones an' I'll be in them! That's what He meant t' Peter! (*He sighs heavily—a pause*) Stones. I picked 'em up an' piled 'em into walls. Ye kin read the years of my life in them walls, every day a hefted stone, climbin' over the hills up and down, fencin' in the fields that was mine, whar I'd made thin's grow out o' nothin'—like the will o' God, like the servant o' His hand. It wa'n't easy. It was hard an' He made me hard fur it. (*He pauses*) All the time I kept gittin' lonesomer. I tuk a wife. She bore Simeon an' Peter. She was a good woman. She wuked hard. We was married twenty year. She never knowed me. She helped but she never knowed what she was helpin'. I was allus lonesome. She died. After that it wa'n't so lonesome fur a spell. (*A pause*) I lost count o' the years. I had no time t' fool away countin' 'em. Sim an' Peter helped. The farm growed. It was all mine! When I thought o' that I didn't feel lonesome. (*A pause*) But ye can't hitch yer mind t' one thin' day an' night. I tuk another wife—Eben's Maw. Her folks was contestin' me at law over my deeds t' the farm—my farm! That's why Eben keeps a-talkin' his fool talk o' this bein' his Maw's farm. She bore Eben. She was purty—but soft. She tried t' be hard. She couldn't. She never knowed me nor nothin'. It was lonesomer 'n hell with her. After a matter o' sixteen odd years, she died. (*A pause*) I lived with the boys. They hated me 'cause I was hard. I hated them 'cause they was soft. They coveted the farm without knowin' what it meant. It made me bitter 'n wormwood. It aged me—them coveting what I'd made fur mine. Then this spring the call come—the voice o' God cryin' in my wilderness, in my lonesomeness—t' go out an' seek an' find! (*Turning to her with strange passion*) I sought ye an' I found ye! Yew air my Rose o' Sharon! Yer eyes air like. . . . (*She has turned a blank face, resentful eyes to his. He stares at her for a moment—then harshly*) Air ye any the wiser fur all I've told ye?

ABBIE. (*confusedly*) Mebbe.

CABOT. (*pushing her away from him—angrily*) Ye don't know nothin'—nor never will. If ye don't hev a son t' redeem ye. . . . (*This in a tone of cold threat.*)

ABBIE. (*resentfully*) I've prayed, hain't I?

CABOT. (*bitterly*) Pray agen—fur understandin'!

ABBIE. (*a veiled threat in her tone*) Ye'll have a son out o' me, I promise ye.

CABOT. How kin ye promise?

ABBIE. I got second-sight mebbe. I kin foretell. (*She gives a queer smile.*)

CABOT. I believe ye have. Ye give me the chills sometimes. (*He shivers*) It's cold in this house. It's oneasy. They's thin's pokin' about in the dark—in the corners. (*He pulls on his trousers, tucking in his night shirt, and pulls on his boots.*)

ABBIE. (*surprised*) Whar air ye goin'?

CABOT. (*queerly*) Down whar it's restful—whar it's warm—down t' the barn. (*Bitterly*) I kin talk t' the cows. They know. They know the farm an' me. They'll give me peace. (*He turns to go out the door.*)

ABBIE. (*a bit frightenedly*) Air ye ailin' tonight, Ephraim?

CABOT. Growin'. Growin' ripe on the bough. (*He turns and goes, his boots clumping down the stairs.* EBEN *sits up with a start, listening.*

ABBIE *is conscious of his movement and stares at the wall.* CABOT *comes out of the house around the corner and stands by the gate, blinking at the sky. He stretches up his hands in a tortured gesture*) God A'mighty, call from the dark! (*He listens as if expecting an answer. Then his arms drop, he shakes his head and plods off toward the barn.* EBEN *and* ABBIE *stare at each other through the wall.* EBEN *sighs heavily and* ABBIE *echoes it. Both become terribly nervous, uneasy. Finally* ABBIE *gets up and listens, her ear to the wall. He acts as if he saw every move she was making, he becomes resolutely still. She seems driven into a decision—goes out the door in rear determinedly. His eyes follow her. Then as the door of his room is opened softly, he turns away, waits in an attitude of strained fixity.* ABBIE *stands for a second staring at him, her eyes burning with desire. Then with a little cry she runs over and throws her arms about his neck, she pulls his head back and covers his mouth with kisses. At first, he submits dumbly; then he puts his arms about her neck and returns her kisses, but finally, suddenly aware of his hatred, he hurls her away from him, springing to his feet. They stand speechless and breathless, panting like two animals.*)

ABBIE. (*at last—painfully*) Ye shouldn't, Eben—ye shouldn't—I'd make ye happy!

EBEN. (*harshly*) I don't want t' be happy—from yew!

ABBIE. (*helplessly*) Ye do, Eben! Ye do! Why d'ye lie?

EBEN. (*viciously*) I don't take t'ye, I tell ye! I hate the sight o' ye!

ABBIE. (*with an uncertain troubled laugh*) Waal, I kissed ye anyways—an' ye kissed back—yer lips was burnin'—ye can't lie 'bout that! (*Intensely*) If ye don't care, why did ye kiss me back—why was yer lips burnin'?

EBEN. (*wiping his mouth*) It was like pizen on 'em. (*Then tauntingly*) When I kissed ye back, mebbe I thought 'twas someone else.

ABBIE. (*wildly*) Min?

EBEN. Mebbe.

ABBIE. (*torturedly*) Did ye go t' see her? Did ye r'ally go? I thought ye mightn't. Is that why ye throwed me off jest now?

EBEN. (*sneeringly*) What if it be?

ABBIE. (*raging*) Then ye're a dog, Eben Cabot!

EBEN. (*threateningly*) Ye can't talk that way t' me!

ABBIE. (*with a shrill laugh*) Can't I? Did ye think I was in love with ye—a weak thin' like yew? Not much! I on'y wanted ye fur a purpose o' my own—an' I'll hev ye fur it yet 'cause I'm stronger'n yew be!

EBEN. (*resentfully*) I knowed well it was on'y part o' yer plan t' swaller everythin'!

ABBIE. (*tauntingly*) Mebbe!

EBEN. (*furious*) Git out o' my room!

ABBIE. This air my room an' ye're on'y hired help!

EBEN. (*threateningly*) Git out afore I murder ye!

ABBIE. (*quite confident now*) I hain't a mite afeerd. Ye want me, don't ye? Yes, ye do! An' yer Paw's son'll never kill what he wants! Look at yer eyes! They's lust fur me in 'em, burnin' 'em up! Look at yer lips now! They're tremblin' an' longin' t' kiss me, an' yer teeth t' bite! (*He is watching her now with a horrible fascination. She laughs a crazy triumphant laugh*) I'm a-goin' t' make all o' this hum my hum! They's one room hain't mine yet, but it's a-goin' t' be tonight. I'm a-goin' down now an' light up! (*She makes him a mocking bow*) Won't ye come courtin' me in the best parlor, Mister Cabot?

EBEN. (*staring at her—horribly confused—dully*) Don't ye dare! It hain't been opened since Maw died an' was laid out thar! Don't ye. . . ! (*But her eyes are fixed on his so burningly that his will seems to wither before hers. He stands swaying toward her helplessly.*)

ABBIE. (*holding his eyes and putting all her will into her words as she backs out the door*) I'll expect ye afore long, Eben.

EBEN. (*stares after her for a while, walking toward the door. A light appears in the parlor window. He murmurs*) In the parlor? (*This seems to arouse connotations, for he comes back and puts on his white shirt, collar, half ties the tie mechanically, puts on coat, takes his hat, stands barefooted looking about him in bewilderment, mutters wonderingly*) Maw! Whar air yew? (*Then goes slowly toward the door in rear.*)

SCENE THREE

A FEW *minutes later. The interior of the parlor is shown. A grim, repressed room like a tomb in which the family has been interred alive.* ABBIE *sits on the edge of the horsehair sofa. She has lighted all the candles and the room is revealed in all its preserved ugliness. A change has come over the woman. She looks awed and frightened now, ready to run away.*

The door is opened and EBEN *appears. His face wears an expression of obsessed confusion. He stands staring at her, his arms hanging disjointedly from his shoulders, his feet bare, his hat in his hand.*

ABBIE. (*after a pause—with a nervous, formal politeness*) Won't ye set?

EBEN. (*dully*) Ay-eh. (*Mechanically he places his hat carefully on the floor near the door and sits stiffly beside her on the edge of the sofa. A pause. They both remain rigid, looking straight ahead with eyes full of fear.*)

ABBIE. When I fust come in—in the dark—they seemed somethin' here.

EBEN. (*simply*) Maw.

ABBIE. I kin still feel—somethin'. . . .

EBEN. It's Maw.

ABBIE. At fust I was feered o' it. I wanted t' yell an' run. Now—since yew come—seems like it's growin' soft an' kind t' me. (*Addressing the air—queerly*) Thank yew.

EBEN. Maw allus loved me.

ABBIE. Mebbe it knows I love yew, too. Mebbe that makes it kind t' me.

EBEN. (*dully*) I dunno. I should think she'd hate ye.

ABBIE. (*with certainty*) No. I kin feel it don't—not no more.

EBEN. Hate ye fur stealin' her place—here in her hum—settin' in her parlor whar she was laid— (*He suddenly stops, staring stupidly before him.*)

ABBIE. What is it, Eben?

EBEN. (*in a whisper*) Seems like Maw didn't want me t' remind ye.

ABBIE. (*excitedly*) I knowed, Eben! It's kind t' me! It don't b'ar me no grudges fur what I never knowed an' couldn't help!

EBEN. Maw b'ars him a grudge.

ABBIE. Waal, so does all o' us.

EBEN. Ay-eh. (*With passion*) I does, by God!

ABBIE. (*taking one of his hands in hers and patting it*) Thar! Don't git riled thinkin' o' him. Think o' yer Maw who's kind t' us. Tell me about yer Maw, Eben.

EBEN. They hain't nothin' much. She was kind. She was good.

ABBIE. (*putting one arm over his shoulder. He does not seem to notice—passionately*) I'll be kind an' good t' ye!

EBEN. Sometimes she used t' sing fur me.

ABBIE. I'll sing fur ye!

EBEN. This was her hum. This was her farm.

ABBIE. This is my hum! This is my farm!

EBEN. He married her t' steal 'em. She was soft an' easy. He couldn't 'preciate her.

ABBIE. He can't 'preciate me!

EBEN. He murdered her with his hardness.

ABBIE. He's murderin' me!

EBEN. She died. (*A pause*) Sometimes she used to sing fur me. (*He bursts into a fit of sobbing.*)

ABBIE. (*both her arms around him—with wild passion*) I'll sing fur ye! I'll die fur ye! (*In spite of her overwhelming desire for him, there is a sincere maternal love in her manner and voice—a horribly frank mixture of lust and mother love*) Don't cry, Eben! I'll take yer Maw's place! I'll be everythin' she was t' ye! Let me kiss ye, Eben! (*She pulls his head around. He makes a bewildered pretense of resistance. She is tender*) Don't be afeered! I'll kiss ye pure, Eben —same 's if I was a Maw t' ye—an' ye kin kiss me back 's if yew was my son—my boy—sayin' good-night t' me! Kiss me, Eben. (*They kiss in restrained fashion. Then suddenly wild passion overcomes her. She kisses him lustfully again and again and he flings his arms about her and returns her kisses. Suddenly, as in the bedroom, he frees himself from her violently and springs to his feet. He is trembling all over, in a strange state of terror.* ABBIE *strains her arms toward him with fierce pleading*) Don't ye leave me, Eben! Can't ye see it hain't enuf—lovin' ye like a Maw—can't ye see it's got t' be that an' more—much more—a hundred times more—fur me t' be happy—fur yew t' be happy?

EBEN. (*to the presence he feels in the room*) Maw! Maw! What d'ye want? What air ye tellin' me?

ABBIE. She's tellin' ye t' love me. She knows I love ye an' I'll be good t' ye. Can't ye feel it? Don't ye know? She's tellin' ye t' love me, Eben!

EBEN. Ay-eh. I feel—mebbe she—but—I can't figger out—why—when ye've stole her place—here in her hum—in the parlor whar she was—

ABBIE. (*fiercely*) She knows I love ye!

EBEN. (*his face suddenly lighting up with a fierce, triumphant grin*) I see it! I sees why. It's her vengeance on him—so's she kin rest quiet in her grave!

ABBIE. (*wildly*) Vengeance o' God on the hull o' us! What d'we give a durn? I love ye, Eben! God knows I love ye! (*She stretches out her arms for him.*)

EBEN. (*throws himself on his knees beside the sofa and grabs her in his arms—releasing all his pent-up passion*) An' I love ye, Abbie!—now I kin say it! I been dyin' fur want o' ye—every hour since ye come! I love ye! (*Their lips meet in a fierce, bruising kiss.*)

SCENE FOUR

EXTERIOR *of the farmhouse. It is just dawn. The front door at right is opened and* EBEN *comes out and walks around to the gate. He is dressed in his working clothes. He seems changed. His face wears a bold and confident expression, he is grinning to himself with evident satisfaction. As he gets near the gate, the window of the parlor is heard opening and the shutters are flung back and* ABBIE *sticks her head out. Her hair tumbles over her shoulders in disarray, her face is flushed, she looks at* EBEN *with tender, langourous eyes and calls softly.*)

ABBIE. Eben. (*As he turns—playfully*) Jest one more kiss afore ye go. I'm goin' to miss ye fearful all day.

EBEN. An' me yew, ye kin bet! (*He goes to her. They kiss several times. He draws away, laughingly*) Thar. That's enuf, hain't it? Ye won't hev none left fur next time.

ABBIE. I got a million o' 'em left fur yew! (*Then a bit anxiously*) D'ye r'ally love me, Eben?

EBEN. (*emphatically*) I like ye better'n any gal I ever knowed! That's gospel!

ABBIE. Likin' hain't lovin'.

EBEN. Waal then—I love ye. Now air yew satisfied?

ABBIE. Ay-eh, I be. (*She smiles at him adoringly.*)

EBEN. I better git t' the barn. The old critter's liable t' suspicion an' come sneakin' up.

ABBIE. (*with a confident laugh*) Let him! I kin allus pull the wool over his eyes. I'm goin' t' leave the shutters open and let in the sun 'n' air. This room's been dead long enuf. Now it's goin' t' be my room!

EBEN. (*frowning*) Ay-eh.

ABBIE. (*hastily*) I meant—our room.

EBEN. Ay-eh.

ABBIE. We made it our'n last night, didn't we? We give it life—our lovin' did. (*A pause.*)

EBEN. (*with a strange look*) Maw's gone back t' her grave. She kin sleep now.

ABBIE. May she rest in peace! (*Then tenderly rebuking*) Ye oughtn't t' talk o' sad thin's—this mornin'.

EBEN. It jest come up in my mind o' itself.

ABBIE. Don't let it. (*He doesn't answer. She yawns*) Waal, I'm a-goin' t' steal a wink o' sleep. I'll tell the Old Man I hain't feelin' pert. Let him git his own vittles.

EBEN. I see him comin' from the barn. Ye better look smart an' git upstairs.

ABBIE. Ay-eh. Good-by. Don't ferget me. (*She throws him a kiss. He grins—then squares his shoulders and awaits his father confidently.* CABOT *walks slowly up from the left, staring up at the sky with a vague face.*)

EBEN. (*jovially*) Mornin', Paw. Star-gazin' in daylight?

CABOT. Purty, hain't it?

EBEN. (*looking around him possessively*) It's a durned purty farm.

CABOT. I mean the sky.

EBEN. (*grinning*) How d'ye know? Them eyes o' your'n can't see that fur. (*This tickles his humor and he slaps his thigh and laughs*) Ho-ho! That's a good un!

CABOT. (*grimly sarcastic*) Ye're feelin' right chipper, hain't ye? Whar'd ye steal the likker?

EBEN. (*good-naturedly*) 'Tain't likker. Jest life. (*Suddenly holding out his hand—soberly*) Yew 'n' me is quits. Let's shake hands.

CABOT. (*suspiciously*) What's come over ye?

EBEN. Then don't. Mebbe it's jest as well. (*A moment's pause*) What's come over me? (*Queerly*) Didn't ye feel her passin'—goin' back t' her grave?

CABOT. (*dully*) Who?

EBEN. Maw. She kin rest now an' sleep content. She's quits with ye.

CABOT. (*confusedly*) I rested. I slept good—down with the cows. They know how t' sleep. They're teachin' me.

EBEN. (*suddenly jovial again*) Good fur the cows! Waal—ye better git t' work.

CABOT. (*grimly amused*) Air yew bossin' me, ye calf?

EBEN. (*beginning to laugh*) Ay-eh! I'm bossin' yew! Ha-ha-ha! See how ye like it! Ha-ha-ha! I'm the prize rooster o' this roost. Ha-ha-ha! (*He goes off toward the barn laughing.*)

CABOT. (*looks after him with scornful pity*) Soft-headed. Like his Maw. Dead spit 'n' image. No hope in him! (*He spits with contemptuous disgust*) A born fool! (*Then matter-of-factly*) Waal—I'm gittin' peckish. (*He goes toward door.*)

CURTAIN

PART THREE—SCENE ONE

A NIGHT *in late spring the following year. The kitchen and the two bedrooms upstairs are shown. The two bedrooms are dimly lighted by a tallow candle in each.* EBEN *is sitting on the side of the bed in his room, his chin propped on his fists, his face a study of the struggle he is making to understand his conflicting emotions. The noisy laughter and music from below where a kitchen dance is in progress annoy and distract him. He scowls at the floor.*

In the next room a cradle stands beside the double bed.

In the kitchen all is festivity. The stove has been taken down to give more room to the dancers. The chairs, with wooden benches added, have been pushed back against the walls. On these are seated, squeezed in tight against one another, farmers and their wives and their young folks of both sexes from the neighboring farms. They are all chattering and laughing loudly. They evidently have some secret joke in common. There is no end of winking, of nudging, of meaning nods of the head toward CABOT *who, in a state of extreme hilarious excitement increased by the amount he has drunk, is standing near the rear door where there is a small keg of whisky and serving drinks to all the men. In the left corner, front, dividing the attention with her husband,* ABBIE *is sitting in a rocking chair, a shawl wrapped about her shoulders. She is very pale, her face is thin and drawn, her eyes are fixed anxiously on the open door in rear as if waiting for someone.*

The musician is tuning up his fiddle, seated in the far right corner. He is a lanky young fellow with a long, weak face. His pale eyes blink incessantly and he grins about him slyly with a greedy malice.

ABBIE. (*suddenly turning to a young girl on her right*) Whar's Eben?

YOUNG GIRL. (*eyeing her scornfully*) I dunno, Mrs. Cabot. I hain't seen Eben in ages. (*Meaningly*) Seems like he's spent most o' his time t' hum since yew come.

ABBIE. (*vaguely*) I tuk his Maw's place.

YOUNG GIRL. Ay-eh. So I've heerd. (*She turns away to retail this bit of gossip to her mother sitting next to her.* ABBIE *turns to her left to a big stoutish middle-aged man whose flushed face and starting eyes show the amount of "likker" he has consumed.*)

ABBIE. Ye hain't seen Eben, hev ye?

MAN. No, I hain't. (*Then he adds with a wink*) If yew hain't, who would?

ABBIE. He's the best dancer in the county. He'd ought t' come an' dance.

MAN. (*with a wink*) Mebbe he's doin' the dutiful an' walkin' the kid t' sleep. It's a boy, hain't it?

ABBIE. (*nodding vaguely*) Ay-eh—born two weeks back—purty's a picter.

MAN. They all is—t' their Maws. (*Then in a whisper, with a nudge and a leer*) Listen, Abbie—if ye ever git tired o' Eben, remember me! Don't fergit now! (*He looks at her uncomprehending face for a second—then grunts disgustedly*) Waal—guess I'll likker agin. (*He goes over and joins* CABOT *who is arguing noisily with an old farmer over cows. They all drink.*)

ABBIE. (*this time appealing to nobody in particular*) Wonder what Eben's a-doin'? (*Her remark is repeated down the line with many a guffaw and titter until it reaches the fiddler. He fastens his blinking eyes on* ABBIE.)

FIDDLER. (*raising his voice*) Bet I kin tell ye, Abbie, what Eben's doin'! He's down t' the church offerin' up prayers o' thanksgivin'. (*They all titter expectantly.*)

A MAN. What fur? (*Another titter.*)

FIDDLER. 'Cause unto him a— (*He hesitates just long enough*) brother is born! (*A roar of laughter. They all look from* ABBIE *to*

CABOT. *She is oblivious, staring at the door.* CABOT, *although he hasn't heard the words, is irritated by the laughter and steps forward, glaring about him. There is an immediate silence.*)

CABOT. What're ye all bleatin' about—like a flock o' goats? Why don't ye dance, damn ye? I axed ye here t' dance—t' eat, drink an' be merry—an' thar ye set cacklin' like a lot o' wet hens with the pip! Ye've swilled my likker an' guzzled my vittles like hogs, hain't ye? Then dance fur me, can't ye? That's fa'r an' squar', hain't it? (*A grumble of resentment goes around but they are all evidently in too much awe of him to express it openly.*)

FIDDLER. (*slyly*) We're waitin' fur Eben. (*A suppressed laugh.*)

CABOT. (*with a fierce exultation*) T'hell with Eben! Eben's done fur now! I got a new son! (*His mood switching with drunken suddenness*) But ye needn't t' laugh at Eben, none o' ye! He's my blood, if he be a dumb fool. He's better nor any o' yew! He kin do a day's work a'most up t' what I kin—an' that'd put any o' yew pore critters t' shame!

FIDDLER. An' he kin do a good night's work, too! (*A roar of laughter.*)

CABOT. Laugh, ye damn fools! Ye're right jist the same, Fiddler. He kin work day an' night too, like I kin, if need be!

OLD FARMER. (*from behind the keg where he is weaving drunkenly back and forth—with great simplicity*) They hain't many t' touch ye, Ephraim—a son at seventy-six. That's a hard man fur ye! I be on'y sixty-eight an' I couldn't do it. (*A roar of laughter in which* CABOT *joins uproariously.*)

CABOT. (*slapping him on the back*) I'm sorry fur ye, Hi. I'd never suspicion sech weakness from a boy like yew!

OLD FARMER. An' I never reckoned yew had it in ye nuther, Ephraim. (*There is another laugh.*)

CABOT (*suddenly grim*) I got a lot in me—a hell of a lot—folks don't know on. (*Turning to the fiddler*) Fiddle 'er up, durn ye!

Give 'em somethin' t' dance t'! What air ye, an ornament? Hain't this a celebration? Then grease yer elbow an' go it!

FIDDLER. (*seizes a drink which the* OLD FARMER *holds out to him and downs it*) Here goes! (*He starts to fiddle "Lady of the Lake." Four young fellows and four girls form in two lines and dance a square dance. The* FIDDLER *shouts directions for the different movements, keeping his words in the rhythm of the music and interspersing them with jocular personal remarks to the dancers themselves. The people seated along the walls stamp their feet and clap their hands in unison.* CABOT *is especially active in this respect. Only* ABBIE *remains apathetic, staring at the door as if she were alone in a silent room.*)

FIDDLER. Swing your partner t' the right! That's it, Jim! Give her a b'ar hug. Her Maw hain't lookin'. (*Laughter*) Change partners! That suits ye, don't it, Essie, now ye got Reub afore ye? Look at her redden up, will ye? Waal, life is short an' so's love, as the feller says. (*Laughter.*)

CABOT. (*excitedly, stamping his foot*) Go it, boys! Go it, gals!

FIDDLER. (*with a wink at the others*) Ye're the spryest seventy-six ever I sees, Ephraim! Now if ye'd on'y good eye-sight . . . ! (*Suppressed laughter. He gives* CABOT *no chance to retort but roars*) Promenade! Ye're walkin' like a bride down the aisle, Sarah! Waal, while they's life they's allus hope, I've heerd tell. Swing your partner to the left! Gosh A'mighty, look at Johnny Cook high-steppin'! They hain't goin' t' be much strength left fur howin' in the corn lot t'morrow. (*Laughter.*)

CABOT. Go it! Go it! (*Then suddenly, unable to restrain himself any longer, he prances into the midst of the dancers, scattering them, waving his arms about wildly*) Ye're all hoofs! Git out o' my road! Give me room! I'll show ye dancin'. Ye're all too soft! (*He pushes them roughly away. They crowd back toward the walls, muttering, looking at him resentfully.*)

FIDDLER. (*jeeringly*) Go it, Ephraim! Go it! (*He starts "Pop, Goes *the Weasel," increasing the tempo with every verse until at the end he is fiddling crazily as fast as he can go.)*

CABOT. (*starts to dance, which he does very well and with tremendous vigor. Then he begins to improvise, cuts incredibly grotesque capers, leaping up and cracking his heels together, prancing around in a circle with body bent in an Indian war dance; then suddenly straightening up and kicking as high as he can with both legs. He is like a monkey on a string. And all the while he intersperses his antics with shouts and derisive comments*) Whoop! Here's dancin' fur ye! Whoop! See that! Seventy-six, if I'm a day! Hard as iron yet! Beatin' the young 'uns like I allus done! Look at me! I'd invite ye t' dance on my hundredth birthday on'y ye'll all be dead by then. Ye're a sickly generation! Yer hearts air pink, not red! Yer veins is full o' mud an' water! I be the on'y man in the county! Whoop! See that! I'm a Injun! I've killed Injuns in the West afore ye was born—an' skulped 'em too! They's a arrer wound on my backside I c'd show ye! The hull tribe chased me. I outrun 'em all—with the arrer stuck in me! An' I tuk vengeance on 'em. Ten eyes fur an eye, that was my motter! Whoop! Look at me! I kin kick the ceilin' off the room! Whoop!

FIDDLER. (*stops playing—exhaustedly*) God A'mighty, I got enuf. Ye got the devil's strength in ye.

CABOT. (*delightedly*) Did I beat yew, too? Waal, ye played smart. Hev a swig. (*He pours whisky for himself and* FIDDLER. *They drink. The others watch* CABOT *silently with cold, hostile eyes. There is a dead pause. The* FIDDLER *rests.* CABOT *leans against the keg, panting, glaring around him confusedly. In the room above,* EBEN *gets to his feet and tiptoes out the door in rear, appearing a moment later in the other bedroom. He moves silently, even frightenedly, toward the cradle and stands there looking down at the baby. His face is as vague as his reactions are confused, but there is a trace of tenderness, of interested discovery. At the same moment that he reaches the cradle,*

ABBIE *seems to sense something. She gets up weakly and goes, to* CABOT.)

ABBIE. I'm goin' up t' the baby.

CABOT. (*with real solicitation*) Air ye able fur the stairs? D'ye want me t' help ye, Abbie?

ABBIE. No. I'm able. I'll be down agen soon.

CABOT. Don't ye git wore out! He needs ye, remember—our son does! (*He grins affectionately, patting her on the back. She shrinks from his touch.*)

ABBIE. (*dully*) Don't—tech me. I'm goin'—up. (*She goes.* CABOT *looks after her. A whisper goes around the room.* CABOT *turns. It ceases. He wipes his forehead streaming with sweat. He is breathing pantingly.*)

CABOT. I'm a-goin' out t' git fresh air. I'm feelin' a mite dizzy. Fiddle up thar! Dance, all o' ye! Here's likker fur them as wants it. Enjoy yerselves. I'll be back. (*He goes, closing the door behind him.*)

FIDDLER. (*sarcastically*) Don't hurry none on our account! (*A suppressed laugh. He imitates* ABBIE) Whar's Eben? (*More laughter.*)

A WOMAN. (*loudly*) What's happened in this house is plain as the nose on yer face! (ABBIE *appears in the doorway upstairs and stands looking in surprise and adoration at* EBEN *who does not see her.*)

A MAN. Ssshh! He's li'ble t' be listenin' at the door. That'd be like him. (*Their voices die to an intensive whispering. Their faces are concentrated on this gossip. A noise as of dead leaves in the wind comes from the room.* CABOT *has come out from the porch and stands by the gate, leaning on it, staring at the sky blinkingly.* ABBIE *comes across the room silently.* EBEN *does not notice her until quite near.*)

EBEN. (*starting*) Abbie!

ABBIE. Ssshh! (*She throws her arms around him. They kiss—then bend over the cradle together*) Ain't he purty?—dead spit 'n' image o' yew!

EBEN. (*pleased*) Air he? I can't tell none.

ABBIE. E-zactly like!

EBEN. (*frowningly*) I don't like this. I don't like lettin' on what's mine's his'n. I been doin' that all my life. I'm gittin' t' the end o' b'arin' it!

ABBIE. (*putting her finger on his lips*) We're doin' the best we kin. We got t' wait. Somethin's bound t' happen. (*She puts her arms around him*) I got t' go back.

EBEN. I'm goin' out. I can't b'ar it with the fiddle playin' an' the laughin'.

ABBIE. Don't git feelin' low. I love ye, Eben. Kiss me. (*He kisses her. They remain in each other's arms.*)

CABOT. (*at the gate, confusedly*) Even the music can't drive it out—somethin'. Ye kin feel it droppin' off the elums, climbin' up the roof, sneakin' down the chimney, pokin' in the corners! They's no peace in houses, they's no rest livin' with folks. Somethin's always livin' with ye. (*With a deep sigh*) I'll go t' the barn an' rest a spell. (*He goes wearily toward the barn.*)

FIDDLER. (*tuning up*) Let's celebrate the old skunk gittin' fooled! We kin have some fun now he's went. (*He starts to fiddle "Turkey in the Straw." There is real merriment now. The young folks get up to dance.*)

SCENE TWO

A HALF *hour later—Exterior—*EBEN *is standing by the gate looking up at the sky, an expression of dumb pain bewildered by itself on his face.* CABOT *appears, returning from the barn, walking wearily, his eyes on the ground. He sees* EBEN *and his whole mood immediately changes. He becomes excited, a cruel, triumphant grin comes to his lips, he strides up and slaps* EBEN *on the back. From within comes the whining of the fiddle and the noise of stamping feet and laughing voices.*

CABOT. So har ye be!

EBEN. (*startled, stares at him with hatred for a moment—then dully*) Ay-eh.

CABOT. (*surveying him jeeringly*) Why hain't ye been in t' dance? They was all axin' fur ye.

EBEN. Let 'em ax!

CABOT. They's a hull passel o' purty gals.

EBEN. T' hell with 'em!

CABOT. Ye'd ought t' be marryin' one o' 'em soon.

EBEN. I hain't marryin' no one.

CABOT. Ye might 'arn a share o' a farm that way.

EBEN. (*with a sneer*) Like yew did, ye mean? I hain't that kind.

CABOT. (*stung*) Ye lie! 'Twas yer Maw's folks aimed t' steal my farm from me.

EBEN. Other folks don't say so. (*After a pause—defiantly*) An' I got a farm, anyways!

CABOT. (*derisively*) Whar?

EBEN. (*stamps a foot on the ground*) Har!

CABOT. (*throws his head back and laughs coarsely*) Ho-ho! Ye hev, hev ye? Waal, that's a good un!

EBEN. (*controlling himself—grimly*) Ye'll see!

CABOT. (*stares at him suspiciously, trying to make him out—a pause —then with scornful confidence*) Ay-eh. I'll see. So'll ye. It's ye that's blind—blind as a mole underground. (EBEN *suddenly laughs, one short sardonic bark: "Ha." A pause.* CABOT *peers at him with renewed suspicion*) What air ye hawin' 'bout? (EBEN *turns away without answering.* CABOT *grows angry*) God A'mighty, yew air a dumb dunce! They's nothin' in that thick skull o' your'n but noise—like a empty keg it be! (EBEN *doesn't seem to hear.* CABOT'*s rage grows*) Yewr farm! God A'mighty! If ye wa'n't a born donkey ye'd know ye'll never own stick nor stone on it, specially now arter him bein' born. It's his'n, I tell ye—his'n arter I die—but I'll live a hundred jest t' fool ye all—an' he'll be growed then—yewr age a'most! (EBEN *laughs again his sardonic "Ha." This drives* CABOT *into a fury*) Ha? Ye think ye kin git 'round that someways, do ye? Waal, it'll be her'n, too—Abbie's—ye won't git 'round her—she knows yer tricks—she'll be too much fur ye—she wants the farm her'n—she was afeerd o' ye—she told me ye was sneakin' 'round tryin' t' make love t' her t' git her on yer side . . . ye . . . ye mad fool, ye! (*He raises his clenched fists threateningly.*)

EBEN. (*is confronting him, choking with rage*) Ye lie, ye old skunk! Abbie never said no sech thing!

CABOT. (*suddenly triumphant when he sees how shaken* EBEN *is*) She did. An' I says, I'll blow his brains t' the top o' them elums—an' she says no, that hain't sense, who'll ye git t'help ye on the farm in his place—an' then she says yew'n me ought t' have a son—I know we kin, she says—an' I says, if we do, ye kin have anythin' I've got ye've a mind t'. An' she says, I wants Eben cut off so's this farm'll be mine when ye die! (*With terrible gloating*) An' that's what's happened, hain't it? An' the farm's her'n! An' the dust o' the road—that's you'rn! Ha! Now who's hawin'?

EBEN. (*has been listening, petrified with grief and rage—suddenly laughs wildly and brokenly*) Ha-ha-ha! So that's her sneakin' game—all along!—like I suspicioned at fust—t' swaller it all—an' me, too . . . ! (*Madly*) I'll murder her! (*He springs toward the porch but* CABOT *is quicker and gets in between.*)

CABOT. No, ye don't!

EBEN. Git out o' my road! (*He tries to throw* CABOT *aside. They grapple in what becomes immediately a murderous struggle. The old man's concentrated strength is too much for* EBEN. CABOT *gets one hand on his throat and presses him back across the stone wall. At the same moment,* ABBIE *comes out on the porch. With a stifled cry she runs toward them.*)

ABBIE. Eben! Ephraim! (*She tugs at the hand on* EBEN's *throat*) Let go, Ephraim! Ye're chokin' him!

CABOT. (*removes his hand and flings* EBEN *sideways full length on the grass, gasping and choking. With a cry,* ABBIE *kneels beside him, trying to take his head on her lap, but he pushes her away.* CABOT *stands looking down with fierce triumph*) Ye needn't t've fret, Abbie, I wa'n't aimin' t' kill him. He hain't wuth hangin' fur—not by a hell of a sight! (*More and more triumphantly*) Seventy-six an' him not thirty yit—an' look whar he be fur thinkin' his Paw was easy! No, by God, I hain't easy! An' him upstairs, I'll raise him t' be like me! (*He turns to leave them*) I'm goin' in an' dance!—sing an' celebrate! (*He walks to the porch—then turns with a great grin*) I don't calc'late it's left in him, but if he gits pesky, Abbie, ye jest sing out. I'll come a-runnin' an' by the Etarnal, I'll put him across my knee an' birch him! Ha-ha-ha! (*He goes into the house laughing. A moment later his loud "whoop" is heard.*)

ABBIE. (*tenderly*) Eben. Air ye hurt? (*She tries to kiss him but he pushes her violently away and struggles to a sitting position.*)

EBEN. (*gaspingly*) T'hell—with ye!

ABBIE. (*not believing her ears*) It's me, Eben—Abbie—don't ye know me?

EBEN. (*glowering at her with hatred*) Ay-eh—I know ye—now! (*He suddenly breaks down, sobbing weakly.*)

ABBIE. (*fearfully*) Eben—what's happened t' ye—why did ye look at me 's if ye hated me?

EBEN. (*violently, between sobs and gasps*) I do hate ye! Ye're a whore—a damn trickin' whore!

ABBIE. (*shrinking back horrified*) Eben! Ye don't know what ye're sayin'!

EBEN. (*scrambling to his feet and following her—accusingly*) Ye're nothin' but a stinkin' passel o' lies! Ye've been lyin' t' me every word ye spoke, day an' night, since we fust—done it. Ye've kept sayin' ye loved me. . . .

ABBIE. (*frantically*) I do love ye! (*She takes his hand but he flings hers away.*)

EBEN. (*unheeding*) Ye've made a fool o' me—a sick, dumb fool—

a-purpose! Ye've been on'y playin' yer sneakin', stealin' game all along—gittin' me t' lie with ye so's ye'd hev a son he'd think was his'n, an' makin' him promise he'd give ye the farm and let me eat dust, if ye did git him a son! (*Staring at her with anguished, bewildered eyes*) They must be a devil livin' in ye! T'ain't human t' be as bad as that be!

ABBIE. (*stunned—dully*) He told yew . . . ?

EBEN. Hain't it true? It hain't no good in yew lyin'.

ABBIE. (*pleadingly*) Eben, listen—ye must listen—it was long ago —afore we done nothin'—yew was scornin' me—goin' t' see Min— when I was lovin' ye—an' I said it t' him t' git vengeance on ye!

EBEN. (*unheedingly. With tortured passion*) I wish ye was dead! I wish I was dead along with ye afore this come! (*Ragingly*) But I'll git my vengeance too! I'll pray Maw t' come back t' help me—t' put her cuss on yew an' him!

ABBIE. (*brokenly*) Don't ye, Eben! Don't ye! (*She throws herself on her knees before him, weeping*) I didn't mean t' do bad t'ye! Fergive me, won't ye?

EBEN. (*not seeming to hear her—fiercely*) I'll git squar' with the old skunk—an' yew! I'll tell him the truth 'bout the son he's so proud o'! Then I'll leave ye here t' pizen each other—with Maw comin' out o' her grave at nights—an' I'll go t' the gold fields o' Californi-a whar Sim an' Peter be!

ABBIE. (*terrified*) Ye won't—leave me? Ye can't!

EBEN. (*with fierce determination*) I'm a-goin', I tell ye! I'll git rich thar an' come back an' fight him fur the farm he stole—an' I'll kick ye both out in the road—t' beg an' sleep in the woods—an' yer son along with ye—t' starve an' die! (*He is hysterical at the end.*)

ABBIE. (*with a shudder—humbly*) He's yewr son, too, Eben.

EBEN. (*torturedly*) I wish he never was born! I wish he'd die this minit! I wish I'd never sot eyes on him! It's him—yew havin' him— a-purpose t' steal—that's changed everythin'!

ABBIE. (*gently*) Did ye believe I loved ye—afore he come?

EBEN. Aye-eh—like a dumb ox!

ABBIE. An' ye don't believe no more?

EBEN. B'lieve a lyin' thief! Ha!

ABBIE. (*shudders—then humbly*) An' did ye r'ally love me afore?

EBEN. (*brokenly*) Ay-eh—an' ye was trickin' me!

ABBIE. An' ye don't love me now!

EBEN. (*violently*) I hate ye, I tell ye!

ABBIE. An' ye're truly goin' West—goin' t' leave me—all account o' him being born?

EBEN. I'm a-goin' in the mornin'—or may God strike me t' hell!

ABBIE. (*after a pause—with a dreadful cold intensity—slowly*) If that's what his comin's done t' me—killin' yewr love—takin' yew away—my on'y joy—the on'y joy I ever knowed—like heaven t' me—purtier'n heaven—then I hate him, too, even if I be his Maw!

EBEN. (*bitterly*) Lies! Ye love him! He'll steal the farm fur ye! (*Brokenly*) But t'ain't the farm so much—not no more—it's yew foolin' me—gittin' me t' love ye—lyin' yew loved me—jest t' git a son t' steal!

ABBIE. (*distractedly*) He won't steal! I'd kill him fust! I do love ye! I'll prove t' ye . . . !

EBEN. (*harshly*) T'ain't no use lyin' no more. I'm deaf t' ye! (*He turns away*) I hain't seein' ye agen. Good-by!

ABBIE. (*pale with anguish*) Hain't ye even goin' t' kiss me—not once—arter all we loved?

EBEN. (*in a hard voice*) I hain't wantin' t' kiss ye never agen! I'm wantin' t' forgit I ever sot eyes on ye!

ABBIE. Eben!—ye mustn't—wait a spell—I want t' tell ye. . . .

EBEN. I'm a-goin' in t' git drunk. I'm a-goin' t' dance.

ABBIE. (*clinging to his arm—with passionate earnestness*) If I could make it—'s if he'd never come up between us—if I could prove t' ye I wa'n't schemin' t' steal from ye—so's everythin' could be jest the same with us, lovin' each other jest the same, kissin' an' happy the same's we've been happy afore he come—if I could do it—ye'd love me agen, wouldn't ye? Ye'd kiss me agen? Ye wouldn't never leave me, would ye?

EBEN. (*moved*) I calc'late not. (*Then shaking her hand off his arm —with a bitter smile*) But ye hain't God, be ye?

ABBIE. (*exultantly*) Remember ye've promised! (*Then with strange intensity*) Mebbe I kin take back one thin' God does!

EBEN. (*peering at her*) Ye're gittin' cracked, hain't ye? (*Then going towards door*) I'm a-goin' t' dance.

ABBIE. (*calls after him intensely*) I'll prove t' ye! I'll prove I love ye better'n. . . . (*He goes in the door, not seeming to hear. She remains standing where she is, looking after him—then she finishes desperately*) Better'n everythin' else in the world!

SCENE THREE

Just before dawn in the morning—shows the kitchen and CABOT'S *bedroom. In the kitchen, by the light of a tallow candle on the table,* EBEN *is sitting, his chin propped on his hands, his drawn face blank and expressionless. His carpetbag is on the floor beside him. In the bedroom, dimly lighted by a small whale-oil lamp,* CABOT *lies asleep.* ABBIE *is bending over the cradle, listening, her face full of terror yet with an undercurrent of desperate triumph. Suddenly, she breaks down and sobs, appears about to throw herself on her knees beside the cradle; but the old man turns restlessly, groaning in his sleep, and she controls herself, and, shrinking away from the cradle with a gesture of horror, backs swiftly toward the door in rear and goes out. A moment later she comes into the kitchen and, running to* EBEN, *flings her arms about his neck and kisses him wildly. He hardens himself, he remains unmoved and cold, he keeps his eyes straight ahead.*

ABBIE. (*hysterically*) I done it, Eben! I told ye I'd do it! I've proved I love ye—better'n everythin'—so's ye can't never doubt me no more!

EBEN. (*dully*) Whatever ye done, it hain't no good now.

ABBIE. (*wildly*) Don't ye say that! Kiss me, Eben, won't ye? I need ye t' kiss me arter what I done! I need ye t' say ye love me!

EBEN. (*kisses her without emotion—dully*) That's fur good-by. I'm a-goin' soon.

ABBIE. No! No! Ye won't go—not now!

EBEN. (*going on with his own thoughts*) I been a-thinkin'—an' I hain't goin' t' tell Paw nothin'. I'll leave Maw t' take vengeance on ye. If I told him, the old skunk'd jest be stinkin' mean enuf to take it out on that baby. (*His voice showing emotion in spite of him*) An' I don't want nothin' bad t' happen t' him. He hain't t' blame fur yew. (*He adds with a certain queer pride*) An' he looks like me! An' by God, he's mine! An' some day I'll be a-comin' back an' . . . !

ABBIE. (*too absorbed in her own thoughts to listen to him—pleadingly*) They's no cause fur ye t' go now—they's no sense—it's all the same's it was—they's nothin' come b'tween us now—arter what I done!

EBEN. (*something in her voice arouses him. He stares at her a bit frightenedly*) Ye look mad, Abbie. What did ye do?

ABBIE. I—I killed him, Eben.

EBEN. (*amazed*) Ye killed him?

ABBIE. (*dully*) Ay-eh.

EBEN. (*recovering from his astonishment—savagely*) An' serves him right! But we got t' do somethin' quick t' make it look s'if the old skunk'd killed himself when he was drunk. We kin prove by 'em all how drunk he got.

ABBIE. (*wildly*) No! No! Not him! (*Laughing distractedly*) But that's what I ought t' done, hain't it? I oughter killed him instead! Why didn't ye tell me?

EBEN. (*appalled*) Instead? What d'ye mean?

ABBIE. Not him.

EBEN. (*his face grown ghastly*) Not—not that baby!

ABBIE. (*dully*) Ay-eh!

EBEN. (*falls to his knees as if he'd been struck—his voice trembling with horror*) Oh, God A'mighty! A'mighty God! Maw, whar was ye, why didn't ye stop her?

ABBIE. (*simply*) She went back t' her grave that night we fust done it, remember? I hain't felt her about since. (*A pause.* EBEN *hides his head in his hands, trembling all over as if he had the ague. She goes on dully*) I left the piller over his little face. Then he killed himself. He stopped breathin'. (*She begins to weep softly.*)

EBEN. (*rage beginning to mingle with grief*) He looked like me. He was mine, damn ye!

ABBIE. (*slowly and brokenly*) I didn't want t' do it. I hated myself fur doin' it. I loved him. He was so purty—dead spit 'n' image o' yew. But I loved yew more—an' yew was goin' away—far off whar I'd never see ye agen, never kiss ye, never feel ye pressed agin me agen—an' ye said ye hated me fur havin' him—ye said ye hated him an' wished he was dead—ye said if it hadn't been fur him comin' it'd be the same's afore between us.

EBEN. (*unable to endure this, springs to his feet in a fury, threatening her, his twitching fingers seeming to reach out for her throat*) Ye lie! I never said—I never dreamed ye'd—I'd cut off my head afore I'd hurt his finger!

ABBIE. (*piteously, sinking on her knees*) Eben, don't ye look at me like that—hatin' me—not after what I done fur ye—fur us—so's we could be happy agen—

EBEN. (*furiously now*) Shut up, or I'll kill ye! I see yer game now—the same old sneakin' trick—ye're aimin' t' blame me fur the murder ye done!

ABBIE. (*moaning—putting her hands over her ears*) Don't ye, Eben! Don't ye! (*She grasps his legs.*)

EBEN. (*his mood suddenly changing to horror, shrinks away from her*) Don't ye tech me! Ye're pizen! How could ye—t' murder a pore little critter— Ye must've swapped yer soul t' hell! (*Suddenly raging*) Ha! I kin see why ye done it! Not the lies ye jest told—but 'cause ye wanted t' steal agen—steal the last thin' ye'd left me—my part o' him—no, the hull o' him—ye saw he looked like me—ye knowed he was all mine—an' ye couldn't b'ar it—I know ye! Ye killed him fur bein' mine! (*All this has driven him almost insane. He makes a rush past her for the door—then turns—shaking both fists at her, violently*) But I'll take vengeance now! I'll git the Sheriff! I'll tell him everythin'! Then I'll sing "I'm off to Californi-a!" an' go —gold—Golden Gate—gold sun—fields o' gold in the West! (*This last he half shouts, half croons incoherently, suddenly breaking off passionately*) I'm a-goin' fur the Sheriff t' come an' git ye! I want ye tuk away, locked up from me! I can't stand t' luk at ye! Murderer an' thief 'r not, ye still tempt me! I'll give ye up t' the Sheriff! (*He turns and runs out, around the corner of house, panting and sobbing, and breaks into a swerving sprint down the road.*)

ABBIE. (*struggling to her feet, runs to the door, calling after him*) I love ye, Eben! I love ye! (*She stops at the door weakly, swaying, about to fall*) I don't care what ye do—if ye'll on'y love me agen— (*She falls limply to the floor in a faint.*)

SCENE FOUR

ABOUT *an hour later. Same as Scene Three. Shows the kitchen and* CABOT'S *bedroom. It is after dawn. The sky is brilliant with the sunrise. In the kitchen,* ABBIE *sits at the table, her body limp and exhausted, her head bowed down over her arms, her face hidden. Upstairs,* CABOT *is still asleep but awakens with a start. He looks toward the window and gives a snort of surprise and irritation—throws back the covers and begins hurriedly pulling on his clothes.*

Without looking behind him, he begins talking to ABBIE *whom he supposes beside him.*

CABOT. Thunder 'n' lightin', Abbie! I hain't slept this late in fifty year! Looks 's if the sun was full riz a'most. Must've been the dancin' an' likker. Must be gittin' old. I hope Eben's t' wuk. Ye might've tuk the trouble t' rouse me, Abbie. (*He turns—sees no one there—surprised*) Waal—whar air she? Gittin' vittles, I calc'late. (*He tiptoes to the cradle and peers down—proudly*) Mornin', sonny. Purty's a picter! Sleepin' sound. He don't beller all night like most o' 'em. (*He goes quietly out the door in rear—a few moments later enters kitchen —sees* ABBIE*—with satisfaction*) So thar ye be. Ye got any vittles cooked?

ABBIE. (*without moving*) No.

CABOT. (*coming to her, almost sympathetically*) Ye feelin' sick?

ABBIE. No.

CABOT. (*pats her on shoulder. She shudders*) Ye'd best lie down a spell. (*Half jocularly*) Yer son'll be needin' ye soon. He'd ought t' wake up with a gnashin' appetite, the sound way he's sleepin'.

ABBIE. (*shudders—then in a dead voice*) He hain't never goin' t' wake up.

CABOT. (*jokingly*) Takes after me this mornin'. I hain't slept so late in . . .

ABBIE. He's dead.

CABOT. (*stares at her—bewilderedly*) What. . . .

ABBIE. I killed him.

CABOT. (*stepping back from her—aghast*) Air ye drunk—'r crazy—'r . . . !

ABBIE. (*suddenly lifts her head and turns on him—wildly*) I killed him, I tell ye! I smothered him. Go up an' see if ye don't b'lieve me! (CABOT *stares at her a second, then bolts out the rear door, can be heard bounding up the stairs, and rushes into the bedroom and over to the cradle.* ABBIE *has sunk back lifelessly into her former position.*

CABOT *puts his hand down on the body in the crib. An expression of fear and horror comes over his face.*)

CABOT. (*shrinking away—tremblingly*) God A'mighty! God A'mighty. (*He stumbles out the door—in a short while returns to the kitchen—comes to* ABBIE, *the stunned expression still on his face—hoarsely*) Why did ye do it? Why? (*As she doesn't answer, he grabs her violently by the shoulder and shakes her*) I ax ye why ye done it! Ye'd better tell me 'r . . . !

ABBIE. (*gives him a furious push which sends him staggering back and springs to her feet—with wild rage and hatred*) Don't ye dare tech me! What right hev ye t' question me 'bout him? He wa'n't yewr son! Think I'd have a son by yew? I'd die fust! I hate the sight o' ye an' allus did! It's yew I should've murdered, if I'd had good sense! I hate ye! I love Eben. I did from the fust. An' he was Eben's son—mine an' Eben's—not your'n!

CABOT. (*stands looking at her dazedly—a pause—finding his words with an effort—dully*) That was it—what I felt—pokin' round the corners—while ye lied—holdin' yerself from me—sayin' ye'd a'ready conceived— (*He lapses into crushed silence—then with a strange emotion*) He's dead, sart'n. I felt his heart. Pore little critter! (*He blinks back one tear, wiping his sleeve across his nose.*)

ABBIE. (*hysterically*) Don't ye! Don't ye! (*She sobs unrestrainedly.*)

CABOT. (*with a concentrated effort that stiffens his body into a rigid line and hardens his face into a stony mask—through his teeth to himself*) I got t' be—like a stone—a rock o' jedgment! (*A pause. He gets complete control over himself—harshly*) If he was Eben's, I be glad he air gone! An' mebbe I suspicioned it all along. I felt they was somethin' onnateral—somewhars—the house got so lonesome—an' cold—drivin' me down t' the barn—t' the beasts o' the field. . . . Ay-eh. I must've suspicioned—somethin'. Ye didn't fool me—not altogether, leastways—I'm too old a bird—growin' ripe on the bough. . . . (*He becomes aware he is wandering, straightens again, looks at* ABBIE *with a cruel grin*) So ye'd liked t' hev murdered me 'stead o' him, would ye? Waal, I'll live to a hundred! I'll live t' see ye hung! I'll deliver ye up t' the jedgment o' God an' the law! I'll git the Sheriff now. (*Starts for the door.*)

ABBIE. (*dully*) Ye needn't. Eben's gone fur him.

CABOT. (*amazed*) Eben—gone fur the Sheriff?

ABBIE. Ay-eh.

CABOT. T' inform agen ye?

ABBIE. Ay-eh.

CABOT. (*considers this—a pause—then in a hard voice*) Waal, I'm thankful fur him savin' me the trouble. I'll git t' wuk. (*He goes to the door—then turns—in a voice full of strange emotion*) He'd ought t' been my son, Abbie. Ye'd ought t' loved me. I'm a man. If ye'd loved me, I'd never told no Sheriff on ye no matter what ye did, if they was t' brile me alive!

ABBIE. (*defensively*) They's more to it nor yew know, makes him tell.

CABOT. (*dryly*) Fur yewr sake, I hope they be. (*He goes out—comes around to the gate—stares up at the sky. His control relaxes. For a moment he is old and weary. He murmurs despairingly*) God A'mighty, I be lonesomer'n ever! (*He hears running footsteps from the left, immediately is himself again.* EBEN *runs in, panting exhaustedly, wild-eyed and mad looking. He lurches through the gate.* CABOT *grabs him by the shoulder.* EBEN *stares at him dumbly*) Did ye tell the Sheriff?

EBEN. (*nodding stupidly*) Ay-eh.

CABOT. (*gives him a push away that sends him sprawling—laughing with withering contempt*) Good fur ye! A prime chip o' yer Maw ye be! (*He goes toward the barn, laughing harshly.* EBEN *scrambles to his feet. Suddenly* CABOT *turns—grimly threatening*) Git off this farm when the Sheriff takes her—or, by God, he'll have t' come back an' git me fur murder, too! (*He stalks off.* EBEN *does not appear to have heard him. He runs to the door and comes into the kitchen.*

ABBIE *looks up with a cry of anguished joy.* EBEN *stumbles over and throws himself on his knees beside her sobbing brokenly.*)

EBEN. Fergive me!

ABBIE. (*happily*) Eben! (*She kisses him and pulls his head over against her breast.*)

EBEN. I love ye! Fergive me!

ABBIE. (*ecstatically*) I'd fergive ye all the sins in hell fur sayin' that! (*She kisses his head, pressing it to her with a fierce passion of possession.*)

EBEN. (*brokenly*) But I told the Sheriff. He's comin' fur ye!

ABBIE. I kin b'ar what happens t' me—now!

EBEN. I woke him up. I told him. He says, wait 'til I git dressed. I was waiting. I got to thinkin' o' yew. I got to thinkin' how I'd loved ye. It hurt like somethin' was bustin' in my chest an' head. I got t' cryin'. I knowed sudden I loved ye yet, an' allus would love ye!

ABBIE. (*caressing his hair—tenderly*) My boy, hain't ye?

EBEN. I begun t' run back. I cut across the fields an' through the woods. I thought ye might have time t' run away—with me—an' . . .

ABBIE. (*shaking her head*) I got t' take my punishment—t' pay fur my sin.

EBEN. Then I want t' share it with ye.

ABBIE. Ye didn't do nothin'.

EBEN. I put it in yer head. I wisht he was dead! I as much as urged ye t' do it!

ABBIE. No. It was me alone!

EBEN. I'm as guilty as yew be! He was the child o' our sin.

ABBIE. (*lifting her head as if defying God*) I don't repent that sin! I hain't askin' God t' fergive that!

EBEN. Nor me—but it led up t' the other—an' the murder ye did, ye did 'count o' me—an' it's my murder, too, I'll tell the Sheriff—an' if ye deny it, I'll say we planned it t'gether—an' they'll all b'lieve me, fur they suspicion everythin' we've done, an' it'll seem likely an' true to 'em. An' it is true—way down. I did help ye—somehow.

ABBIE. (*laying her head on his—sobbing*) No! I don't want yew t' suffer!

EBEN. I got t' pay fur my part o' the sin! An' I'd suffer wuss leavin' ye, goin' West, thinkin' o' ye day an' night, bein' out when yew was in— (*Lowering his voice*) 'r bein' alive when yew was dead. (*A pause*) I want t' share with ye, Abbie—prison 'r death 'r hell 'r anythin'! (*He looks into her eyes and forces a trembling smile*) If I'm sharin' with ye, I won't feel lonesome, leastways.

ABBIE. (*weakly*) Eben! I won't let ye! I can't let ye!

EBEN. (*kissing her—tenderly*) Ye can't he'p yerself. I got ye beat fur once!

ABBIE. (*forcing a smile—adoringly*) I hain't beat—s'long's I got ye!

EBEN. (*hears the sound of feet outside*) Ssshh! Listen! They've come t' take us!

ABBIE. No, it's him. Don't give him no chance to fight ye, Eben. Don't say nothin'—no matter what he says. An' I won't neither. (*It is* CABOT. *He comes up from the barn in a great state of excitement and strides into the house and then into the kitchen.* EBEN *is kneeling beside* ABBIE, *his arm around her, hers around him. They stare straight ahead.*)

CABOT. (*stares at them, his face hard. A long pause—vindictively*) Ye make a slick pair o' murderin' turtle doves! Ye'd ought t' be both hung on the same limb an' left thar t' swing in the breeze an' rot—a warnin' t' old fools like me t' b'ar their lonesomeness alone—an' fur young fools like ye t' hobble their lust. (*A pause. The excitement returns to his face, his eyes snap, he looks a bit crazy*) I couldn't work today. I couldn't take no interest. T' hell with the farm! I'm leavin' it! I've turned the cows an' other stock loose! I've druv 'em into the woods whar they kin be free! By freein' 'em, I'm freein' myself! I'm quittin' here today! I'll set fire t' house an' barn an' watch 'em burn, an' I'll leave yer Maw t' haunt the ashes, an' I'll will the fields back t'

God, so that nothin' human kin never touch 'em! I'll be a-goin' to Californi-a—t' jine Simeon an' Peter—true sons o' mine if they be dumb fools—an' the Cabots'll find Solomon's Mines t'gether! (*He suddenly cuts a mad caper*) Whoop! What was the song they sung? "Oh, Californi-a! That's the land fur me." (*He sings this—then gets on his knees by the floor-board under which the money was hid*) An' I'll sail thar on one o' the finest clippers I kin find! I've got the money! Pity ye didn't know whar this was hidden so's ye could steal. . . . (*He has pulled up the board. He stares—feels—stares again. A pause of dead silence. He slowly turns, slumping into a sitting position on the floor, his eyes like those of a dead fish, his face the sickly green of an attack of nausea. He swallows painfully several times—forces a weak smile at last*) So—ye did steal it!

EBEN. (*emotionlessly*) I swapped it t' Sim an' Peter fur their share o' the farm—t' pay their passage t' Californi-a.

CABOT. (*with one sardonic*) Ha! (*He begins to recover. Gets slowly to his feet—strangely*) I calc'late God give it to 'em—not yew! God's hard, not easy! Mebbe they's easy gold in the West but it hain't God's gold. It hain't fur me. I kin hear His voice warnin' me agen t' be hard an' stay on my farm. I kin see his hand usin' Eben t' steal t' keep me from weakness. I kin feel I be in the palm o' His hand, His fingers guidin' me. (*A pause—then he mutters sadly*) It's a-goin' t' be lonesomer now than ever it war afore—an' I'm gittin' old, Lord—ripe on the bough. . . . (*Then stiffening*) Waal—what d'ye want? God's lonesome, hain't He? God's hard an' lonesome! (*A pause. The Sheriff with two men comes up the road from the left. They move cautiously to the door. The Sheriff knocks on it with the butt of his pistol.*)

SHERIFF. Open in the name o' the law! (*They start.*)

CABOT. They've come fur ye. (*He goes to the rear door*) Come in, Jim! (*The three men enter.* CABOT *meets them in doorway*) Jest a minit, Jim. I got 'em safe here. (*The Sheriff nods. He and his companions remain in the doorway.*)

EBEN. (*suddenly calls*) I lied this mornin', Jim. I helped her to do it. Ye kin take me, too.

ABBIE. (*brokenly*) No!

CABOT. Take 'em both. (*He comes forward—stares at* EBEN *with a trace of grudging admiration*) Purty good—fur yew! Waal, I got t' round up the stock. Good-by.

EBEN. Good-by.

ABBIE. Good-by. (CABOT *turns and strides past the men—comes out and around the corner of the house, his shoulders squared, his face stony, and stalks grimly toward the barn. In the meantime the Sheriff and men have come into the room.*)

SHERIFF. (*embarrassedly*) Waal—we'd best start.

ABBIE. Wait. (*Turns to* EBEN) I love ye, Eben.

EBEN. I love ye, Abbie. (*They kiss. The three men grin and shuffle embarrassedly.* EBEN *takes* ABBIE's *hand. They go out the door in rear, the men following, and come from the house, walking hand in hand to the gate.* EBEN *stops there and points to the sunrise sky*) Sun's a-rizin'. Purty, hain't it?

ABBIE. Ay-eh. (*They both stand for a moment looking up raptly in attitudes strangely aloof and devout.*)

SHERIFF. (*looking around at the farm enviously—to his companions*) It's a jim-dandy farm, no denyin'. Wished I owned it!

CURTAIN

LAZARUS LAUGHED

CHARACTERS

LAZARUS OF BETHANY
HIS FATHER
HIS MOTHER
MARTHA, MARY — *his sisters*
MIRIAM, *his wife*
SEVEN GUESTS, *neighbors of Lazarus*
CHORUS OF OLD MEN
AN ORTHODOX PRIEST
CHORUS OF LAZARUS' FOLLOWERS
A CENTURION
GAIUS CALIGULA
CRASSUS, *a Roman General*
CHORUS OF GREEKS
SEVEN CITIZENS OF ATHENS
CHORUS OF ROMAN SENATORS
SEVEN SENATORS
CHORUS OF LEGIONARIES
FLAVIUS, *a centurion*
MARCELLUS, *a patrician*
CHORUS OF THE GUARD
TIBERIUS CÆSAR
POMPEIA
CHORUS OF YOUTHS AND GIRLS
CHORUS OF THE ROMAN POPULACE
CROWDS

SCENES

ACT ONE

Scene I: Lazarus' home in Bethany—a short time after the miracle.
Scene II: Months later. Outside the House of Laughter in Bethany. Late evening.

ACT TWO

Scene I: A street in Athens. A night months later.
Scene II: A temple immediately inside the walls of Rome. Midnight. Months later.

ACT THREE

Scene I: Garden of Tiberius' palace. A night a few days later.
Scene II: Inside the palace. Immediately after.

ACT FOUR

Scene I: The same. A while after.
Scene II: Interior of a Roman theatre. Dawn of the same night.

LAZARUS LAUGHED

ACT ONE—SCENE ONE

SCENE: *Exterior and interior of* LAZARUS' *home at Bethany. The main room at the front end of the house is shown—a long, low-ceilinged, sparely furnished chamber, with white walls gray in the fading daylight that enters from three small windows at the left. To the left of center several long tables placed lengthwise to the width of the room, around which many chairs for guests have been placed. In the rear wall, right, a door leading into the rest of the house. On the left, a doorway opening on a road where a crowd of men has gathered. On the right, another doorway leading to the yard where there is a crowd of women.*

Inside the house, on the men's side, seven male Guests are grouped by the door, watching LAZARUS *with frightened awe, talking hesitantly in low whispers. The Chorus of Old Men, seven in number, is drawn up in a crescent, in the far corner, right, facing* LAZARUS.

(All of these people are masked in accordance with the following scheme: There are seven periods of life shown: Boyhood (or Girlhood), Youth, Young Manhood (or Womanhood), Manhood (or Womanhood), Middle Age, Maturity and Old Age; and each of these periods is represented by seven different masks of general types of character as follows: The Simple, Ignorant; the Happy, Eager; the Self-Tortured, Introspective; the Proud, Self-Reliant; the Servile, Hypocritical; the Revengeful, Cruel; the Sorrowful, Resigned. Thus in each crowd (this includes among the men the Seven Guests who are composed of one male of each period-type as period one—type one, period two—type two, and so on up to period seven—type seven)

there are forty-nine different combinations of period and type. Each type has a distinct predominant color for its costumes which varies in kind according to its period. The masks of the Chorus of Old Men are double the size of the others. They are all seven in the Sorrowful, Resigned type of Old Age.)

On a raised platform at the middle of the one table placed lengthwise at center sits LAZARUS, *his head haloed and his body illumined by a soft radiance as of tiny phosphorescent flames.*

LAZARUS, *freed now from the fear of death, wears no mask.*

In appearance LAZARUS *is tall and powerful, about fifty years of age, with a mass of gray-black hair and a heavy beard. His face recalls that of a statue of a divinity of Ancient Greece in its general structure and particularly in its quality of detached serenity. It is dark-complected, ruddy and brown, the color of rich earth upturned by the plow, calm but furrowed deep with the marks of former suffering endured with a grim fortitude that had never softened into resignation. His forehead is broad and noble, his eyes black and deep-set. Just now he is staring straight before him as if his vision were still fixed beyond life.*

Kneeling beside him with bowed heads are his wife, MIRIAM, *his sisters,* MARTHA *and* MARY, *and his* FATHER *and* MOTHER.

MIRIAM *is a slender, delicate woman of thirty-five, dressed in deep black, who holds one of his hands in both of hers, and keeps her lips pressed to it. The upper part of her face is covered by a mask which conceals her forehead, eyes and nose, but leaves her mouth revealed. The mask is the pure pallor of marble, the expression that of a statue of Woman, of her eternal acceptance of the compulsion of motherhood, the inevitable cycle of love into pain into joy and new love into separation and pain again and the loneliness of age. The eyes of the mask are almost closed. Their gaze turns within, oblivious to the life outside, as they dream down on the child forever in memory at her breast. The mouth of* MIRIAM *is sensitive and sad, tender with an eager, understanding smile of self-forgetful love, the lips still fresh and young. Her skin, in contrast to the mask, is sunburned and earth-*

colored like that of LAZARUS. MARTHA, MARY *and the two parents all wear full masks which broadly reproduce their own characters.* MARTHA *is a buxom middle-aged housewife, plain and pleasant.* MARY *is young and pretty, nervous and high-strung. The* FATHER *is a small, thin, feeble old man of over eighty, meek and pious. The* MOTHER *is tall and stout, over sixty-five, a gentle, simple woman.*

All the masks of these Jews of the first two scenes of the play are pronouncedly Semitic.

A background of twilight sky. A dissolving touch of sunset still lingers on the horizon.

It is some time after the miracle and Jesus has gone away.

CHORUS OF OLD MEN. (*in a quavering rising and falling chant—their arms outstretched toward* LAZARUS)

Jesus wept!
Behold how he loved him!
He that liveth,
He that believeth,
Shall never die!

CROWD. (*on either side of house, echo the chant*)

He that believeth
Shall never die!
Lazarus, come forth!

FIRST GUEST. (*a Simple Boy—in a frightened whisper after a pause of dead silence*) That strange light seems to come from within him! (*With awe*) Think of it! For four days he lay in the tomb! (*Turns away with a shudder.*)

SECOND GUEST. (*a Happy Youth—with reassuring conviction*) It is a holy light. It came from Jesus.

FIFTH GUEST. (*an Envious Middle-Aged Man*) Maybe if the truth were known, our friend there never really died at all!

FOURTH GUEST. (*a Defiant Man, indignantly*) Do you doubt the miracle? I tell you I was here in this house when Lazarus died!

SEVENTH GUEST. (*an Aged, Sorrowful Man*) And I used to visit him every day. He knew himself his hour was near.

FOURTH GUEST. He wished for death! He said to me one day: "I have known my fill of life and the sorrow of living. Soon I shall know peace." And he smiled. It was the first time I had seen him smile in years.

THIRD GUEST. (*a Self-Tortured Man—gloomily*) Yes, of late years his life had been one long misfortune. One after another his children died—

SIXTH GUEST. (*a Mature Man with a cruel face—with a harsh laugh*) They were all girls. Lazarus had no luck.

SEVENTH GUEST. The last was a boy, the one that died at birth. You are forgetting him.

THIRD GUEST. Lazarus could never forget. Not only did his son die but Miriam could never bear him more children.

FIFTH GUEST. (*practically*) But he could not blame bad luck for everything. Take the loss of his father's wealth since he took over the management. That was his own doing. He was a bad farmer, a poor breeder of sheep, and a bargainer so easy to cheat it hurt one's conscience to trade with him!

SIXTH GUEST. (*with a sneer—maliciously*) You should know best about that! (*A suppressed laugh from those around him.*)

FIRST GUEST. (*who has been gazing at* LAZARUS*—softly*) Ssssh! Look at his face! (*They all stare. A pause.*)

SECOND GUEST. (*with wondering awe*) Do you remember him, neighbors, before he died? He used to be pale even when he worked in the fields. Now he seems as brown as one who has labored in the earth all day in a vineyard beneath the hot sun! (*A pause.*)

FOURTH GUEST. The whole look of his face has changed. He is like a stranger from a far land. There is no longer any sorrow in his eyes. They must have forgotten sorrow in the grave.

FIFTH GUEST. (*grumblingly*) I thought we were invited here to eat—and all we do is stand and gape at him!

FOURTH GUEST. (*sternly*) Be silent! We are waiting for him to speak.

THIRD GUEST. (*impressively*) He did speak once. And he laughed!

ALL THE GUESTS. (*amazed and incredulous*) Laughed?

THIRD GUEST. (*importantly*) Laughed! I heard him! It was a moment after the miracle—

MIRIAM. (*her voice, rich with sorrow, exultant now*) Jesus cried, "Lazarus, come forth!" (*She kisses his hand. He makes a slight movement, a stirring in his vision. The* GUESTS *stare. A frightened pause.*)

FIFTH GUEST. (*nudging the* SECOND*—uneasily*) Go on with your story!

THIRD GUEST. Just as he appeared in the opening of the tomb, wrapped in his shroud—

SECOND GUEST. (*excitedly—interrupting*) My heart stopped! I fell on my face! And all the women screamed! (*Sceptically*) You must have sharp ears to have heard him laugh in that uproar!

THIRD GUEST. I helped to pry away the stone so I was right beside him. I found myself kneeling, but between my fingers I watched Jesus and Lazarus. Jesus looked into his face for what seemed a long time and suddenly Lazarus said "Yes" as if he were answering a question in Jesus' eyes.

ALL THE GUESTS. (*mystified*) Yes? What could he mean by yes?

THIRD GUEST. Then Jesus smiled sadly but with tenderness, as one who from a distance of years of sorrow remembers happiness. And then Lazarus knelt and kissed Jesus' feet and both of them smiled and Jesus blessed him and called him "My Brother" and went away; and Lazarus, looking after Him, began to laugh softly like a man in love with God! Such a laugh I never heard! It made my ears drunk! It was like wine! And though I was half-dead with fright I found myself laughing, too!

MIRIAM. (*with a beseeching summons*) Lazarus, come forth!

CHORUS. (*chanting*) Lazarus! Come forth!

CROWD. (*on either side of the house—echoing the chant*) Come forth! Come forth!

LAZARUS. (*suddenly in a deep voice—with a wonderful exultant acceptance in it*) Yes! (*The* GUESTS *in the room, the* CROWDS *outside all cry out in fear and joy and fall on their knees.*)

CHORUS. (*chanting exultantly*)

The stone is taken away!
The spirit is loosed!
The soul let go!

LAZARUS. (*rising and looking around him at everyone and everything—with an all-embracing love—gently*) Yes! (*His family and the* GUESTS *in the room now throng about* LAZARUS *to embrace him. The* CROWDS *of men and women on each side push into the room to stare at him. He is in the arms of his* MOTHER *and* MIRIAM *while his* SISTERS *and* FATHER *kiss and press his hands. The five are half hysterical with relief and joy, sobbing and laughing.*)

FATHER. My son is reborn to me!

CHORUS. Hosannah!

ALL. (*with a great shout*) Hosannah!

FATHER. Let us rejoice! Eat and drink! Draw up your chairs, friends! Music! Bring wine! (*Music begins in the room off right, rear—a festive dance tune. The company sits down in their places, the* FATHER *and* MOTHER *at* LAZARUS' *right and left.* MIRIAM *next to the* MOTHER, MARTHA *and* MARY *beside the* FATHER. *But* LAZARUS *remains standing. And the* CHORUS OF OLD MEN *remain in their formation at the rear. Wine is poured and all raise their goblets toward* LAZARUS*—then suddenly they stop, the music dies out, and an awed and frightened stillness prevails, for* LAZARUS *is a strange, majestic figure whose understanding smile seems terrible and enigmatic to them.*)

FATHER. (*pathetically uneasy*) You frighten us, my son. You are strange—standing there— (*In the midst of a silence more awkward than before he rises to his feet, goblet in hand—forcing his voice, falteringly*) A toast, neighbors!

CHORUS. (*in a forced echo*) A toast!

ALL. (*echoing them*) A toast!

FATHER. To my son, Lazarus, whom a blessed miracle has brought back from death!

LAZARUS. (*suddenly laughing softly out of his vision, as if to himself, and speaking with a strange unearthly calm in a voice that is like a loving whisper of hope and confidence*) No! There is no death! (*A moment's pause. The people remain with goblets uplifted, staring at him. Then all repeat after him questioningly and frightenedly.*)

ALL. There—is—no—death?

SIXTH GUEST. (*suddenly blurts out the question which is in the minds of all*) What did you find beyond there, Lazarus? (*A pause of silence.*)

LAZARUS. (*smiles gently and speaks as if to a group of inquisitive children*) O Curious Greedy Ones, is not one world in which you know not how to live enough for you?

SIXTH GUEST. (*emboldened*) Why did you say yes, Lazarus?

FOURTH GUEST. Why did you laugh?

ALL THE GUESTS. (*with insistent curiosity but in low awed tones*) What is beyond there, Lazarus?

CHORUS. (*in a low murmur*) What is beyond there? What is beyond?

CROWD. (*carrying the question falteringly back into silence*) What is beyond?

LAZARUS. (*suddenly again—now in a voice of loving exaltation*) There is only life! I heard the heart of Jesus laughing in my heart; "There is Eternal Life in No," it said, "and there is the same Eternal Life in Yes! Death is the fear between!" And my heart reborn to love of life cried "Yes!" and I laughed in the laughter of God! (*He begins to laugh, softly at first—a laugh so full of a complete acceptance of life, a profound assertion of joy in living, so devoid of all self-consciousness or fear, that it is like a great bird song trium-*

phant in depths of sky, proud and powerful, infectious with love, casting on the listener an enthralling spell. The crowd in the room are caught by it. Glancing sideways at one another, smiling foolishly and self-consciously, at first they hesitate, plainly holding themselves in for fear of what the next one will think.)

CHORUS. (*in a chanting murmur*)
Lazarus laughs!
Our hearts grow happy!
Laughter like music!
The wind laughs!
The sea laughs!
Spring laughs from the earth!
Summer laughs in the air!
Lazarus laughs!

LAZARUS. (*on a final note of compelling exultation*)
Laugh! Laugh with me! Death is dead! Fear is no more!
There is only life! There is only laughter!

CHORUS. (*chanting exultingly now*)
Laugh! Laugh!
Laugh with Lazarus!
Fear is no more!
There is no death!

(*They laugh in a rhythmic cadence dominated by the laughter of* LAZARUS.)

CROWD. (*who, gradually, joining in by groups or one by one—including* LAZARUS' *family with the exception of* MIRIAM, *who does not laugh but watches and listens to his laughter with a tender smile of being happy in his happiness—have now all begun to laugh in rhythm with the* CHORUS—*in a great, full-throated pæan as the laughter of* LAZARUS *rises higher and higher*)
Laugh! Laugh!
Fear is no more!
There is no death!

CHORUS.

Laugh! Laugh!
There is only life!
There is only laughter!
Fear is no more!
Death is dead!

CROWD. (*in a rhythmic echo*)

Laugh! Laugh!
Death is dead!
There is only laughter! (*The room rocks, the air outside throbs with the rhythmic beat of their liberated laughter—still a bit uncertain of its freedom, harsh, discordant, frenzied, desperate and drunken, but dominated and inspired by the high, free, aspiring, exulting laughter of* LAZARUS.)

CURTAIN

SCENE TWO

SCENE: *Some months later. Exterior of* LAZARUS' *home in Bethany, now known as the House of Laughter. It is a clear, bright night, the sky sparkling with stars. At the extreme front is a road. Between this and the house is a small raised terrace. The house is low, of one story only, its walls white. Four windows are visible with a closed door in the middle of the wall. Steps lead up to this door, and to the left of door a flight of stairs goes up to the balustraded roof. The windows shine brilliantly with the flickering light of many candles which gives them a throbbing star-like effect. From within comes the sound of flutes and dance music. The dancers can be seen whirling swiftly by the windows. There is continually an overtone of singing laughter emphasizing the pulsing rhythm of the dance. On the road in the foreground, at left and right, two separate groups of Jews are gathered. They are not divided according to sex as in the previous scene. Each is composed about equally of men and women, forty-nine in each, masked and costumed as before. It is religious belief that now divides them. The adherents of Jesus, the Nazarenes, among whom may be noted* MARTHA *and* MARY, *are on the left; the Orthodox, among whom are* LAZARUS' FATHER *and* MOTHER *and a* PRIEST, *are at right. Between the two hostile groups is the same* CHORUS OF OLD MEN, *in a formation like a spearhead, whose point is placed at the foot of the steps leading to the terrace. All these people are staring fascinatedly at the house, listening entranced, their feet moving, their bodies swaying to the music's beat, stiffly, constrainedly, compelled against their wills. Then the music suddenly stops and the chant of youthful voices is heard:*

FOLLOWERS OF LAZARUS. (*from within the house*)

Laugh! Laugh!
There is only life!
There is only laughter.

CHORUS OF OLD MEN. (*as if they were subjects moved by hypnotic suggestion—miserably and discordantly*)

Ha-ha-ha-ha!
There is only laughter!
Ha-ha—

CROWD. (*in the same manner*) Ha-ha—

MARY. Ha— (*Then frantically—half-weeping with indignant rage—to the Nazarenes*) Stop! Oh, how can we laugh! We are betraying Jesus! My brother Lazarus has become a devil!

THE ORTHODOX PRIEST. (*his mask is that of a religious fanatic. He is sixty or so*) Ha—ha— (*Tearing his beard and stamping with rage*) Stop it, you fools! It is a foul sin in the sight of Jehovah! Why do you come here every night to listen and watch their abominations? The Lord God will punish you!

MARY. (*echoing him—to her people*) Jesus will never forgive you!

THE PRIEST. (*angrily*) Jesus? (*He turns to look at the Nazarenes disdainfully and spits on the ground insultingly. The members of the two groups begin to glare at each other. The* CHORUS *falls back, three on each side, leaving one neutral figure before the steps. The* PRIEST *goes on tauntingly*) Did you hear her, friends? These renegade Nazarenes will soon deny they are Jews at all! They will begin to worship in filthy idolatry the sun and stars and man's body—as Lazarus in there (*points to the house*), the disciple of their Jesus, has so well set them the example! (*This is followed by an outburst of insulting shouts of accusation and denial from both sides.*)

A NAZARENE. (*the* FOURTH GUEST *of Scene One*) You lie! Lazarus is no disciple! He is a traitor to Jesus! We scorn him!

PRIEST. (*sneeringly*) But your pretended Messiah did not scorn him. According to your stupid lies, he raised him from the dead! And answer me, has your Jesus ever denied Lazarus, or denounced his laughter? No! No doubt he is laughing, too, at all you credulous fools—for if Lazarus is not his disciple, in the matter of the false miracle he was his accomplice! (*This provokes a furious protest from the Nazarenes and insulting hoots and jeers from the Orthodox, penetrated by a piercing scream from* LAZARUS' MOTHER, *who, crushed in the crowd, sinks fainting to the ground. The* FATHER *bends over her. The group of the Orthodox falls back from them. With frightened cries* MARTHA *and* MARY *run from the group of Nazarenes and kneel beside her.*)

FATHER. (*pitifully*) Rachel! Darling! Speak to me!

MARTHA. (*practically*) She has only fainted.

MARY. She is opening her eyes! Mother, dear!

MOTHER. (*weakly*) Did I fall? (*Recognizing* MARTHA *and* MARY) Martha—and Mary—my dear ones! (*They embrace her, weeping*) I have not kissed you since you left home to follow that Jesus— Oh, if we were only at home again—and if, also, my poor boy, Lazarus— (*She sobs.*)

FATHER. (*gruffly*) You must not speak of him!

MARTHA. Do not worry your head about Lazarus. He is not worth it!

MARY. (*with surprising vindictiveness*) He is accursed! He has betrayed our Lord!

PRIEST. (*to those around him—mockingly*) Do you hear? They already call the Nazarene "Lord!" A Lord who is in the common prison at Jerusalem, I heard today! A fine Lord whom our High Priests have had arrested like a thief!

MARY. (*with fanatic fervor*) He is a king! Whenever He chooses He will gather a great army and He will seize His kingdom and all who deny Him shall be crucified!

PRIEST. (*tauntingly*) Now their jail-bird is a king, no less! Soon they will make him a god, as the Romans do their Cæsars!

MARY. (*her eyes flashing*) He is the Messiah!

PRIEST. (*furiously*) The Messiah! May Jehovah smite you in your lies! Step back among your kind! You defile us! (*As she stands defiantly he appeals to the* FATHER) Have you no authority? She called him the Messiah—that common beggar, that tramp! Curse her!

FATHER. (*confused, pitifully harried, collecting his forces*) Wait! Go back, Mary! You chose to follow that impostor—

MARY. (*defiantly*) The Messiah!

MARTHA. (*trying to calm her*) Ssssh! Remember he is our father!

MARY. (*fanatically*) I deny him! I deny all who deny Jesus!

MOTHER. (*tearfully*) And me, darling?

MARY. You must come to us, Mother! You must believe in Jesus and leave all to follow Him!

FATHER. (*enraged*) So! You want to steal your mother away, to leave me lonely in my old age! You are an unnatural daughter! I disown you! Go, before I curse—

MOTHER. (*beseechingly*) Father!

MARTHA. (*pulling* MARY *away*) Mary! Jesus teaches to be kind.

MARY. (*hysterically*) He teaches to give up all and follow Him! I want to give Him everything! I want my father to curse me!

FATHER. (*frenziedly*) Then I do curse you! No—not you—but the devil in you! And the devil in Martha! And the great mocking devil that dwells in Lazarus and laughs from his mouth! I curse these devils and that Prince of Devils, that false prophet, Jesus! It is he who has brought division to my home and many homes that were happy before. I curse him! I curse the day he called my good son, Lazarus, from the grave to walk again with a devil inside him! It was not my son who came back but a devil! My son is dead! And you, my daughters, are dead! I am the father only of devils! (*His voice has risen to a wailing lament*) My children are dead!

LAZARUS. (*his voice rings from within the house in exultant denial*) Death is dead! There is only laughter! (*He laughs. The voices of all his* FOLLOWERS *echo his laughter. They pour in a laughing rout from the doorway onto the terrace. At the same moment the* CHORUS OF FOLLOWERS *appears on the roof and forms along the balustrade, facing front. These* FOLLOWERS OF LAZARUS, *forty-nine in number, composed about equally of both sexes, wear a mask that, while recognizably Jewish, is a* LAZARUS *mask, resembling him in its expression of fearless faith in life, the mouth shaped by laughter. The* CHORUS OF FOLLOWERS, *seven in number, all men, have identical masks of double size, as before. The Period of all these masks is anywhere between Youth and Manhood (or Womanhood). The music continues to come from within. Laughing, the* FOLLOWERS *dance to it in weaving patterns on the terrace. They are dressed in bright-colored diaphanous robes. Their chorused laughter, now high and clear, now dying to a humming murmur, stresses the rhythmic flow of the dance.*)

CHORUS OF FOLLOWERS.

Laugh! Laugh!
There is no death!
There is only laughter!

FOLLOWERS.

There is only laughter!
Death is dead!
Laugh! Laugh!

CROWD. (*the two groups of Nazarenes and Orthodox, on the appearance of the* FOLLOWERS, *immediately forget their differences and form into one mob, led by their* CHORUS OF OLD MEN, *whose jeering howls they echo as one voice*) Yaah! Yaah! Yaah! (*But they cannot keep it up. The music and laughter rise above their hooting. They fall into silence. Then they again begin to feel impelled by the rhythm and laughter, their feet move, their bodies sway. Their lips quiver, their mouths open as if to laugh. Their* CHORUS OF OLD MEN *are the first to be affected. It is as if this reaction were transmitted through the* CHORUS *to the* CROWD.)

PRIEST. (*his mouth twitching—fighting against the compulsion in him—stammers*) Brothers—listen—we must unite—in one cause—to—stamp out—this abomination! (*It is as if he can no longer control his speech. He presses his hand over his mouth convulsively.*)

AN AGED ORTHODOX JEW. (*the* SEVENTH GUEST *of Scene One—starts to harangue the crowd. He fights the spell but cannot control his jerking body nor his ghastly, spasmodic laughter*) Neighbors! Our young people are corrupted! They are leaving our farms—to dance and sing! To laugh! Ha—! Laugh at everything! Ha-ha—! (*He struggles desperately to control himself.*)

CHORUS OF OLD MEN. (*a barking laugh forced from them*) Ha-ha—!

CROWD. (*echoing this*) Ha-ha—!

THE AGED JEW. They have no respect for life! When I said in kindness, "You must go back to work," they laughed at me! Ha—! "We desire joy. We go to Lazarus," they said—and left my fields! I begged them to stay—with tears in my eyes! I even offered them more money! They laughed! "What is money? Can the heart eat gold?" They laughed at money! Ha-ha—! (*He chokes with exasperated rage.*)

CHORUS OF OLD MEN. (*echoing him*) Ha-ha—!

CROWD. (*echoing the* CHORUS) Ha-ha—!

AGED JEW. (*shaking his fist at* LAZARUS' FOLLOWERS) That loafer taught them that! They come to him and work for nothing! For nothing! And they are glad, these undutiful ones! While they sow, they dance! They sing to the earth when they are plowing! They tend his flocks and laugh toward the sun! Ha-ha-ha—! (*He struggles again.*)

CHORUS OF OLD MEN. (*as before*) Ha-ha-ha—

CROWD. (*as before*) Ha-ha-ha—

AGED JEW. How can we compete with labor for laughter! We will have no harvest. There will be no food! Our children will starve! Our race will perish! And he will laugh! Ha-ha-ha-ha! (*He howls with furious, uncontained laughter.*)

CHORUS OF OLD MEN. (*echoing his tone*)

Our children will starve!
Our race will perish!
Lazarus laughs!
Ha-ha-ha-ha! Ha-ha-ha-ha!

CROWD. (*as before*) Ha-ha-ha-ha! Ha-ha-ha-ha! (*Their former distinctions of Nazarenes and Orthodox are now entirely forgotten. The members of* LAZARUS' *family are grouped in the center as if nothing had ever happened to separate them. The* CHORUS OF OLD MEN *is again joined in its spearhead formation at the stairs. Apparent first in this* CHORUS, *a queer excitement begins to pervade this mob. They begin to weave in and out, clasping each other's hands now and then, moving mechanically in jerky steps to the music in a grotesque sort of marionettes' country dance. At first this is slow but it momentarily becomes more hectic and peculiar. They raise clenched fists or hands distended into threatening talons. Their voices sound thick and harsh and animal-like with anger as they mutter and growl, each one aloud to himself or herself.*)

CHORUS OF OLD MEN. (*threateningly, gradually rising to hatred*)
Hear them laugh!
See them dance!
Shameless! Wanton!
Dirty! Evil!
Infamous! Bestial!
Madness! Blood!
Adultery! Murder!
We burn!
We kill!
We crucify!
Death! Death!
Beware, Lazarus! (*This last in a wild frenzy.*)

CROWD. (*frenziedly*)
Beware, Lazarus!
We burn! We kill!
We crucify!
Death! Death!

(*They crowd toward the gateway, their arms stretched out as if demanding* LAZARUS *for a sacrificial victim. Meanwhile they never cease to hop up and down, to mill around, to twist their bodies toward and away from each other in bestial parody of the dance of the* FOLLOWERS. *The tall figure of* LAZARUS, *dressed in a white robe, suddenly appears on the roof of the house. He stands at the balustrade in the middle of the* CHORUS. *Beside him, a little behind,* MIRIAM *appears dressed in black, her face upturned, her lips praying. She appears to have grown older, to be forty now.* LAZARUS' *body is softly illumined by its inner light. The change in him is marked. He seems ten years younger, at the prime of forty. His body has become less angular and stiff. His movements are graceful and pliant. The change is even more noticeable in his face, which has filled out, become purer in outline, more distinctly Grecian. His complexion is the red-brown of rich earth, the gray in his black, curly beard has almost disap-*

peared. He makes a sign and the music ceases. His FOLLOWERS *remain fixed in their dancing attitudes like figures in a frieze. Each member of the mob remains frozen in a distorted posture. He stares down at the mob pityingly, his face calm.)*

LAZARUS. (*speaks amid a profound silence. His voice releases his own dancers and the mob from their fixed attitudes. The music begins to play again within the house, very soft and barely audible, swelling up and down like the sound of an organ from a distant church*) You laugh, but your laughter is guilty! It laughs a hyena laughter, spotted, howling its hungry fear of life! That day I returned did I not tell you your fear was no more, that there is no death? You believed then—for a moment! You laughed—discordantly, hoarsely, but with a groping toward joy. What! Have you so soon forgotten, that now your laughter curses life again as of old? (*He pauses—then sadly*) That is your tragedy! You forget! You forget the God in you! You wish to forget! Remembrance would imply the high duty to live as a son of God—generously!—with love! —with pride!—with laughter! This is too glorious a victory for you, too terrible a loneliness! Easier to forget, to become only a man, the son of a woman, to hide from life against her breast, to whimper your fear to her resigned heart and be comforted by her resignation! To live by denying life! (*Then exhortingly*) Why are your eyes always either fixed on the ground in weariness of thought, or watching one another with suspicion? Throw your gaze upward! To Eternal Life! To the fearless and deathless! The everlasting! To the stars! (*He stretches out his arms to the sky—then suddenly points*) See! A new star has appeared! It is the one that shone over Bethlehem! (*His voice becomes a little bitter and mocking*) The Master of Peace and Love has departed this earth. Let all stars be for you henceforth symbols of Saviors—Sons of God who appeared on worlds like ours to tell the saving truth to ears like yours, inexorably deaf! (*Then exaltedly*) But the greatness of Saviors is that they may not save! The greatness of Man is that no god can save him—until he becomes a god! (*He stares up at the stars, rapt in contemplation, oblivious to all around him now. Rapidly approaching from the left a man's voice jarring in high-pitched cruel laughter is heard. They all listen, huddled together like sheep.*)

MESSENGER. (*the* THIRD GUEST *of Scene One rushes in breathlessly, shouting*) The Nazarene has been crucified!

PRIEST. (*with fierce triumph*) Jehovah is avenged! Hosannah!

ORTHODOX. Hosannah! The false prophet is dead! The pretended Messiah is dead! (*They jump and dance, embracing one another. The* NAZARENES *stand paralyzed and stunned. The two groups mechanically separate to right and left again, the* CHORUS OF OLD MEN *dividing itself as before.*)

MARY. (*in a frenzy of grief*) Do not believe him! Jesus could not die! (*But at this moment a Nazarene youth, exhausted by grief and tears, staggers in from the left.*)

MESSENGER. (SECOND GUEST *of Scene One*) Jesus is dead! Our Lord is murdered! (*He sinks on his knees sobbing. All the* NAZARENES *do likewise, wailing, rending their garments, tearing their hair, some even beating their heads on the ground in the agony of their despair.*)

MARY. (*insane with rage now*) They have murdered Him! (*To her followers—savagely*) An eye for an eye! Avenge the Master! (*Their frenzy of grief turned into rage, the* NAZARENES *leap to their feet threateningly. Concealed swords and knives are brought out by both sides.*)

MIRIAM. (*leaning over the balustrade—in a voice of entreaty*) Mary! Brothers! (*But none heed her or seem to see her.* LAZARUS *and his* FOLLOWERS *remain oblivious to men, arms upstretched toward the stars, their heads thrown back.*)

MARY. (*wildly*) Vengeance! Death to His murderers!

PRIEST. (*fiercely to his followers*) Death to the Nazarenes! (*With cries of rage the two groups rush on one another. There is a confused tumult of yells, groans, curses, the shrieks of women, the sounds of blows as they meet in a pushing, whirling, struggling mass *in which individual figures are indistinguishable. Knives and swords flash above the heads of the mass, hands in every tense attitude of striking, clutching, tearing are seen upraised. As the fight is at its height a* ROMAN CENTURION *and a squad of eight* SOLDIERS *come tramping up at the double-quick. They all are masked. These Roman masks now and henceforth in the play are carried out according to the same formula of Seven Periods, Seven Types, as those of the Jews seen previously, except that the basis of each face is Roman—heavy, domineering, self-complacent, the face of a confident dominant race. The* CENTURION *differs from his soldiers only in being more individualized. He is middle-aged, his soldiers belong to the Period of Manhood. All are of the Simple, Ignorant Type.*)

CENTURION. (*shouts commandingly*) Disperse! (*But no one hears him—with angry disgust to his* SOLDIERS) Charge! Cut them down! (*The* SOLDIERS *form a wedge and charge with a shout. They soon find it necessary to use their swords, and strike down everyone in their way.*)

MIRIAM. Mercy, Romans! (*As they pay no attention to her, in desperation she embraces* LAZARUS *beseechingly, forcing his attention back to earth*) Lazarus! Mercy!

LAZARUS. (*looks down upon the struggling mass and cries in a ringing voice*) Hold! (*Each person stands transfixed, frozen in the last movement, even the* ROMAN SOLDIERS *and the* CENTURION *himself. Ten dead and mortally wounded lie on the ground, trampled by the feet of friend and foe alike.* LAZARUS *looks at the* CROWD. *To each he seems to look at him or her alone. His eyes are accusing and stern. As one head, the heads of all are averted. Even the* CENTURION *stares at the ground humbly, in spite of himself. Finally* LAZARUS *speaks in a voice of infinite disdain*) Sometimes it is hard to laugh—even *at* men! (*He turns his eyes from them, staring straight before him. This seems to release them from their fixed positions. The* NAZARENES *and the* ORTHODOX *separate and slink guiltily apart. The* CHORUS OF OLD MEN *forms again, the apex at the center of the steps as before. A low wail of lamentation arises from them. The two crowds of* NAZARENES *and* ORTHODOX *echo this.*)

CHORUS OF OLD MEN. (*in a wailing chant*)

Woe unto Israel!
Woe unto thee, Jerusalem!
O divided house,
Thou shalt crumble to dust,
And swine shall root
Where thy Temple stood!
Woe unto us!

CROWD. (*in a great echoing cry*) Woe unto us!

CENTURION. (*gruffly to hide his embarrassment at being awed by* LAZARUS) Here, you! Drag your carcasses away! (*From each side men and women come forward to identify and mourn their dead. The wail of lamentation rises and falls. The* CENTURION *looks up at* LAZARUS*—harshly*) You, there! Are you he whom they call the Laugher?

LAZARUS. (*without looking at him—his voice seeming to come from some dream within him*) I am Lazarus.

CENTURION. Who was brought back from death by enchantment?

LAZARUS. (*looking down at him now—with a smile, simply*) No. There is no death!

CHORUS OF FOLLOWERS. (*chanting joyously*)

There is no death!

FOLLOWERS. (*echoing*)

There is no death!

AN ORTHODOX MAN. (*bending beside the body of* LAZARUS' FATHER) Here is your father, Lazarus. He is dead.

AN ORTHODOX WOMAN. This is your mother, Lazarus. She is dead.

A NAZARENE. Here is your sister, Martha, Lazarus. She is dead.

A NAZARENE WOMAN. And this is Mary, Lazarus. She is dead.

MIRIAM. (*suddenly—with deep grief*) And Jesus who was the Son of Man, who loved you and gave you life again has died, Lazarus—has died!

LAZARUS. (*in a great triumphant voice*) Yes! Yes! Yes!!! Men die! Even a Son of Man must die to show men that Man may live! But there is no death!

CENTURION. (*at first in a tone of great awe—to his* SOLDIERS) Is he a god? (*Then gruffly, ashamed of his question*) Come down, Jew! I have orders to bring you to Rome to Cæsar!

LAZARUS. (*as if he were answering not the* CENTURION *but the command of his fate from the sky*) Yes! (*He walks down the narrow stairs and,* MIRIAM *following him, comes down the path to the road. He goes and kneels for a moment each beside the bodies of his* FATHER, MOTHER, *and* SISTERS *and kisses each in turn on the forehead. For a moment the struggle with his grief can be seen in his face. Then he looks up to the stars and, as if answering a question, again says simply and acceptingly*) Yes! (*Then exultantly*) Yes!! (*And begins to laugh from the depths of his exalted spirit. The laughter of his* CHORUS *and then of his* FOLLOWERS *echoes his. The music and dancing begin again. The* CENTURION *grins sheepishly. The* SOLDIERS *chuckle. The* CENTURION *laughs awkwardly. The* SOLDIERS *laugh. The music from the house and the laughter of the* FOLLOWERS *grow louder. The infection spreads to the* CHORUS OF OLD MEN *whose swaying grief falls into the rhythm of the laughter and music as does that of the mourners.*)

LAZARUS' FOLLOWERS. (*led by their* CHORUS)

Laugh! Laugh!

CHORUS OF OLD MEN. (*torn by the conflict—torturedly*)

Ha-ha-ha—
Woe to us, woe!

CROWD. (*beside the bodies*)

Woe to us, woe!
Ha-ha—!

CENTURION. (*laughingly*) You are brave, you Laugher! Remember Tiberius never laughs! And boast not to Cæsar there is no death, or he will invent a new one for you!

LAZARUS. (*with a smile*) But all death is men's invention! So laugh! (*He laughs and the* CENTURION *and* SOLDIERS *laugh with him, half dancing clumsily now to the beat of the music.*)

CHORUS OF LAZARUS' FOLLOWERS.

Laugh! Laugh!
Fear is no more!
There is no death!
There is only life!
There is only laughter!

FOLLOWERS. (*dancing*)

Laugh! Laugh!
Fear is no more!
Death is dead!

CHORUS OF OLD MEN. (*forgetting their grief—their eyes on* LAZARUS *now, their arms outstretched to him as are those of the crowd grouped around the bodies but forgetting them*)

Death is no more!
Death is dead!
Laugh!

CROWD.

Laugh! Laugh!
Death is no more!

CENTURION. (*laughing, to his laughing* SOLDIERS) Forward! (*They tramp, dancing, off.* LAZARUS *and* MIRIAM *start to follow.*)

MIRIAM. (*suddenly pointing to his* FOLLOWERS *who are dancing and laughing obliviously—pityingly*) But your faithful ones who love you, Lazarus?

LAZARUS. (*simply, with a trace of a sad sternness*) This is their test. Their love must remember—or it must forget. Come! (*With a last gesture back like a blessing on all he is leaving, he goes. The laughter of the* SOLDIERS *recedes. That of the* CHORUS OF OLD MEN *and of the* CROWD *falters and breaks into lamenting grief again, guilt-stricken because of its laughter.*)

CHORUS OF OLD MEN.

Laugh! Laugh!
Death is dead!
Laugh!—But woe!
There lie our dead!
Oh, shame and guilt!
We forget our dead!

CROWD. (*with fierce remorseful grief*)

Woe to us, woe!
There lie our dead!

CHORUS OF LAZARUS' FOLLOWERS. (*their voices and the music growing more and more hesitating and faint*)

Laugh! Laugh!
There is only life!
There is only—
Laugh—

(*Their dance is faltering and slow now*)

Fear is no—
Death is—
Laugh—

(*The music and dancing and voices cease. The lights in the windows, which have been growing dim, go out. There is a second of complete, death-like silence. The mourning folk in the foreground are frozen figures of grief. Then a sudden swelling chorus of forlorn bewilderment, a cry of lost children comes from the* CHORUS OF FOLLOWERS *and the* FOLLOWERS *themselves. They huddle into groups on the roof and on the terrace. They stretch their arms out in every direction supplicatingly.*)

CHORUS OF FOLLOWERS.

Oh, Lazarus, laugh!
Do not forsake us!
We forget!
Where is thy love fled?
Give back thy laughter,
Thy fearless laughter!
We forget!

FOLLOWERS.

Give back thy laughter!
We forget!

CHORUS OF FOLLOWERS. (*with dull, resigned terror now*)

Death slinks out
Of his grave in the heart!
Ghosts of fear
Creep back in the brain!
We remember fear!
We remember death!

FOLLOWERS.

Death in the heart!
Fear in the brain!
We remember fear!
We remember death!

CHORUS OF FOLLOWERS. (*wailing hopelessly now*)

Forgotten is laughter!
We remember
Only death!
Fear is God!
Forgotten is laughter!
Life is death!

FOLLOWERS.

Forgotten is laughter!
Life is death!

ALL. (*the* CHORUS OF OLD MEN *and the* CROWD *joining in*)
Life is a fearing,
A long dying,
From birth to death!
God is a slayer!
Life is death!

CURTAIN

ACT TWO—SCENE ONE

SCENE: *Some months later. A square in Athens about ten o'clock at night. In the rear, pure and beautiful in the light of a full moon, is the façade of a temple. An excited crowd of Greeks of both sexes is gathered in the square as if for some public festival. They are masked according to the scheme of Seven Periods in Seven Types of Character for each sex. Here, of course, the foundation of the mask is the Grecian type of face.*

On the left, the CHORUS OF GREEKS *is grouped, seven in number, facing front, in the spearhead formation. As before the* CHORUS *wears masks double the life size of the* CROWD *masks. They are all of the Proud Self-Reliant type, in the period of Young Manhood.*

These seven are clad in goat skins, their tanned bodies and masks daubed and stained with wine lees, in imitation of the old followers of Dionysus. Rumor has led them to hope and believe that LAZARUS *may be the reincarnation of this deity.*

The people in the crowd are holding themselves in restraint with difficulty, they stir and push about restlessly with an eager curiosity and impatience. All eyes are fixed off left. A buzz of voices hums in the air.

Acting as police, a number of Roman legionaries (masked like the soldiers of Scene Two) armed with staves, keep back the crowd from the line of the street that runs from left to right, front. They resent this duty, which has already kept them there for a long time, and are surly and quick-tempered with the Greeks.

At front, pacing impatiently up and down, is a young Roman noble of twenty-one, clad richly, wearing beautifully wrought armor and helmet. This is GAIUS, *the heir of Tiberius Cæsar, nicknamed* CALIGULA *by the soldiers in whose encampments he was born and where he spent his childhood. His body is bony and angular, almost malformed, with wide, powerful shoulders and long arms and hands, and short, skinny, hairy legs like an ape's. He wears a half-mask of crimson, dark with a purplish tinge, that covers the upper part of his face to below the nose. This mask accentuates his bulging, prematurely wrinkled forehead, his hollow temples and his bulbous, sensual nose. His large troubled eyes, of a glazed greenish-blue, glare out with a shifty feverish suspicion at everyone. Below his mask his own skin is of an anæmic transparent pallor. Above it, his hair is the curly blond hair of a child of six or seven. His mouth also is childish, the red lips soft and feminine in outline. Their expression is spoiled, petulant and self-obsessed, weak but domineering. In combination with the rest of the face there is an appalling morbid significance to his mouth. One feels that its boyish cruelty, encouraged as a manly attribute in the coarse brutality of camps, has long ago become naïvely insensitive to any human suffering but its own.*

Walking with CALIGULA *is* CNEIUS CRASSUS, *a Roman general—a squat, muscular man of sixty, his mask that of a heavy battered face full of coarse humor.*

CHORUS OF GREEKS. (*intoning solemnly*)
Soon the God comes!
Redeemer and Savior!
Dionysus, Son of Man and a god!

GREEK CROWD. (*echoing*)
Soon the God comes!
Redeemer and Savior!
Dionysus!

FIRST GREEK. They say an unearthly flame burns in this Lazarus!

SECOND GREEK. The sacred fire! He must be the Fire-born, the son of Zeus!

THIRD GREEK. Many who have seen him swear he is Dionysus, rearisen from Hades!

FOURTH GREEK. (*importantly*) I saw Lazarus at Antioch where the galley on which they were taking him to Rome had been thrice blown back by a storm. Fear of this warning omen is why they now march with him by land.

FIRST GREEK. Does he truly resemble a god?

FOURTH GREEK. (*impressively*) One look in his eyes while his laughter sings in your ears and you forget sorrow! You dance! You laugh! It is as if a heavy weight you had been carrying all your life without knowing it suddenly were lifted. You are like a cloud, you can fly, your mind reels with laughter, you are drunk with joy! (*Solemnly*) Take my word for it, he is indeed a god. Everywhere the people have acclaimed him. He heals the sick, he raises the dead, by laughter.

SEVENTH GREEK. But I have heard that when he has gone people cannot remember his laughter, that the dead are dead again and the sick die, and the sad grow more sorrowful.

FIFTH GREEK. Well, we shall soon see with our own eyes. But why should the God return in the body of a Jew?

SIXTH GREEK. What better disguise if he wishes to remain unknown? The fools of Romans will never suspect him!

THIRD GREEK. (*laughing*) Never! They are beginning to claim he is a Roman!

FIFTH GREEK. So much the better! He will be in their confidence!

FOURTH GREEK. He will lead us against Rome! He will laugh our tyrants into the sea! Ha! (*He turns toward the Romans and laughs sneeringly. This is taken up by the* CROWD*—unpleasant, resentful laughter. They push forward aggressively and almost sweep the soldiers from their feet.*)

CRASSUS. (*angrily*) Drive them back!

CALIGULA. (*suddenly with a distorted warped smile*) Order them to use their swords, Cneius. Let the scum look at their dead and learn respect for us!

SOLDIERS. (*shoving and whacking*) Back! Step back! Back there!

(*The crowd push back to their former line. There are muttered curses, groans, protests, which subside into the former hum of expectancy.*)

CALIGULA. (*with the same smile*) The sword, my old hyena! Corpses are so educational!

CRASSUS. (*surlily*) I would like to, I promise you! When I see how they hate us—!

CALIGULA. (*carelessly*) Let them hate—so long as they fear us! We must keep death dangling (*He makes the gesture of doing so*) before their eyes! (*He gives a soft, cruel laugh*) Will you not sacrifice in my honor? What are a few Greeks? (*Queerly*) I like to watch men die.

CRASSUS. I dare not, Caligula. Cæsar has forbidden bloodshed.

CALIGULA. Tiberius is a miser. He wants to hoard all of death for his own pleasure! (*He laughs again.*)

CRASSUS. (*with rough familiarity*) I wager no one will make that complaint against you when you are Cæsar! (*He chuckles.*)

CALIGULA. (*with the sudden grandiose posturing of a bad actor unintentionally burlesquing grandeur*) When I, Gaius Caligula, am Cæsar, I— (*Then superstitiously looking up at the sky with cringing foreboding*) But it brings bad luck to anticipate fate. (*He takes off his helmet and spits in it—then with a grim smile*) The heirs of a Cæsar take sick so mysteriously! Even with you who used to ride me on your knee, I do not eat nor drink until you have tasted first.

CRASSUS. (*nodding approvingly*) You are sensible. I suppose I, too, have my price—if they were only clever enough to discover it! (*He laughs hoarsely.*)

CALIGULA. (*steps back from him with an uneasy shudder*) You are honest, at least—too honest, Cneius! (*Grimly*) If my father Germanicus had had you for his counselor, he might have escaped their poison. (*Then gloomily*) I must fear everyone. The world is my enemy.

CRASSUS. Kill it then! (*He laughs again.*)

CHORUS. (*stretching out their arms in the direction from which* LAZARUS *is expected—supplicatingly*)

Son of the Lightning!
Deadly thy vengeance!
Swift thy deliverance!
Beholding thy Mother,
Greece, our Mother,
Her beauty in bondage,
Her pride in chains!
Hasten, Redeemer!

CROWD. (*as before—echoing the chant*)

Hasten, Redeemer!
Son of the Lightning!
Deadly thy vengeance!
Swift thy deliverance!

CALIGULA. (*disdainfully*) What clods! Mob is the same everywhere, eager to worship any new charlatan! They have already convinced themselves this Lazarus is a reincarnation of Dionysus! A Jew become a god! By the breasts of Venus that *is* a miracle! (*He laughs.*)

CRASSUS. (*seriously*) But he must be expert in magic. He was buried four days and came out unharmed. Maybe he is not a Jew. Some say his father was really a legionary of our garrison in Judea. And he teaches people to laugh at death. That smacks of Roman blood!

CALIGULA. (*ironically*) Better still! He tells them there is no death at all! Hence the multitude of fools who have acclaimed him everywhere since he left his own country—and why Tiberius has begun to fear his influence.

CRASSUS. (*sententiously*) Whom Cæsar fears—disappears!

CALIGULA. Yes, the dupes who follow Lazarus will be killed. But Tiberius believes this Lazarus may know a cure for death or for renewing youth, and the old lecher hopes he can worm the secret out of him—before he kills him. (*He laughs ironically, then dis-*

gustedly) That is why I must escort this Jew to Rome—as a special honor! (*With fierce, haughty resentment*) I, the heir of Cæsar! (*Savagely*) Oh, if I were Cæsar—!

CRASSUS. (*with a coarse, meaning smirk*) Patience. Tiberius is old.

CALIGULA. (*suddenly becoming terribly uneasy at some thought*) Cneius! What if this Lazarus has really discovered a cure for old age and should reveal it to Tiberius! (*His lips tremble, his eyes are terrified, he shrinks against* CRASSUS *for protection—with boyish pleading*) Oh, Cneius, what could I do then?

CRASSUS. (*matter-of-factly*) Kill him before Cæsar can talk to him.

CALIGULA. (*almost in tears*) But if he knows a charm against death how could he be slain, old fool?

CRASSUS. (*gruffly*) Bah! (*Then with grim humor*) Death in bed I suspect, but when men are killed I know they stay dead! (*Disgustedly*) A moment ago you were laughing at him! (*Scornfully*) Do you fear him now?

CALIGULA. (*rather shamefacedly pulls himself together—then broodingly*) I fear everyone who lives. Even you. As you advised me. (*He turns away.*)

CRASSUS. (*contemptuously*) Well, maybe he can teach you to laugh at fear. You would welcome him then, eh, cry baby?

CALIGULA. (*with sudden passionate intensity but only half aloud as if to himself*) I would love him, Cneius! As a father! As a god! (*He stands staring before him strangely. There is a new stir from the crowd who again push forward.*)

CRASSUS. (*pointing off right*) Look! I see a great crowd! Your Lazarus must be coming at last!

CHORUS. (*chanting in a deep, rhythmic monotone like the rising and falling cadences of waves on a beach*)

He comes, the Redeemer and Savior!
Laughing along the mountains!
To give back our lost laughter

To raise from the dead our freedom
To free us from Rome!

CROWD. (*echoing this chant*)
Fire-born! Redeemer! Savior!
Raise from the dead our freedom!
Give back our lost laughter!
Free us from Rome!

(*They have been pushing forward, more and more fiercely and defiantly. The* ROMAN SOLDIERS *in spite of their efforts are pushed backward step by step.*)

SOLDIERS. (*angrily*) Back! Back! (*The* SOLDIERS *work with a will, dealing out blows with their staves at everyone in reach. But now these blows seem only to infuriate the* CROWD *which steadily pushes them back into the street. At the same time the distant sound of exultant music, singing and laughter becomes steadily louder. Both* SOLDIERS *and* CROWD *are inspired to battle by these strains without their knowing it.* CALIGULA *is listening spell-bound, his mouth open, his body swaying and twitching. Even* CRASSUS *stares off at the oncomers, forgetful of the growing plight of his* SOLDIERS.)

CROWD. (*led by their* CHORUS—*angrily*)
Cowards! Pigs!
Strike! Hit!
Stones! Knives!
Stab! Kill!
Death to the Romans!
Death!

A SOLDIER. (*alarmed, calls to* CRASSUS) General! Let us use our swords!

SOLDIERS. (*enraged—eagerly*) Yes! Swords!

CROWD. Death!

CRASSUS. (*turning—uneasy but afraid to give any drastic order*) Bah! Staves are enough. Crack their skulls!

CROWD. (*led by the* CHORUS—*defiantly*)

Death to Crassus!
Drunkard! Coward!
Death to him!

(*They continue to push forward, hooting and jeering.*)

CRASSUS. (*exploding for a second*) By the gods—! (*to the* SOLDIERS) Draw your swords! (*The troops do so eagerly. The* CROWD *sag back momentarily with exclamations of fear.*)

CALIGULA. (*listening as in a trance to the music and what is going on behind him—in a queer whisper*) Kill, Cneius! Let me dance! Let me sing! (*The music and crashing of cymbals and the ferment of passions around him cause him to lose all control over himself. He gives a crazy leap in the air and begins to dance grotesquely and chant in a thick voice*) He is coming! Death, the Deliverer! Kill, soldiers! I command you! I, Caligula! I will be Cæsar! Death!

CROWD. (*led by the* CHORUS—*savage now*)

Beast! Cur!
Death to Caligula!

(*They crowd forward.*)

CALIGULA. (*drawing his sword and flourishing it drunkenly—his eyes glazed*) Death!

CRASSUS. (*drawing his own sword in a frenzy*) Strike! Death! (*His* SOLDIERS *raise their swords. The* CROWD *have raised whatever weapons they have found—knives, clubs, daggers, stones, bare fists.*)

CHORUS. (*chanting fiercely*)

Death!

ALL. (ROMANS *and* GREEKS *alike as one great voice*)

Death!

(*The chorused word beats down all sound into a stricken silence. The wild joyous music ceases. The* ROMANS *and* GREEKS *seem to lean back from one another and collect strength to leap forward. At this moment the voice of* LAZARUS *comes ringing through the air like a command from the sky.*)

LAZARUS. There is no death! (*The* SOLDIERS *and* GREEKS *remain frozen in their attitudes of murderous hate. Following his words the laughter of* LAZARUS *is heard, exultant and gaily mocking, filling them with the sheepish shame of children caught in mischief. Their heads hang, their arms sink to their sides. The music starts once more with a triumphant clash of cymbals,* LAZARUS' *laughter is echoed from the throats of the multitude of his* FOLLOWERS *who now come dancing into the square, preceded by a band of masked musicians and by their* CHORUS. *This* CHORUS *wears, in double size, the laughing mask of* LAZARUS' FOLLOWERS *in the same Period and Type as in the preceding scene, except that here the mask of each member of the* CHORUS *has a different racial basis—Egyptian, Syrian, Cappadocian, Lydian, Phrygian, Cilician, Parthian. The* FOLLOWERS *are costumed and masked as in the preceding scene, seven Types in seven Periods, except that, as in the* CHORUS, *racially there are many nations represented. All have wreaths of ivy in their hair and flowers in their hands which they scatter about. They whirl in between the* SOLDIERS *and* CROWD, *forcing them back from each other, teasing them, sifting into the* CROWD, *their* CHORUS *in a half circle, confronting the* CHORUS *of* GREEKS.)

CHORUS OF FOLLOWERS.

Laugh! Laugh!
There is no death!
There is only life!
There is only laughter!

FOLLOWERS. (*echoing*)

Laugh! Laugh!
There is no death!

(CALIGULA *and* CRASSUS *are swept to one side, left. Then the cries and laughter of all become mingled into one exclamation.*)

ALL.

Lazarus! Lazarus!

(*The squad of* ROMAN SOLDIERS *led by the* CENTURION, *who had taken* LAZARUS *prisoner, march in with dancers' steps, like a proud guard of honor now, laughing, pulling a chariot in which* LAZARUS *stands dressed in a tunic of white and gold, his bronzed face and limbs radiant in the halo of his own glowing light.* LAZARUS *now looks less than thirty-five. His countenance now might well be that of the positive masculine Dionysus, closest to the soil of the Grecian gods, a Son of Man, born of a mortal. Not the coarse, drunken Dionysus, nor the effeminate god, but Dionysus in his middle period, more comprehensive in his symbolism, the soul of the recurring seasons, of living and dying as processes in eternal growth, of the wine of life stirring forever in the sap and blood and loam of things.* MIRIAM *is beside him, dressed in black, smiling the same sad tender smile, holding* LAZARUS' *arm as if for protection and in protection. She appears older, a woman over forty-five.)*

CHORUS OF GREEKS. *(rushing to* LAZARUS' *car)*

Hail, Dionysus!
Iacchus!
Lazarus!
Hail!

(They surround him, throw over his shoulders and head the finely dressed hide of a bull with great gilded horns, force into his right hand the mystic rod of Dionysus with a pine cone on top, then prostrate themselves)

Hail, Savior!
Redeemer!
Conqueror of Death!

ALL. *(in a repeated chorus which finally includes even the* ROMAN SOLDIERS, *raising their arms to him)*

Hail, Lazarus!
Redeemer!
Hail!

(They are silent. LAZARUS *looks at them, seeming to see each and all at the same time, and his laughter, as if in answer to their greetings, is heard rising from his lips like a song.)*

CRASSUS. (*awed*) Look! He is more than man!

CALIGULA. (*trembling, in a queer agitation*) I dare not look!

CRASSUS. Do you hear his laughter?

CALIGULA. (*chokingly—puts his hands over his ears*) I will not hear!

CRASSUS. But you must welcome him in Cæsar's name!

CALIGULA. (*his teeth chattering*) I must kill him!

LAZARUS. (*looking directly at him—gaily mocking*) Death is dead, Caligula! (*He begins to laugh again softly.*)

CALIGULA. (*with an hysterical cry of defiant terror*) You lie! (*Sword in hand he whirls to confront* LAZARUS, *but at the first sight of his face he stops in his tracks, trembling, held fascinated by* LAZARUS' *eyes, mumbling with a last pitiful remainder of defiance*) But—you lie—whatever you are! I say there *must* be death! (*The sword has fallen to his side. He stares open-mouthed at* LAZARUS. *There is something of a shy, wondering child about his attitude now.* LAZARUS *looks at him, laughing with gentle understanding.* CALIGULA *suddenly drops his sword and covering his face with his hands weeps like a boy who has been hurt*) You have murdered my only friend, Lazarus! Death would have been my slave when I am Cæsar. He would have been my jester and made me laugh at fear! (*He weeps bitterly.*)

LAZARUS. (*gaily*) Be your own jester instead, O Caligula! Laugh at yourself, O Cæsar-to-be! (*He laughs. The* CROWD *now all join in with him,* CALIGULA *suddenly uncovers his face, grins his warped grin, gives a harsh cackle which cracks through the other laughter with a splitting discord, cuts a hopping caper like some grotesque cripple which takes him to the side of* LAZARUS' *chariot where he squats on his hams and, stretching out his hand, fingers* LAZARUS' *robe inquisitively and stares up into his face in the attitude of a chained monkey.*)

CALIGULA. (*with a childish, mischievous curiosity*) Then if there is no death, O Teacher, tell me why I love to kill?

LAZARUS. Because you fear to die! (*Then gaily mocking*) But what do you matter, O Deathly-Important One? Put yourself that question—as a jester! (*Exultantly*) Are you a speck of dust danced in the wind? Then laugh, dancing! Laugh yes to your insignificance! Thereby will be born your new greatness! As Man, Petty Tyrant of Earth, you are a bubble pricked by death into a void and a mocking silence! But as dust, you are eternal change, and everlasting growth, and a high note of laughter soaring through chaos from the deep heart of God! Be proud, O Dust! Then you may love the stars as equals! (*Then mockingly again*) And then perhaps you may be brave enough to love even your fellow men without fear of their vengeance!

CALIGULA. (*dully*) I cannot understand. I hate men. I am afraid of their poison and their swords and the cringing envy in their eyes that only yields to fear!

LAZARUS. (*gaily mocking*) Tragic is the plight of the tragedian whose only audience is himself! Life is for each man a solitary cell whose walls are mirrors. Terrified as Caligula by the faces he makes! But I tell you to laugh in the mirror, that seeing your life gay, you may begin to live as a guest, and not as a condemned one! (*Raising his hands for silence—with a playful smile*) Listen! In the dark peace of the grave the man called Lazarus rested. He was still weak, as one who recovers from a long illness—for, living, he had believed his life a sad one! (*He laughs softly, and softly they all echo his laughter*) He lay dreaming to the croon of silence, feeling as the flow of blood in his own veins the past re-enter the heart of God to be renewed by faith into the future. He thought: "Men call this death"—for he had been dead only a little while and he still remembered. Then, of a sudden, a strange gay laughter trembled from his heart as though his life, so long repressed in him by fear, had found at last its voice and a song for singing. "Men call this death," it sang. "Men call life death and fear it. They hide from it in horror. Their lives are spent in hiding. Their fear becomes their living. They worship life as death!"

CHORUS OF FOLLOWERS. (*in a chanting echo*)

Men call life death and fear it.
They hide from it in horror.

Their lives are spent in hiding.
Their fear becomes their living.
They worship life as death!

LAZARUS. And here the song of Lazarus' life grew pitiful. "Men must learn to live," it mourned. "Before their fear invented death they knew, but now they have forgotten. They must be taught to laugh again!" And Lazarus answered "Yes!" (*He now addresses the crowd—especially* CALIGULA, *directly, laughingly*) Thus sang his life to Lazarus while he lay dead! Man must learn to live by laughter! (*He laughs.*)

CHORUS OF FOLLOWERS.

Laugh! Laugh!
There is only life!
Their is only laughter!
Fear is no more!
Death is dead!

CHORUS OF GREEKS.

Laugh! Laugh!
Hail, Dionysus!
Fear is no more!
Thou hast conquered death!

ALL. (*laughing—in a great laughing chorus*)

Laugh! Laugh!
Fear is no more!
Death is dead!

LAZARUS. (*as to a crowd of children—laughingly*) Out with you! Out into the woods! Upon the hills! Cities are prisons wherein man locks himself from life. Out with you under the sky! Are the stars too pure for your sick passions? Is the warm earth smelling of night too desirous of love for your pale introspective lusts? Out! Let laughter be your new clean lust and sanity! So far man has only learned to snicker meanly at his neighbor! Let a laughing away of self be your new right to live forever! Cry in your pride, "I am

Laughter, which is Life, which is the Child of God!" (*He laughs and again his voice leads and dominates the rhythmic chorus of theirs. The music and dancing begin again.*)

THE TWO CHORUSES. (*chanting in unison*)

Laugh! Laugh!
There is only God!
We are His Laughter!

ALL. (*echoing*)

There is only God!
We are His Laughter!
Laugh! Laugh!

(*They take hold of his chariot traces, and as he had come in the midst of a happy multitude, now augmented by all the* GREEKS, *and the* ROMAN SOLDIERS *who had awaited him, dancing, playing, singing, laughing, he is escorted off. The noise of their passing recedes.* CALIGULA *and* CRASSUS *are left in the empty square, the former squatting on his hams, monkey-wise, and brooding somberly.*)

CRASSUS. (*is swaying and staggering, like a man in a drunken stupor, in a bewildered, stubborn struggle to control himself. He stammers after the* SOLDIERS) Ha-ha-ha— Halt! Halt, I say! No use—they are gone—mutiny—Halt! (*He continues to stumble toward left*) Ha-ha— Stop it, curse you! Am I laughing? Where am I going? After Lazarus? Thirty years of discipline and I— Halt, traitor! Remember Cæsar! Remember Rome! Halt, traitor! (*He faints with the violence of his struggle and falls in a limp heap.*)

CALIGULA. (*startled by his fall, terrified, hops to his feet and snatches up his sword defensively, glancing over his shoulder and whirling around as if he expected someone to stab him in the back. Then, forcing a twisted grin of self-contempt—harshly.*) Coward! What do I fear—if there is no death? (*As if he had to cut something, he snatches up a handful of flowers—desperately*) You must laugh, Caligula! (*He starts to lop off the flowers from their stems with a savage intentness*) Laugh! Laugh! Laugh! (*Finally, impatiently, he *cuts off all the remaining with one stroke*) Laugh! (*He grinds the petals under his feet and breaks out into a terrible hysterical giggle*) Ha-ha—

CURTAIN

SCENE TWO

SCENE: *A midnight, months later. Immediately inside the walls of Rome. In the foreground is the portico of a temple between whose massive columns one looks across a street on a lower level to the high wall of Rome at the extreme rear. In the center of the wall is a great metal gate. The night is thick and oppressive. In the sky overhead lightning flashes and thunder rumbles and crashes but there is no rain.*

Within the portico on rows of chairs placed on a series of wide steps which are on each side, members of the Senate are seated in their white robes. High hanging lamps cast a wan light over their faces. They are all masked in the Roman mask, refined in them by nobility of blood but at the same time with strength degenerated, corrupted by tyranny and debauchery to an exhausted cynicism. The three periods of Middle Age, Maturity and Old Age are represented in the types of the Self-Tortured, Introspective; Proud, Self-Reliant; the Servile, Hypocritical; the Cruel, Revengeful; and the Resigned, Sorrowful. The SENATORS *are divided into two groups on each side, thirty in each. Seated in the middle of the lower of the three high broad stairs that lead to the level from which the columns rise is the* CHORUS OF SENATORS, *seven in number, facing front, in double-sized masks of the Servile, Hypocritical type of Old Age.*

LAZARUS, *in his robe of white and gold, the aura of lights surrounding his body seeming to glow more brightly than ever, stands in the rear at the edge of the portico, center, gazing upward into the pall of sky beyond the wall. His figure appears in its immobility to be the statue of the god of the temple. Near him, but to the rear and to the left of him, facing right,* MIRIAM *is kneeling in her black robes, swaying backward and forward, praying silently with moving lips like a nun who asks mercy for the sins of the world. She has grown much older, her hair is gray, her shoulders are bowed.*

On the other side, placed similarly in relation to LAZARUS *and facing* MIRIAM, CALIGULA *is squatting on his hams on a sort of throne-chair of ivory and gold. He is dressed with foppish richness in extreme bright colors, a victory wreath around his head. He stares blinkingly and inquisitively at* LAZARUS, *then at* MIRIAM. *He is half-drunk. A large figured goblet of gold is in his hand. A slave with an amphora of wine crouches on the steps by his chair. The slave wears a black negroid mask.*

At the opening of the scene there is heard the steady tramp of departing troops, whose masks, helmets and armored shoulders can be seen as they pass through the street before LAZARUS *to the gate beyond. Finally with a metallic clash the gate is shut behind them and there is a heavy and oppressive silence in which only the murmured prayers of* MIRIAM *are heard.*

CHORUS OF THE SENATE. (*intones wearily, as if under a boring compulsion*)

The Roman Senate
Is the Roman Senate
The Mighty Voice
Of the Roman People
As long as Rome is Rome.

CALIGULA. (*as if he hadn't heard—sings hoarsely an old camp song of the Punic Wars, pounding with his goblet*)

A bold legionary am I!
March, oh march on!
A Roman eagle was my daddy,

My mother was a drunken drabby
Oh, march on to the wars!

Since lived that lady Leda
March, oh march on!
Women have loved high-fliers
And we are eagles of Rome!
Oh, march on to the wars!

Comrades, march to the wars!
There's pretty girls in Carthage
And wine to swill in Carthage,
So we must capture Carthage
And fight for Mother Rome!

(*Holds out his goblet to be refilled. There is silence again. He stares at* LAZARUS *with a somber intentness. He says thickly*) The legions have gone, Lazarus. (LAZARUS *gives no evidence of having heard him.* CALIGULA *gulps at his wine. The* SENATORS *begin to talk to each other in low voices.*)

FIRST SENATOR. How does that Jew make that light come from him, I wonder? It is a well-contrived bit of magic.

SECOND SENATOR. What are we waiting for? A messenger came to me with Cæsar's command that the Senate meet here at midnight.

THIRD SENATOR. (*bored*) Some new whim of Tiberius, naturally— (*With a meaning titter*)—or rather I should say, unnaturally!

FOURTH SENATOR. Perhaps Cæsar has decided to abolish our august body by a massacre in mass!

THIRD SENATOR. (*yawning*) There was a feast at Cinna's last night that lasted until this evening. I could welcome my own murder as an excuse for sleeping!

FIFTH SENATOR. (*pompously*) Tiberius would not dare harm the

Senate. He may mistreat individual Senators, but the Roman Senate is the Roman Senate!

CHORUS OF THE SENATE. (*as before—wearily as if under a boring compulsion—intones*)

While Rome is Rome
The Senate is the Senate
The Mighty Voice of the Roman People.

FIRST SENATOR. (*with the ghost of a laugh—wearily.*) The Senate is an empty name—a pack of degenerate cowards with no trace of their ancient nobility or courage remaining—that and no more!

THIRD SENATOR. (*flippantly*) You are too severe with yourself, Lucius! (*A titter of laughter.*)

FIRST SENATOR. (*wearily*) A degenerate coward. I am, I confess it. So are you too, Sulpicius—a hundred fold!—whether you admit it or not. (SULPICIUS *laughs weakly without taking offense.*)

SIXTH SENATOR. (*after a pause—sighing*) In truth, the Senate is not what it used to be. I can remember—

FIRST SENATOR. Let us forget, if we can! (*Then impatiently*) What are we doing here?

SECOND SENATOR. I imagine it has something to do with the followers of this Lazarus encamped outside the wall. Probably the legions are to butcher them in their sleep.

SEVENTH SENATOR. And what part do we play—official witnesses? But how can we witness at night and through a wall? (*With bored resignation.*) Ah, well, the moods of Tiberius are strange, to say the least. But Cæsar is Cæsar.

CHORUS. (*again with bored weariness as before*)

Hail!
Cæsar is Cæsar
The August One
Prince of the Senate
Tribune over Tribunes
Consul of Consuls

Supreme Pontiff
Emperor of Rome
God among Gods
Hail!

FIRST SENATOR. (*after a pause of silence—dryly*) Cæsar is a beast—and a madman!

FIFTH SENATOR. (*pompously*) Respect, sir! More respect for Cæsar!

THIRD SENATOR. (*mockingly*) Or caution, Lucius. One of us might repeat your opinion to him.

FIRST SENATOR. You would if it would pay you. But all my money is squandered. My death is worthless to Tiberius. He would not reward you. Moreover, you would not be revenged on me, for I long for death.

THIRD SENATOR. (*dryly*) Your stomach must be out of order.

FIRST SENATOR. The times are out of order. But let us change the subject. Is it true Tiberius has fled to Capri?

FOURTH SENATOR. Yes. He was terrified by the multitude of laughing idiots who appeared today with that charlatan. (*He points to* LAZARUS.)

SECOND SENATOR. There are thousands of them outside the wall. Cæsar refused to let them enter the city. The story is, this Lazarus was dead four days and then restored himself to life by magic.

FIRST SENATOR. I have a mind to question him. (*Calls as to a slave*) You, there! Jew, turn round! In the name of the Senate! (LAZARUS *seems not to hear him.* LUCIUS *remarks with a weary smile*) So much for our authority!

SIXTH SENATOR. (*with injured dignity*) What insolence! (*In a rage*) Ho, barbarian cur, turn round! The Senate commands you! (LAZARUS *does not seem to hear, but* CALIGULA *turns on them fiercely.*)

CALIGULA. Silence! Leave him alone! (*With insulting scorn*) I, Caligula, command *you!* (*The* SENATORS *seem to shrink back from him in fear, all but* LUCIUS, *who answers with a mocking servility.*)

FIRST SENATOR. At least, grant us the boon to see this corpse's face, O Gracious Gaius!

CALIGULA. (*fixing his cruel, burning eyes on him—softly*) I heard you wish for death, Lucius. When I am Cæsar you shall scream and pray for it!

FIRST SENATOR. (*dryly and haughtily*) You were bred in camp, Gaius. You should have learned more courage there along with your coarseness. But accept my gratitude for your warning. I shall take care to die before you become Cæsar—and life becomes too idiotic!

CALIGULA. (*his grin becoming ferocious with cruelty*) No. You are too weak to kill yourself. Look at me, Lucius! I am imagining what I shall have done to you! (*The* SENATORS *are now trembling. Even* LUCIUS *cannot repress a shudder of horror at the face glaring at him. Suddenly* CALIGULA *throws the cup from him and springs to his feet*) What good is wine if it cannot kill thought? Lazarus! It is time. I must give the signal! The legions are waiting. It is Cæsar's command that they spare none of your followers. (*He has walked toward* LAZARUS.)

MIRIAM. (*stretches out her hands to* CALIGULA *imploringly*) Mercy! Spare them who are so full of life and joy!

CALIGULA. (*harshly*) For their joy I will revenge myself upon them! Mercy? If there is no death, then death is a mercy! Ask that man! (*He points accusingly to* LAZARUS) And why should you plead for them, Jewess? There are few Jews among them. They are mostly those whom your people call idolaters and would gladly see murdered.

MIRIAM. (*with deep grief*) I am a mother of dead children. I plead for the mothers of those about to die.

CALIGULA. (*contemptuously*) Pah! (*He turns from her and puts his hand on* LAZARUS' *shoulder*) Lazarus! Do you hear? I must signal to the legions!

LAZARUS. (*turns. He has grown more youthful. He seems no more than thirty. His face is exalted and calm and beautiful. His eyes shine with an unearthly glory. The* SENATORS *lean forward in their seats, fascinated by his face. A low murmur of admiration comes from them.* LAZARUS *speaks commandingly*) Wait! I will awaken my beloved ones that their passing may be a symbol to the world that there is no death! (*He turns, throwing back his head and stretching up his arms, and begins to laugh low and tenderly, like caressing music at first but gradually gaining in volume, becoming more and more intense and insistent, finally ending up on a triumphant, blood-stirring call to that ultimate attainment in which all prepossession with self is lost in an ecstatic affirmation of Life. The voices of his* FOLLOWERS *from beyond the wall, at first one by one, then several at a time, then multitudes, join in his laughter. Even the* SENATORS *are drawn into it. Now every one of these is standing up, stretching out his arms toward* LAZARUS, *laughing harshly and discordantly and awkwardly in his attempt to laugh. Terrific flashes of lightning and crashes of thunder seem a responsive accompaniment from the heavens to this laughter of thousands which throbs in beating waves of sound in the air. Mingled with the laughing from beyond the wall comes the sound of singing and the music of flutes and cymbals.* MIRIAM *has crawled on her knees to the edge of the portico where her black figure of grief is outlined below and to the left of* LAZARUS, *her arms raised outward like the arms of a cross.*)

FOLLOWERS OF LAZARUS. (*in a great chanting singing chorus*)

Laugh! Laugh!
There is only God!
Life is His Laughter!
We are His Laughter!
Fear is no more!
Death is dead!

CHORUS OF SENATORS. (*taking it up in a tone between chanting and their old solemn intoning*)

Laugh! Laugh!

Fear is no more!
Death is dead!

ALL. (*the multitude beyond the wall, all the* SENATORS, *everyone except the never-laughing* MIRIAM *and* CALIGULA *and the* MEN OF THE LEGIONS)

Laugh! Laugh!
Death is dead!

CALIGULA. (*in a queer state of mingled exaltation and fear—hopping restlessly about from foot to foot—shouting*) The signal! Shall I give the signal to kill, Lazarus?

MEN OF THE LEGIONS. (*following a brazen trumpet call, are suddenly heard from beyond the wall beginning to laugh their hoarse, bass laughter, a deeper note than all the others*) Laugh! Laugh!

CALIGULA. (*listening—with dismay*) I hear the legions, Lazarus! They are laughing with them! (*He cries with a strange pitifulness and beseeching*) You are playing me false, Lazarus! You are trying to evade death! You are trying to spare your people! You are small and weak like other men when the test comes! You give way to pity! Your great laughter becomes pitiful! (*Working himself into a rage*) You are a traitor, Lazarus! You betray Cæsar! Have you forgotten I will be Cæsar? You betray me, Lazarus! (*He rushes to the edge and, making a megaphone of his hands, bellows*) You on the wall! Sentry! It is I, Caligula! Kill! (*The brazen trumpets of the* LEGIONS *sound from beyond the wall. He springs near* LAZARUS *again, in a fiendish ecstasy, dancing a hopping grotesque sword dance behind him, chanting as he does so*) Kill! Kill laughter! Kill those who deny Cæsar! I will be Cæsar! Kill those who deny Death! I will be Death! My face will be bright with blood! My laughing face, Lazarus! Laughing because men fear me! My face of victorious Fear! Look at me! I am laughing, Lazarus! *My* laughter! Laughter of gods and Cæsars! Ha-ha-ha-ha! (*He laughs, his laughter fanatically cruel and savage, forced from his lips with a desperate, destroying abandon. For a moment, above all the chorus of other sounds, his voice fights to overcome that of* LAZARUS, *whose laughter seems now to have attained the most exultant heights of spiritual affirmation. Then* CALIGULA *breaks into a cry of fear and a sob, and, casting his sword aside, he hides his face in his hands and cries beseechingly*) Forgive me! I love you, Lazarus! Forgive me! (*At this second the blaring trumpets of the* LEGIONS *are heard approaching and their great bass chorus of marching tramping laughter.*)

MEN OF THE LEGIONS. (*chanting*)

Laugh! Laugh! Laugh!
Fear, no more!
Death, no more!
Death is dead!

(*There is now no sound of the singing or the laughter or music of* LAZARUS' FOLLOWERS. MIRIAM *rocks to and fro and raises a low wail of lamentation. The* SENATORS *cheer and shout as at a triumph.*)

CHORUS OF SENATORS. (*saluting* LAZARUS)

Hail, Victor!
Hail, Divine One!
Thou hast slain fear!
Thou hast slain death!
Hail! Triumph!

SENATORS.

Hail! Hail!
Slayer of Fear!
Slayer of Death!

(*The gate in the wall is clanged open. The returning* LEGIONS *burst through and gather in a dense mob in the street below* LAZARUS, *who looks down upon them, silent but smiling gently now. They stare at him with admiration. Only a sea of their masks can be seen, their eyes shining exultantly.* CRASSUS, *their general, ascends the steps until he stands a little below* LAZARUS. *Their* CHORUS OF LEGIONARIES *in double-sized masks climb to the step below* CRASSUS, *forming behind him. They are in the Period of Manhood, of the Simple, Ignorant*

Type. No weapons can be seen—only their masks and helmets and armor gleaming in the lightning flashes and in the flickering light of torches. Their laughter seems to shake the walls and make the pillars of the temple dance.)

CHORUS OF THE LEGIONS.

Fear, no more!
Death, no more!
Death is dead!

LEGIONARIES. (*echoing*)

Laugh! Laugh! Laugh!
Death is dead!

CRASSUS. (*raising his hand*) Silence! (*They obey. He turns to* LAZARUS *and bows his head, falling on one knee, raising his right arm*) Hail!

LEGIONARIES. (*as one man—raising their arms.*) Hail!

CALIGULA. (*suddenly pushes forward impudently and strikes a grandiose attitude*) I am here, my brave ones! (*There is a roar of mocking laughter from the* LEGIONARIES.)

CRASSUS. (*not unkindly*) Not you, Little Killer! We hail the Great Laugher!

CALIGULA. (*harshly*) Have you killed all his followers?

CRASSUS. No. They died. They did not wait for our attack. They charged upon us, laughing! They tore our swords away from us, laughing, and we laughed with them! They stabbed themselves, dancing as though it were a festival! They died, laughing, in one another's arms! We laughed, too, with joy because it seemed it was not they who died but death itself they killed! (*He stops uncertainly, bowing to* LAZARUS, *awkwardly*) I do not understand this. I am a soldier. But there is a god in it somewhere! For I know they were drunk, and so were we, with a happiness no mortal ever felt on earth before! And death was dead! (*In a sudden outburst as if he were drunk with excitement, he takes off his helmet and waves it*) Hail, Deliverer! Death is dead! We left our swords with them! What virtue in killing when there is no death? Your foe laughs. The joke is on you. What a fool's game, eh? One can only laugh! Now we want peace to laugh in—to laugh at war! Let Cæsars fight—that is all they are good for—and not much good for that!

CALIGULA. (*frenziedly*) Silence, impious traitor!

CRASSUS. (*smiling drunkenly*) Shut up, yourself, camp-brat! Though you were Cæsar this minute I would laugh at you! Your death is dead! We will make Lazarus Cæsar! What say you? (*He appeals to the* SOLDIERS.)

CALIGULA. No!

CHORUS OF THE LEGIONS. (*with laughing intoxication*) Hail, Lazarus Cæsar! Hail!

LEGIONARIES. Lazarus Cæsar, hail!

CRASSUS. (*appealing to* SENATE) And you, Senators!

CHORUS OF SENATORS. (*with the same joyous intoxication as the* SOLDIERS) Hail, Lazarus Cæsar! Hail!

SENATORS. Lazarus Cæsar, hail!

CALIGULA. (*piteously*) No, Lazarus! Say no for my sake!

LAZARUS. (*with gay mockery*) What is—Cæsar? (*He begins to laugh with mockery. All except* CALIGULA *and* MIRIAM *join in this laughter.*)

CRASSUS. Ha-ha! What is Cæsar? You are right! You deserve better from us. A god? How is that? We will build you a temple, Lazarus, and make you a god!

LAZARUS. (*laughingly*) When men make gods, there is no God! (*He laughs. They all laugh.*)

CRASSUS. (*with puzzled good-nature*) I do not understand. But there is a god in it somewhere—a god of peace—a god of happiness! Perhaps you are already he, eh? Are you? Well, never mind now, remember our offer. Give us your answer tomorrow. Good night to you!

LAZARUS. (*as the* SOLDIERS *start to march away behind* CRASSUS, *and the* SENATORS *turn to retire, he stops them all for a moment with a gesture—with a deep earnestness*) Wait! When you awake tomorrow, try to remember! Remember that death is dead! Remember to laugh!

ALL. (*as if taking an oath with one voice*) We will remember, Lazarus!

CRASSUS. (*making a sign to the regimental musicians jovially*) And we will laugh! Play there! (*The bands crash out. The* LEGIONS *tramp away.*)

CHORUS OF THE LEGIONS. (*chanting to the music*)

Laugh! Laugh! Laugh!
Cæsar, no more!
War, no more!
Wounds, no more!
Death is dead!
Dead! Dead! Dead!

LEGIONARIES.

Laugh! Laugh! Laugh!
Death is dead!
Dead! Dead! Dead!

CHORUS OF SENATORS. (*following them*)

Cæsar, no more!
Fear, no more!
Death, no more!
Laugh! Laugh! Laugh!

SENATE. (*elated, excited as a crowd of schoolboys going on a vacation. Marching after them*)

Laugh! Laugh! Laugh!
Death is dead!

(LAZARUS, MIRIAM *and* CALIGULA *remain.*)

LAZARUS. (*with a great yearning*) If men would remember! If they could! (*He stares after them compassionately.*)

CALIGULA. (*crouching beside* LAZARUS. *Plucks at his robe humbly*) You will not laugh at Cæsar, Lazarus, will you—when I am Cæsar? You will not laugh at gods when they make me a god? (LAZARUS *does not answer.* CALIGULA *forces a cruel vindictive smile*) I swear you shall not laugh at death when I am Death! Ha-ha— (*He starts to laugh harshly—then suddenly, terrified, slinks away and sidles off at right.*)

MIRIAM. (*from where she kneels bowed with grief—brokenly*) Those who have just died were like your children, Lazarus. They believed in you and loved you.

LAZARUS. And I loved them!

MIRIAM. Then how could you laugh when they were dying?

LAZARUS. (*exultingly*) Did they not laugh? That was their victory and glory! (*With more and more of a passionate, proud exultation*) Eye to eye with the Fear of Death, did they not laugh with scorn? "Death to old Death," they laughed! "Once as squirming specks we crept from the tides of the sea. Now we return to the sea! Once as quivering flecks of rhythm we beat down from the sun. Now we re-enter the sun! Cast aside is our pitiable pretense, our immortal egohood, the holy lantern behind which cringed our Fear of the Dark! Flung off is that impudent insult to life's nobility which gibbers: 'I, this Jew, this Roman, this noble or this slave, must survive in my pettiness forever!' Away with such cowardice of spirit! We will to die! We will to change! Laughing we lived with our gift, now with laughter give we back that gift to become again the Essence of the Giver! Dying we laugh with the Infinite. We are the Giver and the Gift! Laughing, we will our own annihilation! Laughing, we give our lives for Life's sake!" (*He laughs up to heaven ecstatically*) This must Man will as his end and his new beginning! He must conceive and desire his own passing as a mood of eternal laughter and cry with pride, "Take back, O God, and accept in turn a gift from me, my grateful blessing for Your gift—and see, O God, now I am laughing with You! I am Your laughter—and You are mine!" (*He laughs again, his laughter dying lingeringly and tenderly on his lips like a strain of music receding into the silence over still waters.*)

MIRIAM. (*with a sigh—meekly*) I cannot understand, Lazarus.

(*Sadly*) They were like your children—and they have died. Must you not mourn for them?

LAZARUS. (*gently*) Mourn? When they laughed?

MIRIAM. (*sadly*) They are gone from us. And their mothers weep.

LAZARUS. (*puts his arm around her and raises her to her feet—tenderly*) But God, their Father, laughs! (*He kisses her on the forehead.*)

CURTAIN

ACT THREE—SCENE ONE

SCENE: *Some days later—exterior of* TIBERIUS' *villa-palace at Capri. It is about two in the morning of a clear black night. In the rear, the walls of the villa, which is built entirely of marble on the brow of a cliff, loom up with a startling clarity against the sky. The rear foreground is a marble terrace at the middle of which is a triumphal arch. On each side, leading up to it, are massive marble columns standing like the mummies of legionaries at attention. In the exact centre of the arch itself a cross is set up on which a full grown male lion has been crucified. A lamp reflecting downward has been fixed at the top of the cross to light up an inscription placed over the lion's head. Below the steps to the terrace, in a line facing front, on each side of the cross, is the* CHORUS OF THE GUARD *in their double masks and gorgeous uniforms and armor. Their masks are the same as the* LEGIONARY CHORUS *of the previous scene.*

The windows of the palace glow crimson-purple with the reflection of many shaded lamps. The sound of music in a strained theme of that joyless abandon which is vice is heard above a confused drunken clamor of voices, punctuated by the high, staccato laughter of women and youths. A squad of the GUARD *in the same uniforms as the* CHORUS, *masked as all the* ROMAN SOLDIERS *previously, enter from the left, front, climbing up from the beach below. They are commanded by a Centurion,* FLAVIUS. *His mask is that of a typical young patrician officer. They are followed by* LAZARUS *and* MIRIAM. CALIGULA *walks behind, his drawn sword in his hand. He is in a state of queer conflicting emotion, seeming to be filled with a nervous dread and terror of everything about him, while at the same time perversely excited and elated by his own morbid tension.* LAZARUS, *looking no more than twenty-five, haloed in his own mystic light, walks in a deep, detached serenity.*

MIRIAM, *in black, her hair almost white now, her figure bowed and feeble, seems more than ever a figure of a sad, resigned mother of the dead. The soldiers form in line with the columns.*

FLAVIUS. (*saluting* CALIGULA—*with an awed glance at* LAZARUS) I will announce your coming— (*As if in spite of himself he bows awkwardly to* LAZARUS)—and that of this man. Cæsar was not expecting you so soon, I think.

CALIGULA. (*forcing a light tone*) Lazarus laughed and the galley slaves forgot their fetters and made their oars fly as if they were bound for the Blessed Isles of Liberty! (*Then with an ironic smile*) But you need not tell Tiberius that, good Flavius. Say it was due to my extreme zeal.

FLAVIUS. (*smiles with respectful understanding.* CALIGULA *nods in dismissal.* FLAVIUS *turns to go—apologetically*) You may have to wait. I dare not speak before he questions me. (FLAVIUS *salutes and hastens to the villa, walking under an arm of the cross unconcernedly without an upward glance. As they follow him with their eyes* CALIGULA *and* MIRIAM *see the lion for the first time. He steps back with a startled exclamation. She gives a cry of horror and covers her eyes with her hands to shut out the sight.*)

LAZARUS. (*immediately puts his arms around her protectingly*) What is it, Beloved? (*She hides her face on his breast, pointing toward the lion with a trembling hand.*)

CALIGULA. (*pointing—curiously now, but with entire callousness*) This lion they have crucified. Are you frightened, Jewess? (*With a cruel laugh*) My grandfather frequently plants whole orchards of such trees, but usually they bear human fruit!

MIRIAM. (*with a shudder*) Monster!

CALIGULA. (*with genuine surprise—turning to her*) Who? Why? (*He approaches the cross and stares at it moodily*) But why did he have it placed here where he knew you must pass? Tiberius does not go to such pains to frighten women. (*His eyes fasten on the inscription above the lion's head*) Aha! I see! (*He reads*) "From the East, land of false gods and superstition, this lion was brought to Rome to amuse Cæsar." (*A silence.* CALIGULA *shrugs his shoulders, turning away—lightly*) A lesson for you, Lazarus. An example for other lions—not to roar—or laugh—at Cæsar! (*He gives a harsh laugh*) Tiberius must be terribly afraid of you. (*Then somberly*) You should never have come here. I would have advised you not to—but what are you to me? My duty, if I wish to become Cæsar, is to Cæsar. Besides, you are no fool. Evidently you must desire your own death. Last night *you* might have been Cæsar. The legions were yours.

LAZARUS. (*smiling without bitterness—with a sad comprehension*) But this morning the legions had forgotten. They only remembered—to go out and pick up their swords! They also pillaged the bodies a little, as their right, believing now that they had slain them! (*This last a bit bitterly.*)

CALIGULA. (*tauntingly*) The legions did slay them! It was only by some magician's trick you made them think your followers killed themselves.

LAZARUS. (*not answering him—ironically to himself*) It is too soon. Men still need their swords to slash at ghosts in the dark. Men, those haunted heroes! (*He laughs softly.*)

CALIGULA. (*irritably*) What are you laughing at?

LAZARUS. At Lazarus when I find him feeling wronged because men are men! (*He laughs again, softly and musically.*)

CALIGULA. (*again taunting brutally*) You may be in his place soon! (*He points to the lion*) Will you laugh then? (MIRIAM *gives a cry of terror.*)

LAZARUS. (*calmly*) Yes. (*Then humbly, bowing his head*) I will laugh with the pride of a beggar set upon the throne of Man!

CALIGULA. (*sneeringly*) You boast. (*Then as* LAZARUS *does not answer, touching the lion with intentional provoking brutality*) This one from Africa seems almost gone. They do not last as long as men.

LAZARUS. (*walks up the steps to the cross and, stretching to his full height, gently pushes the lion's hair out of its eyes—tenderly*) Poor brother! Cæsar avenges himself on you because of me. Forgive me your suffering!

CALIGULA. (*with a start backward—with frightened awe*) Gods! He licks your hand! I could swear he smiles—with his last breath! (*Then with relief*) Now he is dead!

LAZARUS. (*gently*) There is no death.

CALIGULA. (*pointing to the lion*) What is that then?

LAZARUS. Your fear of life.

CALIGULA. (*impatiently*) Bah! (*Then somberly*) A little fear is useful even for lions—or teachers of laughter if they wish to laugh long! (*Then with a sudden exasperation*) Escape now, you fool, while there is still time!

LAZARUS. (*laughing softly*) Escape—what?

CALIGULA. (*in a frenzy*) You know, you ass, you lunatic! Escape death! Death! Death! (*To* MIRIAM) You, woman! Talk to him! Do you want him nailed up like that?

MIRIAM. (*with a pitiful cry*) Lazarus! Come! Caligula will help us!

CALIGULA. (*harshly*) You presume, Jewess! I have no wish to die! (*Then with his wry smile*) But I will turn my back—and shut my eyes—(*He walks away to left.*)

MIRIAM. (*beseechingly*) Lazarus! I could not bear that aching hunger of my empty heart if you should die again!

LAZARUS. (*coming to her—tenderly*) I will not leave you! Believe in me! (*He kisses her forehead tenderly.*)

MIRIAM. (*after a pause—slowly and lamentingly*) I wish we were home, Lazarus. This Roman world is full of evil. These skies threaten. These hearts are heavy with hatred. There is a taint of blood in the air that poisons the breath of the sea. These columns and arches and thick walls seem waiting to fall, to crush these rotten men and then to crumble over the bones that raised them until both are dust. It is a world deadly to your joy, Lazarus. Its pleasure is a gorging of dirt, its fulfilled desire a snoring in a sty in the mud among swine. Its will is so sick that it must kill in order to be aware of life at all. I wish we were home, Lazarus. I begin to feel horror gnawing at my breast. I begin to know the torture of the fear of death, Lazarus—not of my death but of yours—not of the passing of your man's body but of the going away from me of your laughter which is to me as my son, my little boy!

LAZARUS. (*soothing her*) Be comforted, Beloved. Your fear shall never be!

MIRIAM. On the hills near Bethany you might pray at noon and laugh your boy's laughter in the sun and there would be echoing laughter from the sky and up from the grass and distantly from the shining sea. We would adopt children whose parents the Romans had butchered, and their laughter would be around me in my home where I cooked and weaved and sang. And in the dawn at your going out, and in the evening on your return, I would hear in the hushed air the bleating of sheep and the tinkling of many little bells and your voice. And my heart would know peace.

LAZARUS. (*tenderly*) Only a little longer! There is God's laughter on the hills of space, and the happiness of children, and the soft healing of innumerable dawns and evenings, and the blessing of peace!

CALIGULA. (*looks around at* LAZARUS *impatiently. Then he makes a beckoning gesture to* MIRIAM) Ssstt! (*Wonderingly she leaves* LAZARUS' *side and follows him.* LAZARUS *remains, his eyes fixed on the cross, directly in front of it.* CALIGULA *speaks gruffly to* MIRIAM *with a sneer*) Jewess, your Lazarus is mad, I begin to think. (*Then confusedly but helplessly inquisitive and confiding—bursting out*) What is it troubles me about him? What makes me dream of him?

Why should I—love him, Jewess? Tell me! You love him, too. I do not understand this. Why, wherever he goes, is there joy? You heard even the galley slaves laugh and clank time with their chains! (*Then with exasperation*) And yet why can I not laugh, Jewess?

MIRIAM. (*in a tone of hushed grief*) I may not laugh either. My heart remains a little dead with Lazarus in Bethany. The miracle could not revive all his old husband's life in my wife's heart.

CALIGULA. (*disgustedly*) What answer is that to me? (*Then brusquely*) But I called you to put you on your guard. (*He points*) There is death in there—Tiberius' death, a kind from which no miracles can recall one! (*He smiles his twisted smile*) Since Lazarus will not help himself, you must protect him. I will not, for once in there I am (*Mockingly*) the heir of Cæsar, and you are scum whom I will kill at his order as I would two beetles! So keep watch! Taste first of what he eats—even were I the one to give it to him!

LAZARUS. (*suddenly laughs softly*) Why do you delight in believing evil of yourself, Caligula?

CALIGULA. (*flying into a queer rage*) You lie! I am what I am! (*With grandiose pride*) What could you know of a Cæsar?

LAZARUS. (*still laughing with an affectionate understanding*) What—I know! (*As he finishes speaking all the sound of music and voices from the house ceases abruptly and there is a heavy silence.*)

MIRIAM. (*shaking her head and turning away sadly*) That is too far, Lazarus. Let us go home.

CALIGULA. (*harshly*) Sst! Do you hear? Flavius has told Cæsar. (*Grimly forcing a harsh snicker*) Now we will soon know— (*There is the sudden blaring of a trumpet from within the palace. A wide door is flung open and a stream of reddish light comes out against which the black figures of several men are outlined. The door is shut again quickly. Several* SLAVES *bearing lamps on poles escort the patrician,* MARCELLUS, *forward to the arch. He passes under the crucified lion without a glance—then stands, cool and disdainful, to look about him. He is a man of about thirty-five, wearing the type mask of a Roman patrician to which are added the dissipated courtier's characteristics of one who leans to evil more through weakness than any instinctive urge. He is dressed richly. His smile is hypocritical and his eyes are hard and cold but when they come to rest on* LAZARUS *he gives a start of genuine astonishment.*)

CALIGULA. (*who has moved to* LAZARUS' *side defensively—in a quick whisper*) Beware of this man, Lazarus! (*Then advancing—with a condescending hauteur*) Greeting, Marcellus!

MARCELLUS. (*in an ingratiating tone*) Greeting, Gaius. I have a message from Cæsar for the man called Lazarus.

LAZARUS. (*calmly*) I am Lazarus.

MARCELLUS. (*makes a deep bow—flatteringly*) I had surmised it, sir. Although I cannot pretend to virtue in myself at least I may claim the merit of recognizing it in others. (*He advances toward* LAZARUS, *smiling, with one hand kept hidden beneath his cloak.*)

CALIGULA. (*stepping between them—sharply*) What is your message?

MARCELLUS. (*surprised—placatingly*) I am sorry, Gaius, but it was Cæsar's command I speak to Lazarus alone.

CALIGULA. (*fiercely*) And then, Marcellus? (MARCELLUS *shrugs his shoulders and smiles deprecatingly.*)

LAZARUS. (*with a compelling dignity*) Let him speak. (*Inclining his head to* MARCELLUS*—strangely*) Over here where it is dark you will not be seen—nor see yourself. (*He walks to the darkness at right.*)

CALIGULA. (*turning his back on them, with angry boyish resentfulness that is close to tears*) Idiot! Go and die, then!

MIRIAM. (*with a terrified cry*) Lazarus! (*She starts to go to him.*)

LAZARUS. (*motioning her to remain where she is—gently*) Believe, Beloved! (*He turns his back on them all and stands waiting.*)

MARCELLUS. (*stares at* LAZARUS*—then over his shoulder at* CALIGULA

—uncertainly) What does he mean, Gaius? (*Then suddenly putting on a brave front, he strides up behind* LAZARUS) Cæsar wished me to bid you welcome, to tell you how much regard he has for you, but he desired me to ask whether you propose to laugh here—in Cæsar's palace? He has heard that you laugh at death—that you have caused others to laugh—even his legionaries. (*A pause,* MARCELLUS *remains behind* LAZARUS' *back, the latter standing like a victim*) Briefly, Cæsar requires your pledge that you will not laugh. Will you give it? (*He frees his dagger from under his robe. A pause. Arrogantly*) I am waiting! Answer when Cæsar commands! (*Then angrily, baffled*) I will give you while I count three—or take your silence as a refusal! One! Two! Three! (*He raises his hand to stab* LAZARUS *in the back.* MIRIAM *stifles a scream. At the same instant,* LAZARUS *begins to laugh, softly and affectionately.* MARCELLUS *stops, frozen in mid-action, the dagger upraised.* CALIGULA *has whirled around and stands staring, a smile gradually coming to his face.* LAZARUS *turns, his laughter grown a trifle louder, and faces* MARCELLUS. *The latter steps back from him, staring open-mouthed, fascinated. His arm sinks to his side. The dagger falls from his fingers. He smiles back at* LAZARUS*—the curious, sheepish, bashful smile of one who has fallen in love and been discovered.*)

LAZARUS. (*going to him, puts both hands on his shoulders and looks in his eyes, laughing affectionately—then quizzically*) Here is another one who believes in death! But soon you will laugh with life! I see it in your eyes. Farewell, Marcellus! (*He turns away from him and walks, laughing, toward the arch in rear. With bowed head the black-robed figure of* MIRIAM *follows him.* MARCELLUS *hides his face in his hands, half-sobbing, and half-laughing hysterically.* LAZARUS *pauses before the cross for a moment—raises his hand as if blessing the dead lion, then passes below it, moving slowly on toward the palace in the rear. His laughter rises with more and more summoning power. The files of the* GUARD, *as he passes them, two by two join in his laughter, saluting him as if in spite of themselves.*)

CALIGULA. (*sidling up to* MARCELLUS, *cruel and mocking*) Are you weeping, Marcellus? Laugh at that blundering fool, yourself! What will Cæsar say? Will he laugh when he has your body broken one bone at a time with hammers? Why did you not kill? For shame! A patrician exposed to laughter by a Jew! Poor craven! Why could you not strike? There *must* be death! Coward! Why did you not stab? (*Then in a queer awed whisper*) I know! Was it not because of a sudden you loved him and could not?

MARCELLUS. (*suddenly—eagerly*) Yes! That was it! I loved him!

CALIGULA. (*craftily and cruelly*) You were about to murder him!

MARCELLUS. (*tortured with remorse*) No! No! How could I? What infamy! (*Cries tearfully*) Forgive me, Lazarus!

CALIGULA. (*with vindictive insistence*) Judge yourself! (*He takes up the dagger*) Here is your dagger! Avenge him on yourself!

MARCELLUS. (*trying to laugh*) Ha-ha— Yes! (*He stabs himself and falls. Suddenly his laughter is released*) I laugh! You are a fool, Caligula! There is no death! (*He dies, laughing up at the sky.*)

CALIGULA. (*kicks his body with savage cruelty*) You lie! (*Then suddenly kneels and bends over it imploringly*) Tell me you lie, Marcellus! Do me that mercy!—and when I am Cæsar, I— (*He begins to weep like a frightened boy, his head in his hands. Meanwhile* LAZARUS *has arrived with* MIRIAM *at the steps before the door of the palace. As he starts to ascend these, the crimson-purple lights of the many windows of the palace go out one by one as if fleeing in terror from the laughter which now beats at the walls.*)

CHORUS OF THE GUARD.

Fear, no more!
Death, no more!
Laugh! Laugh! Laugh!
Death is dead!

ALL THE GUARDS. (*now all in a great chorus, raising their spears aloft and saluting* LAZARUS *as if they were his own triumphal body guard.*)

Laugh! Laugh! Laugh!
Death is dead!

(LAZARUS *has ascended the steps. He walks into the black archway of the darkened palace, his figure radiant and unearthly in his own light.* MIRIAM *follows him. They disappear in the darkness. There is a pause of dead silence.*)

CALIGULA. (*raises his head uneasily, looks back toward the palace, jumps to his feet in a panic of terror, and runs toward the palace door, calling*) Lazarus! Wait! I will defend you! There is death inside there—death! Beware, Lazarus!

CHORUS OF THE GUARD. (*as the laughter of* LAZARUS *is heard again from the dark palace.*)

Laugh! Laugh! Laugh!
Death is dead!

ALL THE GUARDS.

Dead! Dead! Dead!
Death is dead!

CURTAIN

SCENE TWO

SCENE: *The banquet hall in the palace of* TIBERIUS*—an immense high-ceilinged room. In the rear, center, is a great arched doorway. Smaller arches in the middle of the side walls lead into other rooms. Long couches are placed along the walls at right and left, and along the rear wall on either side of the arch. Before these couches, a series of narrow tables is set. In the center of the room on a high dais is the ivory and gold chair of* CÆSAR, *a table in front of it; couches for him to recline on at either side. On this table, and on all the tables for his guests, gold lamps with shades of crimson-purple are placed,*

Reclining on the couches on the right are young women and girls, on the left, youths of an equal number.

(The masks are based on the Roman masks of the periods of Boyhood (or Girlhood), Youth, and Young Manhood (or Womanhood) and there are seven individuals of each period and sex in each of the three types of the Introspective, Self-Tortured; the Servile, Hypocritical; and the Cruel, Revengeful—a crowd of forty-two in all. There is a distinctive character to the masks of each sex, the stamp of an effeminate corruption on all the male, while the female have a bold, masculine expression. The male masks are a blotched heliotrope in shade. These youths wear female wigs of curled wire like frizzed hair of a yellow gold. They are dressed in women's robes of pale heliotrope, they wear anklets and bracelets and necklaces. The women are dressed as males in crimson or deep purple. They also wear wire wigs but of straight hair cut in short boyish mode, dyed either deep purple or crimson. Those with crimson hair are dressed in purple, and vice versa. The female voices are harsh, strident, mannish—those of the youths affected, lisping, effeminate. The whole effect of these two groups is of sex corrupted and warped, of invented lusts and artificial vices.

The CHORUS *in this scene and the next is composed of three males and four females—the males in the period of Youth, one in each of the types represented, and three of the females in similar type-period masks. The fourth female is masked in the period of Womanhood in the Proud, Self-Reliant type. They sit, facing front in their double-sized masks, on the side steps of the dais, four on right, three on left.)*

POMPEIA, *a Roman noblewoman, the favorite mistress of* CÆSAR, *sits at front, right.*

She wears a half-mask on the upper part of her face, olive-colored with the red of blood smoldering through, with great, dark, cruel eyes—a dissipated mask of intense evil beauty, of lust and perverted passion. Beneath the mask, her own complexion is pale, her gentle, girlish mouth is set in an expression of agonized self-loathing and weariness of spirit. Her body is strong and beautiful. Her wig and dress are purple.

TIBERIUS CÆSAR *stands on the dais, dressed in deep purple, fringed and ornamented with crimson and gold. An old man of seventy-six, tall, broad and corpulent but of great muscular strength still despite his age, his shiny white cranium rises like a polished shell above his half-masked face. This mask is a pallid purple blotched with darker color, as if the imperial blood in his veins had been sickened by age and debauchery. The eyes are protuberant, leering, cynical slits, the long nose, once finely modeled, now gross and thickened, the forehead lowering and grim. Beneath the mask, his own mouth looks as incongruous as* CALIGULA'S. *The lips are thin and stern and self-contained—the lips of an able soldier-statesman of rigid probity. His chin is forceful and severe. The complexion of his own skin is that of a healthy old campaigner.*

As the curtain rises, slaves are hurriedly putting out the many lamps. From outside, the laughter of LAZARUS *rises on the deep ground swell of the* GUARD'S *laughter. The walls and massive columns seem to reverberate with the sound. In the banquet room all are listening fascinatedly. Every reaction, from the extreme of panic fear or hypnotized ecstasy to a feigned cynical amusement or a pretended supercilious indifference, is represented in their frozen attitudes.* TIBERIUS *stands, shrinking back, staring at the doorway in the rear with superstitious dread. A squad of the* GUARD *surround the dais, commanded by* FLAVIUS.

TIBERIUS. (*in a strained voice shaken by apprehension and awe*) Marcellus! Strike him down! Stab him!

SOLDIERS OF THE GUARD. (*from without*)

Laugh! Laugh! Laugh!
Death is dead!

TIBERIUS (*as he suddenly sees the shining figure of* LAZARUS *appear at the end of the dark hall beyond the archway*) Gods! Flavius, look! (*He points with a shaking finger.* FLAVIUS *has leaped up to his side.*)

FLAVIUS. (*not without dread himself*) That is the man, Cæsar.

TIBERIUS. Man? Say a dæmon! (*To the slaves who are turning out the few remaining lamps*) Quick! Darkness! (*He puts out the lamp on his table himself. Then as nothing is seen but the light from the approaching* LAZARUS) Flavius! Stand here in my place! It will think you are Cæsar! (*He clumps heavily down the steps of the dais*) Guards! Here! Cover me with your shields! (*He goes to the extreme right corner, front, and crouches there. His* GUARDS *follow him. They hold their shields so that they form a wall around him and half over him. Then* CALIGULA'S *voice is heard screaming above the chorus of laughter as he enters the hall behind* LAZARUS.)

CALIGULA. Beware of death! I will defend you, Lazarus! (*He is seen to rush past* LAZARUS, *flourishing his sword and comes running into the room, shouting*) Cæsar! Dare not to murder Lazarus! (*He leaps to the dais and up its steps in a frenzy*) Dare not, I say! (*He stabs* FLAVIUS *with a savage cry*) Ah! (*Then, as the body of* FLAVIUS *falls heavily and rolls down the steps at right, he begins to laugh, at first a clear laughter of selfless joy, sounding startlingly incongruous from him*) I have saved you, Lazarus—at the risk of my own life—and now, hear me, I can laugh! (LAZARUS *appears in the archway,* MIRIAM *behind him. He stops laughing and immediately there is silence, except for* CALIGULA. LAZARUS *casts a luminous glow over the whole room in which the masked faces appear distorted and livid.* CALIGULA *stands with upraised sword by the chair of* CÆSAR. *Suddenly his laughter cracks, changes, becomes full of his old fear and blood-lust.*)

CALIGULA. Ha-ha-ha! See, Lazarus! (*He points to the body of* FLAVIUS *with his sword*) Welcome in the name of Cæsar, now Cæsar is slain and I am Cæsar! (*He assumes the absurd grandiose posture of his imperial posing. No one looks at him or hears him. Their eyes are on* LAZARUS *as he moves directly to where* TIBERIUS *crouches behind the shields of the* GUARDS. MIRIAM *follows him.* CALIGULA *turns and stares toward him, and then down at the body of* FLAVIUS *and back, in a petrified, bewildered stupor.* LAZARUS *steps up beside* TIBERIUS. *The* GUARDS *make way for him fearfully.*)

TIBERIUS. (*feeling his nearness—straightening himself with a certain dignity*) Strike! I have been a soldier. Thou canst not make me fear death, Dæmon! (*He draws his toga over his face.*)

LAZARUS. (*smiling gently*) Then fear not fear, Tiberius! (*He reaches out and pulls back the toga from his face.* TIBERIUS *looks into his eyes, at first shrinkingly, then with growing reassurance, his own masked face clearly revealed now in the light from* LAZARUS.)

TIBERIUS. (*at first falteringly*) So—thou art not evil? Thou art not come to contrive my murder? (*As* LAZARUS *smilingly shakes his head,* TIBERIUS *frowns*) Then why dost thou laugh against Cæsar? (*Then bitterly—with a twisted attempt at a smile*) Yet I like thy laughter. It is young. Once I laughed somewhat like that—so I pardon thee. I will even laugh at thee in return. Ha-ha! (*His laughter is cold, cruel and merciless as the grin of a skeleton.*)

CALIGULA. (*who has been staring in a bewildered stupor from* TIBERIUS, *whom he thought he had killed, to the body of* FLAVIUS—*quaking with terror now as if this laugh was meant for him, drops to his knees, his sword clattering down the steps to the floor.*) Mercy, Tiberius! I implore you forgive your Caligula!

TIBERIUS. (*not understanding. Fixing his eyes on* CALIGULA *with a malevolent irony*) Come down from my throne, Caligula. (CALIGULA *slinks down warily*) You are too impatient. But I must pardon you, too—for where could I find another heir so perfect for serving my spite upon mankind? (*He has walked toward the throne while he is speaking,* CALIGULA *backing away from him.* LAZARUS *remains where he is,* MIRIAM *beside and to the rear of him.* TIBERIUS, *his eyes fixed on* CALIGULA, *stumbles against the body of* FLAVIUS. *He gives a startled gasp and shrinks back, calling*) Lights! A light here! (*A crowd of masked slaves obey his orders. One runs to him with a lantern. He looks down at* FLAVIUS' *corpse—half to himself*) I did wisely to stand him in my place. (*To* CALIGULA—*with sinister emphasis*) Too impatient, my loving grandchild! Take care lest I become impatient also—with your impatience! (CALIGULA *shudders and backs away to the extreme left corner, front, where he crouches on his haunches as inconspicuously as possible.* TIBERIUS *suddenly whirls around as if he felt a dagger at his back.*)

TIBERIUS. Where—? (*Seeing* LAZARUS *where he had been—with relief—staring at his face now that the room is flooded with the purplish-crimson glow from all the lamps*) Ah, you are there. More lights! Darkness leads men into error. My heir mistakes a man for Cæsar and Cæsar, it appears, has mistaken a man for a dæmon! (*Scrutinizing him—with sinister finality*) I can deal with men. I know them well. Too well! (*He laughs grimly*) Therefore I hate them. (*He mounts the steps of the dais and sits on the couch at left of table—staring at* LAZARUS, *wonderingly*) But you seem—something other than man! That light! (*Then he forces a harsh laugh*) A trick! I had forgotten you are a magician. (*Arrogantly*) Stand there, Jew. I would question you about your magic. (*Smilingly* LAZARUS *ascends to where* TIBERIUS *points at the top of the dais.* MIRIAM *remains standing at the foot.* TIBERIUS *stares for a while with somber intensity at* LAZARUS) They say you died and have returned from death?

LAZARUS. (*smiling—as if he were correcting a child*) There is no death, Cæsar.

TIBERIUS. (*with a sneer of scepticism but with an underlying eagerness*) I have heard you teach that folly. (*Then threateningly*) You shall be given full opportunity to prove it! (*A pause—then in a low voice, bending down toward* LAZARUS) Do you foretell the future? (*Trembling but with a pretense of carelessness*) Must I die soon?

LAZARUS. (*simply*) Yes, Cæsar.

TIBERIUS. (*jumping up with a shuddering start*) Soon? Soon? (*Then his fear turning to rage*) What do you say? Vile Jew, do you dare threaten me with death! (LAZARUS, *looking into his eyes, begins to laugh softly.* TIBERIUS *sinks back on his couch, fighting to control himself—confusedly*) Laugh not, I ask you. I am old. It is not seemly. (LAZARUS *ceases his low laughter. A pause.* TIBERIUS *broods—then suddenly*) And you were really dead? (*He shudders*) Come nearer. I need to watch your face. I have learned to read the lies in faces. A Cæsar gets much practice—from childhood on—too much! (*With awe*) Your eyes are dark with death. While I watch them, answer me, what cured thee of death?

LAZARUS. (*gently*) There is only life, Cæsar. (*Then gaily mocking but compellingly*) And laughter! Look! Look well into my eyes, old Reader of Lies, and see if you can find aught in them that is not life—and laughter! (*He laughs softly. A ripple of soft laughter from the motionless figures about the room echoes his.* TIBERIUS *stares into his eyes. In the silence that ensues* POMPEIA *gets up and walks over to the dais. She stops to stare for a moment with cruel contempt at* MIRIAM, *then stands and looks up at* LAZARUS, *trying in vain to attract his or* CÆSAR'S *attention. Failing in this, she passes over and sits beside* CALIGULA, *whose attention is concentrated on* LAZARUS.)

POMPEIA. I admire your strange magician, Caligula.

CALIGULA. (*without looking at her*) He is no magician. He is something like a god.

POMPEIA. (*longingly*) His laughter is like a god's. He is strong. I love him.

CALIGULA. (*turning to her—coarsely*) Do not waste your lust. He is faithful to his wife, I warn you.

POMPEIA. (*she points to* MIRIAM) Not that ugly slave?

CALIGULA. Yes. And yet, on our journey, whole herds of women—and many as beautiful as you, Pompeia—threw themselves on him and begged for his love.

POMPEIA. (*her voice hardening*) And he?

CALIGULA. He laughed—and passed on. (*She starts.* CALIGULA *goes on wonderingly*) But they seemed as happy as if his laughter had possessed them! You are a woman. Tell me, how could that be?

POMPEIA. (*her voice cruel*) He shall not laugh at me!

CALIGULA. (*tauntingly*) I will bet a string of pearls against your body for a night that he does.

POMPEIA. (*defiantly*) Done! (*Then she laughs—a low, cruel laugh —staring at* MIRIAM) So he loves that woman?

CALIGULA. (*curiously*) What are you planning?

POMPEIA. I shall offer her the fruit Cæsar preserves for those he fears.

CALIGULA. (*with a careless shrug*) You will not win his love by killing her.

POMPEIA. I no longer want his love. I want to see him suffer, to hear his laughter choke in his throat with pain! (*She speaks with more and more voluptuous satisfaction*) Then *I* shall laugh! (*She laughs softly and steps forward.*)

CALIGULA. (*concernedly*) Stop. I am his protector. (*Then suddenly*) But what is the Jewess to me? (*With more and more of a spirit of perverse cruelty*) Do it, Pompeia! His laughter is too cruel to us! We must save death from him!

POMPEIA. (*walks to the dais which she ascends slowly until she stands by* CÆSAR'S *couch behind him, confronting* LAZARUS. *But the two men remain unmindful of her presence.* TIBERIUS *continues to stare into* LAZARUS' *eyes. His whole body is now relaxed, at rest, a dreamy smile softens his thin, compressed mouth.* POMPEIA *leans over and takes a peach from the bowl of fruit on* CÆSAR'S *table and, taking* TIBERIUS' *hand in her other, she kisses it and calls insistently*) Cæsar. It is I, Pompeia. (LAZARUS *does not look at her. She stares at him defiantly.* TIBERIUS *blinks his eyes in a daze.*)

TIBERIUS. (*dreamily*) Yes! A cloud came from a depth of sky—around me, softly, warmly, and the cloud dissolved into the sky, and the sky into peace! (*Suddenly springing to his feet and staring about him in a confused rage—clutching* POMPEIA *by the shoulder and forcing her to her knees*) What are you doing here?

POMPEIA. Forgive your loving slave! I grew afraid this magician had put you under a spell. (*She stares at* LAZARUS, *her words challenging him.*)

TIBERIUS. (*confusedly, sinking back on his couch and releasing her*) A spell? Could it be he laid a dream of death upon me, leading me to death? (*He trembles timorously—appealing to* LAZARUS) Whatever magic thou didst to me, Dæmon, I beseech thee undo it!

LAZARUS. (*smiling*) Do you fear peace?

POMPEIA. (*harshly and insolently*) Mock not at Cæsar, dog! (LAZARUS *continues to smile. His eyes remain on* CÆSAR. *He seems absolutely unaware of* POMPEIA. *This enrages her the more against him. She speaks tauntingly to* TIBERIUS) Surely, Cæsar, this magician must have powerful charms since he dares to mock Tiberius to his face!

TIBERIUS. (*stung*) Be still! (*Then in a low tone to her*) Do you not know this Lazarus died and then by his magic rose from his tomb?

POMPEIA. (*scornfully*) To believe that, I must have seen it, Cæsar!

TIBERIUS. (*impatiently*) Do you think I would believe without good evidence? I have had them take the statements of many witnesses. The miracle was done in conjunction with another Jew acting as this man's tool. This other Jew, the report states, could not possibly have possessed any magic power Himself, for Pilate crucified Him a short time after and He died in pain and weakness within a few hours. But this Lazarus laughs at death!

LAZARUS. (*looks up, smiling with ironical bitterness*) Couldst Thou but hear, Jesus! And men shall keep on in panic nailing Man's soul to the cross of their fear until in the end they do it to avenge Thee, for Thine Honor and Glory! (*He sighs sadly—then after a struggle overcoming himself—with exultance*) Yes! (*His eyes fall again to* TIBERIUS *and he smiles*) Yes! Yes to the stupid as to the wise! To what is understood and to what cannot be understood! Known and unknown! Over and over! Forever and ever! Yes! (*He laughs softly to himself.*)

TIBERIUS. (*with superstitious dread*) What dost thou mean, Dæmon?

POMPEIA. (*with indignant scorn*) Let him prove there is no death, Cæsar! (*She appeals to the company who straighten up on their couches with interest.*)

CHORUS. (*chant demandingly*)

Let him prove there is no death!
We are bored!

CROWD. (*echoing*)

Prove there is no death!
We are bored, Cæsar!

TIBERIUS. (*waits to see what* LAZARUS *will say—then as he says nothing, plucking up his courage—his cruelty aroused*) Do you hear, Lazarus?

POMPEIA. Make him perform his miracle again!

CHORUS (*as before*)

Let him perform a miracle!
We are bored, Cæsar!

CROWD. (*they now stand up and coming from behind their tables, move forward toward the dais.*)

A miracle!
We are bored!

POMPEIA. Let him raise someone from the dead!

CHORUS. (*chanting with a pettish insistence.*)

Raise the dead!
We are bored!

CROWD. (*echoing—grouping in a big semicircle as of spectators in a theatre, around and to the sides of the dais, one sex on each side.* CALIGULA *moves in from the left in front of them. They form in three ranks, the first squatting on their hams like savages (as*

CALIGULA *does*), *the second rank crouching over them, the third leaning over the second, all with a hectic, morbid interest.*)

We are bored!

Raise the dead!

POMPEIA. (*with a cruel smile*) I have thought of a special test for him, Cæsar. (*She whispers in* CÆSAR'S *ear and points to* MIRIAM *and the fruit in her hand*) And he must laugh!

TIBERIUS. (*with a harsh, cruel chuckle*) Yes, I shall command him to laugh! (*Then disgustedly*) But she is sad and old. I will be only doing him a favor.

CALIGULA. (*rocking back and forth on his haunches—looking at* LAZARUS *with taunting cruelty*) No, Cæsar! I know he loves her!

LAZARUS. Yes! (*He steps down from the dais to* MIRIAM'S *side and taking her head in both his hands, he kisses her on the lips.*)

TIBERIUS. (*with a malignant grin*) Give her the fruit!

POMPEIA. (*advances and offers the peach to* MIRIAM—*with a hard, cruel little laugh*) Cæsar invites you to eat!

MIRIAM. (*to* LAZARUS—*requesting meekly but longingly*) May I accept, Lazarus? Is it time at last? My love has followed you over long roads among strangers and each league we came from home my heart has grown older. Now it is too old for you, a heart too weary for your loving laughter. Ever your laughter has grown younger, Lazarus! Upward it springs like a lark from a field, and sings! Once I knew your laughter was my child, my son of Lazarus; but then it grew younger and I felt at last it had returned to my womb—and ever younger and younger—until, tonight, when I spoke to you of home, I felt new birth-pains as your laughter, grown too young for me, flew back to the unborn—a birth so like a death! (*She sobs and wipes her eyes with her sleeve—then humbly, reaching out for the fruit*) May I accept it, Lazarus? You should have newborn laughing hearts to love you. My old one labors with memories and its blood is sluggish with the past. Your home on the hills of space is too far away. My heart longs for the warmth of close walls of earth baked in the sun. Our home in Bethany, Lazarus, where you and my children lived and died. Our tomb near our home, Lazarus, in which you and my children wait for me. Is it time at last?

LAZARUS. (*deeply moved*) Poor lonely heart! It has been crueler for you than I remembered. Go in peace—to peace! (*His voice trembles in spite of himself*) I shall be lonely, dear one. (*With a note of pleading*) You have never laughed with my laughter. Will you call back—Yes!—when you know—to tell me you understand and laugh with me at last?

MIRIAM. (*not answering him, to* POMPEIA, *taking the peach and making a humble courtesy before her*) I thank you, pretty lady. (*She raises the peach toward her mouth. Involuntarily one of* LAZARUS' *hands half-reaches out as if to stop her.*)

POMPEIA. (*with savage triumph, pointing*) See! He would stop her! He is afraid of death!

CHORUS. (*pointing—jeeringly*) He is afraid of death! Ha-ha-ha-ha!

CROWD. (*jeeringly*) Ha-ha-ha-ha!

MIRIAM. (*bites into the peach and, chewing, begins, as if immediately affected, to talk like a garrulous old woman, her words coming quicker and quicker as her voice becomes fainter and fainter*) Say what you like, it is much better I should go home first, Lazarus. We have been away so long, there will be so much to attend to about the house. And all the children will be waiting. You would be as helpless as a child, Lazarus. Between you and the children, things would soon be in a fine state! (*More and more confused*) No, no! You cannot help me, dearest one. You are only in my way. No, I will make the fire. When you laid it the last time, we all had to run for our lives, choking, the smoke poured from the windows, the neighbors thought the house was burning! (*She laughs—a queer, vague little inward laugh*) You are so impractical. The neighbors all get the best of you. Money slips through your fingers. If it was not for me— (*She sighs—then brightly and lovingly*) But, dearest husband, why do you take it so to heart? Why do you feel guilty because you are not like other men? That is why I love you so much. Is it a sin to be born a dreamer? But God, He must be a dreamer, too, or how would we be on earth? Do not keep saying to yourself so bitterly, you are a failure in life! Do not sit brooding on the hilltop in the evening like a black figure of Job against the sky! (*Her voice trembling*) Even if God has taken our little ones—yes, in spite of sorrow—have you not a good home I make for you, and a wife who loves you? (*She forces a chuckle*) Be grateful, then—for me! Smile, my sad one! Laugh a little once in a while! Come home, bringing me laughter of the wind from the hills! (*Swaying, looking at the peach in her hand*) What a mellow, sweet fruit! Did you bring it home for me? (*She falls back into his arms. Gently he lets her body sink until it rests against the steps of the dais.* TIBERIUS *rises from his couch to bend over with cruel gloating.* POMPEIA *steps nearer to* LAZARUS, *staring at him mockingly.* CALIGULA *hops to her side, looking from* LAZARUS *to* MIRIAM. *The half-circle of masked figures moves closer, straining forward and downward as if to overwhelm the two figures at the foot of the dais with their concentrated death wish.*)

TIBERIUS. (*thickly*) She is dead, and I do not hear you laugh!

LAZARUS. (*bending down—supplicatingly*) Miriam! Call back to me! Laugh! (*He pauses. A second of dead silence. Then, with a sound that is very like a sob, he kisses her on the lips*) I am lonely!

POMPEIA. (*with savage malice—jeeringly*) See! He weeps, Cæsar! (*She bursts into strident laughter*) Ha-ha-ha-ha!

CHORUS. (*echoing her laughter*)

Ha-ha-ha-ha!
There is fear!
There is death!

CROWD.

There is death!
Ha-ha-ha-ha!

CALIGULA. (*in a frenzy of despairing rage, hopping up and down*)

Liar! Charlatan! Weakling! How you have cheated Caligula! (*He suddenly slaps* LAZARUS *viciously across the face*) There is death! Laugh, if you dare!

TIBERIUS. (*standing—in a sinister cold rage, the crueler because his dream of a cure for death is baffled, yet feeling his power as* CÆSAR *triumphant nevertheless*) And I thought you might be a dæmon. I thought you might have a magic cure— (*With revengeful fury*) But death is, and death is mine! I shall make you pray for death! And I shall make Death laugh at you! Ha-ha-ha-ha! (*In a frenzy as* LAZARUS *neither makes a sound nor looks up*) Laugh, Lazarus! Laugh at yourself! Laugh with me! (*Then to his soldiers*) Scourge him! Make him laugh!

CALIGULA. (*running to soldiers—fiercely*) Give me a scourge!

POMPEIA. (*running to the soldiers—hysterically*) Ha-ha-ha-ha! Let me beat him, Cæsar! (*They group behind him. The rods and scourges are uplifted over his back to strike, when in the dead expectant silence,* MIRIAM'S *body is seen to rise in a writhing tortured last effort.*)

MIRIAM. (*in a voice of unearthly sweetness*) Yes! There is only life! Lazarus, be not lonely! (*She laughs and sinks back and is still. A shuddering murmur of superstitious fear comes from them as they shrink back swiftly from* LAZARUS, *remaining huddled one against the other.* POMPEIA *runs to the feet of* TIBERIUS *and crouches down on the steps below him, as if for protection, her terrified eyes on* MIRIAM. CALIGULA *runs to her and crouches beside and beneath her.*)

LAZARUS. (*kisses* MIRIAM *again and raises his head. His face is radiant with new faith and joy. He smiles with happiness and speaks to himself with a mocking affection as if to an amusing child*) That much remained hidden in me of the sad old Lazarus who died of self-pity—his loneliness! Lonely no more! Man's loneliness is but his fear of life! Lonely no more! Millions of laughing stars there are around me! And laughing dust, born once of woman on this earth, now freed to dance! New stars are born of dust eternally! The old, grown mellow with God, burst into flaming seed! The fields of infinite space are sown—and grass for sheep springs up on the hills of earth! But there is no death, nor fear, nor loneliness! There is only God's Eternal Laughter! His Laughter flows into the lonely heart! (*He begins to laugh, his laughter clear and ringing—the laughter of a conqueror arrogant with happiness and the pride of a new triumph. He bends and picks up the body of* MIRIAM *in his arms and, his head thrown back, laughing, he ascends the dais and places her on the table as on a bier. He touches one hand on her breast, as if he were taking an oath to life on her heart, looks upward and laughs, his voice ringing more and more with a terrible unbearable power and beauty that beats those in the room into an abject submissive panic.* TIBERIUS *grovels half under the table, his hands covering his ears, his face on the floor; he is laughing with the agony and terror of death.* POMPEIA *lies face down on the first step and beats it with her fist; she is laughing with horror and self-loathing.* CALIGULA, *his hands clutching his head, pounds it against the edge of the steps; he is laughing with grief and remorse. The rest, soldiers, slaves and the prostitutes of both sexes, writhe and twist distractedly, seeking to hide their heads against each other, beating each other and the floor with clenched hands. An agonized moan of supplicating laughter comes from them all.*)

ALL.

Ha-ha-ha-ha! Ha-ha-ha-ha!
Let us die, Lazarus!
Mercy, Laughing One!
Mercy of death!
Ha-ha-ha-ha! Ha-ha-ha-ha!

(*But the laughter of* LAZARUS *is as remote now as the laughter of a god.*)

CURTAIN

ACT FOUR—SCENE ONE

SCENE: *The same as previous Scene—the same night a short while later. All the lamps are out except the one on the table on the dais which, placed beside the head of* MIRIAM, *shines down upon the white mask of her face. In the half-darkness, the walls are lost in shadow, the room seems immense, the dais nearer.*

LAZARUS *sits on the couch at the right on the dais. His face is strong and proud although his eyes are fixed down on the face of* MIRIAM. *He seems more youthful still now, like a young son who keeps watch by the body of his mother, but at the same time retaining the aloof serenity of the statue of a god. His face expresses sorrow and a happiness that transcends sorrow.*

On the other side of the table, at the end of the couch, TIBERIUS *sits facing front, his elbows on his knees, his large hands with bloated veins hanging loosely. He keeps his gaze averted from the corpse. He talks to* LAZARUS *half over his shoulder.*

On the top step, POMPEIA *sits, facing right, her hands clasped about one knee, the other leg stretched down to the lower step. Her head is thrown back and she is gazing up into* LAZARUS' *face.*

On the step below her, CALIGULA *squats on his haunches, his arms on his knees, his fists pressed to his temples. He is staring straight before him.*

Only these four people are in the room now.

TIBERIUS. (*gloomily*) Was she dead, Dæmon, and was it thy power that recalled life to her body for that moment? Or was she still living and her words only the last desire of her love to comfort you, Lazarus? (LAZARUS *does not reply*) If thou dost not tell me, I must always doubt thee, Dæmon.

POMPEIA. (*with a sigh of bewildered happiness, turns to* CALIGULA) I am glad he laughed, Caligula! Did I say I loved him before? Then it was only my body that wanted a slave. Now it is my heart that desires a master! Now I know love for the first time in my life!

CALIGULA. (*bitterly*) Fool! What does he care for love? (*Somberly*) He loves everyone—but no one—not even me! (*He broods frowningly.*)

POMPEIA. (*following her own thoughts*) And now that hag is dead he will need a woman, young and beautiful, to protect and comfort him, to make him a home and bear his children! (*She dreams, her eyes again fixed on* LAZARUS*—then suddenly turning to* CALIGULA) I am glad I lost our bet. But you must accept some other payment. Now I know love, I may not give myself to any man save him!

CALIGULA. I do not want you! What are you but another animal! Faugh! (*With a grimace of disgust*) Pleasure is dirty and joyless! Or we who seek it are, which comes to the same thing. (*Then grimly*) But our bet can rest. This is not the end. There may still be a chance for you to laugh at him!

POMPEIA. No! Now I could not! I should weep for his defeat!

TIBERIUS. (*gloomily arguing, half to himself*) His laughter triumphed over me, but he has not brought her back to life. I think he knows no cure for another's death, as I had hoped. And I must always doubt that it was not some trick—(*Harshly*) until I have tested him with his own life! He cannot cheat me then! (*A pause—arguing to himself*) But he was dead—that much has been proved—and before he died he was old and sad. What did he find beyond there? (*Suddenly—turning to* LAZARUS *now*) What did you find beyond death, Lazarus?

LAZARUS. (*exaltedly*) Life! God's Eternal Laughter!

TIBERIUS. (*shaking his head*) I want hope—for me, Tiberius Cæsar.

LAZARUS. What is—you? But there is hope for Man! Love is Man's hope—love for his life on earth, a noble love above suspicion and distrust! Hitherto Man has always suspected his life, and in revenge and self-torture his love has been faithless! He has even betrayed Eternity, his mother, with his slave he calls Immortal Soul! (*He laughs softly, gaily, mockingly—then to* TIBERIUS *directly*) Hope for you, Tiberius Cæsar? Then dare to love Eternity without your fear desiring to possess her! Be brave enough to be possessed!

TIBERIUS. (*strangely*) My mother was the wife of Cæsar. (*Then dully*) I do not understand.

LAZARUS. Men are too cowardly to understand! And so the worms of their little fears eat them and grow fat and terrible and become their jealous gods they must appease with lies!

TIBERIUS. (*wearily*) Your words are meaningless, Lazarus. You are a fool. All laughter is malice, all gods are dead, and life is a sickness.

LAZARUS. (*laughs pityingly*) So say the race of men, whose lives are long dyings! They evade their fear of death by becoming so sick of life that by the time death comes they are too lifeless to fear it! Their disease triumphs over death—a noble victory called resignation! "We are sick," they say, "therefore there is no God in us, therefore there is no God!" Oh, if men would but interpret that first cry of man fresh from the womb as the laughter of one who even then says to his heart, "It is my pride as God to become Man. Then let it be my pride as Man to recreate the God in me!" (*He laughs softly but with exultant pride.*)

POMPEIA. (*laughing with him—proudly*) He will create a god in me! I shall be proud!

CALIGULA. (*pounding his temples with his fists—tortured*) I am Caligula. I was born in a camp among soldiers. My father was Germanicus, a hero, as all men know. But I do not understand this—and though I burst with pride, I cannot laugh with joy!

TIBERIUS. (*gloomily*) Obscurities! I have found nothing in life that merits pride. I am not proud of being Cæsar—and what is a god but a Cæsar over Cæsars? If fools kneel and worship me because they fear me, should I be proud? But Cæsar is a fact, and Tiberius, a man, is one, and I cling to these certainties—and I do not wish to die! If I were sure of eternal sleep beyond there, deep rest and forgetfulness of all I have ever seen or heard or hated or loved on earth, I would gladly die! But surely, Lazarus, nothing is sure—peace the least sure of all—and I fear there is no rest beyond there, that one remembers there as here and cannot sleep, that the mind goes on eternally the same—a long insomnia of memories and regrets and the ghosts of dreams one has poisoned to death passing with white bodies spotted by the leprous fingers of one's lusts. (*Bitterly*) I fear the long nights now in which I lie awake and listen to Death dancing round me in the darkness, prancing to the drum beat of my heart! (*He shudders*) And I am afraid, Lazarus—afraid that there is no sleep beyond there, either!

LAZARUS. There is peace! (*His words are like a benediction he pronounces upon them. Soothed in a mysterious, childlike way, they repeat the word after him, wonderingly.*)

POMPEIA. Peace?

CALIGULA. Peace?

TIBERIUS. Peace? (*For a long moment there is complete silence. Then* TIBERIUS *sighs heavily, shaking his head*) Peace! Another word blurred into a senseless sigh by men's longing! A bubble of froth blown from the lips of the dying toward the stars! No! (*He grins bitterly—then looks at* LAZARUS*—somberly contemptuous and threatening*) You are pleased to act the mysterious, Jew, but I shall solve you! (*Then with a lawyer-like incisiveness*) There is one certainty about you and I must know the cause—for there must be a cause and a rational explanation! You were fifty when you died—

LAZARUS. (*smiling mockingly*) Yes. When I died.

TIBERIUS. (*unheeding*) And now your appearance is of one younger by a score. Not alone your appearance! You *are* young. I see the fact, the effect. And I demand an explanation of the cause without mystic nonsense or evasion. (*Threateningly*) And I warn you to answer directly in plain words—and not to laugh, you understand!—not to dare!—or I shall lose patience with you—and—(*With a grim smile*) I can be terrible! (LAZARUS *smiles gently at him. He turns away with confused annoyance, then back to* LAZARUS, *resuming his lawyer-like manner*) What was it restored your youth? How did you contrive that your body reversed the natural process and grows younger? Is it a charm by which you invoke a supernatural force? Or is it a powder you dissolve in wine? Or a liquid? Or an unguent you rub into the skin to revitalize the old bones and tissues? Or—what is it, Lazarus?

LAZARUS. (*gently*) I know that age and time are but timidities of thought.

TIBERIUS. (*broodingly—as if he had not heard—persuasively*) Perhaps you ask yourself, what would Tiberius do with youth? Then, because you must have heard rumors of my depravity, you will conclude the old lecher desires youth for his lusts! (*He laughs harshly*) Ha! Why, do not my faithful subjects draw pictures of an old buck goat upon the walls and write above them, Cæsar? And they are just. In self-contempt of Man I have made this man, myself, the most swinish and contemptible of men! Yes! In all this empire there is no man so base a hog as I! (*He grins bitterly and ironically*) My claim to this excellence, at least, is not contested! Everyone admits therein Tiberius is by right their Cæsar! (*He laughs bitterly*) Ha! So who would believe Tiberius if he said, I want youth again because I loathe lust and long for purity!

LAZARUS. (*gently*) I believe you, Cæsar.

TIBERIUS. (*stares at him—deeply moved*) You—believe—? (*Then gruffly*) You lie! You are not mad—and only a madman would believe another man! (*Then confidingly, leaning over toward* LAZARUS) I know it is folly to speak—but—one gets old, one becomes talkative, one wishes to confess, to say the thing one has always kept hidden, to reveal one's unique truth—and there is so little time left—and one is alone! Therefore the old—like children—talk to themselves, for they have reached that hopeless wisdom of experience which knows that though one were to cry it in the streets to multitudes, or whisper it in the kiss to one's beloved, the only ears that can ever hear one's secret are one's own! (*He laughs bitterly*) And so I talk aloud, Lazarus! I talk to my loneliness!

LAZARUS. (*simply*) I hear, Tiberius.

TIBERIUS. (*again moved and confused—forcing a mocking smile*) Liar! Eavesdropper! You merely—listen! (*Then he turns away*) My mother, Livia, that strong woman, giving birth to me, desired not a child, but a Cæsar—just as, married to Augustus, she loved him not but loved herself as Cæsar's wife. She made me feel, in the proud questioning of her scornful eyes, that to win her mother love I must become Cæsar. She poisoned Prince Marcellus and young Gaius and Lucius that the way might be clear for me. I used to see their blood dance in red specks before my eyes when I looked at the sky. Now— (*He brushes his hand before his eyes*) it is all a red blot! I cannot distinguish. There have been too many. My mother—her blood is in that blot, for I revenged myself on her. I did not kill her, it is true, but I deprived her of her power and she died, as I knew she must, that powerful woman who bore me as a weapon! The murder was subtle and cruel—how cruel only that passionate, deep-breasted woman unslaked by eighty years of devoured desires could know! Too cruel! I did not go to her funeral. I was afraid her closed eyes might open and look at me! (*Then with almost a cry*) I want youth, Lazarus, that I may play again about her feet with the love I felt for her before I learned to read her eyes! (*He half sobs, bowing his head. A pause.*)

CALIGULA. (*nudging* POMPEIA—*with a crafty whisper*) Do you hear? The old lecher talks to himself. He is becoming senile. He will soon die. And I shall be Cæsar. Then I shall laugh!

POMPEIA. (*staring up at* LAZARUS' *face, hearing only* CALIGULA'S *words without their meaning*) No. My Lazarus does not laugh now. See. His mouth is silent—and a little sad, I think.

LAZARUS. (*gently and comfortingly*) I hear, Tiberius.

TIBERIUS. (*harshly*) I hated that woman, my mother, and I still hate her! Have you ever loved, Lazarus? (*Then with a glance at* MIRIAM's *body and a shuddering away from it—vaguely*) I was forgetting her. I killed your love, too, did I not? Well, I must! I envy those who are loved. Where I can, I kill love—for retribution's sake—but much of it escapes me. (*Then harshly again*) I loved Agrippina. We were married. A son was born to us. We were happy. Then that proud woman, my mother, saw my happiness. Was she jealous of my love? Or did she know no happy man would wish to be Cæsar? Well, she condemned my happiness to death. She whispered to Augustus and he ordered me to divorce Agrippina. I should have opened her veins and mine, and died with her. But my mother stayed by me, Agrippina was kept away, my mother spoke to me and spoke to me and even wept, that tall woman, strong as a great man, and I consented that my love be murdered. Then my mother married me to a whore. Why? The whore was Cæsar's daughter, true—but I feel that was not all of it, that my mother wished to keep me tortured that I might love her alone and long to be Cæsar! (*He laughs harshly*) Ha! In brief, I married the whore, she tortured me, my mother's scheming prospered—that subtle and crafty woman!—and many years passed in being here and there, in doing this and that, in growing full of hate and revengeful ambition to be Cæsar. At last, Augustus died. I was Cæsar. Then I killed that whore, my wife, and I starved my mother's strength to death until she died, and I began to take pleasure in vengeance upon men, and pleasure in taking vengeance on myself. (*He grins horribly*) It is all very simple, as you see! (*He suddenly starts to his feet—with harsh arrogance and pride, threateningly*) Enough! Why do I tell you these old tales? Must I explain to you why I want youth? It is my whim! I am Cæsar! And now I must lie down and try to sleep! And it is my command that you reveal the secret of your youth to me when I awake, or else— (*With malignant cruelty*) I will have to revenge the death of a hope on you—and a hope at my age demands a terrible expiation on its slayer! (*He walks down and starts to go off, right—then turns and addresses* LAZARUS *with grim irony*) Good night to you, Lazarus. And remember there shall be death while I am Cæsar! (*He turns to go.*)

LAZARUS. (*smiling affectionately at him, shakes his head*) Cæsar must believe in death. But does the husband of Agrippina?

TIBERIUS. (*stops short and stares at* LAZARUS, *confused and stuttering*) What—what—do you mean, Lazarus?

LAZARUS. I have heard your loneliness.

TIBERIUS. (*cruelly and grimly again*) So much the more reason why my pride should kill you! Remember that! (*He turns and strides off into the darkness at right.*)

CALIGULA. (*peers after him until sure he is gone—then gets up and begins a grotesque, hopping dance, singing a verse of the legionary's song*)

A bold legionary am I
March, oh march on!
A Roman eagle was my daddy
My mother was a drunken drabby
Oh march on to the wars!

(*He laughs gratingly, posturing and gesticulating up at* LAZARUS) Ha-ha-ha! He is gone! I can breathe! His breath in the same air suffocates me! The gods grant mine do the same for him! But he is failing! He talks to himself like a man in second childhood. His words are a thick babble I could not hear. They well from his lips like clots of blood from a reopened wound. I kept listening to the beating of his heart. It sounded slow, slower than when I last heard it. Did you detect that, Lazarus? Once or twice I thought it faltered—(*He draws in his breath with an avid gasp—then laughs gratingly*) Ha-ha-ha— (*Grandiloquently*) Tiberius, the old buck goat, will soon be gone, my friends, and in his place you will be blessed with the beautiful young god, Caligula! Hail to Caligula! Hail! Ha-ha-ha— (*His laughter suddenly breaks off into a whimper and he stands staring around him in a panic of fear that he has been overheard. He slinks noiselessly up the steps of the dais and squats coweringly at*

LAZARUS' *feet, blinking up at his face monkey-wise, clutching* LAZARUS' *hand in both of his. His teeth can be heard chattering together in nervous fear.* POMPEIA, *whose gaze has remained fixed on* LAZARUS *throughout, has gradually moved closer to him until she, too, is at his feet, half-kneeling beneath the table on which* MIRIAM *lies, side by side with* CALIGULA *but as oblivious of him as he is of her. Having grown calmer now,* CALIGULA *speaks again—mournful and bewildered.*)

CALIGULA. Why should I love you, Lazarus? Your laughter taunts me! It insults Cæsar! It denies Rome! But I will warn you again. Escape! Tonight Tiberius' mood is to play sentimental, but tomorrow he will jeer while hyenas gnaw at your skull and lick your brain. And then—there is pain, Lazarus! There is pain!

POMPEIA. (*pressing her hand to her own heart—with a shudder*) Yes, there is pain!

LAZARUS. (*smiling down on them—gently*) If you can answer Yes to pain, there is no pain!

POMPEIA. (*passionately*) Yes! Yes! I love Lazarus!

CALIGULA. (*with a bitter grin*) Do not take pain away from us! It is our one truth. Without pain there is nothing—a nothingness in which even your laughter, Lazarus, is swallowed at one gulp like a whining gnat by the cretin's silence of immensity! Ha-ha! No, we must keep pain! Especially Cæsar must! Pain must twinkle with a mad mirth in a Cæsar's eyes—men's pain—or they would become dissatisfied and disrespectful! Ha-ha! (*He stops his grating laughter abruptly and continues mournfully*) I am sick, Lazarus, sick of cruelty and lust and human flesh and all the imbecilities of pleasure—the unclean antics of half-witted children! (*With a mounting agony of longing*) I would be clean! If I could only laugh your laughter, Lazarus! That would purify my heart. For I could wish to love all men, as you love them—as I love you! If only I did not fear them and despise them! If I could only believe—believe in them—in life—in myself!—believe that one man or woman in the world knew and loved the real Caligula—then I might have faith in Caligula myself—then I might laugh your laughter!

LAZARUS. (*suddenly, in a quiet but compelling voice*) I, who know you, love you, Caligula. (*Gently patting his head*) I love Caligula.

CALIGULA. (*staring up at him in pathetic confusion*) You? You? You, Lazarus? (*He begins to tremble all over as if in a seizure—chokingly*) Beware! It is not good—not just—to make fun of me—to laugh at my misery—saying you love— (*In a frenzy, he jumps to his feet threatening* LAZARUS) Are you trying to fool me, hypocrite? Do you think I have become so abject that you dare—? Because I love you, do you presume—? Do you think I am your slave, dog of a Jew, that you can—insult—to my face—the heir of Cæsar— (*He stutters and stammers with rage, hopping up and down grotesquely, shaking his fist at* LAZARUS, *who smiles at him affectionately as at a child in a tantrum.*)

LAZARUS. (*catching his eyes and holding them with his glance—calmly*) Believe, Caligula!

CALIGULA. (*again overcome—stuttering with strange terror*) Believe? But I cannot! I must not! You cannot know me, if— You are a holy man! You are a god in a mortal body—you can laugh with joy to be alive—while I— Oh, no, you cannot love me! There is nothing in me at bottom but a despising and an evil eye! You cannot! You are only being kind! (*Hysterically*) I do not want your kindness! I hate your pity! I am too proud! I am too strong! (*He collapses weepingly, kneeling and clutching* LAZARUS' *hand in both of his.*)

LAZARUS. (*smiling*) You are so proud of being evil! What if there is no evil? What if there are only health and sickness? Believe in the healthy god called Man in you! Laugh at Caligula, the funny clown who beats the backside of his shadow with a bladder and thinks thereby he is Evil, the Enemy of God! (*He suddenly lifts the face of* CALIGULA *and stares into his eyes*) Believe! What if you are a man and men are despicable? Men are also unimportant! Men pass! Like rain into the sea! The sea remains! Man remains! Man slowly arises from the past of the race of men that was his tomb of death! For Man death is not! Man, Son of God's Laughter, *is!* (*He begins to laugh triumphantly, staring deep into* CALIGULA'S *eyes*) *Is,* Caligula! Believe in the laughing god within you!

CALIGULA. (*bursting suddenly into choking, joyful laughter—like a visionary.*) I believe! I believe there is love even for Caligula! I can laugh—now—Lazarus! Free laughter! Clean! No sickness! No lust for death! My corpse no longer rots in my heart! The tomb is full of sunlight! I am alive! I who love Man, I who can love and laugh! Listen, Lazarus! I dream! When I am Cæsar, I will devote my power to your truth. I will decree that there must be kindness and love! I will make the Empire one great Blessed Isle! Rome shall know happiness, it shall believe in life, it shall learn to laugh your laughter, Lazarus, or I— (*He raises his hand in an imperial autocratic gesture.*)

LAZARUS. (*gaily mocking*) Or you will cut off its head?

CALIGULA. (*fiercely*) Yes! I will—! (*Then meeting* LAZARUS' *eyes, he beats his head with his fists crazily*) Forgive me! I forget! I forget!

LAZARUS. Go out under the sky! Let your heart climb on laughter to a star! Then make it look down at earth, and watch Caligula commanding Life under pain of death to do his will! (*He laughs.*)

CALIGULA. (*laughing*) I will! I do! I laugh at him! Caligula is a trained ape, a humped cripple! Now I take him out under the sky, where I can watch his monkey tricks, where there is space for laughter and where this new joy, your love of me, may dance! (*Laughing clearly and exultantly, he runs out through the arched doorway at rear.*)

LAZARUS. (*stops laughing—shaking his head, almost sadly*) They forget! It is too soon for laughter! (*Then grinning at himself*) What, Lazarus? Are you, too, thinking in terms of time, old fool so soon to re-enter infinity? (*He laughs with joyous self-mockery.*)

POMPEIA. (*who has crept to his feet, kisses his hand passionately*) I love you, Lazarus!

LAZARUS. (*stops laughing, and looks down at her gently*) And I love you, woman.

POMPEIA. (*with a gasp of delight*) You? (*She stares up into his eyes doubtingly, raising her face toward his*) Then—put your arms around me. (*He does so, smiling gently*) And hold me to you. (*He presses her closer to him*) And kiss me. (*He kisses her on the forehead*) No, on the lips! (*He kisses her. She flings her arms about his neck passionately and kisses him again and again—then slowly draws away—remains looking into his eyes a long time, shrinking back from him with bewildered pain which speedily turns to rage and revengeful hatred*) No! No! It is *my* love, not Love! I want you to know *my* love, to give me back love—for me—only for me—Pompeia—my body, my heart—me, a woman—not Woman, women! Do I love Man, men? I hate men! I love you, Lazarus—a man—a lover—a father to children! I want love—as you loved that woman there (*She points to* MIRIAM) that I poisoned for love of you! But did you love her—or just Woman, wife and mother of men? (*She stares—then as if reading admission in his eyes, she springs to her feet*) Liar! Cheat! Hypocrite! Thief! (*Half hysterical with rage, pain and grief, she bends over* MIRIAM *and smooths the hair back from her forehead*) Poor wife! Poor woman! How he must have tortured you! Now I remember the pity in your eyes when you looked at me! Oh, how his soothing gray words must have pecked at the wound in your heart like doves with bloody beaks! (*Then with sudden harshness*) But perhaps you were too dull to understand, too poor and tired and ugly and old to care, too slavish—! Pah! (*She turns away with contempt and faces* LAZARUS *with revengeful hatred*) Did you think I would take her place—become your slave, wait upon you, give you love and passion and beauty in exchange for phrases about man and gods—you who are neither a man nor a god but a dead thing without desire! You dared to hope I would give my body, my love, to you! (*She spits in his face and laughs harshly*) You insolent fool! I shall punish you! You shall be tortured as you have tortured! (*She laughs wildly—then steps down from the dais and goes off right, crying distractedly*) Cæsar! This man has made you a fool before all the world! Torture him, Cæsar! Now! Let the people witness! Send heralds to wake them! Torture him, Cæsar, the man who laughs at you! Ha-ha-ha-ha! (*Her laughter is caught up by all the* GIRLS *and* YOUTHS *of the palace, who, as she disappears, led by their* CHORUS, *pour in from each side of the room and dance forward to group themselves around the dais as in the previous scene, staring at* LAZARUS, *laughing cruelly, falsely, stridently*.)

CHORUS. (*tauntingly*)
Ha-ha-ha-ha!
Laugh now, Lazarus!
Let us see you laugh!
Ha-ha-ha-ha!

CROWD. (*echoing*)
Ha-ha-ha-ha!
Ha-ha-ha-ha!

LAZARUS. (*moves, and immediately there is silence. He bends down and kisses* MIRIAM *and picks her up in his arms. Talking down to her face—with a tender smile*) Farewell! You are home! And now I will take your body home to earth! Space is too far away, you said! Home in the earth! There will be so much for you to do there! Home! Earth! (*His voice trembling a bit*) Farewell, body of Miriam. My grief is a lonely cry wailing in the home in my heart that you have left forever! (*Then exultantly*) But what am I? Now your love has become Eternal Love! Now, since your life passed, I feel Eternal Life made nobler by your selflessness! Love has grown purer! The laughter of God is more profoundly tender! (*He looks up in an ecstasy and descends the dais, carrying her*) Yes, that is it! That is it, my Miriam! (*Laughing softly and tenderly, he walks around the dais and carries the body out through the doorway in rear. The* CHORUS *and* YOUTHS *and* GIRLS *make way for him in awed silence—then scurry around to right and left, forming an aisle through which he passes—then after he has gone out through the arch, they close into a semicircular group again, staring after him, and a whisper of strange, bewildered, tender laughter comes from them.*)

CHORUS. (*in this whisper*)

That is it!
Love is pure!
Laughter is tender!
Laugh!

CROWD. (*echoing*)

Laugh! Laugh!

CURTAIN

SCENE TWO

SCENE: *The arena of an amphitheatre. It is just before dawn of the same night. Cæsar's throne is on the left at the extreme front, facing right, turned a little toward front. It is lighted by four immense lamps. In front of the throne is a marble railing that tops the wall that encloses the arena. In the rear the towering pile of the circular amphitheatre is faintly outlined in deeper black against the dark sky.*

TIBERIUS *sits on the throne, his eyes fixed on the middle of the arena off right, where, bound to a high stake after he had been tortured,* LAZARUS *is now being burnt alive over a huge pile of faggots. The crackling of the flames is heard. Their billowing rise and fall is reflected on the masked faces of the multitude who sit on the banked tiers of marble behind and to the rear of the throne, with their* CHORUS, *seven men masked in Middle Age in the Servile, Hypocritical type, grouped on each side of the throne of* CÆSAR *on a lower tier.*

Half-kneeling before TIBERIUS, *her chin resting on her hands on top of the marble rail,* POMPEIA *also stares at* LAZARUS.

Before the curtain, the crackle of the flames and an uproar of human voices from the multitude, jeering, hooting, laughing at LAZARUS *in cruel mockery of his laughter. This sound has risen to its greatest volume as the curtain rises.*

CHORUS. (*chanting mockingly*)
Ha-ha-ha-ha!
Burn and laugh!
Laugh now, Lazarus!
Ha-ha-ha-ha!

CROWD. (*chanting with revengeful mockery*) Ha-ha-ha-ha!

TIBERIUS. Who laughs now, Lazarus—thou or Cæsar? Ha-ha—! (*With awe*) His flesh melts in the fire but his eyes shine with peace!

POMPEIA. How he looks at me! (*Averting her eyes with a shudder*) Command them to put out his eyes, Cæsar!

TIBERIUS. (*harshly*) No. I want to read his eyes when they see death! (*Then averting his face—guiltily*) He is looking at me, not you. I should not have listened to your cries for his death.

POMPEIA. (*turning to him again with a shudder of agony—beseechingly*) Have them put out his eyes, Cæsar! They call to me!

TIBERIUS. (*as if not hearing her—to himself*) Why do I feel remorse? His laughter dies and is forgotten, and the hope it raised dies— (*With sudden excitement*) And yet—he must know something—and if he would—even now he could tell— (*Suddenly rising to his feet he calls imploringly*) Lazarus!

CHORUS. (*chanting in a great imploring chorus now*) Lazarus!

CROWD. (*echoing*) Lazarus!

SOLDIER'S VOICE. (*calling from off beside the stake*) You had us gag him, Cæsar, so he might not laugh. Shall we cut away the gag?

POMPEIA. (*in terror*) No, Cæsar! He will laugh! And I will go to him! (*Desperately*) He will laugh at you, Cæsar—and the mob will laugh with him!

TIBERIUS. (*struggles with himself—then calls*) Lazarus! If you hear let your eyes answer, and I will grant the mercy of death to end your agony! Is there hope of love somewhere for men on earth?

CHORUS. (*intoning as before*)

Is there hope of love
For us on earth?

CROWD.

Hope of love
For us on earth!

SOLDIER'S VOICE. His eyes laugh, Cæsar!

TIBERIUS. (*in a strange frenzy now*) Hear me, thou Dæmon of Laughter! Hear and answer, I beseech thee, who alone hath known joy! (*More and more wildly*) How must we live? Wherein lies happiness?

CHORUS. Wherein lies happiness?

CROWD. Wherein, happiness?

TIBERIUS. Why are we born? To what end must we die?

CHORUS. Why are we born to die?

CROWD. Why are we born?

SOLDIER'S VOICE. His eyes laugh, Cæsar! He is dying! He would speak!

CHORUS AND CROWD. (*in one great cry*) Cæsar! Let Lazarus speak!

POMPEIA. (*terrified*) No, Cæsar! He will laugh—and you will die—and I will go to him!

TIBERIUS. (*torn—arguing with his fear*) But—he may know some hope— (*Then making his decision, with grim fatalism*) Hope—or nothing! (*Calls to the* SOLDIERS) Let him speak!

CHORUS AND CROWD. (*cheering*) Hail, Cæsar!

LAZARUS. (*his voice comes, recognizably the voice of* LAZARUS, *yet with a strange, fresh, clear quality of boyhood, gaily mocking with life*) Hail, Cæsar!

CROWD. (*frantic with hope*) Hail, Lazarus!

TIBERIUS. Pull away the fire from him! I see death in his eyes! (*The flaming reflections in the banked, massed faces dance madly, as the* SOLDIERS *rake back the fire from the stake. With a forced, taunting mockery*) What do you say now, Lazarus? You are dying!

CHORUS AND CROWD. (*taking his tone—mockingly*) You are dying, Lazarus!

LAZARUS. (*his voice a triumphant assertion of the victory of life over pain and death*) Yes!

TIBERIUS. (*triumphant yet disappointed—with scorn and rage*) Ha! You admit it, do you, coward! Craven! Knave! Duper of fools! Clown! Liar! Die! I laugh at you! Ha-ha-ha-ha— (*His voice breaks chokingly.*)

CROWD. (*led by their* CHORUS—*in the same frenzy of disappointment, with all sorts of grotesque and obscene gestures and noises, thumbing their fingers to their noses, wagging them at their ears, sticking out their tongues, slapping their behinds, barking, crowing like roosters, howling, and hooting in every conceivable manner*) Yah! Yah! Yellow Gut! Bungkisser! Muckheel! Scumwiper! Liar! Pig! Jackal! Die! We laugh at you! Ha-ha-ha—(*Their voices, too, break.*)

POMPEIA. (*rising to her feet like one in a trance, staring toward* LAZARUS) They are tormenting him. I hear him crying to me! (*She moves to the top of the steps leading to the arena.*)

LAZARUS. (*his voice thrilling with exultance*) O men, fear not life! You die—but there is no death for Man! (*He begins to laugh, and at the sound of his laughter, a great spell of silence settles upon all his hearers—then as his laughter rises, they begin to laugh with him.*)

POMPEIA. (*descending the steps like a sleep-walker*) I hear his laughter calling. I must go to him.

TIBERIUS. (*as if he realized something was happening that was against his will—trying feebly to be imperial*) I command you not to laugh! Cæsar commands— (*Calling feebly to the* SOLDIERS) Put back—the gag! Stop his laughter! (*The laughter of* LAZARUS *gaily and lovingly mocks back at him.*)

SOLDIER'S VOICE. (*his voice gently remonstrating*) We may not, Cæsar. We love his laughter! (*They laugh with him.*)

CHORUS AND CROWD. (*in a soft, dreamy murmur*)

We love his laughter!
We laugh!

TIBERIUS. (*dreamily*) Then—pile the fire back around him. High and higher! Let him blaze to the stars! I laugh with him!

SOLDIER'S VOICE. (*gently and gravely*) That is just, Cæsar. We love men flaming toward the stars! We laugh with him!

CHORUS AND CROWD. (*as the flames, piled back and fed anew by the* SOLDIERS, *flare upward and are reflected on their masks in dancing waves of light*)

We love men flaming toward the stars!
We laugh!

POMPEIA. (*in the arena*) The fire calls me. My burning heart calls for the fire! (*She laughs softly and passes swiftly across the arena toward* LAZARUS.)

TIBERIUS. (*in a sort of childish complaint*) You must pardon me, Lazarus. This is my Cæsar's duty—to kill you! You have no right to laugh—before all these people—at Cæsar. It is not kind. (*He sobs snuffingly—then begins to laugh at himself. Suddenly the flames waver, die down, then shoot up again and* POMPEIA'S *laughter is heard for a moment, rising clear and passionately with that of* LAZARUS, *then dying quickly out.*)

SOLDIER'S VOICE. A woman has thrown herself in the flames, Cæsar! She laughs with Lazarus!

TIBERIUS. (*in a sudden panicky flurry—feverishly*) Quick, Lazarus! You will soon be silent! Speak!—in the name of man's solitude—his agony of farewell—what is beyond there, Lazarus? (*His voice has risen to a passionate entreaty.*)

CHORUS. (*in a great pleading echo*) What is beyond there, Lazarus?

CROWD. What is beyond?

LAZARUS. (*his voice speaking lovingly, with a surpassing clearness and exaltation*) Life! Eternity! Stars and dust! God's Eternal

Laughter! (*His laughter bursts forth now in its highest pitch of ecstatic summons to the feast and sacrifice of Life, the Eternal. The crowds laugh with him in a frenzied rhythmic chorus. Led by the* CHORUS, *they pour down from the banked walls of the amphitheatre and dance in the flaring reflection of the flames strange wild measures of liberated joy.* TIBERIUS *stands on the raised dais laughing great shouts of clear, fearless laughter.*)

CHORUS. (*chanting as they dance*)

Laugh! Laugh!
We are stars!
We are dust!
We are gods!
We are laughter!

CROWD.

We are dust!
We are gods!
Laugh! Laugh!

CALIGULA. (*enters from behind* TIBERIUS. *His aspect is wild, his hair disheveled, his clothes torn, he is panting as if exhausted by running. He stares toward the flames stupidly—then screams despairingly above the chant*) Lazarus! I come to save you! Do you still live, Lazarus?

TIBERIUS. (*has been speaking. His words are now heard as the tumult momentarily dies down*) I have lived long enough! I will die with Lazarus! I no longer fear death! I laugh! I laugh at Cæsar! I advise you, my brothers, fear not Cæsars! Seek Man in the brotherhood of the dust! Cæsar is your fear of Man! I counsel you, laugh away your Cæsars!

CALIGULA. (*with resentful jealousy and rage—in a voice rising to a scream*) What do I hear, Lazarus? You laugh with your murderer? You give him your laughter? You have forgotten me—my love—you make him love you—you make him laugh at Cæsars—at me! (*Suddenly springs on* TIBERIUS *in a fury and grabbing him by the throat chokes him, forcing him back on the throne—screaming*) Die, traitor! Die! (TIBERIUS' *body relaxes in his hands, dead, and slips from the chair.* CALIGULA *rushes madly down the stairs into the midst of the oblivious, laughing, dancing crowd, screaming*) You have betrayed me, dog of a Jew! You have betrayed Cæsar! (*Beginning to be caught by the contagion of the laughter*) Ha-ah— No! I will not laugh! I will kill you! Give me a spear! (*He snatches a spear from a soldier and fights his way drunkenly toward the flames, like a man half overcome by a poisonous gas, shouting, half-laughing in spite of himself, half-weeping with rage*) Ha-ah— The gods be with Cæsar Caligula! O immortal gods, give thy brother strength! You shall die, Lazarus—die—Ha-ah—! (*He disappears toward the flames, his spear held ready to stab.*)

CHORUS AND CROWD. (*who have been entirely oblivious of him—chanting*)

Laugh! Laugh!
We are gods!
We are dust!

LAZARUS. (*at his first word there is a profound silence in which each dancer remains frozen in the last movement*) Hail, Caligula Cæsar! Men forget! (*He laughs with gay mockery as at a child.*)

CHORUS AND CROWD. (*starting to laugh*) Laugh! Laugh! (*Then there is a fierce cry of rage from* CALIGULA *and* LAZARUS' *laughter ceases, and with it the laughter of the crowd turns to a wail of fear and lamentation.*)

CALIGULA. (*dashes back among them waving his bloody spear and rushing up to the throne stands on it and strikes a grandiose pose*) I have killed God! I am Death! Death is Cæsar!

CHORUS AND CROWD. (*turning and scurrying away—huddled in fleeing groups, crouching close to the ground like a multitude of terrified rats, their voices squeaky now with fright*) Hail, Cæsar! Hail to Death! (*They are gone.*)

CALIGULA. (*keeping his absurd majestic pose, turns and addresses with rhetorical intoning, and flowing gestures, the body of* LAZARUS, *high upon its stake, the flames below it now flickering fitfully*) Hail, Caligula! Hero of heroes, conqueror of the Dæmon, Lazarus, who taught the treason that fear and death were dead! But I am Lord of Fear! I am Cæsar of Death! And you, Lazarus, are carrion! (*Then in a more conversational tone, putting aside his grandiose airs, confidentially*) I had to kill you, Lazarus! Surely your good sense tells you— You heard what the old fool, Tiberius, told the mob. A moment more and there would have been a revolution—no more Cæsars—and my dream—! (*He stops—bewilderedly*) My dream? Did I kill laughter? I had just learned to laugh—with love! (*More confusedly*) I must be a little mad, Lazarus. It was one terror too many, to have been laughing your laughter in the night, to have been dreaming great yearning dreams of all the good my love might do for men when I was Cæsar—and then, to hear the old howling of mob lust, and to run here—and there a high white flame amidst the fire—you, Lazarus!—dying!—laughing with him—Tiberius—betraying me—who loved you, Lazarus! Yes, I became mad! I am mad! And I can laugh my own mad laughter, Lazarus—my own! Ha-ha-ha-ha! (*He laughs with a wild triumphant madness and again rhetorically, with sweeping gestures and ferocious capers*) And all of men are vile and mad, and I shall be their madmen's Cæsar! (*He turns as if addressing an amphitheatre full of his subjects*) O my good people, my faithful scum, my brother swine, Lazarus is dead and we have murdered great laughter, and it befits our madness to have done so, and it is befitting above all to have Caligula for Cæsar! (*Then savagely*) Kneel down! Abase yourselves! I am your Cæsar and your God! Hail! (*He stands saluting himself with a crazy intensity that is not without grandeur. A pause. Suddenly the silence seems to crush down upon him; he is aware that he is alone in the vast arena; he whirls about, looking around him as if he felt an assassin at his back; he lunges with his spear at imaginary foes, jumping, dodging from side to side, yelping*) Ho, there! Help! Help! Your Cæsar calls you! Help, my people! To the rescue! (*Suddenly throwing his spear away and sinking on his knees, his face toward* LAZARUS, *supplicatingly*) Lazarus! Forgive me! Help me! Fear kills me! Save me from death! (*He is groveling in a paroxysm of terror, grinding his face in his fists as if to hide it.*)

LAZARUS. (*his voice is heard in a gentle, expiring sigh of compassion, followed by a faint dying note of laughter that rises and is lost in the sky like the flight of his soul back into the womb of Infinity*) Fear not, Caligula! There is no death!

CALIGULA. (*lifts his head at the first sound and rises with the laughter to his feet, until, as it is finally lost, he is on tip-toes, his arms straining upward to the sky, a tender, childish laughter of love on his lips*) I laugh, Lazarus! I laugh with you! (*Then grief-stricken*) Lazarus! (*He hides his face in his hands, weeping*) No more! (*Then beats his head with his fists*) I will remember! I will! (*Then suddenly, with a return to grotesqueness—harshly*) All the same, I killed him and I proved there is death! (*Immediately overcome by remorse, groveling and beating himself*) Fool! Madman! Forgive me, Lazarus! Men forget!

CURTAIN

THE FOUNTAIN

A Play in Eleven Scenes

CHARACTERS

IBNU ASWAD, *a Moorish chieftain*

JUAN PONCE DE LEON

PEDRO, *his servant*

MARIA DE CORDOVA

LUIS DE ALVAREDO

YUSEF, *a Moorish minstrel*

DIEGO MENENDEZ, *a Franciscan*

VICENTE DE CORDOVA, *Maria's husband*

ALONZO DE OVIEDO }
MANUEL DE CASTILLO } *nobles*
CRISTOVAL DE MENDOZA }

A SOLDIER

FRIAR QUESADA, *a Franciscan*

BEATRIZ DE CORDOVA, *daughter of Maria and Vicente*

NANO, *an Indian chief*

A CHIEF OF THE INDIANS IN FLORIDA

A MEDICINE MAN

A FIGURE

A POET OF CATHAY

AN OLD INDIAN WOMAN OF THE BAHAMAS

A DOMINICAN MONK

FATHER SUPERIOR OF THE DOMINICANS IN CUBA

JUAN, *nephew of Juan Ponce de Leon*

Nobles, Monks, Soldiers, Sailors, Captive Indians of Porto Rico, Indians in Florida.

TIME: *Late Fifteenth and early Sixteenth Centuries.*

SCENES

Part One

Scene I: Courtyard of the house of Ibnu Aswad, Granada, Spain—the night of the Moorish capitulation, 1492.

Scene II: Columbus's flagship on the last day of his second voyage, 1493.

Part Two

Scene III: Courtyard of the Government House, Porto Rico, an afternoon twenty years or more later.

Scene IV: Cabinet of Bishop Menendez in the Government House—an evening three months later.

Scene V: A prisoner's cell in the Government House—the same time.

Scene VI: Same as Scene Three—immediately follows Scene Five.

Part Three

Scene VII: A strip of beach on the Florida coast—a night four months later.

Scene VIII: The same—noon the following day.

Scene IX: A clearing in the forest—that night.

Scene X: The same, some hours later.

Scene XI: Courtyard of a Dominican monastery in Cuba—several months later.

THE FOUNTAIN

SCENE ONE

SCENE. *Courtyard of* IBNU ASWAD'S *palace in Granada.*

The section forms a right triangle, its apex at the rear, right. In the left, center, a massive porte-cochère opens on the street. On the right, a door leading into the house itself. In the center of the courtyard, a large splendid fountain of green marble with human and animal figures in gilt bronze. The peristyle of the gallery running around the court is supported by slender columns of polished marble, partly gilded. The interspaces above the horseshoe arches springing from the columns are filled with arabesques, texts from the Koran, red, blue and gold in color. Above are the latticed windows of the women's apartments. Over the house-top a sky with stars can be seen. It is early night.

As the curtain rises, the court is empty and there is silence except for the splash of the fountain. Then a loud, imperious knocking, as of someone pounding with the hilt of a sword, is heard from the porte-cochère. IBNU ASWAD *enters from the right. He is an elderly, noble-looking Moor, the lower part of his face covered by a long, white beard. His expression is one of great pride borne down by sorrow and humiliation. He goes out through the porte-cochère, and returns ushering in* JUAN PONCE DE LEON *and his servant,* PEDRO. JUAN *is a tall, handsome Spanish noble of thirty-one, dressed in full uniform. His countenance is haughty, full of a romantic adventurousness and courage; yet he gives the impression of disciplined ability, of a confident self-mastery—a romantic dreamer governed by the ambitious thinker in him.* PEDRO *is a dull-looking young fellow.*

JUAN. (*as they enter*) (*To* ASWAD) Your pardon, Sir Moor.

ASWAD. (*haughtily*) You are quartered here? (JUAN *bows in affirmation*) Welcome then, since it is the will of Allah that you should conquer.

JUAN. (*graciously*) I am no conqueror here. I am a stranger grateful for hospitality.

ASWAD. (*unbending a bit*) You are kind. I have seen you in action on the field. You are brave. Defeat loses its bitterness when the foe is noble. (*Moodily and bitterly—staring at the fountain*) The waters of the fountain fall—but ever they rise again, Sir Spaniard. Such is the decree of destiny. (*With fervor*) Blessed be Allah who exalteth and debaseth the kings of the earth, according to his divine will, in whose fulfillment consists eternal justice. (*Fiercely and defiantly*) Whosoever the victor, there is no conqueror but Allah!

JUAN. (*stiffening—coldly*) Your fortitude does you honor. (*By way of dismissing the subject—abruptly*) I am expecting friends. Will that disturb your household? If so—

ASWAD. (*coldly*) My house is your house. It is decreed. (*He bows with stately grace and goes out, right.*)

JUAN. (*makes a movement as if to detain him—then shrugs his shoulders*) What can I do for him? (*Ironically repeating* IBNU's *inflection*) It is decreed by Spain if not by Allah. (*Seeing* PEDRO *lolling against the wall, drowsily staring at the fountain—amused*) Lazy lout! Does the fountain cause you, too, to dream? (*In a tone of command*) Bring the wine. They will be here soon.

PEDRO. Yes, sir. (*He goes.* JUAN *paces back and forth, humming to himself.* PEDRO *returns and approaches his master cautiously—in a mysterious whisper*) A lady, sir.

JUAN. (*frowning*) Is she alone? (PEDRO *nods,* JUAN *smiles cynically*) Surely you have mistaken her calling. Tell her I am not here. (*As* PEDRO *turns to go,* MARIA DE CORDOVA *appears in the arch of the porte-cochère. A heavy black veil is thrown over her face.*)

MARIA. (*her voice forced and trembling*) Juan!

JUAN. (*immediately the gallant cavalier, makes a motion for* PEDRO *to leave, and bows low—mockery in his voice*) Beautiful lady, you do me an unmerited honor.

MARIA. (*wearily*) Spare me your mockery, Juan. (*She throws back her veil. She is a striking-looking woman of thirty-eight or forty, but discontent and sorrow have marked her age clearly on her face.*)

JUAN. (*astonished*) Maria! (*Then with genuine alarm*) In God's name!

MARIA. (*her voice breaking*) Juan, I had to come.

JUAN. (*sternly*) Your husband is my brother in arms. To-night—here—he is to be among my guests. I feel that every word we speak now degrades me in my honor.

MARIA. (*in a tone of great grief*) You are cruel! I had to speak with you alone. This is my one chance. I leave the Court tomorrow.

JUAN. (*with evident relief*) Ah.

MARIA. (*stares at him with a pitiful appeal. He avoids her eyes*) Oh, what a fool I am—(*with a half-sob, as if the confession were wrung from her*)—to love you, Juan! (*She makes a movement toward him, but he steps back, aloof and cold.*)

JUAN. (*frowning*) That word—we have never uttered it before. You have always been—my friend. (*After a pause, with deep earnestness*) Why must you ruin our rare friendship for a word that every minstrel mouths? (*Then with irritation*) Love, love, love we chatter everlastingly. We pretend love alone is why we live! Bah! Life is nobler than the weak lies of poets—or it's nothing!

MARIA. (*wounded and indignant*) If you had had to fight for love as you have fought for glory!—

JUAN. (*struck by the pain in her tone, kneels and kisses her hand—remorsefully*) Forgive me! I would die rather than bring sorrow to a heart as kind as yours. Keep me forever in that heart, I beg—but as a friend—as it has always been.

MARIA. (*with a gasp of pain*) Ah! (*Taking her hand from his—with a deep sigh*) God give you knowledge of the heart!

JUAN. (*rises—plainly endeavoring to change the subject*) You are leaving the Court?

MARIA. The Queen has granted my wish to retire to Cordova. (*Passionately*) I'm sick of the Court! I long for simple things! I pray to become worthy again of that pure love of God I knew as a girl. I must seek peace in Him! (*After a pause*) Granada is ours. The Moors are driven from Spain. The wars are over. What will you do now, Juan?

JUAN. Peace means stagnation—a slack ease of cavaliers and songs and faded roses. I must go on.

MARIA. Where will you go?

JUAN. (*smiles half-whimsically at an idea*) Perhaps with the Genoese, Christopher Columbus, when he sails to find the western passage to Cathay.

MARIA. (*disturbed*) But they say he is mad.

JUAN. (*seriously now*) Mad or not, he dreams of glory. I have heard he plans to conquer for Spain that immense realm of the Great Khan which Marco Polo saw.

MARIA. What! Abandon your career at Court now when your exploits have brought you in such favor? No one would ruin himself so senselessly save in despair! (*Jealously*) It must be from love you are fleeing! (*Fiercely mocking*) Is a woman avenging women? Tell me her name!

JUAN (*with a mocking laugh*) Love, love, and always love! Can no other motive exist for you? God pity women!

MARIA. (*after a pause—sadly*) God pity me—because pity is what you offer me. (*As* JUAN *seems about to protest wearily*) Don't deny it, Juan. It sneers at me in your pretended scorn of love— You wish to comfort my humiliation! Am I a fool? Have you not loved others? I could name ten—

JUAN. Maria!

MARIA. Do you imagine I haven't guessed the truth? Those others had youth—while I— And my love seems to you—pitiable!

JUAN (*kneeling and taking her hand—with passionate earnestness*) No, dear friend, no! I swear to you! (*After a pause*) What you call loves—they were merely moods—dreams of a night or two—lustful adventures—gestures of vanity, perhaps—but I have never loved. Spain is the mistress to whom I give my heart, Spain and my own ambitions, which are Spain's. Now do you understand?

MARIA. (*sadly*) No, Juan. (*He rises*) I understand that I am growing old—that love has passed for me—and that I suffer in my loneliness. Perhaps if God had granted me a child— But His justice punishes. He has seen my secret sin. I have loved you, Juan, for years. But it was only in the last year when my heart, feeling youth die, grew desperate that I dared let you see. And now, farewell, until God's will be done in death. We must not meet again.

JUAN, (*sternly*) No. (*Passionately*) I wish to God you had not told me this!

MARIA. (*gently*) If you are still my friend you will not wish it. It was my final penance—that you should know. And, having told you, I am free, for my heart is dead. There is only my soul left that knows the love of God which blesses and does not torture. Farewell once more, Juan. (*He kneels and kisses her hand. She puts the other on his head as if blessing him*) You are noble, the soul of courage, a man of men. You will go far, soldier of iron—and dreamer. God pity you if those two selves should ever clash! You shall have all my prayers for your success—but I shall add, Dear Saviour, let him know tenderness to recompense him when his hard youth dies! (*She turns quickly and goes out.*)

JUAN. (*looks after her in melancholy thought for a while—then sighs deeply and shrugs his shoulders*) Time tarnishes even the pure, difficult things with common weakness. (LUIS DE ALVAREDO *enters through the porte-cochère. He is a dissipated-looking noble, a few years older than* JUAN. *His face is homely but extremely fetching in its nobility, its expression of mocking fun and raillery. He is dressed carelessly, is slightly drunk.*)

LUIS. (*mockingly*) Lover of glory, beloved of women, hail! (*He comes to the startled* JUAN *as voices are heard from the porte-cochère—in a hurried, cautioning whisper*) The devil, Juan! Have you lost your wits—or has she? I recognized her—and Vicente was only ten paces behind. (*Then again mockingly*) Discretion, my stainless knight, discretion!

JUAN. (*sternly*) Stop! You wrong her and me. (*Sounds of a loud, angry dispute are heard from without*) What is that brawling?

LUIS. My Moor. (*Explaining hurriedly to* JUAN) A fellow poet—a minstrel of their common folk. We found him running amuck about the streets declaiming to the stars that their king, Abdallah, had sold his soul to hell when he surrendered. (*With admiration*) By God, Juan, how he cursed! Oh, he's a precious songster, and as poet to poet I collared him and dragged him with us. Our friend, Diego, would have cut his throat for the Church's glory had I not interfered.

JUAN. (*smiling*) As madman for madman, eh? But why bring him here to howl?

LUIS. He has a lute. It is my whim he should sing some verses. (*With an amused grin*) The dog speaks only Arabic. If he is wily, he will chant such curses on our heads as will blight that fountain dry—and no one of us but me will understand. (*With great glee*) It will be sport, Juan! (*The clamor from outside grows more violent*) By God, Diego will murder my minstrel—after all my pains. (*Starts to hurry out—stops in the entrance*) Remember, Juan. Vicente may have recognized—the lady.

JUAN. (*nods, frowning*) The devil take all women! (LUIS *goes out.* PEDRO *enters, carrying two large baskets full of bottles and sets them down, rear*) Drink and forget sad nonsense. Bring out cushions. We will sit beside the fountain. (PEDRO *goes into the house, right.* LUIS *reënters, holding* YUSEF *by the arm—a wizened old Moor dressed in the clothes of the common people, but wearing the turban signifying that he has made the pilgrimage to Mecca.*

His deep-set eyes smolder with hatred but physically he is so exhausted as to seem resigned to his fate. They are followed by DIEGO MENENDEZ, *a Franciscan monk, about the same age as* JUAN *and* LUIS. *He has a pale, long face, the thin, cruel mouth, the cold, self-obsessed eyes of the fanatic. Just now he is full of helpless fury and indignation. Accompanying him is* VICENTE DE CORDOVA, *a gray-haired, stern, soldierly noble of forty-five. Following them are the three nobles,* OVIEDO, CASTILLO *and* MENDOZA. *They are the type of adventurous cavaliers of the day—cruel, courageous to recklessness, practically uneducated—knights of the true Cross, ignorant of and despising every first principle of real Christianity—yet carrying the whole off with a picturesque air.*)

MENENDEZ. (*angrily*) I protest to you, Juan. It is heresy to suffer this dog's presence when we offer thanks to God for victory.

JUAN. (*stares at the Moor interestedly for a moment—then carelessly*) I see no desecration, Diego—if he will sing, not howl. (*Turning to* VICENTE, *scrutinizing his face keenly—carelessly*) What do you say, Vicente?

VICENTE. (*gives him a dark look of suspicion—coldly and meaningly*) I say nothing—now.

JUAN. Ah! (*He and* LUIS *exchange a look*)

OVIEDO. Well, I say let him remain. We may have sport with him.

CASTILLO. (*with a cruel smile*) Perhaps with a sword-point we can persuade him to sing where the townsfolk hid their gold.

MENDOZA. Your words are inspired, Manuel!

LUIS. (*scornfully*) Materialists! You would sack heaven and melt the moon for silver. Juan, where is your wine? (PEDRO *appears, bringing cushions and goblets for each. He uncorks the bottles and pours their goblets full. Scorning a goblet* LUIS *snatches a bottle from him and drinks from that.*)

JUAN. (*keeping a wary eye on* VICENTE) Let us drink. (*Takes a goblet from* PEDRO) To our most Gracious Sovereigns and to Spain! (*He drinks.*)

MENENDEZ. And to the Church! (*Angrily*) But I will not drink until that infidel is moved apart!

VICENTE. I agree.

JUAN. (*impatiently*) Let the Moor go, Luis—since Diego takes himself so seriously.

VICENTE. (*coldly resentful*) And I? (JUAN *is about to reply irritably when* LUIS *breaks in hurriedly.*)

LUIS. Shhh! I'll sing a song for you. (*Releasing the Moor and pointing to the rear*) Go, brother bard, and take your ease. (*The Moor goes to the right, rear, and squats down in the shadow by the wall.* LUIS *sings*)

Love is a flower
Forever blooming.
Life is a fountain
Forever leaping
Upward to catch the golden sunlight,
Striving to reach the azure heaven;
Failing, falling,
Ever returning
To kiss the earth that the flower may live.

(*They all applaud as he finishes*)

JUAN. Charming, Sir Poet—but a lie. (*Mockingly*) Love, and love, and always love! The devil seize your flower! Do fountains flow only to nourish flowers that bloom a day and die?

LUIS. Roar, lion! You will not wake my dream that life is love!

JUAN. Listen to him, Diego! We know his only love is his old mother; and yet, to judge from his songs, you would think him a greater philanderer than—than—

VICENTE. (*interrupting sneeringly*) Than you, Don Juan?

JUAN. (*turning on him—coldly*) Gossip gives many a false name —but gossip only deludes old women.

VICENTE. (*growing pale*) Do you intend that insult? (*Their hands go to the hilts of their swords. The three nobles quicken to excited interest.* LUIS *leaps between them.*)

LUIS. For God's sake! Is either of you a Moor? (*Raises his bottle*) Let us drink again to Spain!

OVIEDO. And to the next war!

CASTILLO. May it be soon!

MENDOZA. With a world to sack! Sing us a song of that, Luis!

LUIS. I am too thirsty. But come, I was forgetting our infidel. Let me use persuasion— (*He goes back to the Moor, and can be heard talking to him in Arabic.*)

JUAN. We were speaking of wars to come. With whom?

OVIEDO. With anyone!

JUAN. But guess. I think it will be in lands beyond strange seas—Cipango and Cathay—the cities of gold that Marco Polo saw.

OVIEDO. But who will lead us there?

JUAN. Why, Christopher Columbus. (*They all laugh.*)

CASTILLO. That Genoese mongrel!—to lead Spaniards!

MENDOZA. He's mad. He claims the earth is round—like an egg! (*They all laugh.*)

JUAN. (*impressively*) I saw him today. He was riding his flea-bitten mule as if he were a Cæsar in a triumph. His eyes were full of golden cities.

CASTILLO. Bah, Juan, you romance! The man's an idiot!

LUIS. (*coming back*) The more fool you to think so! He will yet find for Spain the Western Passage to the East.

CASTILLO. Or fall off the world's edge! I will wager you would not go with him for all the gold in Indies!

LUIS. You would lose.

JUAN. I'm planning to go. (*All are astonished*) But not on his first voyage. Before I pledge my sword I must have proof that it can serve Spain's glory. There is no profit in staking life for dreams.

LUIS. There is no profit in anything but that! You're from the East, Moor. Tell us of the Great Khan, of Cipango and Cathay and

Cambuluc, of golden roofs and emerald-studded lintels to the doors. Your people must have heard these wonders.

MENDOZA. Yes, let him sing of treasure. (*But the Moor remains silent.*)

LUIS. Wait, I'll talk to him. (*He goes back and speaks to the Moor in Arabic. The latter replies.*)

MENENDEZ. (*furiously*) This is all treasonable. The dog had broken the peace. The punishment is death.

JUAN. (*mockingly*) Let him sing of treasure, Diego. Even the Church loves gold.

LUIS. (*coming back—exultantly*) He consents, Juan—because I am a colleague. He will sing of treasure in the East—a tale told to his father by some wandering poet who came from Cathay with a caravan. (*All except the outraged* DIEGO *and the sullen, preoccupied* VICENTE *quicken to interested attention. The Moor strikes a few notes on his lute*) Hush! (*The Moor begins a crooning chant of verses, accompanying himself on the lute. At first they are all held by its strange rhythm, then they begin to betray impatience.*)

OVIEDO. By God, our wolf turns into a sick shepherd.

LUIS. Hush!

CASTILLO. (*impatiently*) What does he sing?

LUIS. (*enrapt—vaguely*) Hush, hush.

MENENDEZ. (*rising to his feet as the Moor's recitative abruptly ends—harshly*) This is the service in a devil's mass!

LUIS. (*passes his hand across his eyes, then stares into the fountain dreamily*) He sang of treasure—but strange to your longing. There is in some far country of the East—Cathay, Cipango, who knows—a spot that Nature has set apart from men and blessed with peace. It is a sacred grove where all things live in the old harmony they knew before man came. Beauty resides there and is articulate. Each sound is music, and every sight a vision. The trees bear golden fruit. And in the center of the grove, there is a fountain—beautiful beyond human dreams, in whose rainbows all of life is mirrored.

In that fountain's waters, young maidens play and sing and tend it everlastingly for very joy in being one with it. This is the Fountain of Youth, he said. The wise men of that far-off land have known it many ages. They make it their last pilgrimage when sick with years and weary of their lives. Here they drink, and the years drop from them like a worn-out robe. Body and mind know youth again, and these young men, who had been old, leap up and join the handmaid's dance. Then they go back to life, but with hearts purified, and the old discords trouble them no more, but they are holy and the folk revere them. (*With a sigh*) That's his tale, my friends—but he added it is hard to find that fountain. Only to the chosen does it reveal itself.

MENENDEZ. (*furiously*) Idolatry!

OVIEDO. Is this his treasure? By God, he mocks us!

LUIS. Fools! Beauty is lost on you. Your souls clink like coppers. (MENENDEZ *slinks back step by step toward the Moor.* LUIS *grabs a bottle*) Come, let us drink! We'll all to Cathay with Don Christopher. You can burrow for dung there—but I will search for this fountain.

JUAN. (*drinking—a bit tipsily*) Drink and forget sad nonsense! The devil! his song beguiled me until you tricked it into that old woman's mumble. Youth! Is youth a treasure? Then are we all—except Vicente—priceless rich; and yet, God's blood, one has but to look to see how poor we are!

LUIS. Poor in spirit! I understand you, Juan.

JUAN. Fountain of youth, God help us, with love to boot! I wish he'd sung instead of the armies and power of the Great Khan! (*Then half-aside to* LUIS) The tale is always told to the wrong person. There was one here not long ago who would have given pearls for drops from that same fountain!

VICENTE. (*who has crept vengefully toward* JUAN *in time to hear these last words—with cold fury*) A moment ago you taunted me with age—and now you dare— (*He slaps* JUAN *across the face. They draw their swords.*)

LUIS. (*trying to intervene*) For God's sake, friends!

OVIEDO. (*with excited interest*) A duel! (*The others echo this. Suddenly there is a harsh shriek from the rear.* MENENDEZ *appears from the shadow, dagger in hand, a look of fanatical triumph on his face. Forgetting the duel, the others stand appalled.*)

MENENDEZ. (*sheathing the dagger*) I have slain the dog. It was high time.

LUIS. Miserable bigot! (*Raging, he tries to throw himself at the monk, but* JUAN *grasps him and forces him down on a cushion. He breaks down, weeping.*)

MENENDEZ. (*coldly scornful*) What! A soldier of Christ weep for an infidel!

JUAN. (*sternly*) Be still, Diego! (*Then frowning—curtly, in a tone of dismissal which silences all protests*) Our reveling is under an ill star. There is blood upon it. Good-night. (*Turning to* VICENTE) Until tomorrow.

(VICENTE *bows and goes, accompanied by* MENENDEZ. *The young nobles troop out behind, disputing noisily about the coming duel.*)

JUAN. (*comes over and puts his hand on* LUIS' *shoulder—in a mocking, but comforting tone*) Come, Luis. Your brother romancer is dead. Tears will not help him. Perhaps even now he drinks of that Fountain of Youth in Dreamland—if he is not in hell.

LUIS. (*raising his head*) Juan, why do you always sneer at beauty —while your heart calls you liar?

JUAN. (*frowning*) I have Spain in my heart—and my ambition. All else is weakness. (*Changing his tone—carelessly*) Well, you were right. Vicente recognized—and so, a duel. I'll prick him in the thigh and send him home to bed. She will nurse and love him then —and hate me for a murderer. Thus, all works out for the best in this fair world! But—a rare thing dies—and I'm sad, Luis. (*Shaking himself and taking a goblet of wine*) Come, forget sad nonsense. We will drink to voyaging with Don Christopher—and to the battles before those golden cities of Cathay!

LUIS. (*recovering his spirits—grabbing a bottle*) Lucifer fire your cities! I drink to my fountain!

JUAN. Your health, Sir Lying Poet!

LUIS. And yours, Sir Glory-Glutton! (*They laugh, clink goblet and bottle, and drink as the curtain falls.*)

SCENE TWO

SCENE. *About a year later—Columbus's flagship on the last day of his second voyage. The section of the vessel shown reveals the main deck amidships, the mainmast, the mainsail with its Maltese Cross, the two higher decks of the poop, the lateen sail on the mizzenmast, etc. Wooden stairs on the starboard, near the bulwark, are the means of getting from one deck to another.*

It is the time just preceding the dawn. The ship is sailing steadily on a calm sea. There is a large lantern at center of the main deck, another low down in the rigging on the port side, another over the cross which hangs over the stern from the high poop. The ship is crowded with people. On the main deck are the nobles. They are dressed in rich uniforms, in armor. Most of them are asleep, lying sprawled on the deck, wrapped in their cloaks—or huddled in hunched attitudes, their backs propped against the mast or the bulwarks. But one small group has apparently been awake all night. They are sitting cross-legged, throwing dice by the light of the lantern. The faces of the gamesters are haggard and drawn, their eyes feverish. Prominent among them are OVIEDO, CASTILLO, MENDOZA *and* LUIS.

On the first deck of the poop, the monks, all Franciscans, are lying asleep. Here, also, are four of the converted Indians Columbus is bringing back. They are dressed in incongruous costumes, half savage and half civilized. They are huddled in the right corner, not asleep, but frozen in a helpless apathy.

On the highest deck JUAN *is seen standing by the pilot who tends the helm.*

LUIS. (*excitedly*) double or quits!

OVIEDO. Done. (*They play.* LUIS *loses.*)

LUIS. I am ruined again! (*With a comical groan of despair*) Fortune is a damned mercenary wench. She scorns the poor. (*Takes up the dice to throw*) Once more!

OVIEDO. (*grumblingly*) No. You owe me more than you can pay.

LUIS. I will soon be rich as Crœsus. Don Columbus says we will sight land today—the Indies, Isles of Spice, Cipango, Cathay, who knows what? I will stake my future wealth against yours. Come! One more cast for anything you wish.

OVIEDO. (*dryly*) For gold—gold I can see and touch.

LUIS. (*disgustedly*) The devil! I must borrow from Juan then. (*He gets to his feet.*)

OVIEDO. He will not thank you to wake him on a beggar's errand.

LUIS. Do you imagine he sleeps with his Promised Land so near? He is astern on the Admiral's poop keeping a watch of his own—for fear the lookout will miss Cathay!

CASTILLO. Juan is over-eager. He will make the Genoese jealous.

MENDOZA. Has already. It is plain Columbus slights him.

OVIEDO. From policy. He knows Juan is in disgrace at Court since the duel. Our admiral trims his sails to the wind.

CASTILLO. Juan paid dearly for Vicente's wound—a pin-prick that hardly drew blood.

MENDOZA. It was the scandal.

LUIS. (*indignantly*) All false—the malice of envious tongues! Vicente himself apologized to Juan. As for the lady, when I was home in Cordova I saw her with Vicente. You could not find a more married pair. It was even rumored they were to have a child— (JUAN *has come down from the Admiral's poop, passed through the sleeping monks and now appears by the light of the lamp in the rigging at the head of the stairs to the main deck.* LUIS *breaks off suddenly*) Is that you, Juan? Come, be a brother. This son of luck (*he indicates* OVIEDO) has won everything but my skin.

JUAN. (*with a laugh*) Then stake the Fountain of Youth which you will find—tomorrow! Sold by the cask it should make you the richest man in Spain. (*The nobles laugh.*)

LUIS (*with real aversion*) What trader's scheming—from you! (*Then jokingly*) Take care! When the pox of old age is on you will come begging to me! (*Then rattling the dice*) But come, loan me gold for a last cast of revenge. (*Then with a sudden idea*) And you throw for me. My star is behind a cloud.

OVIEDO. Not fair. Juan always wins.

JUAN. (*frowning*) This is no time for gaming.

LUIS. (*insistently*) Just once, Juan.

JUAN. (*consenting unwillingly*) Only once. The stakes are yours. Let the cast be an augury for me. (*He takes gold from his purse. He and* OVIEDO *play.* OVIEDO *wins and there is a murmur of astonishment.*)

OVIEDO. (*exultantly*) I win. The first time I have ever beat you, Juan.

JUAN. (*getting up*) A poor omen. (*Then mockingly*) But here on the under side of earth these signs must run by opposites.

MENDOZA. (*half frightenedly*) Can we be hanging head down and not know it?

CASTILLO. Bah! The Genoese made his first voyage safely. We cannot fall off, it seems.

OVIEDO. Columbus may be a liar.

MENDOZA. (*savagely*) A low-born braggart! He displayed his origin in the hoggish demands he made on the crown. What could the Sovereigns be thinking of—to make this foreign upstart an Admiral and a Viceroy?

JUAN. (*sternly rebuking*) It is not for us to question. (*He pauses—then adds*) His enterprise has served Spain well. He is our commander. That is enough to know. (*He turns his back on them and walks to the port side where he stands by the rigging looking out to sea. The nobles look after him for a moment in an abashed silence.*)

CASTILLO. (*mockingly*) You are a perfect Christian, Juan—to love your enemy.

OVIEDO. (*yawns*) Put out the lantern. Let us sleep. The dawn will wake us. (MENDOZA *puts out the lantern. All except* LUIS *wrap themselves in their robes and lie down on the deck.* LUIS *comes over to* JUAN.)

LUIS. (*scornfully*) Look at those clods. They would snore through the Last Judgment. (*Then as* JUAN *is silent*) What are you dreaming of—Cathay and glory?

JUAN. No. (*Then suddenly*) When I came down I heard Vicente's name—and mention of a child. What were you saying?

LUIS. Gossip of Cordova. My mother told me Maria was having masses said that she might bear an heir—and the rumor was her prayers were answered.

JUAN. (*with deep sincerity*) God grant it. She will be happy then. (*With an ironical laugh*) Did I not tell you that night our duel would reconcile them? (*Soberly*) But I pay. Well, what matter the cost if Maria wins happiness?

LUIS. (*reassuringly*) One exploit and the Court will be at your feet again.

JUAN. (*shaking his head*) We will be far from Spain—out of sight and mind. Columbus will be king here, and he and I are by nature antagonistic. (*There is a noise from the higher deck of the poop. A tall figure can be made out coming up on deck there from the companionway. He moves back until the light from the lantern above the cross reveals him. It is* COLUMBUS. *He is in full uniform but wears no hat on his long, white hair. A commanding figure of noble presence, the face full of the ardent, fixed enthusiasm of the religious devotee.)*

LUIS. (*pulling* JUAN *back into the shadow*) Speak the devil's name! (*They stand, watching and listening, but hidden from the poop.*)

COLUMBUS. (*to the helmsman*) Have you held the course?

HELMSMAN. Southwest by west, sir.

COLUMBUS. (*peering about him*) Will the dawn never come? (*He comes to the edge of the deck and calls down where the monks are—in a low voice*) Father Menendez. Are you awake?

MENENDEZ. (*gets up quickly from among the sleeping monks*) I am here, your Excellency. (*He mounts to the deck above and stands waiting respectfully.*)

COLUMBUS. (*begins in a blunt, perfunctory tone*) Toscanelli's map must be in error. We should have sighted land before. (*A pause. He paces back and forth*) The sun will soon be up. It leaps from the darkness in these parts. (*A pause, then with evident irritation*) A weary voyage, Father! The spirit of these nobles is perverse. They look on this voyage as an escapade in search of easy riches, not as a crusade for the glory of God.

MENENDEZ. (*curtly*) They are brave. Many of them have proven their ability in war—Juan Ponce de Leon, for one.

COLUMBUS. (*resentfully*) A bravo! A duelist!

LUIS. (*in an indignant whisper*) The devil seize him!

JUAN. (*grimly*) Another aftermath of that cursed duel!

MENENDEZ. (*shortly*) You are unjust, Excellency.

COLUMBUS. Oh, I admit he possesses all the attributes but the one which alone gives them virtue—an humble piety. On this great quest there is no place for egotists who seek only selfish ends. We must all feel ourselves unworthy servants of God's Holy Will. (*Then breaking off—abruptly*) But I did not call you to speak of him. (*After a pause—despondently*) My soul is overburdened, Father.

MENENDEZ. (*dryly*) You wish to confess?

COLUMBUS. (*surprised*) Confess? (*Then in a loud, ringing tone*)

Yes, to all men! Their mouths are full of lies against me. They say the demands I made for my share of discovery prove my low-minded avarice. Knaves! What can they know of my heart? Is it for myself I desire wealth? No! But as a chosen instrument of God, Who led me to His Indies, I need the power that wealth can give. I need it for God's glory, not my own! (*More and more exaltedly*) I have a dream, Father! Listen! From my earliest youth I have hated the infidel. I fought on the ships of Genoa against their corsairs and as I saw my city's commerce with the East cut off by their ruthlessness, I prayed for one glorious last Crusade that would reclaim the Mediterranean for Christendom and, most fervent prayer of all, regain from profanation the Holy Sepulchre of our Lord Jesus! (*He blesses himself.* MENENDEZ *also. Then he hurries on exultantly*) And now an answer is granted! With my share of the wealth from Indies, from Cipango and Cathay, I will fit out an army—the Last Crusade! I have promised it to His Holiness, the Pope—fifty thousand men, four thousand horse, with a like force to follow after five years. I shall reconquer the Blessed Tomb of Christ for the True Faith! And to that sacred end I devote my life and all my wealth and power! (*He stands looking up to heaven with the rapt gaze of a devotee.*)

MENENDEZ. (*dryly*) Such a pious ambition does you honor.

JUAN. (*unable to restrain himself, calls mockingly*) The Crusades are dead—and the wealth of the East is still unwon.

COLUMBUS. (*stung—indignantly*) Who dares—?

JUAN. (*proudly*) A noble of Spain who thinks of her greatness while you dream of Genoa and Rome; a soldier of the present, not the ghost of a Crusader! (*Then with exasperated mockery*) God's blood, have all our leaders become half monk? There was a time for that when we fought the Moor, but now a new era of world empire dawns for Spain. By living in the past you will consecrate her future to fanaticism!

COLUMBUS. (*angrily*) Insolent!

JUAN. (*vehemently*) No. I respect you, Columbus—but I have my vision, too. Spain can become the mistress of the world, greater than ancient Rome, if she can find leaders who will weld conquest to her, who will dare to govern with tolerance. (*He laughs a bitter, mocking laugh*) But what a time to speak! Look at the men of this fleet—now when the East dawns for them! I agree with you, Don Christopher—a weary voyage! Adventurers lusting for loot to be had by a murder or two; nobles of Spain dreaming greedy visions of wealth to be theirs by birthright; monks itching for the rack to torture useful subjects of the Crown into slaves of the Church! And for leader to have you, Don Christopher—you who will pillage to resurrect the Crusades! Looters of the land, one and all! There is not one who will see it as an end to build upon! We will loot and loot and, weakened by looting, be easy prey for stronger looters. God pity this land until all looters perish from the earth! (*While he is speaking it has grown perceptibly lighter.*)

COLUMBUS. (*furiously*) Who are you? Stand forth! You dare not!

JUAN. (*jumps up to the lower level of the poop and advances to the ladder to the Admiral's poop—proudly*) It is I—Juan Ponce de Leon! Why should I not dare? Do you want men under your command—or lackeys?

COLUMBUS. (*striving to control his rage*) Silence! (*A wailing cry of "Land Ho" comes from the mainmast head. Immediately the same cry can be heard coming over the water from the other vessels of the fleet. Instantly all is confusion. Everyone jumps to his feet, half awake, peering about bewilderedly. The four Indians sense what has happened and hang over the bulwark, staring over the seas with intense longing. A crowd of half-dressed sailors and rabble pour up from below decks. There is a babble of excited shouts. Columbus looks upward to see where the lookout is pointing, then turns to the horizon off the starboard bow.* JUAN *leaps to the ratlines.*)

THE CROWD. Land! Land! Where? I heard the call. He shouted land! Is it Cathay? Where is he pointing? Look where the Admiral looks. When the sun comes— (*Suddenly the ship is flooded by shafts of golden crimson light. They all cry*) The sun!

JUAN. (*pointing*) There! I see! In a haze of gold and purple—Greater Spain!

ALL. (*crowd to the starboard side and to the front. The Indians are pushed away, jostled, thrown aside contemptuously with imprecations until they are hunched disconsolately in the background in dumb terror and bewilderment*) Where? I see! Where? There! There! Cathay. Cipango. Is it Cathay? Where are the golden cities? Where are the golden roofs? Is it Cipango! The Indies! The Isles of Spice! Marco Polo's land! (*They all crowd, pushing and elbowing each other, craning their necks, the eyes of all, rabble, soldiers, nobles, priests, straining with the same greedy longing, the lust to loot.*)

JUAN. (*exultantly*) Cathay or Cipango or the Isles of Spice, what difference? It shall be Greater Spain! (*The crowd cheers vociferously.*)

COLUMBUS. (*trying to quell the tumult*) Silence, I say! (*Fixing his eyes sternly on* JUAN *with undisguised hostility—rebukingly*) The earth is God's! Give thanks to Him! Kneel, I command you! Raise the cross! (*The monks raise their cross. They kneel but the nobles and soldiers hesitate waiting for* JUAN *as if they saw in him their true commander.*)

JUAN. (*leaps down from the rigging, drawing his sword—with fierce exultance*) This is a cross too, a soldier's cross—the cross of Spain! (*He sticks his sword-point into the deck before him. He kneels before it. All the nobles and soldiers do likewise with a great flourish of gestures and excited shouts. They are all kneeling with their quivering cross swords, hilts rising above their heads.*)

COLUMBUS. (*from his knees—looking up to heaven devoutly*) Te Deum! (*The monks begin to chant. All join in, their pent-up excitement giving to the hymn a hectic, nervous quality.* JUAN *does not sing but stares at the land on the distant horizon.*)

CURTAIN

SCENE THREE

SCENE. *Twenty years or so later—the courtyard of the Governor's palace, Porto Rico. Flowers, shrubs, a coco-palm, orange and banana trees. A large, handsome fountain closely resembling that of Scene One is at center. Two marble benches are at front and rear of fountain. A narrow paved walk encircles the fountain basin, with other walks leading from it to the different entrances. Doors to the interior of the house are at left and right. The main entrance to the courtyard, opening on the road, is at rear center.*

It is in the late, languid hours of a torrid afternoon. The courtyard bakes in the heat, the fountain shimmering in the heat-waves.

JUAN *is seated on the stone bench in front of the basin. He is dressed in the full uniform of his authority as Governor. His face is aged, lined, drawn. His hair and beard are gray. His expression and attitude are full of great weariness. His eyes stare straight before him blankly in a disillusioned dream. The lines about his compressed lips are bitter.*

LUIS *enters from the left, rear. He is dressed in the robe of a Dominican monk. His face shows the years but it has achieved a calm, peaceful expression as if he were at last in harmony with himself. He comes down to* JUAN *and puts a hand on his shoulder.*

JUAN. (*starts—then greets his friend with a smile*) Ah, it's you, reverend Father. (*He accents this last mockingly.*)

LUIS. (*good-naturedly*) Yes, illustrious Governor. (*He sits beside* JUAN*—with a laugh*) You are like a sulky child, Juan. Come, is it not time, after five years, you forgave me for being a Dominican?

JUAN. (*bitterly*) My friend deserting to my enemy!

LUIS. (*protestingly*) Come, come! (*Then after a pause, with a sigh*) You have always had the dream of Cathay. What had I? What had I done with life?—an aimless, posing rake, neither poet nor soldier, without place nor peace! I had no meaning even to myself until God awakened me to His Holy Will. Now I live in truth. You must renounce in order to possess.

JUAN. The world would be stale indeed if that were true! (*After a pause—irritably*) I fight the battles; you monks steal the spoils! I seek to construct; you bind my hands and destroy!

LUIS (*remonstrating*) You speak of Diego and his kind.

JUAN (*frowning*) Whether you convert by clemency or he by cruelty, the result is the same. All this baptizing of Indians, this cramming the cross down their throats has proved a ruinous error. It crushes their spirits and weakens their bodies. They become burdens for Spain instead of valuable servitors.

LUIS. Your army crushed them first—

JUAN. They had to be conquered, but there I would have stopped. (*Then irritably*) God's blood, here we are arguing about this same issue—for the thousandth time! It is too late. Talk is useless. (*With a weary sigh*) We do what we must—and sand covers our bodies and our deeds. (*With a smile*) And the afternoon is too hot, besides. Tell me some news. Will the fleet from Spain make port today?

LUIS. Just now I saw them rounding the point under full sail. They should anchor inside soon. (*They are interrupted by the noise of several people approaching from outside.* OVIEDO *and* FRIAR QUESADA, *a Franciscan, enter, followed by the Indian chief,* NANO, *who is guarded by two soldiers with drawn swords.* QUESADA *is a thin young monk with the sallow, gaunt face and burning eyes of a fanatic.* OVIEDO *is aged but gives no evidence of having changed in character.* NANO *is a tall, powerfully built Indian of fifty or so. Although loaded down with chains, he carries himself erect with an air of aloof, stoical dignity. He wears a headdress of feathers. His face and body are painted, ornaments are about his neck. He is naked except for a breech-clout and moccasins.*)

QUESADA. (*fiercely and arrogantly*) I demand justice on this dog!

JUAN. (*freezing—proudly*) Demand?

QUESADA. (*with ill-concealed hatred but awed by* JUAN'S *manner*) Pardon my zeal in the service of God, Your Excellency. I ask justice. (*Then defiantly*) But it is not the Church's custom to be a suppliant.

JUAN. So much the worse— (*Sternly*) What is this Indian's crime?

QUESADA. His tribe will not pay the tithes—and he himself has dared to refuse baptism!

JUAN. (*coldly*) I'll question him. (*Then as* QUESADA *hesitates, raging inwardly—sternly*) You may go.

QUESADA. (*controlling his rage, bows*) Yes, Your Excellency. (*He goes.*)

JUAN. (*to* OVIEDO *with a certain contempt*) You also have a charge against this Indian?

OVIEDO. (*angrily*) A plea for justice! These dogs will not pay their taxes. And we who own estates cannot get them to work except by force, which you have arbitrarily curtailed. Then why not punish them by leasing their labor to us until their debt's wiped out? Thus the government will be paid, and we will have workers for our mines and fields.

JUAN. (*disgustedly*) Your brain is not inventive, Oviedo! You are well aware that is the same blunder which failed on Espaniola. It means slavery. It defeats its purpose. The Indians die under the lash —and your labor dies with them. (*Contemptuously*) Do you think I am Columbus that you ask this folly of me?

OVIEDO. (*haughtily*) You refuse? (*He goes to the rear where he turns—threateningly*) Take care, Juan! There will come a day of reckoning—when Diego returns from Spain. (*He goes out.*)

JUAN. (*frowning*) Diego? What do you mean?

OVIEDO. (*with a revengeful smile*) Nothing. Adios, Don Juan. (*He goes out.*)

JUAN. (*with a bitter laugh*) There you have it! Bah! What use—?

(*He suddenly seems to see* NANO *for the first time. They stare at each other*) I was forgetting you. Are you not Nano, chief of the last tribe I conquered? (*As the Indian is silent—imperiously*) Speak!

NANO. The devils were with you. Our villages were burned. Women and children were killed—my wives, my children!

JUAN. (*frowning*) Contrary to my command. But, again, what use? The dead are dead. It is too late. (*After a pause—with a sort of weary self-mockery*) Have you ever heard of Cathay—Cipango? Do you know of vast countries to the west—many peoples—great villages with high walls—much gold?

NANO. I have heard.

JUAN. (*surprised—eagerly*) Ah! Where are they? (NANO *points west.*)

LUIS. (*amusedly*) Where the Fountain of Youth of my drunken days is located—in dreamland!

JUAN. (*with a certain seriousness*) Do you know, they say there is a similar fountain legend among these tribes. (*Then to* NANO *with a mocking smile*) My friend here is growing impatient waiting for immortality in heaven and would rather gain it here on earth—

LUIS. Juan!

JUAN. So tell him, O Mighty Chief, if there is not over there—a fountain—a spring—in which old men bathe or drink and become young warriors again?

NANO. (*to both their surprise*) The tale is told. Not here. In my home—a land that never ends. Our priests told the tale. I was young then. I was captured in war and brought here. I was adopted. I have never returned.

JUAN. (*lost in thought*) So? Where is this land, your home? (NANO *points as before*) Where Cathay is? And the fountain—the spring—is there?

NANO. (*after a moment's hesitation*) Yes. My people call it the Spring of Life.

LUIS. (*whimsically*) A pretty title, indeed. (*Sceptically*) But none can find it, I suppose?

NANO. Those the Gods love can find it.

JUAN. (*scornfully*) Aha, that old trick of poets—evasion of facts! (*Turning to* LUIS) Do you remember the Moor that night in Granada? "Only to the chosen." Here is the echo! Bah! What jugglery! (*Then thoughtfully*) But it is strange. Where there is so much smoke, there must be a spark of fire. The Moor traced his myth back to the East—Cathay—and now we discover it again—still in Cathay—circling the world— (*Then, as if ashamed of himself for taking it so seriously—carelessly*) At all events, it is added evidence that Cathay is near. (*The boom of a cannon comes from the harbor.*)

LUIS. The fleet is anchored. Diego will soon be here. If you can give this Indian into my keeping I will attempt his conversion.

JUAN. (*impatiently*) Until his case is investigated, he must go to prison. You may see him there. (*To* NANO, *sternly*) If it is proven you have encouraged rebellion against Spain, you will be hung. Against any other charge I will try to save you. (*Summoning the soldiers*) Guard. (*They salute and lead* NANO *out, left.* JUAN *paces up and down in frowning thought*) Diego! Did you hear Oviedo threaten me with him? What mischief will he bring from Spain this time, I wonder? The cursed spider! His intriguing will destroy all my work here— (*With impotent anger*) And the fight is hopeless. His weapons are whispers. A man of honor stands disarmed. (*Intensely*) Would to God this fleet brought me the King's patent to discover new lands! I would sail tomorrow for Cathay—or for the moon!

LUIS. (*firmly*) Fight your battle here! This is your land. You conquered it.

JUAN. Columbus discovered it; and I still feel his influence, like a black fog, stifling me!

LUIS. (*mollifyingly*) He is dead. Forgive. He suffered too much injustice to be just.

JUAN. How can my pride forgive? For years I held his solitary outposts; I suffered wounds and fevers; I fought the Indians for him while he went sailing for the Garden of Eden, the mines of Solomon, his Bible-crazed chimeras! He knew my honor would not permit my conspiring against him as others did. So he ignored my services and deliberately condemned me to obscurity! Never one mention of my name in his reports to Spain! It is only since his downfall—(*Breaking off*) But this, too, is an old story. (*Then with sudden exasperation*) Why should I not sail to find Cathay? He failed in that—but I would succeed! I am no visionary chasing rainbows. (*Desperately*) I tell you I loathe this place! I loathe my petty authority! By God, I could sink all Porto Rico under the sea for one glimpse of Cathay!

LUIS. (*alarmed*) Juan!

JUAN. (*after a pause—ironically*) Well, do not fear that I will leave your precious island. The patent will never come—and if it did, there is a flaw— (*Despondently, with a great weariness*) It is too late. Cathay is too far. I am too weary. I have fought small things so long that I am small. My spirit has rusted in chains for twenty years. Now it tends to accept them—to gain peace. (*With passionate yearning*) If I could only feel again my old fire, my energy of heart and mind! If I could be once more the man who fought before Granada—! But the fire smolders. It merely warms my will to dream of the past. It no longer catches flame in deeds. (*With a desolate smile of self-pity*) I begin to dread—another failure. I am too old to find Cathay.

(MENENDEZ *appears in rear in time to hear this last. He is dressed in a Bishop's robes. He looks his years, but his expression of rabid fanaticism has changed to one, not less cruel, of the crafty schemer made complacent by a successful career, the oily intriguer of Church politics. He hesitates with a suspicious, inquisitive glance from one to the other—then advances with a forced air of joviality*) What is this I hear? Too old? Tut-tut! This is hearsay, Juan. (*The two turn, startled.* JUAN *stares at him resentfully.* MENENDEZ *exchanges a cold bow of condescension with* LUIS, *then comes to* JUAN *with outstretched hands, smiling oilily*) Have you no greeting for me, old friend?

JUAN. (*takes his hands perfunctorily—then sarcastically*) Who would expect you unattended—like any eavesdropping monk?

MENENDEZ. (*unruffled*) My eagerness to see you. I have great news. I often spoke to the King about you. He now holds you in the highest esteem, and as a proof of his favor I bring you— (*Then with a sly smile*) But, on second thought, I should not say, I bring you. That is reserved for a worthier hand!

JUAN. (*impatiently*) I dislike mysteries.

MENENDEZ. (*provokingly*) I will give you this hint out of respect for the old age you were lamenting! Prepare to welcome youth—and a prize you have sought for all your life in the Indies—a gift more welcome to you than wine was to Luis before he repented! (*With this parting gibe, he turns away*) Pardon me if I leave you. I must make preparations—for this event. (*He bows mockingly and goes off right.*)

JUAN. (*angrily*) Schemer! (*He paces up and down.*)

LUIS. (*after pondering a moment—suddenly*) I have it! It must be your patent to explore! He has obtained it from the King—because he wishes to get rid of you here! You stand in his way—your policy of clemency. He wants to be dictator to introduce torture and slavery! Yet he is afraid to fight you openly, so what craftier scheme than to send you away contented, grateful for a gift, bribed without knowing it?

JUAN. (*resentfully*) Then I will fool the fox! There is no compulsion in such a patent. (*Then confused*) But—it would be my highest hope come true—too late! Too late! I am too old. (*With an attempt at a railing tone*) God's blood, I need to find Cathay—if your Fountain of Youth is there!

LUIS. I hear a crowd coming. I must go. It adds to their spleen to find us together. (*He presses* JUAN's *hand*) Whatever comes, be firm, old friend. (*He goes out left. The murmur of the crowd increases.* JUAN *sinks on the bench before the fountain, oblivious to it, lost in gloomy thought.* BEATRIZ DE CORDOVA *appears, attended by her duenna and a crowd of richly dressed nobles. She is a beautiful young girl of eighteen or so, the personification of youthful vitality, charm and grace. The nobles point out* JUAN *to her. She dismisses them, motioning for them to be quiet—then comes in and approaches* JUAN, *keeping the fountain between them. She holds a sealed document in her hand. Finally she calls in a trembling, eager voice.*)

BEATRIZ. Don Juan! (JUAN *whirls on his bench and stares through the fountain at her. He utters a stunned exclamation as if he saw a ghost. His eyes are held fascinated by her beauty. Then suddenly she laughs—a gay, liquid, clear note—and coming quickly around confronts him*) It is I, Don Juan.

JUAN. (*stares at her still fascinated—then, reminded, springs to his feet and bows low with his old mocking gallantry*) Pardon! I am bewitched! I thought you were the spirit of the fountain. (*Then more mockingly*) Beautiful lady, you do me unmerited honor!

BEATRIZ (*hurt and confused by his tone*) You don't know me? Why, I'm Beatriz. (*As he bows but shows no recognition*) Has Bishop Menendez not told you—?

JUAN. (*suspiciously*) Nothing of you, my lady.

BEATRIZ. I am Beatriz de Cordova—

JUAN. (*guessing—amazed, stares at her—a pause, slowly*) Maria's child!—you!

BEATRIZ. (*letting it all pour forth regardless*) She died a year ago—and—I am your ward now. It was her last wish. My father was dead. There was no near relative whom she would trust. I asked the King to send me here to you. He bade me wait until the Bishop could escort me. He made me the bearer of this gift for you—your dearest wish, he said. (*She gives him the document.*)

JUAN. (*unrolls it—a pause as he stares at it dully, then bitterly*) The patent—to find Cathay!

BEATRIZ. Yes! And you can find it where the others failed, I know! You were my dear mother's ideal of Spanish chivalry, of a true knight of the Cross! That was her prophecy, that you would be the first to reach Cathay!

JUAN. She spoke of the man she knew. (*Staring at her fascinatedly —eagerly*) She sends me you—and you are youth! Is it in mockery?

BEATRIZ. (*suddenly*) Oh, Don Juan, I recall something she said I must remember when we should meet. "Bring him tenderness," she said. "That will repay the debt I owe him for saving me for you." She said these words were secrets to tell you alone. What did she mean, Don Juan?

JUAN. (*deeply moved*) Tenderness? Do you bring me that, Beatriz? (*Then as if recalling himself*) No, do not—for it means weakness. Bring me the past instead. Give me back—the man your mother knew.

BEATRIZ. (*who has been scrutinizing him without paying attention to his words*) You are older than I dreamed, Don Juan.

JUAN. (*wounded—with harsh violence*) No tenderness there! Youth! A cuirass of shining steel! A glittering sword! Laughter above the battle! (*Then seeing her look of frightened astonishment at his wild words, he controls himself and adds with a melancholy bitterness*) It was so long ago, Beatriz—that night in Granada—a dimly-remembered dream— (*Then with a sudden return of his mockingly gallant manner*) Forgive me. I have become a savage lost to manners. (*He kneels and kisses her hand with all his old-time gallantry*) Welcome, dear ward, to Porto Rico! (*She looks down at his bowed head, blushing with pleasure and naïve embarrassment, as the curtain falls.*)

SCENE FOUR

SCENE. *Three months later*—MENENDEZ' *official study in the palace—a large, high-ceilinged, bare room with a heavy table at center. The color scheme is dark and gloomy, the atmosphere that of a rigid, narrow ecclesiasticism. In one corner is an altar with high candles burning before it. Heavy hangings shut out the light from the lofty, arched windows. An enormous crucifix hangs on the wall in rear. The room is like an exaggerated monk's cell, but it possesses a somber power over the imagination by the force of its concentration. There is a main entrance at rear, center, and a smaller side door at left, hidden by curtains.*

It is early evening. MENENDEZ *is seated at the table. He is frowningly impatient, listening and waiting for someone. There is the sound of approaching footsteps.* MENENDEZ *turns eagerly in his chair.* QUESADA *enters through the hangings on the left. His face is ominous and set. He wears a sword and pistols over his robe which is tucked up over high riding boots and spurs. He is covered with dust, and has evidently been riding hard. He bows respectfully to* MENENDEZ.

MENENDEZ. I had begun to think you would never come. (*Then with anxiety*) What news?

QUESADA. The meeting is being held. They have gathered in the fort outside the town.

MENENDEZ. Good! It is moving according to my plan, then.

QUESADA. They all agree that Don Juan must resign his patent.

MENENDEZ. Unless he sails to find Cathay at once?

QUESADA. Yes. They are all mad for the gold (*with a sneer*) over there, the report of which I have had rumored about, as you directed.

MENENDEZ. Good. Then we shall be rid of Juan and all the discontented spirits on the island at one stroke!

QUESADA (*excitedly*) But they also demand that first the Indian, Nano, must be burned at the stake. They believe he has bewitched the Governor. They know of Don Juan's secret interviews with him.

MENENDEZ. (*angrily*) Who told them?

QUESADA. (*after a moment's hesitation—defiantly*) I did.

MENENDEZ. (*angrily*) Fool!

QUESADA. (*alarmed—humbly*) But the dog still refuses baptism.

MENENDEZ. (*sternly*) Is this a time to consider one Indian? Idiot! You know as well as I that my intention has been to attack Juan on one issue, and only one—his failure to sail for Cathay now that he has the King's patent. What have all the Nanos, hung or unhung, to do with that?

QUESADA. Much! If Don Juan were not bewitched by Nano's spells, he would have sailed long since.

MENENDEZ. And you told the rabble that? God pardon you! Was it any part of my orders that you should play upon the mob's lust for blood? I have worked for a peaceable revolt that would awaken Juan to his weakness and shame him into leaving. You have dared to evoke a madness which might easily sweep away all recognized authority. Quick! What was the rabble's mood when you left? (QUESADA *avoids his eyes.* MENENDEZ *pounds the table*) Answer me.

QUESADA. (*evasively*) They had been drinking—

MENENDEZ. (*furiously, a note of alarm creeping in*) Ah!

QUESADA. (*now thoroughly cowed*) They were clamoring to march on the palace. Don Oviedo was trying to restrain them—

MENENDEZ. (*fiercely—with bitter scorn*) You cursed blunderer! No, I am the dolt for having trusted you!

QUESADA. (*kneeling—cowed*) Forgive me, Your Grace!

MENENDEZ. Your action was treachery to me! And I shall punish you! When this expedition sails for that golden fable, Cathay, you shall go with it. Then blunder all you like! (*He rises and strides to the window at rear.*)

QUESADA. (*humbly*) I humbly accept my penance.

MENENDEZ. (*bitterly*) Behold the first fruits of your excessive piety! (*He points*) The southern horizon is aflame!

QUESADA. (*rising*) They must have set fire to the Indian villages.

MENENDEZ. Blood and fire! Your merry dance begins well! (*He lets the curtains fall back*) Only Juan can control them now—if he would only promise them to sail at once—but no, he is too proud. He will fight armed rebellion to the last—and we will all go down in the same ruin!

QUESADA. (*scornfully*) He is not the man he was—since Nano bewitched him.

MENENDEZ. (*disgustedly*) Bah! You fool! (*Then intently*) Yet there is truth in what you say. He has grown weak—between Luis' influence and the girl's meddling— (*Abruptly*) Come! There is still a chance. Summon Don Juan to me at once! (*This last in a shout of impatience.*)

JUAN. (*from outside, rear, mockingly*) There is no need for messengers. (*He enters. In the three months he has aged greatly. His hair and beard have grown perceptibly white. Beneath the bitter, mocking mask there is an expression of deep, hidden conflict and suffering on his face as if he were at war with himself.*)

MENENDEZ. (*startled, afraid of what* JUAN *may have overheard*) You heard—?

JUAN. (*scornfully*) Only what you shouted. Am I a monk to listen at keyholes? (*This with a glance at* QUESADA) But I know your intrigues. This meeting of yapping curs—you see, I have heard the rumor—you would have me sail at their bidding, and thus you would be free to rule this island in God's Holy Name! Is it not so?

MENENDEZ. (*controlling his anger*) You have lost your senses. You will not realize that things have reached a crisis! The government has slipped through your fingers while you played at being a loving father—

JUAN. (*stung—fiercely*) It's a lie! (*Controlling himself*) I tell you again, Diego, I will sail at my pleasure, not yours.

MENENDEZ. (*persuasively*) You have kept repeating that—and meanwhile your apathy has ruined us. Your soldiers and sailors are in open mutiny. The mob has risen. (*Urgently*) Juan, do you want rebellion to overwhelm us? You promised them Cathay—

JUAN. (*proudly*) It was you who promised them in my name, you mean, to make certain you would be rid of me!

MENENDEZ. (*tauntingly—noting* JUAN'S *reactions craftily*) I promised because I thought you were still Juan Ponce de Leon. But you are not. You have become merely a slave to a girl's sentimental whims! You are too feeble to govern here and too weak for Cathay. (JUAN'S *hand goes to his sword.* MENENDEZ *continues cuttingly*) Then for the sake of Spain, resign your office and surrender your patent for discovery to someone with the youth and courage to dare!

JUAN. (*infuriated, half drawing his sword*) Take care, Diego! Your cloth cannot condone such insults!

MENENDEZ. (*in a softened, oily tone*) Forgive me, Juan. I insult you for your own sake! Push on to your greatest victory! Do not wait here in a stupor for inglorious defeat!

JUAN. (*shaken*) I shall sail—but first I must know—know for a certainty, beyond all doubt—exactly where— (*He stops abruptly.*)

MENENDEZ. (*inquisitively*) What?

JUAN. (*suspiciously*) Nothing.

QUESADA. (*who has been listening with feverish interest—points to* JUAN *accusingly*) He has gone to Nano every day. Look at his eyes! He is bewitched! (JUAN *starts guiltily but tries to ignore him contemptuously.*)

MENENDEZ. Be still, Quesada! (*He looks at* JUAN) These interviews *are* mysterious, Juan.

JUAN. (*quickly—half turning away and averting his eyes—with forced carelessness*) I need accurate information for my voyage that only Nano can give me. That is why I have delayed.

MENENDEZ. (*looking at him sharply*) So? I had thought it might be affection for Beatriz that held you.

JUAN. (*vehemently*) No!

MENENDEZ. (*keenly*) Why are you so vehement? It would be natural enough. You have lived alone. To find a daughter in your declining years—

JUAN. (*pale with rage and agony*) Daughter? How could she look upon me—?

MENENDEZ. (*soothingly but with a taunting intent*) She used to regard you as her hero, her great commander. She must wonder now at this old man's weakness in you.

JUAN. (*frenziedly*) Do you dare taunt me in her name? I *will* sail, I say! I will sail the very first day after I discover— (*Then distractedly, shaken*) Enough, Diego! I shall do what I wish and when it pleases me! (*He rushes out rear as if furies were hounding him.* MENENDEZ *looks after him, a sneering smile of satisfaction gradually coming over his face as if something were proven to him.*)

MENENDEZ. (*half to himself, half to* QUESADA) I should have guessed it before. Yet, who would have thought— He is bewitched, certainly.

QUESADA. (*eagerly*) Yes!

MENENDEZ. (*dryly*) But you are blaming the wrong witch. The guilty one is sinless. (QUESADA *puzzles over this paradox with open eyes.* MENENDEZ *ponders for a moment, then he turns to* QUESADA) Bring the Lady Beatriz.

QUESADA. Yes, Your Grace. (*He bows and hurries out, left.* MENENDEZ *sits thoughtfully, evidently planning out his campaign. A moment later* BEATRIZ *enters. She bows respectfully.*)

BEATRIZ. (*reservedly*) You wish to see me, Your Grace?

MENENDEZ. (*nods and motions her to a chair. He scrutinizes her face carefully for a moment, then begins in a playful, ironical tone*) Beauty did not leave a stone on stone of ancient Troy. Are you another Helen, Beatriz?

BEATRIZ. (*confused*) I—don't understand.

MENENDEZ. (*coldly and brusquely*) Not understand that rebellion is seething in Porto Rico?—a rebellion that will deal destruction to us all!

BEATRIZ. (*bewildered*) Rebellion? (*Then spiritedly*) Who would dare rebel against Don Juan?

MENENDEZ. (*belittlingly*) Juan is powerless. His own soldiers have taken the lead against him. He is facing ruin! Do you understand? I wish I had words of fire to brand it on your brain! For I tell you on my conscience, as God's minister, you are the one responsible!

BEATRIZ. (*stunned*) I? I? You are jesting! (*Then with haughty resentment*) I harm Don Juan, who is my second father!

MENENDEZ. (*seeming to grow more icy under her anger*) Who has done most in influencing him to softness and lax discipline—

BEATRIZ. (*indignantly*) You mean because I have pitied the suffering of the Indians—?

MENENDEZ. (*dryly*) Let us judge your pity by its results. These heathen no longer fear. They defy our Holy Faith. They sneer at baptism. These Indians shirk their labor. And because Don Juan spends his time with you, he has forgotten not only his duty to govern but his oath to seek Cathay. The soldiers and sailors have waited too long in idleness. Now they revere him no longer as a daring general who will lead them to glory but despise him for a dissembler, delaying because he has lost the courage for action! And so they have conspired. Those are the facts. Will you deny your influence is deep at the root of them? (*Beatriz is too overwhelmed by the ruthlessness of his attack to reply. He pushes his advantage*) And can you deny that a great change has come over Don Juan since your arrival? You cannot have helped noticing this!

BEATRIZ. He has seemed—to become despondent at times.

MENENDEZ. (*vehemently*) Spiritless! Infirm! His thoughts wander like a senile old man's! I believe his mind is failing him!

BEATRIZ. (*horrified*) No! No!

MENENDEZ. You must face the truth! (*Sternly*) When you take a life's ambition from a man like Juan, the man withers away. You have made him forget Cathay. Why? Why have you not urged him to go—for his own sake? When you brought out the patent, you dreamed of him as he dreams of himself—a conqueror and hero!

BEATRIZ. (*hesitatingly*) Father Luis told me we must keep him here—or else his good work would be undone—

MENENDEZ. This uprising will undo it in an hour! (*Then soothingly*) Father Luis is a good man—but blind. You are a girl—and inexperienced— Come. (*He pauses, watching her keenly, then takes her hand, and leading her to the window, pulls back the curtain*) Look!

BEATRIZ. (*with a shudder of horror*) Ah!

MENENDEZ. Now do you believe in the rebellion—in Juan's danger?

BEATRIZ. (*horrified*) Fire!

MENENDEZ. And murder! In the Indian villages. See what your pity for them has done! And it will not stop there. That is only the first spark of revolution. They'll march here! (*Impressively*) Beatriz, you can save Don Juan. He loves you—as his daughter. Urge him to sail at once! Rouse the hero in him! Give him back his sanity! He is my old friend. I implore you for his sake, Beatriz.

BEATRIZ. (*bewilderedly*) Yes—yes—but give me time to think—to pray for guidance— (*She kneels before the altar.*)

MENENDEZ. (*impatiently*) There is no time! (*There is a noise of hurrying steps and* OVIEDO *enters. He is booted, spurred, covered with dust, his face betraying anxiety and alarm.*)

OVIEDO. (*without stopping to see who is there, bursts forth*) Diego!

I tried to check them, but they have gone mad! They are marching on the town! Juan will be lost!

MENENDEZ. (*to* BEATRIZ *who has turned around in terror*) You hear!

OVIEDO. The time has come to abandon that sick fool! We must openly lead this rebellion!

BEATRIZ. (*springs to her feet and faces him—her eyes flashing*) Coward! (*He falls back, his hand on his sword, glaring at her.*)

MENENDEZ. (*urgently*) Go, Beatriz! (*She passes* OVIEDO *with a scathing glance, and goes out rear.* MENENDEZ *turns to* OVIEDO *with an ironical but worried smile.*)

MENENDEZ. If she will but speak to Juan as she did to you, we may still win, my friend!

CURTAIN

SCENE FIVE

SCENE. NANO's *dungeon—a circular cavern, hollowed out by Nature and cut out by man in the solid rock under the Government House. The enclosed space is narrow but lofty, cylindrical in form. A cut-in flight of steps leads from the floor in rear to a trap-door above. The high wall glistens with moisture. A small bench is at right. A lantern stands on one of the lower steps. In the middle of the floor stands a soldier, thick-set, brutal-looking, his sleeves rolled up over his muscular arms. He is blowing with a bellows on a charcoal brazier, glowing red-hot, in which are thrust several irons. On the wall in the rear, his toes barely touching the floor,* NANO *hangs with his arms outstretched over his head, the wrists bound by chains to iron sockets in the rock. His head hangs on one side as if he were in a state of semi-consciousness. His body is thin and wasted.*

The trap-door is opened and a circular patch of gray light falls on the stairs. This is obscured as someone descends. It is JUAN. *He shuts the trap-door behind him and comes down. He stops when he is opposite* NANO's *head, and, leaning over, stares at the savage's face. The latter opens his eyes. His head stiffens proudly erect on his shoulders. He and* JUAN *stare into each other's eyes.* JUAN *drops his guiltily, turns away and descends to the floor, where the soldier is standing at attention.*

JUAN. (*harshly*) Has he spoken?

SOLDIER. Not one word, sir.

JUAN. Then you have not obeyed—

SOLDIER. (*indicates the irons in the fire*) I have tried every trick I know—but he's made of iron.

JUAN. (*looks up at* NANO *with intense hatred*) Dog! (*Then he turns to the soldier*) Go and keep guard above.

SOLDIER. Yes, sir. (*He bends down to pick up the brazier.*)

JUAN. (*harshly*) No.

SOLDIER. (*with a glance at him—understandingly*) Yes, sir. (*He goes up the stairs, opens the trap-door and disappears, letting it fall shut behind him.* JUAN *sinks on the stone bench at right and stares up at* NANO, *who looks back at him with unflinching defiance. A pause.*)

JUAN. (*his eyes now fixed dully on the floor—half-aloud to himself*) Diego did not lie. The storm is gathering. (*With bitter hopelessness*) What matter? I could pray that it might be a deluge annihilating mankind—but for Beatriz. (*He groans, then raises his eyes again to* NANO) Why do you look at me? I can never read your eyes. They see in another world. What are you? Flesh, but not our flesh. Earth. I come after—or before—but lost, blind in a world where my eyes deflect on surfaces. What values give you your loan of life? Answer! I must know the terms in which to make appeal! (*The savage is silent, motionless. A pause. Then* JUAN, *as if suddenly reminded, jumps to his feet in a frenzy of impatience*) Answer me, dog! I must find the will to act—or be dishonored!

NANO. (*solemnly—in a faint voice*) The gods are angry.

JUAN. (*with wild joy*) You speak! At last! Nano, why have you kept dumb while I implored—?

NANO. The gods have stopped your ears.

JUAN. (*going on obsessed, regardless*) Juan Ponce de Leon—to torture a helpless captive! Why did you bring me to such shame? Why would you not answer my question?

NANO. (*with contempt*) My tongue grew weary. For a moon I answered every day.

JUAN. (*fiercely*) But you lied! Tell me the truth now! Where is the fountain?

NANO. (*indifferently, shutting his eyes*) Only the gods know.

JUAN. The same lie! You told me at first that men of your former tribe knew! You must know! This is your revenge—for the death of your wives and children! Must I swear to you again they were killed in spite of my strict orders? Come! Forget them! I will give you your choice of all your women on the island—your freedom—I will petition the King to honor you—give you back your lands—anything if you will answer me! (NANO *remains silent.* JUAN *utters a furious cry and, rushing to the brazier, takes a red-hot coal with the tongs and holds it before the Indian's eyes*) Dog! I will burn that scorn from your eyes! (*The Indian stares at the hot iron immovably.* JUAN *lets it fall to the floor with a desperate groan of misery*) Pardon! Forgiveness in Christ's name! It is you who torture me! Nano, I burn to hell! I love! (*He suddenly stops, chilled to despair by the implacable isolation in the savage's face. He throws himself down on the bench in an apathy. Finally he slowly draws his sword and speaks in a dead voice*) Either you speak or you die. I swear it.

NANO. (*with aloof contempt*) What is death?

JUAN. (*dully*) I will die, too. Perhaps in the grave there is oblivion and peace. (*After a pause*) You are a fool, Nano. If you would help me I could make you pilot of the fleet to guide us to your land. The fountain once found, you would be free. No harm should come to your people. Do you never long for your old home?

NANO. (*who has been listening with quickened interest*) Home? To the land of flowers. My home of many warriors. (*After a pause*) You will let me guide the great winged canoes—to my home?

JUAN. (*eagerly*) Yes. (*In great suspense*) Will you help me? Tell me! (*He has sprung to his feet.*)

NANO. Only the gods— (*He checks himself abruptly.*)

JUAN. (*frenziedly*) Ah! (*He raises his sword as if to run the savage through.*)

NANO. (*looking into Juan's eyes without noticing the threat*) The tongues of the white devils are false. How can I trust your word?

JUAN. I take my sacred oath! (*He raises his hand.*)

NANO. Your God is a God of lies.

JUAN. (*wildly*) By your God then—since mine has forsaken me!

NANO. (*lifts his head and murmurs some supplication, as if begging forgiveness—then looks at* JUAN *with savage triumph*) I will guide you—but remember the way is long!

JUAN. (*triumphantly*) At last! What does it matter how long or difficult! (*Raising his arms*) Ah, God's blood, I already feel new life, the will to live! I can conquer now! (*A pounding of a sword-butt on the trap-door. Then it is flung open.*)

SOLDIER. Pardon, Excellency—

BEATRIZ' VOICE. (*calls down*) Don Juan! Don Juan!

JUAN. (*exultantly*) Her voice! A happy omen! (*He hurries up the stairs.*)

NANO. (*again lifting his eyes to heaven—with religious fervor*) Great Spirit, forgive my lie. His blood shall atone!

CURTAIN

SCENE SIX

SCENE. *Same as Scene Three—Courtyard of the Governor's House—a stifling twilight. The sky is darkening with clouds.*

BEATRIZ' *voice—from the left—calls down as at the end of preceding scene.*

BEATRIZ. Don Juan! Don Juan! (*His voice is heard, "Beatriz." She enters, pale and agitated, runs to rear and looks for signs of the insurrection—then hurries back just in time to meet* JUAN, *who enters, left. He is in a tense state of hectic excitement, his face ghastly pale, his obsessed eyes burning feverishly, his drawn sword still in his hand. She starts back from him, frightened by his appearance.*)

JUAN. (*in a strained, high-pitched tone*) Was it the fountain called —or you, Beatriz? You, for you are the fountain! (*He takes her hand impetuously and kisses it.*)

BEATRIZ. (*flurriedly*) I came to warn you—

JUAN. (*with a sharp glance*) Warn? Then you have seen Diego? Bah! (*He makes a gesture of contempt with his sword as if brushing all revolutions aside*) When the hour comes, I shall be strong. The will breathes in me again. Forget all else, Beatriz. Give me your thoughts! Have you been happy here with me?

BEATRIZ. (*not knowing what to say or do*) Yes—yes. (*Trying to return to her mission*) But—

JUAN. You came as a benediction—that cursed me. (*Abruptly*) Have you not noticed how much older I have grown?

BEATRIZ. (*convinced he is out of his head—resolved to humor him —frightened but pityingly*) You can become young again.

JUAN. (*exultantly*) I will! (*Then mysteriously*) This is a strange world with many wonders still undiscovered.

BEATRIZ. (*seeing a chance to bring in her point—quickly*) Then discover them. The search will make you young.

JUAN. (*deeply and superstitiously impressed*) From your own lips! It is another blessed augury! (*Eagerly*) But pretend I am young. What then?

BEATRIZ. Why, then you would be happy.

JUAN. (*intensely*) You promise—? Have you never loved?

BEATRIZ. (*bewildered*) Loved?

JUAN. Since you speak of happiness.

BEATRIZ. I loved my mother—my father—I love you, Don Juan.

JUAN. (*avidly*) Ah, say that again! Those words are blood to my heart!

BEATRIZ. (*earnestly*) I love you as I loved my father—

JUAN. (*brusquely—wounded to the quick*) Has love never stolen into your dreams? You are no nun. Come, tell me the image of the one you dream of as a lover.

BEATRIZ. (*resolved to pass this off jestingly*) It is a great secret. You insist? Well then it is your double— (JUAN *utters a cry of joy, bending toward her. She adds hastily*) You as my mother described you in the wars before Granada.

JUAN. (*bitterly*) When I had youth. But I loved only glory then. Did she not tell you that?

BEATRIZ. Why then—that is why she said, bring him tenderness.

JUAN. (*somberly*) You have fulfilled her wish—or was it her revenge? (*Then abruptly*) And what if I should myself become that double?—the knight of Granada with your gift of tenderness—what then?

BEATRIZ. (*frightened by his strangeness*) Ah, now, you are jesting, Don Juan. (*She forces a laugh.*)

JUAN. (*passionately*) No, Beatriz! (*She instinctively shrinks away from him. He calms himself*) No more now. I fear your laughter.

First let the consummation— Then you will not laugh. You— (*Trying to read her mystified eyes—miserably uncertain*) What will you do?

BEATRIZ. (*controlling her timidity—softly persuasive*) You are ill, Don Juan. Will you listen to my cure for you?

JUAN. Yes.

BEATRIZ (*with energy*) Sail and find Cathay!

JUAN. (*with a start, tormentedly*) You, too, condemn me! But I swear to you I have longed to go! I have hated my own cowardice! I have played the traitor to every dream, every great hope— But, Beatriz, when I go, I will leave my life behind with you. So—until I knew—I was afraid of losing what I have— (*Then with a quick change to something approaching triumphant decision*) But that is past! My will has risen from the dead. It is decreed by your own lips. I shall sail at once!

BEATRIZ. Oh, I am glad!

JUAN. (*sadly*) Glad I am leaving you?

BEATRIZ. No, I shall be sad and lonely. It is for your own welfare—

JUAN. But promise me one boon——

BEATRIZ. (*eagerly*) Anything!

JUAN. Promise you will not marry until I return—or you hear I am dead?

BEATRIZ. (*confused*) I have never even thought of marrying.

JUAN. (*in deadly earnest in spite of his pitiful pretense at a joking tone*) Until I present my double to you—?

BEATRIZ. (*relieved and laughing easily*) Why, I might change my mind then, Don Juan.

JUAN. Will you seal that pledge with a kiss? (*He forces a smile to conceal his longing.*)

BEATRIZ. (*uncertainly—forcing a laugh*) Yes, Don Juan. (*She lifts her face to him. He starts to kiss her on the lips but something in her face stops him and he ends by kissing her reverentially on the forehead—forcing a smile.*)

JUAN. There—upon your forehead—for remembrance. The other —for tenderness—is still a promise of my dream. (*There is a sound of hurrying steps and* JUAN *moves away from* BEATRIZ *guiltily.* LUIS *enters from the rear. His face is agitated, full of alarm and anxiety.*)

BEATRIZ. (*greeting him eagerly, glad of the interruption*) Father Luis.

LUIS. Juan! I bring you terrible news. (*He sees* JUAN'S *drawn sword*) Ah, you know! It is time you drew your sword.

JUAN. (*scornfully*) You mean the scum rises? When I tell them the fleet sails tomorrow—

LUIS. Will you give them Nano to burn at the stake? That is their first demand. (BEATRIZ *gives a horrified cry.*)

JUAN. (*stunned—unbelievingly*) Surrender Nano? No, it is impossible. You have heard rumors—

LUIS. Quesada has roused their cruelty to frenzy. (*He points to where a red glow is mounting up in the sky*) See! They are burning the Indian quarter. May God have mercy!

JUAN. (*in a rage*) Kill Nano? The curs! I shall order a company of my guard—

LUIS. (*looking at him pityingly*) Your guard is leading the mob! (*Reproachfully*) Juan, Juan, why have you lived in a dream! I warned you time after time. If you had been governor in anything but name—

JUAN. (*sinking on the bench—stupidly*) Call the guard. I must order them to disperse.

BEATRIZ. (*pityingly*) His mind is sick—

LUIS. (*rather peremptorily*) Will you leave us, Beatriz?

BEATRIZ. (*obediently*) Yes, Father. (*Then excitedly*) I must see Bishop Menendez— (*She hurries out, right.*)

LUIS. (*comes and slaps* JUAN *on the back—sternly*) Juan! Awake, in God's name!

JUAN. (*startled to action, springs to his feet*) I shall protect his life with my own!

LUIS. In order to torture him yourself?

JUAN. (*vehemently but guiltily*) A lie! (*Suspicious—resentfully*) Have you seen him? I gave orders—

LUIS. It is weeks since I was permitted to see him; and you have avoided meeting me. Why?

JUAN. (*harshly*) I have no patience with your converting. I need Nano as he is.

LUIS. Because you prefer his heathen myths—

JUAN. (*controlling an outburst of rage*) Myths? Why myths? Cathay is there. (*He points.*)

LUIS. I was not speaking of Cathay. You are sailing tomorrow? Does this mean you have finally wrung from this poor Indian's agonies a faith in magic fountains—?

JUAN. (*losing control of himself—raging*) Fool! You are like those dullards who, when Columbus said the earth was round, brayed at him for blaspheming! Listen to me! I do not believe Nano, I believe in Nature. Nature is part of God. She can perform miracles. Since this land was discovered have we not found wonders undreamed of before? The points in Nano's story hold true to the facts we know. His home is a beautiful mainland—"A land of flowers," in his own words. Is not Cathay also known as the "Flowery Land"? There are great walled cities with roofs of gold inland to the West. Is not that Marco Polo's land beyond all doubt? And the fountain is in Cathay. All the evidence from around the world proves that! And I shall find it!

LUIS. (*pityingly*) But this evidence is merely fable, legend, the dreams of poets!

JUAN. (*furiously*) Have praying and fasting made you an imbecile? What evidence had Columbus? And you—you believe Christ lived and died. Well, have you talked with men who saw Him in the manger, or on the cross?

LUIS. Juan, this is blasphemy!

JUAN. (*with bitter despair*) Then let it be! I have prayed to Him in vain.

LUIS. Juan!

JUAN. (*with all the power of his will in the words*) Let me be damned forever if Nature will only grant me youth upon this earth again!

LUIS. (*horrified*) Juan! You defy your God!

JUAN. There is no God but Love—no heaven but youth!

LUIS. (*looks at his tortured face intently—suddenly realizes—in a tone of great pity*) So that is it—I have been blind. I thought your love saw in her—a child, a daughter!

JUAN. (*intensely*) A child—yes—for a time—but one morning standing by the fountain she was a woman. More than a woman! She was the Spirit of Youth, Hope, Ambition, Power to dream and dare! She was all that I had lost. She was Love and the Beauty of Love! So I loved her, loved her with all the intensity of Youth's first love—when youth was dead! Oh, it was monstrous folly, I admit. I called myself a senile fool! I suffered with the damned. I lived in hell without the recompense of being dead! And I loved her more—and more! (*His head sinks down on his hands. A great sob racks his whole body.*)

LUIS. (*overcome by compassion, his voice trembling*) Old friend—God in His Mercy have pity on you! (*He is interrupted by the hurried entrance of* BEATRIZ *from the right.*)

BEATRIZ. (*indignantly*) Bishop Menendez says he can do nothing—that you must give Nano up! (*The angry tumult of a mob marching is heard from the distance. Frightenedly*) Listen! Oh, Don Juan, you will save him, will you not?

JUAN. (*starting up—in a voice in which rage and apprehension are blended*) I must! (*He listens to the rising murmur of the mob. As he does so his whole body stiffens into defiant determination. He becomes in an instant the commander again*) Cowardly rabble! (*He springs to the entrance on the left and shouts to the soldier on guard*) Bring Nano! (*He comes back to where* BEATRIZ *and* LUIS *are standing and looks around the courtyard as if measuring his position*) I shall face them here. Take Beatriz away, Luis.

BEATRIZ. I wish to stay with you!

MENENDEZ. (*enters from the right*) Juan! (*Seeing his drawn sword —apprehensively*) What? You will defy them? Then you are lost! Yield to them, I advise you. Give Nano to justice. (*While he is speaking* NANO *is half carried in by the soldiers. He is limp and exhausted.*)

JUAN. (*with wild scorn*) Ah, High Priest! Deliver him up, eh?

MENENDEZ. Juan! You are impious! (*Angrily*) It is sacrilege—to compare this Indian dog—you mock our Blessed Saviour! You are cursed—I wash my hands—His will be done! (*He turns and strides back into the house, right.*)

LUIS. (*at a nearer roar from the mob*) Juan! Escape! There is still time—

JUAN. Run from jackals! Is my honor dead?

LUIS. (*as a smashing battering sounds from outside*) They are at the outer gate! Come, Beatriz, in God's name! (*She struggles but he succeeds in getting her as far as the entrance, right. A last crashing smash is heard as the outer gate gives way. A moment later the advance guard of the mob pour in—all of the lower rabble, these. Some wave torches above their heads. All are armed with pikes, knives, and various crude weapons that they have picked up or stolen.*)

JUAN. (*in a roar of command*) Back! (*They hesitate for a moment. Then they see* NANO *and with yells of fury rush for him around the fountain.* JUAN *springs to meet them. With quick thrusts and cuts of his sword he kills or wounds four of the foremost, who drop to the ground. The rest fall back frightened and awed for the moment. In this lull the remainder of the mob pour in from the rear, crowding and jostling each other. They are a nondescript crowd, ranging from nobles, richly dressed, soldiers, sailors, to the riffraff of the criminal element in bright-colored rags. There are a number of monks among them, Franciscans who urge them on, a few Dominicans who plead for restraint.*)

THE MOB. Don Juan! It's the Governor—push back there!—To the flames with the Indian dog! Seize him! Stand aside, Don Juan! Heretic! He's bewitched! The dog refused baptism! Torture!

JUAN. (*sternly*) I will kill the man who touches this Indian! (*He walks up and down before them, his sword ready to thrust, looking from eye to eye—scathingly*) Scoundrels! Where is your valor now? Prick up your courage! (*Mockingly*) Come! Who wishes to die?

A NOBLE. We demand justice! (*Yells of approval from the crowd. They push in closer.* JUAN *levels his sword at the breast of the nearest who springs back with a frightened cry. The mob sways and surges, close packed and indecisive, cowed by* JUAN'S *eyes.*)

QUESADA. (*suddenly pushing his way to the front of the crowd—pointing at* NANO, *frantically*) Give him up! You are bewitched! (*The mob are again aroused. There are cries of "To the stake! Torture!" etc.*)

JUAN. No! (*Yells of rage. The mob surges forward.* JUAN *raises his sword*) I will kill the first one who— (*They recoil again, all but* QUESADA. *With his free hand* JUAN *sweeps him to one side contemptuously—then fiercely threatening the crowd*) Will you rebel against the Governor of your King? Then you are traitors to Spain! And, by God's blood, I will hang one of you on every tree! (*The crowd gives way by inches, sullenly, their yells reduced for the moment to a rebellious muttering: "The King will remove you! Hang the Indians! Hang them! Hang Nano!" etc.*)

A SOLDIER. We mean no harm to you, Don Juan. Keep your word to us. Order the fleet to sail. (*A yell of acclamation from the soldiers and sailors.*)

QUESADA. And give over that dog! The Inquisition shall know you protect infidels!

JUAN. I am Spain's soldier, not the Inquisition's! Soldiers and sailors! I tell you it is in Spain's service this Indian's life is spared. The fleet sails tomorrow—and we need Nano to pilot our voyage! (*A tumult from the bewildered crowd. Shouts of various nature: "The fleet sails! Tomorrow! Hurrah! He jokes! He mocks us! Spare him? No luck with a heathen on board! What does he mean? Guide us? No! The curse of the Church!" But the mob is puzzled, blundering, and* JUAN *continues with a sort of condescension as if he were speaking to children*) Silence! Since you are so stupid, I must explain. This Nano was born on the mainland—Cathay!—our goal, do you understand?—and I have put off sailing while I questioned him. We must have his knowledge. He must be our pilot. (*With a fierce glance at* NANO *as if to let his threat strike home*) And if he fails in his promise to me, I will gladly give him to you for punishment.

QUESADA. (*furiously*) You say this to save him!

JUAN. Soldiers, sailors, I appeal to you! Can this mad monk lead you to conquest? You must decide between us. (*The crowd are all turning his way, becoming greedily enthusiastic.* JUAN *sees the psychological moment to play a trump card*) But to convince you finally, listen to Nano. Speak, Nano! Tell them what you told me—of the golden cities. Speak! (*Then under cover of the crowd's shouts of "Down with the dog! Torture! Hear! Let him speak! Don Juan says let him!" etc., he adds in a fierce whisper to the Indian*) If you wish ever to see your home again!

NANO. (*mechanically, in a clear monotonous voice, with expressionless face*) A big land—far mighty cities—gold—

JUAN. You hear? The cities of gold! (*The crowd murmurs excitedly.*)

NANO. There is much gold. The houses have gold on them.

A SOLDIER. Cipango! We'll storm their cities for them!

A SAILOR. Loot, my bullies!

JUAN. Glory and gold for all of you! And now go! (*The crowd are jubilant. Shouts of "Up anchor! Ahoy Cathay! At last! We sail! Sack! Riches! Gold!" etc.* JUAN *shouts above the tumult*) Go! Disperse! Tomorrow we sail! (*A voice cries, "Long live Don Juan!" The whole mob takes it up.* JUAN *begins to give way under the strain—wearily*) Go. Go.

THE MOB. (*led by a sailor, takes up a sort of chanty song in mighty chorus, dancing wildly, waving their torches, crowding out, rear.*)

The Cities of Gold
In far Cathay—
Their great Khan is old,
And his wealth untold
In prize for our bold
Who sail away.
Aye!
His gold for our bold who sail away!!

BEATRIZ. (*as the last of the mob disappear—rushing up to* JUAN *with great admiration*) You have saved him! What they have said of you is true indeed—lion by nature as well as name!

JUAN. (*bitterly*) Lion? No! Tricky politician! If I had been the Juan of long ago, I would not have pled or bargained with such curs. I would have— (*He raises his sword threateningly—then lets his arm sink limply. The sword slips from his fingers and falls to the ground.*)

BEATRIZ. (*kneels quickly and presents its hilt to him*) I give you back your sword—to bring good fortune. Now you must find the golden cities!

JUAN. (*taking it—longingly*) I care only for the one, Beatriz—the golden city of Youth, where you are queen. (*She looks into his face smilingly, mystified as the curtain falls.*)

SCENE SEVEN

SCENE. *Four months later—a strip of beach on the Florida coast—a bright, moonlight night. The forest runs diagonally from right, front, to left, rear—a wall of black shadow. The sand gleams a pallid white in the moonlight. The rhythmic ebb and flow of waves is heard—their voice on a windless night of calm.*

As the curtain rises, an INDIAN *is discovered, standing in the moonlight, just out of the shadow of the forest. He is old, but still erect and warrior-like, a chief by his demeanor. His body, naked save for a piece of deerskin at his waist, is elaborately painted, as is his face. A knot of feathers is in his hair. A tomahawk and flint knife are at his waist. He is motionless and silent as a statue, one hand clasping his unslung bow as if it were a staff, but he peers intently at some object in the ocean before him. Finally, he gives an ejaculation of surprise and makes a motion of summons to the forest behind him. The* MEDICINE MAN *glides out of the darkness to his side. This latter is incredibly old and shrunken, daubed with many insignia in paint, wearing many ornaments of bone and shell. They confer together in low tones with much pantomime. A man is evidently swimming toward them from some strange object out at sea. Other* INDIANS *steal from the forest, form a group in the shadow behind the two, point out to sea, gesticulate. At a sharp command from the* CHIEF, *they unsling their bows, fit arrows to strings, crouch in an ambush in the shadow. The* CHIEF *does likewise and stands waiting, prepared for what may come.* NANO *walks up the beach from front, left. His naked body glistens with drops of water. He sees the* CHIEF *and stops, raising his right hand above his head. The* CHIEF *makes a sign. The other* INDIANS *dart from their ambush and surround* NANO.

CHIEF. Bind him.

NANO. (*calmly*) Is a brother an enemy? (*They all start with surprise at hearing their own language.* NANO *goes on*) This is the land of my fathers. I am Nano, a son of Boanu, who was a chief. (*They all stare at him. The* CHIEF *makes a sign to the* MEDICINE MAN, *who comes forward and examines* NANO's *face intently.*)

MEDICINE MAN. His words are truth. He is Nano—or an evil spirit in his body. (*He shakes a charm at him*) Are you from the Land of the Dead?

NANO. I am of the living. They did not chain me. They think I fear the sea. I come to warn you. I swam from the great canoes. They are the warships of the Spaniards.

CHIEF. (*mystified*) What are Spaniards? Their winged canoes are like the boats of gods.

NANO. These are no gods. They are men who die from wounds. Their faces are white, but they are evil. They wear shirts that arrows cannot pierce. They have strange sticks that spit fire and kill. Their devils make them strong. But they are not true warriors. They are thieves and rapers of women.

CHIEF. Have they no God?

NANO. (*with scorn*) Their God is a thing of earth! It is this! (*He touches a gold ornament that the* CHIEF *wears*)

MEDICINE MAN. (*mystified*) Gold? Gold is sacred to the Sun. It can be no god itself.

NANO. (*contemptuously*) They see only things, not the spirit behind things. Their hearts are muddy as a pool in which deer have trampled. Listen. Their Medicine Men tell of a God who came to them long ago in the form of a man. He taught them to scorn things. He taught them to look for the spirit behind things. In revenge, they killed him. They tortured him as a sacrifice to their Gold Devil. They crossed two big sticks. They drove little sticks through his hands and feet and pinned him on the others—thus. (*He illustrates. A murmur of horror and indignation goes up among them.*)

MEDICINE MAN. To torture a God! How did they dare?

NANO. Their devils protected them. And now each place they go, they carry that figure of a dying God. They do this to strike fear. They command you to submit when you see how even a God who fought their evil was tortured. (*Proudly*) But I would not.

MEDICINE MAN. (*suspiciously*) If you defied them, how are you alive?

NANO. I am craftier than they. They have an old chief who is cursed with madness. Him I told of the Spring of Life. I said I would find it for him.

MEDICINE MAN. Only the gods can reveal it. Why have you told this lie?

NANO (*fiercely*) Revenge! I have made a plan. Is there a spring near?

CHIEF. (*mystified*) Yes. In the forest.

NANO. (*with satisfaction*) Good! Listen. This mad chief is the mightiest among them. Without him they would turn cowards. Tomorrow night I will lead him to the spring. You must lie hidden. We will kill him there. Is this clear?

CHIEF. Yes.

NANO. I will swim back now. I escaped to tell you of my plan and warn you. They would lay waste your land as they did mine. They killed my wives and children. They burned. They tortured. They chained warriors neck to neck. They beat them with a whip to dig in the fields like squaws. This old chief led them. My heart is fire. Until he dies, it will know no peace.

CHIEF. I begin to feel your hatred.

NANO. Then remember to hide by the spring.

CHIEF. We will not forget.

NANO. It is well. (*He turns and strides down to the sea. They stand watching him in silence.*)

MEDICINE MAN. (*uneasily, thoughtful*) Only devils could build great canoes that fly with wings. My brothers, they are evil spirits. Nano has made war with them. They have beaten him. Can we trust his plan?

CHIEF. What is your counsel?

MEDICINE MAN. I have heard the voice of the Great Spirit speaking in the night. Let us first try to propitiate their devils.

CHIEF. I do not know how to war with devils. That is your duty. Let us summon the council. (*He makes a sign at which his followers disappear silently into the wood. He and the* MEDICINE MAN *follow as the curtain falls.*)

SCENE EIGHT

SCENE. *The same. High noon of the following day—glaring sunlight on the beach, an atmosphere of oppressive heat and languor. The earth seems dead, preserved in some colorless, molten fluid. The forest is a matted green wall. The sound of the sea has the quality of immense exhaustion.*

On the beach, a sort of makeshift altar is being erected—two round boulders supporting a flat slab of rock. On top of the slab is placed a shallow bowl made of bark. A group of INDIANS, *under the direction of the* MEDICINE MAN, *are hurriedly putting on the finishing touches to this shrine. They keep casting awed apprehensive glances seaward. The* MEDICINE MAN *is binding two branches of a tree together in the form of a cross. All the* INDIANS *are feathered and painted as for an unusually solemn occasion.*

THE INDIANS. (*their eyes on the sea as they work—frightenedly*) The small canoes leave the great winged ones. They are coming! The sun gleams on their shirts that arrows cannot pierce. Their fire-sticks glitter in the sun. Their faces are turned. Their faces are pale! They are watching us!

MEDICINE MAN. (*finishing his work*) Keep your hearts brave! (*Giving the cross to two* INDIANS) Here. This is their totem pole. Stand it there. (*They dig a hole in the sand before the altar and set the cross there; but they make the mistake of setting it head down. The* MEDICINE MAN *grunts with satisfaction*) They will think we adore the same devil. They will leave us in peace.

INDIAN. (*his eyes on the sea*) The last canoe has left the great ships. (*He gives a cry of fear echoed by the others*) Aie! Fire and smoke! (*They cower. The hollow boom of a cannon fired in salute reverberates over the sea. They all shrink with terror, bowing their heads.*)

INDIAN. (*awe-struck*) The Thunder fights with them!

INDIAN. They are white gods!

MEDICINE MAN. (*frightened himself, but rallying his followers sternly*) You have the hearts of squaws. Quick! Where is the gold? (*An* INDIAN *comes to him with an earthenware vessel. He empties it out on the bowl on the top of the altar. It is full of gold nuggets of different sizes. They form a heap glowing in the sun.*)

INDIANS. They come! They come!

MEDICINE MAN. (*sternly*) Pretend to worship their gold devil but pray to our Great Father, the Sun. He can defeat all devils. Pray to him. (*An* INDIAN *starts to beat rhythmically on the small drum. The* MEDICINE MAN *lifts his shrill voice in the first strains of the chant. Immediately the others all join in as if hypnotized*) Great Father, Mighty One, Ruler of Earth. Maker of Days. Ripener of the Corn. Creator of Life. Look down upon us out of your Sky-Tent. Let our song rise to you. Let it enter your heart. Mighty One, hear us. Hide not your face in clouds. Bless us at the dawn. And at the day's end. (*They form a circle and dance about the altar, their eyes raised to the sun overhead. Their chant hides the noise of the* SPANIARDS *landing. Then the* SPANIARDS *appear from the left, front. First comes* JUAN, *his face wild and haggard, his eyes obsessed. He is accompanied by* LUIS. *Following him are a squad of* SOLDIERS, *guarding* NANO, *who is in chains. Then come four* FRANCISCAN MONKS, *led by* QUESADA, *who wears a sword and pistol over his robe. The others carry crosses. Following them is a group of* NOBLES, *richly dressed. Then come ranks of* SOLDIERS. *They all stare at this Indian ceremony with contemptuous scorn.*)

JUAN. (*irritably*) Make them cease their accursed noise, Luis. Let Nano speak to them.

LUIS. (*advancing toward the* INDIANS—*in a loud but friendly voice, raising his right hand*) Peace, brothers. (*The* INDIANS *stop, petrified, staring with awe at the white men. The* MEDICINE MAN *lifts his right hand and advances a step toward* LUIS. QUESADA *notices the cross, utters a furious exclamation, strides forward to verify his suspicion. When he sees that it is indeed upside down his face grows livid with fury.*)

QUESADA. The cross head down! The black mass! (*He pulls out his pistol*) Blaspheming dog! (*He fires. The* MEDICINE MAN *falls. The other* INDIANS *who have shrunk back toward the woods in terror at his first move, now turn tail in panic and flee.*)

LUIS. (*in horror*) Stop, Quesada! (QUESADA *pulls up the cross and is setting it back upright when the* MEDICINE MAN, *by a last dying effort, draws his knife, and writhing to his feet, plunges it into* QUESADA'S *back. They both fall together, the* INDIAN *dead.* QUESADA *shudders and is still. A yell of rage goes up from the* SPANIARDS. *They rush forward toward the woods as if to pursue the* INDIANS *but* JUAN *shouts a command.*)

JUAN. Halt! Fools! (*They stop prudently but sullenly.* JUAN *turns to* LUIS, *who is kneeling beside* QUESADA) Is he dead?

LUIS. Yes. (*Crossing himself*) May his soul rest in peace. (*All echo this, crossing themselves.*)

JUAN. An eye for an eye, a tooth for a tooth. (*Mockingly*) And now it is his eye, his tooth. (*Then with a shudder*) Take him away. This is a bloody baptism for Cathay. (*Turning to* NANO *as the* SOLDIERS *carry the bodies aside*) Is this the land, Nano?

NANO. (*his eyes smoldering with hate*) Yes.

JUAN. You said it was a wonder land—a land of flowers. I see no flowers.

NANO. (*in a sinister tone*) In the forest—flowers grow by a spring—

JUAN. (*harshly—with an apprehensive glance about*) Silence!

A NOBLE. (*from the group that has been stirring impatiently*) Your Excellency. The banners of Castile and Aragon wait on your pleasure.

JUAN. (*making a confused gesture as if wiping cobwebs from his brain*) Yes—yes—I must take possession. Bring the banners. (*He kneels on one knee. They all do likewise*) In the name of Jesus Christ, Our Lord, and of his most gracious Majesty, the sovereign of Castile and Aragon, I do hereby annex to his dominions this land and all its environs. And I call the land Florida. (*He bends and kisses the sand. The banners are planted in the ground, where they hang motionless from their poles.* JUAN, *having made this effort, seems to fall into a stupor.*)

A NOBLE. (*in a mocking whisper*) A pretty name!

A NOBLE. He has grown imbecile. Will he go spring-hunting here, too? My faith, with all the water he has drunk in the past four months, he must be flooded. (*They all snicker at this.*)

A NOBLE. (*impatiently*) Will he never get off his knees and let us rise?

LUIS. (*sensing what is going on behind their backs—to* JUAN—*who seems to be praying with bowed head—plucking his sleeve*) Juan! Come!

JUAN. (*vaguely*) I was praying—to what God, who knows? (*He rises to his feet weakly. At this, they all rise.*)

A NOBLE. (*pointing excitedly*) Look! In that bowl on the stones. Is it not gold? (*They all rush forward to the altar. The* NOBLE *picks up a piece of it—his voice hoarse with greedy triumph*) Gold! (*They all grab at the bowl, upsetting its contents on the sand. They bend down and clutch for it crying*) Gold! This must be a rich land! There must be more! The Golden Cities are near! Cathay at last! (*The* SOLDIERS *forget discipline, break ranks, form a disorderly, pushing crowd about their leaders. Even the* MONKS *edge forward inquisitively.*)

LUIS. (*urgently*) Juan! Look! This is disgraceful!

JUAN. (*coming to himself with a start—in a furious tone of command*) Get back to your ranks! A brave example you set, nobles of Spain! (*His personality is compelling. They all slink to their former order again, muttering rebelliously.* JUAN *seems suddenly seized with a wild exultation*) Cathay! We have found Cathay! This is the land—the Flowery Land! Our dreams lie hidden here! Sing the Te Deum! Sing! (*There is an oppressive silence for a moment, in which the heat, the sun glaring on the beach, the green of the forest, all nature seems to lay upon these men a mysterious spell, a sudden exhausted recognition of their own defeat. Then the* FRANCISCAN MONKS *raise their voices mechanically and spiritlessly in the Te Deum. Other listless voices gradually join theirs as the curtain falls.*)

SCENE NINE

SCENE. *About midnight—in the forest. Gigantic tree-trunks, entwined with vines in flower, are in the foreground. Festoons of Spanish moss hang clear to the ground from the branches. Through the network one sees a circular clearing, grass-grown, flooded with moonlight. There is the soft murmur of a spring which bubbles from the ground in the center of this open space.* INDIANS *are crouched in ambush among the trees, motionless, their eyes fixed on the clearing.*

The stillness is broken by the whistled call of a bird. The INDIANS *stir alertly. One of them whistles in answer to the call. An* INDIAN *creeps swiftly in from the left. The* CHIEF *comes from his place of ambush to meet him.*

CHIEF. He comes?

INDIAN. He has entered the forest.

CHIEF. I will give Nano the signal when we are ready. Go. Hide. (*The* INDIAN *takes a place with the others. The* CHIEF *fits an arrow to his bow and crouches in the shadow. There is a pause of silence—then the noise of someone pushing his way through the woods at the rear of the clearing.* NANO *appears there, followed by* JUAN.)

JUAN. Why do you stop?

NANO. This is the place.

JUAN. (*looking around him disappointedly*) This?

NANO. There is the spring.

JUAN. (*stepping forward to look at it—with growing anger*) It looks a common spring like any other. Beware, dog! In these past months you have shown me many springs—

NANO. (*quickly*) The voyage was long. There were many islands. You forced me to lead you to a spring on each. But I told you the Spring of Life was here.

JUAN. I feared your revenge might lie. (*Relapsed into a mood of somber preoccupation—bitterly*) I drank of every one. I closed my eyes. I felt the stirring of rebirth. Fool! Always the mirror in the spring showed me the same loathsome blighted face— (*He groans —then with a harsh laugh*) A sacred grove, the legend says! Some of those springs bubbled from sandy water! Beautiful maidens? There were none. At one place I found an old hag filling her bowl, who drank and mumbled at me. (*Then in a harsh tone of command*) Nano! I command you to tell me if you have lied. (*Distractedly*) I must have certainty, be it of faith or despair!

NANO. This is the spring.

JUAN. (*looking around him*) But where are the trees with golden fruit, the maidens, the fountain—? (*Bewildered, staring—grasping at hope*) And yet—this spot has singular beauty. I feel enchantment. But why do I shudder? (*A low whistled signal comes from the* CHIEF *hidden on the edge of the clearing.* JUAN *starts*) Sssh! What was that?

NANO. A bird. (*Insistently*) It is a magic spring. Drink!

JUAN. (*bending over the spring*) A mirror of moonlight. The dead eyes of a corpse stare back in mine. (*He kneels by the spring as if fascinated*) I dare not drink. To whom can I pray? Beatriz! Oh, to hear your voice once more, to see your face! And yet I see you everywhere. Your spirit inspires all things wherever there is beauty. I hear you call in the song of the waves, the wind is your breath, the trees reach out with your arms, the dawn and sunset promise with your lips! You are everywhere and nowhere—part of all life but mine! (*He breaks off, turning distrustful, harried eyes on the impatient* NANO*—bitterly*) I am a spectacle for laughter, eh? A grotesque old fool!

NANO. (*in a fierce tone of command*) Drink!

JUAN. (*hectically—goading himself to action*) The test. Spirit of Eternal Youth, I pray to you! Beatriz! (*He bends down and drinks. As he does so* NANO *darts away from him to the woods in front.*)

NANO. (*hurriedly*) Kill when he stands again! (*The* INDIANS *can be seen raising their bows, taking aim.*)

JUAN. (*having drunk, remains kneeling by the spring—in a trembling tone of hesitating joy*) New life thrills in me! Is it youth? Do I dream? Then let me never wake till the end of time! (*Then harshly*) Coward! How often have you looked death in the face. Are you afraid of life? Open! Open and see! (*He opens his eyes and stares down into the spring. A terrible groan tears from his breast*) O God! (*His grief is turned immediately into a frenzy of rage*) Treacherous dog. You betrayed me. (*He leaps to his feet, drawing his sword. There is a twanging of many bows, the whiz of a flight of arrows.* JUAN *falls, clutches at the grass, is still. The* INDIANS *pour out into the clearing but keep a cautious distance from* JUAN.)

NANO. (*with more courage than they, he bends down over the body*) He wore no shining shirt. He is dead. (*He does a wild dance of savage triumph beside the body—then stops as suddenly*) Quick. To their camp. The great Spirit has made them helpless. Be brave and kill! (*He runs swiftly into the woods, followed by the whole band, brandishing their weapons. There is a pause. Then the fierce yells of the savages as they fall upon the sleeping camp, the howls of terror of the* SPANIARDS, *the screams of the dying, a few futile musket-shots.*)

CURTAIN

SCENE TEN

SCENE. *The same clearing in the woods some hours later. There is no intervening fringe of trees in this scene, the open space is in full view. The Spring is at center. The wall of forest forms a semi-circular background. As the curtain rises, there is a pitch-blackness and silence except for the murmur of the Spring. Then the sound of someone struggling to rise from the ground, falling back again with a groan of pain.* JUAN'S *voice comes out of the darkness.*

JUAN. (*as if he had just regained consciousness—then with a groan of rage and pain as memory returns*) Fool! Why did I look? I might have died in my dream. (*A pause—weakly*) Sleep seems humming in my ears. Or is it—death!—death, the Merciful One! (*He stirs and his voice suddenly grows strident*) No, no! Why have I lived? To die alone like a beast in the wilderness? (*With a bitter mocking despair*) O Son of God, is this Thy justice? Does not the Saviour of Man know magnanimity? True, I prayed for a miracle which was not Thine. Let me be damned then, but (*Passionately*) let me believe in Thy Kingdom! Show me Thy miracle—a sign—a word—a second's vision of what I am that I should have lived and died! A test, Lord God of Hosts! (*He laughs with a scornful bravado*) Nothing! (*But even as he speaks a strange unearthly light begins to flood down upon a spot on the edge of the clearing on the right. Startled in spite of himself*) This light—the moon has waned— (*Beneath the growing light a form takes shape—a tall woman's figure, like a piece of ancient sculpture, shrouded in long draperies of a blue that is almost black. The face is a pale mask with features indistinguishable save for the eyes that stare straight ahead with a stony penetration that sees through and beyond things. Her arms are rigid at her sides, the palms of the hands turned outward.* JUAN *stares at her, defiance striving with his awe*) What are you? (*Forcing a sneer*) An angel in answer to my prayer? (*He cannot control a shudder—tries to calm himself. He stares at the figure—after a pause, boldly*) Or are you Death? Why then I have often laughed in your eyes! (*Tauntingly*) Off with your mask, coward! (*Mockingly but uneasy*) Delightful Lady, you are enigmatic. One must embrace you with bold arms, tear off your masquerade. That was my pastime once—to play at love as gaming. Were I the Juan of long ago—but you see I am old now and wounded. (*He pauses. The figure is frozen. He asks a bit falteringly*) Are you—Death? Then wait— (*In passionate invocation*) O Beatriz! Let me hear your voice again in mercy of farewell! (*As if in answer to this the voice of* BEATRIZ *sings from the darkness*)

VOICE. Love is a flower
Forever blooming
Life is a fountain
Forever leaping
Upward to catch the golden sunlight
Upward to reach the azure heaven
Failing, falling,
Ever returning,
To kiss the earth that the flower may live.

JUAN. (*raptly*) Youth! (*As the song is sung, the same mystical light floods down slowly about the spring, which is transformed into a gigantic fountain, whose waters, arched with rainbows, seem to join earth and sky, forming a shimmering veil, which hides the background of forest.* JUAN *and the* FIGURE *are left at the edge of this, on the outside. The form of* BEATRIZ *appears within as if rising from the spring. She dances in ecstasy—the personified spirit of the fountain.* JUAN *cries with a voice trembling with joy*) The Fountain! Let me drink! (*He tries to drag himself to it but cannot—in anguish*) Must I die—? (*Making a furious gesture of defiance at the* FIGURE *and struggling to rise*) No! I defy you! (*Exhausted, he sinks back crying beseechingly*) Beatriz! (*But she seems not to see or hear him.* JUAN *half sobs in despair*) She will not see! She will not hear! Fountain, cruel as the heart of youth, what mercy have you for the old and wounded? (*He sinks down overcome by weakness.* BEATRIZ *vanishes from the fountain. In her place appears the form of a Chinese poet. He is a venerable old man with the mild face of a dreamer and scholar. He carries a block and writes upon it with a brush, absorbed in contemplation.* JUAN *looking up and seeing him—startled*) What are you? (*Groping at some clue in his memory*) I know—that night in Granada—the Moor's tale—(*Excitedly*) Of the poet from the East who told his father the Fountain lie! Are you not that poisoner of life? (*The* POET *raises his hand as if in summons. The form of the Moorish minstrel of Scene One appears at his side*) The Moor! (*Raging*) Infidel Dog! Your lie has cursed me! (*The form of* NANO *appears at the other side of the Chinese poet.* JUAN *struggles to reach his sword in a fury*) Murderer! (*Then his eyes are caught by a fourth figure which materializes beside the Moor. It is* LUIS *as he was in Scene One. With a cry of joy*) Luis—old friend— (*Then as* LUIS *seems neither to see nor hear him, he sinks back helplessly*) No—another mocking phantom! (*He watches the Chinese poet, who seems to be reading what he has written to all of them*) See! The dead lie to the living. It passes on—from East to West—round the round world—from old worlds to new—cheating the old and wounded—Ha! (*He laughs harshly and wildly. The Chinese poet takes the Indian by one hand, the Moor by the other. These latter stretch out their hands to* LUIS, *who takes them, thus completing the circle.* BEATRIZ' *voice can be heard singing*)

VOICE. Life is a field
Forever growing
Beauty a fountain
Forever flowing
Upward beyond the source of sunshine
Upward beyond the azure heaven,
Born of God but
Ever returning
To merge with earth that the field may live.

(*As she sings, the four forms disappear as if they were dissolved in the fountain.*)

JUAN. (*lost in the ecstasy of her song*) Sing on, Youth! (*With a start as the song stops—stupidly*) The ghosts are gone. What is the answer to their riddle? I am no poet. I have striven for what the hand can grasp. What is left when Death makes the hand powerless? (*Addresses the* FIGURE *pitifully, trying to mock*) O Mighty Relaxer of hands, have you no vision for the graspers of earth? (*The* FIGURE *raises a summoning hand. One by one, within the fountain, solemn figures materialize. First the Chinese poet, now robed as a Buddhist priest; then the Moorish minstrel, dressed as a priest of Islam; and then the* MEDICINE MAN *as he was in Scene Eight, decked out in all the paint and regalia of his office; lastly,* LUIS, *the Dominican monk of the present. Each one carries the symbol of his religion before him. They appear clearly for a moment, then fade from sight, seeming to dissolve in the fountain.* JUAN *has stared at them with straining eyes —in a bewildered voice*) All faiths—they vanish—are one and equal—within— (*Awe and reverence creeping into his voice*) What are you, Fountain? That from which all life springs and to which it must return—God! Are all dreams of you but the one dream? (*Bowing his head miserably*) I do not know. Come back, Youth. Tell me this secret! (*For a moment the voice of* BEATRIZ *is heard from the darkness*)

Death is a mist
Veiling sunrise.

(JUAN *seems to fall into a rapt spell. The form of an old Indian woman appears from the left. She falters forward, a wooden bowl under her arm, as if she were going to fill it at the fountain.*)

JUAN. (*recognizing her aghast*) Damned hag! I remember you waited beside a spring to mock me! Begone! (*But the old woman stretches out her hands to him with a mysterious beseeching.* JUAN *shudders—then after a struggle with himself, gets to his feet painfully*) So be it. Sit here by me. I am old, too—and, poor woman, you cannot fill your bowl there. Come. (*He grasps her hands. In a flash her mask of age disappears. She is* BEATRIZ. JUAN *gazes at her in an ecstasy—faltering, his mind groping*) Beatriz! Age—Youth— They are the same rhythm of eternal life! (*Without his noticing it,* BEATRIZ *recedes from him and vanishes in the fountain. He raises his face to the sky—with halting joy*) Light comes! Light creeps into my soul! (*Then he sees the* FIGURE *walk slowly from its place and vanish in the fountain*) Death is no more! (*The* FIGURE *materializes again within the fountain but this time there is no mask, the face is that of* BEATRIZ, *her form grown tall, majestic, vibrant with power. Her arms are raised above her head. Her whole body soars upward. A radiant, dancing fire, proceeding from the source of the fountain, floods over and envelops her until her figure is like the heart of its flame.* JUAN *stares at this vision for a moment, then sinks on his knees—exultantly*) I see! Fountain Everlasting, time without end! Soaring flame of the spirit transfiguring Death! All is within! All things dissolve, flow on eternally! O aspiring fire of life, sweep the dark soul of man! Let us burn in thy unity! (BEATRIZ' *voice rises triumphantly*)

VOICE. God is a flower
Forever blooming
God is a fountain
Forever flowing.

(*The song ceases. The light fades. There is darkness.* JUAN'S *voice is heard sobbing with happiness.*)

JUAN. O God, Fountain of Eternity, Thou art the All in One, the One in All—the Eternal Becoming which is Beauty! (*He falls unconscious. A pause. Then the faint misty light of the dawn floats over the clearing.* JUAN *is seen lying where he had fallen. There is the noise of someone approaching from the woods in the rear.* LUIS *and a brother* DOMINICAN *enter from the forest.*)

LUIS. (*seeing* JUAN) God be praised! (*He rushes forward and kneels by* JUAN's *body.* JUAN *stirs and groans*) He moves! Juan! It's Luis! Our friends were murdered. A boat from the fleet is waiting—

JUAN. (*in a dreaming ecstasy*) God—Thou art all—

DOMINICAN. He prays.

LUIS. Delirium. Let us carry him. We'll sail for the nearest settlement—

JUAN. (*as they raise him*) Light! I see and know!

LUIS. It is the dawn, Juan.

JUAN. (*exultantly*) The dawn! (*They carry him out as the curtain falls.*)

SCENE ELEVEN

SCENE. *Some months later. The courtyard of a Dominican monastery in Cuba. A crude little home-made fountain is in center. This is the only adornment of the quadrangle of bald, sunbaked earth, enclosed on the left and in the rear by a high white wall, on the right by the monastery building itself. The entrance to this is an arched doorway surmounted by a crucifix of carved wood. Two niches on either side of this door shelter primitive wooden figures of the Holy Family and Saint Dominic. In the wall, center, is another arched door with a cross above it. Beyond the wall nature can be seen and felt—vivid, colorful, burgeoning with the manifold, compelling life of the tropics. Palm trees lean over the wall casting their graceful shadows within. Vines in flower have climbed to the top and are starting to creep down inside.*

A sunset sky of infinite depth glows with mysterious splendor.

As the curtain rises, JUAN *and the* FATHER SUPERIOR *are discovered.* JUAN *is asleep, reclining on a sort of improvised invalid's chair, his cloak wrapped around him, facing the fountain. He is pale and emaciated but his wasted countenance has gained an entirely new quality, the calm of a deep spiritual serenity. The* FATHER SUPERIOR *is a portly monk with a simple round face, gray hair and beard. His large eyes have the opaque calm of a ruminating cow's. The door in the rear is opened and* LUIS *enters. He closes the door carefully and tiptoes forward.*

LUIS. (*in a whisper*) He is sleeping?

FATHER SUPERIOR. As you see, Father.

LUIS. (*looking down at* JUAN) How calm his face is—as if he saw a vision of peace.

FATHER SUPERIOR. It is a blessed miracle he has lived so long.

LUIS. He has been waiting. (*Sadly*) And now, I am afraid his desire is fulfilled—but not as he dreamed. Rather the cup of gall and wormwood—

FATHER SUPERIOR. (*mystified*) You mean the caravel brings him bad tidings?

LUIS. Yes; and I must wake him to prepare his mind.

FATHER SUPERIOR. I will leave you with him. It is near vesper time. (*He turns and goes into the monastery.*)

LUIS. (*touching* JUAN *on the arm—gently*) Juan, awake. (JUAN *opens his eyes*) The caravel has anchored.

JUAN. From Porto Rico?

LUIS. Yes.

JUAN. (*with an air of certainty—with exultant joy*) Then Beatriz is here!

LUIS. (*disturbed—evasively*) There has been a frightful insurrection of the Indians. Diego was killed. (*Hastily*) But I will not trouble you with that. (*Then slowly*) Beatriz comes to nurse you—(*With warning emphasis*)—her second father, those were her words.

JUAN. (*smiling*) You need not emphasize. I know her heart. (*Then earnestly*) But I must tell her my truth. (*Then with a sort of pleading for assurance*) It is for that I have waited, to tell her of the love I bore her—now—as farewell—when she cannot misunderstand. (*Proudly*) My love was no common thing. It was the one time Beauty touched my life. I wish to live in her memory as what she was to me. (*Sinking back—with a flickering smile, weakly*) Come, old friend, are you grown so ascetic you deny my right to lay this Golden City—the only one I ever conquered—at the feet of Beauty?

LUIS. (*kindly persuasive*) Silence is better, Juan. You should renounce—

JUAN. (*gently*) All is renounced. But do you begrudge a traveler if he begs a flower from this earth, a last token of the world's grace, to lend farewell the solace of regret?

LUIS. (*more and more troubled*) Juan—I—I speak because—you have suffered—and now—I would not have you suffer more, dear friend. (*Then blurting out most brusquely*) The caravel brings you a surprise. Your nephew, Juan, has arrived from Spain and comes from Porto Rico to greet you.

JUAN. (*vaguely*) My nephew? (*The sound of voices comes from inside the monastery*) Beatriz! (*The* FATHER SUPERIOR *appears in the doorway ushering in* BEATRIZ *and* JUAN'S *nephew. They are followed by the Duenna and the nephew's* SERVANT, *who carries his master's cloak and a lute. During the following scene these two remain standing respectfully by the doorway for a time, then go back into the monastery, the* SERVANT *leaving the cloak and lute on the ground beside the doorway. The* FATHER SUPERIOR *retires immediately.* LUIS, *after a clasp of* JUAN'S *hand, also withdraws, exchanging greetings as he passes the* NEPHEW *and* BEATRIZ. BEATRIZ *glows with fulfillment, is very apparently deeply in love. The* NEPHEW *is a slender, graceful young cavalier. He is dressed richly.*)

BEATRIZ. (*halting a moment with a shocked exclamation as she sees* JUAN'S *wasted face—then rushing forward and flinging herself on her knees beside his chair. Hastily*) Don Juan! Oh, this is happiness—to find you still—recovered from your wounds! Oh, I'll say prayers of thanksgiving! (*Impulsively she kisses him.*)

JUAN. (*thrilled—choked—unable to say but one word*) Beatriz! Beatriz!

NEPHEW. (*kneels and kisses* JUAN'S *hand. Startled,* JUAN'S *eyes search his face keenly, apprehensive of what he, too, plainly sees there*) I greet you, sir. God grant you may soon be strong again.

JUAN. (*weakly*) Soon—I shall be strong—against all wounds. (*After a pause*) And so your name is Juan, too?

NEPHEW. In your honor. Though I can add no honor to it, I hope to bear it worthily.

JUAN. (*hostility creeping into his tone*) You come out here adventuring?

NEPHEW. I come to serve Spain!

JUAN. (*harshly*) A heart as steeled as your sword. Have you that?

BEATRIZ. (*eagerly—somewhat hurt by* JUAN'S *reception*) Oh, he is brave! When the mob tried to storm the palace it was Juan who led the defenders.

JUAN. (*more and more agitated—trying to hide his growing resentment under effusive amiability*) Bravely done! But you have doubtless heard great tales of mountains of jewels—Golden Cities of Cathay—you hope to grow rich.

NEPHEW. (*proudly*) I do not care for riches; and as for Golden Cities, I only wish to plant Spain's banner on their citadels.

JUAN. (*inspired by respect in spite of himself*) Brave dreams! Echoes blown down the wind of years.

BEATRIZ. (*looking at the* NEPHEW *with great pride as* JUAN *searches her face*) He is as you were in my mother's tales. (*She and the* NEPHEW *are held by each other's eyes.*)

JUAN. (*after a conquering struggle with his bitterness—fatalistically*) So—thus old heart—in silence. (*Then rousing himself—in-*

tensely) But with joy! with joy! (*They look at him in puzzled alarm. He smiles gently at* BEATRIZ) Then you have found him at last—my double?

BEATRIZ. (*blushing, confusedly*) I—I do not know, Don Juan.

JUAN. Then I know. (*Musing a bit sadly*) You have stolen my last gesture. An old man had a tale to tell you—oh, so brave a tale!—but now he sees that if youth cannot, age must keep its secrets! A sad old ghost to haunt your memory, that would be a poor wedding gift. (*They again look from him to each other, mystified and apprehensive,* JUAN *suddenly looks up at them—with a startling directness*) You love each other! (*He hurries on with feverish gayety*) Forgive—I'm a rough soldier—and there is need for haste. Quick. Do you not ask my blessing?

BEATRIZ. (*falling on her knees beside him—happily*) Oh, yes, good Don Juan! (*The* NEPHEW *kneels beside her.*)

JUAN. (*he raises his hands over their heads*) Youth of this earth——love—hail—and farewell! May you be blessed forever! (*He touches their heads with his hands—then sinks back, closing his eyes. They rise and stand looking down at him uncertainly.*)

NEPHEW. (*after a pause—in a whisper*) He wishes to sleep.

BEATRIZ. (*as they walk apart, in a whisper, the tears in her eyes*) Oh, Juan, I'm afraid—and yet—I am not sad.

NEPHEW. (*takes her in his arms passionately*) My life! My soul! (*He kisses her.*)

BEATRIZ. My love!

NEPHEW. Life is beautiful! The earth sings for us! Let us sing, too! (*He strides over to where the lute is and picks it up.*)

BEATRIZ. (*happily*) Yes— (*Then reminded*) Ssshh! (*She points at* JUAN.)

NEPHEW. (*urgingly*) He is asleep. We can go out beyond the walls. (*He puts his arm around her and leads her out through the door in rear.*)

JUAN. (*opening his eyes and looking after them, a tender smile on his lips*) Yes! Go where Beauty is! Sing! (*From outside the voices of* BEATRIZ *and his* NEPHEW *are heard mingling in their version of the fountain song*)

Love is a flower
Forever blooming
Beauty a fountain
Forever flowing
Upward into the source of sunshine,
Upward into the azure heaven;
One with God but
Ever returning
To kiss the earth that the flower may live.

(JUAN *listens in an ecstasy, bows his head, weeps. Then he sinks back with closed eyes exhaustedly.* LUIS *enters from the monastery.*)

LUIS. (*hurries forward in alarm*) Juan! (*He hears the song and is indignant*) Have they lost all feeling? I will soon stop— (*He starts for the door in rear.*)

JUAN. (*in a ringing voice*) No! I am that song! One must accept, absorb, give back, become oneself a symbol! Juan Ponce de Leon is past! He is resolved into the thousand moods of beauty that make up happiness—color of the sunset, of tomorrow's dawn, breath of the great Trade wind—sunlight on grass, an insect's song, the rustle of leaves, an ant's ambitions. (*In an ecstasy*) Oh, Luis, I begin to know eternal youth! I have found my Fountain! O Fountain of Eternity, take back this drop, my soul! (*He dies.* LUIS *bows his head and weeps.*)

FATHER SUPERIOR. (*enters from the right*) Vespers. (*Then in a voice of awe as he stares at* JUAN) Is he—dead?

LUIS. (*aroused—exaltedly*) No! He lives in God! Let us pray. (LUIS *sinks on his knees beside* JUAN'S *body, the* FATHER SUPERIOR *beside him. He lifts his eyes and clasped hands to heaven and prays fervently. The voices of* BEATRIZ *and the* NEPHEW *in the fountain song seem to rise to an exultant pitch. Then the chant of the monks swells out, deep and vibrant. For a moment the two strains blend into harmony, fill the air in an all-comprehending hymn of the mystery of life as the curtain falls.*)

"S.S. GLENCAIRN"

The Moon of the Caribbees

Bound East for Cardiff

The Long Voyage Home

In the Zone

THE MOON OF THE CARIBBEES

A Play in One Act

CHARACTERS

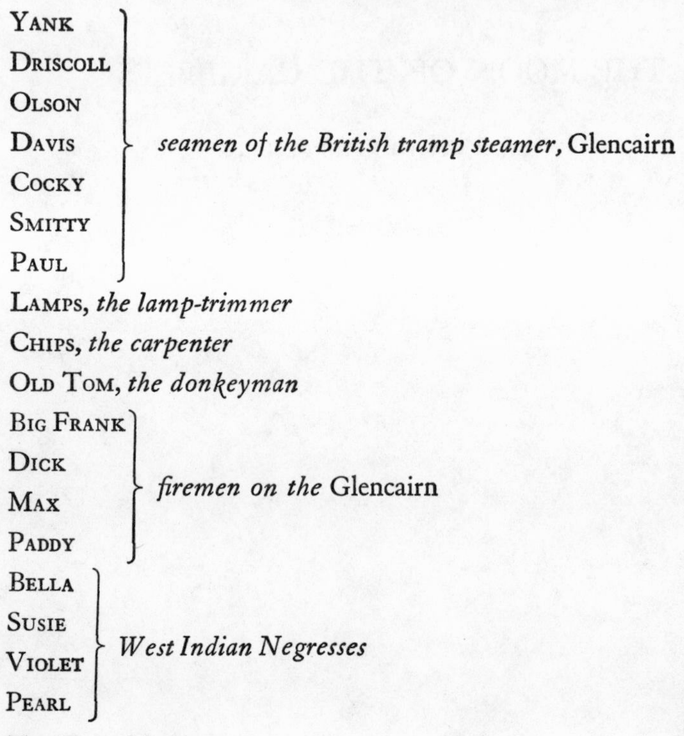

Yank, Driscoll, Olson, Davis, Cocky, Smitty, Paul — *seamen of the British tramp steamer,* Glencairn

Lamps, *the lamp-trimmer*

Chips, *the carpenter*

Old Tom, *the donkeyman*

Big Frank, Dick, Max, Paddy — *firemen on the* Glencairn

Bella, Susie, Violet, Pearl — *West Indian Negresses*

The First Mate

Two other seamen—Scotty and Ivan—and several other members of the stokehole-engine-room crew.

Note.—With the exception of "In the Zone," the action of all the plays following takes place in years preceding the outbreak of the World War.

THE MOON OF THE CARIBBEES

SCENE. *A forward section of the main deck of the British tramp steamer* Glencairn, *at anchor off an island in the West Indies. The full moon, half-way up the sky, throws a clear light on the deck. The sea is calm and the ship motionless.*

On the left two of the derrick booms of the foremast jut out at an angle of forty-five degrees, black against the sky. In the rear the dark outline of the port bulwark is sharply defined against a distant strip of coral beach, white in the moonlight, fringed with coco-palms whose tops rise clear of the horizon. On the right is the forecastle with an open doorway in the center leading to the seamen's and firemen's compartments. On either side of the doorway are two closed doors opening on the quarters of the bo'sun, the ship's carpenter, the mess-room steward, and the donkeyman—what might be called the petty officers of the ship. Near each bulwark there is also a short stairway, like a section of fire escape, leading up to the forecastle head (the top of the forecastle)—the edge of which can be seen on the right.

In the center of the deck, and occupying most of the space, is the large, raised square of the number one hatch, covered with canvas, battened down for the night.

A melancholy Negro chant, faint and far off, drifts, crooning, over the water.

Most of the seamen and firemen are reclining or sitting on the hatch. PAUL *is leaning against the port bulwark, the upper part of his stocky figure outlined against the sky.* SMITTY *and* COCKY *are sitting on the edge of the forecastle head with their legs dangling over. Nearly all are smoking pipes or cigarettes. The majority are dressed in patched suits of dungaree. Quite a few are in their bare feet and some of them, especially the firemen, have nothing on but a pair of pants and an undershirt. A good many wear caps.*

There is the low murmur of different conversations going on in the separate groups as the curtain rises. This is followed by a sudden silence in which the singing from the land can be plainly heard.

DRISCOLL. (*a powerfully built Irishman who is sitting on the edge of the hatch, front—irritably*) Will ye listen to them naygurs? I wonder now, do they call that keenin' a song?

SMITTY. (*a young Englishman with a blond mustache. He is sitting on the forecastle head looking out over the water with his chin supported on his hands*) It doesn't make a chap feel very cheerful, does it? (*He sighs.*)

COCKY. (*a wizened runt of a man with a straggling gray mustache—slapping* SMITTY *on the back*) Cheero, ole dear! Down't be ser dawhn in the marf, Duke. She loves yer.

SMITTY. (*gloomily*) Shut up, Cocky! (*He turns away from* COCKY *and falls to dreaming again, staring toward the spot on shore where the singing seems to come from.*)

BIG FRANK. (*a huge fireman sprawled out on the right of the hatch —waving a hand toward the land*) They bury somebody—py chimminy Christmas, I tink so from way it sound.

YANK. (*a rather good-looking rough who is sitting beside* DRISCOLL) What d'yuh mean, bury? They don't plant 'em down here, Dutchy. They eat 'em to save fun'ral expenses. I guess this guy went down the wrong way an' they got indigestion.

COCKY. Indigestion! Ho yus, not 'arf! Down't yer know as them blokes 'as two stomacks like a bleedin' camel?

DAVIS. (*a short, dark man seated on the right of hatch*) An' you seen the two, I s'pect, ain't you?

COCKY. (*scornfully*) Down't be showin' yer igerance be tryin' to make a mock o' me what has seen more o' the world than yeself ever will.

MAX. (*a Swedish fireman—from the rear of hatch*) Spin dat yarn, Cocky.

COCKY. It's Gawd's troof, what I tole yer. I 'eard it from a bloke what was captured pris'ner by 'em in the Solomon Islands. Shipped wiv 'im one voyage. 'Twas a rare treat to 'ear 'im tell what 'appened to 'im among 'em. (*Musingly*) 'E was a funny bird, 'e was—'ailed from Mile End, 'e did.

DRISCOLL. (*with a snort*) Another lyin' cockney, the loike av yourself!

LAMPS. (*a fat Swede who is sitting on a camp stool in front of his door talking with* CHIPS) Where you meet up with him, Cocky?

CHIPS. (*a lanky Scotchman—derisively*) In New Guinea, I'll lay my oath!

COCKY. (*defiantly*) Yus! It *was* in New Guinea, time I was shipwrecked there. (*There is a perfect storm of groans and laughter at this speech.*)

YANK. (*getting up*) Yuh know what we said yuh'd get if yuh sprung any of that lyin' New Guinea dope on us again, don't yuh? Close that trap if yuh don't want a duckin' over the side.

COCKY. Ow, I was on'y tryin' to edicate yer a bit. (*He sinks into dignified silence.*)

YANK. (*nodding toward the shore*) Don't yuh know this is the West Indies, yuh crazy mut? There ain't no cannibals here. They're only common niggers.

DRISCOLL. (*irritably*) Whativir they are, the divil take their cryin'. It's enough to give a man the jigs listenin' to 'em.

YANK. (*with a grin*) What's the matter, Drisc? Yuh're as sore as a boil about somethin'.

DRISCOLL. I'm dyin' wid impatience to have a dhrink; an' that blarsted bumboat naygur woman took her oath she'd bring back rum enough for the lot av us whin she came back on board tonight.

BIG FRANK. (*overhearing this—in a loud eager voice*) You say the bumboat voman vill bring booze?

DRISCOLL. (*sarcastically*) That's right—tell the Old Man about ut, an' the Mate, too. (*All of the crew have edged nearer to* DRISCOLL *and are listening to the conversation with an air of suppressed excitement.* DRISCOLL *lowers his voice impressively and addresses them all*) She said she cud snake ut on board in the bottoms av thim baskets av fruit they're goin' to bring wid 'em to sell to us for'ard.

THE DONKEYMAN. (*an old gray-headed man with a kindly, wrinkled face. He is sitting on a camp stool in front of his door, right front*) She'll be bringin' some black women with her this time—or times has changed since I put in here last.

DRISCOLL. She said she wud—two or three—more, maybe, I dunno. (*This announcement is received with great enthusiasm by all hands.*)

COCKY. What a bloody lark!

OLSON. Py yingo, we have one hell of a time!

DRISCOLL. (*warningly*) Remimber ye must be quiet about ut, ye scuts—wid the dhrink, I mane—ivin if the bo'sun is ashore. The Old Man ordered her to bring no booze on board or he wudn't buy a thing off av her for the ship.

PADDY. (*a squat, ugly Liverpool Irishman*) To the divil wid him!

BIG FRANK. (*turning on him*) Shud up, you tamn fool, Paddy! You vant make trouble? (*To* DRISCOLL) You und me, ve keep dem quiet, Drisc.

DRISCOLL. Right ye are, Dutchy. I'll split the skull av the first wan av ye starts to foight. (*Three bells are heard striking.*)

DAVIS. Three bells. When's she comin', Drisc?

DRISCOLL. She'll be here any minute now, surely. (*To* PAUL, *who has returned to his position by the bulwark after hearing* DRISCOLL'S *news*) D'you see 'em comin', Paul?

PAUL. I don't see anyting like bumboat. (*They all set themselves to wait, lighting pipes, cigarettes, and making themselves comfortable.*

There is a silence broken only by the mournful singing of the Negroes on shore.)

SMITTY. (*slowly—with a trace of melancholy*) I wish they'd stop that song. It makes you think of—well—things you ought to forget. Rummy go, what?

COCKY. (*slapping him on the back*) Cheero, ole love! We'll be 'avin' our rum in arf a mo', Duke. (*He comes down to the deck, leaving* SMITTY *alone on the forecastle head.*)

BIG FRANK. Sing someting, Drisc. Den ve don't hear dot yelling.

DAVIS. Give us a chanty, Drisc.

PADDY. Wan all av us knows.

MAX. We all sing in on chorus.

OLSON. "Rio Grande," Drisc.

BIG FRANK. No, ve don't know dot. Sing "Viskey Johnny."

CHIPS. "Flyin' Cloud."

COCKY. Now! Guv us "Maid o' Amsterdam."

LAMPS. "Santa Anna" iss a good one.

DRISCOLL. Shut your mouths, all av you. (*Scornfully*) A chanty is ut ye want? I'll bet me whole pay day there's not wan in the crowd 'ceptin' Yank here, an' Ollie, an' meself, an' Lamps an' Cocky, maybe, wud be sailors enough to know the main from the mizzen on a windjammer. Ye've heard the names of chanties but divil a note av the tune or a loine av the words do ye know. There's hardly a rale deep-water sailor lift on the seas, more's the pity.

YANK. Give us "Blow the Man Down." We all know some of that. (*A chorus of assenting voices*) Yes!—Righto!—Let 'er drive! Start 'er, Drisc (*etc.*)

DRISCOLL. Come in then, all av ye. (*He sings*) As I was a-roamin' down Paradise Street—

ALL. Wa-a-ay, blow the man down!

DRISCOLL. As I was a-roamin' down Paradise Street—

ALL. Give us some time to blow the man down!

CHORUS

Blow the man down, boys, oh, blow the man down!
Wa-a-ay, blow the man down!
As I was a-roamin' down Paradise Street—
Give us some time to blow the man down!

DRISCOLL. A pretty young maiden I chanced for to meet.

ALL. Wa-a-ay, blow the man down!

DRISCOLL. A pretty young maiden I chanced for to meet.

ALL. Give us some time to blow the man down!

CHORUS

Blow the man down, boys, oh, blow the man down!
Wa-a-ay, blow the man down!
A pretty young maiden I chanced for to meet.
Give us some time to blow the man down!

PAUL. (*just as* DRISCOLL *is clearing his throat preparatory to starting the next verse*) Hay, Drisc! Here she come, I tink. Some bumboat comin' dis way. (*They all rush to the side and look toward the land.*)

YANK. There's five or six of them in it—and they paddle like skirts.

DRISCOLL. (*wildly elated*) Hurroo, ye scuts! 'Tis thim right enough. (*He does a few jig steps on the deck.*)

OLSON. (*after a pause during which all are watching the approaching boat*) Py yingo, I see six in boat, yes, sir.

DAVIS. I kin make out the baskets. See 'em there amidships.

BIG FRANK. Vot kind booze dey bring—viskey?

DRISCOLL. Rum, foine West Indy rum wid a kick in ut loike a mule's hoind leg.

LAMPS. Maybe she don't bring any; maybe skipper scare her.

DRISCOLL. Don't be throwin' cold water, Lamps. I'll skin her black hoide off av her if she goes back on her worrd.

YANK. Here they come. Listen to 'em gigglin'. (*Calling*) Oh, you kiddo! (*The sound of women's voices can be heard talking and laughing.*)

DRISCOLL. (*calling*) Is ut you, Mrs. Old Black Joe?

A WOMAN'S VOICE. 'Ullo, Mike! (*There is loud feminine laughter at this retort.*)

DRISCOLL. Shake a leg an' come abord thin.

THE WOMAN'S VOICE. We're a-comin'.

DRISCOLL. Come on, Yank. You an' me'd best be goin' to give 'em a hand wid their truck. 'Twill put 'em in good spirits.

COCKY. (*as they start off left*) Ho, you ain't 'arf a fox, Drisc. Down't drink it all afore we sees it.

DRISCOLL. (*over his shoulder*) You'll be havin' yours, me sonny bye, don't fret. (*He and* YANK *go off left.*)

COCKY. (*licking his lips*) Gawd blimey, I can do wiv a wet.

DAVIS. Me, too!

CHIPS. I'll bet there ain't none of us'll let any go to waste.

BIG FRANK. I could trink a whole barrel mineself, py chimminy Christmas!

COCKY. I 'opes all the gels ain't as bloomin' ugly as 'er. Looked like a bloody organ-grinder's monkey, she did. Gawd, I couldn't put up wiv the likes of 'er!

PADDY. Ye'll be lucky if any of thim looks at ye, ye squint-eyed runt.

COCKY. (*angrily*) Ho, yus? You ain't no bleedin' beauty prize yeself, me man. A 'airy ape, I calls yer.

PADDY. (*walking toward him—truculently*) Whot's thot? Say ut again if ye dare.

COCKY. (*his hand on his sheath-knife—snarling*) 'Airy ape! That's wot I says! (PADDY *tries to reach him but the others keep them apart.*)

BIG FRANK. (*pushing* PADDY *back*) Vot's the matter mit you, Paddy. Don't you hear vat Driscoll say—no fighting?

PADDY. (*grumblingly*) I don't take no back-talk from that deck-scrubbin' shrimp.

COCKY. Blarsted coal-puncher! (DRISCOLL *appears wearing a broad grin of satisfaction. The fight is immediately forgotten by the crowd, who gather around him with exclamations of eager curiosity.* How is it, Drisc? Any luck? Vot she bring, Drisc? Where's the gels? *etc.*)

DRISCOLL. (*with an apprehensive glance back at the bridge*) Not so loud, for the love av hivin! (*The clamor dies down*) Yis, she has ut wid her. She'll be here in a minute wid a pint bottle or two for each wan av ye—three shillin's a bottle. So don't be impashunt.

COCKY. (*indignantly*) Three bob! The bloody cow!

SMITTY. (*with an ironic smile*) Grand larceny, by God! (*They all turn and look up at him surprised to hear him speak.*)

OLSON. Py yingo, we don't pay so much.

BIG FRANK. Tamn black tief!

PADDY. We'll take ut away from her and give her nothin'.

THE CROWD. (*growling*) Dirty thief! Dot's right! Give her nothin'! Not a bloomin' 'apenny! (*etc.*)

DRISCOLL. (*grinning*) Ye can take ut or lave ut, me sonny byes. (*He casts a glance in the direction of the bridge and then reaches inside his shirt and pulls out a pint bottle*) 'Tis foine rum, the rale stuff. (*He drinks*) I slipped this wan out av wan of the baskets whin they wasn't lookin'. (*He hands the bottle to* OLSON *who is nearest him*) Here ye are, Ollie. Take a small sup an' pass ut to the nixt. 'Tisn't much but 'twill serve to take the black taste out av your mouths if ye go aisy wid ut. An' there's buckets more av ut comin'. (*The bottle passes from hand to hand, each man taking a sip and smacking his lips with a deep "Aa-ah" of satisfaction.*)

DAVIS. Where's she now, Drisc?

DRISCOLL. Up havin' a worrd wid the skipper, makin' arrangements about the money, I s'pose.

DAVIS. An' where's the other gels?

DRISCOLL. Wid her. There's foive av thim she took aboard—two swate little slips av things, near as white as you an' me are, for that gray-whiskered auld fool, an' the mates—an' the engineers too, maybe. The rist of thim'll be comin' for'ard whin she comes.

COCKY. 'E ain't 'arf a funny ole bird, the skipper. Gawd blimey! 'Member when we sailed from 'ome 'ow 'e stands on the bridge lookin' like a bloody ole sky pilot? An' 'is missus dawhn on the bloomin' dock 'owlin' fit to kill 'erself? An' 'is kids 'owlin' an' wavin' their 'andkerchiefs? (*With great moral indignation*) An' 'ere 'e is makin' up to a bleedin' nigger! There's a captain for yer! Gawd blimey! Bloody crab, I calls 'im!

DRISCOLL. Shut up, ye insect! Sure, it's not you should be talkin', an' you wid a woman an' childer weepin' for ye in iviry divil's port in the wide worrld, if we can believe your own tale av ut.

COCKY. (*still indignant*) I ain't no bloomin' captain. I ain't. I ain't got no missus—reg'lar married, I means. I ain't—

BIG FRANK. (*putting a huge paw over* COCKY'S *mouth*) You ain't going talk so much, you hear? (COCKY *wriggles away from him*) Say, Drisc, how ve pay dis voman for booze? Ve ain't got no cash.

DRISCOLL. It's aisy enough. Each girl'll have a slip av paper wid her an' whin you buy anythin' you write ut down and the price beside ut and sign your name. If ye can't write have some one who can do ut for ye. An' rimimber this: Whin ye buy a bottle av dhrink or (*with a wink*) somethin' else forbid, ye must write down tobaccy or fruit or somethin' the loike av that. Whin she laves the skipper'll pay what's owin' on the paper an' take ut out av your pay. Is ut clear to ye now?

ALL. Yes—Clear as day—Aw right, Drisc—Righto—Sure (*etc.*)

DRISCOLL. An' don't forgit what I said about bein' quiet wid the dhrink, or the Mate'll be down on our necks an' spile the fun. (*A chorus of assent.*)

DAVIS. (*looking aft*) Ain't this them comin'? (*They all look in that direction. The silly laughter of a woman is heard.*)

DRISCOLL. Look at Yank, wud ye, wid his arrm around the middle av wan av thim. That lad's not wastin' any toime. (*The four women enter from the left, giggling and whispering to each other. The first three carry baskets on their heads. The youngest and best-looking comes last.* YANK *has his arm about her waist and is carrying her basket in his other hand. All four are distinct Negro types. They wear light-colored, loose-fitting clothes and have bright bandana handkerchiefs on their heads. They put down their baskets on the hatch and sit down beside them. The men crowd around, grinning.*)

BELLA. (*she is the oldest, stoutest, and homeliest of the four—grinning back at them*) 'Ullo, boys.

THE OTHER GIRLS. 'Ullo, boys.

THE MEN. Hello, yourself—Evenin'—Hello—How are you? (*etc.*)

BELLA. (*genially*) Hope you had a nice voyage. My name's Bella, this here's Susie, yander's Violet, and her there (*pointing to the girl with* YANK) is Pearl. Now we all knows each other.

PADDY. (*roughly*) Never mind the girls. Where's the dhrink?

BELLA. (*tartly*) You're a hawg, ain't you? Don't talk so loud or you don't git any—you nor no man. Thinks I wants the ole captain to put me off the ship, do you?

YANK. Yes, nix on hollerin', you! D'yuh wanta queer all of us?

BELLA. (*casting a quick glance over her shoulder*) Here! Some of you big strapping boys sit back of us on the hatch there so's them officers can't see what we're doin'. (DRISCOLL *and several of the others sit and stand in back of the girls on the hatch.* BELLA *turns to* DRISCOLL) Did you tell 'em they gotter sign for what they gits—and *how* to sign?

DRISCOLL. I did—what's your name again—oh, yis—Bella, darlin'.

BELLA. Then it's all right; but you boys has gotter go inside the fo'castle when you gits your bottle. No drinkin' out here on deck. I ain't takin' no chances. (*An impatient murmur of assent goes up from the crowd*) Ain't that right, Mike?

DRISCOLL. Right as rain, darlin'. (BIG FRANK *leans over and says something to him in a low voice.* DRISCOLL *laughs and slaps his thigh*) Listen, Bella, I've somethin' to ask ye for my little friend here who's bashful. Ut has to do wid the ladies so I'd best be whisperin' ut to ye meself to kape them from blushin'. (*He leans over and asks her a question.*)

BELLA. (*firmly*) Four shillin's.

DRISCOLL. (*laughing*) D'you hear that, all av ye? Four shillin's ut is.

PADDY. (*angrily*) To hell wid this talkin'. I want a dhrink.

BELLA. Is everything all right, Mike?

DRISCOLL. (*after a look back at the bridge*) Sure. Let her droive!

BELLA. All right, girls. (*The girls reach down in their baskets in under the fruit which is on top and each pulls out a pint bottle. Four of the men crowd up and take the bottles*) Fetch a light, Lamps, that's a good boy. (LAMPS *goes to his room and returns with a candle. This is passed from one girl to another as the men sign the sheets of paper for their bottles*) Don't you boys forget to mark down cigarettes or tobacco or fruit, remember! Three shillin's is the price. Take it into the fo'castle. For Gawd's sake, don't stand out here drinkin' in the moonlight. (*The four go into the forecastle. Four more take their places.* PADDY *plants himself in front of* PEARL *who is sitting by* YANK *with his arm still around her.*)

PADDY. (*gruffly*) Gimme thot! (*She holds out a bottle which he snatches from her hand. He turns to go away.*)

YANK. (*sharply*) Here, you! Where d'yuh get that stuff? You ain't signed for that yet.

PADDY. (*sullenly*) I can't write me name.

YANK. Then I'll write it for yuh. (*He takes the paper from* PEARL *and writes*) There ain't goin' to be no welchin' on little Bright Eyes here—not when I'm around, see? Ain't I right, kiddo?

PEARL. (*with a grin*) Yes, suh.

BELLA. (*seeing all four are served*) Take it into the fo'castle, boys. (PADDY *defiantly raises his bottle and gulps down a drink in the full moonlight.* BELLA *sees him*) Look at 'im! Look at the dirty swine! (PADDY *slouches into the forecastle*) Wants to git me in trouble. That settles it! We all got to git inside, boys, where we won't git caught.

Come on, girls. (*The girls pick up their baskets and follow* BELLA. YANK *and* PEARL *are the last to reach the doorway. She lingers behind him, her eyes fixed on* SMITTY, *who is still sitting on the forecastle head, his chin on his hands, staring off into vacancy.*)

PEARL. (*waving a hand to attract his attention*) Come ahn in, pretty boy. Ah likes you.

SMITTY. (*coldly*) Yes; I want to buy a bottle, please. (*He goes down the steps and follows her into the forecastle. No one remains on deck but* THE DONKEYMAN, *who sits smoking his pipe in front of his door. There is the subdued babble of voices from the crowd inside but the mournful cadence of the song from the shore can again be faintly heard.* SMITTY *reappears and closes the door to the forecastle after him. He shudders and shakes his shoulders as if flinging off something which disgusted him. Then he lifts the bottle which is in his hand to his lips and gulps down a long drink.* THE DONKEYMAN *watches him impassively.* SMITTY *sits down on the hatch facing him. Now that the closed door has shut off nearly all the noise, the singing from shore comes clearly over the moonlit water.*)

SMITTY. (*listening to it for a moment*) Damn that song of theirs. (*He takes another big drink*) What do you say, Donk?

THE DONKEYMAN. (*quietly*) Seems nice an' sleepy-like.

SMITTY. (*with a hard laugh*) Sleepy! If I listened to it long—sober—I'd never go to sleep.

THE DONKEYMAN. 'Tain't sich bad music, is it? Sounds kinder pretty to me—low an' mournful—same as listenin' to the organ outside o' church of a Sunday.

SMITTY. (*with a touch of impatience*) I didn't mean it was bad music. It isn't. It's the beastly memories the damn thing brings up—*for some reason.* (*He takes another pull at the bottle.*)

THE DONKEYMAN. Ever hear it before?

SMITTY. No; never in my life. It's just a something about the rotten thing which makes me think—of—well, oh, the devil! (*He forces a laugh.*)

THE DONKEYMAN. (*spitting placidly*) Queer things, mem'ries. I ain't ever been bothered much by 'em.

SMITTY. (*looking at him fixedly for a moment—with quiet scorn*) No, you wouldn't be.

THE DONKEYMAN. Not that I ain't had my share o' things goin' wrong; but I puts 'em out o' me mind, like, an' fergets 'em.

SMITTY. But suppose you couldn't put them out of your mind? Suppose they haunted you when you were awake and when you were asleep—what then?

THE DONKEYMAN. (*quietly*) I'd git drunk, same's you're doin'.

SMITTY. (*with a harsh laugh*) Good advice. (*He takes another drink. He is beginning to show the effects of the liquor. His face is flushed and he talks rather wildly*) We're poor little lambs who have lost our way, eh, Donk? Damned from here to eternity, what? God have mercy on such as we! True, isn't it, Donk?

THE DONKEYMAN. Maybe; I dunno. (*After a slight pause*) What ever set you goin' to sea? You ain't made for it.

SMITTY. (*laughing wildly*) My old friend in the bottle here, Donk.

THE DONKEYMAN. I done my share o' drinkin' in my time. (*Regretfully*) Them was good times, those days. Can't hold up under drink no more. Doctor told me I'd got to stop or die. (*He spits contentedly*) So I stops.

SMITTY. (*with a foolish smile*) Then I'll drink one for you. Here's your health, old top! (*He drinks.*)

THE DONKEYMAN. (*after a pause*) S'pose there's a gel mixed up in it some place, ain't there?

SMITTY. (*stiffly*) What makes you think so?

THE DONKEYMAN. Always is when a man lets music bother 'im. (*After a few puffs at his pipe*) An' she said she threw you over 'cause you was drunk; an' you said you was drunk 'cause she threw you over. (*He spits leisurely*) Queer thing, love, ain't it?

SMITTY. (*rising to his feet with drunken dignity*) I'll trouble you not to pry into my affairs, Donkeyman.

THE DONKEYMAN. (*unmoved*) That's everybody's affair, what I said. I been through it many's the time. (*Genially*) I always hit 'em a whack on the ear an' went out and got drunker'n ever. When I come home again they always had somethin' special nice cooked fur me to eat. (*Puffing at his pipe*) That's the on'y way to fix 'em when they gits on their high horse. I don't s'pose you ever tried that?

SMITTY. (*pompously*) Gentlemen don't hit women.

THE DONKEYMAN. (*placidly*) No; that's why they has mem'ries when they hears music. (SMITTY *does not deign to reply to this but sinks into a scornful silence.* DAVIS *and the girl* VIOLET *come out of the forecastle and close the door behind them. He is staggering a bit and she is laughing shrilly.*)

DAVIS. (*turning to the left*) This way, Rose, or Pansy, or Jessamine, or black Tulip, or Violet, or whatever the hell flower your name is. No one'll see us back here. (*They go off left.*)

THE DONKEYMAN. There's love at first sight for you—an' plenty more o' the same in the fo'c's'tle. No mem'ries jined with that.

SMITTY. (*really repelled*) Shut up, Donk. You're disgusting. (*He takes a long drink.*)

THE DONKEYMAN. (*philosophically*) All depends on how you was brung up, I s'pose. (PEARL *comes out of the forecastle. There is a roar of voices from inside. She shuts the door behind her, sees* SMITTY *on the hatch, and comes over and sits beside him and puts her arm over his shoulder.*)

THE DONKEYMAN. (*chuckling*) There's love for you, Duke.

PEARL. (*patting* SMITTY'S *face with her hand*) 'Ullo, pretty boy. (SMITTY *pushes her hand away coldly*) What you doin' out here all alone by yourself?

SMITTY. (*with a twisted grin*) Thinking and—(*he indicates the bottle in his hand*)—drinking to stop thinking. (*He drinks and laughs maudlinly. The bottle is three-quarters empty.*)

PEARL. You oughtn't drink so much, pretty boy. Don't you know that? You have big, big headache come mawnin'.

SMITTY. (*dryly*) Indeed?

PEARL. That's true. Ah knows what Ah say. (*Cooingly*) Why you run 'way from me, pretty boy? Ah likes you. Ah don' like them other fellahs. They act too rough. You ain't rough. You're a genelman. Ah knows. Ah can tell a genelman fahs Ah can see 'im.

SMITTY. Thank you for the compliment; but you're wrong, you see. I'm merely—a ranker. (*He adds bitterly*) And a rotter.

PEARL. (*patting his arm*) No, you ain't. Ah knows better. You're a genelman. (*Insinuatingly*) Ah wouldn't have nothin' to do with them other men, but (*she smiles at him enticingly*) you is diff'rent. (*He pushes her away from him disgustedly. She pouts*) Don' you like me, pretty boy?

SMITTY. (*a bit ashamed*) I beg your pardon. I didn't mean to be rude, you know, really. (*His politeness is drunkenly exaggerated*) I'm a bit off color.

PEARL. (*brightening up*) Den you do like me—little ways?

SMITTY. (*carelessly*) Yes, yes, why shouldn't I? (*He suddenly laughs wildly and puts his arm around her waist and presses her to him*) Why not? (*He pulls his arm back quickly with a shudder of disgust, and takes a drink.* PEARL *looks at him curiously, puzzled by his strange actions. The door from the forecastle is kicked open and* YANK *comes out. The uproar of shouting, laughing and singing voices has increased in violence.* YANK *staggers over toward* SMITTY *and* PEARL.)

YANK. (*blinking at them*) What the hell—oh, it's you, Smitty the Duke. I was goin' to turn one loose on the jaw of any guy'd cop my dame, but seein' it's you— (*Sentimentally*) Pals is pals and any pal of mine c'n have anythin' I got, see? (*Holding out his hand*) Shake, Duke. (SMITTY *takes his hand and he pumps it up and down*) You'n me's frens. Ain't I right?

SMITTY. Right it is, Yank. But you're wrong about this girl. She isn't with me. She was just going back to the fo'c's'tle to you. (PEARL *looks at him with hatred gathering in her eyes.*)

YANK. Tha' right?

SMITTY. On my word!

YANK. (*grabbing her arm*) Come on then, you, Pearl! Le's have a drink with the bunch. (*He pulls her to the entrance where she shakes off his hand long enough to turn on* SMITTY *furiously.*)

PEARL. You swine! You can go to hell! (*She goes into the forecastle, slamming the door.*)

THE DONKEYMAN. (*spitting calmly*) There's love for you. They're all the same—white, brown, yeller 'n' black. A whack on the ear's the only thing'll learn 'em. (SMITTY *makes no reply but laughs harshly and takes another drink; then sits staring before him, the almost empty bottle tightly clutched in one hand. There is an increase in volume of the muffled clamor from the forecastle and a moment later the door is thrown open and the whole mob, led by Driscoll, pours out on deck. All of them are very drunk and several of them carry bottles in their hands.* BELLA *is the only one of the women who is absolutely sober. She tries in vain to keep the men quiet.* PEARL *drinks from* YANK'S *bottle every moment or so, laughing shrilly, and leaning against* YANK, *whose arm is about her waist.* PAUL *comes out last carrying an accordion. He staggers over and stands on top of the hatch, his instrument under his arm.*)

DRISCOLL. Play us a dance, ye square-head swab!—a rale, God-forsaken son av a turkey trot wid guts to ut.

YANK. Straight from the old Barbary Coast in Frisco!

PAUL. I don't know. I try. (*He commences tuning up.*)

YANK. Attaboy! Let 'er rip! (DAVIS *and* VIOLET *come back and join the crowd.* THE DONKEYMAN *looks on them all with a detached, indulgent air.* SMITTY *stares before him and does not seem to know there is anyone on deck but himself.*)

BIG FRANK. Dance? I don't dance. I trink! (*He suits the action to the word and roars with meaningless laughter.*)

DRISCOLL. Git out av the way thin, ye big hulk, an' give us some room. (BIG FRANK *sits down on the hatch, right. All of the others who are not going to dance either follow his example or lean against the port bulwark.*)

BELLA. (*on the verge of tears at her inability to keep them in the forecastle or make them be quiet now they are out*) For Gawd's sake, boys, don't shout so loud! Want to git me in trouble?

DRISCOLL. (*grabbing her*) Dance wid me, me cannibal quane. (*Someone drops a bottle on deck and it smashes.*)

BELLA. (*hysterically*) There they goes! There they goes! Captain'll hear that! Oh, my Lawd!

DRISCOLL. Be damned to him! Here's the music! Off ye go! (PAUL *starts playing "You Great Big Beautiful Doll" with a note left out every now and then. The four couples commence dancing—a jerk-shouldered version of the old Turkey Trot as it was done in the sailor-town dives, made more grotesque by the fact that all the couples are drunk and keep lurching into each other every moment. Two of the men start dancing together, intentionally bumping into the others.* YANK *and* PEARL *come around in front of* SMITTY *and, as they pass him,* PEARL *slaps him across the side of the face with all her might, and laughs viciously. He jumps to his feet with his fists clenched but sees who hit him and sits down again smiling bitterly.* YANK *laughs boisterously.*)

YANK. Wow! Some wallop! One on you, Duke.

DRISCOLL. (*hurling his cap at* PAUL) Faster, ye toad! (PAUL *makes frantic efforts to speed up and the music suffers in the process.*)

BELLA. (*puffing*) Let me go. I'm wore out with you steppin' on my toes, you clumsy Mick. (*She struggles but* DRISCOLL *holds her tight.*)

DRISCOLL. God blarst you for havin' such big feet, thin. Aisy, aisy, Mrs. Old Black Joe! 'Tis dancin'll take the blubber off ye. (*He whirls her around the deck by main force.* COCKY, *with* SUSIE, *is dancing near the hatch, right, when* PADDY, *who is sitting on the edge with* BIG FRANK, *sticks his foot out and the wavering couple stumble over it and fall flat on the deck. A roar of laughter goes up.* COCKY *rises to his feet, his face livid with rage, and springs at* PADDY, *who promptly knocks him down.* DRISCOLL *hits* PADDY *and* BIG FRANK *hits* DRISCOLL. *In a flash a wholesale fight has broken out and the deck is a surging crowd of drink-maddened men hitting out at each other indiscriminately, although the general idea seems to be a battle between seamen and firemen. The women shriek and take refuge on top of the hatch, where they huddle in a frightened group. Finally there is the flash of a knife held high in the moonlight and a loud yell of pain.*)

DAVIS. (*somewhere in the crowd*) Here's the Mate comin'! Let's git out o' this! (*There is a general rush for the forecastle. In a moment there is no one left on deck but the little group of women on the hatch;* SMITTY, *still dazedly rubbing his cheek;* THE DONKEYMAN *quietly smoking on his stool; and* YANK *and* DRISCOLL, *their faces battered up considerably, their undershirts in shreds, bending over the still form of* PADDY, *which lies stretched out on the deck between them. In the silence the mournful chant from the shore creeps slowly out to the ship.*)

DRISCOLL. (*quickly—in a low voice*) Who knoifed him?

YANK. (*stupidly*) I didn't see it. How do I know? Cocky, I'll bet. (*The* FIRST MATE *enters from the left. He is a tall, strongly-built man dressed in a plain blue uniform.*)

THE MATE. (*angrily*) What's all this noise about? (*He sees the man lying on the deck*) Hello! What's this? (*He bends down on one knee beside* PADDY.)

DRISCOLL. (*stammering*) All av us—was in a bit av a harmless foight, sir—an' I dunno— (*The* MATE *rolls* PADDY *over and sees a knife wound on his shoulder.*)

THE MATE. Knifed, by God. (*He takes an electric flash from his pocket and examines the cut*) Lucky it's only a flesh wound. He must have hit his head on deck when he fell. That's what knocked him out. This is only a scratch. Take him aft and I'll bandage him up.

DRISCOLL. Yis, sor. (*They take* PADDY *by the shoulders and feet and carry him off left. The* MATE *looks up and sees the women on the hatch for the first time.*)

THE MATE. (*surprised*) Hello! (*He walks over to them*) Go to the cabin and get your money and clear off. If I had my way, you'd never— (*His foot hits a bottle. He stoops down and picks it up and smells of it*) Rum, by God! So that's the trouble! I thought their breaths smelled damn queer. (*To the women, harshly*) You needn't go to the skipper for any money. You won't get any. That'll teach you to smuggle rum on a ship and start a riot.

BELLA. But, Mister—

THE MATE. (*sternly*) You know the agreement—rum—no money.

BELLA. (*indignantly*) Honest to Gawd, Mister, I never brung no—

THE MATE (*fiercely*) You're a liar! And none of your lip or I'll make a complaint ashore tomorrow and have you locked up.

BELLA. (*subdued*) Please, Mister—

THE MATE. Clear out of this, now! Not another word out of you! Tumble over the side damn quick! The others are waiting for you. Hop, now! (*They walk quickly—almost run—off to the left.* THE MATE *follows them, nodding to* THE DONKEYMAN, *and ignoring the oblivious* SMITTY. *There is absolute silence on the ship for a few moments. The melancholy song of the Negroes drifts crooning over the water.* SMITTY *listens to it intently for a time; then sighs heavily, a sigh that is half a sob.*)

SMITTY. God! (*He drinks the last drop in the bottle and throws it behind him on the hatch.*)

THE DONKEYMAN. (*spitting tranquilly*) More mem'ries? (SMITTY *does not answer him. The ship's bell tolls four bells.* THE DONKEYMAN *knocks out his pipe*) I think I'll turn in. (*He opens the door to his cabin, but turns to look at* SMITTY—*kindly*) You can't hear it in the fo'c's'tle—the music, I mean—an' there'll likely be more drink in there, too. Good-night. (*He goes in and shuts the door.*)

SMITTY. Good-night, Donk. (*He gets wearily to his feet and walks with bowed shoulders, staggering a bit, to the forecastle entrance and goes in. There is silence for a second or so, broken only by the haunted, saddened voice of that brooding music, faint and far-off, like the mood of the moonlight made audible.*)

CURTAIN

BOUND EAST FOR CARDIFF

A Play in One Act

CHARACTERS

YANK

DRISCOLL

COCKY

DAVIS

SCOTTY

OLSON

PAUL

SMITTY

IVAN

THE CAPTAIN

THE SECOND MATE

BOUND EAST FOR CARDIFF

SCENE. *The seamen's forecastle of the British tramp steamer* Glencairn *on a foggy night midway on the voyage between New York and Cardiff. An irregular-shaped compartment, the sides of which almost meet at the far end to form a triangle. Sleeping bunks about six feet long, ranged three deep with a space of three feet separating the upper from the lower, are built against the sides. On the right above the bunks three or four port-holes can be seen. In front of the bunks, rough wooden benches. Over the bunks on the left, a lamp in a bracket. In the left foreground, a doorway. On the floor near it, a pail with a tin dipper. Oilskins are hanging from a hook near the doorway.*

The far side of the forecastle is so narrow that it contains only one series of bunks.

In under the bunks a glimpse can be had of sea-chests, suitcases, sea-boots, etc., jammed in indiscriminately.

At regular intervals of a minute or so the blast of the steamer's whistle can be heard above all the other sounds.

Five men are sitting on the benches talking. They are dressed in dirty patched suits of dungaree, flannel shirts, and all are in their stocking feet. Four of the men are pulling on pipes and the air is heavy with rancid tobacco smoke. Sitting on the top bunk in the left foreground, a Norwegian, PAUL, *is softly playing some folk-song on a battered accordion. He stops from time to time to listen to the conversation.*

In the lower bunk in the rear a dark-haired, hard-featured man is lying apparently asleep. One of his arms is stretched limply over the side of the bunk. His face is very pale, and drops of clammy perspiration glisten on his forehead.

It is nearing the end of the dog-watch—about ten minutes to eight in the evening.

COCKY. (*a weazened runt of a man. He is telling a story. The others are listening with amused, incredulous faces, interrupting him at the end of each sentence with loud derisive guffaws*) Makin' love to me, she was! It's Gawd's truth! A bloomin' nigger! Greased all over with cocoanut oil, she was. Gawd blimey, I couldn't stand 'er. Bloody old cow, I says; and with that I fetched 'er a biff on the ear wot knocked 'er silly, an'— (*He is interrupted by a roar of laughter from the others.*)

DAVIS. (*a middle-aged man with black hair and mustache*) You're a liar, Cocky.

SCOTTY. (*a dark young fellow*) Ho-ho! Ye werr neverr in New Guinea in yourr life, I'm thinkin'.

OLSON. (*a Swede with a drooping blond mustache—with ponderous sarcasm*) Yust tink of it! You say she wass a cannibal, Cocky?

DRISCOLL. (*a brawny Irishman with the battered features of a prize-fighter*) How cud ye doubt ut, Ollie? A quane av the naygurs she musta been surely. Who else wud think herself aqual to fallin' in love wid a beauthiful, divil-may-care rake av a man the loike av Cocky? (*A burst of laughter from the crowd.*)

COCKY. (*indignantly*) Gawd strike me dead if it ain't true, every bleedin' word of it. 'Appened ten year ago come Christmas.

SCOTTY. 'Twas a Christmas dinner she had her eyes on.

DAVIS. He'd a been a tough old bird.

DRISCOLL. 'Tis lucky for both av ye ye escaped; for the quane av the cannibal isles wad a died av the bellyache the day afther Christmas, divil a doubt av ut. (*The laughter at this is long and loud.*)

COCKY. (*sullenly*) Blarsted fat-'eads! (*The sick man in the lower bunk in the rear groans and moves restlessly. There is a hushed silence. All the men turn and stare at him.*)

DRISCOLL. Ssshh! (*In a hushed whisper*) We'd best not be talkin' so loud and him tryin' to have a bit av a sleep. (*He tiptoes softly to the side of the bunk*) Yank! You'd be wantin' a drink av wather, maybe? (YANK *does not reply.* DRISCOLL *bends over and looks at him*) It's asleep he is, sure enough. His breath is chokin' in his throat loike wather gurglin' in a poipe. (*He comes back quietly and sits down. All are silent, avoiding each other's eyes.*)

COCKY. (*after a pause*) Pore devil! It's over the side for 'im, Gawd 'elp 'im.

DRISCOLL. Stop your croakin'! He's not dead yet and, praise God, he'll have many a long day yet before him.

SCOTTY. (*shaking his head doubtfully*) He's bod, mon, he's verry bod.

DAVIS. Lucky he's alive. Many a man's light woulda gone out after a fall like that.

OLSON. You saw him fall?

DAVIS. Right next to him. He and me was goin' down in number two hold to do some chippin'. He puts his leg over careless-like and misses the ladder and plumps straight down to the bottom. I was scared to look over for a minute, and then I heard him groan and I scuttled down after him. He was hurt bad inside, for the blood was drippin' from the side of his mouth. He was groanin' hard, but he never let a word out of him.

COCKY. An' you blokes remember when we 'auled 'im in 'ere? Oh, 'ell, 'e says, oh, 'ell—like that, and nothink else.

OLSON. Did the captain know where he iss hurted?

COCKY. That silly ol' josser! Wot the 'ell would 'e know abaht anythink?

SCOTTY. (*scornfully*) He fiddles in his mouth wi' a bit of glass.

DRISCOLL. (*angrily*) The divil's own life ut is to be out on the lonely sea wid nothin' betune you and a grave in the ocean but a spindle-shanked, gray-whiskered auld fool the loike av him. 'Twas enough to make a saint shwear to see him wid his gold watch in his hand, tryin' to look as wise as an owl on a tree, and all the toime he not knowin' whether 'twas cholery or the barber's itch was the matther with Yank.

SCOTTY. (*sardonically*) He gave him a dose of salts, na doot?

DRISCOLL. Divil a thing he gave him at all, but looked in the book he had wid him, and shook his head, and walked out widout sayin' a word, the second mate afther him no wiser than himself, God's curse on the two av thim!

COCKY. (*after a pause*) Yank was a good shipmate, pore beggar. Lend me four bob in Noo Yark, 'e did.

DRISCOLL. (*warmly*) A good shipmate he was and is, none betther. Ye said no more than the truth, Cocky. Five years and more ut is since first I shipped wid him, and we've stuck together iver since through good luck and bad. Fights we've had, God help us, but 'twas only when we'd a bit av drink taken, and we always shook hands the nixt mornin'. Whativer was his was mine, and many's the toime I'd a been on the beach or worse, but for him. And now— (*His voice trembles as he fights to control his emotion*) Divil take me if I'm not startin' to blubber loike an auld woman, and he not dead at all, but goin' to live many a long year yet, maybe.

DAVIS. The sleep'll do him good. He seems better now.

OLSON. If he wud eat something—

DRISCOLL. Wud ye have him be eatin' in his condishun? Sure it's hard enough on the rest av us wid nothin' the matther wid our insides to be stomachin' the skoff on this rusty lime-juicer.

SCOTTY. (*indignantly*) It's a starvation ship.

DAVIS. Plenty o' work and no food—and the owners ridin' around in carriages!

OLSON. Hash, hash! Stew, stew! Marmalade, py damn! (*He spits disgustedly.*)

COCKY. Bloody swill! Fit only for swine is wot I say.

DRISCOLL. And the dish-wather they disguise wid the name av tea! And the putty they call bread! My belly feels loike I'd swalleyed a dozen rivets at the thought av ut! And sea-biscuit that'd break the teeth av a lion if he had the misfortune to take a bite at one! (*Unconsciously they have all raised their voices, forgetting the sick man in their sailor's delight at finding something to grumble about.*)

PAUL. (*swings his feet over the side of his bunk, stops playing his accordion, and says slowly*) And rot-ten po-tay-toes! (*He starts in playing again. The sick man gives a groan of pain.*)

DRISCOLL. (*holding up his hand*) Shut your mouths, all av you. 'Tis a hell av a thing for us to be complainin' about our guts, and a sick man maybe dyin' listenin' to us. (*Gets up and shakes his fist at the Norwegian*) God stiffen you, ye square-head scut! Put down that organ av yours or I'll break your ugly face for you. Is that banshee schreechin' fit music for a sick man? (*The Norwegian puts his accordion in the bunk and lies back and closes his eyes.* DRISCOLL *goes over and stands beside* YANK. *The steamer's whistle sounds particularly loud in the silence.*)

DAVIS. Damn this fog! (*Reaches in under a bunk and yanks out a pair of sea-boots, which he pulls on*) My lookout next, too. Must be nearly eight bells, boys. (*With the exception of* OLSON, *all the men sitting up put on oilskins, sou'westers, sea-boots, etc., in preparation for the watch on deck.* OLSON *crawls into a lower bunk on the right.*)

SCOTTY. My wheel.

OLSON. (*disgustedly*) Nothin' but yust dirty weather all dis voyage. I yust can't sleep when weestle blow. (*He turns his back to the light and is soon fast asleep and snoring.*)

SCOTTY. If this fog keeps up, I'm tellin' ye, we'll no be in Cardiff for a week or more.

DRISCOLL. 'Twas just such a night as this the auld Dover wint down. Just about this toime ut was, too, and we all sittin' round in the fo'c'stle, Yank beside me, whin all av a suddint we heard a great slitherin' crash, and the ship heeled over till we was all in a heap on wan side. What came afther I disremimber exactly, except 'twas a hard shift to get the boats over the side before the auld teakittle sank. Yank was in the same boat wid me, and sivin morthal days we drifted wid scarcely a drop of wather or a bite to chew on. 'Twas Yank here that held me down whin I wanted to jump into the ocean, roarin' mad wid the thirst. Picked up we were on the same day wid only Yank in his senses, and him steerin' the boat.

COCKY. (*protestingly*) Blimey but you're a cheerful blighter, Driscoll! Talkin' abaht shipwrecks in this 'ere blushin' fog. (YANK *groans and stirs uneasily, opening his eyes.* DRISCOLL *hurries to his side.*)

DRISCOLL. Are ye feelin' any betther, Yank?

YANK. (*in a weak voice*) No.

DRISCOLL. Sure, you must be. You look as sthrong as an ox. (*Appealing to the others*) Am I tellin' him a lie?

DAVIS. The sleep's done you good.

COCKY. You'll be 'avin your pint of beer in Cardiff this day week.

SCOTTY. And fish and chips, mon!

YANK. (*peevishly*) What're yuh all lyin' fur? D'yuh think I'm scared to— (*He hesitates as if frightened by the word he is about to say.*)

DRISCOLL. Don't be thinkin' such things! (*The ship's bell is heard heavily tolling eight times. From the forecastle head above the voice of the lookout rises in a long wail:* Aaall's welll. *The men look uncertainly at* YANK *as if undecided whether to say good-by or not.*)

YANK. (*in an agony of fear*) Don't leave me, Drisc! I'm dyin', I tell yuh. I won't stay here alone with everyone snorin'. I'll go out on deck. (*He makes a feeble attempt to rise, but sinks back with a sharp groan. His breath comes in wheezy gasps*) Don't leave me, Drisc! (*His face grows white and his head falls back with a jerk.*)

DRISCOLL. Don't be worryin', Yank. I'll not move a step out av here —and let that divil av a bosun curse his black head off. You speak a word to the bosun, Cocky. Tell him that Yank is bad took and I'll be stayin' wid him a while yet.

COCKY. Right-o. (COCKY, DAVIS, *and* SCOTTY *go out quietly.*)

COCKY. (*from the alleyway*) Gawd blimey, the fog's thick as soup.

DRISCOLL. Are ye satisfied now, Yank? (*Receiving no answer, he bends over the still form*) He's fainted, God help him! (*He gets a tin dipper from the bucket and bathes* YANK's *forehead with the water.* YANK *shudders and opens his eyes.*)

YANK. (*slowly*) I thought I was goin' then. Wha' did yuh wanta wake me up fur?

DRISCOLL. (*with a forced gayety*) It is wishful for heaven ye are?

YANK. (*gloomily*) Hell, I guess.

DRISCOLL. (*crossing himself involuntarily*) For the love av the saints don't be talkin' loike that! You'd give a man the creeps. It's chippin' rust on deck you'll be in a day or two wid the best av us. (YANK *does not answer, but closes his eyes wearily. The seaman who has been on lookout,* SMITTY, *a young Englishman, comes in and takes off his dripping oilskins. While he is doing this the man whose turn at the wheel has been relieved enters. He is a dark burly fellow with a round stupid face. The Englishman steps softly over to* DRISCOLL. *The other crawls into a lower bunk.*)

SMITTY. (*whispering*) How's Yank?

DRISCOLL. Betther. Ask him yourself. He's awake.

YANK. I'm all right, Smitty.

SMITTY. Glad to hear it, Yank. (*He crawls to an upper bunk and is soon asleep.*)

IVAN. (*the stupid-faced seaman, who comes in after* SMITTY, *twists his head in the direction of the sick man*) You feel gude, Jank?

YANK. (*wearily*) Yes, Ivan.

IVAN. Dot's gude. (*He rolls over on his side and falls asleep immediately.*)

YANK. (*after a pause broken only by snores—with a bitter laugh*) Good-by and good luck to the lot of you!

DRISCOLL. Is ut painin' you again?

YANK. It hurts like hell—here. (*He points to the lower part of his chest on the left side*) I guess my old pump's busted. Ooohh! (*A spasm of pain contracts his pale features. He presses his hand to his side and writhes on the thin mattress of his bunk. The perspiration stands out in beads on his forehead.)*

DRISCOLL. (*terrified*) Yank! Yank! What is ut? (*Jumping to his feet*) I'll run for the captain. (*He starts for the doorway.*)

YANK. (*sitting up in his bunk, frantic with fear*) Don't leave me, Drisc! For God's sake don't leave me alone! (*He leans over the side of his bunk and spits.* DRISCOLL *comes back to him*) Blood! Ugh!

DRISCOLL. Blood again! I'd best be gettin' the captain.

YANK. No, no, don't leave me! If yuh do I'll git up and follow you. I ain't no coward, but I'm scared to stay here with all of them asleep and snorin'. (DRISCOLL, *not knowing what to do, sits down on the bench beside him. He grows calmer and sinks back on the mattress*) The captain can't do me no good, yuh know it yourself. The pain ain't so bad now, but I thought it had me then. It was like a buzz-saw cuttin' into me.

DRISCOLL. (*fiercely*) God blarst ut!

(*The* CAPTAIN *and the* SECOND MATE *of the steamer enter the forecastle. The* CAPTAIN *is an old man with gray mustache and whiskers. The* MATE *is clean-shaven and middle-aged. Both are dressed in simple blue uniforms.*)

THE CAPTAIN. (*taking out his watch and feeling* YANK'S *pulse*) And how is the sick man?

YANK. (*feebly*) All right, sir.

THE CAPTAIN. And the pain in the chest?

YANK. It still hurts, sir, worse than ever.

THE CAPTAIN. (*taking a thermometer from his pocket and putting it into* YANK'S *mouth*) Here. Be sure and keep this in under your tongue, not over it.

THE MATE. (*after a pause*) Isn't this your watch on deck, Driscoll?

DRISCOLL. Yes, sorr, but Yank was fearin' to be alone, and—

THE CAPTAIN. That's all right, Driscoll.

DRISCOLL. Thank ye, sorr.

THE CAPTAIN. (*stares at his watch for a moment or so; then takes the thermometer from* YANK'S *mouth and goes to the lamp to read it. His expression grows very grave. He beckons the* MATE *and* DRISCOLL *to the corner near the doorway.* YANK *watches them furtively. The* CAPTAIN *speaks in a low voice to the* MATE) Way up, both of them. (*To* DRISCOLL) He has been spitting blood again?

DRISCOLL. Not much for the hour just past, sorr, but before that—

THE CAPTAIN. A great deal?

DRISCOLL. Yes, sorr.

THE CAPTAIN. He hasn't eaten anything?

DRISCOLL. No, sorr.

THE CAPTAIN. Did he drink that medicine I sent him?

DRISCOLL. Yes, sorr, but it didn't stay down.

THE CAPTAIN. (*shaking his head*) I'm afraid—he's very weak. I can't do anything else for him. It's too serious for me. If this had only happened a week later we'd be in Cardiff in time to—

DRISCOLL. Plaze help him some way, sorr!

THE CAPTAIN. (*impatiently*) But, my good man, I'm not a doctor. (*More kindly as he sees* DRISCOLL'S *grief*) You and he have been shipmates a long time?

DRISCOLL. Five years and more, sorr.

THE CAPTAIN. I see. Well, don't let him move. Keep him quiet and we'll hope for the best. I'll read the matter up and send him some medicine, something to ease the pain, anyway. (*Goes over to* YANK) Keep up your courage! You'll be better tomorrow. (*He breaks down lamely before* YANK'S *steady gaze*) We'll pull you through all right—and—hm—well—coming, Robinson? Dammit! (*He goes out hurriedly, followed by the* MATE.)

DRISCOLL. (*trying to conceal his anxiety*) Didn't I tell you you wasn't half as sick as you thought you was? The Captain'll have you out on deck cursin' and swearin' loike a trooper before the week is out.

YANK. Don't lie, Drisc. I heard what he said, and if I didn't I c'd tell by the way I feel. I know what's goin' to happen. I'm goin' to—

(*He hesitates for a second—then resolutely*) I'm goin' to die, that's what, and the sooner the better!

DRISCOLL. (*wildly*) No, and be damned to you, you're not. I'll not let you.

YANK. It ain't no use, Drisc. I ain't got a chance, but I ain't scared. Gimme a drink of water, will yuh, Drisc? My throat's burnin' up. (DRISCOLL *brings the dipper full of water and supports his head while he drinks in great gulps.*)

DRISCOLL. (*seeking vainly for some word of comfort*) Are ye feelin' more aisy-loike now?

YANK. Yes—now—when I know it's all up. (*A pause*) You mustn't take it so hard, Drisc. I was just thinkin' it ain't as bad as people think—dyin'. I ain't never took much stock in the truck them sky-pilots preach. I ain't never had religion; but I know whatever it is what comes after it can't be no worser'n this. I don't like to leave you, Drisc, but—that's all.

DRISCOLL. (*with a groan*) Lad, lad, don't be talkin'.

YANK. This sailor life ain't much to cry about leavin'—just one ship after another, hard work, small pay, and bum grub; and when we git into port, just a drunk endin' up in a fight, and all your money gone, and then ship away again. Never meetin' no nice people; never gittin' outa sailor-town, hardly, in any port; travelin' all over the world and never seein' none of it; without no one to care whether you're alive or dead. (*With a bitter smile*) There ain't much in all that that'd make yuh sorry to lose it, Drisc.

DRISCOLL. (*gloomily*) It's a hell av a life, the sea.

YANK. (*musingly*) It must be great to stay on dry land all your life and have a farm with a house of your own with cows and pigs and chickens, 'way in the middle of the land where yuh'd never smell the sea or see a ship. It must be great to have a wife, and kids to play with at night after supper when your work was done. It must be great to have a home of your own, Drisc.

DRISCOLL. (*with a great sigh*) It must, surely; but what's the use av thinkin' av ut? Such things are not for the loikes av us.

YANK. Sea-farin' is all right when you're young and don't care, but we ain't chickens no more, and somehow, I dunno, this last year has seemed rotten, and I've had a hunch I'd quit—with you, of course—and we'd save our coin, and go to Canada or Argentine or some place and git a farm, just a small one, just enough to live on. I never told yuh this, 'cause I thought you'd laugh at me.

DRISCOLL. (*enthusiastically*) Laugh at you, is ut? When I'm havin' the same thoughts myself, toime afther toime. It's a grand idea and we'll be doin' ut sure if you'll stop your crazy notions—about—about bein' so sick.

YANK. (*sadly*) Too late. We shouldn'ta made this trip, and then—How'd all the fog git in here?

DRISCOLL. Fog?

YANK. Everything looks misty. Must be my eyes gittin' weak, I guess. What was we talkin' of a minute ago? Oh, yes, a farm. It's too late. (*His mind wandering*) Argentine, did I say? D'yuh remember the times we've had in Buenos Aires? The moving pictures in Barracas? Some class to them, d'yuh remember?

DRISCOLL. (*with satisfaction*) I do that; and so does the piany player. He'll not be forgettin' the black eye I gave him in a hurry.

YANK. Remember the time we was there on the beach and had to go to Tommy Moore's boarding house to git shipped? And he sold us rotten oilskins and sea-boots full of holes, and shipped us on a skysail-yarder round the Horn, and took two months' pay for it. And the days we used to sit on the park benches along the Paseo Colon with the vigilantes lookin' hard at us? And the songs at the Sailor's Opera where the guy played ragtime—d'yuh remember them?

DRISCOLL. I do, surely.

YANK. And La Plata—phew, the stink of the hides! I always liked

Argentine—all except that booze, caña. How drunk we used to git on that, remember?

DRISCOLL. Cud I forget ut? My head pains me at the menshun av that divil's brew.

YANK. Remember the night I went crazy with the heat in Singapore? And the time you was pinched by the cops in Port Said? And the time we was both locked up in Sydney for fightin'?

DRISCOLL. I do so.

YANK. And that fight on the dock at Cape Town— (*His voice betrays great inward perturbation.*)

DRISCOLL. (*hastily*) Don't be thinkin' av that now. 'Tis past and gone.

YANK. D'yuh think He'll hold it up against me?

DRISCOLL. (*mystified*) Who's that?

YANK. God. They say He sees everything. He must know it was done in fair fight, in self-defense, don't yuh think?

DRISCOLL. Av course. Ye stabbed him, and be damned to him, for the skulkin' swine he was, afther him tryin' to stick you in the back, and you not suspectin'. Let your conscience be aisy. I wisht I had nothin' blacker than that on my sowl. I'd not be afraid av the angel Gabriel himself.

YANK. (*with a shudder*) I c'd see him a minute ago with the blood spurtin' out of his neck. Ugh!

DRISCOLL. The fever, ut is, that makes you see such things. Give no heed to ut.

YANK. (*uncertainly*) You don't think He'll hold it up agin me— God, I mean.

DRISCOLL. If there's justice in hiven, no! (YANK *seems comforted by this assurance.*)

YANK. (*after a pause*) We won't reach Cardiff for a week at least. I'll be buried at sea.

DRISCOLL. (*putting his hands over his ears*) Ssshh! I won't listen to you.

YANK. (*as if he had not heard him*) It's as good a place as any other, I s'pose—only I always wanted to be buried on dry land. But what the hell'll I care—then? (*Fretfully*) Why should it be a rotten night like this with that damned whistle blowin' and people snorin' all round? I wish the stars was out, and the moon, too; I c'd lie out on deck and look at them, and it'd make it easier to go—somehow.

DRISCOLL. For the love av God don't be talkin' loike that!

YANK. Whatever pay's comin' to me yuh can divvy up with the rest of the boys; and you take my watch. It ain't worth much, but it's all I've got.

DRISCOLL. But have you no relations at all to call your own?

YANK. No, not as I know of. One thing I forgot: You know Fanny the barmaid at the Red Stork in Cardiff?

DRISCOLL. Sure, and who doesn't?

YANK. She's been good to me. She tried to lend me half a crown when I was broke there last trip. Buy her the biggest box of candy yuh c'n find in Cardiff. (*Breaking down—in a choking voice*) It's hard to ship on this voyage I'm goin' on—alone! (DRISCOLL *reaches out and grasps his hand. There is a pause, during which both fight to control themselves*) My throat's like a furnace. (*He gasps for air*) Gimme a drink of water, will yuh, Drisc? (DRISCOLL *gets him a dipper of water*) I wish this was a pint of beer. Oooohh! (*He chokes, his face convulsed with agony, his hands tearing at his shirt-front. The dipper falls from his nerveless fingers.*)

DRISCOLL. For the love av God, what is ut, Yank?

YANK. (*speaking with tremendous difficulty*) S'long, Drisc! (*He stares straight in front of him with eyes starting from their sockets*) Who's that?

DRISCOLL. Who? What?

YANK. (*faintly*) A pretty lady dressed in black. (*His face twitches and his body writhes in a final spasm, then straightens out rigidly.*)

DRISCOLL. (*pale with horror*) Yank! Yank! Say a word to me for the love av hiven! (*He shrinks away from the bunk, making the sign of the cross. Then comes back and puts a trembling hand on* YANK'S *chest and bends closely over the body.*)

COCKY. (*from the alleyway*) Oh, Driscoll! Can you leave Yank for arf a mo' and give me a 'and?

DRISCOLL. (*with a great sob*) Yank! (*He sinks down on his knees beside the bunk, his head on his hands. His lips move in some half-remembered prayer.*)

COCKY. (*enters, his oilskins and sou'wester glistening with drops of water*) The fog's lifted. (COCKY *sees* DRISCOLL *and stands staring at him with open mouth.* DRISCOLL *makes the sign of the cross again.*)

COCKY. (*mockingly*) Sayin' 'is prayers! (*He catches sight of the still figure in the bunk and an expression of awed understanding comes over his face. He takes off his dripping sou'wester and stands, scratching his head.*)

COCKY. (*in a hushed whisper*) Gawd blimey!

CURTAIN

THE LONG VOYAGE HOME

A Play in One Act

CHARACTERS

FAT JOE, *proprietor of a dive*

NICK, *a crimp*

MAG, *a barmaid*

OLSON, DRISCOLL, COCKY, IVAN — *seamen of the British tramp steamer* Glencairn

KATE

FREDA

TWO ROUGHS

THE LONG VOYAGE HOME

SCENE. *The bar of a low dive on the London water-front—a squalid, dingy room dimly lighted by kerosene lamps placed in brackets on the walls. On the left, the bar. In front of it, a door leading to a side room. On the right, tables with chairs around them. In the rear, a door leading to the street.*

A slovenly barmaid with a stupid face sodden with drink is mopping off the bar. Her arm moves back and forth mechanically and her eyes are half shut as if she were dozing on her feet. At the far end of the bar stands FAT JOE, *the proprietor, a gross bulk of a man with an enormous stomach. His face is red and bloated, his little piggish eyes being almost concealed by rolls of fat. The thick fingers of his big hands are loaded with cheap rings, and a gold watch-chain of cable-like proportions stretches across his checked waistcoat.*

At one of the tables, front, a round-shouldered young fellow is sitting, smoking a cigarette. His face is pasty, his mouth weak, his eyes shifting and cruel. He is dressed in a shabby suit, which must have once been cheaply flashy, and wears a muffler and a cap.

It is about nine o'clock in the evening.

JOE. (*yawning*) Blimey if bizness ain't 'arf slow tonight. I donnow wot's 'appened. The place is like a bleedin' tomb. Where's all the sailormen, I'd like to know? (*Raising his voice*) Ho, you Nick! (NICK *turns around listlessly*) Wot's the name o' that wessel put in at the dock below jest arter noon?

NICK. (*laconically*) *Glencairn*—from Bewnezerry. [Buenos Aires.]

JOE. Ain't the crew been paid orf yet?

NICK. Paid orf this arternoon, they tole me. I 'opped on board of 'er an' seen 'em. 'Anded 'em some o' yer cards, I did. They promised faithful they'd 'appen in tonight—them as whose time was done.

JOE. Any two-year men to be paid orf?

NICK. Four—three Britishers an' a square-'ead.

JOE. (*indignantly*) An' yer popped orf an' left 'em? An' me a-payin' yer to 'elp an' bring 'em in 'ere!

NICK. (*grumbling*) Much you pays me! An' I ain't slingin' me 'ook abaht the 'ole bleedin' town fur now man. See?

JOE. I ain't speakin' on'y fur meself. Down't I always give yer yer share, fair an' square, as man to man?

NICK. (*with a sneer*) Yus—b'cause you 'as to.

JOE. 'As to? Listen to 'im! There's many'd be 'appy to 'ave your berth, me man!

NICK. Yus? Wot wiv the peelers li'ble to put me away in the bloody jail fur crimpin', an' all?

JOE. (*indignantly*) We down't do no crimpin'.

NICK. (*sarcastically*) Ho, now! Not arf!

JOE. (*a bit embarrassed*) Well, on'y a bit now an' agen when there ain't no reg'lar trade. (*To hide his confusion he turns to the barmaid angrily. She is still mopping off the bar, her chin on her breast, half-asleep*) 'Ere, me gel, we've 'ad enough o' that. You been a-moppin', an' a-moppin', an' a-moppin' the blarsted bar fur a 'ole 'our. 'Op it aht o' this! You'd fair guv a bloke the shakes a-watchin' yer.

MAG. (*beginning to sniffle*) Ow, you do frighten me when you 'oller at me, Joe. I ain't a bad gel, I ain't. Gawd knows I tries to do me best fur you. (*She bursts into a tempest of sobs.*)

JOE. (*roughly*) Stop yer grizzlin'! An' 'op it aht of 'ere!

NICK. (*chuckling*) She's drunk, Joe. Been 'ittin' the gin, eh, Mag?

MAG. (*ceases crying at once and turns on him furiously*) You little crab, you! Orter wear a muzzle, you ort! A-openin' of your ugly mouth to a honest woman what ain't never done you no 'arm. (*Commencing to sob again*) H'abusin' me like a dawg cos I'm sick an' orf me oats, an' all.

JOE. Orf yer go, me gel! Go hupstairs and 'ave a sleep. I'll wake yer if I wants yer. An' wake the two gels when yer goes hup. It's 'arpas' nine an' time as some one was a-comin' in, tell 'em. D'yer 'ear me?

MAG. (*stumbling around the bar to the door on left—sobbing*) Yus, yus, I 'ears you. Gawd knows wot's goin' to 'appen to me, I'm that sick. Much you cares if I dies, down't you? (*She goes out.*)

JOE. (*still brooding over* NICK'S *lack of diligence—after a pause*) Four two-year men paid orf wiv their bloody pockets full o' sovereigns —an' yer lorst 'em. (*He shakes his head sorrowfully.*)

NICK. (*impatiently*) Stow it! They promised faithful they'd come, I tells yer. They'll be walkin' in in 'arf a mo'. There's lots o' time yet. (*In a low voice*) 'Ave yer got the drops? We might wanter use 'em.

JOE. (*taking a small bottle from behind the bar*) Yus; 'ere it is.

NICK. (*with satisfaction*) Righto! (*His shifty eyes peer about the room searchingly. Then he beckons to* JOE, *who comes over to the table and sits down*) Reason I arst yer about the drops was 'cause I seen the capt'n of the *Amindra* this arternoon.

JOE. The *Amindra?* Wot ship is that?

NICK. Bloody windjammer—skys'l-yarder—full-rigged—painted white—been layin' at the dock above 'ere fur a month. You knows 'er.

JOE. Ho, yus. I knows now.

NICK. The capt'n says as 'e wants a man special bad—ter-night. They sails at daybreak ter-morrer.

JOE. There's plenty o' 'ands lyin' abaht waitin' fur ships, I should fink.

NICK. Not fur this ship, ole buck. The capt'n an' mate are bloody slave-drivers, an' they're bound down round the 'Orn. They 'arf starved the 'ands on the larst trip 'ere, an' no one'll dare ship on 'er. (*After a pause*) I promised the capt'n faithful I'd get 'im one, and ter-night.

JOE. (*doubtfully*) An' 'ow are yer goin' to git 'im?

NICK. (*with a wink*) I was thinkin' as one of 'em from the *Glencairn*'d do—them as was paid orf an' is comin' 'ere.

JOE. (*with a grin*) It'd be a good 'aul, that's the troof. (*Frowning*) If they comes 'ere.

NICK. They'll come, an' they'll all be rotten drunk, wait an' see. (*There is the noise of loud, boisterous singing from the street*) Sounds like 'em, now. (*He opens the street door and looks out*) Gawd blimey if it ain't the four of 'em! (*Turning to* JOE *in triumph*) Naw, what d'yer say? They're lookin' for the place. I'll go aht an' tell 'em. (*He goes out.* JOE *gets into position behind the bar, assuming his most oily smile. A moment later the door is opened, admitting* DRISCOLL, COCKY, IVAN *and* OLSON. DRISCOLL *is a tall, powerful Irishman;* COCKY, *a wizened runt of a man with a straggling gray mustache;* IVAN, *a hulking oaf of a peasant;* OLSON, *a stocky, middle-aged Swede with round, childish blue eyes. The first three are all very drunk, especially* IVAN, *who is managing his legs with difficulty.* OLSON *is perfectly sober. All are dressed in their ill-fitting shore clothes and look very uncomfortable.* DRISCOLL *has unbuttoned his stiff collar and its ends stick out sideways. He has lost his tie.* NICK *slinks into the room after them and sits down at a table in rear. The seamen come to the table, front.*)

JOE. (*with affected heartiness*) Ship ahoy, mates! 'Appy to see yer 'ome safe an' sound.

DRISCOLL. (*turns round, swaying a bit, and peers at him across the bar*) So ut's you, is ut? (*He looks about the place with an air of recognition*) 'An the same damn rat's-hole, sure enough. I remimber foive or six years back 'twas here I was sthripped av me last shillin' whin I was aslape. (*With sudden fury*) God stiffen ye, come none av your dog's thricks on me this trip or I'll— (*He shakes his fist at* JOE.)

JOE. (*hastily interrupting*) Yer must be mistaken. This is a honest place, this is.

COCKY. (*derisively*) Ho, yus! An' you're a bleedin' angel, I s'pose?

IVAN. (*vaguely taking off his derby hat and putting it on again—plaintively*) I don' li-ike dis place.

DRISCOLL. (*going over to the bar—as genial as he was furious a moment before*) Well, no matther, 'tis all past an' gone an' forgot. I'm not the man to be holdin' harrd feelin's on me first night ashore, an' me dhrunk as a lord. (*He holds out his hand, which* JOE *takes very gingerly*) We'll all be havin' a dhrink, I'm thinkin'. Whiskey for the three av us—*Irish* whiskey!

COCKY. (*mockingly*) An' a glarse o' ginger beer fur our blarsted love-child 'ere. (*He jerks his thumb at* OLSON.)

OLSON. (*with a good-natured grin*) I bane a good boy dis night, for one time.

DRISCOLL. (*bellowing, and pointing to* NICK *as* JOE *brings the drinks to the table*) An' see what that crimpin' son av a crimp'll be wantin' —an' have your own pleasure. (*He pulls a sovereign out of his pocket and slams it on the bar.*)

NICK. Guv me a pint o' beer, Joe. (JOE *draws the beer and takes it down to the far end of the bar.* NICK *comes over to get it and* JOE *gives him a significant wink and nods toward the door on the left.* NICK *signals back that he understands.*)

COCKY. (*drink in hand—impatiently*) I'm that bloody dry! (*Lifting his glass to* DRISCOLL) Cheero, ole dear, cheero!

DRISCOLL. (*pocketing his change without looking at it*) A toast for ye: Hell roast that divil av a bo'sun! (*He drinks.*)

COCKY. Righto! Gawd strike 'im blind! (*He drains his glass.*)

IVAN. (*half-asleep*) Dot's gude. (*He tosses down his drink in one gulp.* OLSON *sips his ginger ale.* NICK *takes a swallow of his beer and then comes round the bar and goes out the door on left.*)

COCKY. (*producing a sovereign*) Ho there, you Fatty! Guv us another!

JOE. The saime, mates?

COCKY. Yus.

DRISCOLL. No, ye scut! I'll be havin' a pint av beer. I'm dhry as a loime kiln.

IVAN. (*suddenly getting to his feet in a befuddled manner and nearly upsetting the table*) I don' li-ike dis place! I wan' see girls—plenty girls. (*Pathetically*) I don' li-ike dis place. I wan' dance with girl.

DRISCOLL. (*pushing him back on his chair with a thud*) Shut up, ye Rooshan baboon! A foine Romeo you'd make in your condishun. (IVAN *blubbers some incoherent protest—then suddenly falls asleep.*)

JOE. (*bringing the drinks—looks at* OLSON) An' you, matey?

OLSON. (*shaking his head*) Noting dis time, thank you.

COCKY. (*mockingly*) A-savin' of 'is money, 'e is! Goin' back to 'ome an' mother. Goin' to buy a bloomin' farm an' punch the blarsted dirt, that's wot 'e is! (*Spitting disgustedly*) There's a funny bird of a sailorman for yer, Gawd blimey!

OLSON. (*wearing the same good-natured grin*) Yust what I like, Cocky. I wus on farm long time when I wus kid.

DRISCOLL. Lave him alone, ye bloody insect! 'Tis a foine sight to see a man wid some sense in his head instead av a damn fool the loike av us. I only wisht I'd a mother alive to call me own. I'd not be dhrunk in this divil's hole this minute, maybe.

COCKY. (*commencing to weep dolorously*) Ow, down't talk, Drisc! I can't bear to 'ear you. I ain't never 'ad no mother, I ain't—

DRISCOLL. Shut up, ye ape, an' don't be makin' that squealin'. If ye cud see your ugly face, wid the big red nose av ye all screwed up in a knot, ye'd never shed a tear the rist av your loife. (*Roaring into song*) We ar're the byes av We-e-exford who fought wid hearrt an' hand! (*Speaking*) To hell wid Ulster! (*He drinks and the others follow his example*) An' I'll strip to any man in the city av London won't dhrink to that toast. (*He glares truculently at* JOE, *who immediately downs his beer.* NICK *enters again from the door on the left and comes up to* JOE *and whispers in his ear. The latter nods with satisfaction.*)

DRISCOLL. (*glowering at them*) What divil's thrick are ye up to now, the two av ye? (*He flourishes a brawny fist*) Play fair wid us or ye deal wid me!

JOE. (*hastily*) No trick, shipmate! May Gawd kill me if that ain't troof!

NICK. (*indicating* IVAN, *who is snoring*) On'y your mate there was arskin' fur gels an' I thorght as 'ow yer'd like 'em to come dawhn and 'ave a wet wiv yer.

JOE. (*with a smirking wink*) Pretty, 'olesome gels they be, ain't they, Nick?

NICK. Yus.

COCKY. Aar! I knows the gels you 'as, not 'arf! They'd fair blind yer, they're that 'omely. None of yer bloomin' gels fur me, ole Fatty. Me an' Drisc knows a place, down't we, Drisc?

DRISCOLL. Divil a lie, we do. An' we'll be afther goin' there in a minute. There's music there an' a bit av a dance to liven a man.

JOE. Nick, 'ere, can play yer a tune, can't yer, Nick?

NICK. Yus.

JOE. An' yer can 'ave a dance in the side room 'ere.

DRISCOLL. Hurroo! Now you're talkin'. (*The two women,* FREDA *and* KATE, *enter from the left.* FREDA *is a little, sallow-faced blonde.* KATE *is stout and dark.*)

COCKY. (*in a loud aside to* DRISCOLL) Gawd blimey, look at 'em! Ain't they 'orrible? (*The women come forward to the table, wearing their best set smiles.*)

FREDA. (*in a raspy voice*) 'Ullo, mates.

KATE. 'Ad a good voyage?

DRISCOLL. Rotten; but no matther. Welcome, as the sayin' is, an' sit down, an' what'll ye be takin' for your thirst? (*To* KATE) You'll be sittin' by me, darlin'—what's your name?

KATE. (*with a stupid grin*) Kate. (*She stands by his chair.*)

DRISCOLL. (*putting his arm around her*) A good Irish name, but you're English by the trim av ye, an' be damned to you. But no matther. Ut's fat ye are, Katy dear, an' I never cud endure skinny wimin. (FREDA *favors him with a viperish glance and sits down by* OLSON) What'll ye have?

OLSON. No, Drisc. Dis one bane on me. (*He takes out a roll of notes from his inside pocket and lays one on the table.* JOE, NICK, *and the women look at the money with greedy eyes.* IVAN *gives a particularly violent snore.*)

FREDA. Waike up your fren'. Gawd, 'ow I 'ates to 'ear snorin'.

DRISCOLL. (*springing to action, smashes* IVAN'S *derby over his ears*) D'you hear the lady talkin' to ye, ye Rooshan swab? (*The only reply to this is a snore.* DRISCOLL *pulls the battered remains of the derby off* IVAN'S *head and smashes it back again*) Arise an' shine, ye dhrunken swine! (*Another snore. The women giggle.* DRISCOLL *throws the beer left in his glass into* IVAN'S *face. The Russian comes to in a flash, spluttering. There is a roar of laughter.*)

IVAN. (*indignantly*) I tell you—dot's someting I don' li-ike!

COCKY. Down't waste good beer, Drisc.

IVAN. (*grumblingly*) I tell you—dot is not ri-ight.

DRISCOLL. Ut's your own doin', Ivan. Ye was moanin' for girrls an' whin they come you sit gruntin' loike a pig in a sty. Have ye no manners? (IVAN *seems to see the women for the first time and grins foolishly.*)

KATE. (*laughing at him*) Cheero, ole chum, 'ows Russha?

IVAN. (*greatly pleased—putting his hand in his pocket*) I buy a drink.

OLSON. No; dis one bane on me. (*To* JOE) Hey, you faller!

JOE. Wot'll it be, Kate?

KATE. Gin.

FREDA. Brandy.

DRISCOLL. An' Irish whiskey for the rist av us—wid the excipshun av our timperance friend, God pity him!

FREDA. (*to* OLSON) You ain't drinkin'?

OLSON. (*half-ashamed*) No.

FREDA. (*with a seductive smile*) I down't blame yer. You got sense, you 'ave. I on'y tike a nip o' brandy now an' agen fur my 'ealth. (JOE *brings the drinks and* OLSON's *change.* COCKY *gets unsteadily to his feet and raises his glass in the air.*)

COCKY. 'Ere's a toff toast for yer: The ladies, Gawd— (*He hesitates—then adds in a grudging tone*)—bless 'em.

KATE. (*with a silly giggle*) Oo-er! That wasn't what you was goin' to say, you bad Cocky, you! (*They all drink.*)

DRISCOLL. (*to* NICK) Where's the tune ye was promisin' to give us?

NICK. Come ahn in the side 'ere an' you'll 'ear it.

DRISCOLL. (*getting up*) Come on, all av ye. We'll have a tune an' a dance if I'm not too dhrunk to dance, God help me. (COCKY *and* IVAN *stagger to their feet.* IVAN *can hardly stand. He is leering at* KATE *and snickering to himself in a maudlin fashion. The three, led by* NICK, *go out the door on the left.* KATE *follows them.* OLSON *and* FREDA *remain seated.*)

COCKY. (*calling over his shoulder*) Come on an' dance, Ollie.

OLSON. Yes, I come. (*He starts to get up. From the side room comes the sound of an accordion and a boisterous whoop from* DRISCOLL, *followed by a heavy stamping of feet.*)

FREDA. Ow, down't go in there. Stay 'ere an' 'ave a talk wiv me. They're all drunk an' you ain't drinkin'. (*With a smile up into his face*) I'll think yer don't like me if yer goes in there.

OLSON. (*confused*) You wus wrong, Miss Freda. I don't—I mean I do like you.

FREDA. (*smiling—puts her hand over his on the table*) An' I likes you. Yer a gentleman. You don't get drunk an' hinsult poor gels wot 'as a 'ard an' uneppy life.

OLSON. (*pleased but still more confused—wriggling his feet*) I bane drunk many time, Miss Freda.

FREDA. Then why ain't yer drinkin' now? (*She exchanges a quick, questioning glance with* JOE, *who nods back at her—then she continues persuasively*) Tell me somethin' abaht yeself.

OLSON. (*with a grin*) There ain't noting to say, Miss Freda. I bane poor devil sailorman, dat's all.

FREDA. Where was you born—Norway? (OLSON *shakes his head*) Denmark?

OLSON. No. You guess once more.

FREDA. Then it must be Sweden.

OLSON. Yes. I wus born in Stockholm.

FREDA. (*pretending great delight*) Ow, ain't that funny! I was born there, too—in Stockholm.

OLSON. (*astonished*) You wus born in Sweden?

FREDA. Yes; you wouldn't think it, but it's Gawd's troof. (*She claps her hands delightedly.*)

OLSON. (*beaming all over*) You speak Swedish?

FREDA. (*trying to smile sadly*) No. Y'see my ole man an' woman come 'ere to England when I was on'y a baby an' they was speakin' English b'fore I was old enough to learn. Sow I never knew Swedish. (*Sadly*) Wisht I 'ad! (*With a smile*) We'd 'ave a bloomin' lark of it if I 'ad, wouldn't we?

OLSON. It sound nice to hear the old talk yust once in a time.

FREDA. Righto! No place like yer 'ome, I says. Are yer goin' up to —to Stockholm b'fore yer ships away agen?

OLSON. Yes. I go home from here to Stockholm. (*Proudly*) As passenger!

FREDA. An' you'll git another ship up there arter you've 'ad a vacation?

OLSON. No. I don't never ship on sea no more. I got all sea I want for my life—too much hard work for little money. Yust work, work, work on ship. I don't want more.

FREDA. Ow, I see. That's why you give up drinkin'.

OLSON. Yes. (*With a grin*) If I drink I yust get drunk and spend all money.

FREDA. But if you ain't gointer be a sailor no more, what'll yer do? You been a sailor all yer life, ain't yer?

OLSON. No. I work on farm till I am eighteen. I like it, too—it's nice—work on farm.

FREDA. But ain't Stockholm a city same's London? Ain't no farms there, is there?

OLSON. We live—my brother and mother live—my father iss dead —on farm yust a little way from Stockholm. I have plenty money, now. I go back with two years' pay and buy more land yet; work on farm. (*Grinning*) No more sea, no more bum grub, no more storms—yust nice work.

FREDA. Ow, ain't that luv'ly! I s'pose you'll be gittin' married, too?

OLSON. (*very much confused*) I don't know. I like to, if I find nice girl, maybe.

FREDA. Ain't yer got some gel back in Stockholm? I bet yer 'as.

OLSON. No. I got nice girl once before I go on sea. But I go on ship, and I don't come back, and she marry other faller. (*He grins sheepishly.*)

FREDA. Well, it's nice for yer to be goin' 'ome, anyway.

OLSON. Yes. I tank so. (*There is a crash from the room on left and the music abruptly stops. A moment later* COCKY *and* DRISCOLL *appear, supporting the inert form of* IVAN *between them. He is in the last stage of intoxication, unable to move a muscle.* NICK *follows them and sits down at the table in rear.*)

DRISCOLL. (*as they zigzag up to the bar*) Ut's dead he is, I'm thinkin', for he's as limp as a blarsted corpse.

COCKY. (*puffing*) Gawd, 'e ain't 'arf 'eavy!

DRISCOLL. (*slapping* IVAN'S *face with his free hand*) Wake up, ye divil, ye. Ut's no use. Gabriel's trumpet itself cudn't rouse him. (*To* JOE) Give us a dhrink, for I'm perishing wid the thirst. 'Tis harrd worrk, this.

JOE. Whiskey?

DRISCOLL. *Irish* whiskey, ye swab. (*He puts down a coin on the bar.* JOE *serves* COCKY *and* DRISCOLL. *They drink and then swerve over to* OLSON'S *table.*)

OLSON. Sit down and rest for time, Drisc.

DRISCOLL. No, Ollie, we'll be takin' this lad home to his bed. Ut's late for wan so young to be out in the night. An' I'd not trust him in this hole as dhrunk as he is, an' him wid a full pay day on him. (*Shaking his fist at* JOE) Oho, I know your games, me sonny bye!

JOE. (*with an air of grievance*) There ye goes again—hinsultin' a honest man!

COCKY. Ho, listen to 'im! Guv 'im a shove in the marf, Drisc.

OLSON. (*anxious to avoid a fight—getting up*) I help you take Ivan to boarding house.

FREDA. (*protestingly*) Ow, you ain't gointer leave me, are yer? An' we 'avin' sech a nice talk, an' all.

DRISCOLL. (*with a wink*) Ye hear what the lady says, Ollie. Ye'd best stay here, me timperance lady's man. An' we need no help. 'Tis only a bit av a way and we're two strong men if we are dhrunk. Ut's no hard shift to take the remains home. But ye can open the door for us, Ollie. (OLSON *goes to the door and opens it*) Come on, Cocky, an' don't be fallin' aslape yourself. (*They lurch toward the door. As they go out* DRISCOLL *shouts back over his shoulder*) We'll be comin' back in a short time, surely. So wait here for us, Ollie.

OLSON. All right. I wait here, Drisc. (*He stands in the doorway uncertainly.* JOE *makes violent signs to* FREDA *to bring him back. She goes over and puts her arms around* OLSON'S *shoulder.* JOE *motions to* NICK *to come to the bar. They whisper together excitedly.*)

FREDA. (*coaxingly*) You ain't gointer leave me, are yer, dearie? (*Then irritably*) Fur Gawd's sake, shet that door! I'm fair freezin' to death wiv the fog. (OLSON *comes to himself with a start and shuts the door.*)

OLSON. (*humbly*) Excuse me, Miss Freda.

FREDA. (*leading him back to the table—coughing*) Buy me a drink o' brandy, will yer? I'm sow cold.

OLSON. All you want, Miss Freda, all you want. (*To* JOE, *who is still whispering instructions to* NICK) Hey, Yoe! Brandy for Miss Freda. (*He lays a coin on the table.*)

JOE. Righto! (*He pours out her drink and brings it to the table*) 'Avin' somethink yeself, shipmate?

OLSON. No. I don' tank so. (*He points to his glass with a grin*) Dis iss only belly-wash, no? (*He laughs.*)

JOE. (*hopefully*) 'Ave a man's drink.

OLSON. I would like to—but no. If I drink one I want drink one tousand. (*He laughs again.*)

FREDA. (*Responding to a vicious nudge from* JOE'S *elbow*) Ow, tike somethin'. I ain't gointer drink all be meself.

OLSON. Den give me a little yinger beer—small one. (JOE *goes back of the bar, making a sign to* NICK *to go to their table.* NICK *does so and stands so that the sailor cannot see what* JOE *is doing.*)

NICK. (*to make talk*) Where's yer mates popped orf ter? (JOE *pours the contents of the little bottle into* OLSON'S *glass of ginger beer.*)

OLSON. Dey take Ivan, dat drunk faller, to bed. They come back. (JOE *brings* OLSON'S *drink to the table and sets it before him.*)

JOE. (*to* NICK—*angrily*) 'Op it, will yer? There ain't no time to be dawdlin'. See? 'Urry!

NICK. Don't worry, ole bird, I'm orf. (*He hurries out the door.* JOE *returns to his place behind the bar.*)

OLSON. (*after a pause—worriedly*) I tank I should go after dem. Cocky iss very drunk, too, and Drisc—

FREDA. Aar! The big Irish is all right! Don't yer 'ear 'im say as 'ow they'd surely come back 'ere, an' fur you to wait fur 'em?

OLSON. Yes; but if dey don't come soon I tank I go see if dey are in boarding house all right.

FREDA. Where is the boardin' 'ouse?

OLSON. Yust little way back from street here.

FREDA. You stayin' there, too?

OLSON. Yes—until steamer sail for Stockholm—in two day.

FREDA. (*she is alternately looking at* JOE *and feverishly trying to keep* OLSON *talking so he will forget about going away after the others*) Yer mother won't be arf glad to see yer agen, will she? (OLSON *smiles*) Does she know yer comin'?

OLSON. No. I tought I would yust give her surprise. I write to her from Bonos Eres but I don't tell her I come home.

FREDA. Must be old, ain't she, yer ole lady?

OLSON. She iss eighty-two. (*He smiles reminiscently*) You know, Miss Freda, I don't see my mother or my brother in—let me tank— (*He counts laboriously on his fingers*) must be more than ten year. I write once in while and she write many time; and my brother he write me, too. My mother say in all letter I should come home right away. My brother he write same ting, too. He want me to help him on farm. I write back always I come soon; and I mean all time to go back home at end of voyage. But I come ashore, I take one drink, I take many drinks, I get drunk, I spend all money, I have to ship away for other voyage. So dis time I say to myself: Don't drink one drink, Ollie, or, sure, you don't get home. And I want go home dis time. I feel homesick for farm and to see my people again. (*He smiles*) Yust like little boy, I feel homesick. Dat's why I don't drink noting tonight but dis—belly-wash! (*He roars with childish laughter, then suddenly becomes serious*) You know, Miss Freda, my mother get very old, and I want see her. She might die and I would never—

FREDA. (*moved a lot in spite of herself*) Ow, don't talk like that! I jest 'ates to 'ear anyone speakin' abaht dyin'. (*The door to the street is opened and* NICK *enters, followed by two rough-looking, shabbily-dressed men, wearing mufflers, with caps pulled down over their eyes. They sit at the table nearest to the door.* JOE *brings them three beers, and there is a whispered consultation, with many glances in the direction of* OLSON.)

OLSON. (*starting to get up—worriedly*) I tank I go round to boarding house. I tank someting go wrong with Drisc and Cocky.

FREDA. Ow, down't go. They kin take care of theyselves. They ain't babies. Wait 'arf a mo'. You ain't 'ad yer drink yet.

JOE (*coming hastily over to the table, indicates the men in the rear with a jerk of his thumb*) One of them blokes wants yer to 'ave a wet wiv 'im.

FREDA. Righto! (*To* OLSON) Let's drink this. (*She raises her glass. He does the same*) 'Ere's a toast fur yer: Success to yer bloomin' farm an' may yer live long an' 'appy on it. Skoal! (*She tosses down her brandy. He swallows half his glass of ginger beer and makes a wry face.*)

OLSON. Skoal! (*He puts down his glass.*)

FREDA. (*with feigned indignation*) Down't yer like my toast?

OLSON. (*grinning*) Yes. It iss very kind, Miss Freda.

FREDA. Then drink it all like I done.

OLSON. Well— (*He gulps down the rest*) Dere! (*He laughs.*)

FREDA. Done like a sport!

ONE OF THE TOUGHS. (*with a laugh*) *Amindra,* ahoy!

NICK (*warningly*) Sssshh!

OLSON. (*turns around in his chair*) *Amindra?* Iss she in port? I sail on her once long time ago—three mast, full rig, skys'l-yarder? Iss dat ship you mean?

THE ROUGH. (*grinning*) Yus; right you are.

OLSON. (*angrily*) I know dat damn ship—worst ship dat sail to sea. Rotten grub and dey make you work all time—and the Captain and Mate wus Bluenose devils. No sailor who know anyting ever ship on her. Where iss she bound from here?

THE ROUGH. Round Cape 'Orn—sails at daybreak.

OLSON. Py yingo, I pity poor fallers make dat trip round Cape Stiff dis time year. I bet you some of dem never see port once again. (*He passes his hand over his eyes in a dazed way. His voice grows weaker*) Py golly, I feel dizzy. All the room go round and round like I wus drunk. (*He gets weakly to his feet*) Good-night, Miss Freda. I bane feeling sick. Tell Drisc—I go home. (*He takes a step forward and suddenly collapses over a chair, rolls to the floor, and lies there unconscious.*)

JOE (*from behind the bar*) Quick, nawh! (NICK *darts forward with* JOE *following.* FREDA *is already beside the unconscious man and has taken the roll of money from his inside pocket. She strips off a note furtively and shoves it into her bosom, trying to conceal her action, but* JOE *sees her. She hands the roll to* JOE, *who pockets it.* NICK *goes through all the other pockets and lays a handful of change on the table.*)

JOE. (*impatiently*) 'Urry, 'urry 'an't yer? The other blokes'll be 'ere in 'arf a mo'. (*The two roughs come forward*) 'Ere, you two, tike 'im in under the arms like 'e was drunk. (*They do so*) Tike 'im to the *Amindra*—yer knows that, don't yer?—two docks above. Nick'll show yer. An' you, Nick, down't yer leave the bleedin' ship till the capt'n guvs yer this bloke's advance—full month's pay—five quid, d'yer 'ear?

NICK. I knows me bizness, ole bird. (*They support* OLSON *to the door.*)

THE ROUGH. (*as they are going out*) This silly bloke'll 'ave the s'prise of 'is life when 'e wakes up on board of 'er. (*They laugh. The door closes behind them.* FREDA *moves quickly for the door on the left but* JOE *gets in her way and stops her.*)

JOE. (*threateningly*) Guv us what yer took!

FREDA. Took? I guv yer all 'e 'ad.

JOE. Yer a liar! I seen yer a-playin' yer sneakin' tricks, but yer can't fool Joe. I'm too old a 'and. (*Furiously*) Guv it to me, yer bloody cow! (*He grabs her by the arm.*)

FREDA. Lemme alone! I ain't got no—

JOE. (*hits her viciously on the side of the jaw. She crumples up on the floor*) That'll learn yer! (*He stoops down and fumbles in her bosom and pulls out the banknote, which he stuffs into his pocket with a grunt of satisfaction.* KATE *opens the door on the left and looks in—then rushes to* FREDA *and lifts her head up in her arms.*)

KATE. (*gently*) Pore dearie! (*Looking at* JOE *angrily*) Been 'ittin' 'er agen, 'ave yer, yer cowardly swine!

JOE. Yus; an' I'll 'it you, too, if yer don't keep yer marf shut. Tike 'er aht of 'ere! (KATE *carries* FREDA *into the next room.* JOE *goes behind the bar. A moment later the outer door is opened and* DRISCOLL *and* COCKY *come in.*)

DRISCOLL. Come on, Ollie. (*He suddenly sees that* OLSON *is not there, and turns to* JOE) Where is ut he's gone to?

JOE. (*with a meaning wink*) 'E an' Freda went aht t'gether 'bout five minutes past. 'E's fair gone on 'er, 'e is.

DRISCOLL. (*with a grin*) Oho, so that's ut, is ut? Who'd think Ollie'd be sich a divil wid the wimin? 'Tis lucky he's sober or she'd have him stripped to his last ha'penny. (*Turning to* COCKY, *who is blinking sleepily*) What'll ye have, ye little scut? (*To* JOE) Give me whiskey, *Irish* whiskey!

CURTAIN

IN THE ZONE

A Play in One Act

CHARACTERS

SMITTY DAVIS SWANSON SCOTTY IVAN PAUL JACK DRISCOLL COCKY	*seamen on the British tramp steamer* Glencairn

IN THE ZONE

SCENE. *The seamen's forecastle. On the right above the bunks three or four portholes covered with black cloth can be seen. On the floor near the doorway is a pail with a tin dipper. A lantern in the middle of the floor, turned down very low, throws a dim light around the place. Five men,* SCOTTY, IVAN, SWANSON, SMITTY *and* PAUL, *are in their bunks apparently asleep. It is about ten minutes of twelve on a night in the fall of the year 1915.*

SMITTY *turns slowly in his bunk and, leaning out over the side, looks from one to another of the men as if to assure himself that they are asleep. Then he climbs carefully out of his bunk and stands in the middle of the forecastle fully dressed, but in his stocking feet, glancing around him suspiciously. Reassured, he leans down and cautiously pulls out a suitcase from under the bunks in front of him.*

Just at this moment DAVIS *appears in the doorway, carrying a large steaming coffee-pot in his hand. He stops short when he sees* SMITTY. *A puzzled expression comes over his face, followed by one of suspicion, and he retreats farther back in the alleyway, where he can watch* SMITTY *without being seen.*

All the latter's movements indicate a fear of discovery. He takes out a small bunch of keys and unlocks the suitcase, making a slight noise as he does so. SCOTTY *wakes up and peers at him over the side of the bunk.* SMITTY *opens the suitcase and takes out a small black tin box, carefully places this under his mattress, shoves the suitcase back under the bunk, climbs into his bunk again, closes his eyes and begins to snore loudly.*

DAVIS *enters the forecastle, places the coffee-pot beside the lantern, and goes from one to the other of the sleepers and shakes them vigorously, saying to each in a low voice:* Near eight bells, Scotty. Arise and shine, Swanson. Eight bells, Ivan. SMITTY *yawns loudly with a great pretense of having been dead asleep. All of the rest of the men tumble out of their bunks, stretching and gaping, and commence to pull on their shoes. They go one by one to the cupboard near the open door, take out their cups and spoons, and sit down together on the benches. The coffee-pot is passed around. They munch their biscuits and sip their coffee in dull silence.*

DAVIS. (*suddenly jumping to his feet—nervously*) Where's that air comin' from? (*All are startled and look at him wonderingly.*)

SWANSON. (*a squat, surly-faced Swede—grumpily*) What air? I don't feel nothing.

DAVIS. (*excitedly*) I kin feel it—a draft. (*He stands on the bench and looks around—suddenly exploding*) Damn fool square-head! (*He leans over the upper bunk in which* PAUL *is sleeping and slams the porthole shut*) I got a good notion to report him. Serve him bloody well right! What's the use o' blindin' the ports when that thick-head goes an' leaves 'em open?

SWANSON. (*yawning—too sleepy to be aroused by anything—carelessly*) Dey don't see what little light go out yust one port.

SCOTTY. (*protestingly*) Dinna be a loon, Swanson! D'ye no ken the dangerr o' showin' a licht wi' a pack o' submarrines lyin' aboot?

IVAN. (*shaking his shaggy ox-like head in an emphatic affirmative*) Dot's right, Scotty. I don't li-ike blow up, no, by devil!

SMITTY. (*his manner slightly contemptuous*) I don't think there's much danger of meeting any of their submarines, not until we get into the war zone, at any rate.

DAVIS (*he and* SCOTTY *look at* SMITTY *suspiciously—harshly*) You don't, eh? (*He lowers his voice and speaks slowly*) Well, we're in the war zone right this minit if you wants to know. (*The effect of this speech is instantaneous. All sit bolt upright on their benches and stare at* DAVIS.)

SMITTY. How do you know, Davis?

DAVIS. (*angrily*) 'Cos Drisc heard the First send the Third below to wake the skipper when we fetched the zone—'bout five bells, it was. Now whata y' got to say?

SMITTY. (*conciliatingly*) Oh, I wasn't doubting your word, Davis; but you know they're not pasting up bulletins to let the crew know when the zone is reached—especially on ammunition ships like this.

IVAN. (*decidedly*) I don't li-ike dees voyage. Next time I ship on windjammer Boston to River Plate, load with wood only so it float, by golly!

SWANSON. (*fretfully*) I hope British navy blow 'em to hell, those submarines, py damn!

SCOTTY. (*looking at* SMITTY, *who is staring at the doorway in a dream, his chin on his hands. Meaningly*) It is no the submarrines only we've to fear, I'm thinkin'.

DAVIS (*assenting eagerly*) That's no lie, Scotty.

SWANSON. You mean the mines?

SCOTTY. I wasna thinkin' o' mines eitherr.

DAVIS. There's many a good ship blown up and at the bottom of the sea, what never hit no mine or torpedo.

SCOTTY. Did ye neverr read of the Gerrman spies and the dirrty work they're doin' all the war? (*He and* DAVIS *both glance at* SMITTY, *who is deep in thought and is not listening to the conversation.*)

DAVIS. An' the clever way they fool you!

SWANSON. Sure; I read it in paper many time.

DAVIS. Well—(*he is about to speak, but hesitates and finishes lamely*) You got to watch out, that's all I says.

IVAN. (*drinking the last of his coffee and slamming his fist on the bench explosively*) I tell you dis rotten coffee give me belly-ache, yes! (*They all look at him in amused disgust.*)

SCOTTY. (*sardonically*) Dinna fret about it, Ivan. If we blow up ye'll no be mindin' the pain in your middle. (JACK *enters. He is a young American with a tough, good-natured face. He wears dungarees and a heavy jersey.*)

JACK. Eight bells, fellers.

IVAN. (*stupidly*) I don't hear bell ring.

JACK. No, and yuh won't hear any ring, yuh boob—(*lowering his voice unconsciously*) now we're in the war zone.

SWANSON. (*anxiously*) Is the boats all ready?

JACK. Sure; we can lower 'em in a second.

DAVIS. A lot o' good the boats'll do, with us loaded deep with all kinds o' dynamite and stuff the like o' that! If a torpedo hits this hooker we'll all be in hell b'fore you could wink your eye.

JACK. They ain't goin' to hit us, see? That's my dope. Whose wheel is it?

IVAN. (*sullenly*) My wheel. (*He lumbers out.*)

JACK. And whose lookout?

SWANSON. Mine, I tink. (*He follows* IVAN.)

JACK. (*scornfully*) A hell of a lot of use keepin' a lookout! We couldn't run away or fight if we wanted to. (*To* SCOTTY *and* SMITTY) Better look up the bo'sun or the Fourth, you two, and let 'em see you're awake. (SCOTTY *goes to the doorway and turns to wait for* SMITTY, *who is still in the same position, head on hands, seemingly unconscious of everything.* JACK *slaps him roughly on the shoulder and he comes to with a start*) Aft and report, Duke! What's the matter with yuh—in a dope dream? (SMITTY *goes out after* SCOTTY *without answering.* JACK *looks after him with a frown*) He's a queer guy. I can't figger him out.

DAVIS. Nor no one else. (*Lowering his voice—meaningly*) An' he's liable to turn out queerer than any of us think if we ain't careful.

JACK. (*suspiciously*) What d'yuh mean? (*They are interrupted by the entrance of* DRISCOLL *and* COCKY.)

COCKY. (*protestingly*) Blimey if I don't fink I'll put in this 'ere watch ahtside on deck. (*He and* DRISCOLL *go over and get their cups*) I down't want to be caught in this 'ole if they 'its us. (*He pours out coffee.*)

DRISCOLL. (*pouring his*) Divil a bit ut wud matther where ye arre.

Ye'd be blown to smithereens b'fore ye cud say your name. (*He sits down, overturning as he does so the untouched cup of coffee which* SMITTY *had forgotten and left on the bench. They all jump nervously as the tin cup hits the floor with a bang.* DRISCOLL *flies into an unreasonable rage*) Who's the dirty scut left this cup where a man 'ud sit on ut?

DAVIS. It's Smitty's.

DRISCOLL. (*kicking the cup across the forecastle*) Does he think he's too much av a bloody gentleman to put his own away loike the rist av us? If he does I'm the bye'll beat that noshun out av his head.

COCKY. Be the airs 'e puts on you'd think 'e was the Prince of Wales. Wot's 'e doin' on a ship, I arsks yer? 'E ain't no good as a sailor, is 'e? —dawdlin' abaht on deck like a chicken wiv 'is 'ead cut orf!

JACK. (*good-naturedly*) Aw, the Duke's all right. S'posin' he did ferget his cup—what's the dif? (*He picks up the cup and puts it away—with a grin*) This war zone stuff's got yer goat, Drisc—and yours too, Cocky—and I ain't cheerin' much fur it myself, neither.

COCKY. (*with a sigh*) Blimey, it ain't no bleedin' joke, yer first trip, to know as there's a ship full of shells li'ble to go orf in under your bloomin' feet, as you might say, if we gets 'it be a torpedo or mine. (*With sudden savagery*) Calls theyselves 'uman bein's, too! Blarsted 'Uns!

DRISCOLL. (*gloomily*) 'Tis me last trip in the bloody zone, God help me. The divil take their twenty-foive per cent. bonus—and be drowned like a rat in a trap in the bargain, maybe.

DAVIS. Wouldn't be so bad if she wasn't carryin' ammunition. Them's the kind the subs is layin' for.

DRISCOLL. (*irritably*) Fur the love av hivin, don't be talkin' about ut. I'm sick wid thinkin' and jumpin' at iviry bit av a noise. (*There is a pause during which they all stare gloomily at the floor.*)

JACK. Hey, Davis, what was you sayin' about Smitty when they come in?

DAVIS. (*with a great air of mystery*) I'll tell you in a minit. I want to wait an' see if he's comin' back. (*Impressively*) You won't be callin' him all right when you hears what I seen with my own eyes. (*He adds with an air of satisfaction*) An' you won't be feelin' no safer, neither. (*They all look at him with puzzled glances full of a vague apprehension.*)

DRISCOLL. God blarst ut! (*He fills his pipe and lights it. The others, with an air of remembering something they had forgotten, do the same.* SCOTTY *enters.*)

SCOTTY. (*in awed tones*) Mon, but it's clear outside the nicht! Like day.

DAVIS. (*in low tones*) Where's Smitty, Scotty?

SCOTTY. Out on the hatch starin' at the moon like a mon half-daft.

DAVIS. Can you see him from the doorway?

SCOTTY (*goes to doorway and carefully peeks out*) Aye; he's still there.

DAVIS. Keep your eyes on him for a moment. I've got something I want to tell the boys and I don't want him walkin' in in the middle of it. Give a shout if he starts this way.

SCOTTY. (*with suppressed excitement*) Aye, I'll watch him. And I've somethin' myself to tell aboot his Lordship.

DRISCOLL. (*impatiently*) Out wid ut! You're talkin' more than a pair av auld women wud be standin' in the road, and gittin' no further along.

DAVIS. Listen! You 'member when I went to git the coffee, Jack?

JACK. Sure, I do.

DAVIS. Well, I brings it down here same as usual and got as far as the door there when I sees him.

JACK. Smitty?

DAVIS. Yes, Smitty! He was standin' in the middle of the fo'c's'tle there. (*Pointing*) Lookin' around sneakin'-like at Ivan and Swanson and the rest 's if he wants to make certain they're asleep. (*He pauses significantly, looking from one to the other of his listeners.* SCOTTY *is nervously dividing his attention between* SMITTY *on the hatch outside and* DAVIS' *story, fairly bursting to break in with his own revelations.*)

JACK. (*impatiently*) What of it?

DAVIS. Listen! He was standin' right there—(*pointing again*) in his stockin' feet—no shoes on, mind, so he wouldn't make no noise!

JACK. (*spitting disgustedly*) Aw!

DAVIS. (*not heeding the interruption*) I seen right away somethin' on the queer was up so I slides back into the alleyway where I kin see him but he can't see me. After he makes sure they're all asleep he goes in under the bunks there—bein' careful not to raise a noise, mind!—an' takes out his bag there. (*By this time everyone,* JACK *included, is listening breathlessly to his story*) Then he fishes in his pocket an' takes out a bunch o' keys an' kneels down beside the bag an' opens it.

SCOTTY. (*unable to keep silent longer*) Mon, didn't I see him do that same thing wi' these two eyes. 'Twas just that moment I woke and spied him.

DAVIS. (*surprised, and a bit nettled to have to share his story with anyone*) Oh, you seen him, too, eh? (*To the others*) Then Scotty kin tell you if I'm lyin' or not.

DRISCOLL. An' what did he do whin he'd the bag opened?

DAVIS. He bends down and reaches out his hand sort o' scared-like, like it was somethin' dang'rous he was after, an' feels round in under his duds—hidden in under his duds an' wrapped up in 'em, it was—an' he brings out a black iron box!

COCKY. (*looking around him with a frightened glance*) Gawd blimey! (*The others likewise betray their uneasiness, shuffling their feet nervously.*)

DAVIS. Ain't that right, Scotty?

SCOTTY. Right as rain, I'm tellin' ye!

DAVIS. (*to the others with an air of satisfaction*) There you are! (*Lowering his voice*) An' then what d'you suppose he did? Sneaks to his bunk an' slips the black box in under his mattress—in under his mattress, mind!

JACK. And it's there now?

DAVIS. Course it is! (JACK *starts toward* SMITTY'S *bunk*. DRISCOLL *grabs him by the arm.*)

DRISCOLL. Don't be touchin' ut, Jack!

JACK. Yuh needn't worry. I ain't goin' to touch it. (*He pulls up* SMITTY'S *mattress and looks down. The others stare at him, holding their breaths. He turns to them, trying hard to assume a careless tone*) It's there, aw right.

COCKY. (*miserably upset*) I'm gointer 'op it aht on deck. (*He gets up but* DRISCOLL *pulls him down again.* COCKY *protests*) It fair guvs me the trembles sittin' still in 'ere.

DRISCOLL. (*scornfully*) Are ye frightened, ye toad? 'Tis a hell av a thing fur grown men to be shiverin' loike childer at a bit av a black box. (*Scratching his head in uneasy perplexity*) Still, ut's damn queer, the looks av ut.

DAVIS. (*sarcastically*) A bit of a black box, eh? How big d'you think them—(*he hesitates*)—things has to be—big as this fo'c's'tle?

JACK. (*in a voice meant to be reassuring*) Aw, hell! I'll bet it ain't nothin' but some coin he's saved he's got locked up in there.

DAVIS. (*scornfully*) That's likely, ain't it? Then why does he act so s'picious? He's been on ship near two year, ain't he? He knows damn well there ain't no thiefs in this fo'c'stle, don't he? An' you know's well's I do he didn't have no money when he came on board an' he ain't saved none since. Don't you? (JACK *doesn't answer*) Listen! D'you know what he done after he put that thing under his mattress?—an' Scotty'll tell you if I ain't speakin' truth. He looks round to see if anyone's woke up—

SCOTTY. I clapped my eyes shut when he turned round.

DAVIS. An' then he crawls into his bunk an' shuts his eyes, an' starts in snorin', *pretendin'* he was asleep, mind!

SCOTTY. Aye, I could hear him.

DAVIS. An' when I goes to call him I don't even shake him. I just says, "Eight bells, Smitty," in almost a whisper-like, an' up he gets yawnin' an' stretchin' fit to kill hisself 's if he'd been dead asleep.

COCKY. Gawd blimey!

DRISCOLL. (*shaking his head*) Ut looks bad, divil a doubt av ut.

DAVIS. (*excitedly*) An' now I come to think of it, there's the porthole. How'd it come to git open, tell me that? I know'd well Paul never opened it. Ain't he grumblin' about bein' cold all the time?

SCOTTY. The mon that opened it meant no good to this ship, whoever he was.

JACK. (*sourly*) What porthole? What're yuh talkin' about?

DAVIS. (*pointing over* PAUL's *bunk*) There. It was open when I come in. I felt the cold air on my neck an' shut it. It would'a been clear's a lighthouse to any sub that was watchin'—an' we s'posed to have all the ports blinded! Who'd do a dirty trick like that? It wasn't none of us, nor Scotty here, nor Swanson, nor Ivan. Who would it be, then?

COCKY. (*angrily*) Must'a been 'is bloody Lordship.

DAVIS. For all's we know he might'a been signalin' with it. They does it like that by winkin' a light. Ain't you read how they gets caught doin' it in London an' on the coast?

COCKY. (*firmly convinced now*) An' wot's 'e doin' aht alone on the 'atch—keepin' isself clear of us like 'e was afraid?

DRISCOLL. Kape your eye on him, Scotty.

SCOTTY. There's no a move oot o' him.

JACK. (*in irritated perplexity*) But, hell, ain't he an Englishman? What'd he wanta—

DAVIS. English? How d'we know he's English? Cos he talks it? That ain't no proof. Ain't you read in the papers how all them German spies they been catchin' in England has been livin' there for ten, often as not twenty years, an' talks English as good's anyone? An' look here, ain't you noticed he don't talk natural? He talks it too damn good, that's what I mean. He don't talk exactly like a toff, does he, Cocky?

COCKY. Not like any toff as I ever met up wiv.

DAVIS. No; an' he don't talk it like us, that's certain. An' he don't look English. An' what d'we know about him when you come to look at it? Nothin'! He ain't ever said where he comes from or why. All we know is he ships on here in London 'bout a year b'fore the war starts, as an A. B.—stole his papers most lik'ly—when he don't know how to box the compass, hardly. Ain't that queer in itself? n' was he ever open with us like a good shipmate? No; he's always had that sly air about him 's if he was hidin' somethin'.

DRISCOLL. (*slapping his thigh—angrily*) Divil take me if I don't think ye have the truth av ut, Davis.

COCKY. (*scornfully*) Lettin' on be 'is silly airs, and all, 'e's the son of a blarsted earl or somethink!

DAVIS. An' the name he calls hisself—Smith! I'd risk a quid of my next pay day that his real name is Schmidt, if the truth was known.

JACK. (*evidently fighting against his own conviction*) Aw, say, you guys give me a pain! What'd they want puttin' a spy on this old tub for?

DAVIS. (*shaking his head sagely*) They're deep ones, an' there's a lot o' things a sailor'll see in the ports he puts in ought to be useful to 'em. An' if he kin signal to 'em an' they blows us up it's one ship less, ain't it? (*Lowering his voice and indicating* SMITTY's *bunk*) Or if he blows us up hisself.

SCOTTY. (*in alarmed tones*) Hush, mon! Here he comes! (SCOTTY *hurries over to a bench and sits down. A thick silence settles over the forecastle. The men look from one to another with uneasy glances.* SMITTY *enters and sits down beside his bunk. He is seemingly unaware of the dark glances of suspicion directed at him from all sides. He slides his hand back stealthily over his mattress and his fingers move, evidently feeling to make sure the box is still there. The others follow this movement carefully with quick looks out of the corners of their eyes. Their attitudes grow tense as if they were about to spring at him. Satisfied the box is safe,* SMITTY *draws his hand away slowly and utters a sigh of relief.)*

SMITTY. (*in a casual tone which to them sounds sinister*) It's a good light night for the subs if there's any about. (*For a moment he sits staring in front of him. Finally he seems to sense the hostile atmosphere of the forecastle and looks from one to the other of the men in surprise. All of them avoid his eyes. He sighs with a puzzled expression and gets up and walks out of the doorway. There is silence for a moment after his departure and then a storm of excited talk breaks loose.*)

DAVIS. Did you see him feelin' if it was there?

COCKY. 'E ain't arf a sly one wiv 'is talk of submarines, Gawd blind 'im!

SCOTTY. Did ye see the sneakin' looks he gave us?

DRISCOLL. If ivir I saw black shame on a man's face 'twas on his whin he sat there!

JACK. (*thoroughly convinced at last*) He looked bad to me. He's a crook, aw right.

DAVIS. (*excitedly*) What'll we do? We gotter do somethin' quick or— (*He is interrupted by the sound of something hitting against the port side of the forecastle with a dull, heavy thud. The men start to their feet in wild-eyed terror and turn as if they were going to rush for the deck. They stand that way for a strained moment, scarcely breathing and listening intently.*)

JACK. (*with a sickly smile*) Hell! It's on'y a piece of driftwood or a floatin' log. (*He sits down again.*)

DAVIS. (*sarcastically*) Or a mine that didn't go off—that time—or a piece o' wreckage from some ship they've sent to Davy Jones.

COCKY. (*mopping his brow with a trembling hand*) Blimey! (*He sinks back weakly on a bench.*)

DRISCOLL. (*furiously*) God blarst ut! No man at all cud be puttin' up wid the loike av this—an' I'm not wan to be fearin' anything or any man in the worrld'll stand up to me face to face; but this divil's trickery in the darrk— (*He starts for* SMITTY'S *bunk*) I'll throw ut out wan av the portholes an' be done wid ut. (*He reaches toward the mattress.*)

SCOTTY. (*grabbing his arm—wildly*) Arre ye daft, mon?

DAVIS. Don't monkey with it, Drisc. I knows what to do. Bring the bucket o' water here, Jack, will you? (JACK *gets it and brings it over to* DAVIS) An' you, Scotty, see if he's back on the hatch.

SCOTTY. (*cautiously peering out*) Aye, he's sittin' there the noo.

DAVIS. Sing out if he makes a move. Lift up the mattress, Drisc—careful now! (DRISCOLL *does so with infinite caution*) Take it out, Jack—careful—don't shake it now, for Christ's sake! Here—put it in the water—easy! There, that's fixed it! (*They all sit down with great sighs of relief*) The water'll git in and spoil it.

DRISCOLL. (*slapping* DAVIS *on the back*) Good wurrk for ye, Davis, ye scut! (*He spits on his hands aggressively*) An' now what's to be done wid that black-hearted thraitor?

COCKY. (*belligerently*) Guv 'im a shove in the marf and 'eave 'im over the side!

DAVIS. An' serve him right!

JACK. Aw, say, give him a chance. Yuh can't prove nothin' till you find out what's in there.

DRISCOLL. (*heatedly*) Is ut more proof ye'd be needin' afther what we've seen an' heard? Then listen to me—an' ut's Driscoll talkin'—if there's divilmint in that box an' we see plain 'twas his plan to murrdher his own shipmates that have served him fair— (*He raises his fist*) I'll choke his rotten hearrt out wid me own hands, an' over the side wid him, and one man missin' in the mornin'.

DAVIS. An' no one the wiser. He's the balmy kind what commits suicide.

COCKY. They 'angs spies ashore.

JACK. (*resentfully*) If he's done what yuh think I'll croak him myself. Is that good enough for yuh?

DRISCOLL. (*looking down at the box*) How'll we be openin' this, I wonder?

SCOTTY. (*from the doorway—warningly*) He's standin' up.

DAVIS. We'll take his keys away from him when he comes in. Quick, Drisc! You an' Jack get beside the door and grab him. (*They get on either side of the door.* DAVIS *snatches a small coil of rope from one of the upper bunks*) This'll do for me an' Scotty to tie him.

SCOTTY. He's turrnin' this way—he's comin'! (*He moves away from door.*)

DAVIS. Stand by to lend a hand, Cocky.

COCKY. Righto. (*As* SMITTY *enters the forecastle he is seized roughly from both sides and his arms pinned behind him. At first he struggles fiercely, but seeing the uselessness of this, he finally stands calmly and allows* DAVIS *and* SCOTTY *to tie up his arms.*)

SMITTY. (*when they have finished—with cold contempt*) If this is your idea of a joke I'll have to confess it's a bit too thick for me to enjoy.

COCKY. (*angrily*) Shut yer marf, 'ear!

DRISCOLL. (*roughly*) Ye'll find ut's no joke, me bucko, b'fore we're done wid you. (*To* SCOTTY) Kape your eye peeled, Scotty, and sing out if anyone's comin'. (SCOTTY *resumes his post at the door.*)

SMITTY. (*with the same icy contempt*) If you'd be good enough to explain—

DRISCOLL. (*furiously*) Explain, is ut? 'Tis you'll do the explainin'—an' damn quick, or we'll know the reason why. (*To* JACK *and* DAVIS) Bring him here, now. (*They push* SMITTY *over to the bucket*) Look here, ye murrdherin' swab. D'you see ut? (SMITTY *looks down with an expression of amazement which rapidly changes to one of anguish.*)

DAVIS. (*with a sneer*) Look at him! S'prised, ain't you? If you wants to try your dirty spyin' tricks on us you've gotter git up earlier in the mornin'.

COCKY. Thorght yer weren't 'arf a fox, didn't yer?

SMITTY. (*trying to restrain his growing rage*) What—what do you mean? That's only— How dare— What are you doing with my private belongings?

COCKY. (*sarcastically*) Ho yus! Private b'longings!

DRISCOLL. (*shouting*) What is ut, ye swine? Will you tell us to our faces? What's in ut?

SMITTY. (*biting his lips—holding himself in check with a great effort*) Nothing but— That's my business. You'll please attend to your own.

DRISCOLL. Oho, ut is, is ut? (*Shaking his fist in* SMITTY's *face*) Talk aisy now if ye know what's best for you. Your business. Your business, indade! Then we'll be makin' ut ours, I'm thinkin'. (*To* JACK *and* DAVIS) Take his keys away from him an' we'll see if there's one'll open ut, maybe. (*They start in searching* SMITTY, *who tries to resist and kicks out at the bucket.* DRISCOLL *leaps forward and helps them push him away*) Try to kick ut over, wud ye? Did ye see him then? Tryin' to murrdher us all, the scut! Take that pail out av his way, Cocky. (SMITTY *struggles with all of his strength and keeps them busy for a few seconds. As* COCKY *grabs the pail* SMITTY *makes a final effort and, lunging forward, kicks again at the bucket but only succeeds in hitting* COCKY *on the shin.* COCKY *immediately sets down the pail with a bang and, clutching his knee in both hands, starts hopping around the forecastle, groaning and swearing.*)

COCKY. Ooow! Gawd strike me pink! Kicked me, 'e did! Bloody, bleedin', rotten Dutch 'og! (*Approaching* SMITTY, *who has given up the fight and is pushed back against the wall near the doorway with* JACK *and* DAVIS *holding him on either side—wrathfully, at the top of his lungs*) Kick me, will yer? I'll show yer what for, yer bleedin' sneak! (*He draws back his fist.* DRISCOLL *pushes him to one side.*)

DRISCOLL. Shut your mouth! D'you want to wake the whole ship? (COCKY *grumbles and retires to a bench, nursing his sore shin.*)

JACK. (*taking a small bunch of keys from* SMITTY's *pocket*) Here yuh are, Drisc.

DRISCOLL. (*taking them*) We'll soon be knowin'. (*He takes the pail and sits down, placing it on the floor between his feet.* SMITTY *again tries to break loose but he is too tired and is easily held back against the wall.*)

SMITTY. (*breathing heavily and very pale*) Cowards!

JACK. (*with a growl*) Nix on the rough talk, see! That don't git yuh nothin'.

DRISCOLL. (*looking at the lock on the box in the water and then scrutinizing the keys in his hand*) This'll be ut, I'm thinkin'. (*He selects one and gingerly reaches his hand in the water.*)

SMITTY. (*his face grown livid—chokingly*) Don't you open that box, Driscoll. If you do, so help me God, I'll kill you if I hang for it.

DRISCOLL. (*pausing—his hand in the water*) Whin I open this box I'll not be the wan to be kilt, me sonny bye! I'm no dirty spy.

SMITTY. (*his voice trembling with rage. His eyes are fixed on* DRISCOLL'S *hand*) Spy? What are you talking about? I only put that box there so I could get it quick in case we were torpedoed. Are you all mad? Do you think I'm— (*Chokingly*) You stupid curs! You cowardly dolts! (DAVIS *claps his hand over* SMITTY'S *mouth.*)

DAVIS. That'll be enough from you! (DRISCOLL *takes the dripping box from the water and starts to fit in the key.* SMITTY *springs forward furiously, almost escaping from their grasps, and drags them after him half-way across the forecastle.*)

DRISCOLL. Hold him, ye divils! (*He puts the box back in the water and jumps to their aid.* COCKY *hovers on the outskirts of the battle, mindful of the kick he received.*)

SMITTY. (*raging*) Cowards! Damn you! Rotten curs! (*He is thrown to the floor and held there*) Cowards! Cowards!

DRISCOLL. I'll shut your dirty mouth for you. (*He goes to his bunk and pulls out a big wad of waste and comes back to* SMITTY.)

SMITTY. Cowards! Cowards!

DRISCOLL. (*with no gentle hand slaps the waste over* SMITTY'S *mouth*) That'll teach you to be misnamin' a man, ye sneak. Have ye a handkerchief, Jack? (JACK *hands him one and he ties it tightly around* SMITTY's *head over the waste*) That'll fix your gab. Stand him up, now, and tie his feet, too, so he'll not be movin'. (*They do so and leave him with his back against the wall near* SCOTTY. *Then they all sit down beside* DRISCOLL, *who again lifts the box out of the water and sets it carefully on his knees. He picks out the key, then hesitates, looking from one to the other uncertainly*) We'd best be takin' this to the skipper, d'you think, maybe?

JACK. (*irritably*) To hell with the Old Man. This is our game and we c'n play it without no help.

COCKY. No bleedin' horficers, I says!

DAVIS. They'd only be takin' all the credit and makin' heroes of themselves.

DRISCOLL. (*boldly*) Here goes, thin! (*He slowly turns the key in the lock. The others instinctively turn away. He carefully pushes the cover back on its hinges and looks at what he sees inside with an expression of puzzled astonishment. The others crowd up close. Even* SCOTTY *leaves his post to take a look*) What is ut, Davis?

DAVIS. (*mystified*) Looks funny, don't it? Somethin' square tied up in a rubber bag. Maybe it's dynamite—or somethin'—you can't never tell.

JACK. Aw, it ain't got no works, so it ain't no bomb, I'll bet.

DAVIS. (*dubiously*) They makes them all kinds, they do.

JACK. Open it up, Drisc.

DAVIS. Careful now! (DRISCOLL *takes a black rubber bag resembling a large tobacco pouch from the box and unties the string which is wound tightly around the top. He opens it and takes out a small packet of letters also tied up with string. He turns these over in his hands and looks at the others questioningly.*)

JACK. (*with a broad grin*) On'y letters! (*Slapping* DAVIS *on the back*) Yuh're a hell of a Sherlock Holmes, ain't yuh? Letters from his best girl too, I'll bet. Let's turn the Duke loose, what d'yuh say? (*He starts to get up.*)

DAVIS. (*fixing him with a withering look*) Don't be so damn smart, Jack. Letters, you says, 's if there never was no harm in 'em. How d'you s'pose spies gets their orders and sends back what they finds out if it ain't by letters and such things? There's many a letter is worser'n any bomb.

COCKY. Righto! They ain't as innercent as they looks, I'll take me oath, when you read 'em. (*Pointing at* SMITTY) Not 'is Lordship's letters; not be no means!

JACK. (*sitting down again*) Well, read 'em and find out. (DRISCOLL *commences untying the packet. There is a muffled groan of rage and protest from* SMITTY.)

DAVIS. (*triumphantly*) There! Listen to him! Look at him tryin' to git loose! Ain't that proof enough? He knows well we're findin' him out. Listen to me! Love letters, you says, Jack, 's if they couldn't harm nothin'. Listen! I was readin' in some magazine in New York on'y two weeks back how some German spy in Paris was writin' love letters to some woman spy in Switzerland who sent 'em on to Berlin, Germany. To read 'em you wouldn't s'pect nothin'—just mush and all. (*Impressively*) But they had a way o' doin' it—a damn sneakin' way. They had a piece o' plain paper with pieces cut out of it an' when they puts it on top o' the letter they sees on'y the words what tells them what they wants to know. An' the Frenchies gets beat in a fight all on account o' that letter.

COCKY. (*awed*) Gawd blimey! They ain't 'arf smart bleeders!

DAVIS. (*seeing his audience is again all with him*) An' even if these letters of his do sound all right they may have what they calls a code. You can't never tell. (*To* DRISCOLL, *who has finished untying the packet*) Read one of 'em, Drisc. My eyes is weak.

DRISCOLL. (*takes the first one out of its envelope and bends down to the lantern with it. He turns up the wick to give him a better light*) I'm no hand to be readin' but I'll try ut. (*Again there is a muffled groan from* SMITTY *as he strains at his bonds.*)

DAVIS. (*gloatingly*) Listen to him! He knows. Go ahead, Drisc!

DRISCOLL. (*his brow furrowed with concentration*) Ut begins: Dearest Man— (*His eyes travel down the page*) An' thin there's a lot av blarney tellin' him how much she misses him now she's gone away to singin' school—an' how she hopes he'll settle down to rale worrk an' not be skylarkin' around now that she's away loike he used to before she met up wid him—and ut ends: "I love you betther than anythin' in the worrld. You know that, don't you, dear? But b'fore I can agree to live out my life wid you, you must prove to me that the black shadow—I won't menshun uts hateful name but you know what I mean—which might wreck both our lives, does not exist for you. You can do that, can't you, dear? Don't you see you must for my sake?" (*He pauses for a moment—then adds gruffly*) Ut's signed: "Edith." (*At the sound of the name* SMITTY, *who has stood tensely with his eyes shut as if he were undergoing torture during the reading, makes a muffled sound like a sob and half turns his face to the wall.*)

JACK. (*sympathetically*) Hell! What's the use of readin' that stuff even if—

DAVIS. (*interrupting him sharply*) Wait! What's that letter from, Drisc?

DRISCOLL. There's no address on the top av ut.

DAVIS. (*meaningly*) What'd I tell you? Look at the postmark, Drisc—on the envelope.

DRISCOLL. The name that's written is Sidney Davidson, wan hundred an'—

DAVIS. Never mind that. O' course it's a false name. Look at the postmark.

DRISCOLL. There's a furrin' stamp on ut by the looks av ut. The mark's blurred so it's hard to read. (*He spells it out laboriously* B-e-r—the nixt is an l, I think—i—an' an n.

DAVIS. (*excitedly*) Berlin! What did I tell you? I knew them letters was from Germany.

COCKY. (*shaking his fist in* SMITTY's *direction*) Rotten 'ound! (*The others look at* SMITTY *as if this last fact had utterly condemned him in their eyes.*)

DAVIS. Give me the letter, Drisc. Maybe I kin make somethin' out of it. (DRISCOLL *hands the letter to him*) You go through the others, Drisc, and sing out if you sees anythin' queer. (*He bends over the first letter as if he were determined to figure out its secret meaning.* JACK, COCKY *and* SCOTTY *look over his shoulder with eager curiosity.* DRISCOLL *takes out some of the other letters, running his eyes quickly down the pages. He looks curiously over at* SMITTY *from time to time, and sighs frequently with a puzzled frown.*)

DAVIS. (*disappointingly*) I gotter give it up. It's too deep for me, but we'll turn 'em over to the perlice when we docks at Liverpool to look through. This one I got was written a year before the war started anyway. Find anythin' in yours, Drisc?

DRISCOLL. They're all the same as the first—lovin' blarney, an' how her singin' is doin', and the great things the Dutch teacher says about her voice, an' how glad she is that her Sidney bye is worrkin' harrd an' makin' a man av himself for her sake. (SMITTY *turns his face completely to the wall.*)

DAVIS. (*disgustedly*) If we on'y had the code!

DRISCOLL. (*taking up the bottom letter*) Hullo! Here's wan addressed to this ship—s. s. *Glencairn,* ut says—whin we was in Cape Town sivin months ago— (*Looking at the postmark*) Ut's from London.

DAVIS. (*eagerly*) Read it. (*There is another choking groan from* SMITTY.)

DRISCOLL. (*reads slowly—his voice becomes lower and lower as he goes on*) Ut begins wid simply the name Sidney Davidson—no dearest or sweetheart to this wan. "Ut is only from your chance meetin' with Harry—whin you were drunk—that I happen to know where to reach you. So you have run away to sea loike the coward you are because you knew I had found out the truth—the truth you have covered over with your mean little lies all the time I was away in

Berlin and blindly trusted you. Very well, you have chosen. You have shown that your drunkenness means more to you than any love or faith av mine. I am sorry—for I loved you, Sidney Davidson—but this is the end. I lave you—the mem'ries; an' if ut is any satisfaction to you I lave you the real-i-zation that you have wrecked my loife as you have wrecked your own. My one remainin' hope is that nivir in God's worrld will I ivir see your face again. Good-by. Edith." (*As he finishes there is a deep silence, broken only by* SMITTY'S *muffled sobbing. The men cannot look at each other.* DRISCOLL *holds the rubber bag limply in his hand and some small white object falls out of it and drops noiselessly on the floor. Mechanically* DRISCOLL *leans over and picks it up, and looks at it wonderingly.*)

DAVIS. (*in a dull voice*) What's that?

DRISCOLL. (*slowly*) A bit av a dried-up flower—a rose, maybe. (*He drops it into the bag and gathers up the letters and puts them back. He replaces the bag in the box, and locks it and puts it back under* SMITTY'S *mattress. The others follow him with their eyes. He steps softly over to* SMITTY *and cuts the ropes about his arms and ankles with his sheath-knife, and unties the handkerchief over the gag.* SMITTY *does not turn around but covers his face with his hands and leans his head against the wall. His shoulders continue to heave spasmodically but he makes no further sound.*)

DRISCOLL. (*stalks back to the others—there is a moment of silence, in which each man is in agony with the hopelessness of finding a word he can say—then* DRISCOLL *explodes*) God stiffen us, are we never goin' to turn in fur a wink av sleep? (*They all start as if awakening from a bad dream and gratefully crawl into their bunks, shoes and all, turning their faces to the wall, and pulling their blankets up over their shoulders.* SCOTTY *tiptoes past* SMITTY *out into the darkness. . . .* DRISCOLL *turns down the light and crawls into his bunk as the curtain falls.*)

ILE

A Play in One Act

CHARACTERS

Ben, *the cabin boy*

The Steward

Captain Keeney

Slocum, *second mate*

Mrs. Keeney

Joe, *a harpooner*

Members of the crew of the steam whaler Atlantic Queen

ILE

SCENE. CAPTAIN KEENEY's *cabin on board the steam whaling ship* Atlantic Queen—*a small, square compartment about eight feet high with a skylight in the center looking out on the poop deck. On the left (the stern of the ship) a long bench with rough cushions is built in against the wall. In front of the bench, a table. Over the bench, several curtained portholes.*

In the rear, left, a door leading to the CAPTAIN's *sleeping quarters. To the right of the door a small organ, looking as if it were brand-new, is placed against the wall.*

On the right, to the rear, a marble-topped sideboard. On the sideboard, a woman's sewing basket. Farther forward, a doorway leading to the companionway, and past the officers' quarters to the main deck.

In the center of the room, a stove. From the middle of the ceiling a hanging lamp is suspended. The walls of the cabin are painted white.

There is no rolling of the ship, and the light which comes through the skylight is sickly and faint, indicating one of those gray days of calm when ocean and sky are alike dead. The silence is unbroken except for the measured tread of someone walking up and down on the poop deck overhead.

It is nearing two bells—one o'clock—in the afternoon of a day in the year 1895.

At the rise of the curtain there is a moment of intense silence. Then the STEWARD *enters and commences to clear the table of the few dishes which still remain on it after the* CAPTAIN's *dinner. He is an old, grizzled man dressed in dungaree pants, a sweater, and a woolen cap with ear-flaps. His manner is sullen and angry. He stops stacking up the plates and casts a quick glance upward at the skylight; then tiptoes over to the closed door in rear and listens with his ear pressed to the crack. What he hears makes his face darken and he mutters a furious curse. There is a noise from the doorway on the right and he darts back to the table.*

BEN *enters. He is an overgrown, gawky boy with a long, pinched face. He is dressed in sweater, fur cap, etc. His teeth are chattering with the cold and he hurries to the stove, where he stands for a moment shivering, blowing on his hands, slapping them against his sides, on the verge of crying.*

THE STEWARD. (*in relieved tones—seeing who it is*) Oh, 'tis you, is it? What're ye shiverin' 'bout? Stay by the stove where ye belong and ye'll find no need of chatterin'.

BEN. It's c-c-cold. (*Trying to control his chattering teeth—derisively*) Who d'ye think it were—the Old Man?

THE STEWARD. (*makes a threatening move—*BEN *shrinks away*) None o' your lip, young un, or I'll learn ye. (*More kindly*) Where was it ye've been all o' the time—the fo'c's'tle?

BEN. Yes.

THE STEWARD. Let the Old Man see ye up for'ard monkey-shinin' with the hands and ye'll get a hidin' ye'll not forget in a hurry.

BEN. Aw, he don't see nothin'. (*A trace of awe in his tones—he glances upward*) He just walks up and down like he didn't notice nobody—and stares at the ice to the no'the'ard.

THE STEWARD. (*the same tone of awe creeping into his voice*) He's always starin' at the ice. (*In a sudden rage, shaking his fist at the skylight*) Ice, ice, ice! Damn him and damn the ice! Holdin' us in for nigh on a year—nothin' to see but ice—stuck in it like a fly in molasses!

BEN. (*apprehensively*) Ssshh! He'll hear ye.

THE STEWARD. (*raging*) Aye, damn him, and damn the Arctic seas, and damn this stinkin' whalin' ship of his, and damn me for a fool to ever ship on it! (*Subsiding as if realizing the uselessness of this outburst—shaking his head—slowly, with deep conviction*) He's a hard man—as hard a man as ever sailed the seas.

BEN. (*solemnly*) Aye.

THE STEWARD. The two years we all signed up for are done this day. Blessed Christ! Two years o' this dog's life, and no luck in the fishin', and the hands half starved with the food runnin' low, rotten as it is; and not a sign of him turnin' back for home! (*Bitterly*) Home! I begin to doubt if ever I'll set foot on land again. (*Excitedly*) What is it he thinks he's goin' to do? Keep us all up here after our time is worked out till the last man of us is starved to death or frozen? We've grub enough hardly to last out the voyage back if we started now. What are the men goin' to do 'bout it? Did ye hear any talk in the fo'c's'tle?

BEN. (*going over to him—in a half-whisper*) They said if he don't put back south for home today they're goin' to mutiny.

THE STEWARD. (*with grim satisfaction*) Mutiny? Aye, 'tis the only thing they can do; and serve him right after the manner he's treated them—'s if they weren't no better nor dogs.

BEN. The ice is all broke up to s'uth'ard. They's clear water 's far 's you can see. He ain't got no excuse for not turnin' back for home, the men says.

THE STEWARD. (*bitterly*) He won't look nowheres but no'the'ard where they's only the ice to see. He don't want to see no clear water. All he thinks on is gittin' the ile—'s if it was our fault he ain't had good luck with the whales. (*Shaking his head*) I think the man's mighty nigh losin' his senses.

BEN. (*awed*) D'you really think he's crazy?

THE STEWARD. Aye, it's the punishment o' God on him. Did ye ever hear of a man who wasn't crazy do the things he does? (*Pointing to the door in rear*) Who but a man that's mad would take his woman —and as sweet a woman as ever was—on a stinkin' whalin' ship to the Arctic seas to be locked in by the rotten ice for nigh on a year, and maybe lose her senses forever—for it's sure she'll never be the same again.

BEN. (*sadly*) She useter be awful nice to me before— (*his eyes grow wide and frightened*) —she got—like she is.

THE STEWARD. Aye, she was good to all of us. 'Twould have been hell on board without her; for he's a hard man—a hard, hard man—a driver if there ever was one. (*With a grim laugh*) I hope he's satisfied now—drivin' her on till she's near lost her mind. And who could blame her? 'Tis a God's wonder we're not a ship full of crazed people—with the damned ice all the time, and the quiet so thick you're afraid to hear your own voice.

BEN. (*with a frightened glance toward the door on right*) She don't never speak to me no more—jest looks at me 's if she didn't know me.

THE STEWARD. She don't know no one—but him. She talks to him —when she does talk—right enough.

BEN. She does nothin' all day long now but sit and sew—and then she cries to herself without makin' no noise. I've seen her.

THE STEWARD. Aye, I could hear her through the door a while back.

BEN. (*tiptoes over to the door and listens*) She's cryin' now.

THE STEWARD. (*furiously—shaking his fist*) God send his soul to hell for the devil he is! (*There is the noise of someone coming slowly down the companionway stairs.* THE STEWARD *hurries to his stacked-up dishes. He is so nervous from fright that he knocks off the top one, which falls and breaks on the floor. He stands aghast, trembling with dread.* BEN *is violently rubbing off the organ with a piece of cloth which he has snatched from his pocket.* CAPTAIN KEENEY *appears in the doorway on right and comes into the cabin, removing his fur cap as he does so. He is a man of about forty, around five-ten in height but looking much shorter on account of the enormous proportions of his shoulders and chest. His face is massive and deeply lined, with gray-blue eyes of a bleak hardness, and a tightly clenched, thin-lipped mouth. His thick hair is long and gray. He is dressed in a heavy blue jacket and blue pants stuffed into his sea-boots.*

He is followed into the cabin by the SECOND MATE, *a rangy six-footer with a lean weather-beaten face. The* MATE *is dressed about the same as the* CAPTAIN. *He is a man of thirty or so.*)

KEENEY. (*comes toward* THE STEWARD—*with a stern look on his face.* THE STEWARD *is visibly frightened and the stack of dishes rattles in his trembling hands.* KEENEY *draws back his fist and* THE STEWARD *shrinks away. The fist is gradually lowered and* KEENEY *speaks slowly*) 'Twould be like hitting a worm. It is nigh on two bells, Mr. Steward, and this truck not cleared yet.

THE STEWARD. (*stammering*) Y-y-yes, sir.

KEENEY. Instead of doin' your rightful work ye've been below here gossipin' old woman's talk with that boy. (*To* BEN, *fiercely*) Get out o' this, you! Clean up the chart-room. (BEN *darts past the* MATE *to the open doorway*) Pick up that dish, Mr. Steward!

THE STEWARD. (*doing so with difficulty*) Yes, sir.

KEENEY. The next dish you break, Mr. Steward, you take a bath in the Bering Sea at the end of a rope.

THE STEWARD. (*tremblingly*) Yes, sir. (*He hurries out. The* SECOND MATE *walks slowly over to the* CAPTAIN.)

MATE. I warn't 'specially anxious the man at the wheel should catch what I wanted to say to you, sir. That's why I asked you to come below.

KEENEY. (*impatiently*) Speak your say, Mr. Slocum.

MATE. (*unconsciously lowering his voice*) I'm afeard there'll be trouble with the hands by the look o' things. They'll likely turn ugly, every blessed one o' them, if you don't put back. The two years they signed up for is up today.

KEENEY. And d'you think you're tellin' me somethin' new, Mr. Slocum? I've felt it in the air this long time past. D'you think I've not seen their ugly looks and the grudgin' way they worked? (*The door in rear is opened and* MRS. KEENEY *stands in the doorway. She is a slight, sweet-faced little woman primly dressed in black. Her eyes are red from weeping and her face drawn and pale. She takes in the cabin with a frightened glance and stands as if fixed to the spot by some nameless dread, clasping and unclasping her hands nervously. The two men turn and look at her.*)

KEENEY. (*with rough tenderness*) Well, Annie?

MRS. KEENEY. (*as if awakening from a dream*) David, I— (*She is silent. The* MATE *starts for the doorway.*)

KEENEY. (*turning to him—sharply*) Wait!

MATE. Yes, sir.

KEENEY. D'you want anything, Annie?

MRS. KEENEY. (*after a pause, during which she seems to be endeavoring to collect her thoughts*) I thought maybe—I'd go on deck, David, to get a breath of fresh air. (*She stands humbly awaiting his permission. He and the* MATE *exchange a significant glance.*)

KEENEY. It's too cold, Annie. You'd best stay below today. There's nothing to look at on deck—but ice.

MRS. KEENEY. (*monotonously*) I know—ice, ice, ice! But there's nothing to see down here but these walls. (*She makes a gesture of loathing.*)

KEENEY. You can play the organ, Annie.

MRS. KEENEY. (*dully*) I hate the organ. It puts me in mind of home.

KEENEY. (*a touch of resentment in his voice*) I got it jest for you.

MRS. KEENEY. (*dully*) I know. (*She turns away from them and walks slowly to the bench on left. She lifts up one of the curtains and looks through a porthole; then utters an exclamation of joy*) Ah, water! Clear water! As far as I can see! How good it looks after all these months of ice! (*She turns round to them, her face transfigured with joy*) Ah, now I must go up on the deck and look at it, David.

KEENEY. (*frowning*) Best not today, Annie. Best wait for a day when the sun shines.

MRS. KEENEY. (*desperately*) But the sun never shines in this terrible place.

KEENEY. (*a tone of command in his voice*) Best not today, Annie.

MRS. KEENEY. (*crumbling before this command—abjectly*) Very well, David. (*She stands there staring straight before her as if in a daze. The two men look at her uneasily.*)

KEENEY. (*sharply*) Annie!

MRS. KEENEY. (*dully*) Yes, David.

KEENEY. Me and Mr. Slocum has business to talk about—ship's business.

MRS. KEENEY. Very well, David. (*She goes slowly out, rear, and leaves the door three-quarters shut behind her.*)

KEENEY. Best not have her on deck if they's goin' to be any trouble.

MATE. Yes, sir.

KEENEY. And trouble they's going to be. I feel it in my bones. (*Takes a revolver from the pocket of his coat and examines it*) Got your'n?

MATE. Yes, sir.

KEENEY. Not that we'll have to use 'em—not if I know their breed of dog—jest to frighten 'em up a bit. (*Grimly*) I ain't never been forced to use one yit; and trouble I've had by land and by sea 's long as I kin remember, and will have till my dyin' day, I reckon.

MATE. (*hesitatingly*) Then you ain't goin'—to turn back?

KEENEY. Turn back? Mr. Slocum, did you ever hear o' me pointin' s'uth for home with only a measly four hundred barrel of ile in the hold?

MATE. (*hastily*) No, sir—but the grub's gittin' low.

KEENEY. They's enough to last a long time yit, if they're careful with it; and they's plenty o' water.

MATE. They say it's not fit to eat—what's left; and the two years they signed on fur is up today. They might make trouble for you in the courts when we git home.

KEENEY. To hell with 'em! Let them make what law trouble they kin. I don't give a damn 'bout the money. I've got to git the ile! (*Glancing sharply at the* MATE) You ain't turnin' no damned sea-lawyer, be you, Mr. Slocum?

MATE. (*flushing*) Not by a hell of a sight, sir.

KEENEY. What do the fools want to go home fur now? Their share o' the four hundred barrel wouldn't keep 'em in chewin' terbacco.

MATE. (*slowly*) They wants to git back to their folks an' things, I s'pose.

KEENEY. (*looking at him searchingly*) 'N you want to turn back, too. (*The* MATE *looks down confusedly before his sharp gaze*) Don't lie, Mr. Slocum. It's writ down plain in your eyes. (*With grim sarcasm*) I hope, Mr. Slocum, you ain't agoin' to jine the men again me.

MATE. (*indignantly*) That ain't fair, sir, to say sich things.

KEENEY. (*with satisfaction*) I warn't much afeard o' that, Tom. You been with me nigh on ten year and I've learned ye whalin'. No man kin say I ain't a good master, if I be a hard one.

MATE. I warn't thinkin' of myself, sir—'bout turnin' home, I mean. (*Desperately*) But Mrs. Keeney, sir—seems like she ain't jest satisfied up here, ailin' like—what with the cold an' bad luck an' the ice an' all.

KEENEY. (*his face clouding—rebukingly but not severely*) That's my business, Mr. Slocum. I'll thank you to steer a clear course o' that. (*A pause*) The ice'll break up soon to no'th'ard. I could see it startin' today. And when it goes and we git some sun Annie'll perk up. (*Another pause—then he bursts forth*) It ain't the damned money what's keepin' me up in the Northern seas, Tom. But I can't go back to Homeport with a measly four hundred barrel of ile. I'd die fust. I ain't never come back home in all my days without a full ship. Ain't that truth?

MATE. Yes, sir; but this voyage you been icebound, an'—

KEENEY. (*scornfully*) And d'you s'pose any of 'em would believe that—any o' them skippers I've beaten voyage after voyage? Can't you hear 'em laughin' and sneerin'—Tibbots 'n' Harris 'n' Simms and the rest—and all o' Homeport makin' fun o' me? "Dave Keeney what boasts he's the best whalin' skipper out o' Homeport comin' back with a measly four hundred barrel of ile?" (*The thought of this drives him into a frenzy, and he smashes his fist down on the marble top of the sideboard*) Hell! I got to git the ile, I tell you.

How could I figger on this ice? It's never been so bad before in the thirty year I been acomin' here. And now it's breakin' up. In a couple o' days it'll be all gone. And they's whale here, plenty of 'em. I know they is and I ain't never gone wrong yit. I got to git the ile! I got to git it in spite of all hell, and by God, I ain't agoin' home till I do git it! (*There is the sound of subdued sobbing from the door in the rear. The two men stand silent for a moment, listening. Then* KEENEY *goes over to the door and looks in. He hesitates for a moment as if he were going to enter—then closes the door softly.* JOE, *the harpooner, an enormous six-footer with a battered, ugly face, enters from right and stands waiting for the captain to notice him.*)

KEENEY. (*turning and seeing him*) Don't be standin' there like a gawk, Harpooner. Speak up!

JOE. (*confusedly*) We want—the men, sir—they wants to send a depitation aft to have a word with you.

KEENEY. (*furiously*) Tell 'em to go to— (*Checks himself and continues grimly*) Tell 'em to come. I'll see 'em.

JOE. Aye, aye, sir. (*He goes out.*)

KEENEY. (*with a grim smile*) Here it comes, the trouble you spoke of, Mr. Slocum, and we'll make short shift of it. It's better to crush such things at the start than let them make headway.

MATE. (*worriedly*) Shall I wake up the First and Fourth, sir? We might need their help.

KEENEY. No, let them sleep. I'm well able to handle this alone, Mr. Slocum. (*There is the shuffling of footsteps from outside and five of the crew crowd into the cabin, led by* JOE. *All are dressed alike—sweaters, sea-boots, etc. They glance uneasily at the* CAPTAIN, *twirling their fur caps in their hands.*)

KEENEY. (*after a pause*) Well? Who's to speak fur ye?

JOE. (*stepping forward with an air of bravado*) I be.

KEENEY. (*eyeing him up and down coldly*) So you be. Then speak your say and be quick about it.

JOE. (*trying not to wilt before the* CAPTAIN's *glance and avoiding his eyes*) The time we signed up for is done today.

KEENEY. (*icily*) You're tellin' me nothin' I don't know.

JOE. You ain't pintin' fur home yit, far 's we kin see.

KEENEY. No, and I ain't agoin' to till this ship is full of ile.

JOE. You can't go no further no'the with the ice afore ye.

KEENEY. The ice is breaking up.

JOE. (*after a slight pause during which the others mumble angrily to one another*) The grub we're gittin' now is rotten.

KEENEY. It's good enough fur ye. Better men than ye are have eaten worse. (*There is a chorus of angry exclamations from the crowd.*)

JOE. (*encouraged by this support*) We ain't agoin' to work no more 'less you puts back for home.

KEENEY. (*fiercely*) You ain't, ain't you?

JOE. No; and the law courts'll say we was right.

KEENEY. To hell with your law courts! We're at sea now and I'm the law on this ship. (*Edging up toward the harpooner*) And every mother's son of you what don't obey orders goes in irons. (*There are more angry exclamations from the crew.* MRS. KEENEY *appears in the doorway in rear and looks on with startled eyes. None of the men notice her.*)

JOE. (*with bravado*) Then we're agoin' to mutiny and take the old hooker home ourselves. Ain't we, boys? (*As he turns his head to look at the others,* KEENEY's *fist shoots out to the side of his jaw.* JOE *goes down in a heap and lies there.* MRS. KEENEY *gives a shriek and hides her face in her hands. The men pull out their sheath-knives and start a rush, but stop when they find themselves confronted by the revolvers of* KEENEY *and the* MATE.)

KEENEY. (*his eyes and voice snapping*) Hold still! (*The men stand huddled together in a sullen silence.* KEENEY's *voice is full of mockery*) You've found out it ain't safe to mutiny on this ship, ain't you? And now git for'ard where ye belong, and— (*He gives* JOE's *body a contemptuous kick*) Drag him with you. And remember the first man of ye I see shirkin' I'll shoot dead as sure as there's a sea under us, and you can tell the rest the same. Git for'ard now! Quick! (*The men leave in cowed silence, carrying* JOE *with them.* KEENEY *turns to the* MATE *with a short laugh and puts his revolver back in his pocket*) Best get up on deck, Mr. Slocum, and see to it they don't try none of their skulkin' tricks. We'll have to keep an eye peeled from now on. I know 'em.

MATE. Yes, sir. (*He goes out, right.* KEENEY *hears his wife's hysterical weeping and turns around in surprise—then walks slowly to her side.*)

KEENEY. (*putting an arm around her shoulder—with gruff tenderness*) There, there, Annie. Don't be afeard. It's all past and gone.

MRS. KEENEY. (*shrinking away from him*) Oh, I can't bear it! I can't bear it any longer!

KEENEY. (*gently*) Can't bear what, Annie?

MRS. KEENEY. (*hysterically*) All this horrible brutality, and these brutes of men, and this terrible ship, and this prison cell of a room, and the ice all around, and the silence. (*After this outburst she calms down and wipes her eyes with her handkerchief.*)

KEENEY. (*after a pause during which he looks down at her with a puzzled frown*) Remember, I warn't hankerin' to have you come on this voyage, Annie.

MRS. KEENEY. I wanted to be with you, David, don't you see? I didn't want to wait back there in the house all alone as I've been doing these last six years since we were married—waiting, and watching, and fearing—with nothing to keep my mind occupied—not able to go back teaching school on account of being Dave Keeney's wife. I used to dream of sailing on the great, wide, glorious ocean. I wanted to be by your side in the danger and vigorous life of it all. I wanted to see you the hero they make you out to be in Homeport. And instead— (*Her voice grows tremulous*) All I find is ice and cold—and brutality! (*Her voice breaks.*)

KEENEY. I warned you what it'd be, Annie. "Whalin' ain't no ladies' tea-party," I says to you, and "you better stay to home where you've got all your woman's comforts." (*Shaking his head*) But you was so set on it.

MRS. KEENEY. (*wearily*) Oh, I know it isn't your fault, David. You see, I didn't believe you. I guess I was dreaming about the old Vikings in the story-books and I thought you were one of them.

KEENEY. (*protestingly*) I done my best to make it as cozy and comfortable as could be. (MRS. KEENEY *looks around her in wild scorn*) I even sent to the city for that organ for ye, thinkin' it might be soothin' to ye to be playin' it times when they was calms and things was dull-like.

MRS. KEENEY. (*wearily*) Yes, you were very kind, David. I know that. (*She goes to left and lifts the curtains from the porthole and looks out—then suddenly bursts forth*) I won't stand it—I can't stand it—pent up by these walls like a prisoner. (*She runs over to him and throws her arms around him, weeping. He puts his arm protectingly over her shoulders*) Take me away from here, David! If I don't get away from here, out of this terrible ship, I'll go mad! Take me home, David! I can't think any more. I feel as if the cold and the silence were crushing down on my brain. I'm afraid. Take me home!

KEENEY. (*holds her at arm's length and looks at her anxiously*) Best go to bed, Annie. You ain't yourself. You got fever. Your eyes look so strange-like. I ain't never seen you look this way before.

MRS. KEENEY. (*laughing hysterically*) It's the ice and the cold and the silence—they'd make anyone look strange.

KEENEY. (*soothingly*) In a month or two, with good luck, three at the most, I'll have her filled with ile and then we'll give her everything she'll stand and pint for home.

MRS. KEENEY. But we can't wait for that—I can't wait. I want to get home. And the men won't wait. They want to get home. It's cruel, it's brutal for you to keep them. You must sail back. You've got no excuse. There's clear water to the south now. If you've a heart at all you've got to turn back.

KEENEY. (*harshly*) I can't, Annie.

MRS. KEENEY. Why can't you?

KEENEY. A woman couldn't rightly understand my reason.

MRS. KEENEY. (*wildly*) Because it's a stupid, stubborn reason. Oh, I heard you talking with the second mate. You're afraid the other captains will sneer at you because you didn't come back with a full ship. You want to live up to your silly reputation even if you do have to beat and starve men and drive me mad to do it.

KEENEY. (*his jaw set stubbornly*) It ain't that, Annie. Them skippers would never dare sneer to my face. It ain't so much what any-one'd say—but— (*He hesitates, struggling to express his meaning*) You see—I've always done it—since my first voyage as skipper. I always come back—with a full ship—and—it don't seem right not to —somehow. I been always first whalin' skipper out o' Homeport, and— Don't you see my meanin', Annie? (*He glances at her. She is not looking at him but staring dully in front of her, not hearing a word he is saying*) Annie! (*She comes to herself with a start*) Best turn in, Annie, there's a good woman. You ain't well.

MRS. KEENEY. (*resisting his attempts to guide her to the door in rear*) David! Won't you please turn back?

KEENEY. (*gently*) I can't, Annie—not yet awhile. You don't see my meanin'. I got to git the ile.

MRS. KEENEY. It'd be different if you needed the money, but you don't. You've got more than plenty.

KEENEY. (*impatiently*) It ain't the money I'm thinkin' of. D'you think I'm as mean as that?

MRS. KEENEY. (*dully*) No—I don't know—I can't understand— (*Intensely*) Oh, I want to be home in the old house once more and see my own kitchen again, and hear a woman's voice talking to me and be able to talk to her. Two years! It seems so long ago—as if I'd been dead and could never go back.

KEENEY. (*worried by her strange tone and the far-away look in her eyes*) Best go to bed, Annie. You ain't well.

MRS. KEENEY. (*not appearing to hear him*) I used to be lonely when you were away. I used to think Homeport was a stupid, monotonous place. Then I used to go down on the beach, especially when it was windy and the breakers were rolling in, and I'd dream of the fine free life you must be leading. (*She gives a laugh which is half a sob*) I used to love the sea then. (*She pauses; then continues with slow intensity*) But now—I don't ever want to see the sea again.

KEENEY. (*thinking to humor her*) 'Tis no fit place for a woman, that's sure. I was a fool to bring ye.

MRS. KEENEY. (*after a pause—passing her hand over her eyes with a gesture of pathetic weariness*) How long would it take us to reach home—if we started now?

KEENEY. (*frowning*) 'Bout two months, I reckon, Annie, with fair luck.

MRS. KEENEY. (*counts on her fingers—then murmurs with a rapt smile*) That would be August, the latter part of August, wouldn't it? It was on the twenty-fifth of August we were married, David, wasn't it?

KEENEY. (*trying to conceal the fact that her memories have moved him—gruffly*) Don't *you* remember?

MRS. KEENEY. (*vaguely—again passes her hand over her eyes*) My memory is leaving me—up here in the ice. It was so long ago. (*A pause—then she smiles dreamily*) It's June now. The lilacs will be all in bloom in the front yard—and the climbing roses on the trellis to the side of the house—they're budding. (*She suddenly covers her face with her hands and commences to sob.*)

KEENEY. (*disturbed*) Go in and rest, Annie. You're all wore out cryin' over what can't be helped.

MRS. KEENEY. (*suddenly throwing her arms around his neck and clinging to him*) You love me, don't you, David?

KEENEY. (*in amazed embarrassment at this outburst*) Love you? Why d'you ask me such a question, Annie?

MRS. KEENEY. (*shaking him—fiercely*) But you do, don't you, David? Tell me!

KEENEY. I'm your husband, Annie, and you're my wife. Could there be aught but love between us after all these years?

MRS. KEENEY. (*shaking him again—still more fiercely*) Then you do love me. Say it!

KEENEY. (*simply*) I do, Annie!

MRS. KEENEY. (*gives a sigh of relief—her hands drop to her sides.* KEENEY *regards her anxiously. She passes her hand across her eyes and murmurs half to herself*) I sometimes think if we could only have had a child. (KEENEY *turns away from her, deeply moved. She grabs his arm and turns him around to face her—intensely*) And I've always been a good wife to you, haven't I, David?

KEENEY. (*his voice betraying his emotion*) No man has ever had a better, Annie.

MRS. KEENEY. And I've never asked for much from you, have I, David? Have I?

KEENEY. You know you could have all I got the power to give ye, Annie.

MRS. KEENEY. (*wildly*) Then do this this once for my sake, for God's sake—take me home! It's killing me, this life—the brutality and cold and horror of it. I'm going mad. I can feel the threat in the air. I can hear the silence threatening me—day after gray day and every day the same. I can't bear it. (*Sobbing*) I'll go mad, I know I will. Take me home, David, if you love me as you say. I'm afraid. For the love of God, take me home! (*She throws her arms around him, weeping against his shoulder. His face betrays the tremendous struggle going on within him. He holds her out at arm's length, his expression softening. For a moment his shoulders sag, he becomes old, his iron spirit weakens as he looks at her tear-stained face.*)

KEENEY. (*dragging out the words with an effort*) I'll do it, Annie—for your sake—if you say it's needful for ye.

MRS. KEENEY. (*with wild joy—kissing him*) God bless you for that,

David! (*He turns away from her silently and walks toward the companionway. Just at that moment there is a clatter of footsteps on the stairs and the* SECOND MATE *enters the cabin.*)

MATE. (*excitedly*) The ice is breakin' up to no'the'ard, sir. There's a clear passage through the floe, and clear water beyond, the lookout says. (KEENEY *straightens himself like a man coming out of a trance.* MRS. KEENEY *looks at the* MATE *with terrified eyes.*)

KEENEY. (*dazedly—trying to collect his thoughts*) A clear passage? To no'the'ard?

MATE. Yes, sir.

KEENEY. (*his voice suddenly grim with determination*) Then get her ready and we'll drive her through.

MATE. Aye, aye, sir.

MRS. KEENEY. (*appealingly*) David!

KEENEY. (*not heeding her*) Will the men turn to willin' or must we drag 'em out?

MATE. They'll turn to willin' enough. You put the fear o' God into 'em, sir. They're meek as lambs.

KEENEY. Then drive 'em—both watches. (*With grim determination*) They's whale t'other side o' this floe and we're going to git 'em.

MATE. Aye, aye, sir. (*He goes out hurriedly. A moment later there is the sound of scuffling feet from the deck outside and the* MATE'*s voice shouting orders.*)

KEENEY (*speaking aloud to himself—derisively*) And I was agoin' home like a yaller dog!

MRS. KEENEY. (*imploringly*) David!

KEENEY. (*sternly*) Woman, you ain't adoin' right when you meddle in men's business and weaken 'em. You can't know my feelin's. I got to prove a man to be a good husband for ye to take pride in. I got to git the ile, I tell ye.

MRS. KEENEY. (*supplicatingly*) David! Aren't you going home?

KEENEY. (*ignoring this question—commandingly*) You ain't well. Go and lay down a mite. (*He starts for the door*) I got to git on deck. (*He goes out. She cries after him in anguish*) David! (*A pause. She passes her hand across her eyes—then commences to laugh hysterically and goes to the organ. She sits down and starts to play wildly an old hymn.* KEENEY *re-enters from the doorway to the deck and stands looking at her angrily. He comes over and grabs her roughly by the shoulder.*)

KEENEY. Woman, what foolish mockin' is this? (*She laughs wildly and he starts back from her in alarm*) Annie! What is it? (*She doesn't answer him.* KEENEY'S *voice trembles*) Don't you know me, Annie? (*He puts both hands on her shoulders and turns her around so that he can look into her eyes. She stares up at him with a stupid expression, a vague smile on her lips. He stumbles away from her, and she commences softly to play the organ again.*)

KEENEY. (*swallowing hard—in a hoarse whisper, as if he had difficulty in speaking*) You said—you was agoin' mad—God! (*A long wail is heard from the deck above*) Ah bl-o-o-o-ow! (*A moment later the* MATE'S *face appears through the skylight. He cannot see* MRS. KEENEY.)

MATE. (*in great excitement*) Whales, sir—a whole school of 'em —off the star'b'd quarter 'bout five miles away—big ones!

KEENEY. (*galvanized into action*) Are you lowerin' the boats?

MATE. Yes, sir.

KEENEY. (*with grim decision*) I'm acomin' with ye.

MATE. Aye, aye, sir. (*Jubilantly*) You'll git the ile now right enough, sir. (*His head is withdrawn and he can be heard shouting orders.*)

KEENEY. (*turning to his wife*) Annie! Did you hear him? I'll git the ile. (*She doesn't answer or seem to know he is there. He gives a hard laugh, which is almost a groan*) I know you're foolin' me, Annie. You ain't out of your mind— (*anxiously*) be you? I'll git the ile now right enough—jest a little while longer, Annie—then we'll turn hom'ard. I can't turn back now, you see that, don't ye? I've got to git the ile. (*In sudden terror*) Answer me! You ain't mad, be you? (*She keeps on playing the organ, but makes no reply. The* MATE's *face appears again though the skylight.)*

MATE. All ready, sir. (KEENEY *turns his back on his wife and strides to the doorway, where he stands for a moment and looks back at her in anguish, fighting to control his feelings.)*

MATE. Comin', sir?

KEENEY. (*his face suddenly grown hard with determination*) Aye. (*He turns abruptly and goes out.* MRS. KEENEY *does not appear to notice his departure. Her whole attention seems centered in the organ. She sits with half-closed eyes, her body swaying a little from side to side to the rhythm of the hymn. Her fingers move faster and faster and she is playing wildly and discordantly as the curtain falls.)*

WHERE THE CROSS IS MADE

A Play in One Act

CHARACTERS

CAPTAIN ISAIAH BARTLETT

NAT BARTLETT, *his son*

SUE BARTLETT, *his daughter*

DOCTOR HIGGINS

SILAS HORNE, *mate*	
CATES, *bo'sun*	*of the schooner* Mary Allen
JIMMY KANAKA, *harpooner*	

WHERE THE CROSS IS MADE

SCENE. CAPTAIN BARTLETT'S *"cabin"—a room erected as a lookout post at the top of his house situated on a high point of land on the California coast. The inside of the compartment is fitted up like the captain's cabin of a deep-sea sailing vessel. On the left, forward, a porthole. Farther back, the stairs of the companionway. Still farther, two more portholes. In the rear, left, a marble-topped sideboard with a ship's lantern on it. In the rear, center, a door opening on stairs which lead to the lower house. A cot with a blanket is placed against the wall to the right of the door. In the right wall, five portholes. Directly under them, a wooden bench. In front of the bench, a long table with two straight-backed chairs, one in front, the other to the left of it. A cheap, dark-colored rug is on the floor. In the ceiling, midway from front to rear, a skylight extending from opposite the door to above the left edge of the table. In the right extremity of the skylight is placed a floating ship's compass. The light from the binnacle sheds over this from above and seeps down into the room, casting a vague globular shadow of the compass on the floor.*

The time is an early hour of a clear windy night in the fall of the year 1900. Moonlight, winnowed by the wind which moans in the stubborn angles of the old house, creeps wearily in through the portholes and rests like tired dust in circular patches upon the floor and table. An insistent monotone of thundering surf, muffled and far-off, is borne upward from the beach below.

After the curtain rises the door in the rear is opened slowly and the head and shoulders of NAT BARTLETT *appear over the sill. He casts a quick glance about the room, and seeing no one there, ascends the remaining steps and enters. He makes a sign to someone in the darkness beneath: "All right, Doctor."* DOCTOR HIGGINS *follows him into the room and, closing the door, stands looking with great curiosity around him. He is a slight, medium-sized professional-looking man of about thirty-five.* NAT BARTLETT *is very tall, gaunt, and loose-framed. His right arm has been amputated at the shoulder and the sleeve on that side of the heavy mackinaw he wears hangs flabbily or flaps against his body as he moves. He appears much older than his thirty years. His shoulders have a weary stoop as if worn down by the burden of his massive head with its heavy shock of tangled black hair. His face is long, bony, and sallow, with deep-set black eyes, a large aquiline nose, a wide thin-lipped mouth shadowed by an unkempt bristle of mustache. His voice is low and deep with a penetrating, hollow, metallic quality. In addition to the mackinaw, he wears corduroy trousers stuffed down into high laced boots.*

NAT. Can you see, Doctor?

HIGGINS (*in the too-casual tones which betray an inward uneasiness*) Yes—perfectly—don't trouble. The moonlight is so bright—

NAT. Luckily. (*Walking slowly toward the table*) He doesn't want any light—lately—only the one from the binnacle there.

HIGGINS. He? Ah—you mean your father?

NAT. (*impatiently*) Who else?

HIGGINS. (*a bit startled—gazing around him in embarrassment*) I suppose this is all meant to be like a ship's cabin?

NAT. Yes—as I warned you.

HIGGINS. (*in surprise*) Warned me? Why, warned? I think it's very natural—and interesting—this whim of his.

NAT. (*meaningly*) Interesting, it may be.

HIGGINS. And he lives up here, you said—never comes down?

NAT. Never—for the past three years. My sister brings his food up to him. (*He sits down in the chair to the left of the table*) There's a lantern on the sideboard there, Doctor. Bring it over and sit down. We'll make a light. I'll ask your pardon for bringing you to this room on the roof—but—no one'll hear us here; and by seeing for yourself the mad way he lives— Understand that I want you to get all the facts—just that, facts!—and for that light is necessary. Without that —they become dreams up here—dreams, Doctor.

HIGGINS. (*with a relieved smile carries over the lantern*) It is a trifle spooky.

NAT. (*not seeming to notice this remark*) He won't take any note of this light. His eyes are too busy—out there. (*He flings his left arm in a wide gesture seaward*) And if he does notice—well, let him come down. You're bound to see him sooner or later. (*He scratches a match and lights the lantern.*)

HIGGINS. Where is—he?

NAT. (*pointing upward*) Up on the poop. Sit down, man! He'll not come—yet awhile.

HIGGINS. (*sitting gingerly on the chair in front of table*) Then he has the roof too rigged up like a ship?

NAT. I told you he had. Like a deck, yes. A wheel, compass, binnacle light, the companionway there (*he points*), a bridge to pace up and down on—*and keep watch.* If the wind wasn't so high you'd hear him now—back and forth—all the live-long night. (*With a sudden harshness*) Didn't I tell you he's mad?

HIGGINS. (*with a professional air*) That was nothing new. I've heard that about him from all sides since I first came to the asylum yonder. You say he only walks at night—up there?

NAT. Only at night, yes. (*Grimly*) The things he wants to see can't be made out in daylight—dreams and such.

HIGGINS. But just what is he trying to see? Does anyone know? Does he tell?

NAT. (*impatiently*) Why, everyone knows what Father looks for, man! The ship, of course.

HIGGINS. What ship?

NAT. His ship—the *Mary Allen*—named for my dead mother.

HIGGINS. But—I don't understand— Is the ship long overdue—or what?

NAT. Lost in a hurricane off the Celebes with all on board—three years ago!

HIGGINS. (*wonderingly*) Ah. (*After a pause*) But your father still clings to a doubt—

NAT. There is no doubt for him or anyone else to cling to. She was sighted bottom up, a complete wreck, by the whaler *John Slocum*. That was two weeks after the storm. They sent a boat out to read her name.

HIGGINS. And hasn't your father ever heard—

NAT. He was the first to hear, naturally. Oh, he *knows* right enough, if that's what you're driving at. (*He bends toward the doctor—intensly*) He *knows*, Doctor, he *knows*—but he won't *believe*. He can't—and keep living.

HIGGINS. (*impatiently*) Come, Mr. Bartlett, let's get down to brass tacks. You didn't drag me up here to make things more obscure, did you? Let's have the facts you spoke of. I'll need them to give sympathetic treatment to his case when we get him to the asylum.

NAT. (*anxiously—lowering his voice*) And you'll come to take him away tonight—for sure?

HIGGINS. Twenty minutes after I leave here I'll be back in the car. That's positive.

NAT. And you know your way through the house?

HIGGINS. Certainly, I remember—but I don't see—

NAT. The outside door will be left open for you. You must come right up. My sister and I will be here—with him. And you understand— Neither of us knows anything about this. The authorities have been complained to—not by us, mind—but by someone. He must never know—

HIGGINS. Yes, yes—but still I don't— Is he liable to prove violent?

NAT. No—no. He's quiet always—too quiet; but he might do something—anything—if he knows—

HIGGINS. Rely on me not to tell him, then; but I'll bring along two attendants in case— (*He breaks off and continues in matter-of-fact tones*) And now for the facts in this case, if you don't mind, Mr. Bartlett.

NAT. (*shaking his head—moodily*) There are cases where facts—Well, here goes—the brass tacks. My father was a whaling captain as his father before him. The last trip he made was seven years ago. He expected to be gone two years. It was four before we saw him again. His ship had been wrecked in the Indian Ocean. He and six others managed to reach a small island on the fringe of the Archipelago—an island barren as hell, Doctor—after seven days in an open boat. The rest of the whaling crew never were heard from again—gone to the sharks. Of the six who reached the island with my father only three were alive when a fleet of Malay canoes picked them up, mad from thirst and starvation, the four of them. These four men finally reached Frisco. (*With great emphasis*) They were my father; Silas Horne, the mate; Cates, the bo'sun, and Jimmy Kanaka, a Hawaiian harpooner. Those four! (*With a forced laugh*) There are facts for you. It was in all the papers at the time—my father's story.

HIGGINS. But what of the other three who were on the island?

NAT. (*harshly*) Died of exposure, perhaps. Mad and jumped into the sea, perhaps. That was the told story. Another was whispered—killed and eaten, perhaps! But gone—vanished—that, undeniably. That was the fact. For the rest—who knows? And what does it matter?

HIGGINS. (*with a shudder*) I should think it would matter—a lot.

NAT. (*fiercely*) We're dealing with facts, Doctor! (*With a laugh*) And here are some more for you. My father brought the three down to this house with him—Horne and Cates and Jimmy Kanaka. We hardly recognized my father. He had been through hell and looked it. His hair was white. But you'll see for yourself—soon. And the others—they were all a bit queer, too—mad, if you will. (*He laughs again*) So much for the facts, Doctor. They leave off there and the dreams begin.

HIGGINS. (*doubtfully*) It would seem—the facts are enough.

NAT. Wait. (*He resumes deliberately*) One day my father sent for me and in the presence of the others told me the dream. I was to be heir to the secret. Their second day on the island, he said, they discovered in a sheltered inlet the rotten, water-logged hulk of a Malay prau—a proper war-prau such as the pirates used to use. She had been there rotting—God knows how long. The crew had vanished—God knows where, for there was no sign on the island that man had ever touched there. The Kanakas went over the prau—they're devils for staying under water, you know—and they found—in two chests—(*He leans back in his chair and smiles ironically*) Guess what, Doctor?

HIGGINS. (*with an answering smile*) Treasure, of course.

NAT. (*leaning forward and pointing his finger accusingly at the other*) You see! The root of belief is in you, too! (*Then he leans back with a hollow chuckle*) Why, yes. Treasure, to be sure. What else? They landed it and—you can guess the rest, too—diamonds, emeralds, gold ornaments—innumerable, of course. Why limit the stuff of dreams? Ha-ha! (*He laughs sardonically as if mocking himself.*)

HIGGINS. (*deeply interested*) And then?

NAT. They began to go mad—hunger, thirst, and the rest—and they began to forget. Oh, they forgot a lot, and lucky for them they did, probably. But my father realizing, as he told me, what was happening to them, insisted that while they still knew what they were doing they should—guess again now, Doctor. Ha-ha!

HIGGINS. Bury the treasure?

NAT. (*ironically*) Simple, isn't it? Ha-ha. And then they made a map—the same old dream, you see—with a charred stick, and my father had care of it. They were picked up soon after, mad as hatters, as I have told you, by some Malays. (*He drops his mocking and adopts a calm, deliberate tone again*) But the map isn't a dream, Doctor. We're coming back to facts again. (*He reaches into the pocket of his mackinaw and pulls out a crumpled paper*) Here. (*He spreads it out on the table.*)

HIGGINS. (*craning his neck eagerly*) Dammit! This is interesting. The treasure, I suppose, is where—

NAT. Where the cross is made.

HIGGINS. And here are the signatures, I see. And that sign?

NAT. Jimmy Kanaka's. He couldn't write.

HIGGINS. And below? That's yours, isn't it?

NAT. As heir to the secret, yes. We all signed it here the morning the *Mary Allen,* the schooner my father had mortgaged this house to fit out, set sail to bring back the treasure. Ha-ha.

HIGGINS. The ship he's still looking for—that was lost three years ago?

NAT. The *Mary Allen,* yes. The other three men sailed away on her. Only father and the mate knew the approximate location of the island—and I—as heir. It's—(*He hesitates, frowning*) No matter. I'll keep the mad secret. My father wanted to go with them—but my mother was dying. I dared not go either.

HIGGINS. Then you wanted to go? You believed in the treasure then?

NAT. Of course. Ha-ha. How could I help it? I believed until my mother's death. Then *he* became mad, entirely mad. He built this cabin—to wait in—and he suspected my growing doubt as time went on. So, as final proof, he gave me a thing he had kept hidden from them all—a sample of the richest of the treasure. Ha-ha. Behold! (*He takes from his pocket a heavy bracelet thickly studded with stones and throws it on the table near the lantern.*)

HIGGINS. (*picking it up with eager curiosity—as if in spite of himself*) Real jewels?

NAT. Ha-ha! You want to believe, to. No—paste and brass—Malay ornaments.

HIGGINS. You had it looked over?

NAT. Like a fool, yes. (*He puts it back in his pocket and shakes his head as if throwing off a burden*) Now you know why he's mad—waiting for that ship—and why in the end I had to ask you to take him away where he'll be safe. The mortgage—the price of that ship—is to be foreclosed. We have to move, my sister and I. We can't take him with us. She is to be married soon. Perhaps away from the sight of the sea he may—

HIGGINS. (*perfunctorily*) Let's hope for the best. And I fully appreciate your position. (*He gets up, smiling*) And thank you for the interesting story. I'll know how to humor him when he raves about treasure.

NAT. (*somberly*) He is quiet always—too quiet. He only walks to and fro—watching—

HIGGINS. Well, I must go. You think it's best to take him tonight?

NAT. (*persuasively*) Yes, Doctor. The neighbors—they're far away but—for my sister's sake—you understand.

HIGGINS. I see. It must be hard on her—this sort of thing— Well—(*He goes to the door, which* NAT *opens for him*) I'll return presently. (*He starts to descend.*)

NAT. (*urgently*) Don't fail us, Doctor. And come right up. He'll be here. (*He closes the door and tiptoes carefully to the companionway. He ascends it a few steps and remains for a moment listening for some sound from above. Then he goes over to the table, turning the lantern very low, and sits down, resting his elbow, his chin on his hand, staring somberly before him. The door in the rear is slowly opened. It creaks slightly and* NAT *jumps to his feet—in a thick voice of terror*) Who's there? (*The door swings wide open, revealing* SUE BARTLETT. *She ascends into the room and shuts the door behind her. She is a tall, slender woman of twenty-five, with a pale, sad face framed in a mass of dark red hair. This hair furnishes the only touch of color about her. Her full lips are pale; the blue of her wistful wide eyes is fading into a twilight gray. Her voice is low and melancholy. She wears a dark wrapper and slippers.*)

SUE. (*stands and looks at her brother accusingly*) It's only I. What are you afraid of?

NAT. (*averts his eyes and sinks back on his chair again*) Nothing. I didn't know—I thought you were in your room.

SUE. (*comes to the table*) I was reading. Then I heard someone come down the stairs and go out. Who was it? (*With sudden terror*) It wasn't—Father?

NAT. No. He's up there—watching—as he always is.

SUE. (*sitting down—insistently*) Who was it?

NAT. (*evasively*) A man—I know.

SUE. What man? What is he? You're holding something back. Tell me.

NAT. (*raising his eyes defiantly*) A doctor.

SUE. (*alarmed*) Oh! (*With quick intuition*) You brought him up here—so that I wouldn't know!

NAT. (*doggedly*) No. I took him up here to see how things were—to ask him about Father.

SUE. (*as if afraid of the answer she will get*) Is he one of them—from the asylum? Oh, Nat, you haven't—

NAT. (*interrupting her—hoarsely*) No, no! Be still.

SUE. That would be—the last horror.

NAT. (*defiantly*) Why? You always say that. What could be more horrible than things as they are? I believe—it would be better for him—away—where he couldn't see the sea. He'll forget his mad idea of waiting for a lost ship and a treasure that never was. (*As if trying to convince himself—vehemently*) I believe this!

SUE. (*reproachfully*) You don't, Nat. You know he'd die if he hadn't the sea to live with.

NAT. (*bitterly*) And you know old Smith will foreclose the mortgage. Is that nothing? We cannot pay. He came yesterday and talked with me. He knows the place is his—to all purposes. He talked as if we were merely his tenants, curse him! And he swore he'd foreclose immediately unless—

SUE. (*eagerly*) What?

NAT. (*in a hard voice*) Unless we have—Father—taken away.

SUE. (*in anguish*) Oh, but why, why? What is Father to him?

NAT. The value of the property—our home which is his, Smith's. The neighbors are afraid. They pass by on the road at nights coming back to their farms from the town. They see *him* up there walking back and forth—waving his arms against the sky. They're afraid. They talk of a complaint. They say for his own good he must be taken away. They even whisper the house is haunted. Old Smith is afraid of his property. He thinks that *he* may set fire to the house—do anything—

SUE. (*despairingly*) But you told him how foolish that was, didn't you? That Father is quiet, always quiet.

NAT. What's the use of telling—when they believe—when they're afraid? (SUE *hides her face in her hands—a pause—*NAT *whispers hoarsely*) I've been afraid myself—at times.

SUE. Oh, Nat! Of what?

NAT. (*violently*) Oh, him and the sea he calls to! Of the damned sea he forced me on as a boy—the sea that robbed me of my arm and made me the broken thing I am!

SUE. (*pleadingly*) You can't blame Father—for your misfortune.

NAT. He took me from school and forced me on his ship, didn't he? What would I have been now but an ignorant sailor like him if he had had his way? No. It's the sea I should not blame, that foiled him by taking my arm and then throwing me ashore—another one of *his* wrecks!

SUE. (*with a sob*) You're bitter, Nat—and hard. It was so long ago. Why can't you forget?

NAT. (*bitterly*) Forget! You can talk! When Tom comes from this voyage you'll be married and out of this with life before you—a captain's wife as our mother was. I wish you joy.

SUE. (*supplicatingly*) And you'll come with us, Nat—and Father, too—and then—

NAT. Would you saddle your young husband with a madman and

a cripple? (*Fiercely*) No, no, not I! (*Vindictively*) And not him, either! (*With sudden meaning—deliberately*) I've got to stay here. My book is three-fourths done—my book that will set me free! But I know, I feel, as sure as I stand here living before you, that I must finish it here. It could not live for me outside of this house where it was born. (*Staring at her fixedly*) So I will stay—in spite of hell! (SUE *sobs hopelessly. After a pause he continues*) Old Smith told me I could live here indefinitely without paying—as caretaker—if—

SUE. (*fearfully—like a whispered echo*) If?

NAT. (*staring at her—in a hard voice*) If I have *him* sent—where he'll no longer harm himself—nor others.

SUE. (*with horrified dread*) No—no, Nat! For our dead mother's sake.

NAT. (*struggling*) Did I say I had? Why do you look at me—like that?

SUE. Nat! Nat! For our mother's sake!

NAT. (*in terror*) Stop! Stop! She's dead—and at peace. Would you bring her tired soul back to him again to be bruised and wounded?

SUE. Nat!

NAT. (*clutching at his throat as though to strangle something within him—hoarsely*) Sue! Have mercy! (*His sister stares at him with dread foreboding.* NAT *calms himself with an effort and continues deliberately*) Smith said he would give two thousand, cash if I would sell the place to him—and he would let me stay, rent-free, as caretaker.

SUE. (*scornfully*) Two thousand! Why, over and above the mortgage it's worth—

NAT. It's not what it's worth. It's what one can get, cash—for my book—for freedom!

SUE. So that's why he wants Father sent away, the wretch! He must know the will Father made—

NAT. Gives the place to me. Yes, he knows. I told him.

SUE. (*dully*) Ah, how vile men are!

NAT. (*persuasively*) If it were to be done—if it were, I say—there'd be half for you for your wedding portion. That's fair.

SUE. (*horrified*) Blood-money! Do you think I could touch it?

NAT. (*persuasively*) It would be only fair. I'd give it you.

SUE. My God, Nat, are you trying to bribe me?

NAT. No. It's yours in all fairness. (*With a twisted smile*) You forget I'm heir to the treasure, too, and can afford to be generous. Ha-ha.

SUE. (*alarmed*) Nat! You're so strange. You're sick, Nat. You couldn't talk this way if you were yourself. Oh, we must go away from here—you and father and I! Let Smith foreclose. There'll be something over the mortgage; and we'll move to some little house—by the sea so that father—

NAT. (*fiercely*) Can keep up his mad game with me—whispering dreams in my ear—pointing out to sea—mocking me with stuff like this! (*He takes the bracelet from his pocket. The sight of it infuriates him and he hurls it into a corner, exclaiming in a terrible voice*) No! No! It's too late for dreams now. It's too late; I've put them behind me tonight—forever!

SUE. (*looks at him and suddenly understands that what she dreads has come to pass—letting her head fall on her outstretched arms with a long moan*) Then—you've done it! You've sold him! Oh, Nat, you're cursed!

NAT. (*with a terrified glance at the roof above*) Ssshh! What are you saying? He'll be better off—away from the sea.

SUE. (*dully*) You've sold him.

NAT. (*wildly*) No! No! (*He takes the map from his pocket*) Listen, Sue! For God's sake, listen to me! See! The map of the island (*He spreads it out on the table*) And the treasure—where the cross is made (*He gulps and his words pour out incoherently*) I've carried it about for years. Is that nothing? You don't know what it means. It stands between me and my book. It's stood between me and life—driving me mad! *He* taught me to wait and hope with him—wait and hope—day after day. He made me doubt my brain and give the lie to my eyes—when hope was dead—when I knew it was all a dream—I couldn't kill it! (*His eyes starting from his head*) God forgive me, I still believe! And that's mad—mad, do you hear?

SUE. (*looking at him with horror*) And that is why—you hate him!

NAT. No, I don't— (*Then in a sudden frenzy*) Yes! I do hate him! He's stolen my brain! I've got to free myself, can't you see, from him—and his madness.

SUE. (*terrified—appealingly*) Nat! Don't! You talk as if—

NAT. (*with a wild laugh*) As if I were mad? You're right—but I'll be mad no more! See! (*He opens the lantern and sets fire to the map in his hand. When he shuts the lantern again it flickers and goes out. They watch the paper burn with fascinated eyes as he talks*) See how I free myself and become sane. And now for facts, as the doctor said. I lied to you about him. He was a doctor from the asylum. See how it burns! It must all be destroyed—this poisonous madness. Yes, I lied to you—see—it's gone—the last speck—and the only other map is the one Silas Horne took to the bottom of the sea with him. (*He lets the ash fall to the floor and crushes it with his foot*) Gone! I'm free of it—at last! (*His face is very pale, but he goes on calmly*) Yes, I sold him, if you will—to save my soul. They're coming from the asylum to get him— (*There is a loud, muffled cry from above, which sounds like "Sail-ho," and a stamping of feet. The slide to the companionway above is slid back with a bang. A gust of air tears down into the room.* NAT *and* SUE *have jumped to their feet and stand petrified.* CAPTAIN BARTLETT *tramps down the stairs.*)

NAT. (*with a shudder*) God! Did he hear?

SUE. Ssshh! (CAPTAIN BARTLETT *comes into the room. He bears a striking resemblance to his son, but his face is more stern and formidable, his form more robust, erect and muscular. His mass of hair is pure white, his bristly mustache the same, contrasting with the weather-beaten leather color of his furrowed face. Bushy gray brows overhang the obsessed glare of his fierce dark eyes. He wears a heavy, double-breasted blue coat, pants of the same material, and rubber boots turned down from the knee.*)

BARTLETT. (*in a state of mad exultation strides toward his son and points an accusing finger at him.* NAT *shrinks backward a step*) Bin thinkin' me mad, did ye? Thinkin' it for the past three years, ye bin—ever since them fools on the *Slocum* tattled their damn lie o' the *Mary Allen* bein' a wreck.

NAT. (*swallowing hard—chokingly*) No— Father—I—

BARTLETT. Don't lie, ye whelp! You that I'd made my heir—aimin' to git me out o' the way! Aimin' to put me behind the bars o' the jail for mad folk!

SUE. Father—no!

BARTLETT (*waving his hand for her to be silent*) Not you, girl, not you. You're your mother.

NAT. (*very pale*) Father—do you think—I—

BARTLETT. (*fiercely*) A lie in your eyes! I bin a-readin' 'em. My curse on you!

SUE. Father! Don't!

BARTLETT. Leave me be, girl. He believed, didn't he? And ain't he turned traitor—mockin' at me and sayin' it's all a lie—mockin' at himself, too, for bein' a fool to believe in dreams, as he calls 'em.

NAT. (*placatingly*) You're wrong, Father. I do believe.

BARTLETT. (*triumphantly*) Aye, now ye do! Who wouldn't credit their own eyes?

NAT. (*mystified*) Eyes?

BARTLETT. Have ye not seen her, then? Did ye not hear me hail?

NAT. (*confusedly*) Hail? I heard a shout. But—hail what?—seen what?

BARTLETT. (*grimly*) Aye, now's your punishment, Judas. (*Explosively*) The *Mary Allen,* ye blind fool, come back from the Southern Seas—come back as I swore she must!

SUE. (*trying to soothe him*) Father! Be quiet. It's nothing.

BARTLETT. (*not heeding her—his eyes fixed hypnotically on his son's*)

Turned the pint a half-hour back—the *Mary Allen* loaded with gold as I swore she would be—carryin' her lowers—not a reef in 'em—makin' port, boy, as I swore she must—too late for traitors, boy, too late!—droppin' her anchor just when I hailed her.

NAT. (*a haunted, fascinated look in his eyes, which are fixed immovably on his father's*) The *Mary Allen!* But how do you know?

BARTLETT. Not know my own ship! 'Tis you're mad!

NAT. But at night—some other schooner—

BARTLETT. No other, I say! The *Mary Allen*—clear in the moonlight. And heed this: D'you call to mind the signal I gave to Silas Horne if he made this port o' a night?

NAT. (*slowly*) A red and a green light at the mainmast-head.

BARTLETT. (*triumphantly*) Then look out if ye dare! (*He goes to the porthole, left forward*) Ye can see it plain from here. (*Commandingly*) Will ye believe your eyes? Look—and then call me mad! (NAT *peers through the porthole and starts back, a dumbfounded expression on his face.*)

NAT. (*slowly*) A red and a green at the mainmast-head. Yes—clear as day.

SUE. (*with a worried look at him*) Let me see. (*She goes to the porthole.*)

BARTLETT. (*to his son with fierce satisfaction*) Aye, ye see now clear enough—too late for you. (NAT *stares at him spellbound*) And from above I saw Horne and Cates and Jimmy Kanaka plain on the deck in the moonlight lookin' up at me. Come! (*He strides to the companionway, followed by* NAT. *The two of them ascend.* SUE *turns from the porthole, an expression of frightened bewilderment on her face. She shakes her head sadly. A loud* "Mary Allen, *ahoy!*" *comes from above in* BARTLETT'S *voice, followed like an echo by the same hail from* NAT. SUE *covers her face with her hands, shuddering.* NAT *comes down the companionway, his eyes wild and exulting.*)

SUE. (*brokenly*) He's bad tonight, Nat. You're right to humor him. It's the best thing.

NAT. (*savagely*) Humor him? What in hell do you mean?

SUE (*pointing to the porthole*) There's nothing there, Nat. There's not a ship in harbor.

NAT. You're a fool—or blind! The *Mary Allen's* there in plain sight of anyone, with the red and the green signal-lights. Those fools lied about her being wrecked. And I've been a fool, too.

SUE. But, Nat, there's nothing. (*She goes over to the porthole again*) Not a ship. See.

NAT. I saw, I tell you. From above it's all plain. (*He turns from her and goes back to his seat by the table.* SUE *follows him, pleading frightenedly.*)

SUE. Nat! You mustn't let this— You're all excited and trembling, Nat. (*She puts a soothing hand on his forehead.*)

NAT. (*pushing her away from him roughly*) You blind fool! (*Bartlett comes down the steps of the companionway. His face is transfigured with the ecstasy of a dream come true.*)

BARTLETT. They've lowered a boat—the three—Horne and Cates and Jimmy Kanaka. They're a-rowin' ashore. I heard the oars in the locks. Listen! (*A pause.*)

NAT. (*excitedly*) I hear!

SUE. (*who has taken the chair by her brother—in a warning whisper*) It's the wind and sea you hear, Nat. Please!

BARTLETT. (*suddenly*) Hark! They've landed. They're back on earth again as I swore they'd come back. They'll be a-comin' up the path now. (*He stands in an attitude of rigid attention.* NAT *strains forward in his chair. The sound of the wind and sea suddenly ceases and there is a heavy silence. A dense green glow floods slowly in rhythmic waves like a liquid into the room—as of great depths of the sea faintly penetrated by light.*)

NAT. (*catching at his sister's hand—chokingly*) See how the light changes! Green and gold! (*He shivers*) Deep under the sea! I've been drowned for years! (*Hysterically*) Save me! Save me!

SUE. (*patting his hand comfortingly*) Only the moonlight, Nat. It hasn't changed. Be quiet, dear, it's nothing. (*The green light grows deeper and deeper.*)

BARTLETT. (*in a crooning, monotonous tone*) They move slowly—slowly. They're heavy, I know, heavy—the two chests. Hark! They're below at the door. You hear?

NAT. (*starting to his feet*) I hear! I left the door open.

BARTLETT. For them?

NAT. For them.

SUE. (*shuddering*) Ssshh! (*The sound of a door being heavily slammed is heard from way down in the house.*)

NAT. (*to his sister—excitedly*) There! You hear?

SUE. A shutter in the wind.

NAT. There is no wind.

BARTLETT. Up they come! Up, bullies! They're heavy—heavy! (*The padding of bare feet sounds from the floor below—then comes up the stairs.*)

NAT. You hear them now?

SUE. Only the rats running about. It's nothing, Nat.

BARTLETT. (*rushing to the door and throwing it open*) Come in, lads, come in!—and welcome home! (*The forms of* SILAS HORNE, CATES, *and* JIMMY KANAKA *rise noislessly into the room from the stairs. The last two carry heavy inlaid chests.* HORNE *is a parrot-nosed, angular old man dressed in gray cotton trousers and a singlet torn open across his hairy chest.* JIMMY *is a tall, sinewy, bronzed young Kanaka. He wears only a breechcloth.* CATES *is squat and stout and is dressed in dungaree pants and a shredded white sailor's blouse, stained with iron-rust. All are in their bare feet. Water drips from their soaked and rotten clothes. Their hair is matted, intertwined with slimy strands of seaweed. Their eyes, as they glide silently into the room, stare frightfully wide at nothing. Their flesh in the green light has the suggestion of decomposition. Their bodies sway limply, nervelessly, rhythmically as if to the pulse of long swells of the deep sea.*)

NAT. (*making a step toward them*) See! (*Frenziedly*) Welcome home, boys.

SUE. (*grabbing his arm*) Sit down, Nat. It's nothing. There's no one there. Father—sit down!

BARTLETT. (*grinning at the three and putting his finger to his lips*) Not here, boys, not here—not before him. (*He points to his son*) He has no right, now. Come. The treasure is ours only. We'll go away with it together. Come. (*He goes to the companionway. The three follow. At the foot of it* HORNE *puts a swaying hand on his shoulder and with the other holds out a piece of paper to him.* BARTLETT *takes it and chuckles exultantly*) That's right—for him—that's right! (*He ascends. The figures sway up after him.*)

NAT. (*frenziedly*) Wait! (*He struggles toward the companionway.*)

SUE. (*trying to hold him back*) Nat—don't! Father—come back!

NAT. Father! (*He flings her away from him and rushes up the companionway. He pounds against the slide, which seems to have been shut down on him.*)

SUE. (*hysterically—runs wildly to the door in rear*) Help! help! (*As she gets to the door* DOCTOR HIGGINS *appears, hurrying up the stairs.*)

HIGGINS. (*excitedly*) Just a moment, Miss. What's the matter?

SUE. (*with a gasp*) My father—up there!

HIGGINS. I can't see—where's my flash. Ah. (*He flashes it on her terror-stricken face, then quickly around the room. The green glow disappears. The wind and sea are heard again. Clear moonlight floods through the portholes.* HIGGINS *springs to the companionway.* NAT *is still pounding*) Here, Bartlett. Let me try.

NAT. (*coming down—looking dully at the doctor*) They've locked it. I can't get up.

HIGGINS. (*looks up—in an astonished voice*) What's the matter, Bartlett? It's all open. (*He starts to ascend.*)

NAT. (*in a voice of warning*) Look out, man. Look out for them!

HIGGINS. (*calls down from above*) Them? Who? There's no one here. (*Suddenly—in alarm*) Come up! Lend a hand here! He's fainted! (NAT *goes up slowly.* SUE *goes over and lights the lantern, then hurries back to the foot of the companionway with it. There is a scuffling noise from above. They reappear, carrying* CAPTAIN BARTLETT's *body.*)

HIGGINS. Easy now! (*They lay him on the couch in rear.* SUE *sets the lantern down by the couch.* HIGGINS *bends and listens for a heartbeat. Then he rises, shaking his head*). I'm sorry—

SUE. (*dully*) Dead?

HIGGINS. (*nodding*) Heart failure, I should judge. (*With an attempt at consolation*) Perhaps it's better so, if—

NAT. (*as if in a trance*) There was something Horne handed him. Did you see?

SUE. (*wringing her hands*) Oh, Nat, be still! He's dead. (*To* HIGGINS *with pitiful appeal*) Please go—go—

HIGGINS. There's nothing I can do?

SUE. Go—please— (HIGGINS *bows stiffly and goes out.* NAT *moves slowly to his father's body, as if attracted by some irresistible fascination.*)

NAT. Didn't you see? Horne handed him something.

SUE. (*sobbing*) Nat! Nat! Come away! Don't touch him, Nat! Come away. (*But her brother does not heed her. His gaze is fixed on his father's right hand, which hangs downward over the side of the couch. He pounces on it and forcing the clenched fingers open with a great effort, secures a crumpled ball of paper.*)

NAT. (*flourishing it above his head with a shout of triumph*) See! (*He bends down and spreads it out in the light of the lantern*) The map of the island! Look! It isn't lost for me after all! There's still a chance—*my* chance! (*With mad, solemn decision*) When the house is sold I'll go—and I'll find it! Look! It's written here in his handwriting: "The treasure is buried where the cross is made."

SUE. (*covering her face with her hands—brokenly*) Oh, God! Come away, Nat! Come away!

CURTAIN

THE ROPE

A Play in One Act

CHARACTERS

ABRAHAM BENTLEY

ANNIE, *his daughter*

PAT SWEENEY, *her husband*

MARY, *their child*

LUKE BENTLEY, *Abe's son by a second marriage*

THE ROPE

SCENE. *The interior of an old barn situated on top of a high headland of the seacoast. In the rear, to the left, a stall in which lumber is stacked up. To the right of it, an open double doorway looking out over the ocean. Outside the doorway, the faint trace of what was once a road leading to the barn. Beyond the road, the edge of a cliff which rises sheer from the sea below. On the right of the doorway, three stalls with mangers and hay-ricks. The first of these is used as a woodbin and is half full of piled-up cordwood. Near this bin, a chopping-block with an ax driven into the top of it.*

The left section of the barn contains the hayloft, which extends at a height of about twelve feet from the floor as far to the right as the middle of the doorway. The loft is bare except for a few scattered mounds of dank-looking hay. From the edge of the loft, half-way from the door, a rope about five feet long with an open running noose at the end, is hanging. A rusty plow and various other farming implements, all giving evidence of long disuse, are lying on the floor near the left wall. Farther forward an old cane-bottomed chair is set back against the wall.

In front of the stalls on the right stands a long, roughly constructed carpenter's table, evidently home-made. Saws, a lathe, a hammer, chisel, a keg containing nails and other tools of the carpentry trade are on the table. Two benches are placed, one in front, one to the left of it.

The right side of the barn is a bare wall.

It is between six and half-past in the evening of a day in early spring. At the rising of the curtain some trailing clouds near the horizon, seen through the open doorway, are faintly tinged with gold by the first glow of the sunset. As the action progresses this reflected light gradually becomes brighter, and then slowly fades into a smoky crimson. The sea is a dark slate color. From the rocks below the headland sounds the muffled monotone of breaking waves.

As the curtain rises MARY *is discovered squatting cross-legged on the floor, her back propped against the right side of the doorway, her face in profile. She is a skinny, overgrown girl of ten, with thin, carroty hair worn in a pigtail. She wears a shabby gingham dress. Her face is stupidly expressionless. Her hands flutter about aimlessly in relaxed, flabby gestures.*

She is staring fixedly at a rag doll which she has propped up against the doorway opposite her. She hums shrilly to herself.

At a sudden noise from outside she jumps to her feet, peeks out, and quickly snatches up the doll, which she hugs fiercely to her breast. Then, after a second's fearful hesitation, she runs to the carpenter's table and crawls under it.

As she does so ABRAHAM BENTLEY *appears in the doorway and stands, blinking into the shadowy barn. He is a tall, lean, stoop-shouldered old man of sixty-five. His thin legs, twisted by rheumatism, totter feebly under him as he shuffles slowly along by the aid of a thick cane. His face is gaunt, chalky-white, furrowed with wrinkles, surmounted by a shiny bald scalp fringed with scanty wisps of white hair. His eyes peer weakly from beneath bushy, black brows. His mouth is a sunken line drawn in under his large, beak-like nose. A two weeks' growth of stubby patches of beard covers his jaws and chin. He has on a threadbare brown overcoat but wears no hat.*

BENTLEY. (*comes slowly into the barn, peering around him suspiciously. As he reaches the table and leans one hand on it for support,* MARY *darts from underneath and dashes out through the doorway.* BENTLEY *is startled; then shakes his cane after her*) Out o' my sight, you Papist brat! Spawn o' Satan! Spyin' on me! They set her to it. Spyin' to watch me! (*He limps to the door and looks out cautiously. Satisfied, he turns back into the barn*) Spyin' to see—

what they'll never know. (*He stands staring up at the rope and taps it testingly several times with his stick, talking to himself as he does so*) It's tied strong—strong as death— (*He cackles with satisfaction*) They'll see, then! They'll see! (*He laboriously creeps over to the bench and sits down wearily. He looks toward the sea and his voice quavers in a doleful chant*) "Woe unto us! for the day goeth away, for the shadows of the evening are stretched out." (*He mumbles to himself for a moment—then speaks clearly*) Spyin' on me! Spawn o' the Pit! (*He renews his chant*) "They hunt our steps that we cannot go in our streets: our end is near, our days are fulfilled; for our end is come."

(*As he finishes* ANNIE *enters. She is a thin, slovenly, worn-out-looking woman of about forty with a drawn, pasty face. Her habitual expression is one of a dulled irritation. She talks in a high-pitched, sing-song whine. She wears a faded gingham dress and a torn sunbonnet.*)

ANNIE. (*comes over to her father but warily keeps out of range of his stick*) Paw! (*He doesn't answer or appear to see her*) Paw! You ain't fergittin' what the doctor told you when he was here last, be you? He said you was to keep still and not go a-walkin' round. Come on back to the house, Paw. It's gittin' near supper-time and you got to take your medicine b'fore it, like he says.

BENTLEY. (*his eyes fixed in front of him*) "The punishment of thine iniquity is accomplished, O daughter of Zion: he will visit thine iniquity, O daughter of Edom; he will discover thy sins."

ANNIE. (*waiting resignedly until he has finished—wearily*) You better take watch on your health, Paw, and not be sneakin' up to this barn no more. Lord sakes, soon 's ever my back is turned you goes sneakin' off agen. It's enough to drive a body outa their right mind.

BENTLEY. "Behold, every one that useth proverbs shall use this proverb against thee, saying, As is the mother, so is her daughter!" (*He cackles to himself*) So is her daughter!

ANNIE. (*her face flushing with anger*) And if I am, I'm glad I take after her and not you, y' old wizard! (*Scornfully*) A fine one you be to be shoutin' Scripture in a body's ears all the live-long day—you that druv Maw to her death with your naggin', and pinchin', and miser stinginess. If you've a mind to pray, it's down in the medder you ought to go, and kneel down by her grave, and ask God to forgive you for the meanness you done to her all her life.

BENTLEY. (*mumbling*) "As is the mother, so is her daughter."

ANNIE. (*enraged by the repetition of this quotation*) *You* quotin' Scripture! Why, Maw wasn't cold in the earth b'fore you was down in the port courtin' agen—courtin' that harlot that was the talk o' the whole town! And then you disgraces yourself and me by marryin' her—*her*—and bringin' her back home with you; and me still goin' every day to put flowers on Maw's grave that you'd fergotten. (*She glares at him vindictively, pausing for breath*) And between you you'd have druv me into the grave like you done Maw if I hadn't married Pat Sweeney so's I could git away and live in peace. Then you took on so high and mighty 'cause he was a Cath'lic—*you* gittin' religion all of a moment just for spite on me 'cause I'd left—and b'cause she egged you on against me; *you* sayin' it was a sin to marry a Papist, after not bein' at Sunday meetin' yourself for more'n twenty years!

BENTLEY. (*loudly*) "He will visit thine iniquity—"

ANNIE. (*interrupting*) And the carryin's-on you had the six years at home after I'd left you—the shame of the whole county! Your wife, indeed, with a child she *claimed* was your'n, and her goin' with this farmer and that, and even men off the ships in the port, and you blind to it! And then when she got sick of you and ran away—only to meet her end at the hands of God a year after—she leaves you alone with that—*your* son, Luke, *she* called him—and him only five years old!

BENTLEY. (*babbling*) Luke? Luke?

ANNIE. (*tauntingly*) Yes, Luke! "As is the mother, so is her son"—that's what you ought to preach 'stead of puttin' curses on me. You was glad enough to git me back home agen, and Pat with me, to tend the place, and help bring up that brat of hers. (*Jealously*) You was fond enough of him all them years—and how did he pay you back? Stole your money and ran off and left you just when he was sixteen and old enough to help. Told you to your face he'd stolen and was leavin'. He only laughed when you was took crazy and cursed him; and he only laughed harder when you hung up that silly rope there (*she points*) and told him to hang himself on it when he ever came home agen.

BENTLEY. (*mumbling*) You'll see, then. You'll see!

ANNIE. (*wearily—her face becoming dull and emotionless again*) I s'pose I'm a bigger fool than you be to argy with a half-witted body. But I tell you agen that Luke of yours ain't comin' back; and if he does he ain't the kind to hang himself, more's the pity. He's like her. He'd hang *you* more likely if he s'pected you had any money. So you might 's well take down that ugly rope you've had tied there since he run off. He's probably dead anyway by this.

BENTLEY. (*frightened*) No! No!

ANNIE. Them as bad as him comes to a sudden end. (*Irritably*) Land sakes, Paw, here I am argyin' with your lunatic notions and the supper not ready. Come on and git your medicine. You can see no one ain't touched your old rope. Come on! You can sit 'n' read your Bible. (*He makes no movement. She comes closer to him and peers into his face—uncertainly*) Don't you hear me? I do hope you ain't off in one of your fits when you don't know nobody. D'you know who's talkin'? This is Annie—your Annie, Paw.

BENTLEY. (*bursting into senile rage*) None o' mine! Spawn o' the Pit! (*With a quick movement he hits her viciously over the arm with his stick. She gives a cry of pain and backs away from him, holding her arm.*)

ANNIE. (*weeping angrily*) That's what I git for tryin' to be kind to you, you ugly old devil! (*The sound of a man's footsteps is heard from outside, and* SWEENEY *enters. He is a stocky, muscular, sandy-*

haired Irishman dressed in patched corduroy trousers shoved down into high laced boots, and a blue flannel shirt. The bony face of his bullet head has a pressed-in appearance except for his heavy jaw, which sticks out pugnaciously. There is an expression of mean cunning and cupidity about his mouth and his small, round, blue eyes. He has evidently been drinking and his face is flushed and set in an angry scowl.)

SWEENEY. Have ye no supper at all made, ye lazy slut? (*Seeing that she has been crying*) What're you blubberin' about?

ANNIE. It's all his fault. I was tryin' to git him home but he's that set I couldn't budge him; and he hit me on the arm with his cane when I went near him.

SWEENEY. He did, did he? I'll soon learn him better. (*He advances toward* BENTLEY *threateningly.*)

ANNIE. (*grasping his arm*) Don't touch him, Pat. He's in one of his fits and you might kill him.

SWEENEY. An' good riddance!

BENTLEY. (*hissing*) Papist! (*Chants*) "Pour out thy fury upon the heathen that know thee not, and upon the families that call not on thy name: for they have eaten up Jacob, and devoured him, and consumed him, and made his habitation desolate."

SWEENEY. (*instinctively crosses himself—then scornfully*) Spit curses on me till ye choke. It's not likely the Lord God'll be listenin' to a wicked auld sinner the like of you. (*To* ANNIE) What's got into him to be roamin' up here? When I left for the town he looked too weak to lift a foot.

ANNIE. Oh, it's the same crazy notion he's had ever since Luke left. He wanted to make sure the rope was still here.

BENTLEY. (*pointing to the rope with his stick*) He-he! Luke'll come back. Then you'll see. You'll see!

SWEENEY. (*nervously*) Stop that mad cacklin', for the love of heaven! (*With a forced laugh*) It's great laughter I should be havin' at you, mad as you are, for thinkin' that thief of a son of yours would come back to hang himself on account of your curses. It's five years he's been gone, and not a sight of him; an' you cursin' an' callin' down the wrath o' God on him by day an' by night. That shows you what God thinks of your curses—an' Him deaf to you!

ANNIE. It's no use talkin' to him, Pat.

SWEENEY. I've small doubt but that Luke is hung long since—by the police. He's come to no good end, that lad. (*His eyes on the rope*) I'll be pullin' that thing down, so I will; an' the auld loon'll stay in the house, where he belongs, then, maybe. (*He reaches up for the rope as if to try and yank it down.* BENTLEY *waves his stick frantically in the air, and groans with rage.*)

ANNIE. (*frightened*) Leave it alone, Pat. Look at him. He's liable to hurt himself. Leave his rope be. It don't do no harm.

SWEENEY. (*reluctantly moves away*) It looks ugly hangin' there open like a mouth. (*The old man sinks back into a relieved immobility.* SWEENEY *speaks to his wife in a low tone*) Where's the child? Get her to take him out o' this. I want a word with you he'll not be hearin'. (*She goes to the door and calls out*) Ma-ry! Ma-ry! (*A faint, answering cry is heard and a moment later* MARY *rushes breathlessly into the barn.* SWEENEY *grabs her roughly by the arm. She shrinks away, looking at him with terrified eyes*) You're to take your grandfather back to the house—an' see to it he stays there.

ANNIE. And give him his medicine.

SWEENEY. (*as the child continues to stare at him silently with eyes stupid from fear, he shakes her impatiently*) D'you hear me, now? (*To his wife*) It's soft-minded she is, like I've always told you, an' stupid; and you're not too firm in the head yourself at times, God help you! An' look at him! It's the curse is in the wits of your family, not mine.

ANNIE. You've been drinkin' in town or you wouldn't talk that way.

MARY. (*whining*) Maw! I'm skeered!

SWEENEY. (*lets go of her arm and approaches* BENTLEY) Get up out o' this, ye auld loon, an' go with Mary. She'll take you to the house. (BENTLEY *tries to hit him with the cane*) Oho, ye would, would ye? (*He wrests the cane from the old man's hands*) Bad cess to ye, you're the treach'rous one! Get up, now! (*He jerks the old man to his feet*) Here, Mary, take his hand. Quick now! (*She does so tremblingly*) Lead him to the house.

ANNIE. Go on, Paw! I'll come and git your supper in a minute.

BENTLEY. (*stands stubbornly and begins to intone*) "O Lord, thou hast seen my wrong; judge thou my cause. Thou hast seen all their vengeance and all their imaginations against me—"

SWEENEY. (*pushing him toward the door.* BENTLEY *tries to resist.* MARY *pulls at his hand in a sudden fit of impish glee, and laughs shrilly*) Get on now an' stop your cursin'.

BENTLEY. "Render unto them a recompense, O Lord, according to the work of their hands."

SWEENEY. Shut your loud quackin'! Here's your cane. (*He gives it to the old man as they come to the doorway and quickly steps back out of reach*) An' mind you don't touch the child with it or I'll beat you to a jelly, old as ye are.

BENTLEY. (*resisting* MARY's *efforts to pull him out, stands shaking his stick at* SWEENEY *and his wife*) "Give them sorrow of heart, thy curse unto them. Persecute and destroy them in anger from under the heavens of the Lord."

MARY. (*tugging at his hand and bursting again into shrill laughter*) Come on, Gran'paw. (*He allows himself to be led off, right.*)

SWEENEY. (*making the sign of the cross furtively—with a sigh of relief*) He's gone, thank God! What a snake's tongue he has in him! (*He sits down on the bench to the left of table*) Come here, Annie, till I speak to you. (*She sits down on the bench in front of table.* SWEENEY *winks mysteriously*) Well, I saw him, sure enough.

ANNIE. (*stupidly*) Who?

SWEENEY. (*sharply*) Who? Who but Dick Waller, the lawyer, that I went to see. (*Lowering his voice*) An' I've found out what we was wishin' to know. (*With a laugh*) Ye said I'd been drinkin'—which was true; but 'twas all in the plan I'd made. I've a head for strong drink, as ye know, but he hasn't. (*He winks cunningly*) An' the whiskey loosened his tongue till he'd told all he knew.

ANNIE. He told you—about Paw's will?

SWEENEY. He did. (*Disappointedly*) But for all the good it does us we might as well be no wiser than we was before. (*He broods for a moment in silence—then hits the table furiously with his fist*) God's curse on the auld miser!

ANNIE. What did he tell you?

SWEENEY. Not much at the first. He's a cute one, an' he'd be askin' a fee to tell you your own name, if he could get it. His practice is all dribbled away from him lately on account of the drink. So I let on I was only payin' a friendly call, havin' known him for years. Then I asked him out to have a drop o' drink, knowin' his weakness; an' we had rashers of them, an' I payin' for it. Then I come out with it straight and asked him about the will—because the auld man was crazy an' on his last legs, I told him, an' he was the lawyer made out the will when Luke was gone. So he winked at me an' grinned—he was drunk by this—an' said: "It's no use, Pat. He left the farm to the boy." "To hell with the farm," I spoke back. "It's mortgaged to the teeth; but how about the money?" "The money?" an' he looks at me in surprise, "What money?" "The cash he has," I says. "You're crazy," he says. "There wasn't any cash—only the farm." "D'you mean to say he made no mention of money in his will?" I asked. You could have knocked me down with a feather. "He did not—on my oath," he says. (SWEENEY *leans over to his wife—indignantly*) Now what d'you make o' that? The auld divil!

ANNIE. Maybe Waller was lyin'.

SWEENEY. He was not. I could tell by his face. He was surprised to hear me talkin' of money.

ANNIE. But the thousand dollars Paw got for the mortgage just before that woman ran away—

SWEENEY. An' that I've been slavin' me hands off to pay the int'rist on!

ANNIE. What could he have done with that? He ain't spent it. It was in twenty-dollar gold pieces he got it, I remember Mr. Kellar of the bank tellin' me once.

SWEENEY. Divil a penny he's spent. Ye know as well as I do if it wasn't for my hammerin', an' sawin', an' nailin', he'd be in the poorhouse this minute—or the madhouse, more likely.

ANNIE. D'you suppose that harlot ran off with it?

SWEENEY. I do not; I know better—an' so do you. D'you not remember the letter she wrote tellin' him he could support Luke on the money he'd got on the mortgage she'd signed with him; for he'd made the farm over to her when he married her. An' where d'you suppose Luke got the hundred dollars he stole? The auld loon must have had cash with him then, an' it's only five years back.

ANNIE. He's got it hid some place in the house most likely.

SWEENEY. Maybe you're right. I'll dig in the cellar this night when he's sleepin'. He used to be down there a lot recitin' Scripture in his fits.

ANNIE. What else did Waller say?

SWEENEY. Nothin' much; except that we should put notices in the papers for Luke, an' if he didn't come back by sivin years from when he'd left—two years from now, that'd be—the courts would say he was dead an' give us the farm. Divil a lot of use it is to us now with no money to fix it up; an' himself ruinin' it years ago by sellin' everythin' to buy that slut new clothes.

ANNIE. Don't folks break wills like his'n in the courts?

SWEENEY. Waller said 'twas no use. The auld divil was plain in his full senses when he made it; an' the courts cost money.

ANNIE. (*resignedly*) There ain't nothin' we can do then.

SWEENEY. No—except wait an' pray that young thief is dead an' won't come back; an' try an' find where it is the auld man has the gold hid, if he has it yet. I'd take him by the neck an' choke him till

he told it, if he wasn't your father. (*He takes a full quart flask of whiskey from the pocket of his coat and has a big drink*) Aahh! If we'd on'y the thousand we'd stock the farm good an' I'd give up this dog's game (*He indicates the carpentry outfit scornfully*) an' we'd both work hard with a man or two to help, an' in a few years we'd be rich; for 'twas always a payin' place in the auld days.

ANNIE. Yes, yes, it was always a good farm then.

SWEENEY. He'll not last long in his senses, the doctor told me. His next attack will be very soon an' after it he'll be a real lunatic with no legal claims to anythin'. If we on'y had the money— 'Twould be the divil an' all if the auld fool should forget where he put it, an' him takin' leave of his senses altogether. (*He takes another nip at the bottle and puts it back in his pocket—with a sigh*) Ah, well, I'll save what I can an' at the end of two years, with good luck in the trade, maybe we'll have enough. (*They are both startled by the heavy footsteps of someone approaching outside. A shrill burst of* MARY'S *laughter can be heard and the deep voice of a man talking to her.*)

SWEENEY. (*uneasily*) It's Mary; but who could that be with her? It's not himself. (*As he finishes speaking* LUKE *appears in the doorway, holding the dancing* MARY *by the hand. He is a tall, strapping young fellow about twenty-five with a coarse-featured, rather handsome face bronzed by the sun. What his face lacks in intelligence is partly forgiven for his good-natured, half-foolish grin, his hearty laugh, his curly dark hair, a certain devil-may-care recklessness and irresponsible youth in voice and gesture. But his mouth is weak and characterless; his brown eyes are large but shifty and acquisitive. He wears a dark blue jersey, patched blue pants, rough sailor shoes, and a gray cap. He advances into the stable with a mocking smile on his lips until he stands directly under the rope. The man and woman stare at him in petrified amazement.*)

ANNIE. Luke!

SWEENEY. (*crossing himself*) Glory be to God—it's him!

MARY. (*hopping up and down wildly*) It's Uncle Luke, Uncle

Luke, Uncle Luke! (*She runs to her mother, who pushes her away angrily.*)

LUKE. (*regarding them both with an amused grin*) Sure, it's Luke—back after five years of bummin' round the rotten old earth in ships and things. Paid off a week ago—had a bust-up—and then took a notion to come out here—bummed my way—and here I am. And you're both of you tickled to death to see me, ain't yuh?—like hell! (*He laughs and walks over to* ANNIE) Don't yuh even want to shake flippers with your dear, long-lost brother, Annie? I remember you and me used to git on so fine together—like hell!

ANNIE. (*giving him a venomous look of hatred*) Keep your hands to yourself.

LUKE. (*grinning*) You ain't changed, that's sure—on'y yuh're homelier'n ever. (*He turns to the scowling* SWEENEY) How about you, brother Pat?

SWEENEY. I'd not lower myself to take the hand of a—

LUKE. (*with a threat in his voice*) Easy goes with that talk! I'm not so soft to lick as I was when I was a kid; and don't forget it.

ANNIE. (*to* MARY, *who is playing catch with a silver dollar which she has had clutched in her hand—sharply*) Mary! What have you got there? Where did you get it? Bring it here to me this minute! (MARY *presses the dollar to her breast and remains standing by the doorway in stubborn silence.*)

LUKE. Aw, let her alone! What's bitin' yuh? That's on'y a silver dollar I give her when I met her front of the house. She told me you was up here; and I give her that as a present to buy candy with. I got it in Frisco—cart-wheels, they call 'em. There ain't none of them in these parts I ever seen, so I brung it along on the voyage.

ANNIE. (*angrily*) I don't know or care where you got it—but I know you ain't come by it honest. Mary! Give that back to him this instant! (*As the child hesitates, she stamps her foot furiously*) D'you hear me? (MARY *starts to cry softly, but comes to* LUKE *and hands him the dollar.*)

LUKE. (*taking it—with a look of disgust at his half-sister*) I was right when I said you ain't changed, Annie. You're as stinkin' mean as ever. (*To* MARY, *consolingly*) Quit bawlin', kid. You 'n' me'll go out on the edge of the cliff here and chuck some stones in the ocean same's we useter, remember? (MARY's *tears immediately cease. She looks up at him with shining eyes, and claps her hands.*)

MARY. (*pointing to the dollar he has in his hand*) Throw that! It's flat 'n' it'll skip.

LUKE. (*with a grin*) That's the talk, kid. That's all it's good for—to throw away; not buryin' it like your miser folks'd tell you. Here! You take it and chuck it away. It's your'n. (*He gives her the dollar and she hops to the doorway. He turns to* PAT *with a grin*) I'm learnin' your kid to be a sport, Tight-Wad. I hope you ain't got no objections.

MARY. (*impatiently*) Come on, Uncle Luke. Watch me throw it.

LUKE. Aw right. (*To* PAT) I'll step outside a second and give you two a chanct to git all the dirty things yuh're thinkin' about me off your chest. (*Threateningly*) And then I'm gointer come and talk turkey to you, see? I didn't come back here for fun, and the sooner you gets that in your beans, the better.

MARY. Come on and watch me!

LUKE. Aw right, I'm comin'. (*He walks out and stands, leaning his back against the doorway, left.* MARY *is about six feet beyond him on the other side of the road. She is leaning down, peering over the edge of the cliff and laughing excitedly.*)

MARY. Can I throw it now? Can I?

LUKE. Don't git too near the edge, kid. The water's deep down there, and you'd be a drowned rat if you slipped. (*She shrinks back a step*) You chuck it when I say three. Ready, now! (*She draws back her arm*) One! Two! Three! (*She throws the dollar away and bends down to see it hit the water.*)

MARY. (*clapping her hands and laughing*) I seen it! I seen it splash! It's deep down now, ain't it?

LUKE. Yuh betcher it is! Now watch how far I kin chuck rocks. (*He picks up a couple and goes to where she is standing. During the following conversation between* SWEENEY *and his wife he continues to play this way with* MARY. *Their voices can be heard but the words are indistinguishable.*)

SWEENEY. (*glancing apprehensively toward the door—with a great sigh*) Speak of the divil an' here he is! (*Furiously*) Flingin' away dollars, the dirty thief, an' us without—

ANNIE. (*interrupting him*) Did you hear what he said? A thief like him ain't come back for no good. (*Lowering her voice*) D'you s'pose he knows about the farm bein' left to him?

SWEENEY. (*uneasily*) How could he? An' yet—I dunno— (*With sudden decision*) You'd best lave him to me to watch out for. It's small sense you have to hide your hate from him. You're as loony as the rist of your breed. An' he needs to be blarneyed round to fool him an' find out what he's wantin'. I'll pritind to make friends with him, God roast his soul! An' do you run to the house an' break the news to the auld man; for if he seen him suddin it's likely the little wits he has left would leave him; an' the thief could take the farm from us tomorrow if himself turned a lunatic.

ANNIE. (*getting up*) I'll tell him a little at a time till he knows.

SWEENEY. Be careful, now, or we'll lose the farm this night. (*She starts towards the doorway.* SWEENEY *speaks suddenly in a strange, awed voice*) Did you see Luke when he first came in to us? He stood there with the noose of the rope almost touchin' his head. I was almost wishin'— (*He hesitates.*)

ANNIE. (*viciously*) I was wishin' it was round his neck chokin' him, that's what I was—hangin' him just as Paw says.

SWEENEY. Ssshh! He might hear ye. Go along, now. He's comin' back.

MARY. (*pulling at* LUKE'S *arm as he comes back to the doorway*) Lemme throw 'nother! Lemme throw 'nother!

LUKE. (*enters just as* ANNIE *is going out and stops her*) Goin' to the house? Do we get any supper? I'm hungry.

ANNIE. (*glaring at him but restraining her rage*) Yes.

LUKE. (*jovially*) Good work! And tell the old man I'm here and I'll see him in a while. He'll be glad to see me, too—like hell! (*He comes forward.* ANNIE *goes off, right.*)

MARY. (*in an angry whine, tugging at his hand*) Lemme throw 'nother. Lemme—

LUKE. (*shaking her away*) There's lots of rocks, kid. Throw them. Dollars ain't so plentiful.

MARY. (*screaming*) No! No! I don' wanter throw rocks. Lemme throw 'nother o' them.

SWEENEY. (*severely.*) Let your uncle in peace, ye brat! (*She commences to cry*) Run help your mother now or I'll give ye a good hidin'. (MARY *runs out of the door, whimpering.* PAT *turns to* LUKE *and holds out his hand.*)

LUKE. (*looking at it in amazement*) Ahoy, there! What's this?

SWEENEY. (*with an ingratiating smile*) Let's let bygones be bygones. I'm harborin' no grudge agen you these past years. Ye was only a lad when ye ran away an' not to be blamed for it. I'd have taken your hand a while back, an' glad to, but for her bein' with us. She has the divil's own tongue, as ye know, an' she can't forget the rowin' you an' her used to be havin'.

LUKE. (*still looking at* SWEENEY's *hand*) So that's how the wind blows! (*With a grin*) Well, I'll take a chanct. (*They shake hands and sit down by the table,* SWEENEY *on the front bench and* LUKE *on the left one.*)

SWEENEY. (*pulls the bottle from his coat pocket—with a wink*) Will ye have a taste? It's real stuff.

LUKE. Yuh betcher I will! (*He takes a big gulp and hands the bottle back.*)

SWEENEY. (*after taking a drink himself, puts bottle on table*) I wasn't wishin' herself to see it or I'd have asked ye sooner. (*There is a pause, during which each measures the other with his eyes.*)

LUKE. Say, how's the old man now?

SWEENEY. (*cautiously*) Oh, the same as ivir—older an' uglier, maybe.

LUKE. I thought he might be in the bug-house by this time.

SWEENEY. (*hastily*) Indeed not; he's foxy to pritind he's loony, but he's his wits with him all the time.

LUKE. (*insinuatingly*) Is he as stingy with his coin as he used to be?

SWEENEY. If he owned the ocean he wouldn't give a fish a drink; but I doubt if he's any money left at all. Your mother got rid of it all I'm thinkin'. (LUKE *smiles a superior, knowing smile*) He has on'y the farm, an' that mortgaged. I've been payin' the int'rist an' supportin' himself an' his doctor bills by the carpentryin' these five years past.

LUKE. (*with a grin*) Huh! Yuh're slow. Yuh oughter get wise to yourself.

SWEENEY. (*inquisitively*) What d'ye mean by that?

LUKE. (*aggravatingly*) Aw, nothin'. (*He turns around and his eyes fix themselves on the rope*) What the hell— (*He is suddenly convulsed with laughter and slaps his thigh*) Haha! If that don't beat the Dutch! The old nut!

SWEENEY. What?

LUKE. That rope. Say, has he had that hangin' there ever since I skipped?

SWEENEY. (*smiling*) Sure; an' he thinks you'll be comin' home to hang yourself.

LUKE. Hahaha! Not this chicken! And you say he ain't crazy! Gee, that's too good to keep. I got to have a drink on that. (SWEENEY *pushes the bottle toward him. He raises it toward the rope*) Here's how, old chum! (*He drinks.* SWEENEY *does likewise*) Say, I'd almost forgotten about that. Remember how hot he was that day when he hung that rope up and cussed me for pinchin' the hundred? He was standin' there shakin' his stick at me, and I was laughin' 'cause he looked so funny with the spit dribblin' outa his mouth like he was a mad dog. And when I turned round and beat it he shouted after me: "Remember, when you come home again there's a rope waitin' for yuh to hang yourself on, yuh bastard!" (*He spits contemptuously*) What a swell chanct. (*His manner changes and he frowns*) The old slave-driver! That's a hell of a fine old man for a guy to have!

SWEENEY. (*pushing the bottle toward him*) Take a sup an' forgit it. 'Twas a long time past.

LUKE. But the rope's there yet, ain't it? And he keeps it there. (*He takes a large swallow.* SWEENEY *also drinks*) But I'll git back at him aw right, yuh wait 'n' see. I'll git every cent he's got this time.

SWEENEY. (*slyly*) If he has a cent. I'm not wishful to discourage ye, but— (*He shakes his head doubtfully, at the same time fixing* LUKE *with a keen glance out of the corner of his eye.*)

LUKE. (*with a cunning wink*) Aw, he's got it aw right. You watch me! (*He is beginning to show the effects of the drink he has had. He pulls out tobacco and a paper and rolls a cigarette and lights it. As he puffs he continues boastfully*) You country jays oughter wake up and see what's goin' on. Look at me. I was green as grass when I left here, but bummin' round the world, and bein' in cities, and meetin' all kinds, and keepin' your two eyes open—that's what'll learn yuh a cute trick or two.

SWEENEY. No doubt but you're right. Us country folks is stupid in most ways. We've no chance to learn the things a travelin' lad like you'd be knowin'.

LUKE. (*complacently*) Well, you watch me and I'll learn yuh. (*He snickers*) So yuh thinks the old man's flat broke, do yuh?

SWEENEY. I do so.

LUKE. Then yuh're simple; that's what—simple! Yuh're lettin' him kid yuh.

SWEENEY. If he has any, it's well hid, I know that. He's a sly old bird.

LUKE. And I'm a slyer bird. D'yuh hear that? I c'n beat his game any time. You watch me! (*He reaches out his hand for the bottle. They both drink again.* SWEENEY *begins to show signs of getting drunk. He hiccoughs every now and then and his voice grows uncertain and husky.*)

SWEENEY. It'd be a crafty one who'd find where he'd hidden it, sure enough.

LUKE. You watch me! I'll find it. I betcher anything yuh like I find it. You watch me! Just wait till he's asleep and I'll show yuh—ter-night. (*There is a noise of shuffling footsteps outside and* ANNIE'S *whining voice raised in angry protest.*)

SWEENEY. Ssshh! It's himself comin' now. (LUKE *rises to his feet and stands, waiting in a defensive attitude, a surly expression on his face. A moment later* BENTLEY *appears in the doorway, followed by* ANNIE. *He leans against the wall, in an extraordinary state of excitement, shaking all over, gasping for breath, his eyes devouring* LUKE *from head to foot.*)

ANNIE. I couldn't do nothin' with him. When I told him *he'd* come back there was no holdin' him. He was a'most frothin' at the mouth till I let him out. (*Whiningly*) You got to see to him, Pat, if you want any supper. I can't—

SWEENEY. Shut your mouth! We'll look after him.

ANNIE. See that you do. I'm goin' back. (*She goes off, right.* LUKE *and his father stand looking at each other. The surly expression disappears from* LUKE'S *face, which gradually expands in a broad grin.*)

LUKE. (*jovially*) Hello, old sport! I s'pose yuh're tickled to pieces to see me—like hell! (*The old man stutters and stammers incoherently as if the very intensity of his desire for speech had paralyzed all power of articulation.* LUKE *turns to* PAT) I see he ain't lost the old stick. Many a crack on the nut I used to get with that.

BENTLEY. (*suddenly finding his voice—chants*) "Bring forth the best robe, and put it on him; and put a ring on his hand, and shoes on his feet: And bring hither the fatted calf, and kill it; and let us eat and be merry: For this my son was dead, and is alive again; he was lost, and is found." (*He ends up with a convulsive sob.*)

LUKE. (*disapprovingly*) Yuh're still spoutin' the rotten old Word o' God same's ever, eh? Say, give us a rest on that stuff, will yuh? Come on and shake hands like a good sport. (*He holds out his hand. The old man totters over to him, stretching out a trembling hand.* LUKE *seizes it and pumps it up and down*) That's the boy!

SWEENEY. (*genuinely amazed*) Look at that, would ye—the two-faced auld liar. (BENTLEY *passes his trembling hand all over* LUKE, *feeling of his arms, his chest, his back. An expression of overwhelming joy suffuses his worn features.*)

LUKE. (*grinning at* SWEENEY) Say, watch this. (*With tolerant good-humor*) On the level I b'lieve the old boy's glad to see me at that. He looks like he was tryin' to grin; and I never seen him grin in my life, I c'n remember. (*As* BENTLEY *attempts to feel of his face*) Hey, cut it out! (*He pushes his hand away, but not roughly*) I'm all here, yuh needn't worry. Yuh needn't be scared I'm a ghost. Come on and sit down before yuh fall down. Yuh ain't got your sea-legs workin' right. (*He guides the old man to the bench at left of table*) Squat here for a spell and git your wind. (BENTLEY *sinks down on the bench.* LUKE *reaches for the bottle*) Have a drink to my makin' port. It'll buck yuh up.

SWEENEY. (*alarmed*) Be careful, Luke. It might likely end him.

LUKE. (*holds the bottle up to the old man's mouth, supporting his head with the other hand.* BENTLEY *gulps, the whiskey drips over his chin, and he goes into a fit of convulsive coughing.* LUKE *laughs*) Ha-haha! Went down the wrong way, did it? I'll show yuh the way to do it. (*He drinks*) There yuh are—smooth as silk. (*He hands the bottle to* SWEENEY, *who drinks and puts it back on the table.*)

SWEENEY. He must be glad to see ye or he'd not drink. 'Tis dead against it he's been these five years past. (*Shaking his head*) An' him cursin' you day an' night! I can't put head or tail to it. Look out he ain't meanin' some bad to ye underneath. He's crafty at pretendin'.

LUKE. (*as the old man makes signs to him with his hand*) What's he after now? He's lettin' on he's lost his voice again. What d'yuh want? (BENTLEY *points with his stick to the rope. His lips move convulsively as he makes a tremendous effort to utter words.*)

BENTLEY. (*mumbling incoherently*) Luke—Luke—rope—Luke—hang.

SWEENEY. (*appalled*) There ye are! What did I tell you? It's to see you hang yourself he's wishin', the auld fiend!

BENTLEY. (*nodding*) Yes—Luke—hang.

LUKE. (*taking it as a joke—with a loud guffaw*) Hahaha! If that don't beat the Dutch! The old nanny-goat! Aw right, old sport. Anything to oblige. Hahaha! (*He takes the chair from left and places it under the rope. The old man watches him with eager eyes and seems to be trying to smile.* LUKE *stands on the chair.*)

SWEENEY. Have a care, now! I'd not be foolin' with it in your place.

LUKE. All out for the big hangin' of Luke Bentley by hisself. (*He puts the noose about his neck with an air of drunken bravado and grins at his father. The latter makes violent motions for him to go on*) Look at him, Pat. By God, he's in a hurry. Hahaha! Well, old sport, here goes nothin'. (*He makes a movement as if he were going to jump and kick the chair from under him.*)

SWEENEY. (*half starts to his feet—horrified*) Luke! Are ye gone mad?

LUKE. (*stands staring at his father, who is still making gestures for him to jump. A scowl slowly replaces his good-natured grin*) D'yuh really mean it—that yuh want to see me hangin' myself? (BENTLEY *nods vigorously in the affirmative.* LUKE *glares at him for a moment in silence*) Well, I'll be damned! (*To* PAT) An' I thought he was only kiddin'. (*He removes the rope gingerly from his neck. The old man stamps his foot and gesticulates wildly, groaning with disappointment.* LUKE *jumps to the floor and looks at his father for a second. Then his face grows white with a vicious fury*) I'll fix your hash, you stinkin' old murderer! (*He grabs the chair by its back and swings it over his head as if he were going to crush* BENTLEY'S *skull with it. The old man cowers on the bench in abject terror.*)

SWEENEY. (*jumping to his feet with a cry of alarm*) Luke! For the love of God! (LUKE *hesitates; then hurls the chair in back of him under the loft, and stands menacingly in front of his father, his hands on his hips.*)

LUKE. (*grabbing* BENTLEY'S *shoulder and shaking him—hoarsely*) Yuh wanted to see me hangin' there in real earnest, didn't yuh? You'd hang me yourself if yuh could, wouldn't yuh? And you my own father! Yuh damned son-of-a-gun! Yuh would, would yuh? I'd smash your brains out for a nickel! (*He shakes the old man more and more furiously.*)

SWEENEY. Luke! Look out! You'll be killin' him next.

LUKE. (*giving his father one more shake, which sends him sprawling on the floor*) Git outa here! Git outa this b'fore I kill yuh dead! (SWEENEY *rushes over and picks the terrified old man up*) Take him outa here, Pat! (*His voice rises to a threatening roar*) Take him outa here or I'll break every bone in his body! (*He raises his clenched fists over his head in a frenzy of rage.*)

SWEENEY. Ssshh! Don't be roarin'! I've got him. (*He steers the whimpering, hysterical* BENTLEY *to the doorway*) Come out o' this, now. Get down to the house! Hurry now! Ye've made enough trouble for one night! (*They disappear off right.* LUKE *flings himself on a bench, breathing heavily. He picks up the bottle and takes a long swallow.* SWEENEY *re-enters from rear. He comes over and sits down in his old place*) Thank God he's off down to the house, scurryin' like a frightened hare as if he'd never a kink in his legs in his life. He was moanin' out loud so you could hear him a long ways. (*With a sigh*) It's a murd'rous auld loon he is, sure enough.

LUKE. (*thickly*) The damned son-of-a-gun!

SWEENEY. I thought you'd be killin' him that time with the chair.

LUKE. (*violently*) Serve him damn right if I done it.

SWEENEY. An' you laughin' at him a moment sooner! I thought 'twas jokin' ye was.

LUKE. (*suddenly*) So I was kiddin'; but I thought he was tryin' to kid me, too. And then I seen by the way he acted he really meant it. (*Banging the table with his fist*) Ain't that a hell of a fine old man for yuh!

SWEENEY. He's a mean auld swine.

LUKE. He meant it aw right, too. Yuh shoulda seen him lookin' at me. (*With sudden lugubriousness*) Ain't he a hell of a nice old man for a guy to have? Ain't he?

SWEENEY. (*soothingly*) Hush! It's all over now. Don't be thinkin' about it.

LUKE. (*on the verge of drunken tears*) How kin I help thinkin'—and him my own father? After me bummin' and starvin' round the rotten earth, and workin' myself to death on ships and things—and when I come home he tries to make me bump off—wants to see me a corpse—my own father, too! Ain't he a hell of an old man to have? The rotten son-of-a-gun!

SWEENEY. It's past an' done. Forgit it. (*He slaps* LUKE *on the shoulder and pushes the bottle toward him*) Let's take a drop more. We'll be goin' to supper soon.

LUKE. (*takes a big drink—huskily*) Thanks. (*He wipes his mouth on his sleeve with a snuffle*) But I'll tell yuh something you can put in your pipe and smoke. It ain't past and done, and it ain't goin' to be! (*More and more aggressively*) And I ain't goin' to fergit it, either! Yuh kin betcher life on that, pal. And *he* ain't goin' to ferget it—not if he lives a million—not by a damned sight! (*With sudden fury*) I'll fix his hash! I'll git even with him, the old skunk! You watch me! And this very night, too!

SWEENEY. How'd you mean?

LUKE. You just watch me, I tell yuh! (*Banging the table*) I said I'd git even and I will git even—this same night, with no long waits, either! (*Frowning*) Say, you don't stand up for him, do yuh?

SWEENEY. (*spitting—vehemently*) That's child's talk. There's not a day passed I've not wished him in his grave.

LUKE. (*excitedly*) Then we'll both git even on him—you 'n' me. We're pals, ain't we?

SWEENEY. Sure.

LUKE. And yuh kin have half what we gits. That's the kinda feller I am! That's fair enough, ain't it?

SWEENEY. Surely.

LUKE. I don't want no truck with this rotten farm. You kin have my share of that. I ain't made to be no damned dirt-puncher—not me! And I ain't goin' to loaf round here more'n I got to, and when I goes this time I ain't never comin' back. Not me! Not to punch dirt and milk cows. You kin have the rotten farm for all of me. What I wants is cash—regular coin yuh kin spend—not dirt. I want to show the gang a real time, and then ship away to sea agen or go bummin' agen. I want coin yuh kin throw away—same's your kid chucked that dollar of mine overboard, remember? A real dollar, too! She's a sport, aw right!

SWEENEY. (*anxious to bring him back to the subject*) But where d'you think to find his money?

LUKE. (*confidently*) Don't yuh fret. I'll show yuh. You watch me! I know his hidin' places. I useter spy on him when I was a kid—Maw used to make me—and I seen him many a time at his sneakin'. (*Indignantly*) He used to hide stuff from the old lady. What d'yuh know about him—the mean skunk.

SWEENEY. That was a long time back. You don't know—

LUKE. (*assertively*) But I do know, see! He's got two places. One was where I swiped the hundred.

SWEENEY. It'll not be there, then.

LUKE. No; but there's the other place; and he never knew I was wise to that. I'd have left him clean on'y I was a kid and scared to pinch more. So you watch me! We'll git even on him, you 'n' me, and go halfs, and yuh kin start the rotten farm goin' agen and I'll beat it where there's some life.

SWEENEY. But if there's no money in that place, what'll you be doin' to find out where it is, then?

LUKE. Then you 'n' me 'ull make him tell!

SWEENEY. Oho, don't think it! 'Tis not him'd be tellin'.

LUKE. Aw, say, you're simple! You watch me! I know a trick or two about makin' people tell what they don't wanter. (*He picks up the chisel from the table*) Yuh see this? Well, if he don't answer up nice and easy we'll show him! (*A ferocious grin settles over his face*) We'll git even on him, you 'n' me—and he'll tell where it's hid. We'll just shove this into the stove till it's red-hot and take off his shoes and socks and warm the bottoms of his feet for him. (*Savagely*) He'll tell then—anything we wants him to tell.

SWEENEY. But Annie?

LUKE. We'll shove a rag in her mouth so's she can't yell. That's easy.

SWEENEY. (*his head lolling drunkenly—with a cruel leer*) 'Twill serve him right to heat up his hoofs for him, the limpin' auld miser! —if ye don't hurt him too much.

LUKE. (*with a savage scowl*) We won't hurt him—more'n enough. (*Suddenly raging*) I'll pay him back aw right! He won't want no more people to hang themselves when I git through with him. I'll fix his hash! (*He sways to his feet, the chisel in his hand*) Come on! Let's git to work. Sooner we starts the sooner we're rich. (SWEENEY *rises. He is steadier on his feet than* LUKE. *At this moment* MARY *appears in the doorway.*)

MARY. Maw says supper's ready. I had mine. (*She comes into the room and jumps up, trying to grab hold of the rope*) Lift me, Uncle Luke. I wanter swing.

LUKE. (*severely*) Don't yuh dare touch that rope, d'yuh hear?

MARY. (*whining*) I wanter swing.

LUKE. (*with a shiver*) It's bad, kid. Yuh leave it alone, take it from me.

SWEENEY. She'll get a good whalin' if I catch her jumpin' at it.

LUKE. Come on, pal. T'hell with supper. We got work to do first. (*They go to the doorway.*)

SWEENEY. (*turning back to the sulking* MARY) And you stay here, d'you hear, ye brat, till we call ye—or I'll skin ye alive.

LUKE. And termorrer mornin', kid, I'll give yuh a whole handful of them shiny, bright things yuh chucked in the ocean—and yuh kin be a real sport.

MARY. (*eagerly*) Gimme 'em now! Gimme 'em now, Uncle Luke. (*As he shakes his head—whiningly*) Gimme one! Gimme one!

LUKE. Can't be done, kid. Termorrer. Me 'n' your old man is goin' to git even now—goin' to make him pay for—

SWEENEY. (*interrupting—harshly*) Hist with your noise! D'you think she's no ears? Don't be talkin' so much. Come on, now.

LUKE. (*permitting himself to be pulled out the doorway*) Aw right! I'm with yuh. We'll git even—you 'n' me. The damned son-of-a-gun! (*They lurch off to the right.*)

(MARY *skips to the doorway and peeps after them for a moment. Then she comes back to the center of the floor and looks around her with an air of decision. She sees the chair in under the loft and runs over to it, pulling it back and setting it on its legs directly underneath the noose of the rope. She climbs and stands on the top of the chair and grasps the noose with both her upstretched hands. Then with a shriek of delight she kicks the chair from under her and launches herself for a swing. The rope seems to part where it is fixed to the beam. A dirty gray bag tied to the end of the rope falls to the floor with a muffled, metallic thud.* MARY *sprawls forward on her hands and knees, whimpering. Straggly wisps from the pile of rank hay fall silently to the floor in a mist of dust.* MARY, *discovering she is unhurt, glances quickly around and sees the bag. She pushes herself along the floor and, untying the string at the top, puts in her hand. She gives an exclamation of joy at what she feels and, turning the bag upside down, pours its contents in her lap. Giggling to herself, she gets to her feet and goes to the doorway, where she dumps what she has in her lap in a heap on the floor just inside the barn. They lie there in a glittering pile, shimmering in the faint sunset glow—fifty twenty-dollar gold pieces.* MARY *claps her hands and sings to herself: "Skip—skip—skip." Then she quickly picks up four or five and runs out to the edge of the cliff. She throws them one after another into the ocean as fast as she can and bends over to see them hit the water. Against the background of horizon clouds still tinted with blurred crimson she hops up and down in a sort of grotesque dance, clapping her hands and laughing shrilly. After the last one is thrown she rushes back into the barn to get more.*)

MARY. (*picking up a handful—giggling ecstatically*) Skip! Skip! (*She turns and runs out to throw them as the curtain falls.*)

THE DREAMY KID

A Play in One Act

CHARACTERS

Mammy Saunders

Abe, *her grandson, "The Dreamy Kid"*

Ceely Ann

Irene

THE DREAMY KID

SCENE. *Mammy Saunders' bedroom in a house just off Carmine Street, New York City. The left of the room, forward, is taken up by a heavy, old-fashioned wooden bedstead with a feather mattress. A gaudy red-and-yellow quilt covers the other bedclothes. In back of the bed, a chest of drawers placed against the left wall. On top of the chest, a small lamp. A rocking-chair stands beside the head of the bed on the right. In the rear wall, toward the right, a low window with ragged white curtains. In the right corner, a washstand with bowl and pitcher. Bottles of medicine, a spoon, a glass, etc., are also on the stand. Farther forward, a door opening on the hall and stairway.*

It is soon after nightfall of a day in early winter. The room is in shadowy half darkness, the only light being a pale glow that seeps through the window from the arc lamp on the nearby corner, and by which the objects in the room can be dimly discerned. The vague outlines of Mammy Saunders' figure lying in the bed can be seen, and her black face stands out in sharp contrast to the pillows that support her head.

MAMMY. (*weakly*) Ceely Ann! (*With faint querulousness*) Light de lamp, will you? Hit's mighty dark in yere. (*After a slight pause*) Ain't you dar, Ceely Ann? (*Receiving no reply she sighs deeply and her limbs move uneasily under the bedclothes. The door is opened and shut and the stooping form of another colored woman appears in the semi-darkness. She goes to the foot of the bed sobbing softly, and stands there evidently making an effort to control her emotion.*)

MAMMY. Dat you, Ceely Ann?

CEELY. (*huskily*) Hit ain't no yuther, Mammy.

MAMMY. Light de lamp, den. I can't see nowhars.

CEELY. Des one second till I finds a match. (*She wipes her eyes with her handkerchief—then goes to the chest of drawers and feels around on the top of it—pretending to grumble*) Hit beat all how dem pesky little sticks done hide umse'fs. Shoo! Yere dey is. (*She fumbles with the lamp.*)

MAMMY. (*suspiciously*) You ain't been cryin', is you?

CEELY. (*with feigned astonishment*) Cryin'? I clar' ter goodness you does git de mos' fool notions lyin' dar.

MAMMY. (*in a tone of relief*) I mos' thought I yeard you.

CEELY. (*lighting the lamp*) 'Deed you ain't. (*The two women are revealed by the light.* MAMMY SAUNDERS *is an old, white-haired Negress about ninety with a weazened face furrowed by wrinkles and withered by old age and sickness. Ceely is a stout woman of fifty or so with gray hair and a round fat face. She wears a loose-fitting gingham dress and a shawl thrown over her head.*)

CEELY. (*with attempted cheeriness*) Bless yo' soul, I ain't got nothin' to cry 'bout. Yere. Lemme fix you so you'll rest mo' easy. (*She lifts the old woman gently and fixes the pillows*) Dere. Now, ain't you feelin' better?

MAMMY. (*dully*) My strenk don' all went. I can't lift a hand.

CEELY. (*hurriedly*) Dat'll all come back ter you de doctor tole me des now when I goes down to de door with him. (*Glibly*) He say you is de mos' strongest 'oman fo' yo years ever he sees in de worl'; and he tell me you gwine ter be up and walkin' agin fo' de week's out. (*As she finds the old woman's eyes fixed on her she turns away confusedly and abruptly changes the subject*) Hit ain't too wa'm in dis room, dat's a fac'.

MAMMY. (*shaking her head—in a half whisper*) No, Ceely Ann. Hit ain't no use'n you tellin' me nothin' but de trufe. I feels mighty poo'ly. En I knows hit's on'y wid de blessin' er God I kin las' de night out.

CEELY. (*distractedly*) Ain't no sich a thing! Hush yo' noise, Mammy!

MAMMY. (*as if she hadn't heard—in a crooning sing-song*) I'se gwine soon fum dis wicked yearth—and may de Lawd have mercy on dis po' ole sinner. (*After a pause—anxiously*) All I'se prayin' fer is dat God don' take me befo' I sees Dreamy agin. Whar's Dreamy, Ceely Ann? Why ain't he come yere? Ain't you done sent him word I'se sick like I tole you?

CEELY. I tole dem boys ter tell him speshul, and dey swar dey would soon's dey find him. I s'pose dey ain't kotch him yit. Don' you pester yo'se'f worryin'. Dreamy 'ull come fo' ve'y long.

MAMMY. (*after a pause—weakly*) Dere's a feelin' in my haid like I was a-floatin' yander whar I can't see nothin', or 'member nothin', or know de sight er any pusson I knows; en I wants ter see Dreamy agin befo'—

CEELY. (*quickly*) Don' waste yo strenk talkin'. You git a wink er sleep en I wake you when he comes, you heah me?

MAMMY. (*faintly*) I does feel mighty drowsy. (*She closes her eyes.* CEELY *goes over to the window and pulling the curtains aside stands looking down into the street as if she were watching for someone coming. A moment later there is a noise of footfalls from the stairs in the hall, followed by a sharp rap on the door.*)

CEELY. (*turning quickly from the window*) Ssshh! Ssshh! (*She hurries to the door, glancing anxiously toward* MAMMY. *The old woman appears to have fallen asleep.* CEELY *cautiously opens the door a bare inch or so and peeks out. When she sees who it is she immediately tries to slam it shut again but a vigorous shove from the outside forces her back and* IRENE *pushes her way defiantly into the room. She is a young, good-looking Negress, highly rouged and powdered, dressed in gaudy, cheap finery.*)

IRENE. (*in a harsh voice—evidently worked up to a great state of nervous excitement*) No you don't, Ceely Ann! I said I was comin' here and it'll take mo'n you to stop me!

CEELY. (*almost speechless with horrified indignation—breathing heavily*) Yo' bad 'oman! Git back ter yo' bad-house whar yo' b'longs!

IRENE. (*raising her clenched hand—furiously*) Stop dat talkin' to me, nigger, or I'll split yo' fool head! (*As* CEELY *shrinks away* IRENE *lowers her hand and glances around the room*) Whar's Dreamy?

CEELY. (*scornfully*) Yo' ax me dat! Whar's Dreamy? Ax yo'se'f. Yo's de one ought ter know whar he is.

IRENE. Den he ain't come here?

CEELY. I ain't tellin' de likes er you wedder he is or not.

IRENE. (*pleadingly*) Tell me, Ceely Ann, ain't he been here? He'd be sure to come here 'count of Mammy dyin', dey said.

CEELY. (*pointing to* MAMMY*—apprehensively*) Ssshh! (*Then lowering her voice to a whisper—suspiciously*) Dey said? Who said?

IRENE. (*equally suspicious*) None o' your business who said. (*Then pleading again*) Ceely Ann, I jest got ter see him dis minute, dis secon'! He's in bad, Dreamy is, and I knows somep'n I gotter tell him, somep'n I jest heard—

CEELY. (*uncomprehendingly*) In bad? What you jest heah?

IRENE. I ain't tellin' no one but him. (*Desperately*) For Gawd's sake, tell me whar he is, Ceely!

CEELY. I don' know no mo'n you.

IRENE. (*fiercely*) You's lyin', Ceely! You's lyin' jest 'cause I'se bad.

CEELY. De good Lawd bar witness I'se tellin' you de trufe!

IRENE. (*hopelessly*) Den I gotter go find him, high and low, somewheres. (*Proudly*) You ain't got de right not ter trust me, Ceely, where de Dreamy's mixed in it. I'd go ter hell for Dreamy!

CEELY. (*indignantly*) Hush yo' wicked cussin'! (*Then anxiously*) Is Dreamy in trouble?

IRENE. (*with a scornful laugh*) Trouble? Good Lawd, it's worser'n dat! (*Then in surprise*) Ain't you heerd what de Dreamy done last night, Ceely?

CEELY. (*apprehensively*) What de Dreamy do? Tell me, gal. Somep'n bad?

IRENE. (*with the same scornful laugh*) Bad? Worser'n bad, what he done!

CEELY. (*lamenting querulously*) Oh good Lawd, I knowed it! I knowed with all his carryin's-on wid dat passel er tough young niggers—him so uppity 'cause he's de boss er de gang—sleepin' all de day 'stead er workin' an' Lawd knows what he does in de nights —fightin' wid white folks, an' totin' a pistol in his pocket—(*With a glance of angry resentment at* IRENE)—an' as fo' de udder company he's been keepin'—

IRENE. (*fiercely*) Shut your mouth, Ceely! Dat ain't your business.

CEELY. Oh, I knowed Dreamy'd be gittin' in trouble fo' long! De lowflung young trash! An' here's his ole Mammy don' know no dif'frunt but he's de mos' innercent young lamb in de worl'. (*In a strained whisper*) What he do? Is he been stealin' somep'n?

IRENE. (*angrily*) You go ter hell, Ceely Ann! You ain't no fren' of de Dreamy's, you talk dat way, and I ain't got no time ter waste argyin' wid your fool notions. (*She goes to the door*) Dreamy'll go ter his death sho's yo' born, if I don't find him an' tell him quick!

CEELY. (*terrified*) Oh Lawd!

IRENE. (*anxiously*) He'll sho'ly try ter come here and see his ole Mammy befo' she dies, don't you think, Ceely?

CEELY. Fo' Gawd I hopes so! She's been a-prayin' all de day—

IRENE. (*opening the door*) You hopes so, you fool nigger! I tells you it's good-by to de Dreamy, he come here! I knows! I gotter find an' stop him. If he come here, Ceely, you tell him git out quick and hide, he don't wanter git pinched. You hear? You tell him dat, Ceely, for Gawd's sake! I'se got ter go—find him—high an' low. (*She goes out leaving* CEELY *staring at her in speechless indignation*.)

CEELY. (*drawing a deep breath*) Yo' street gal! I don' b'lieve one word you says—stuffin' me wid yo' bad lies so's you kin keep de Dreamy frum leavin' you! (MAMMY SAUNDERS *awakes and groans faintly*. CEELY *hurries to her bedside*) Is de pain hurtin' agin, Mammy?

MAMMY. (*vaguely*) Dat you, Dreamy?

CEELY. No, Mammy, dis is Ceely. Dreamy's comin' soon. Is you restin' easy?

MAMMY. (*as if she hadn't heard*) Dat you, Dreamy?

CEELY. (*sitting down in the rocker by the bed and taking one of the old woman's hands in hers*) No. Dreamy's comin'.

MAMMY. (*after a pause—suddenly*) Does you 'member yo' dead Mammy, chile?

CEELY. (*mystified*) My dead Mammy?

MAMMY. Didn' I heah yo' talkin' jest now, Dreamy?

CEELY. (*very worried*) I clar ter goodness, she don' know me ary bit. Dis is Ceely Ann talkin' ter yo', Mammy.

MAMMY. Who was yo' talkin' wid, Dreamy?

CEELY. (*shaking her head—in a trembling voice*) Hit can't be long befo' de en'. (*In a louder tone*) Hit was me talkin' wid a pusson fum ovah de way. She say tell you Dreamy comin' heah ter see yo' right away. You heah dat, Mammy? (*The old woman sighs but does not answer. There is a pause.*)

MAMMY. (*suddenly*) Does yo' 'member yo' dead Mammy, chile? (*Then with a burst of religious exaltation*) De Lawd have mercy!

CEELY. (*like an echo*) Bless de Lawd! (*Then in a frightened half-whisper to herself*) Po' thing! Her min's done leavin' her jest like de doctor said. (*She looks down at the old woman helplessly. The door on the right is opened stealthily and the* DREAMY KID *slinks in.*)

CEELY. (*hearing a board creak, turns quickly toward the door and gives a frightened start*) Dreamy!

DREAMY. (*puts his fingers to his lips—commandingly*) Ssshh! (*He bends down to a crouching position and holding the door about an inch open, peers out into the hallway in an attitude of tense waiting, one hand evidently clutching some weapon in the side pocket of his coat. After a moment he is satisfied of not being followed, and, after closing the door carefully and locking it, he stands up and walks to the center of the room casting a look of awed curiosity at the figure in the bed. He is a well-built, good-looking young Negro, light in color. His eyes are shifty and hard, their expression one of tough, scornful defiance. His mouth is cruel and perpetually drawn back at the corners into a snarl. He is dressed in well-fitting clothes of a flashy pattern. A light cap is pulled down on the side of his head.*)

CEELY. (*coming from the bed to meet him*) Bless de Lawd, here you is at las'!

DREAMY. (*with a warning gesture*) Nix on de loud talk! Talk low, can't yuh! (*He glances back at the door furtively—then continues with a sneer*) Yuh're a fine nut, Ceely Ann! What for you sendin' out all ober de town for me like you was crazy! D'yuh want ter git me in de cooler? Don' you know dey're after me for what I done last night?

CEELY. (*fearfully*) I heerd somep'n—but—what you done, Dreamy?

DREAMY. (*with an attempt at a careless bravado*) I croaked a guy, dat's what! A white man.

CEELY. (*in a frightened whisper*) What you mean—croaked?

DREAMY. (*boastfully*) I shot him dead, dat's what! (*As* CEELY *shrinks away from him in horror—resentfully*) Aw say, don' gimme none o' dem looks o' yourn. 'Twarn't my doin' nohow. He was de one lookin' for trouble. I wasn't seekin' for no mess wid him dat I could help. But he told folks he was gwine ter git me for a fac', and dat fo'ced my hand. I had ter git him ter pertect my own life. (*With cruel satisfaction*) And I got him right, you b'lieve me!

CEELY. (*putting her hands over her face with a low moan of terror*) May de good Lawd pardon yo' wickedness! Oh Lawd! What yo' po' ole Mammy gwine say if she hear tell—an' she never knowin' how bad you's got.

DREAMY. (*fiercely*) Hell! You ain't tole her, is you?

CEELY. Think I want ter kill her on the instant? An' I didn' know myse'f—what you done—till you tells me. (*Frightenedly*) Oh, Dreamy, what you gwine do now? How you gwine git away? (*Almost wailing*) Good Lawd, de perlice do' kotch you shuah!

DREAMY. (*savagely*) Shut yo' loud mouth, damn yo'! (*He stands tensely listening for some sound from the hall. After a moment he points to the bed*) Is Mammy sleepin'?

CEELY. (*tiptoes to the bed*) Seems like she is. (*She comes back to him*) Dat's de way wid her—sleep fo' a few minutes, den she wake, den sleep again.

DREAMY. (*scornfully*) Aw, dere ain't nothin' wrong wid her 'ceptin' she's ole. What yuh wanter send de word tellin' me she's croakin', and git me comin' here at de risk o' my life, and den find her sleepin'. (*Clenching his fist threateningly*) I gotter mind ter smash yo' face for playin' de damn fool and makin' me de goat. (*He turns toward the door*) Ain't no us'en me stayin' here when dey'll likely come lookin' for me. I'm gwine out where I gotta chance ter make my git-away. De boys is all fixin' it up for me. (*His hand on the door-knob*) When Mammy wakes, you tell her I couldn't wait, you hear?

CEELY. (*hurrying to him and grabbing his arm—pleadingly*) Don' yo' go now, Dreamy—not jest yit. Fo' de good Lawd's sake, don' you go befo' you speaks wid her! If yo' knew how she's been a-callin' an' a-prayin' for yo' all de day—

DREAMY. (*scornfully but a bit uncertainly*) Aw, she don' need none o' me. What good kin I do watchin' her do a kip? It'd be dif'frunt if she was croakin' on de level.

CEELY. (*in an anguished whisper*) She's gwine wake up in a secon' an' den she call: "Dreamy. Whar's Dreamy?"—an' what I gwine tell her den? An' yo' Mammy is dyin', Dreamy, sho's fate! Her min' been wanderin' an' she don' even recernize me no mo', an' de doctor say when dat come it ain't but a sho't time befo' de en'. Yo' gotter stay wid yo' Mammy long 'nuff ter speak wid her, Dreamy. Yo' jest gotter stay wid her in her las' secon's on dis yearth when she's callin' ter yo'. (*With conviction as he hesitates*) Listen heah, yo' Dreamy! Yo' don' never git no bit er luck in dis worril ary agin, yo' leaves her now. Der perlice gon' kotch yo' shuah.

DREAMY. (*with superstitious fear*) Ssshh! Can dat bull, Ceely! (*Then boastfully*) I wasn't pinin' to beat it up here, git me? De boys was all persuadin' me not ter take de chance. It's takin' my life in my hands, dat's what. But when I heerd it was ole Mammy croakin' and axin' ter see me, I says ter myse'f: "Dreamy, you gotter make good wid old Mammy no matter what come—or you don' never git a bit of luck in yo' life no mo'." And I was game and come, wasn't I? Nary body in dis worril kin say de Dreamy ain't game ter de core, n'matter what. (*With sudden decision walks to the foot of the bed and stands looking down at* MAMMY. *A note of fear creeps into his voice*) Gawd, she's quiet 'nuff. Maybe she done passed away in her sleep like de ole ones does. You go see, Ceely; an' if she's on'y sleepin', you wake her up. I wanter speak wid her quick—an' den I'll make a break outa here. You make it fast, Ceely Ann, I tells yo'.

CEELY. (*bends down beside the bed*) Mammy! Here's de Dreamy.

MAMMY. (*opens her eyes—drowsily and vaguely, in a weak voice*) Dreamy?

DREAMY. (*shuffling his feet and moving around the bed*). Here I is, Mammy.

MAMMY. (*fastening her eyes on him with fascinated joy*) Dreamy! Hit's yo'! (*Then uncertainly*) I ain't dreamin' nor seein' ha'nts, is I?

DREAMY. (*coming forward and taking her hand*) 'Deed I ain't no ghost. Here I is, sho' 'nuff.

MAMMY. (*clutching his hand tight and pulling it down on her breast—in an ecstasy of happiness*) Didn' I know you'd come! Didn' I say: "Dreamy ain't gwine let his ole Mammy die all lone by he'se'f an' him not dere wid her." I knows yo'd come. (*She starts to laugh joyously, but coughs and sinks back weakly.*)

DREAMY. (*shudders in spite of himself as he realizes for the first time how far gone the old woman is—forcing a tone of joking reassurance*) What's dat foolishness I hears you talkin', Mammy? Wha' d'yuh mean pullin' dat bull 'bout croakin' on me? Shoo! Tryin' ter kid me, ain't yo'? Shoo! You live ter plant de flowers on my grave, see if you don'.

MAMMY. (*sadly and very weakly*) I knows! I knows! Hit ain't long now. (*Bursting into a sudden weak hysteria*) Yo' stay heah, Dreamy! Yo' stay heah by me, yo' stay heah—till de good Lawd takes me home. Yo' promise me dat! Yo' do dat fo' po' ole Mammy, won't yo'?

DREAMY. (*uneasily*) 'Deed I will, Mammy, 'deed I will.

MAMMY. (*closing her eyes with a sigh of relief—calmly*) Bless de Lawd for dat. Den I ain't skeered no mo'. (*She settles herself comfortably in the bed as if preparing for sleep.*)

CEELY. (*in a low voice*) I gotter go home fo' a minute, Dreamy. I ain't been dere all de day and Lawd knows what happen. I'll be back yere befo' ve'y long.

DREAMY. (*his eyes fixed on* MAMMY) Aw right, beat it if yuh wanter. (*Turning to her—in a fierce whisper*) On'y don' be long. I can't stay here an' take dis risk, you hear?

CEELY. (*frightenedly*) I knows, chile. I come back, I swar! (*She goes out quietly.* DREAMY *goes quickly to the window and cautiously searches the street below with his eyes.*)

MAMMY. (*uneasily*) Dreamy. (*He hurries back and takes her hand again*) I got de mos' 'culiar feelin' in my head. Seems like de years done all roll away an' I'm back down home in de ole place whar yo' was bo'n. (*A short pause*) Does yo' 'member yo' own mammy, chile?

DREAMY. No.

MAMMY. Yo' was too young, I s'pec'. Yo' was on'y a baby w'en she tuck 'n' die. My Sal was a mighty fine 'oman, if I does say hit m'se'f.

DREAMY. (*fidgeting nervously*) Don' you talk, Mammy. Better you'd close yo' eyes an' rest.

MAMMY. (*with a trembling smile—weakly*) Shoo! W'at is I done come ter wid my own gran'chile bossin' me 'bout? I wants ter talk. You knows you ain't give me much chance ter talk wid yo' dese las' years.

DREAMY. (*sullenly*) I ain't had de time, Mammy; but you knows I was always game ter give you anything I got. (*A note of appeal in his voice*) You knows dat, don' you, Mammy?

MAMMY. Sho'ly I does. Yo' been a good boy, Dreamy; an' if dere's one thing more'n 'nother makes me feel like I mighter done good in de sight er de Lawd, hit's dat I raised yo' fum a baby.

DREAMY. (*clearing his throat gruffly*) Don' talk so much, Mammy.

MAMMY. (*querulously*) I gotter talk, chile. Come times—w'en I git thinkin' yere in de bed—w'at's gwine ter come ter me a'mos' b'fore I knows hit—like de thief in de night—en den I gits skeered. But w'en I talks wid yo' I ain't skeered a bit.

DREAMY. (*defiantly*) You ain't got nothin' to be skeered of—not when de Dreamy's here.

MAMMY. (*after a slight pause, faintly*) Dere's a singin' in my ears all de time. (*Seized by a sudden religious ecstasy*) Maybe hit's de singin' hymns o' de blessed angels I done heah fum above. (*Wildly*) Bless Gawd! Bless Gawd! Pity dis po' ole sinner.

DREAMY. (*with an uneasy glance at the door*) Ssshh, Mammy! Don' shout so loud.

MAMMY. De pictures keep a whizzin' fo' my eyes like de thread in a sewing machine. Seem 's if all my life done fly back ter me all ter once. (*With a flickering smile—weakly*) Does you know how yo' come by dat nickname dey alls call yo'—de Dreamy? Is I ever tole yo' dat?

DREAMY. (*evidently lying*) No, Mammy.

MAMMY. Hit was one mawnin' b'fo' we come No'th. Me an' yo' mammy—yo' was des a baby in arms den—

DREAMY. (*hears a noise from the hall*) Ssshh, Mammy! For God's sake, don't speak for a minute. I hears somep'n. (*He stares at the door, his face hardening savagely, and listens intently.*)

MAMMY. (*in a frightened tone*) W'at's de matter, chile?

DREAMY. Ssshh! Somebody comin'. (*A noise of footsteps comes from the hall stairway.* DREAMY *springs to his feet*) Leggo my hand, Mammy—jest for a secon'. I come right back to you. (*He pulls his hand from the old woman's grip. She falls back on the pillows moaning.* DREAMY *pulls a large automatic revolver from his coat pocket and tiptoes quickly to the door. As he does so there is a sharp rap. He stands listening at the crack for a moment, then noiselessly turns the key, unlocking the door. Then he crouches low down by the wall so that the door, when opened, will hide him from the sight of anyone entering. There is another and louder rap on the door.)*

MAMMY. (*groaning*) W'at's dat, Dreamy? Whar is yo'?

DREAMY. Ssshh! (*Then muffling his voice he calls*) Come in. (*He raises the revolver in his hand. The door is pushed open and Irene enters, her eyes peering wildly about the room. Her bosom is heaving as if she had been running and she is trembling with terrified excitement.*)

IRENE. (*not seeing him calls out questioningly*) Dreamy?

DREAMY. (*lowering his revolver and rising to his feet roughly*) Close dat door!

IRENE. (*whirling about with a startled cry*) Dreamy!

DREAMY. (*shutting the door and locking it—aggressively*) Shut yo' big mouth, gal, or I'll bang it shut for you! You wanter let de whole block know where I is?

IRENE. (*hysterical with joy—trying to put her arms around him*) Bless God, I foun' you at last!

DREAMY. (*pushing her away roughly*) Leggo o' me! Why you come here follerin' me? Ain't yo' got 'nuff sense in yo' fool head ter know de bulls is liable ter shadow you when dey knows you's my gal? Is you pinin' ter git me kotched an' sent to de chair?

IRENE. (*terrified*) No, no!

DREAMY. (*savagely*) I gotter mind ter hand you one you won't ferget! (*He draws back his fist.*)

IRENE. (*shrinking away*) Don' you hit me, Dreamy! Don' you beat me up now! Jest lemme 'xplain, dat's all.

MAMMY. (*in a frightened whimper*) Dreamy! Come yere to me. Whar is yo'? I'se skeered!

DREAMY. (*in a fierce whisper to Irene*) Can dat bull or I'll fix you. (*He hurries to the old woman and pats her hand*) Here I is, Mammy.

MAMMY. Who dat yo's a-talkin' wid?

DREAMY. On'y a fren' o' Ceely Ann's, askin' where she is. I gotter talk wid her some mo' yit. You sleep, Mammy? (*He goes to Irene.*)

MAMMY. (*feebly*) Don' yo' leave me, Dreamy.

DREAMY. I'se right here wid you. (*Fiercely, to Irene*) You git the hell outa here, you Reeny, you heah—quick! Dis ain't no place for de likes o' you wid ole Mammy dyin'.

IRENE. (*with a horrified glance at the bed*) Is she dyin'—honest?

DREAMY. Ssshh! She's croakin', I tells yo'—an' I gotter stay wid her fo' a while—an' I ain't got no time ter be pesterin' wid you. Beat it, now! Beat it outa here befo' I knocks yo' cold, git me?

IRENE. Jest wait a secon' for de love o' Gawd. I got somep'n ter tell you—

DREAMY. I don' wanter hear yo' fool talk. (*He gives her a push toward the door*) Git outa dis, you hear me?

IRENE. I'll go. I'm going soon—soon's ever I've had my say. Lissen, Dreamy! It's about de coppers I come ter tell you.

DREAMY. (*quickly*) Why don' you say dat befo'? What you know?

IRENE. Just befo' I come here to find you de first time, de Madam sends me out to Murphy's ter git her a bottle o' gin. I goes in de side door but I ain't rung de bell yet. I hear yo' name spoken an' I stops ter lissen. Dey was three or four men in de back room. Dey don't hear me open de outside door, an' dey can't see me, 'course. It was Big Sullivan from de Central Office talkin'. He was talkin' 'bout de killin' you done last night and he tells dem odders he's heerd 'bout de ole woman gittin' so sick, and dat if dey don't fin' you none of de udder places dey's lookin', dey's goin' wait for you here. Dey s'pecs you come here say good-by to Mammy befo' you make yo' git-away.

DREAMY. It's aw right den. Dey ain't come yit. Twister Smith done tole me de coast was clear befo' I come here.

IRENE. Dat was den. It ain't now.

DREAMY. (*excitedly*) What you mean, gal?

IRENE. I was comin' in by de front way when I sees some pusson hidin' in de doorway 'cross de street. I gits a good peek at him and when I does—it's a copper. Dreamy, shuah's yo' born, in his plain clo'se, and he's a watchin' de door o' dis house like a cat.

DREAMY. (*goes to the window and stealthily crouching by the dark side peeks out. One glance is enough. He comes quickly back to Irene*) You got de right dope, gal. It's dat Mickey. I knows him even in de dark. Dey're waitin'—so dey ain't wise I'm here yit, dat's suah.

IRENE. But dey'll git wise befo' long.

DREAMY. He don' pipe you comin' in here?

IRENE. I skulked roun' and sneaked in by de back way froo de yard. Dey ain't none o' dem dar yit. (*Raising her voice—excitedly*) But dere will be soon. Dey're boun' to git wise to dat back door. You ain't got no time to lose, Dreamy. Come on wid me now. Git back where yo' safe. It's de cooler for you certain if you stays here. Dey'll git you like a rat in de trap. (*As Dreamy hesitates*) For de love of Gawd, Dreamy, wake up to youse'f!

DREAMY. (*uncertainly*) I can't beat it—wid Mammy here alone. My luck done turn bad all my life, if I does.

IRENE. (*fiercely*) What good's you gittin' pinched and sent to de chair gwine do her? Is you crazy mad? Come wid me, I tells you!

DREAMY. (*half-persuaded—hesitatingly*) I gotter speak wid her. You wait a secon'.

IRENE. (*wringing hands*) Dis ain't no time for fussin' wid her.

DREAMY. (*gruffly*) Shut up! (*He makes a motion for her to remain where she is and goes over to the bed—in a low voice*) Mammy.

MAMMY. (*hazily*) Dat you, Dreamy? (*She tries to reach out her hand and touch him.*)

DREAMY. I'm gwine leave you—jest for a moment, Mammy. I'll send de word for Ceely Ann—

MAMMY. (*wide awake in an instant—with intense alarm*) Don' yo' do dat! Don' yo' move one step out er yere or yo'll be sorry, Dreamy.

DREAMY. (*apprehensively*) I gotter go, I tells you. I'll come back.

MAMMY. (*with wild grief*) O good Lawd! W'en I's drawin' de

las' bre'fs in dis po' ole body—(*Frenziedly*) De Lawd have mercy! Good Lawd have mercy!

DREAMY. (*fearfully*) Stop dat racket, Mammy! You bring all o' dem down on my head! (*He rushes over and crouches by the window to peer out—in relieved tones*) He ain't heerd nothin'. He's dar yit.

IRENE. (*imploringly*) Come on, Dreamy! (*Mammy groans with pain.*)

DREAMY. (*hurrying to the bed*) What's de matter, Mammy?

IRENE. (*stamping her foot*) Dreamy! Fo' Gawd's sake!

MAMMY. Lawd have mercy! (*She groans*) Gimme yo' han', chile. Yo' ain't gwine leave me now, Dreamy? Yo' ain't, is yo'? Yo' ole Mammy won't bodder yo' long. Yo' know w'at yo' promise me, Dreamy! Yo' promise yo' sacred word yo' stay wid me till de en'. (*With an air of somber prophecy—slowly*) If yo' leave me now, yo' ain't gwine git no bit er luck s'long's yo' lives, I tells yo' dat!

DREAMY. (*frightened—pleadingly*) Don' you say dat, Mammy!

IRENE. Come on, Dreamy!

DREAMY. (*slowly*) I can't. (*In awed tones*) Don' you hear de curse she puts on me if I does?

MAMMY. (*her voice trembling with weak tears*) Don' go, chile!

DREAMY. (*hastily*) I won't leave dis room, I swar ter you! (*Relieved by the finality in his tones, the old woman sighs and closes her eyes.* DREAMY *frees his hand from hers and goes to* IRENE. *With a strange calm*) De game's up, gal. You better beat it while de goin's good.

IRENE (*aghast*) You gwine stay?

DREAMY. I gotter, gal. I ain't gwine agin her dyin' curse. No, suh!

IRENE. (*pitifully*) But dey'll git you shuah!

DREAMY. (*slapping the gun in his pocket significantly*) Dey'll have some gittin'. I git some o' dem fust. (*With gloomy determination*) Dey don't git dis chicken alive! Lawd Jesus, no suh. Not de Dreamy!

IRENE (*helplessly*) Oh, Lawdy, Lawdy! (*She goes to the window—with a short cry*) He's talkin' wid someone. Dere's two o' dem. (*Dreamy hurries to her side.*)

DREAMY. I knows him—de udder. It's Big Sullivan. (*Pulling her away roughly*) Come out o' dat! Dey'll see you. (*He pushes her toward the door*) Dey won't wait down dere much longer. Dey'll be comin' up here soon. (*Prayerfully, with a glance at the bed*) I hopes she's croaked by den, 'fo' Christ I does!

IRENE. (*as if she couldn't believe it*) Den you ain't gwine save youse'f while dere's time? (*Pleadingly*) Oh, Dreamy, you can make it yit!

DREAMY. De game's up, I tole you. (*With gloomy fatalism*) I s'pect it hatter be. Yes, suh. Dey'd git me in de long run anyway—and wid her curse de luck'd be agin me. (*With sudden anger*) Git outa here, you Reeny! You ain't aimin' ter get shot up too, is you? Ain't no sense in dat.

IRENE. (*fiercely*) I'se stayin' too, here wid you!

DREAMY. No you isn't! None o' dat bull! You ain't got no mix in dis jam.

IRENE. Yes, I is! Ain't you my man?

DREAMY. Don't make no dif. I don't wanter git you in Dutch more'n you is. It's bad 'nuff fo' me. (*He pushes her toward the door*) Blow while you kin, I tells you!

IRENE. (*resisting him*) No, Dreamy! What I care if dey kills me? I'se gwine stick wid you.

DREAMY. (*gives her another push*) No, you isn't, gal. (*Unlocking the door—relentlessly*) Out wid you!

IRENE. (*hysterically*) You can't gimme no bum's rush. I stays.

DREAMY. (*gloomily*) On'y one thing fo' me ter do den. (*He hits her on the side of the face with all his might knocking her back against the wall where she sways as if about to fall. Then he opens the door and grabs her two arms from behind*) Out wid you, gal!

IRENE. (*moaning*) Dreamy! Dreamy! Lemme stay wid you! (*He pushes her into the hallway and holds her there at arm's length*) Fo' Gawd's sake, Dreamy!

MAMMY. (*whimperingly*) Dreamy! I'se skeered!

IRENE. (*from the hall*) I'se gwine stay right here at de door. You might s'well lemme in.

DREAMY. (*frowning*) Don' do dat, Reeny. (*Then with a sudden idea*) You run roun' and tell de gang what's up. Maybe dey git me outa dis, you hear?

IRENE. (*with eager hope*) You think dey kin?

DREAMY. Never kin tell. You hurry—through de back yard, 'member —an' don' git pinched, now.

IRENE. (*eagerly*) I'm gwine! I'll bring dem back!

DREAMY. (*stands listening to her retreating footsteps—then shuts and locks the door—gloomily to himself*) Ain't no good. Dey dassent do nothin'—but I hatter git her outa dis somehow.

MAMMY. (*groaning*) Dreamy!

DREAMY. Here I is. Jest a secon'. (*He goes to the window.*)

MAMMY. (*weakly*) I feels—like—de en's comin'. Oh, Lawd, Lawd!

DREAMY. (*absent-mindedly*) Yes, Mammy. (*Aloud to himself*) Dey're sneakin' cross de street. Dere's anudder of 'em. Dat's tree. (*He glances around the room quickly—then hurries over and takes hold of the chest of drawers. As he does so the old woman commences to croon shrilly to herself.*)

DREAMY. Stop dat noise, Mammy! Stop dat noise!

MAMMY. (*wanderingly*) Dat's how come yo' got dat—dat nickname —Dreamy.

DREAMY. Yes, Mammy. (*He puts the lamp on the floor to the rear of the door, turning it down low. Then he carries the chest of drawers over and places it against the door as a barricade.*)

MAMMY. (*rambling as he does this—very feebly*) Does yo' know— I gives you dat name—w'en yo's des a baby—lyin' in my arms—

DREAMY. Yes, Mammy.

MAMMY. Down by de crik—under de ole willow—whar I uster take yo'—wid yo' big eyes a-chasin'—de sun flitterin' froo de grass—an' out on de water—

DREAMY. (*takes the revolver from his pocket and puts it on top of the chest of drawers*) Dey don't git de Dreamy alive—not for de chair! Lawd Jesus, no suh!

MAMMY. An' yo' was always—a-lookin'—an' a-thinkin' ter yo'se'f—an' yo' big eyes jest a-dreamin' an' a-dreamin'—an' dat's w'en I gives yo' dat nickname—Dreamy—Dreamy—

DREAMY. Yes, Mammy. (*He listens at the crack of the door—in a tense whisper*) I don' hear dem—but dey're comin' sneakin' up de stairs, I knows it.

MAMMY. (*faintly*) Whar is yo', Dreamy? I can't—ha'dly—breathe—no mo'. Oh, Lawd have mercy!

DREAMY. (*goes over to the bed*) Here I is, Mammy.

MAMMY. (*speaking with difficulty*) Yo'—kneel down—chile—say a pray'r—Oh, Lawd!

DREAMY. Jest a secon', Mammy. (*He goes over and gets his revolver and comes back.*)

MAMMY. Gimme—yo' hand—chile. (*Dreamy gives her his left hand. The revolver is in his right. He stares nervously at the door*) An' yo' kneel down—pray fo' me. (*Dreamy gets on one knee beside the bed. There is a sound from the hallway as if someone had made a misstep on the stairs—then silence. Dreamy starts and half aims his gun in the direction of the door. Mammy groans weakly*) I'm dyin', chile. Hit's de en'. You pray for me—out loud—so's I can heah. Oh, Lawd! (*She gasps to catch her breath.*)

DREAMY. (*abstractedly, not having heard a word she has said*) Yes, Mammy. (*Aloud to himself with an air of grim determination as if he were making a pledge*) Dey don't git de Dreamy! Not while he's 'live! Lawd Jesus, no suh!

MAMMY. (*falteringly*) Dat's right—yo' pray—Lawd Jesus—Lawd Jesus—(*There is another slight sound of movement from the hallway.*)

CURTAIN

BEFORE BREAKFAST

A Play in One Act

BEFORE BREAKFAST

SCENE. *A small room serving both as kitchen and dining room in a flat on Christopher Street, New York City. In the rear, to the right, a door leading to the outer hallway. On the left of the doorway, a sink, and a two-burner gas stove. Over the stove, and extending to the left wall, a wooden closet for dishes, etc. On the left, two windows looking out on a fire escape where several potted plants are dying of neglect. Before the windows, a table covered with oilcloth. Two cane-bottomed chairs are placed by the table. Another stands against the wall to the right of door in rear. In the right wall, rear, a doorway leading into a bedroom. Farther forward, different articles of a man's and a woman's clothing are hung on pegs. A clothes line is strung from the left corner, rear, to the right wall, forward.*

It is about eight-thirty in the morning of a fine, sunshiny day in the early fall.

MRS. ROWLAND *enters from the bedroom, yawning, her hands still busy putting the finishing touches on a slovenly toilet by sticking hairpins into her hair which is bunched up in a drab-colored mass on top of her round head. She is of medium height and inclined to a shapeless stoutness, accentuated by her formless blue dress, shabby and worn. Her face is characterless, with small regular features and eyes of a nondescript blue. There is a pinched expression about her eyes and nose and her weak, spiteful mouth. She is in her early twenties but looks much older.*

She comes to the middle of the room and yawns, stretching her arms to their full length. Her drowsy eyes stare about the room with the irritated look of one to whom a long sleep has not been a long rest. She goes wearily to the clothes hanging on the right and takes an apron from a hook. She ties it about her waist, giving vent to an exasperated "damn" when the knot fails to obey her clumsy fingers. Finally gets it tied and goes slowly to the gas stove and lights one burner. She fills the coffee pot at the sink and sets it over the flame. Then slumps down into a chair by the table and puts a hand over her forehead as if she were suffering from headache. Suddenly her face brightens as though she had remembered something, and she casts a quick glance at the dish closet; then looks sharply at the bedroom door and listens intently for a moment or so.

MRS. ROWLAND. (*in a low voice*) Alfred! Alfred! (*There is no answer from the next room and she continues suspiciously in a louder tone*) You needn't pretend you're asleep. (*There is no reply to this from the bedroom, and, reassured, she gets up from her chair and tiptoes cautiously to the dish closet. She slowly opens one door, taking great care to make no noise, and slides out, from their hiding place behind the dishes, a bottle of Gordon gin and a glass. In doing so she disturbs the top dish, which rattles a little. At this sound she starts guiltily and looks with sulky defiance at the doorway to the next room.*)
(*Her voice trembling*) Alfred!

(*After a pause, during which she listens for any sound, she takes the glass and pours out a large drink and gulps it down; then hastily returns the bottle and glass to their hiding place. She closes the closet door with the same care as she had opened it, and, heaving a great sigh of relief, sinks down into her chair again. The large dose of alcohol she has taken has an almost immediate effect. Her features become more animated, she seems to gather energy, and she looks at the bedroom door with a hard, vindictive smile on her lips. Her eyes glance quickly about the room and are fixed on a man's coat and vest which hang from a hook at right. She moves stealthily over to the open doorway and stands there, out of sight of anyone inside, listening for any movement.*)

(*Calling in a half-whisper*) Alfred!

(*Again there is no reply. With a swift movement she takes the coat and vest from the hook and returns with them to her chair. She sits down and takes the various articles out of each pocket but quickly puts them back again. At last, in the inside pocket of the vest, she finds a letter.*)

(*Looking at the handwriting—slowly to herself*) Hmm! I knew it.

(*She opens the letter and reads it. At first her expression is one of hatred and rage, but as she goes on to the end it changes to one of triumphant malignity. She remains in deep thought for a moment, staring before her, the letter in her hands, a cruel smile on her lips. Then she puts the letter back in the pocket of the vest, and still careful not to awaken the sleeper, hangs the clothes up again on the same hook, and goes to the bedroom door and looks in.*)

(*In a loud, shrill voice*) Alfred! (*Still louder*) Alfred! (*There is a muffled, yawning groan from the next room*) Don't you think it's about time you got up? Do you want to stay in bed all day? (*Turning around and coming back to her chair*) Not that I've got any doubts about your being lazy enough to stay in bed forever. (*She sits down and looks out of the window, irritably*) Goodness knows what time it is. We haven't even got any way of telling the time since you pawned your watch like a fool. The last valuable thing we had, and you knew it. It's been nothing but pawn, pawn, pawn, with you—anything to put off getting a job, anything to get out of going to work like a man. (*She taps the floor with her foot nervously, biting her lips.*)

(*After a short pause*) Alfred! Get up, do you hear me? I want to make that bed before I go out. I'm sick of having this place in a continual muss on your account. (*With a certain vindictive satisfaction*) Not that we'll be here long unless you manage to get some money some place. Heaven knows I do my part—and more—going out to sew every day while you play the gentleman and loaf around barrooms with that good-for-nothing lot of artists from the Square.

(*A short pause during which she plays nervously with a cup and saucer on the table.*)

And where are you going to get money, I'd like to know? The rent's due this week and you know what the landlord is. He won't let us stay a minute over our time. You say you *can't* get a job. That's a lie and you know it. You never even look for one. All you do is moon around all day writing silly poetry and stories that no one will buy—and no wonder they won't. I notice I can always get a position, such as it is; and it's only that which keeps us from starving to death.

(*Gets up and goes over to the stove—looks into the coffee pot to see if the water is boiling; then comes back and sits down again.*)

You'll have to get money today some place. I can't do it all, and I won't do it all. You've got to come to your senses. You've got to beg, borrow, or steal it somewheres. (*With a contemptuous laugh*) But where, I'd like to know? You're too proud to beg, and you've borrowed the limit, and you haven't the nerve to steal.

(*After a pause—getting up angrily*) Aren't you up yet, for heaven's sake? It's just like you to go to sleep again, or pretend to. (*She goes to the bedroom door and looks in*) Oh, you are up. Well, it's about time. You needn't look at me like that. Your airs don't fool me a bit any more. I know you too well—better than you think I do—you and your goings-on. (*Turning away from the door—meaningly*) I know a lot of things, my dear. Never mind what I know, now. I'll tell you before I go, you needn't worry. (*She comes to the middle of the room and stands there, frowning.*)

(*Irritably*) Hmm! I suppose I might as well get breakfast ready —not that there's anything much to get. (*Questioningly*) Unless you have some money? (*She pauses for an answer from the next room which does not come*) Foolish question! (*She gives a short, hard laugh*) I ought to know you better than that by this time. When you left here in such a huff last night I knew what would happen. You can't be trusted for a second. A nice condition you came home in! The fight we had was only an excuse for you to make a beast of yourself. What was the use pawning your watch if all you wanted with the money was to waste it in buying drink?

(*Goes over to the dish closet and takes out plates, cups, etc., while she is talking.*)

Hurry up! It don't take long to get breakfast these days, thanks to you. All we got this morning is bread and butter and coffee; and you wouldn't even have that if it wasn't for me sewing my fingers off. (*She slams the loaf of bread on the table with a bang.*)

The bread's stale. I hope you'll like it. *You* don't deserve any better, but I don't see why *I* should suffer.

(*Going over to the stove*) The coffee'll be ready in a minute, and you needn't expect me to wait for you.

(*Suddenly with great anger*) What on earth are you doing all this time? (*She goes over to the door and looks in*) Well, you're *almost* dressed at any rate. I expected to find you back in bed. That'd be just like you. How awful you look this morning! For heaven's sake, shave! You're disgusting! You look like a tramp. No wonder no one will give you a job. I don't blame them—when you don't even look half-way decent. (*She goes to the stove*) There's plenty of hot water right here. You've got no excuse. (*Gets a bowl and pours some of the water from the coffee pot into it*) Here.

(*He reaches his hand into the room for it. It is a sensitive hand with slender fingers. It trembles and some of the water spills on the floor.*)

(*Tauntingly*) Look at your hand tremble! You'd better give up drinking. You can't stand it. It's just your kind that get the D. T.'s. *That would be* the last straw! (*Looking down at the floor*) Look at the mess you've made of this floor—cigarette butts and ashes all over the place. Why can't you put them on a plate? No, you wouldn't be considerate enough to do that. You never think of me. You don't have to sweep the room and that's all you care about.

(*Takes the broom and commences to sweep viciously, raising a cloud of dust. From the inner room comes the sound of a razor being stropped.*)

(*Sweeping*) Hurry up! It must be nearly time for me to go. If I'm late I'm liable to lose my position, and then I couldn't support you any longer. (*As an afterthought she adds sarcastically*) And then you'd have to go to work or something dreadful like that. (*Sweeping under the table*) What I want to know is whether you're going to look for a job to-day or not. You know your family won't help us any more. They've had enough of you, too. (*After a moment's silent sweeping*) I'm about sick of all this life. I've a good notion to go home, if I wasn't too proud to let them know what a failure you've been—you, the millionaire Rowland's only son, the Harvard graduate, the poet, the catch of the town—Huh! (*With bitterness*) There wouldn't be many of them now envy my catch if they knew the truth. What has our marriage been, I'd like to know? Even before your *millionaire* father died owing everyone in the world money, you certainly never wasted any of your time on your wife. I suppose you thought I'd ought to be glad you were *honorable* enough to marry me—after getting me into trouble. You were ashamed of me with your fine friends because my father's only a grocer, that's what you were. At least he's honest, which is more than anyone could say about yours. (*She is sweeping steadily toward the door. Leans on her broom for a moment.*)

You hoped everyone'd think you'd been forced to marry me, and pity you, didn't you? You didn't hesitate much about telling me you loved me, and making me believe your lies, before it happened, did you? You made me think you didn't want your father to buy me off as he tried to do. I know better now. I haven't lived with you all this time for nothing. (*Somberly*) It's lucky the poor thing was born dead, after all. What a father you'd have been!

(*Is silent, brooding moodily for a moment—then she continues with a sort of savage joy.*)

But I'm not the only one who's got you to thank for being unhappy.

There's one other, at least, and *she* can't hope to marry you now. (*She puts her head into the next room*) How about Helen? (*She starts back from the doorway, half frightened.*)

Don't look at me that way! Yes, I read her letter. What about it? I got a right to. I'm your wife. And I know all there is to know, so don't lie. You needn't stare at me so. You can't bully me with your superior airs any longer. Only for me you'd be going without breakfast this very morning. (*She sets the broom back in the corner—whiningly*) You never did have any gratitude for what I've done. (*She comes to the stove and puts the coffee into the pot*) The coffee's ready. I'm not going to wait for you. (*She sits down in her chair again.*)

(*After a pause—puts her hand to her head—fretfully*) My head aches so this morning. It's a shame I've got to go to work in a stuffy room all day in my condition. And I wouldn't if you were half a man. By rights I ought to be lying on my back instead of you. You know how sick I've been this last year; and yet you object when I take a little something to keep up my spirits. You even didn't want me to take that tonic I got at the drug store. (*With a hard laugh*) I know you'd be glad to have me dead and out of your way; then you'd be free to run after all these silly girls that think you're such a wonderful, misunderstood person—this Helen and the others. (*There is a sharp exclamation of pain from the next room.*)

(*With satisfaction*) There! I knew you'd cut yourself. It'll be a lesson to you. You know you oughtn't to be running around nights drinking with your nerves in such an awful shape. (*She goes to the door and looks in.*)

What makes you so pale? What are you staring at yourself in the mirror that way for? For goodness sake, wipe that blood off your face! (*With a shudder*) It's horrible. (*In relieved tones*) There, that's better. I never could stand the sight of blood. (*She shrinks back from the door a little*) You better give up trying and go to a barber shop. Your hand shakes dreadfully. Why do you stare at me like that?

(*She turns away from the door*) Are you still mad at me about that letter? (*Defiantly*) Well, I had a right to read it. I'm your wife. (*She comes to the chair and sits down again. After a pause.*)

I knew all the time you were running around with someone. Your lame excuses about spending the time at the library didn't fool me. Who is this Helen, anyway? One of those artists? Or does she write poetry, too? Her letter sounds that way. I'll bet she told you your things were the best ever, and you believed her, like a fool. Is she young and pretty? I was young and pretty, too, when you fooled me with your fine, poetic talk; but life with you would soon wear anyone down. What I've been through!

(*Goes over and takes the coffee off the stove*) Breakfast is ready. (*With a contemptuous glance*) Breakfast! (*Pours out a cup of coffee for herself and puts the pot on the table.*) Your coffee'll be cold. What are you doing—still shaving, for heaven's sake? You'd better give it up. One of these mornings you'll give yourself a serious cut. (*She cuts off bread and butters it. During the following speeches she eats and sips her coffee.*)

I'll have to run as soon as I've finished eating. One of us has got to work. (*Angrily*) Are you going to look for a job today or aren't you? I should think some of your fine friends would help you, if they really think you're so much. But I guess they just like to hear you talk. (*Sits in silence for a moment.*)

I'm sorry for this Helen, whoever she is. Haven't you got any feelings for other people? What will her family say? I see she mentions them in her letter. What is she going to do—have the child—or go to one of those doctors? That's a nice thing, I must say. Where can she get the money? Is she rich? (*She waits for some answer to this volley of questions.*)

Hmm! You won't tell me anything about her, will you? Much I care. Come to think of it, I'm not so sorry for her after all. She knew what she was doing. She isn't any schoolgirl, like I was, from the looks of her letter. Does she know you're married? Of course, she must. All your friends know about your unhappy marriage. I know they pity you, but they don't know my side of it. They'd talk different if they did.

(*Too busy eating to go on for a second or so.*)

This Helen must be a fine one, if she knew you were married. What does she expect, then? That I'll divorce you and let her marry you? Does she think I'm crazy enough for that—after all you've made me go through? I guess not! And you can't get a divorce from me and you know it. No one can say *I've* ever done anything wrong. (*Drinks the last of her cup of coffee.*)

She deserves to suffer, that's all I can say. I'll tell you what I think; I think your Helen is no better than a common streetwalker, that's what I think. (*There is a stifled groan of pain from the next room.*)

Did you cut yourself again? Serves you right. (*Gets up and takes off her apron*) Well, I've got to run along. (*Peevishly*) This is a fine life for me to be leading! I won't stand for your loafing any longer. (*Something catches her ear and she pauses and listens intently*) There! You've overturned the water all over everything. Don't say you haven't. I can hear it dripping on the floor. (*A vague expression of fear comes over her face*) Alfred! Why don't you answer me?

(*She moves slowly toward the room. There is the noise of a chair being overturned and something crashes heavily to the floor. She stands, trembling with fright.*)

Alfred! Alfred! Answer me! What is it you knocked over? Are you still drunk? (*Unable to stand the tension a second longer she rushes to the door of the bedroom.*)

Alfred!

(*She stands in the doorway looking down at the floor of the inner room, transfixed with horror. Then she shrieks wildly and runs to the other door, unlocks it and frenziedly pulls it open, and runs shrieking madly into the outer hallway.*)

CURTAIN